THE PIMA INDIANS

Jose Louis Brennan, Papago Indian, who served as interpreter to Frank Russell. This photo was taken at San Xavier del Bac in 1894.

THE PIMA INDIANS

FRANK RUSSELL

Re-edition
with Introduction,
Citation Sources, and Bibliography
by BERNARD L. FONTANA

The University of Arizona Press
Tucson, Arizona

About the Author . . .

FRANK RUSSELL was an early and dedicated member of the anthropological profession whose detailed work on the material culture of the Piman people was accomplished in Arizona virtually on the eve of his death from tuberculosis. A member of the Harvard Faculty of Arts and Sciences, in 1900 Russell was given leave of absence for field work on the Gila River Reservation for the Bureau of American Ethnology. By contrast, his previous investigations had been among the tribes around Great Slave Lake and Herschel Island in the Arctic Sea. Russell's distinction as researcher and author is relatively little known to modern students of anthropology because his career was cut short at age 35. By that time he had completed this standard reference work on the Gila River Pimas, originally published as part of the *Twenty-sixth Annual Report of the Bureau of American Ethnology, 1904–1905.*

THE UNIVERSITY OF ARIZONA PRESS

Reprinted 1980
Re-edition Copyright © 1975
The Arizona Board of Regents
All Rights Reserved
Manufactured in the U.S.A.

ISBN 0-8165-0335-4
L.C. No. 74-78735

This re-edition of *The Pima Indians*
is dedicated to the memory of
JOSÉ LEWIS
O'odham scholar and author,
and to the
modern descendants of the AKIMEL O'ODHAM

CONTENTS OF THE RE-EDITION

INTRODUCTION TO THE RE-EDITION

The Pima Indians of Frank Russell and of Today

What used to be a rough buggy ride between Tucson or Phoenix and the Gila River Indian Reservation in southern Arizona has become a smooth automobile ride over a four-lane superhighway. In 1901–1902, when Harvard anthropologist Frank Russell and his wife spent most of a year visiting with the Pima Indians on this reservation, the pace was slow, and when they arrived they knew they were there. In the 1970s the Gila River Indian Community — the constitutionally-sanctioned governing body of Pima and Maricopa Indians responsible for the management of reservation affairs — found it desirable to erect a huge billboard alongside the superhighway to entice motorists to pause long enough in their headlong flights to visit the Arts and Crafts Center and to have a bite of good Pima cooking in a tribally owned restaurant. If it weren't for the billboard, few people would have had any inkling that they were on Arizona's oldest Indian reservation. From the highway it would simply appear to be more desert, a bit of open space between rapidly growing urban centers to the north and south.

As of 1974 somewhat more than 9,000 Pima Indians of Arizona lived on the 371,933-acre Gila River Reservation and on the nearby Salt River (46,624 acres) and Ak Chin (21,840 acres) reservations. They also lived off-reservation in Phoenix and in other southern Arizona communities, not to mention those who moved out-of-state and who chose at least for the moment to fashion their lives in a non-Pima world. Linguistically, culturally and historically, Arizona's Pimas are related to the Papago Indians and, farther south, to various Piman-speaking groups in the Mexican state of Sonora. But since the nucleus of the first of their reservations was created in 1859, Gila River Pimas have been dealt with by the non-Indian world as a single social entity, as a tribe, and similarities between them and their cultural brethren have been increasingly disregarded while their differences have been emphasized. Indeed, Pimas living on the three different reservations have tended to regard themselves

[ix]

in somewhat different lights, the administrations, particular histories, and unique problems of each being quite separate.

Most outsiders viewing the Pimas of the Gila River Reservation would be tempted to think they are no longer "really Indian." The clothes they wear, the cars and trucks they drive, the music they play and sing — these are as familiar to us as mom and apple pie. Although no one has reliable figures, large numbers of young people no longer learn to speak Pima, and cement block and other "foreign" goods are replacing native building materials in the construction of homes. Like other owners of large tracts of Arizona land, Pimas in the 1970s were selectively leasing parts of their acreage for industrial developments, industrialized farming operations, and for a variety of other uses unheard of seventy years earlier. Their subsistence has become tied wholly to cash economy.

To be misled into believing Pimas are no longer "really Indians," however, is to be misled on the basis of appearances and on the whites' mistaken notion that Pimas inevitably will disappear as a people. What is important is that Pimas continue to think of themselves as a people with their own history, with their own traditions, with their own ways of looking at life and the world around them. Although few particular items in the total cultural inventory of modern Pimas may be attributed solely to them, their arrangement of the parts — whether these parts be Indian or non-Indian in origin — is theirs and theirs alone. They have retained cultural distinctiveness in the face of all outside attempts to bring about their disappearance via assimilation.

Curiously enough, something of this same situation seems to have prevailed in 1901–1902 when Frank Russell did his field work on the Gila River Reservation. Pimas of 1901 were in many ways superficially similar to their non-Indian neighbors — although one would never get that impression from reading Russell's report alone. Presbyterian missionaries, the Indian Department, trading posts and traders, the railroad, the immediate proximity of non-Indian towns like Phoenix — all had shared by 1901 in the alteration of Pima life to such an extent that Pimas active as adults a half century earlier would have felt strangely out of touch. Water from the river had gone dry or had been largely appropriated by non-Indians before 1900, and the entire basis of Pima economy had shifted dramatically. Reasonably self-sufficient farmers had become wage laborers; the keepers of native traditions found their beliefs and practices being assaulted by unsympathetic whites who chose neither to understand nor to appreciate the positive values of Pima culture.

Russell's book on the Pima Indians, then, is really a history. Most of what he described in 1901–02 was already old and disappearing when he described it. In the anthropological tradition of the day, he sought out Pima elders and those comparatively few specialists in various aspects of traditional Pima culture to learn from them what they knew and remembered concerning subjects of interest to anthropologists. And subjects primarily of interest to anthropologists in the late nineteenth and early twentieth centuries were those which they viewed as being threatened by extinction, those of which it was felt to be immediately necessary to make a documentary record lest all knowledge of it disappear forever. This was "salvage anthropology," and it led, as it did in Russell's case, to the compilation of reports written in the "ethnographic present." They are reports, not of whole cultures, but of highly selected fragments of cultures. The result is that *The Pima Indians* provides us with a valuable, if distorted view, of what parts of Pima life may have been in, let us say, the 1860s or 1870s. Read and understood in that context, the book is a classic of its kind. Information of value and interest to living Pimas as well as to non-Pimas is, in fact, preserved for us in the pages of this book, information which may well have been lost to human knowledge had it not been for Russell's endeavors.

If Russell wanted to describe the "aboriginal" life of Pima Indians, he was also interested in a specific historical question, an interest he shared with Pimas themselves. This was the nature of the relationship, if any, between Pimas and the monumental prehistoric remains — ancient irrigation canals, elaborately decorated pottery and huge abandoned adobe structures — everywhere evident in Pima country. As Russell notes, it is a question that intrigued the earliest Spanish and other European missionaries, soldiers, and explorers in the area; it is one which continues to perplex modern cultural historians, Pimans and non-Indians alike (see, for example, Bahr 1971; DiPeso 1956; Ezell 1963; Ferdon 1967; Fontana and others 1962: 84–94; Haury 1967; Hayden 1970; Simpson 1946; and Winter 1973). The prehistoric origins of the Gila River Pima continue to remain a mystery concerning which there are a great many conflicting opinions.

Pima Literature Since 1902

Due in large part, no doubt, to non-Indians' belief that twentieth century Pimas had lost their "Indianness," coupled with the belief that Russell had done essentially all that could be done to describe their "aboriginal" way of life, the years since the publication of *The Pima Indians* in 1908 have seen very little written concerning these people. If anyone thinks the twentieth century bibliography of Pima Indians is long, they have only to compare it, for example, with what has been written concerning the neighboring Papagos. The Papago list of references is at least ten times as extensive.

Discounting the abundant medical bibliography relating to Pimas — their diabetes, tuberculosis, heart disease, cigarette smoking, and cancer rates have long been of concern to U.S. Public Health Service personnel — it is not too difficult to summarize those works written by and about them since Russell's days and which would have interested Russell himself.

There has first of all been a continuing fascination in calendar stick histories for Pimas as well as for Papagos (Arizona. *University of Arizona. Arizona State Museum* n.d.; Breazeale 1927, 1951; Hall 1907; Kilcrease 1939; Lumholtz 1912; 74–75; Papago Tribe of Arizona and others 1972: A1-A11; Smith 1942; Southworth 1931; Underhill 1938). Documentary history of the Pimas, which is to say their past as compiled and interpreted by non-Pimas, has attracted some attention, a part of it the result of the Pimas' successfully prosecuted claims case against the United States for lands wrongfully taken away from them (Ezell 1957, 1961; Hamilton 1948; Kneale 1950: 383–429; Wetzler 1949; Woodward 1949). George Webb (1959), who was a Pima, published some charming reminiscent history, as has Anna Shaw (1974).

A large part of *The Pima Indians* is devoted to material culture. Since 1901 there have been additional publications concerning Pima baskets (Breazeale 1923; Cain 1962; Douglas 1930; Duclos 1939; Field 1969; Hodge 1940; Kissell 1916, 1972; Robinson 1954: 8–53), and Tanner and Leavitt (1965), although concerned with Papago burden baskets, have added to our knowledge of this particular artifact, one equally common among Pimas. Pottery (Douglas 1953; Fontana and others 1962: 116–117; Hayden 1959), houses (Halseth 1933; Van Willigen 1970), wood carving (Douglas 1939), cane pipes and tobacco (Steen 1943), war clubs (Woodward 1933), and various goods found as a result of archaeological excavations in historic Pima sites (Steen 1946; VanValkenburgh 1946) are further Pima tools described in this century. General material culture and trait list summaries are found in Beals (1934) and Drucker (1941), while more information on Pima games than that cited by Russell can be read in Culin (1907: 148–152, 267, 295–296, 339, 355–356, 389, 489, 528, 551–552, 648, 660, 666, 671–672, 717, 724, 806), Underhill (1939: 144–145) and Smith (1945). The latter two described the game of *kinyskut,* played by both Pimas and Papagos.

What Russell included under the headings of "food supply" and "agriculture" have been considerably elaborated upon by Castetter and Bell (1942) and Curtin (1949), while Pima economy, a heading not found in Russell, and including all-important considerations of water supply and water rights, has been the subject of reports by Cormack (1968), Hackenberg (1962, 1964), Hayden (1965), and Weaver (1974). The Bureau of Ethnic Research of the University of Arizona (Arizona. *University of Arizona Bureau of Ethnic Research* 1971) prepared an extensive study under contract to the Gila River Community which concerns itself primarily with modern political organization and business management on the reservation, but the report has not been released for general distribution.

For Pima sociology we have studies by Herzog (1936b), Hill (1936, 1938), Krueger (1971) and Woodward (1938). Pima education, discussed in a single paragraph by Russell under the heading of "schools" (p. 34), has attracted at least some further published interest in more recent times (Kelly 1967; Padfield and others 1966; Smith 1930).

As for linguistics and for "sophiology" (i.e., the "science of human ideas"), or what would be thought of today as religion, mythology, and folklore, there are the published efforts of Bahr (1971), Brown (1906), Curtis (1907–1930: II: 14–23), Grossman (1958), Kroeber (1908), Herzog (1936a, 1960), Lloyd (1911), Neff (1912), Shaw (1968), Walton and Waterman (1925) and Willenbrink (1935). As thorough as he was in his research, Russell failed to note the Pima origin story published in Bancroft (1886: 78–80) and he missed a short but early Piman vocabulary published in *The Historical Magazine* (Anonymous 1862).

Finally, there have been some very general surveys of Pima culture, always brief, which deserve mention (see Curtis 1907–1930: II: 1–14, and 1909; Hrdlička 1906; McClintock 1918; Parsons 1928; Spicer 1962: 146–151; and Underhill n.d.). And for some unexplained reason, Russell chose to ignore Grossman's (1873) pioneer ethnographic sketch of the Gila River Pimas.

In the last six decades a great many accounts of nineteenth century travellers have been published, and diaries and journals of some of the people who accompanied railroad survey and military expeditions cited by Russell are now available. Forty-niners on their way to the California gold fields sometimes passed through the Pima villages, and some of their descriptions have also been printed in the 1900s. Perhaps the most interesting of such materials to come to light have been the drawings, paintings and sketches made by artists accompanying John R. Bartlett's survey of the United States and Mexican boundary between 1850 and 1852. Excellent water color paintings of Pima villages by Henry C. Pratt and Seth Eastman now can be seen in a handsome book (Hine 1968: illustrations 35 and 36).

This summary of twentieth century literature concerning the Pimas is by no means exhaustive, but it includes virtually all the major reports, other than those related to Pima physical anthropology and health. Excluded as well are descriptions of Pimas appearing in travel accounts or in larger discussions of Indians of Arizona or of the Southwest and which are based solely on secondary references.

Frank Russell and José Lewis

The Pima Indians is actually a coauthored work. Its conception, organization, and selection of content are those of Frank Russell, and certainly it was he who was asking most of the questions of the Pimas. But his silent partner, barely mentioned as an "interpreter" in a footnote on page 18, was a remarkable Papago Indian named José Lewis. Born in the 1860s or 1870s at Vainam Kug ("Iron Stands") in what is today the Sells District of the Papago Indian Reservation, Lewis first comes to our written attention when in 1894 he was hired by W. J. McGee, an ethnologist with the Bureau of American Ethnology, to accompany him as interpreter on an expedition through the eastern portions of Papago country in Arizona and Sonora. McGee's diary of this trip, which awaits publication, makes it clear that Lewis was a splendid interpreter of both culture and language, and he became one of McGee's principal informants.

Subsequently, in 1897, José Lewis wrote for the Smithsonian Institution, in both Papago and English, a number of texts relating to Papago life and language. A partial Papago-English dictionary, the berdache and "backward" people (i.e., "contraries"), political organization, and the ritual oratory of salt-gathering expeditions are a few of the topics on which Lewis wrote. Known to the people at the Smithsonian as José Lewis Brennan, some of his material on warfare has been published (Brennan 1959); one of his folktales has been mimeographed and widely circulated (Brennan 1958); and much of what he wrote concerning sickness and curing has now appeared in print (Bahr and others 1974: 66, 114, 120, 243, 272).

As it turns out, however, his real published monument is more than 150 pages of *The Pima Indians,* virtually the entire sections on sophiology and linguistics. These are the kinds of data that could only have been collected by a native speaker of the Piman language — recalling that Pima and Lewis' dialect of Papago are mutually intelligible — and the orthography used in the extensive texts of songs, myths and speeches is precisely that found in Lewis' holograph manuscripts of 1897.

José Lewis still has living relatives among Pimas and Papagos. They recall that he died at Blackwater on the Gila River Reservation, probably in the 1920s, and that he used to sell copies of *The Pima Indians* to his friends and kinsmen. They have been only dimly aware of the kind and degree of his involvement with anthropologists and with the Smithsonian Institution, and until now I doubt that any of them have known that José Lewis was in fact an outstanding ethnographer of his own people. It is only fitting that this new edition of the book for which he wrote so much should be dedicated to him and, by extension, to his fellow Pimans. It turns out that it really has been their book all along.

Frank Russell, probably because he died when he was barely thirty-five years old, is not one of the better-known American anthropologists. Born at Fort Dodge, Iowa, August 26, 1868, his undergraduate college career was at the University of Iowa. In June, 1891, he accompanied Professor C. C. Nutting to the Grand Rapids of Saskatchewan River and to the mouth of the river at Cedar Lake, and the following year he graduated from the University. Still excited about his summer's trip to Canada, after graduation he returned alone to the north country, this time exploring for two-and-a-half years among the Slavey, Dogrib, Yellow Knives, Eskimos, Chipewyans and Crees from Fort Providence and Bathurst Inlet to Great Slave Lake and Herschel Island in the Arctic Sea.

In 1895 the University of Iowa gave Russell the degree of S.M., and a year later he was appointed as instructor of anthropology at Harvard University which gave him an A.B. degree that same year. In 1897 he was awarded his

A.M. at Harvard, and in 1898, after writing a dissertation describing Eskimo crania from Labrador (Russell 1898b), he earned his Ph.D.

In 1899 Russell was appointed a permanent member of the Harvard Faculty of Arts and Sciences, but the following year he was given a leave of absence to do field work in Arizona for the Bureau of American Ethnology. When Russell and his wife arrived on the Gila River Reservation in November of 1901, he was suffering from advanced stages of tuberculosis. His field work carried him through June, and in October, 1902, he was back at work at Harvard. Early in 1903, however, his tuberculosis forced him back to Arizona, and he and his wife were living in Kingman next to the Lower Colorado River when the end came for him on November 7, 1903. His body was taken to Los Angeles and his remains were cremated there (*Mohave County Miner* 1903).

During his short career Russell had been Vice-President of Section "H" of the American Association for the Advancement of Science, President of the American Folk-Lore Society, and a councillor of the American Anthropological Association. He published more than three dozen articles and books (see Russell in the Bibliography), although most of these were book reviews and very short essays. "His genial companionship" wrote Frederick Webb Hodge (1903: 708) on the occasion of his death, "will be missed by all who were honored by his acquaintance."

The Pima Indians, by Frank Russell and José Lewis, continues to be the standard reference work about the Gila River Pimas. The reader should know, however, that he is reading a particular kind of history and that much of the information was already history in 1901–02. It is by no means a balanced picture of Pima life in any period; it certainly is not a description of Pima life today. But viewed in that perspective — and especially considering the contributions of José Lewis to Piman literature and the descriptions of Pima material culture — it remains a fascinating and valuable work.

One would hope, however, that in the near future there will be a new book describing the full range of modern culture of the Pima Indians, one which describes the Pima situation as it is rather than as someone thinks it was or ought to be. One would further hope, moreover, that a Pima will be the author of such a book. So many of us who are non-Pimans have spoken about them, it is time they be given every encouragement to speak for themselves.

BERNARD L. FONTANA
Ethnologist
State Museum
The University of Arizona

THE PIMA INDIANS

BY

FRANK RUSSELL

CONTENTS

8 CONTENTS

ILLUSTRATIONS

PIMA SOUNDS AND THEIR SYMBOLS

a .....as in father.
â .....as in law.
ă .....as in what.
ä .....as in hat.
ɐ .....indeterminate sound between a and ä.
c .....as sh in shall, a rare sound: occurs in vi-shûk (hawk).
d .....as in dread.
e .....as in they.
ĕ .....as in then.
f .....as in fife.
ɟ .....as a mere breathing.
g .....as in good; occurs in foreign words.
ᵹ .....between k and g.
h .....as in he.
i .....as in pique.
ĭ .....as in pick.
k .....as in kick.
l .....as in lull.
ʇ .....as with a faint ɋ following.
m .....as in mum.
n .....as in nun.
ñ .....as ng in sing.
o .....as in note.
ŏ .....as in whole, (German soll).
p .....as in pipe.

r .....an initial uvular r.
s .....as in sauce.
t .....as in touch.
td ....heard now as t, now as d, or between.
u .....as in rule.
ŭ .....as in pull.
û .....as in but.
ɒ .....like the German ö in Göthe.
v .....as in valve.
ʌ .....a synthetic sound, v+w.
w .....as in wish.
y .....as in you.
hy ....as in hue.
ñg ....as in finger.
ny ....as ny in canyon.
tc ....as ch in church.
t' .....an exploded breathing.
d' ....an exploded breathing.
k' ....an exploded breathing.
p' ....an exploded breathing.
x .....a k sound with an expulsion of breath before sounding it.
ɱ .....an m with lips closed.
' =exploded breathing.
' =laryngeal closure.

16

THE PIMA INDIANS

By Frank Russell

INTRODUCTION

From November, 1901, until June, 1902, the writer made his headquarters at Sacaton (see pl. i), on the Gila River reservation, in southern Arizona, where he was engaged in a study of the Pima tribe. With the aid of five native interpreters information was obtained from ten Pima men and women,[a] selected because of their intelligence and special aptitude in certain lines. With so many persons engaged in the investigations, the work of one frequently overlapped and served as a check on that of another. This made it possible to obtain a quite full account of Piman ethnology for the time employed. A house-to-house canvass of the villages, week after week, month after month, led to personal contact with nearly every household on the reservation and visits were made also to the Salt River Pimas and the desert Kwahadk's. One valuable result was the collection of more than 300 specimens illustrative of nearly all Piman arts, gathered from among a people whom poverty had induced to dispose of so many of their

---

[a] The name and a brief sketch of each of the author's informants and interpreters are here given:

Informants. Kâ'mâltkâk, Thin Leather (pl. xliv, b), an old man, is said to be the most popular of the few remaining narrators of myths and speeches, or " speakers." He is an intimate friend of the head chief, Antonio Azul (pl. ii, a), and has always occupied a prominent place in the councils of the tribe. In his prime he exceeded 6 feet in stature and was strong and sturdy of frame. Indeed, his hand grasp is yet vigorous enough to make his silent and friendly greeting somewhat formidable. Intelligent, patient, dignified, his influence must have been helpful to those youths who formerly came to him for instruction. From him was obtained the cosmogonical myth of the tribe, many speeches, songs, and much general information. He also made a model of a loom and a few other specimens for the collection of material pertaining to the Pimas.

Sala Hina, Sarah Fish, or Hina (fig. 51), as she was called by her people, was recommended as one of the most intelligent of the older women. An earnest Christian, she had no scruples about relating all that she knew concerning the religious beliefs of the tribe. She had undergone a long and exacting training in practical botany which rendered her a valuable assistant in gathering information concerning the economic plants of the region. Taught by gaunt Hunger, she and her kind had learned to know and use a large number of vegetal products. She inherited through her father some of the Kwahadk' potters' skill, which enabled her to impart valuable knowledge of the art and to furnish specimens.

Sika'tcu, Dry, an old woman, is the half sister of Antonio Azul and is one of the best known nurses and midwives about the Sacaton settlement. Though unable to speak English, after a few interviews with an interpreter she was quick to understand by means of signs and a few Pima words when to pose for photographs and the like. Among her earliest recollections was the sight of the covered wagons of the emigrant trains that followed the Gila route in such numbers during the early years of the California gold excitement. Her memory therefore extends over a quarter of a century of the period of bitterest

old belongings that for a month or two after going into their midst there seemed but little opportunity of securing anything approaching a representative series. Several specimens that were finally discovered are believed to be the very last of their kind among the Pimas, though of course such a statement must be made with reserve. Prof. J. J. Thornber, of the University of Arizona, accompanied the party on a round trip of 80 miles along the Gila river and to him the collection is indebted for about 50 herbarium specimens, representing the larger portion of the economic plants of the Pimas that are susceptible of preparation in this way. To him also is due the credit of examining and identifying the mass of material gathered by the persons engaged at Casa Blanca and Gila Crossing. As complete a list as possible of the plants used for food, medicine, and the like was made, after which the services of both men and women were enlisted to point out the plants in the course of a trip through the river bottoms or on the hills. Furthermore, a number of sets of seeds was obtained, a portion of which were planted during the summer of 1902 for the purpose of raising plants that could not otherwise be identified. Unfortunately, the season proved too dry for them to germinate and the list is consequently less complete than it should be. The Pima name is given in all cases.

The American people owe the Pimas a lasting debt of gratitude. The California pioneers that traversed the southern route before the

---

warfare between the Pimas and the Apaches. After several months acquaintance with this old woman Mrs Russell obtained from her much information concerning the Pima woman's views of warfare as well as knowledge of facts pertaining to various customs, especially those peculiar to her sex.

Antonio Azul (see pl. II, a) was the head chief of the tribe, and from him much information concerning war customs and recent history was obtained.

Ki'satc, Cheese, an old Santan pariah, had employed such wit as grudging nature had endowed him with in practising the arts of the medicine-man. His contributions, while of a minor character, proved to be of interest.

William Blackwater, an elderly Pima, had taken an active part in the later history of the village of Blackwater, which is situated at the eastern end of the reservation. He was employed but a short time and gave information concerning history and customs.

Ha'hali, or Juan Thomas, a Christian Pima who was formerly a medicine-man, contributed much valuable information concerning the " occult." He also furnished a calendar record and made a number of specimens illustrating the medicine-man's paraphernalia.

Tco'kŭt Nak, Owl Ear (pl. II, b), an old man, lived at the Salt River village and was the first from whom a calendar record was obtained.

Benjamin Thompson, so far as could be learned, kept the only calendar in the central group of villages about Casa Blanca, and he related the events that are commemorated by it.

Kâemâ-â, Rattlesnake Head (pl. II, c), a chief, is known to the whites as Joseph Head. He gave an excellent specimen of a calendar record and stick.

Interpreters. The principal interpreter, who was employed by the month during the entire period of the writer's stay, was José Lewis, a Papago who had lived from childhood among the Pimas. He had once been engaged by the Bureau of American Ethnology to write a vocabulary of his own language and to supply other information, so that he was acquainted with the phonetic alphabet and other approved methods of procedure. He was engaged in linguistic work the greater part of the time.

Melissa Jones, the official interpreter at the agency, was employed to interpret the statements of Sika'tcu, her mother, known to the whites as "Old Mary," and also at intervals on the calendars.

Jacob L. Roberts spoke quite as good English as the average white man of the country and was employed to secure Tco'kŭt Nak's calendar (pl. II, b) and for the final revision of the linguistic material.

Carl Smart, of Sacaton, and Thomas Allison, of Blackwater, were occasionally engaged as temporary interpreters. In addition to these there were half a dozen others who were employed for from one to three days each at the lower villages.

days of transcontinental railroads often owed their lives to the friendly brown-skinned farmers whom they met upon the Gila.[a] This tribe rendered notable assistance as scouts in the long contest with the Apaches. Even had they remained neutral, they would have deserved friendly consideration on the part of the whites, but as they fought bravely in the latter's behalf justice requires that their services be accorded proper recognition.

The Pimas live in two river valleys that are strewn with the ruins of prehistoric buildings and other evidences of the presence of a considerable population that had attained probably the highest degree of civilization or culture to be found north of Mexico. The present race has been variously regarded as the descendants of the one that has disappeared, as having amalgamated with it, and as being entirely independent of it. The determination of the exact relationship of the two groups has been held constantly in mind during the course of these investigations. Closely connected with this principal problem are those problems of the extent and direction of the migrations of men and culture toward the Sierra Madre, the Rio Grande, the Pacific, and the plateau to the northward. Was this a center of culture or was it a halting place in the march of clans?

HISTORY

NAME

The tribe known as the Pimas was so named by the Spaniards early in the history of the relations of the latter with them. The oldest reference to the name within the writer's knowledge is that by Velarde: "The Pima nation, the name of which has been adopted by the Spaniards from the native idiom, call themselves Otama or in the plural Ohotoma; the word pima is repeated by them to express negation."[b] This "negacion" is expressed by such words as pia, "none," piatc, "none remaining," pimatc, "I do not know" or "I do not understand." In the last the sound of tc is often reduced to a faint click. The Americans corrupted this to "Pimos," and while this form of the word is now used only by the illiterate living in the neighborhood of the tribe, it is fairly common in the literature referring to them. They call themselves Ă'-â'tam, "men" or "the people," and when they wish to distinguish themselves from the Papago and other

---

[a] Sylvester Mowry, lieutenant in the Third Artillery, in an address before the American Geographical Society, in New York, February 3, 1859 (Arizona and Sonora, 3d ed., 30), said: "Much as we pride ourselves upon our superior government, no measures [the United States Government have [sic] since, under urgent pressure of the writer, made some small appropriations for the Pima Indians] have been taken to continue our friendly relations with the Pimos; and to our shame be it said, it is only to the forbearance of these Indians that we owe the safety of the life of a single American citizen in central or western Arizona, or the carriage of the mails overland to the Pacific."

[b] "La nacion pima, cuyo nombre han tomado los españoles en su nativo idioma, se llama Otama y en plural Ohotoma, de la palabra Pima repetida en ellos por ser su negacion." Documentos para la Historia de Mexico, 4th ser., I, 345.

divisions of the same linguistic stock they add the word â'kimûlt, "river." "River people" is indeed an apt designation, as evidenced by their dependence on the Gila.

Gatschet has thus defined the Pima linguistic stock in an article entitled "The Indian languages of the Pacific," which was published in the Magazine of American History: [a]

Pima. Dialects of this stock are spoken on the middle course of the Gila river, and south of it on the elevated plains of southern Arizona and northern Sonora (Pimería alta, Pimería baja). The Pima does not extend into California unless the extinct, historical Cajuenches, mentioned in Mexican annals, spoke one of the Pima (or Pijmo, Pimo) dialects. Pima, on Pima reserve, Gila river, a sonorous, root-duplicating idiom; Névome, a dialect probably spoken in Sonora, of which we possess a reliable Spanish grammar, published in Shea's Linguistics; [b] Papago, on Papago reserve, in southwestern Arizona.

VILLAGES

During the early part of the nineteenth century there were eight Pima villages on the Gila, according to statements made by Kâ'mâl tkâk and other old men of the tribe. The numerous accounts by travelers and explorers contain mention of from five to ten pueblos or villages. The names are usually those bestowed by the Spanish missionaries or unrecognizable renderings of the native terms. The villages were principally upon the south bank of the river, along which they extended for a distance of about 30 miles. [c] Some have been abandoned; in other cases the name has been retained, but the site has been moved. The first villages named by Kino were Equituni, Uturituc, and Sutaquison. The last two were situated near the present agency of Sacaton (pl. I). The first may have been the village of Pimas and Kwahadk's, which was situated west of Picacho on the border of the sink of the Santa Cruz river (fig. 1), which was abandoned about a century ago and was known as Akûtcĭny, Creek

---

[a] Vol. I, 156.

[b] The most valuable publication relating to the Pima language is the "Grammar of the Pima or Névome, a language of Sonora, from a manuscript of the XVIII Century." This was edited by Buckingham Smith, and 160 copies were issued in 1862. It is in Spanish-Névome, the latter differing slightly from the true Pima. The grammar has 97 octavo pages with 32 additional pages devoted to a "Doctrina Cristiana y Confesionario en Lengua Névome, ó sea la Pima."

[c] The Rudo Ensayo states that "between these Casas Grandes, the Pimas, called Gileños, inhabit both banks of the river Gila, occupying ranches on beautiful bottom land for 10 leagues farther down, which, as well as some islands, are fruitful and suitable for wheat, Indian corn, etc." Records of the American Catholic Historical Society, v, 128.

"The most important of these ranches are, on this side, Tusonimó, and on the other, Sudacson or the Incarnation, where the principal of their chiefs, called Tavanimó, lived, and farther down, Santa Theresa, where there is a very copious spring." (Ibid., 129.) This "spring" was probably above the present Gila Crossing where the river, after running for many miles underground in the dry season, rises with a strong flow of water that supplies extensive irrigating ditches.

Whipple, Ewbank, and Turner, writing in 1855, enumerate the following Pima villages: San Juan Capistrano, Sutaquison, Atison, Tubuscabor, and San Seferino de Napgub (see Pacific Railroad Reports, III, pt. 3, 123).

In 1858 Lieut. A. B. Chapman, First Dragoons, U. S. Army, completed a census of the Pimas and Maricopas. The names of the villages, leaders, and the population of both tribes are here reprinted

Mouth. The site of this settlement was visited by the writer in April, 1902. It is marked by several acres of potsherds that are scattered about the sand dunes on the south side of the dry river bottom that is scarcely lower than the level of the plain. A few Mexican families have lived in the vicinity for many years, pumping water from a depth of a hundred feet and depending upon crops of corn and beans raised in the summer when a few showers fall upon their fields. These Mexicans plow out stone implements and bits of pottery, but have never found any burial places.[a] There are two medium-sized adobe ruins on the flat river bottom; one of these has walls of the same pisé type that is exhibited by the Casa Grande ruin (pl. III), situated 25 miles to the northward.

from S. Ex. Doc. 1, pt. 1, 559, 35th Cong., 2d sess., 1859. The number of Maricopas is included that the comparatively small importance of that tribe may be appreciated.

MARICOPAS

[Head chief, Juan Chevereah.]

Villages.	Chiefs.	Warriors.	Women and children.	Total.
El Juez Tarado.......	} Juan Jose...	116	198	314
Sacaton...............		76	128	204
		192	326	518

PIMAS

[Head chief, Antonio Soule [Azul].]

Buen Llano...........	Ojo de Buro and Yiela del Arispe...............	132	259	391
Ormejera No. 1........	Miguel and Xavier...........................	140	503	643
Ormejera No. 2........	Cabeza del Aquila	37	175	212
Casa Blanca...........	Chelan	110	425	535
Chemisez..............	Tabacaro.....................................	102	210	312
El Juez Tarado........	Cadrillo del Mundo and Ariba Aqua Bolando...	105	158	263
Arizo del Aqua........	Francisco....................................	235	535	770
Aranca No. 1	La Mano del Mundo...........................	291	700	991
Aranca No. 2	Boca Dulce..................................	....	....	....
		1,152	2,965	4,117

Mr Browne, a member of Commissioner Poston's party that visited the villages in January, 1864, wrote: "The number of Pima villages is 10; Maricopas, 2; separate inclosures, 1,000." (J. Ross Browne, Adventures in the Apache Country, 110.) On a later page (290) he gives the population by villages, of which he names but seven:

Aqua Baiz.....................................	533	Herringuen...................................	514
Cerrito.......................................	259	Llano.......................................	392
Arenal..	616		
Cachunilla....................................	438	Total...................................	3,067
Casa Blanca..................................	315		

"There are 1,200 laboring Pimas and 1,000 warriors."

James F. Rusling (The Great West and the Pacific Coast, 369), who visited the Pimas in 1867, also states that there were then ten Pima villages.

a Font mentions a Pima-Papago village in this vicinity, called "Cuitoa." Manuscript Diary, 35.

The villages known to the oldest Pimas are as follows:

1. Petâ′ĭkuk, Where the Petai (ash tree?) Stands.
2. Tcupatäk, Mortar Stone.
3. Tcu′wutukawutûk, Earth Hill.
4. Os Kâ′kûmûk Tco′tcikäm, Arrow-bush Standing.
5. Ko′-okûp Van′sĭk, Medicine Paraphernalia.
6. Kâ′mĭt, Back.
7. Tco′ûtĭk Wu′tcĭk, Charcoal Laying.

8 and 9. Akûtcĭny, Creek Mouth. One 5 miles west of Picacho and another south-west of Maricopa station. Both depended upon flood waters.

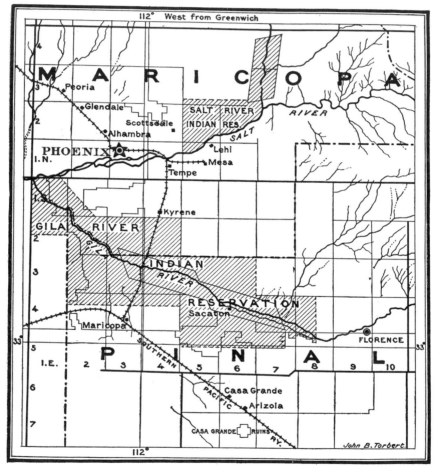

FIG. 1. Map of Pima reservation.

There are two Maricopa villages: Hi′nămâ, Hina Head (hina, a kind of fish) and Tco′ûtcĭk Wu′tcĭk, which is included among the Pima villages, as it was occupied by them after the Maricopas moved down the river to their present location below Gila Crossing. The Hi′nămâ people now reside on the south bank of the Salt, east of the Mormon settlement of Lehi.

The Pimas have a tradition relating the circumstances of the coming of the band of Sobaipuris,[a] whom they call Rsa'rsavinâ, Spotted, from the San Pedro. They are said to have drunk na'vait or cactus liquor together with a village of Pimas of forgotten name, on the north side of the Gila, near the present Blackwater and the Picacho village of Akûtcĭny, before the time when the Apaches forced them to leave their homes on the San Pedro.

Since the settlement of the Gila and Salt river valleys by the whites and the establishment of peace with the Apaches, the Pimas have again manifested a disposition to extend their settlements, principally owing, however, to the scarcity of water on the Gila River reservation. The present villages are as follows:

Os Kuk, Tree Standing, known as Blackwater.

We'tcu(r)t, Opposite, North Blackwater.

Ha'rsanykuk, Saguaro Standing, Sacaton Flats.

S'a'opuk, Many Trees, The Cottonwoods.

Tat'sĭtûk', Place of Fright, the settlement about Cruz's store.

Ku'-u Ki, Big House, Sacaton.

ᴧo'pohiûm, (?), Santan.

Hu'tcĭlttcĭk, Round Clearing, village below Santan on north bank of river.

Va'-aki, Ruin or Ancient House, Casa Blanca.

Stâ'tânnyĭk, Many Ants, a village between the two last preceding, on south bank of Gila.

Pe-ep'tcĭlt'k', Concave (from a family with noses of that shape), northeast of Casa Blanca.

Rso'tûk', Water Standing, northwest of Casa Blanca.

Skâ'kâĭk, Many Rattlesnakes, on north side of Gila, opposite Rso'tûk'.

Rsâ'nûk, Beginning, about a mile east of Sacaton station on Maricopa and Phoenix railroad.

Ka'woltûk' Wutca, Hill Below, west of railroad.

Hi'atam, Sea Sand Place, from Hi'akatcĭk, where the people of this village formerly lived. Hi'atam was just north of Maricopa station.

Kâ'matûk Wu'tcâ, Kâ'matûk Below, Gila Crossing. Kâ'matûk is the Pima name of the Sierra Estrella.

Herm'ho, Once, or Â'mû Â'kimûlt, Salt River, known by last name. This is the settlement on the north side of the river, 3 miles from Mesa.

PREHISTORIC RUINS

The Pimas have long since grown accustomed to being interrogated concerning the builders of the great stone and adobe pueblos that now lie in ruins on the mesas of the Gila and Salt river valleys. However ready they may have been in the past to claim relationship

---

[a] " The most warlike among all the Pimas are those we call the Sobiarpuris, for they are born and reared on the border of the Apaches; but they have become tired of living in constant warfare, and have, during the present year of 1762, abandoned their beautiful and fertile valley, retiring, some to Santa Maria Soanca, and some to San Xavier del Bac and to Tucson, thus leaving to the enemies a free entrance to the high region of the Pimas." Rudo Ensayo, translated by Eusebio Guitéras, Records of the American Catholic Historical Society, v, 192.

with the Hohokam[a] or relate tales of the supernatural origin of the pueblos, they now frankly admit that they do not know anything about the matter.[b] As early as the time of Kino and Mange mention is made of the chief of the former pueblo of Casa Grande, who was called "Siba." Mange in his Diary of November, 1697, translates this word as "bitter" or "cruel." The present pronunciation is sivan[y] and the same name is given to all Hohokam chiefs; no one now knows the meaning of the word. The query arises, Is the similarity of this term to the native name for the Zuñis a mere coincidence? Mr Cushing states that "Cibola equals the 'Chi-vo-la' of Fray Marcus, of Nizza, equals the Zuñi name for themselves, namely, Shiwona, or Shiwina."[c]

Each ruin is called va-aki, ancient house, and in the myths a name is added to distinguish it from other ruins and to it si'van[y] to identify him from other chiefs.

Following is the list of the best known places, with their chiefs:

Tco'-oltûk, Corner, Casa Grande. Ruled by Sĭa'-al Tcu-vtakĭ, Morning Blue.
Â-ât'kam Va-aki, Sandy Ancient House, Santan. Ruled by Kĭa'-atak, Handle.
S'o'am Nyu'ĭ Va-aki, Yellow Vulture Ancient House. Name of chief not known to my informants.

The following names of chiefs are preserved in the myths, but the ruins are referred to simply as va-aki:

Tcuĭ'haowo-o, Dipper, was the sivan[y] at the ruin situated about 4 miles northwest of Santan. (Pl. IV, a, b.)
Ta'-a, Flying, lived at the Sweetwater pueblo. (Pl. IV, c.)
Tco'-otcuk Ta'tai, Black Sinew, at Casa Blanca.[d]
Tcu'narsat, Lizard, at Gila Crossing.
A'-an Hi'tŭpăkĭ, Feather Breathing, at Mesa.
Vi'-ĭk I'alt Ma'kai, Soft Feathers Rolling, ruled the pueblo between Tempe and Phoenix that is now being excavated by the Arizona Antiquarian Society.

When a single chief is referred to, he is usually called Si'van[y], and when the full name is given, Si'van[y] is always added, so that it is not surprising that Mange, Bandelier,[e] and others should have sup-

---

[a] The term Hohokam, That which has Perished, is used by the Pimas to designate the race that occupied the pueblos that are now rounded heaps of ruins in the Salt and Gila river valleys. As there is no satisfactory English term, the Pima name has been adopted throughout this memoir.

[b] " I made frequent inquiries of the Pimos and Coco-Maricopas as to the builders of these (Salt River ruins) and the ruins on the Gila, but could obtain no other than the ever ready, Quien sabe? These, as well as the ruins above the Pimo villages, are known among the Indians as the 'houses of Montezuma,' an idea doubtless derived from the Mexicans, rather than from any tradition of their own. We asked our Indian guide who Montezuma was. He answered, 'Nobody knows who the devil he was; all we know is, that he built these houses.'" Bartlett, Personal Narrative, 1854, II, 248.

[c] Congrès International des Américanistes, 7me sess., 1890, 155.

[d] The ruin at Casa Blanca (pl. V, a) is one of the largest south of the Gila. The adobe walls yet show at the level of the surface of the mound. Sedelmair states in his Relación that there were two houses standing at Casa Blanca in 1744. This and the ruin in Santan are the only ones near which the modern villages are built. Casa Grande is 6 miles from the nearest Pima village, which was, furthermore, quite recently established by families from points farther down the river.

[e] " While in New Mexico the chain of traditional information appears almost unbroken as far down as San Marcial, in Arizona the folk-lore of the Zuñi terminates, according to Mr Cushing, with the northern folds of the Escudilla and of the Sierra Blanca. The remarkable architecture prevalent on the

posed that the Casa Grande pueblo was under the control of "Siba" or "Si'van^y;" indeed it is now frequently designated "Si'van^y Ki" by the Pimas. Fifteen miles southeast of the Casa Grande ruin is the mountain ridge that rises abruptly from the nearly level plains which is known as Ta-a'tûkam or Picacho mountain. Picacho is an isolated peak south of the mountain. The pass between them, through which the main trail ran from the Pima villages to Tucson, and through which the railroad has been built, was one of the most dreaded portions of the overland trail when the Apaches were "out," as they were most of the time. To the northeast of the mountain is a small pueblo ruin that lies about 15 miles from the river, which is apparently the nearest water. It was probably occupied during a part of the year only. East of the mountain is a ruin called Kĭs'tcoĭt Vatcĭk^ʿ, Table Tank; on the north is one known as Mo'-ok^ʿ Vatcĭk^ʿ, Sharp Tank; and at the foot of Ta-a'tûkam, on the west, is A'-alt Vap^{ʿ}tck^ʿ, Small Tanks. Southwest of the mountain were situated the Pima village of Akûtcĭny and the two pueblo ruins previously mentioned. There is another small pueblo ruin a few miles northwest of the site of Akûtcĭny, but no others of similar type are known to the writer at any point in Arizona south of Picacho. A personal examination of all the ruins of the southeastern part of the Territory has shown them to be of a different type from those of the upper and lower Gila and the Salt river valleys. The ruins along the San Pedro, it is true, extend to the southward of the parallel of Picacho, and it is believed to be desirable that some of them be explored. Superficially they resemble the ruins about Solomonsville, where cremation

---

Salado, Gila, and Verde has no light shed upon it by their folk-lore tales. Here the statements of the Pimas, which Mr Walker has gathered, are of special value; and to him I owe the following details: The Pimas claim to have been created where they now reside, and after passing through a disastrous flood—out of which only one man, Cĭ-hö, was saved—they grew and multiplied on the south bank of the Gila until one of their chiefs, Ci-vă-nŏ, built the Casa Grande. They call it to-day 'Ci-vă-nŏ-qi' (house of Ci-vă-nŏ); also 'Văt-qi' (ruin). A son of Ci-vă-nŏ settled on lower Salt river, and built the villages near Phoenix and Tempe. At the same time a tribe with which they were at war occupied the Rio Verde; to that tribe they ascribe the settlements whose ruins I have visited, and which they call 'O-ŏt-gŏm-vătqi' (gravelly ruins). The Casa Blanca and all the ruins south of the Gila were the abodes of the forefathers of the Pimas, designated by them as 'Vĭ-pĭ-sĕt' (great-grandparents), or 'Ho-ho-qŏm' (the extinct ones). (Ci-vă-nŏ had twenty wives, etc. ['Each of whom wore on her head, like a headdress, the peculiar half-hood, half-basket contrivance called Ki'-jo.' Papers Archeol. Inst., IV, 463.]) At one time the Casa Grande was beset by enemies, who came from the east in several bodies, and who caused its abandonment; but the settlements at Zacaton, Casa Blanca, etc., still remained, and there is even a tale ['It is even said that the people of Zacaton made war upon their kindred at Casa Blanca and blockaded that settlement by constructing a thorny hedge around it. Through the artifices of the medicine-men the hedge turned into a circle of snakes.' Papers Archeol. Inst., IV, 464] of intertribal war between the Pimas of Zacaton and those of Casa Blanca after the ruin of Casa Grande. Finally, the pueblos fell one after the other, until the Pimas, driven from their homes, and moreover decimated by a fearful plague, became reduced to a small tribe. A portion of them moved south into Sonora, where they still reside, but the main body remained on the site of their former prosperity. I asked particularly why they did not again build houses with solid walls like those of their ancestors. The reply was that they were too weak in numbers to attempt it, and had accustomed themselves to their present mode of living. But the construction of their winter houses— a regular pueblo roof bent to the ground over a central scaffold—their organization and arts, all bear testimony to the truth of their sad tale, that of a powerful sedentary tribe reduced to distress and decadence in architecture long before the advent of the Spaniards." Bandelier in Fifth Ann. Rep. Archeol. Inst. Am., 1883–84, 80, 81.

was the prevailing mode of disposing of the dead, as it was also on the lower Gila and the Salt river. Nothing was learned to indicate that the Sobaipuris of the San Pedro practised incineration. If some of the clans of the Hopis or Zuñis are to be identified with the Hohokam of the Gila, as is maintained by some of the most able authorities upon Southwestern archeology,[a] how is the total disappearance of this primal custom to be explained?

There is a strong belief among the Pimas that they came from the east. It is in that quarter that the abode of their dead is located. Their gods dwell there. Their beliefs do not seem to have been influenced in this respect in the least through contact with the tribes of Yuman stock who have sought a paradise in the opposite direction. There are vestiges of a tradition that the Pimas were once overwhelmed by a large force of warriors who came from the east and destroyed nearly all the people and devastated the entire Gila valley. This does not appear to be another version of the account of the invasion by the underworld clans. While the majority of the Pimas declare that their people have always lived where they now are, or that they came from the east, there are some who say that the Hohokam were killed by an invasion from the east before the Pimas came.

The Pimas formerly regarded the ruins with the same reverence or aversion which they felt toward their own burial places. After the excavations made by the Hemenway Expedition on the Salt river, as no disasters followed the disturbance of the dead, they grew less scrupulous and can now readily be hired as workmen to excavate the ruins or ancient cemeteries.

CONTACT WITH SPANIARDS

From the meager records of the Coronado Expedition of 1540–1542 it has been surmised that Chichilticalli was the Casa Grande, but this statement lacks verification. After traversing the entire southern and eastern part of Arizona the writer can not but believe that it is extremely improbable that Coronado saw the Casa Grande and the

---

[a] The earliest mention of the Gila origin of the Hopi theory is that of Garcés: "Also they knew that I was padre ministro of the Pimas, who likewise are their enemies. This hostility had been told me by the old Indians of my mission, by the Gileños, and Coco-Maricopas, from which information I have imagined (he discurrido) that the Moqui nation anciently extended to the Rio Gila itself. I take my stand (fundome, ground myself) in this matter on the ruins that are found from this river as far as the land of the Apaches, and that I have seen between the Sierras de la Florida and San Juan Nepomuzeno. Asking a few years ago some Subaipuris Indians who were living in my mission of San Xavier if they knew who had built those houses whose ruins and fragments of pottery (losa for loza) are still visible—as, on the supposition that neither Pimas nor Apaches knew how to make (such) houses or pottery, no doubt it was done by some other nation—they replied to me that the Moquis had built them, for they alone knew how to do such things, and added that the Apaches who are about the missions are neither numerous nor valiant; that toward the north was where there were many powerful people; 'there went we,' they said, 'to fight in former times (antiguamente); and even though we attained unto their lands we did not surmount the mesas whereon they lived.'" Diary in Coues, On the Trail of a Spanish Pioneer, New York, 1900, II, 386, 387.

neighboring Pima villages.   For a century and a half after that invasion no white man is known to have reached the territory of the Pimas Gileños.

The earliest as well as the most important explorer in the history of Pimería Alta was Father Eusebio Francisco Kino, who, between the years 1687 and 1710, journeyed many a dusty, thirsty league in the eager search for souls.   In 1694 he reached the Casa Grande in company with native guides who had informed him of the existence of the ruin.   Absolutely nothing is known about this expedition except that a mass was said within the walls of Casa Grande.   However, it may be safely inferred that Kino visited the near-by Pima villages.   As the Papagos were at that time also called Pimas it is sometimes difficult to determine what part the true Pimas played in the events chronicled by the padres.   Yet it is probable that they are referred to in the account of the religious festival which was observed in 1698 at Remedios, in Pimería Baja.   Among the visitors were "native chieftains from as far north as the Gila valley."   Then as now the Pimas and Papagos were on a friendly footing, and the character and movements of the Spaniards must have been made known to the Pimas before the latter saw Kino or any other white man.

Kino diligently strove to establish missions among the many tribes that he visited, but was much hampered by lack of funds.   He succeeded in interesting the authorities sufficiently to induce them to send a military expedition to the Gila in 1697 for the purpose of ascertaining the disposition of the Pimas.   The party included 20 soldiers, with 3 officers.   Juan Mateo Mange was sent with Kino to write the official reports of the expedition.   On the upper San Pedro river 30 Sobaipuris joined the party, which followed that stream to the Gila.   They reached the Pima villages on the 21st of November, visiting and for the first time describing the Casa Grande.   The return was by the more direct route of the Santa Cruz valley.   It was by this route also that Kino in September, 1698, again descended to the Pimas with a small party of native guides.   He returned by way of Quijotoa (?) and the Gulf.

Early in 1699 Kino, in company with Mange, made his fourth journey to the Pimas by way of Sonoita and the lower Gila.   The return was by way of the Santa Cruz.

A year later Kino again reached the Gila by a new route.   From a point above the Bend, and hence doubtless among the Pimas, he descended to the mouth and returned to Sonora by way of Sonoita.

In 1702 he made his sixth and last journey to the Pimas, going by way of Sonoita and the lower Gila.   Among the "40,000 gentiles" whom he is said to have baptized there were quite a number of Pimas, but as his sojourn among them was never of more than a few days' duration his influence could not have been very great.   Nevertheless, he gave away great quantities of beads, and as the people already valued highly those of their own manufacture it is probable that they readily accepted Kino's statement that magic power resided in the new beads of glass.   At any rate, the writer has found very old glass beads on all Piman shrines and has no doubt that some of them were brought by Kino. The first horses, also, to reach Pimería were brought by these expeditions.   There is no record of any cattle being brought so far north, though they were generally distributed to the Papago rancherias in Kino's time.

After the death of Kino, in 1711, no Spaniard is known to have reached the Gila or even to have entered Arizona for a period of more than twenty years.   In 1731 two missionaries, Father Felipe Segresser and Juan Bautista Grashoffer, took charge of the missions of San Xavier del Bac and San Miguel de Guevavi and became the first permanent Spanish residents of Arizona.   In 1736–37 Padre Ignacio Javier Keller, of Suamca, made two trips to the Pima villages on the Gila, where he found "that many of the rancherias of Kino's time had been broken up." [a]   Again in 1743 Keller went up to the Pimas and endeavored to penetrate the Apache country to the northward. Communications by means of native messengers indicated a desire on the part of the Hopis to have Jesuit missionaries come to them from Sonora.   The point of greatest interest to us is that any communication should have existed at all.   Keller failed in his attempt on account of the hostility of the Apaches, and Sedelmair, who tried to make the journey in the following year, was unable to induce the Pimas or Maricopas to accompany him.   In 1748 Sedelmair reached the Gila near the mouth of the Salt river and journeyed westward. Of his trip to the Gila in 1750 little is known.

Accounts of these earliest missionaries of course preceded them by means of Papago messengers, who doubtless made clear the distinction between the slave-hunting Spanish adventurers and the Jesuits and Franciscans.   Fortunately for the Pimas they were quite beyond the reach of the former and were so remote from the Sonoran settlements that only the most devout and energetic friars ever reached them.

The first military force to be stationed in Arizona was a garrison of 50 men at Tubac, on the Santa Cruz.   This presidio was moved to Tucson about 1776, and in 1780 the garrison was increased to 75 men. Even when at Tucson the influence of this small force on the Pimas could not have been very great.   Between 1768 and 1776 Padre Francisco Garcés made five trips from San Xavier del Bac to the Pimas and beyond.   The fifth entrada was well described in Garcés's Diary (admirably translated and edited by Elliott Coues under the title "On the Trail of a Spanish Pioneer"), though he exhibited a pitiful waste

---

[a] Bancroft, XVII, 362.

of opportunities for ethnological observation while among the Pimas.[a]
From this time forward until the American occupancy of the Gadsden
Purchase in 1853 the Spanish and Mexican population of Tucson
varied from 500 to 2,000, and there was more or less trade with the
Pimas either at the post or through small trading parties that went
from Tucson to the Gila villages.

---

a Pfefferkorn, who published his Beschreibung der Landschaft Sonora in 1794-95, gives a very full
account of the southern Pima-speaking tribes, but dismisses the "unconverted Pimas" in the following words:

"Hierauf folgen den *Gila* hinunter die noch unbekehrten *Pimas*, welche sich auf beyden Seiten des
Flusses ausbreiten. Dieses Volk ist in drey zahlreiche Gemeinden getheilet: wovon die stärkeste ein
anmüthiges mit Bäumen wohl besetzes Land von 14 Meilen bewohnet; welches durch Wasserleitungen,
die sich wegen dem ebenen Boden mit geringer Mühe aus dem Flusse auf das umliegende Land führen
lassen, befeuchtet, und fruchtbar gemacht werden kann." (Vol. I, p. 6.)

Padre Pedro Font, who accompanied Garcés in 1775, wrote an extended diary of the journey, in which
he devotes a few pages to the Pimas. Following is a translation from a copy of the original manuscript,
pages 48-52:

" First of November: Wednesday.—I said mass, which was attended by some Gileños Indians who
happened to be there and who gave evidence of considerable attention, good behaviour, and silence. They
sought to imitate the Christians in crossing themselves, which they did awkwardly enough, and in
other things. We left the Laguna (Lagoon) at half-past nine in the morning, and at one o'clock in the
afternoon we reached the town of San Juan Capistrano de Uturituc, after having travelled four leagues
towards the west-northwest. This town consists of small lodges of the kind that the Gileños use. We
were received by the Indians, whom I estimated to be about a thousand in number. They were drawn
up in two rows, the men on one side and the women on the other. After we had dismounted they all
came in turn to salute us and offered their hand to the Commander and the three Fathers, men and
women, children and adults. Indeed they all gave token of much satisfaction at seeing us, touching
their breast with their hand, naming God, and using many other expressions of benevolence. In short,
their salutation was most lengthy, for almost every one of them bowed to us, saying: "Dios ato m' busi-
boy," as do the Pimas Christians of Pimería alta, which signifies "May God aid us." We, on our part,
must needs return their salutations. They lodged us in a large hut, which they constructed to that end,
and in front of it they placed a large cross, Pagans though they were. The river being somewhat distant, the Governor ordered his wives to bring water, which they straightway carried to his lodge for
the people. These Pimas Gileños are gentle and kind-hearted Indians. In order to fête our arrival
they sought permission of the Commander to dance, and soon the women were moving from mess to
mess, dancing after their fashion with hands clasped. In short, the whole people gave token of great
pleasure at seeing us in their country, and some of them even offered us their little ones to be baptized.
This we did not do, being desirous of proceeding with circumspection, although we sought to comfort
them with good hopes. In the afternoon I went to the town with Father Garcés and the Governor,
Papago de Cojat, to see the fields. These *milpas* are enclosed by stakes, cultivated in sections, with
five canals or draws, and are excessively clean. They are close by the town on the banks of the river,
which is large only in the season of the freshets. At that time its water was so low that an Indian who
entered and crossed it had the water but halfway up his leg. From what they have told me, this is the
reason they had not yet made their sowing, for inasmuch as the river was so low the water could not
enter the canals. They also told me that to remedy this need they were all anxious to come together for a
council, and had already thought of sinking many stakes and branches into the river to raise the water
so that it might enter the drains; this industry on their part is a proof of their devotion to toil and
shows that they are not restless and nomad like other races, for to maintain themselves in their towns
with their fields they themselves have contrived to hold and control the river. I also saw how they
wove cloaks of cotton, a product which they sew and spin; and the greater number of them know
how to weave. They own some large-sized sheep whose wool is good, and also Castilian fowl. These
Indians are somewhat heavy in build, very ugly and dark, the women much more so than the men.
Moreover, perchance on account of their excessive eating of *pechita*, which is the husk of the crushed
mesquite made into a gruel, of screw bean, grass seed, and other coarse foods, a very foul odor may be
noticed when they are gathered in groups. This evening the Commander presented them all with
tobacco, beads, and glass trinkets, wherewith they were highly pleased. The distribution of these
things lasted until night.

2nd Day: Thursday.—We began to say mass very early in the morning, and with the sacred vestments
I carried with me and with those which Father Garcés brought from Tubac to use in Colorado river,
we erected two altars. It being All-Souls day, we three Religious said nine masses. It was, moreover,
a most notable and unheard of thing that in the river Gila so many masses should be said. They were
attended by a goodly number of Indians, who preserved the utmost decorum and silence. We left the
town of Uturituc at eleven o'clock in the morning, and about three in the afternoon we halted on the

RELATIONS WITH AMERICANS

CIVIL AND MILITARY EXPEDITIONS

Early in the nineteenth century American beaver trappers began
to penetrate through the Apache-infested mountains that bordered
Pimería on the north and east. Beaver were then fairly abundant in
the mountain streams and down the Colorado Grande to the very end
in the burning lowlands. The annals of the Pimas make no mention
of these earliest visitors from the United States, but it is known that
several parties reached the "Pimos Gileños," who were found uniformly friendly. The Patties, father and son, journeyed from the
Rio Grande to trap beaver in the Gila country between 1825 and 1828,
and in the latter year pushed on to California.[a] Kit Carson, with a
party of trappers, returned from his first trip to California by this
route during the winter of 1829–30. The famous trapper, Paul
Weaver, inscribed his name on the walls of Casa Grande in 1833.[b]

Besides the self-reliant and well-armed trappers, a few parties of
settlers made their way to California through the Gila valley while it
was yet in the possession of the Mexicans, though the best-known
route was then north of the Colorado canyon. With the opening of
the new era of American ownership began the journeys of surveyors
and explorers. The first military invasion was by General Kearney,
with a party of 200 troopers, in 1846. Emory's excellent Notes of a
Military Reconnoissance and Johnston's Journal give details of this
journey with the first reliable information concerning the Pimas.
Kearney was followed by Lieutenant-Colonel Cooke in command of
the Mormon battalion, which opened a practicable wagon road to
California by way of Tucson and the Pima villages. In his official
report Colonel Cooke states:

> I halted one day near the villages of this friendly, guileless, and singularly inno-
> cent and cheerful people, the Pimos. They were indeed friendly, for they refused
> to surrender supplies that had been left at the villages to be held for the Mormon
> battalion, and they threatened armed resistance to the Mexicans who demanded the
> mules and goods.

---

banks of the river Gila near the town of the Incarnation of Sutaquison, having journeyed more than
four leagues towards the west and a quarter northwest. The Indians of the town came out to receive
us and saluted us with tokens of great joy. Their number I estimated to be five hundred souls. On our
way we passed through two other small towns. In this limited territory lies almost all the land occupied
by the tribe of the Pimas Gileños. The soil here is very poor and raises a very sticky dust, on account of
which and their wretched food the Indians are very ugly, dirty, and repulsive. The river Gila was dry
in this region, so they obtained their water by digging wells in the sand. It is only during the season of
freshets that the river is of any service for the seed lands and fields of the Indians. The banks of the
river are covered with a grove of undersized cottonwood trees. In the evening tobacco was distributed among the Indians and glass beads were promised the women for the following day. We asked
the Indians why they lived so far from the river, for formerly they had their town on its banks. They
replied that they had changed its site because on account of the groves and woods on its banks they
could defend themselves but ill against the Apaches, but that by living apart from the river they were
able to have a clear field for pursuing and killing the Apaches when they came against their town."

a Pattie's Personal Narrative.

b J. R. Browne, Adventures in the Apache Country, New York, 1869, 118.

A battalion of dragoons under Maj. L. P. Graham marched westward to California by way of the Pima villages in 1848. Bancroft states that he has a manuscript diary from Capt. Cave J. Coutts, of this battalion, in which it is recorded that the Pimas were very hospitable and exhibited conspicuous signs of thrift.[a]

The parties of the Boundary Survey Commissioners passed down the Gila in 1851, and the account of the Pimas by J. R. Bartlett, the American commissioner, is by far the best that has been published thus far.[b] Bartlett's party returned eastward through the Pima villages in 1852.

In 1854 Lieuts. J. G. Parke[c] and George Stoneman began at the Pima villages the survey for a railroad which was destined to pass through just a quarter of a century later. In 1855 Lieutenant Parke, with another party, made a second survey and again visited the villages.

From the time of the discovery of gold in California, in 1849, parties of gold seekers, numbering in all many thousand persons each year, followed the Gila route, meeting with hospitality from the Pimas and almost equally uniform hostility from the Apaches. The location of the Pimas in the midst of the 280-mile stretch between Tucson and Yuma was a peculiarly fortunate one for the travelers, who could count upon supplies and if need be protection at a point where their journey otherwise must have been most perilous.[d]

The United States Government first recognized the value of the assistance rendered by the Pimas when by act of Congress of February 28, 1859, $1,000 was appropriated for a survey of their lands and $10,000 for gifts.[e]

---

[a] History of Arizona and New Mexico, 479.

[b] Personal Narrative, 1854, 2 vols.

[c] " Their chiefs and old men were all eloquent in professions of friendship for the Americans and were equally desirous that we should read the certificates of good offices rendered various parties while passing through their country." Pacific Railroad Report, II, 5.

[d] " Since the year 1849 [they] have acted in the capacity of and with even more efficiency than a frontier military. They have protected American emigrants from molestation by Apaches, and when the latter have stolen stock from the emigrants, the Pimos and Maricopas have punished them and recovered their animals. Yet in all this time [ten years] nothing has been done for them by our Government." Extract from a letter in the Alta California, June 28, 1858, quoted in S. Ex. Doc. 1, pt. 1, 556, 35th Cong., 2d sess., 1859.

"A company of nearly one hundred of their best warriors was enlisted into the United States service in the latter part of 1865, which served one year with great credit to themselves and did much good service in quelling our common enemy. Seventy of them have just been mustered out [1867] of the United States service, after having performed six months' duty as spies and scouts, for which service they are invaluable." Report of Commissioner of Indian Affairs, 1867, 163.

[e] Following is a list of the articles distributed among the Pimas and Maricopas, as reported by Mowry:

444 axes.	36 hammers.	3 pairs tongs.
618 shovels.	48 rakes.	1 set stock and dies.
31 hand saws.	48 trowels.	12 file handles.
706 butcher knives.	12 screw-drivers.	36 hatchets.
516 hoes.	1 " carpenter shop."	120 picks.
240 sickles.	15 plows.	7 kegs nails.
48 files.	15 sets plow harness.	9 gross screws.
270 harrow teeth.	1 forge.	1,400 needles.
48 mattocks.	1 anvil.	1 box sheet tin.
72 whetstones.	1 vise.	4,000 pounds barley.
15 grindstones.	1 set sledges.	1 pint turnip seed.
36 hay forks.	1 cast-steel hand hammer.	

Mowry explains that a larger number of plows would have been included in this lot of tools and imple-

Maricopa Wells, near the lower villages, became an important stage station when the overland mails began to pass late in the fifties.[a]

With the advent of the stage, the emigrant and the military trains began the breaking down of the best that was old and the building up of the worst that was new. For a period of thirty years, or from 1850 to 1880, the Pimas were visited by some of the vilest specimens of humanity that the white race has produced. Until 1871 the tribe was without a teacher, missionary, or, to judge from their own story and the records of the Government, a competent agent. Bancroft has thus summarized the conditions prevailing during that period:

In many respects there has been a sad deterioration during forty years of contact with civilization, notably by acquiring habits of intemperance, prostitution, and pilfering; yet they are still vastly superior to most other tribes. For several years, from 1868, serious troubles with them seemed imminent. Presuming on their military services and past immunity from all restraint, they became insolent and aggressive, straying from the reservation, robbing travelers, refusing all satisfaction for inroads of their horses on the settlers' fields, the young men being beyond the chiefs' control. Swindling traders had established themselves near the villages to buy the Indians' grain at their own prices, and even manipulate Government goods, the illegal traffic receiving no check, but rather apparently protection from the Territorial authorities. Whiskey was bought from Adamsville or from itinerant Mexicans; the agents were incompetent, or at least had no influence, the military refused support or became involved in profitless controversies. Worst of all, white settlers on the Gila used so much of the water that the Pimas in dry years had to leave the reservation or starve. General Howard deemed the difficulties insurmountable, and urged removal. Had it not been for dread of the Pima numbers and valor, the Apaches still being hostile, very likely there might have been a disastrous outbreak.[b]

As early as 1859 Lieut. Sylvester Mowry, special agent, Indian Bureau, foresaw danger threatening the interests of the Pimas and wrote:

There are some fine lands on the Gila and any extensive cultivation above the Indian fields will cause trouble about the water for irrigation and inevitably bring about a collision between the settlers and the Indians.[c]

Again in 1862 Poston gave additional warning:

If in the eager rush for farms or embryo cities the land above them should be occupied by Americans, and their supply of water be reduced, it might produce discontent.[d]

---

ments had not the Indian Department distributed a few plows a short time previously. (S. Ex. Doc. 2, 723, 36th Cong., 1st sess., 1859.) The gifts were d'stributed by Lieut. Mowry and the survey was made under his direction by Col. A. B. Gray.

This original survey contained 64,000 acres—much less than the Pimas claimed and actually required for their fields and grazing lands. The commissioners who negotiated with them assured the tribe that the present boundaries were but temporary limits to protect the people in their rights, and that the Government would enlarge the reservation later. This promise was made good by a survey in 1869, which added 81,140.16 acres (U. S. Statutes at Large, 1869, II, 401). In 1876 9,000 acres about the village of Blackwater were added to the eastern end of the reservation.

[a] " In August and September, 1857, the San Antonio and San Diego semimonthly stage line, under the direction of I. C. Woods, was established, James Burch acting as contractor. This continued till the Butterfield semiweekly line was put upon the route, in August, 1858, under a contract of six years with the Postmaster-General, at $600,000 a year." J. R. Browne, Adventures in the Apache Country, 19. The journey of nearly 2,500 miles was made in from twenty to twenty-two days.

[b] Bancroft's Works, XVII, 548.

[c] S. Ex. Doc. 2, 727, 36th Cong., 1st sess., 1859.

[d] Report of Commissioner of Indian Affairs 1863, 386, 1864.

Agent R. G. Wheeler protested against the diversion of the water of the Gila from the Pima reservation at the time the Florence canal was projected in 1886 and succeeded in gaining the attention of the Department of the Interior which instructed the Director of the Geological Survey to investigate the matter. As a result of the investigation the following facts were established:

(1) That the water supply of the Pima and Maricopa reservations under present conditions is no more than sufficient for the wants of the Indians.

(2) That the construction of a dam by the Florence Canal Company of the character represented in the correspondence will give the control substantially of all the waters of the Gila river.

(4) That if the water supply from the river be shut off, the Indian reservation would become uninhabitable.

Other facts were presented, but these are the essential ones that directly concern us here. [a] Notwithstanding the above finding, no effective efforts were made to prevent the water from being diverted from the reservation, and the result was nearly as predicted—a result that should bring a blush of shame to every true American. A thrifty, industrious, and peaceful people that had been in effect a friendly nation rendering succor and assistance to emigrants and troops for many years when they sorely needed it was deprived of the rights inhering from centuries of residence. The marvel is that the starvation, despair, and dissipation that resulted did not overwhelm the tribe.

AGENTS

In 1857 John Walker was appointed Indian agent for the territory embraced in the Gadsden Purchase, with headquarters at Tucson. The Pimas were of course within his territory, though his control over them could not have been very great with the agency separated from the villages by a 90-mile stretch of desert in the scarcely disputed possession of the Apaches. Walker presented no report to his superior at Santa Fé in 1858, but in 1859 gave some account of the condition of the Pimas.

In 1864 Charles D. Poston was appointed superintendent of Indian affairs for Arizona, but he resigned that year. He was succeeded by four others during the next eight years, at the end of which period the office was abolished. Abraham Lyons was appointed agent for the Pimas in 1862, and he also lived at Tucson. Ammi M. White, appointed in 1864, was a resident trader. He had built a mill at Casa Blanca, which was destroyed by the flood of September, 1868. Levi Ruggles, appointed in 1866, administered affairs from Tucson. During 1867 C. H. Lord acted as deputy agent. Fairly adequate adobe buildings were erected for the agent at Sacaton in 1870, and the agents

---

[a] U. S. Geol. Surv., Water-Supply and Irrigation Papers, no. 33, p. 10.

thereafter resided at that place. The present commodious dwelling was erected in 1883. Following is a list of the later agents, with the dates of their appointment:

Capt. F. E. Grossman, 1869.
J. H. Stout, 1871–1875, 1877–78.
Charles Hudson, 1876.
A. B. Ludlam, 1879.
E. B. Townsend, 1881.
R. G. Wheeler, 1881.
A. H. Jackson, 1882.

R. G. Wheeler, 1885.
C. M. Johnson, 1888.
C. W. Crouse, 1889.
J. R. Young, 1893.
Henry J. Cleveland, 1897.
Elwood Hadley, 1898.
J. B. Alexander, 1902.

SCHOOLS

The first school (pl. v, *b*) among the Pimas was opened by Rev. C. H. Cook, in the employ of the Government, February 18, 1871, in an adobe building about 2 miles west of the present agency of Sacaton. This day school had a good attendance from the first, and much of the present beneficial influence of the missionary may be ascribed to the command over the children which he obtained during the seven years that he occupied the position of teacher. The change to a boarding school located at the agency was made in 1881, and a Mr Armstrong was the first superintendent. The school buildings were destroyed by fire in November, 1888, and the mission church was occupied during the remainder of that year. The capacity of the school is now 225, though during our stay at Sacaton more than 300 were crowded in. Two and three children were apportioned to sleep in narrow single beds and even in the hospital the beds were overcrowded. For years the accommodations have been inadequate to receive all the children that desired education. Day schools at Gila Crossing and Salt River take care of a few, and three or four new buildings for day schools have been erected at Blackwater, Lehi, Maricopa, and Casa Blanca.

ANNALS

CHRONOLOGICAL RECORDS

Three chronological records have thus far been preserved from among the many that are supposed to have existed among the American tribes. The first of these to be published was the Walum Olam of the Delawares, the definitive edition of which was published by D. G. Brinton.[a] In 1877 Col. Garrick Mallery brought to light the "Lone-dog winter count" of the Sioux and subsequently secured several other records from the same tribe.[b] Recently James Mooney

---

[a] The Lenape and their Legends, Brinton's Library of Aboriginal American Literature, v, 1885.

[b] A Calendar of the Dakota Nation, Bulletin U. S. Geol. Surv., III, no. 1; also Fourth and Tenth Annual Reports of the Bureau of Ethnology.

has published a series of Kiowa calendars that resemble those of the Sioux, but are more distinctly calendric.[a]

In addition to these published records we have references to yet others that have wholly disappeared; references that can not now be verified. For example, the Iroquois are said [b] to have maintained a record of their exploits in war by means of war posts on which notches indicated the occurrence of campaigns and conventional characters denoted the number of scalps and captives taken. Events of a certain class were thus recorded in chronologic order. Among the Santee Sioux Clark [c] found a notched stick which he was assured represented the history of the tribe for more than a thousand years. Mooney suggests that this must have been used in connection with a chant similar to that accompanying the Walum Olam. However, it seems extremely improbable that any record should have survived the vicissitudes of an Indian camp for so long a period. The use of notched sticks for mere numeration is common enough in all cultures and among all peoples, but such a use as that made by the Santees is not, so far as known, mentioned elsewhere in the literature.

The writer was therefore greatly interested to discover no fewer than five notched calendar sticks among the Pimas. Two sticks were "told" to him by their possessors. The record covers a period of seventy years, dating from the season preceding the meteoric shower of November 13, 1833, as do the oldest of those discovered among the Kiowa. There are traditions of older sticks that have been lost or buried with their keepers. Juan Thomas, of the village of Blackwater, had lost his stick in some inexplicable manner, but he was continuing the history with pencil and paper, thus rendering it more nearly comparable to the calendars of the Plains tribes. It is noteworthy that the change from stick to paper introduced a tendency to use pictorial symbols rather than merely mnemonic characters, such as are most easily incised on the surface of a stick having clearly marked grain. Among the sticks there is an evident increase in the number and elaboration of characters which may be attributed to contact with the whites, though not to their direct influence, as the existence of the calendars has been almost entirely unknown to them.

The year begins with the saguaro harvest, about the month of June. At that time, also, the mesquite beans are ripening, as well as the cultivated crops. It is the season of feasting and rejoicing. No other annual occurrence can compare in importance with these festivities, so that it is not surprising that the years should be counted by harvests. The Lower California tribes, as described by Baegert

---

a Calendar History of the Kiowa, Seventeenth Annual Report of the Bureau of American Ethnology.
b J. E. Seaver, A Narrative of the Life of Mrs. Mary Jemison, 70; cited by Mallery.
c The Indian Sign Language, 211, 1885; cited by Mooney.

more than a century ago, similarly numbered the years.   A space of
three years would be expressed by the term "three pitahayas,"
" yet they seldom make use of such phrases." [a]

THE PIMA CALENDAR

It is said that when Elder Brother was leaving Pimería for the last
time he told the people to count the tail feathers of the little bird,
Gisap, which are twelve in number, and that they should divide the
year into that number of parts.   He gave them names for these
parts, except for the coldest and the hottest months.   The writer is
disposed to regard the recognition of the "moons" as of recent origin.
Not many have any names for them and these do not agree even in
the same village.   For example, the list of months given by the chief is
quite different from that furnished by Kâ'mâl tkâk, and also contains
references to wheat, which is of course modern.

The months according to Kâ'mâl tkâk.	*The months according to Antonio Azul.*
1. Harsany paihitak marsat, Saguaro harvest moon.	1. Peɬkan^y paihitak marsat, Wheat harvest moon.
2. Tcokiapĭk, Rainy.	2. Harsany paihitak, Saguaro harvest.
3. Rsopol usapĭk, Short planting.	3. Tcokiapĭk, Rainy.
4. Varsa kakatak, Dry grass.	4. Rsopol ʋsapĭk, Short planting.
5. Hʋhokiapkʽ, Winter begins.	5. Varsa kakatak, Dry grass.
6. Oam, Yellow.	6. Vi-ihainyĭk, Windy.
7. Kâ-âmak, Leaves falling.	7. Ovalĭk, Smell.
8. Aʋfpa hiâsĭk, Cottonwood flowers.	8. Kʋ-ʋtco sʽhʋpitcĭk, Big winter.
9. Aʋfpa i-ivakitak, Cottonwood leaves.	9. Kâmaki, Gray.
10. Koĭ i-ivakitak, Mesquite leaves.	10. Tcʋ-ʋtaki, Green.
11. Koĭ hiâsĭk, Mesquite flowers.	11. Oam, Yellow.
12. Kai tcokolĭk, Black seeds on saguaros.	12. Kâ-âk, Strong.

As they have no winters the Pimas naturally do not have a "winter
count."   As there are two rainy seasons and neither is of any consequence as a general rule, while both are sometimes wanting alto-
gether, they could not be expected to mark the flight of years by the
recurrence of the rains.   There are but two seasons in the Gila valley,
one of torrid heat [b] and one of ideal weather throughout the remainder
of the year.   The onset of the former coincides with the harvest season
and the new year is therefore adapted, albeit unwittingly, to seasonal
change.   The year mark is invariably a deep notch across the stick.

The records of the early years are memorized and there are few
minor notches to aid in recalling them.   The year notches are exactly
alike, yet on asking a narrator to go back and repeat the story for
a certain year the writer found that he never made a mistake.   Taking the stick in hand he would rake his thumb nail across the year

---

[a] The aboriginal inhabitants of the Californian Peninsula in Smithsonian Report, 1864, 388.
[b] Maximum temperature recorded for a period of nineteen years at Phoenix was 119° F.   Report
of Chief of Weather Bureau, 1900-1901, I.

notch and begin: "That notch means," etc. The interpreter, either through imitation or because of the same mode of thought, would then take the stick and dig his thumb into the same notch before repeating the story in English. Both seemed to endow the stick and the particular notch with a definite personality in their minds. That notch looked exactly like its neighbors but it stood for something different, which was apparently recalled as much by the sense of touch as by that of sight.

Dots or shallow circular pits and short notches are the most common symbols on the sticks. These have no distinctive meaning, and are used for recording a great variety of events. The human figure is freely used, and may signify that a man killed Apaches or was killed by them, that he was bitten by a rattlesnake, struck by lightning, or, in short, any event relating to a man in any manner may be denoted by this symbol. The date of building railways was recorded by an ideogram, representing rails and ties. Only one symbol had come arbitrarily to designate a single event. This is the T which was used to record the "tizwin drunks," or festivals at which saguaro or agave liquor was brewed and freely imbibed.

NATURE OF THE EVENTS

It has been frequently observed that the records of the American Indians contain much that is trivial and oftentimes omit that which is important. There are obvious reasons for this that have been adequately set forth by Mallery,[a] and it must also be borne in mind that the relative importance of an event differs according as it is viewed by Caucasian eyes or by those of the American Indian. Judging by the early portions of the records, the conclusion might be reached that the purpose was to secure chronologic sequence, though the Pimas are not known to have had ceremonies that by their infrequent recurrence would require calendric regulation. However, the later years are so filled with events that the primary purpose is clearly narrative. They are therefore to be designated annals, rather than calendars. Moreover, the years are never named. "In this year the crops failed;" "In this year the floods overspread the whole valley," etc., but never, "This is the famine year" or "This is the flood year." Upon analysis the events recorded are found to be distributed as follows:

Battles or skirmishes.. 66
Infrequent phenomena, eclipses, floods, earthquakes, etc....................... 14
Famines and years of abundance... 5
Epidemics.. 11
Accidents, rattlesnake bite, lightning stroke, etc............................. 13
Events relating to whites, but not to Pimas.................................... 19

---

[a] Tenth Annual Report of the Bureau of Ethnology, 271.

THE NARRATIVE

1833–34

Gila Crossing, Salt River. During the moon preceding the meteoric shower the Yumas, armed with clubs, bows, and arrows, attacked the Maricopa village. The Yumas surprised the Maricopas and captured their women, whom they surrounded and tried to take away with them. They were about to cross the Gila with their captives when the Pimas arrived and attacked them. The women took advantage of the confusion to escape into the chaparral. The Yumas fought bravely, but they were overpowered by numbers and few escaped to tell of their defeat.

In the early winter[a] the meteoric shower took place. This event was followed by heavy rains that caused floods in the Salt and Gila rivers. The spectacle of falling stars was to the Pimas an augury of disaster, and the succeeding floods were regarded as a punishment for sins which they had committed. What the sins might be they did not know, but concluded that they must have offended some medicine-man who possessed great magic power. Many thought it must be the medicine-man Kaku who brought this calamity upon them because they had not shown him the respect that he thought was due him. It is said that when the flood was at its height he climbed a cottonwood tree and thence proclaimed in a loud voice that he would perform certain miracles that would prove disastrous to them if they did not listen to him and show him respect.

Others declared that the floods were caused by the two sons of an old goddess, Takwa-artam. When she saw the flood threatening to overwhelm the Pimas and Maricopas she said to her sons: "Give me back my milk and then you can drown my people. The land is yet what it was when it was new." This puzzled the two brothers. They knew that they could not return the milk that had nourished them in infancy, so they did not allow the flood to rise any higher, but caused it to go down.

1834–35

Salt River. This year was long remembered because of the bountiful crops of wheat, corn, squashes, pumpkins, and watermelons that were raised. The desert mesas were carpeted with flowers and the

---

a November 13, 1833.

bloom of cacti further transformed them into gardens. "Our people worshiped the gods in grateful recognition for their protection; we danced unmolested by the murderous Apaches; we looked after the welfare of our households."

1835–36

Gila Crossing, Salt River. One summer afternoon when only women and old men were at home, the Apaches came and killed two Pimas, a man who was irrigating his field and a boy who was hunting doves. That morning the younger men of the village of Rsânûk had planned to have a rabbit hunt toward the north, but when the crier gave the final announcement it was to hunt toward the south. Thus it was that one side of the village had been left unprotected, and when the fighting men returned it was too late to follow the raiders and the revenge was postponed.

1836–37

Salt River. At the beginning of this year the fruit of the giant cactus was gathered and a large quantity of liquor prepared from it. All the men became intoxicated—too drunk to be on their guard against an attack from the Apaches. Early in the morning a woman started toward the hills to gather cactus fruit. She had not gone far when she saw a man mount a horse and start toward her. She suspected danger and walked backward for some distance before turning to flee. She got halfway to the village before she was overtaken by the Apache, with whom she struggled so desperately as to raise a cloud of dust. Those who were somewhat sober hastened toward the place, but too late to rescue the woman from being roped and dragged to death. However, they overtook the party of Apaches and killed five of them. Upon examining the dead Apaches it was found that their bodies were protected with rawhide armor; then the Pimas understood why their arrows had glanced off or jumped back.

Gila Crossing, Salt River. A year passed without a visit from the marauding Apaches. "We tilled our fields, danced our war dances, sang songs, kept up target practice, and exercised in the use of the shield."

1837–38

Gila Crossing, Salt River. One cold night in the spring a Pima at Rso'tûk was irrigating his wheat field by moonlight. Without thought of enemies he built a fire to warm himself. This the Apaches saw and came about him in the thicket. Hearing the twigs cracking under their feet, he ran to the village and gave the alarm. The Pimas gathered in sufficient numbers to surround the Apaches, who attempted to reach the hills on their horses. Two horses stumbled into a gully, and their riders were killed before they could extricate themselves. The others were followed and all killed. "This was the only event of the year, and our people were undisturbed further in the practice of their customs."

1838–39

Salt River. Late in the spring a party of Pimas went to Tucson to buy clothing and other needed supplies. On their return they were ambushed and barely escaped massacre. The Apaches had concealed themselves on either side of the trail, and when the attack was suddenly made the Pimas were at first panic-stricken, but recovered sufficiently to repel their assailants, with the loss, however, of two men killed and a boy captured. This youth is said to have been a very handsome fellow, skillful in the use of the bow and arrow. Fearing a renewal of the conflict, the Pimas hastened home.

A few months later they obtained their revenge upon a party of Apaches who came to the villages to steal horses. The enemy were seen and chased across the river. On the way they were met by a party of Pimas, returning from a council, who called out to the approaching horsemen to ask who they were; on receiving no answer they shot one of them. An Apache called "Slender Leg" was pushed off his mule and two Pimas jumped off their horses and tried to hold him, but he was too strong for them and they had to tie him. He was taken to the well-swept plaza of the village, according to the Salt River calendar, or to an open alkali flat near the villages, as stated by the Gila Crossing annalist, where the people gathered and danced and sang around him. Two widows of men killed in an ambuscade earlier in the season walked four times around the outside of the circle of dancers, and then passed inside as an avenue was opened for them. They carried long clubs of mesquite, with which they beat the captive into insensibility.

1839–41

There are no events recorded for these two years on either of the two sticks that date back thus far.

1841–42

Gila Crossing, Salt River. The Maricopas of the village of Masakimûlt, accompanied by one Pima, went on a campaign against the Yumas. The enemy gathered to meet them and sent a messenger to tell them that they should leave aside their knives and bows and fight only with sticks. The Maricopas agreed to this, but the Pima said he had made his bow and arrows to use on the enemy and he would keep them in his own hands. The Yuma messenger showed the Maricopas where to cross the Colorado river and conducted them to the assembled Yumas on the farther side. It was agreed that four from each side should engage in the combat, using sharp sticks about 6 feet long (lances) instead of the customary war club.

Four times each squad ran in a semicircle near the enemy's line; four times they approached each other before the fight began. At the first onslaught three Maricopas and two Yumas were killed; the Yumas killed the surviving Maricopa and retired to their line.

Then Pantatûk, "bravest of the Maricopas," ran his horse through the entire party of Yumas, striking many with his lance before being caught in the line of women behind the warriors. Kâûtci Pai, Hawk-tail, also rode through the Yuma lines, and is living to-day (1902).

Tcʊwʊt Hakûtäny, Earth-crack, challenged a Yuma to single combat and was wounded, but recovered.

Then the fight became general, most of the Maricopas being killed. Many Yumas were also killed. The Pima killed so many with his arrows that they could not reach him with their lances, and he escaped, as did some Maricopas, and they reached home in safety. Ââpap Anton, Maricopa Antoine (pl. XLIII, b) also kept his bow and arrows, and when closely pressed by the Yumas exclaimed in the Pima language: "You can not catch me!" which somewhat confused his enemies and enabled him to escape.

1842–43

Salt River. In the autumn the Yumas again came to attack the Maricopa village, but did not attempt to surprise it. They formed in line of battle opposite the line of Maricopas, who were equally courageous. The war chiefs stood between the lines. Each man was armed with a club only. The Yuma chief said to his opponent: "I am ready to have you strike me first if you can." The Maricopa chief answered: "It is for me to let you try your club on me, because you want to kill me, and you have traveled far to satisfy your heart." In the personal combat which ensued the Yuma was killed, the sharp end of his opponent's club piercing his side. Then the fight became general, each attacking the man opposite him in the line. There were some Mohave Apaches with the Yumas who fought with bows and arrows. When they saw the line of Yumas wavering, they deserted them. The Yumas retreated some distance and again made a stand, and the fight ended in an indecisive manner, with perhaps a greater loss to the Maricopas than to the Yumas. After the fight the Mohaves wanted to scalp the dead enemy, but the Yuma chief said no, they might scalp some Yumas by mistake, and they must wait until these had been gathered from the field.

1843–44

Salt River. In the spring the Maricopas, Pimas, and Cocopas went
on a campaign against the Apaches. They were scouting through
the Verde valley west of the Four Peaks one afternoon when they
saw a small band of the enemy. They were unable to overtake the
Apaches, who kept sending up signal smokes. The next morning
the number of Apaches had increased and formed a circular line,
which attacked the allies, who lost two men, father and son.

Four days later a woman went with her daughter to gather cactus
fruit for drying. She was accompanied by her husband, who went
as a guard. While she was busy gathering the spiny cactus, she heard
a step and, turning, saw an Apache. She screamed for help and told
her daughter to run to the village and give the alarm. The husband
was hunting near at hand, but was too far away to rescue his wife.
The little girl brought the men of the village, but they could find no
trace of the enemy.

A few days later the Apaches killed a party of Pimas who had gone
to the mountains to gather mescal. The Pimas had planned to go
to the Kwahadk͓ camp, but changed their minds and camped opposite them. The Apaches sent down scouts from the hills to see how
many there were at the place where the smoke from the mescal pits
was seen. It was a night attack and many Pimas never wakened
to see another day; only one escaped to tell the Kwahadk͓s of the
massacre. They followed the trail of the Apaches but did not overtake them. The dead were buried there by the Kwahadk͓s, who knew
the Pimas well.

In the summer, when the watermelons were ripe, a large force of
Yumas came to attack the Pimas and Maricopas. Their coming was
heralded by messengers, who said they were advancing in great
numbers as gaily as for a dance. The Maricopas were ready to meet
them, but the Pimas were not. The Maricopas went out to engage
the enemy and check their advance while the women got out of the
way. The Yumas were driven back, but the Maricopas lost two of
their bravest warriors.

1844–45

Salt River. The next year the Yumas and Mohaves came to attack
the Maricopa village. The fight was undecided, but the enemy retreated. One Pima and several Maricopas were killed.

Gila Crossing, Salt River. A plague swept through all the tribes
during this year. Those stricken with it usually died within twenty-
four hours, but if they recovered they were well again in three days.
From 4 to 10 died each day. The people of Akûtcĭny came to the
Gila and the Gila villagers fled into the desert. The [cholera or]

tcoko vihâsĭk, "black vomit,"[a] as it was called, brought all the medicine-men not in the best repute under suspicion.   Four were killed,
and the surviving medicine-men were kept busy guarding the camps
against the plague.

¶   *Gila Crossing.* During the winter, when ice was on the water and
snow was evenly sprinkled on the lowlands, the Apaches came to
the village of Rsânûk, where one of the marauders was killed.
The Apaches, accompanied by the Päsĭnâ tribe from the north,
attacked the Papagos at Kihotoak (Quijotoa) in April as the mesquites
were changing from bud to leaf.   The Apaches advanced with drums
beating and with cries like the howl of the coyote.   The Papagos were
few in number, so they concealed their women in a cave and sought
to protect them by fighting outside, but the enemy had firearms and
all the Papagos fell in the futile attempt to preserve their loved ones
from slavery.   There yet lives a Pima who was shot through the
leg and left for dead on the field of this battle.   Many Apaches were
wounded but none were killed.

1845–46

¶   *Gila Crossing.*   A party of Apaches was encamped on Mo'hatûk
mountain, and two of them came to steal corn from the fields
at Gila Crossing.   The theft was discovered and three Pimas lay in
wait for the thieves.   When they again entered the field those lying
in wait sprang upon them and killed one; the other escaped.

Salt River.   During the winter the Pimas went on a campaign
against the Apaches, several of whom were killed.   The attacks were
made at night and the enemy were killed before they could defend
themselves.   One Pima was killed and one wounded so severely that
he died after returning home.

In the spring the Apaches waylaid a party of Pimas who were
returning from a mescal-gathering expedition in the mountains.
Nearly all the party were killed and two girls were made prisoners.
The Apaches were followed, most of them killed, and the girls rescued
by a party from the villages.

1846–47

¶   *Gila Crossing.*   Three Apaches were going toward the Papago village near Mââtcpät, or Table mountain, when a Pima, coming to
the Gila river, crossed it and discovered their trail.   A party went in
pursuit and succeeded in killing all three.   Kâ'mâl tkâk's brother was
in this party of Pimas and was himself killed a few days later in an

---

[a] "Aquellas gentes y sus ministros gozan por lo general de buena salud: entre los naturales pasan
muchos de cien años, excepto los pimas altos que segun se cree por razon de las aguas y sombrío cauce
de sus arroyos, son espuestos á diversos achaques.   El mas temible entre ellos es, el que llaman *saguaı-
dodo* ó vómito amarillo."   Alegre, Historia de la Compañía de Jesus en Nueva-España, II, 213.

ambush into which the Pimas were lured in the Santan hills.   One other Pima was killed in this engagement and many were wounded, but no injury was inflicted on the Apaches.

The Pima Kwakrsân was surrounded by the enemy, who clung to him and to his horse and sought to pull him down; but he had spurs on his feet and striking them deeply into his horse's flank he caused the animal to rear and throw the man who was holding its head, high in the air.   In the confusion he escaped.

Salt River.   The Apaches came one moonlight night to steal horses. Leaving their own mounts tied in the brush, they crept toward the houses near which were the Pima ponies.   They were discovered and pursued to the river, where all were killed in a running fight.

1847-48

ℱ   *Gila Crossing.*   The Rsânûk villagers went to Kâ'matûk to hunt deer.   They were seen coming by the Apaches, who lay in wait at the spring, and two were shot before they could reach cover.

Salt River.   The Apaches came to Santan early one morning and killed four Pimas.   They were chased, overtaken, and five of them killed before pursuit was abandoned.

1848-49

There is no record for this year upon either calendar stick.

1849-50

ℱ   *Gila Crossing.*   Three Apaches were discovered approaching the villages and a party was sent out on horseback to attack them. They fled to a hill near Tempe, where they hastily built up a wall of stone, behind which they maintained themselves until nearly sunset, when a Pima led his party inside the Apache breastwork and the enemy were killed.

1850-51

〉   *Gila Crossing.*   The Yumas came again to attack the Maricopas They surprised the village, killed several, and carried their property to a hill near by, where they sang and danced, saying that they were waiting for the Maricopas to bring their friends, the Pimas, to be defeated next.   But they underestimated the number and valor of the Pimas, who soon put them to flight, leaving many of their dead upon the field.   One of their chiefs, known to the Pimas as Vĭsaki-kitoʌaɪ(t), when he saw most of his men fallen, came back saying he did not wish to escape alone.   He had but a knife in his hand and was killed with arrows.

The remnant of the party took refuge in a thicket near the Estrellas, where the pursuers rushed in upon them with horses and killed all. Many Pimas were wounded but none killed.   A strand of hair was cut from the head of each fallen Yuma, but these have since been lost or buried. There were 134 Yumas killed; their bodies were left on the field.

1851-52

¶ ▌ *Gila Crossing.* Two Apaches were discovered near the Maricopa village by Whycnânâvĭm, a Maricopa warrior, who killed one of them before they could escape.

The Pimas went on a campaign against the Apaches on Salt river, near where the present reservation is located, and one of their number was killed.

Blackwater. In this year the Apaches raided a Papago village near Quijotoa, called Koĭ Tatk' (mesquite root).[a]

1852-53

For three years the Gila Crossing calendar has nothing but the year marks on it, and the keeper could recall no event for that period.

Blackwater. At the hill shaped "like a nose," in the Santans, the Apaches ambushed a party of Pimas and Maricopas. They sent six men to the Maricopa village, near which they discovered and killed some women. The Maricopa and Pima warriors pursued the Apaches, who retreated slowly, thus luring them within reach of the arrows of the waiting Apaches, who killed four Maricopas and one Pima. The survivors retreated to their supports, who were coming up in such numbers that the Apaches withdrew. The dead were burned that day north of the Santan hills.

At about the same time the Pimas killed four Apaches south of the villages.[b]

When the wheat was ripe [June] the Apaches were pursued north of the Santan hills and four of them killed. Three men are yet living who killed Apaches in this fight.

1853-54

Blackwater. The Apaches came to steal horses and brought a live vulture with them. They were discovered and several killed.

1854-55

Blackwater. The Apaches were reported by the Papagos to be stealing horses in their territory and the Pimas were requested to aid in driving the enemy out of the country. In the Rincon mountains, at Tâva Kosuwa, Turkey Neck, the horse thieves were overtaken and many of them killed. The horse's head indicates the purpose of the Apaches.

---

[a] The figure on the Blackwater stick is intended to represent a mesquite root.

[b] At a point about 15 miles from the Gila where the Southern Pacific now runs—just south of the reservation.

Gila Crossing. Skââkoĭk was approached one evening by seven Apaches, who were discovered and surrounded. Six escaped in the darkness, but one was tracked into the arrow bushes, where he dropped his bow. He was soon found to have secreted himself in a hole washed deep in the sand. The Pimas could not see or reach him, so they shook live coals down upon the fugitive, which caused him to yell and suddenly leap out among them. The apparition so startled everyone that no move was made to detain him. As he was passing through their line some asked those around them, "Can we catch him?" but he was such a giant and the peculiar manner of his appearance among them so unnerved for a moment the courage of the men whose deepest instinct was to crush out the life of the Apache, that he made his escape.

Blackwater. The Apaches, whom the Pimas attacked during a raid of this year, were grinding out mesquite beans from the dry pods when the arrows began to fall into their camp. A blind Apache was killed as his companions fled.

Blackwater. The Pimas and Maricopas joined the white soldiers in a campaign against the Apaches under White Hat. Two Pimas were killed and two wounded, but no Apaches were injured. While the Pimas were on their way home still another of their party was killed. The Pimas burned their dead. Later they killed several Apaches who were raising corn on Salt river.

Salt River. About the end of the year a band of Apaches came to the Pima villages one morning. They were discovered and chased 30 miles to Tempe butte, where they were surrounded. They hid themselves at the summit of the butte, but were all killed except one, who escaped into the brush.

In the summer the Yumas came again, accompanied by the Mohaves. They sent scouts ahead, who found the Maricopa women gathering mesquite beans. They killed all the women except one, whom they kept to act as a guide. She was the sister of a well-known Maricopa warrior, and they compelled her to lead them to her brother's home. When they reached it she was killed with a club and the man was chased, but he was as good a runner as he was fighter and they could not catch him. A Yuma told him to stop and die like a man, but he answered that if they could overtake him he would show them how to die like a man. The Maricopas fled from their village and the Yumas burned it. Messengers went to all the villages that day and under cover of the night the Pimas and Maricopas gathered. They kept coming until late the next forenoon. They found the

Yumas encamped near the river at a spot where they had assaulted some women and a Pima had been killed while defending them. The Yumas had spent the night in singing their war songs. Now and again a medicine-man would come forward to puff whiffs of smoke in order that their cause might find favor with the gods. The Pima-Maricopa council ended about noon and it was decided to surround the Yumas and to make special effort to prevent them from reaching the river to obtain water. Formed in a semicircle, the Pimas and Maricopas shot down the Yumas upon three sides. Soon the Yumas began to waver and become exhausted from thirst in the heat of the day. They made several attempts to break through the line, but failed, and finally gathered in a compact body to make a last attempt to reach the river. At that moment the Pimas and Maricopas who were on horseback rushed in upon the enemy and rode them down. After a hand-to-hand combat the Yumas were all killed except one, who was stunned by the blow of a club and lay unconscious under a heap of dead. During the night he recovered his senses and escaped. This was the bloodiest fight known, and the Yumas came here to fight no more.[a]

 Blackwater. During the year Pimas were killed in two places by the Apaches; three south of the river and one north.[b]

1858-59

 Blackwater. The meteor of 1859 was observed by the Pimas, who called it pai-ikam ho-o. During a raid into the Apache country three of the enemy were killed and also one Pima.

---

[a] " In 1857, with Mohave, Cocopa, and Tonto allies, they [the Yumas] attacked the Pimas and Papagos up the river, and in a great battle were almost annihilated." Bancroft, Arizona and New Mexico, 501.

Cremony visited the Pimas as a captain in the California Column in 1862. In his Life Among the Apaches, 148, he mentions this conflict of the Pimas with their old enemies, saying: " The grazing ground to which we resorted during our stay near the Maricopa villages had been the scene of a desperate conflict between that tribe and the Pimos, on one side, and the Yumas, Chimehuevis, and Amohaves on the other. Victory rested with the Maricopas and Pimos, who slew over 400 of the allied tribes, and so humiliated them that no effort has ever been made on their part to renew hostilities. This battle occurred four years before our advent, and the ground was strewed with the skulls and bones of the slaughtered warriors."

For the Yuma side of the story see Lieutenant Ives's Report upon the Colorado River of the West, p. 45.

In a letter from an unnamed correspondent living among the Yumas or at Fort Yuma, to Sylvester Mowry, it is stated that the tribes engaging in this battle were the Yumas, Yampais, Mohaves, and Tonto Apaches, with one or two Dieganos [Diegueños], against the Pimas, Maricopas, and Papagos. One thousand five hundred men were engaged on each side. The Yumas "lost not less than 200 of the flower of their chivalry." See S. Ex. Doc. 11, 588, 35th Cong., 1st sess., 1858.

The Blackwater annalist could give but little information concerning the victory over the Yumas, but he had recorded it upon the calendar stick by a fringed line, in itself meaningless.

[b] The two men in the figure are not meant to represent two killed, but that the events occurred in two places.

1859–60

 Blackwater.   The Pimas attacked a party of Apaches and killed a man and a boy.   A white man who accompanied the Pimas was slightly wounded with an arrow.

1860–61

Gila Crossing.   A plague which killed its victims in a single day prevailed throughout the villages.   Three medicine-men who were suspected of causing the disease by their magic were killed, "and nobody was sick any more."

Blackwater.   The one-armed trader sold his store to Ammi M. White during this year and for some reason unknown to the Pimas threw away his grain sacks.[a]

Two Pimas were killed by Apaches, but the details concerning the event are beyond recall.

1861–62

Gila Crossing.   The trader, Ammi M. White, was captured by the "soldiers from the east."[b]

---

[a] Probably to avoid contagion.

[b] "Early in 1862 a force of two or three hundred Texans, under Captain Hunter, marched westward from Mesilla and in February took possession of Tucson for the Confederacy.   There was, of course, little opposition, Union men, if there were any left, fleeing across the line into Sonora.   Not much is really known of Hunter's operations in Arizona so far as details are concerned, even the date of his arrival being doubtful.   Besides holding Tucson, driving out men suspected of Union sympathies, confiscating a few mines belonging to Northerners, and fighting the Apaches to some extent, he sent a detachment to the Pima villages, and possibly contemplated an attack on Fort Yuma.   But—to say nothing of the recent floods, which had greatly increased the difficulties of the route, destroying Gila and Colorado cities—the news from California was not reassuring, and Hunter deemed it best to retire.

"This news was to the effect that California troops were on the march eastward.   These troops, about 1,800 strong, consisted of several volunteer regiments or parts of regiments organized at the beginning of the war, and which, on receipt of intelligence that Arizona had been invaded, were ordered to Yuma and Tucson, constituting what was known as the California Column, under the command of Colonel James H. Carleton.   The main body of this army in detachments, whose exact movements now and later I do not attempt to follow in detail, left Los Angeles and was concentrated at Yuma in April, and in May followed the Gila route to Tucson.   But previously Lieutenant-Colonel West, commanding the advance, had sent out some parties from Yuma, and these were the only troops that came in contact with the Confederates.   Jones, in February, was sent with dispatches to Tucson and fell into the hands of Hunter, who released and sent him back by another route, bearing the first definite news that Tucson had been occupied.   Captain William McCleave, of Company A, First Cavalry, being sent out to look for Jones, was captured, with three men, at the Pima villages on the 6th of April and was carried to Mesilla, where he was soon exchanged.   Captain William P. Calloway was next sent up the Gila with a stronger force to rescue McCleave.   At the Pima villages he heard of a Confederate detachment of 16 men, under Lieutenant Jack Swilling, and sent Lieutenant James Barrett with 12 men to cut them off.   Pursuing the enemy into a chaparral, Barrett was killed, with two of his men, one or two of the foe being also killed and three taken prisoners.   This was the only skirmish of the campaign with Confederates, and it occurred on the 15th of April at a spot known as El Picacho."
Bancroft, XVII, 514.

Both the Gila Crossing and the Blackwater calendars mention the capture of White, but the calendrists can give no definite information concerning the events related by Bancroft.   The trader was of vastly more interest and importance to the Pimas than the whole Confederate or Union army.   He was agent for the Pimas, an office which he held until 1865.   The writer has not found any account of his capture in the records of the period, but it is probable he was soon released.   As soon as he was taken away, the Pimas took possession of his store and quarreled over the distribution of the stock of wheat on hand.

Blackwater. A man named Thomas [whether given name or surname could not be ascertained], who had been trading at Gila Crossing, took charge of White's store after the latter left. The soldiers from the west fought the soldiers from the east at Picacho and were defeated. Then a white man known to the Pimas as Has Viakam came from the east and traded with them.

[John] Walker[a] came from the west with the California Column and learned the Pima language at the same time that Thomas learned the Maricopa.

1862–63

¶ *Gila Crossing.* The men of Rso'tûk went to the mountains about Prescott in search of Apaches during the summer of 1862. As they were following a mountain trail they caught sight of a man lying on his coat asleep. From his dress they could not be sure if he were an Apache or a Pima, so two men went to waken him. "How did you sleep?" said they. On hearing this the man sprang up and they saw that he was an Apache. One struck him on the head with his club, but he jumped and would have escaped had not the other shot him. Soon afterwards two Apaches came to the village of Akûtcĭny and their trail was discovered by two Pimas who were hunting for their horses. They followed the Apaches, who ran toward the Estrellas. The elder Pima was some distance ahead of the other when the leading Apache climbed the mountain and the other turned back to fight. The two men used their bows, each endeavoring to protect himself behind a clump of bushes. Finally, as they were chasing each other around the same clump of bushes, the Apache getting the better of the conflict, having wounded the Pima in the elbow and side, the other Pima came up and killed the Apache, who was called by the Pimas Whaiemââ.

Two Maricopas dragged the body of the Apache to a hill near Gila Crossing and tied it to a post, where it remained for some time. A friend of the dead Apache led a party of six to the place where he had fallen and followed the trail of the dragged body to where it stood tied. The friend wept and went away without attempting to remove the body. As the party returned up the river they entered an isolated house in which there were two old Maricopa men. They warmed themselves at the fire, but did not molest the old men.

Salt River. Two Apaches came near the villages and were seen by a man working in the fields; he called to his friends to help him and at once set off after the enemy. When the Apache who was farthest away saw that his companion was in danger he turned back and attacked the first pursuer. The other Apache escaped, but the braver one was killed. The Pimas returned home, but the Maricopas dragged

---

[a] See p. 33 for list of Pima agents.

the body to the buttes at the point where the Maricopa and Phoenix railroad now crosses the Gila and left it tied to a post. The Apache who ran away led a party of his people to recover the body, but it was afterwards ascertained from the tracks that they turned back just before reaching the spot.

A Pima was killed by the Apaches while the California Column was at the villages and a squad of soldiers accompanied the pursuing party of Pimas as far as the Estrellas, but the enemy escaped. The raid was in the saguaro fruit season "as shown by the red on the dead Pima" [or the month of June, 1862].

 Blackwater. Two medicine-men, father and son, were killed during the year because of their supposed machinations against the people.

1863–64

Gila Crossing, Salt River. For a short time there was peace between the Pimas and Apaches. During this period the Maricopas killed two old men and captured a boy from a party of Apaches who came to the Maricopa village. The boy was sold to a half-brother of the trader A. M. White [named Cyrus Lennan], known to the Pimas as Satcĭny Vâ, Chin Beard.

This man took the boy with him on an expedition against the Apaches. There was a Mexican in the party who understood the Apache language, so that communication was opened with the enemy as soon as they were discovered. The whites placed flour, sugar, and other rations on blankets, and the Apaches, believing that the food was intended as a peace offering, came up to them. The soldiers were accompanied by three Pimas, but they had concealed them under blankets. They had stacked their guns, but retained their side arms concealed. At a signal from the leader of the party the Apaches were fired upon and nearly all of them were killed. Lennan was killed while following the escaping Apaches, but the Pimas killed the man who had thrust a lance into his breast.[a] The place has since been known as Yatâkit ku Kâkûta, Place where the snare was set.[b]

---

[a] Owl Ear states that Lennan shot the man who struck him and they fell dead together.

[b] As we have independent white testimony, it is interesting to compare it with the Piman account. In his Adventures in the Apache Country J. Ross Browne describes the engagement in which Cyrus Lennan was killed. It was at the "Bloody Tanks" and is known in history as King Woolsey's (infamous) "pinole treaty." A party of 26 whites had been pursuing a band of Apaches with stolen stock for several days until they ran out of provisions and sent to the Pima villages for supplies. They were joined by 14 Maricopas under the leadership of Juan Chivaria and Cyrus Lennan. The entire party under the command of King Woolsey camped on the Salt river in a small valley which could not have been far from the upper end of the Salt River canyon. As soon as the smoke of their camp fire arose they were approached by Apaches to whom "Woolsey sent Tonto Jack, an interpreter, to learn what they had to say, and at the same time to tell them it was not the wish of his party to fight them; that he wanted them to come down and he would give them some pinole." The Apaches were finally prevailed upon to enter the camp to the number of 30 or 35. After the display of some insolence on the part of the Apache chief Woolsey drew his pistol and shot him dead. "This was the signal for the signing of the treaty. Simultaneously the whole party commenced firing upon the Indians, slaughtering them right and left. Lennan stood in advance of the Maricopas and was warned by

Salt River. While peace prevailed between the tribes a party of Apaches came to the Pimas to trade goods for ponies. When near the villages they divided into two parties, one of which came on to trade and the other went around to try to steal horses. The thieves were followed and when it was found that their tracks joined those of the party at the villages the Pimas went back and killed many of those who were trading. Some of the Pima warriors overtook the horse thieves and killed several of them.

 Blackwater. A Pima was killed by Apaches while looking for his horses near Kâ'matûk, the hill between Blackwater and the Sacatons.

1864–65

 Gila Crossing, Salt River. This was the first year in which the Pimas were supplied with firearms (by order of General Carleton) and aided the United States soldiers.[a]

Salt River. The Pimas and Maricopas went on a campaign against the Apaches and met a band that had probably ambushed some American soldiers, for they had arms and other army property. The allies rushed the camp of the enemy and captured all that had been taken from the soldiers. When they returned with their spoils to the villages some whites accused them of having killed the soldiers. They told how they obtained the things, but the whites would not believe them. "That is why I do not think the white man is good enough to trust us," said Owl Ear. When several guides took the whites to the battle ground they were satisfied when they saw the dead Apaches there.

Blackwater. In a raid in this year two Apaches were killed and their ears cut off and nailed on a stick.

In an effort to establish peace with the Apaches, the soldiers and Pima scouts took a wagon loaded with rations to the Superstition mountains. The Apaches took it to be a hostile move and attacked the party, killing the driver of the wagon. The Apaches were pursued and several were killed before the trail was lost.

Woolsey to make sure of a lame Indian with a lance, who was eyeing him suspiciously. 'I'll look out for him,' was Lennan's reply, and the slaughter became general. * * * The fight, if such it could be called, lasted seven or eight minutes. Lennan had incautiously closed upon and shot an Indian near him, forgetting the lame one against whom he had been cautioned, who the next moment ran him through the body with his lance. Dye (a rancher) coming up, killed this Indian. The only person wounded was Tonto Jack, who was shot in the neck with an arrow. * * * Twenty Tontos and four Pinals lay dead upon the ground. Others were seen running off with the blood streaming from their wounds, and it is supposed some of them died." (P. 121.)

a John Walker, the first agent for the Pimas, in his report for the year 1860 stated that the tribe petitioned for more guns, as theirs were "few and old." See Report of Commissioner of Indian Affairs 1860, 168. In the report of J. L. Collins, superintendent of Indian affairs in New Mexico, it is stated that 100 muskets and 10,000 rounds of ammunition had just been given the Pimas. In ibid., 1862, 239, 1863.

1865–66

¶ *Gila Crossing, Salt River.* The Pimas went on a campaign against the Apaches and one of their number was killed. His fellows burned the corpse with the bow and war gear. Dry ironwood was used in the cremation.[a]

In the same engagement another Pima was wounded and came home to die.

Gila Crossing. The Pimas soon afterwards went to the mountains north of Tempe to seek Apaches. Two of their party were killed and a third came home mortally wounded.

Blackwater. Another war party attacked an Apache camp, described as the one at which the children were playing and piling up gourds, and killed several of the enemy.

1866–67

Gila Crossing. Many died this year of a sickness characterized by shooting pains that resembled needle and knife pricks. One day the three medicine-men who were accused of having caused the disease came home drunk from the Gila Bend stage station and were set upon by their fellow-villagers. Two were killed and the other was seriously but not fatally wounded.

Gila Crossing, Salt River. This year was marked by a devastating fever at Rso'tûk and three medicine-men were killed there in the hope of stopping it.

Blackwater. A party of Pimas accompanied the soldiers to the Verde region and there killed a number of Apaches, among whom was a man with a very long foot.

1867–68

Gila Crossing. During this year a disease prevailed that from the description would seem to have been malaria. Many died, and the medicine-men were blamed, as usual, for the calamity. Two were killed before the disease abated.

Blackwater. The Pimas went raiding in the Superstition Mountain region and killed one Apache who was running away with his shield but who stumbled and fell.

1868–69

Gila Crossing. A heavy rain caused a flood which destroyed the store at Casa Blanca.[b]

This was known as the Vamati Tcoki, Snake rain.

---

[a] This custom of burning the dead is occasionally referred to in these annals, though my informants always insisted that this method was never resorted to by their people except in the case of those killed in war.

[b] The store was more than 2 miles south of the channel of the river, but it had been built at the foot of a little rise upon which the present village is located and was within the reach of the flood. This is but one of many instances where the white settlers of Arizona have not profited by the experience

Blackwater. The Pimas went on a campaign against the Apaches with the Papagos, but the parties quarreled and separated. The Pimas killed an Apache woman near Salt river while on their way home.

1869–70

Gila Crossing. A man at Rso'tûk was killed by the accidental discharge of a revolver in the hands of a companion.

Blackwater. An unusually heavy rain occurred during the winter, which gullied the hills deeply.

The Apaches were making tizwin when the soldiers and Pima scouts attacked them; they took the alarm and escaped, leaving the liquor in the hands of the allies.

1870–71

Gila Crossing. The first canal [a] at Tempe was built by the Mormon settlers [1870].

Blackwater. The Apaches had come to the river at Santan for water and some Pimas discovered their trail and set off in pursuit. They failed to inflict any injury upon the enemy and retired with one of their own number mortally wounded.

At this time a Pima was killed at Ta-atûkam by the Apaches. These two corpses were burned.

Another Pima was killed during the year at Tempe by the Apaches, and his body was buried.

1871–72

Gila Crossing. An epidemic of measles prevailed in all the villages during this year. The Indians knew absolutely nothing about treating the disease, and many died.[b]

Salt River. In the winter the Kwahadk's went on the warpath against the Apaches and were accompanied by Na-aputk't. They tried to surprise the enemy at a tank near Picacho, but found no one there. They followed the trail, however, until they came to a point near the present station of Red Rock, where they sent out scouts in the night, who discovered the whereabouts of the enemy by hearing one of them cough. They surrounded the camp and attacked it at

---

of the natives, ancient and modern, who have located their homes beyond the reach of the freshets that transform the shallow beds of blistering sand into irresistible torrents that overrun the bottom lands which may have been untouched by flood for many years. "The flood of September, 1868, was perhaps the most destructive ever known, destroying three of the Pima villages and a large amount of property on the lower Gila." Bancroft, XVII, 536.

a The main canal is less than 2 miles in length. It has been enlarged several times, so that its capacity is now 325 cubic feet per second, irrigating over 30,000 acres.

b The experience of the agency physicians in after years show that the high rate of mortality from this disease has not been due to the lack of acquired immunity, but to the ignorance of the Pimas as to the proper care of patients, and especially those convalescing. The youth who was the only victim at Sacaton in 1899 took a cold water shower bath as soon as he was able to be about and paid the penalty for his rashness.

daylight. The Apaches ran confusedly about without their weapons; fifteen were killed and many guns, bows, and quivers were captured.

Blackwater. At the hill, Kâ'matûk, somewhat detached from the Sacatons on the northeast, a man was bitten by a rattlesnake and died.

At about the same time the Pimas killed an Apache who was known as Vakoa, Canteen, near the Superstition mountains.

1872–73

Gila Crossing, Salt River. For several years the Pimas had had little water to irrigate their fields and were beginning to suffer from actual want when the settlers on Salt river invited them to come to that valley. During this year a large party of Rso'tûk Pimas accepted the invitation and cleared fields along the river bottom south of their present location. Water was plentiful in the Salt and the first year's crop was the best that they had ever known. The motive of the Mormons on the Salt was not wholly disinterested, as they desired the Pimas to act as a buffer against the assaults of the Apaches, who were masters of the country to the north and east.[a]

Salt River. It was during this winter that the United States soldiers and the Pima, Maricopa, and Apache scouts surrounded the Superstition Mountain Apaches at the "Tanks" and rained bullets into their ranks until not a single man remained alive. "It was a sight long to be remembered," said Owl Ear, in narrating the circumstances.[b]

1873–74

Gila Crossing. Ku-ukâmûkam, the Apache chief, and his band were killed by the soldiers and Pima scouts.

Kâmûk Wutcâ Â-âtam, People-under-Kâ'matûk, or the village at Gila Crossing, was settled during this year.[c]

Gila Crossing, Salt River. The telegraph line was run through from west to east during the winter.[d]

---

[a] By Executive order of June 14, 1879, the land occupied by the Pimas on Salt river was set apart as the Salt River reservation. It embraces about three townships on the north side of the river about 30 miles north of the original Pima villages. There are several large ruins and at least one large canal upon the reservation that were built by the Hohokam. By an arrangement with the canal companies the Pimas have insured for themselves a constant supply of water, and the Salt River community is regarded as the most prosperous among the Pimas.

[b] This sharp engagement took place on the 28th of December, 1872, in the canyon of the Salt river, south of the Mazatzal mountains. It has been graphically described by Capt. John G. Bourke in his On the Border with Crook, 191–200. He states that 76 Apaches were killed and 18 captured. One wounded man was overlooked and made his escape. "Lead poured in by the bucketful" and an avalanche of bowlders was hurled down hundreds of feet from above upon the enemy.

[c] There is an unfailing supply of water at this place; the Gila, after flowing 75 miles beneath the surface, rises to form a stream large enough to irrigate several hundred acres.

[d] This was a military telegraph built from funds obtained by special appropriations from Congress. Arizona was fairly well provided with telegraph lines by the time the railroad reached Yuma, in 1877, as there were more than 1,000 miles in operation in the Territory.

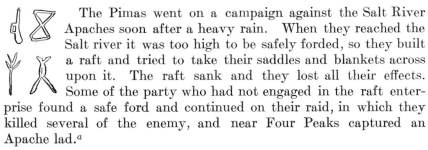

The Pimas went on a campaign against the Salt River Apaches soon after a heavy rain. When they reached the Salt river it was too high to be safely forded, so they built a raft and tried to take their saddles and blankets across upon it. The raft sank and they lost all their effects. Some of the party who had not engaged in the raft enterprise found a safe ford and continued on their raid, in which they killed several of the enemy, and near Four Peaks captured an Apache lad.[a]

1874–75

Gila Crossing. A man trying to catch his pony approached from the rear so that he could reach its tail, which he probably thought it advisable to lay hold on until he could fasten the rope around the animal's neck. One end of the lariat was attached to his waist, the other he tied to the horse's tail. The animal broke away and dragged him to death.[b]

Blackwater. The Apache White Hat killed a Pima.

1875–76

Gila Crossing. In this year sickness prevailed in the village of Rsânûk, apparently the same as in 1866, when the principal symptom of the disease was shooting pains through the body. Two medicine-men were suspected of having caused the trouble by magic means, and they were killed to stop the plague.

Blackwater. For a short time the Pimas were free from Apache attacks, and they ventured into the mountains to gather mescal. While there, a race took place between a man and a woman, in which the woman won.

Later in the season there was a general gathering of the villages to witness a race with the kicking-ball.

1876–77

Gila Crossing. There was an Apache village called Hâvany Kâs at the junction of the Gila and Salt rivers while a truce existed between the Pimas and Apaches. During this year an epidemic of smallpox prevailed in that village, as well as in all those of the Pimas and Maricopas.

---

[a] He afterwards became known as Doctor Montezuma, now a prosperous physician practising in the city of Chicago.

[b] This, the only event of the year in the Gila Crossing record, is unimportant in itself, and yet it illustrates a phase of Pima character that is worthy of notice. In handling horses they exhibit a patient subtlety resembling that of the snake creeping upon its prey, until they have gotten a rope or halter on the animal, when their gentleness disappears. Yet in all their harnessing or saddling they manifest an innate tendency toward carelessness. They always work up on the right instead of the left side of a horse, and they also mount from that side.

In the spring of 1877 the Gila Crossing Pimas and the Gila Maricopa villagers were pitted against each other in a relay race, the first between the two tribes.[a]

 Blackwater. While a party was gathering mescal just before the wheat ripened a mare gave birth to twin colts.

1877-78

 Gila Crossing, Salt River. During the winter a man who had gone a long distance to search for his horses perished from the cold, and his body was found in a sitting position under a tree.[b]

Gila Crossing. A party of Pimas went to the Kwahadk[c] village to drink tizwin, and in the quarrel which ensued the Casa Blancas killed two men of Santan.

Some time afterwards the Gila Crossing people drank tizwin, and one of their number was killed by a man from Salt River.

 Blackwater. A man of Blackwater who was with a party that went to gather mescal sickened from some unknown cause, and died. The corpse was brought back to the village.

1878-79

Gila Crossing, Salt River, Blackwater. The principal event of the year was the building of the Southern Pacific railroad along the southern border of the Gila River reservation.

Salt River (a), Blackwater (b). A feud that had originated in the quarrel at the Kwahadk[c] village during the preceding year reached an acute stage in February, 1879. The majority of the people of Blackwater and the lower villages, which were then known as Santan, conspired to kill the men of a certain faction during a night determined upon several days in advance. A guard was set at Blackwater, who was to watch their movements without giving them any hint of his purpose. One of those who were preparing for the attack at Blackwater had a brother at Casa Blanca, and he feared that this brother might be included in the list of victims at the lower villages, so he went one night to warn him or to get him to return with him to Blackwater. The next day the brother's conscience began to act, and he finally decided that if these men were killed and he did not warn them he would be answerable for their death. He therefore sent a runner to Blackwater, who told one of the intended victims of the conspiracy formed against them.

---

[a] Tcĕrĭkûs, one of the Maricopa runners, afterwards won a six-day race in San Francisco and was a close second in a similar endurance race in New York.

[b] The Pimas believe that he froze to death, and if this be true it indicates an unusually low temperature and that one man at least had very slight power of resistance to cold. The lowest temperature recorded at the Phoenix meteorological station for a period of sixteen years is 11° F. Rept. of Chief of Weather Bureau, 1900-1901, i.

The recipient of the news sent one of his family to inform another of his party, and so the news was spread so quietly that the guard scarcely noticed what was going on until the men began slipping one by one into the mesquite thickets. Before he could reach his friends, who were out in the fields, the whole proscribed party had escaped and were on their way toward Santan, where they and their friends attacked their Santan opponents early the next morning.

Juan Thomas, his two brothers, father, and uncle were in the party attacked. The old man, Iïâs, was the bravest, and fought openly with bow and arrows until they succeeded in driving off their assailants. He was slightly wounded with a bullet in the abdomen and an arrow in the arm, but no one was killed. One of the brothers was irrigating his field when a runner came with the news that his family was being killed and that he was in danger also. He ran toward the Double buttes and soon saw another man running in a course parallel to his own. The other saw him, and both began dodging to escape from the two clumps of mesquite behind which they had halted. Then they discovered that they were brothers, and they debated long as to what they should do. It is also said that they shed tears at the peril of their relatives, to whose aid they could not go without weapons. It was also a cause of grief that their fellows should rise against them. They decided to return to the village, but by that time the fight had ended.

Iïâs had come out of his house and chased those who were trying to shoot him. They fired several shots and some arrows at him, but when he came near they ran away. He called his enemies by name, inviting them to come and get satisfaction if they were bent on killing him. When the attacking party withdrew, the Thomas family went to the Double buttes, and on finding that they were not pursued they went to Blackwater, where their story so aroused their friends that an expedition was organized to seek revenge. They secured two boxes of cartridges from the trader at Blackwater and came down the river.

They formed a skirmish line as they approached the lower settlement and met their opponents at the Government school building. The Santan party hastily knocked a few loopholes in the adobe walls and gathered in and around the building, to withstand an attack. The Blackwater men killed three among those outside the schoolhouse and could have killed many more with their superior weapons, but their thirst for revenge seemed to be satisfied with that number, and they did not pursue those who fled across the mesa like frightened rabbits.

1879—80

Gila Crossing. During this winter there was a heavy fall of snow.[a]

 Blackwater. At an abandoned store above Casa Blanca, the walls of which are yet standing, a white man was killed by two young men, who were caught before they secured the money of the victim, robbery being the motive for the deed. The one who did the shooting was taken to the county jail at Florence.

1880—81

 Gila Crossing. At the beginning of the year a man was bitten and killed by a rattlesnake at Gila Crossing.

 Blackwater. The murderer mentioned in the record of the preceding year was hanged at Florence.

1881—82

Gila Crossing. During a tizwin drunk at Salt River two young men killed each other. The Casa Blanca people went to Gila Crossing to participate in a feast and dance.

 Blackwater. The Pima police were sent from Sacaton to arrest some Kwahadk's living at their village about 50 miles south of the agency. Two were killed.[b]

1882—83

Gila Crossing (a), Blackwater (b). An epidemic of measles prevailed among the Pimas and Maricopas, causing the death of many persons.

(a)   (b)

---

[a] An event of such rarity that it is mentioned but twice in these records of seventy years.

[b] The Kwahadk's had been drinking tizwin, and as they had never been interfered with by the agent they were not conscious of having trangressed any laws. Furthermore, drunkenness was the rule among the few whites with whom they came in contact, and it was a privilege that the Kwahadk's indulged in but once or twice a year. Old inhabitants at Sacaton tell me that the agent was working prisoners upon a reservation farm and selling the crop for his own profit. The Pimas had been committing no misdemeanors or crimes that offered any excuse for imprisoning them and the crops needed attention, but nevertheless he ordered his police to bring in the Kwahadk's dead or alive. One of the young Kwahadk's frankly declared his innocence of any intentional transgression and defied the police to take him from his home. He was promptly shot. As the police were returning to Sacaton they were overtaken by the father of the murdered man, who told them that he had nothing to live for, as they had killed his son and they might as well kill him. The police obligingly complied with his request. "Innocent and unoffending men were shot down or bowie-knifed merely for the pleasure of witnessing their death agonies. Men walked the streets and public squares with double-barreled shotguns, and hunted each other as sportsmen hunt for game. In the graveyard of Tucson there were 47 graves of white men in 1860, and of that number two had died natural deaths, all the rest having been murdered in bar-room quarrels." Life Among the Apaches, by John C. Cremony, 117.

1883–84

T   *Gila Crossing.* The Salt River Pimas went to a fiesta at Gila Crossing.

Blackwater. A drunken Pima while riding on a box car on the Southern Pacific was run over and killed.[a]

1884–85

Gila Crossing. An epidemic during this year among the Kwahadk's caused the execution of two medicine-men who were suspected of bringing the visitation upon the tribe.[b]

Blackwater. The first wagons issued by the Government to the Blackwater people were received this year.

1885–86

Gila Crossing. Hwela, named for the agent Wheeler, was baptized this year as the first Christian convert among the Pimas.[c]

Two youths were thrown from their horses during a rabbit hunt and killed.[d]

Blackwater. Two prominent men of Blackwater died.

1886–87

Gila Crossing. Tizwin was made at Gila Crossing in such quantities that it was passed around in bowl-shaped baskets. One man was killed.

The first adobe houses were built at Gila Crossing, and their owners were thereby entitled to one wagon each.[e]

A man at Salt River was shot by a white man; the particulars were not known to Kâemâ-â.

---

[a] The practice of allowing the Indians to ride free upon freight trains was established when the road was first built and is yet continued. The object of this generosity is said to be the procurement of the good will of the natives, who in return would give warning of washouts, or obstructions intentionally placed on the track and, perhaps, give concessions of rights of way across the reservations in the event of future extensions. Agent Jackson in his report for 1883 stated that six Pimas had been killed that year by falling from trains when drunk.

[b] It will be noticed that such common events as this among the Kwahadk's are recorded by the calendrists, thus showing how closely related the tribe is to the Pimas.

[c] Mr C. H. Cook, a Civil War veteran, had come as a teacher and missionary among the Pimas at the close of the year 1870. A sincere and devout Christian, he labored for nearly fifteen years before the people to whom he has devoted his life began to understand the message that he brought to them. He informs the writer that three or four other men had accepted his teaching before Hwela, but it is probable that this year marks the beginning of the conversion, which thereafter advanced very rapidly. Mr Cook has described his experiences among the Pimas and Apaches in a small volume of 136 pages, entitled, Among the Pimas, 1893. The chapter on "The Pima Indians, their manners and customs," by Rev. Isaac T. Whittemore, is inaccurate and inadequate.

[d] These hunts were frequently made and resulted in the destruction of large numbers of hares and rabbits, two species of the former and one of the latter. They were simply drives by a company of mounted men who surrounded the area to be beaten over and then advanced toward the center, where the animals were shot with arrows or killed with clubs. Such hunts are yet continued.

[e] These wagons were issued to such men as were willing to cut their long hair, build adobe houses of reasonable size, and provide suitable sheds to shelter the wagons from the scorching heat of summer, which is exceedingly severe on vehicles.

Gila Crossing, Salt river. The Maricopa and Phoenix railroad was built during this year, and thus connection was established between the 'fertile districts of the Salt river and the Southern Pacific railroad.[a]

Salt River. The medicine-man Staups gave a great dance at Santan, which was accompanied by races and other ceremonies which attracted many visitors, among whom were a Yuma and his wife.

Blackwater. Juan Thomas was employed as a scout by the troops who pursued Geronimo during his last flight into Mexico. The eight dots on Juan's stick represent the soldiers whom the Pimas accompanied. The minor leaders of the Apaches had entered the Pima camp thinking that they were friends, and had been captured, except seven who broke away. The commanding officer having ordered a fresh party of Pimas who had come up, to pursue the escaping Apaches, thirty-one Pimas and eight soldiers tracked the Apaches for two months, until they doubled back to the White mountains, where they were captured by the white soldiers before the Pimas overtook them.

1887–88

Gila Crossing, Salt river. Special mention is made by two annalists of the severe earthquake of May 3, 1887.[b] Owl Ear declared that "it was noticed by many of our people, if not by all, who wondered why the earth shook so."

Gila Crossing. The stage station at Gila Crossing, no longer needed after the railroad was built from the Southern Pacific to Phoenix, was moved during this year to Maricopa junction.

The Gila Crossing settlement was prosperous, and the Casa Blanca people went down to dance and share the products of their brothers' industry.

During a tizwin carousal which took place later in the year, two Gila Crossing men killed each other.

It was at this time that "a Mexican (sic) counted the bones of the people."[c]

The Maricopas were all living together at Mo'hatûk mountain when a quarrel arose in which a medicine-man was killed. His friends retaliated by killing a medicine-man of the opposite faction. This resulted in a division of the tribe, some going to the Pima settle-

---

[a] The road was completed July 2, 1887.

[b] This is known as the "Sonora earthquake." The shocks were so severe in that state as to be destructive to property and human life. At Tombstone, Ariz., the severe shocks lasted ten seconds, and the vibrations continued for a full minute. The earthquake was felt throughout the southern part of the Territory, and many ranchmen firmly believe that the drought of the last few years, which has transformed the grassy mesas into a desert waste, is due to that earthquake. See Goodfellow in Science, New York, Aug. 12, 1887.

[c] This is the Pima view of the somatological investigations of Dr Herman F. C. ten Kate, who measured 312 Pimas, besides many others among the Maricopas, Papagos, Zuñis, etc. His results are briefly summarized in the Journal of American Ethnology and Archæology, III, 119.

ment on Salt river and the remainder going to their present location on the Gila below the crossing.

Salt River. A white man killed an unknown Pima some time after the earthquake for some unknown reason.

1888–89

§ *Gila Crossing.* The American settlers at Tempe invited the Salt River Pimas to a feast.

⋈ An eclipse of the moon was observed by the Pimas, and as usual was spoken of as the "time when the moon died."[a]

T A prosperous season enabled the Salt River people to hold a dance festival.

○ Tizwin was made at Gila Crossing, but no one was killed in the resulting debauch.

Blackwater. A Papago who knew the bluebird series of songs sang for the Santan people during the festival held by them.

The captain of the native police and the calendrist went to Fort McDowell with three other men to act as scouts for the soldiers stationed there.

During the year an epidemic carried away three prominent men at Blackwater.

1889–90

⋏ *Gila Crossing.* Two tramps killed a man near the Maricopa and Phoenix railroad.

ϙ The Salt River people made tizwin, and during the carousal which followed a man was shot and killed. The murderer was sent to Yuma.

ϙ The Hi'atam villagers who formerly lived at Akûtcĭny, south of Maricopa station, went to Gila Crossing to join in the dance festival held there.

T *Salt River.* In a tizwin drunk at Salt River Santeo was killed. Soon afterwards another general debauch resulted in the death of Hitiraki. These events caused the order prohibiting the Pimas from making tizwin.

 Blackwater. The wife of the head chief died.

1890–91

| *Gila Crossing.* During a tizwin drunk at Gila Crossing a man put poison into the liquor of an enemy, who died in great agony after drinking it.

---

[a] Notwithstanding the fact that several score of partial and total eclipses of the moon were visible in Pimería during the period covered by these annals, which in that clear atmosphere must have been seen, they are mentioned but twice, and that in recent times. As it is known from American testimony that the Pimas were profoundly impressed by such phenomena, the failure of the annalists to note them can be accounted for only by their aversion to even a mention of supernatural events supposed to be threatening in character.

V   At the Salt River settlement a Mexican under the influence
of whisky killed a Pima, but the Indians "were good enough not
to want to kill" the murderer.

H   *Gila Crossing (a), Salt River, Blackwater (b).*   In the spring of
(a)   1891 occurred the last and most disastrous of the Gila floods.
The Maricopa and Phoenix Railroad bridge was swept away and
the channels of both the Gila and Salt rivers were changed in
(b)   many places.   The destruction of cultivated lands led to the
change of the Salt River Pimas from the low bottoms to the mesas.

1891–92

ᠬᠬ   *Gila Crossing.*   A boarding school[a] for Indian children was
established at Phoenix.

|| Two men died at Gila Crossing during the autumn, and it was
supposed that they were poisoned by the tizwin which they had
been drinking.

    In a tizwin drunk on the Salt River reservation a Papago
shot a Pima and fled to escape the consequences, leaving his
wife at the village.

    Blackwater.   The chief and one of the headmen at Black-
water died during the year.

1892–93

Y   *Gila Crossing.*   Two friends went to Maricopa and got drunk
on whisky.   One cut the other's throat; he then went to the
villages on the river above Gila Crossing and in maudlin tones said he
thought he saw himself striking someone under him.[b]

ᠬᠬ   The schoolhouse was moved out of Phoenix to a point 3 miles
north of the city during the summer of this year (1892).

ᦙ   A woman was struck by lightning at Hi'atam, the village above
Gila Crossing.

T·|| A dance at Salt River occurred in which two men, drunk
with whisky, killed each other.

| In the spring of 1892 the Gila Crossing chief, Ato'wâkäm, died.

|| The Government issued barbed wire for fencing at Gila Cross-
ing, and directed the people to make a road across the fields, which
should be fenced to form a lane.

⌇   *Blackwater.*   A woman was gored to death at Blackwater by
a cow.

⧖   The chief, who had been bitten some years before by a rattlesnake but had recovered, died in the spring of 1893.

---

a It was opened in a leased hotel building in September, 1891. Owing to lack of facilities only boys, to
the number of 42, were admitted.

b The passion for distilled liquor had arisen within the last quarter of a century. Lieutenant Emory
wrote, in November, 1846, "Aguardiente (brandy) is known among their chief men only, and the abuse
of this and the vices which it entails are yet unknown."

1893–94

T   *Gila Crossing.*   The village of Hi'atam and the Gila Maricopas had a dance together, but no one was killed.

Tizwin was made secretly at Gila Crossing, but no fatalities occurred.

The "prettiest woman in the village" died at Gila Crossing, and her husband was suspected of having caused her death.

A man was shot by another, who was drunk with whisky.

 Blackwater.   This year the first horse race ever held by the Pimas took place at Blackwater.[a]

1894–95

Gila Crossing.   The Gila Crossing Presbyterian Church was built at the beginning of the year—that is, during the summer of 1894. It was dedicated in December of that year.[b]

A woman was found dead on the Phoenix road. It is supposed that she had been killed by a Maricopa or a Chinaman.

T   The Gila Crossing people held a dance festival.

The Santa Fé railway reached Phoenix.

There was an eclipse of the moon during this year.

Blackwater.   The chief at Gila Crossing favored tizwin drinking and resisted the progress that was beginning to manifest itself. He died in jail at Sacaton.

 In a horse race between animals owned by the Sacaton flats and Blackwater villages, that of the former won.

1895–96

T   *Gila Crossing.*   The Maricopas living on the Gila came to Gila Crossing to attend a dance festival.

Kâemâ-â was elected a chief at the Gila Crossing village. The line is drawn "crooked because I was crooked in my mind whether or not I should accept the responsibility."

Salt River.   Two brothers-in-law got drunk together and in the quarrel that ensued one was seriously injured.

Soon afterwards Juan made some wine and invited a number of his friends to come and drink with him. All became drunk and Luigi killed a man whose name was not known to the calendrist. Luigi was sent to the Territorial prison at Yuma, where he died a year later.

---

a However, this sport has not become popular among them, partly owing to their poverty, which prevents them from feeding a horse well enough to enable it to run and from accumulating property with which to bet on the race, and perhaps partly owing to the growing influence of the church party in the community.

b This church was established by the veteran missionary, Mr C. H. Cook, who successfully awakened an interest in Christianity among the Gila Crossing villages and had a number of converts at the time when it was considered that, owing to its isolation, the settlement should have a resident missionary.

Blackwater. Two Christians died in this year, one at Blackwater and the other at the Cottonwoods.[a]

 During this year a Blackwater youth at the Phoenix school committed suicide by shooting himself.

Gila Crossing. The Kwahadk's indulged in a tizwin drunk in which one man was killed.

Gila Crossing, Salt River. The Gila Crossing chief fell dead in the prisoner's chair when on trial at Sacaton for selling whisky.

1896–97

Gila Crossing. An epidemic of smallpox prevailed and the whites established a quarantine which the calendrist interprets as, "the Pimas were ordered to stay at home."

Blackwater. Square indicates the Gila Crossing church.

Salt River. The Maricopa and Phoenix railroad was extended from Tempe to Mesa [a distance of about 8 miles] during this year.

1897–98

 Gila Crossing. At the beginning of this year the Gila Crossing Catholic and the Casa Blanca Presbyterian churches were being built.

A Papago chief was killed at Maricopa by a companion who was drunk with whisky.

The Rsânikam people went to Akûtcĭny to dance and run a relay race.

In various ways the Spanish-American war was brought to the notice of the Pimas and Kâemâ-â made a record of the event by the sign which might be supposed to be a bush or a yucca plant.

Blackwater. Juan's brother "and another man" died.

1898–99

Gila Crossing. Many children died this year of measles at the Phoenix Indian boarding school.[b]

---

[a] Professing Christians among the Pimas were not so rare at this time that the death of two need have been recorded. This was the time when the long labors of the missionary were beginning to take effect and the converts numbered hundreds each year.

[b] The disease also prevailed at Sacaton. Nearly all the children in the school, about two hundred, were sick, but the indefatigable efforts of the agency physician saved all but one, who disobeyed his orders.

There was a heavy fall of snow that could be rolled into great balls as it was melting.

 Blackwater. There was no crop this year.[a]

1899-1900

 Gila Crossing. During the summer of 1899 a Catholic mission school was established at Gila Crossing.

A Papago was killed by lightning at Gila Crossing.

 Barbed wire was issued from the agency at Sacaton.[b]

 The Indian Department established a day school at Gila Crossing at this time.

 Victor Jackson was struck by lightning as he was returning to Sacaton on the stage road from Casa Grande.[c]

 Blackwater. A woman at Blackwater was fatally bitten by a rattlesnake.[d]

---

[a] The water of the Gila had been so far utilized by white settlers above the reservation, for the most part more than a hundred miles above, that there was none left for the Pimas. It is difficult to obtain accurate information at this time of the number who perished either directly or indirectly by starvation. During this and the following year five persons are known to have died from this cause, and it is probable that there were others. Most of the Pimas will not beg, however desperate their need may be, so that not all cases were reported.

In one case a wood chopper tried during the hot season to cut mesquite for sale, but he was too weak to withstand the heat and the exertion and was found dead in the chaparral. An old couple were found dead in their house with no food of any kind in their storehouse, and it is supposed that they preferred to starve rather than beg. A man riding to Salt River was too weak from hunger to keep his saddle and fell and perished.

[b] The agent wisely stipulated that if they received free wire they must leave a lane for a road through the fields. The width was not prescribed and they made the lane so narrow that two teams can scarcely pass each other in it, and it becomes churned into mud when the adjoining land is flooded for purposes of irrigation. The Pimas have not manifested any striking road-building instinct that would lead an enthusiastic admirer to relate them to the Aztecs or Incas. Year after year they plodded through the slough between the agency and the river without making an effort to put in a bridge or filling. When one of the Government employees was building a bridge for them several passing teamsters preferred risking their teams and wagons in the sea of mud to assisting for a few minutes to put the bridge in place.

The soil of the reservation is well adapted for road making, and a little care would make the thoroughfares as hard and smooth as those to be found anywhere. However, those upon the tillable lands of river silt readily cut into light dust that rises in clouds when disturbed. In a few places this condition has been remedied by resorting to the temporary and shiftless expedient of the white settlers, who cover the road with straw or corral refuse. The mesa roads, which include all those leading any distance from the Gila, pass alternately over loose soil containing coarse sand that gradually accumulates in the ruts and renders the road "heavy," and over "adobe" soil which is hard and firm in dry seasons, and which makes an ideal roadbed. Hill roads are unknown and there are very few traveling sand dunes to be crossed near the reservation.

[c] His horse was killed and its bones are certain to be pointed out to the stage traveler by the loquacious driver, John McCoy.

[d] It may be presumed that such occurrences are rare or they would not be deemed worthy of record. This woman had gone far out on the desert to search for mesquite beans, as she was without food; indeed the whole community was starving because of the failure of the crops owing to the lack of water in the river for their ditches. Rattlesnakes sometimes make their way into the houses and bite the occupants. Repeated inquiries failed to elicit information that would indicate that any remedies were used for snake bites. A common weed (golondrina?) is called snakeweed by a few whites, and is supposed to be used as a remedy by the Pimas, but I have not yet found a native who ever heard of its being so used.

1900–1901

Gila Crossing. It was during this year that the President came to
Phoenix.[a]

❘❘   *Gila Crossing, Salt River.* During the spring the man employed
to carry the mail between Phoenix and Scottsdale became insane
and shot a white man and a Pima youth whom he met on the road
near the latter place.

1901–2

Gila Crossing. In September, 1901, the day school was
started at Masâ′kimûlt, the Gila Maricopa village.

TECHNOLOGY

THE FOOD SUPPLY

The Pimas subsist upon a mixed diet in which vegetable food pre-
dominates. In the past it would seem probable that the proportion
of meat was greater than at present, though they have long been tillers
of the soil. Certain articles of their diet appear to be markedly flesh
producing, and this tendency is at least not diminished by the habits
of life resulting from the semitropical climate of the Gila valley.
They are noticeably heavier than individuals belonging to the tribes
on the Colorado plateau to the north and northeast, and many old
persons exhibit a degree of obesity that is in striking contrast with
the "tall and sinewy" Indian conventionalized in popular thought.
(Fig. 2.)

About every fifth year in primitive times the Gila river failed in
midwinter, the flow diminishing day by day until at length the last
drop of water that could not gain shelter beneath the sands was
licked up by the ever-thirsty sun. The fish gathered in the few pools
that were maintained by the underflow, the ducks and other water
birds took flight, but the deer and antelope could the more readily be
stalked because of their resorting to known watering places. Without water in the river and canals there could be no crops, and neces-
sity drove the people to seek far afield for the native plants that in
some degree produce fruits or seeds even in dry seasons. The fruit
of the saguaro and the seed or bean of the mesquite were the most
abundant and accessible resources. When even these failed the
Pimas were driven to make long journeys into the Apache country—

---

[a] The visit of President McKinley to Phoenix, in May, 1901, made a profound impression upon the
Pimas. Kâemâ-â lives but 20 miles south of the Arizona capital, and was present at the time of the
President's visit. He made no mark upon the calendar stick to commemorate the event, but related
the circumstances as a part of the history.

It is not surprising that the Pimas, who had heard for many years of the Great Chiefs in Washington,
should be desirous of seeing one in the flesh when the opportunity presented itself. The official interpreter at the agency frequently, during the winter of 1901-2, expressed her desire to obtain a good biography
of the late President. After commenting upon the hideous crime of the assassin at Buffalo she made
the truthful and suggestive remark that ' no Pima would do such a thing; he would never kill his chief."

and whenever they got a mile from their own villages they were in the land of the Apache—in search of animal food, roots, berries, and especially the edible agaves.

At other times the very abundance of water proved disastrous;

FIG. 2. Fat Louisa.

floods destroyed the canals and swept away the crops. As early as 1697 Padre Kino reported that owing to the fields having been over-flowed the Pimas could offer him no pinole,[a] but gave mesquite meal instead.[b] The resort to uncultivated products such as their Papago

---

[a] Manuscript, Hemenway Collection, x, p. 6, copy by Bandelier from Doc. His. Mex.

[b] Made by grinding parched corn into meal and mixing it with water to form a thin gruel; wheat is now similarly treated. Pfefferkorn gives the following appreciative description of pinole in his Beschrei-bung der Landschaft Sonora, the second volume of which was published in 1795: "Auch auf dem Felde, und auf der Reise, wo keine Bequemlichkeit zum Kochen ist, haben die Sonorer ihre Nahrung von dem *Mais*. Sie nehmen den nöthigen Vorrath mit: dieser bestehet in dem *Pinole*, den ihnen die Weiber auf folgende Art bereiten. Nachdem der *Mais* im Wasser etwas geweicht, und hernach getrocknet ist; rösten sie denselben in einer irdenen Schüssel, und rühren ihn beständig herum, damit er nicht anbrenne. Währendem Rösten, springen die Körner auf; und das Mark bricht, gleich einer schneeweissen Blume, hervor. Dieses wird *Esquita* genant und ist nicht unangenehm zu essen. Der auf diese Art geröstete *Mais* wird auf dem *Metate* gemahlen; und bekömmt alsdann den Namen *Pinole*. Diese Feld und Reisekost führt der Sonorer in dem Balge von einer wilden Katze, oder einem andern Thiere, mit sich. Sogar die Soldaten, und andere Spanier, haben auf der Reise keine andere Nahrung. Wenn sie essen wollen; so werfen sie zwei oder drei handvoll *Pinole* in eine *Corita*, welche ihnen zu dem Ende allezeit zur Seite hängt; schütten Wasser dazu, rühren beides durcheinander; und nehmen also aus einem Geschiere, zur selbigen Zeit, Speise und Trank. So sehr der *Pinole* von den Amerikanern geschätzet wird; so wenigen Beifall findet sein Geschmack bei dem Europäer; nur Zimmet, und Zucker, können ihm denselben angenehm machen." (Vol. II, p. 132.)

cousins to the southward wholly subsisted upon did not prevent the Pimas from attaining proficiency in agriculture, as will be seen later, and it must many times have preserved them from total extinction. With what success they sought for edible plants may be judged from the subjoined list, which is believed to be fairly complete. It contains 22 plants of which the stems, leaves, or flowers were eaten, 4 that furnished roots or bulbs, 24 with seeds or nuts, and 15 that supplied fruits or berries. And this in a region that appears to the casual visitor to be a desert with but a few thorny shrubs and but one tree that he would deem worthy of the name.

PREPARATION OF FOOD

Very few articles of Pima diet are eaten raw, and many of them are of such a nature as to necessitate thorough cooking; thus the agave and the fruit of some of the cacti are baked for many hours. It may be well, therefore, to describe the methods, so far as they could be ascertained, of preparing the various plants for use. The art of cooking is not well developed among these people; no such elaborate preparations as Mr Cushing found at Zuñi tempt the Pima palate.

In the olden time maize was ground upon the flat metates and formed into loaves, which must have been "sad" indeed, to judge from their modern counterparts. With the advent of the whites came the introduction of a new and quickly accepted cereal, wheat; and the bread made from it also, without leavening agent, is heavy and indigestible. One loaf was obtained (pl. VI, a), said to be a comparatively small one, that weighed 14 pounds and yet was only 3 inches thick and 20 inches in diameter. No knowledge of the pueblo wafer breads exists among the Pimas, who confine their treatment of mesquite, corn, wheat, and other flour to baking as tortillas or as loaves in the ashes, frying in suet, or boiling, either in water to form a gruel or mush, or with other foods in the shape of dumplings.

A large part of the cereal food of the Pimas is parched before it is ground.

The process of parching on, or rather among, the coals is dexterously carried out. The coals are raked into the parching pan (pl. XIX, a) and after the grain has been thrown upon them it is given a series of tosses with a quarter-turn to each which redistributes the light but bulky coals and the heavier grain. A frequent puff of breath carries away the quickly gathering flakes of ashes. The contents of the pan are separated by a few short jerks that carry the coals in a mass to the edge of the dish, whence the larger particles are scraped off and the smaller blown out. Another method of parching seeds is to place over the fire an olla that has been broken so that at least one side is wanting, thus admitting the hand to stir the contents as they are browned.

Meat is roasted on the coals, a favorite method of cooking dried meat or that of small rodents, or it is boiled until well done. In the latter method, according to one informant, it is put on the fire in cold water. The broth is then thrown away lest it cause consumption. A coarse-grained flour is sometimes boiled with the meat to make what a Canadian voyageur would term rubabu.

Occasionally a housewife will be met with among the Pimas who is scrupulously neat and clean in cooking and in the care of the home. Most of the women, however, carry traces of dried dough on their fingers from week's end to week's end, and the cooking vessels know no cleansing except the scraping that seeks the last particle of food that may cling to them, the rasping tongue of the starving dog, or the hasty slopping of a little cold water into them just before using again. The evil effects of slovenliness are reduced, however, by the peculiar conditions, such as the dry air, which saps the moisture from all organic matter, even in the shade; the outdoor cooking place exposed to a sun that withers all germs; and the habit of eating all the food prepared for each meal, which includes the rule of etiquette prescribing that one must eat all that is set before him.

The kitchen is an arrow-bush inclosure, about 4 or 5 meters in diameter (pl. VI, b), containing its set of half a dozen pottery vessels. In the center are the three stones on which the cooking pot rests. Such an inclosure is quite common at the present day, though many have adoped the oval fireplaces of adobe (pl. VI, c), some obtain iron kettle stands from the agency blacksmith, and a few (chiefly those who live in adobe houses) are using modern stoves.

PLANTS USED FOR FOOD

Â'nŭk i'avak, Atriplex bracteosa var.; A. coronata Wats.; A. elegans Dietrich. These saltbushes, with a few others as yet unidentified, are sometimes boiled with other food because of their salty flavor. They are cooked in pits with the fruit of the cactus, Opuntia arborescens, the method of roasting them being described below. The young shoots of some of them are crisp and tender. Commonly known as "sagebrush," these saltbushes are among the most abundant plants in that region. There are both herbaceous and woody species, the former being eaten by stock and the latter being useful for fuel.

A'opa hi'âsĭk, Populus deltoides Marsh. The cottonwood occurs in a thin fringe, with here and there a grove along the Gila and Salt rivers. In February and March the women send some of the barefoot boys into the tree tops to throw down the catkins, which are then gathered in baskets and carried home to be eaten raw by stripping them off the stem between the teeth.

Aot, Agave americana Linn. (possibly a few related species also). Mescal was gathered in times of famine, and it would have been much more extensively used had it not been for the danger from " the enemy," the Apaches, that attended even the shortest journey away from the villages. The plant has ever been a favorite, not only among the Pimas but also with the Papagos, the Apaches, and a score of other tribes. The first day's work after reaching the hills where this plant grows was to seek suitable wood and make digging sticks. Then the men gathered the mescal heads by prying them out with the sticks, and trimmed off the leaves with a knife, leaving one or two, so that the heads might be tied in pairs and slung on a rope for carrying. Thin-leaved specimens were rejected, inasmuch as they not only contain little nourishment, but blister the mouth when eaten. While the men were bringing in the mescal, the women gathered wood for fuel. Pits were dug, and after the fire built in them had died down small stones were placed on the coals. The mescal was then placed on the stones and the whole covered with earth. When it had roasted for twenty-four hours, a small opening was made in the pit and its contents examined; if the cooking was not yet complete, the opening was closed and the pit left undisturbed twelve hours longer. If the roasting was not done when the pit was first opened, it was believed that the incontinence of some members of the party was the cause. The heads of the fruit were opened by removing the envelope on one side; the center was cut out and dried in the sun, when it was ready for use or for storing away.

Mescal is now obtained from the Papagos. It is eaten by chewing until the juice is extracted and rejecting the fiber. It is used alone or together with pinole. Sirup is extracted from the prepared mescal by boiling until the juice is removed, which is then thickened by prolonged boiling until it becomes a black sirup, somewhat similar to sorghum. It is inferior to saguaro sirup.

Ä'păn, Monolepis chenopoides. The roots are washed, boiled in an olla, and cooled in a basket. The water is squeezed out, and they are again put into the olla with a little fat or lard and salt. After cooking for a few moments they are ready to serve with tortillas. This plant is also used in a similar manner by the Mexicans, who are supposed to have learned its value from the natives. The seeds are boiled, partially dried, parched, ground on the metate, and eaten as pinole.

A'taftak, Cucurbita fœtidissima H. B. K. The seeds of this wild gourd are roasted and eaten.

E'ikâfĭ. The root of this small plant is gathered, boiled, and eaten without peeling.

Hait'ʿkam, Olneya tesota. The nuts of the ironwood tree (pl. VII, *a*) are parched in an olla, or, what is more usual, the broken half of one, and eaten without further preparation. The tree grows on the mesas on all sides of the villages, where it is very conspicuous for a few days in May, when it is covered with a mass of purple flowers.

Hâ'kowat, Phoradendron californicum. The berries of the mistletoe that grows on the mesquite are gathered and boiled without stripping from the stem. They are taken in the fingers, and the berries stripped off into the mouth as eaten. Various species of mistletoe are very abundant on the trees along the Gila, but this one only is eaten.

Halt, Cucurbita pepo Linn. The common species of pumpkin grown by the Pimas, as well as by the whites and Mexicans, is cut in strips and dried, when it is known by a number of different names, according to the manner of cutting and the particular variety. This species includes the pumpkins proper, the bush scallop squashes, the summer crook-necks, and the white or yellow warty squashes. The club-shaped, pear-shaped, or long-cylindrical smooth squash is Cucurbita moschata Duchesne. It is extensively grown by the Pimas. The seeds of the pumpkin are parched and eaten. When the dried pumpkin is used, it is softened in water and boiled.

Ha'nûm, Opuntia arborescens. The fruit of this cactus (pl. VIII, *a*) is gathered with an instrument that resembles an enlarged wooden clothespin. It is collected in large quantities and carried home in the kiâhâ, or carrying basket. A pit is dug and a fire built in it, on which stones are heated. As the fire dies down the stones are removed and a layer of the saltbush, Suæda arborescens, is placed over the coals; above this is placed a layer of cactus fruit, then hot stones, and so alternately to the top, over which a thick layer of saltbush is laid with earth outside. The pit is left undisturbed over one night, then its contents are spread out, dried, and the fruit stirred with a stick until the thorns are rubbed off, whereupon it is ready to store away for future use. In its final preparation it must be boiled. It is then salted and eaten with pinole. The acid flavor is usually relieved by the addition of various plants cooked as greens.

Ha'rsany, Cereus giganteus Engelm. The fruit of the giant cactus, or, as it is more generally known in the Southwest, the saguaro (pls. VIII, *b*, and IX, *c*, *d*), is gathered in June, and so important is the harvest that the event marks the beginning of the new year in the Pima calendar. The supply is a large one and only industry is required to make it available throughout the entire year, as both the seeds and the dried fruit may be preserved. Seeds that have passed through the body are sometimes gathered from the dried feces, washed, and treated as those obtained directly from the fruit, though there would seem to be some special value ascribed to them as in the case of the "second harvest" of the Seri.[a]

---

[a] Cf. W J McGee in Seventeenth Annual Report of Bureau of American Ethnology, 212.

The fruit is eaten without preparation when it ripens. It is of a crimson color and contains many black seeds about the size of those of the fig, which fruit it resembles in taste. By a process of boiling and fermentation an intoxicating liquor is obtained from the fresh fruit which has been more highly esteemed than the nutritious food and has rendered this new-year a season of debauchery.[a]

The fruit is dried and preserved in balls 15 or more centimeters in diameter (fig. 3). From either the fresh or dried fruit sirup is extracted by boiling it "all day." The residue is ground on the metate into an oily paste which is eaten without further preparation. The seeds may be separated from the pulp at the time of drying the fruit and may be eaten raw or ground on the metate and treated as any meal—put into water to form a pinole or combined with other meal to bake into bread.

Ha'valt, Yucca bacatta. The fruit is boiled, dried, ground on the mealing-stone, and boiled with flour. It is also eaten raw as a cathartic. The stems are reduced to pulp and used as soap. Y. elata is also used as soap.

Ho'ny, Zea Mays. Corn, the most important crop of the Pueblo tribes, has, in recent years at least, been of less value to the Pimas than wheat. The numerous varieties are all prepared in about the same manner. As the husked corn is brought in by the women, it is piled on a thin layer of brush and roasted by burning the latter, after which it is cut from the cob, dried, and stored away for future use.

---

[a] " I arrived at the Pimas Gileños, accompanied by the governor of the Coco-Maricopas. There was great rejoicement, for there had spread thus far the report that they (the Moquis) had me killed. The governor of the Pimas told me that all the relatives were well content, and wishing to make a feast, all the pueblos together. I agreed to this, but on condition that it should be apart from me, foreseeing in this what would come to pass. In a little while I heard that they were singing 'a heap' (*de monton*); this was stopped presently, but was followed by a great uproar of discordant voices, and shouting, in which they said, 'We are good! We are happy! We know God! We are the fellows to fight the Apaches! We are glad the old man (as they call me) has come, and not been killed!' This extravagant shouting (*exorbitante griteria*), a thing foreign to the seriousness of the Pimas, I knew came from drinking, which produced various effects. Some came and took me by the hand, saluting me. One said, 'I am padre de Pedro.' Another said to me, 'Thou hast to baptize a child.' Another, 'This is thy home—betake not thyself to see the king, nor to Tucson.' Others made the sign of the cross, partly in Spanish, so that though I felt very angry at such general drunkenness, there did not fail me some gusto to l ear the good expressions into which they burst, even when deprived of reason. The next day I complained of these excesses to the governor, who told me that it only happened a few times and in the season of saguaro, and adding that it made his people vomit yellow and kept them in good health. What most pleased me was to see that no woman got drunk; instead of which saw many of them leading by the bridle the horse upon which her husband was mounted, gathering up at the same time the clothes and beads that the men scattered about, in order that none should be lost." (Garcés's Diary, 438.) "The three pitahaya months," says Father Salva-Tierra [describing the saguaro harvest in California], "resemble the carnival in some parts of Europe, when the men arc in a great measure stupified or mad. The natives here also throw aside what reason they have, giving themselves up to feastings, dancings, entertainments of the neighboring rancherias, buffooneries, and comedies, such as they are; and in these, whole nights are spent to the high diversion of the audience. The actors are selected for their talent of imitation; and they execute their parts admirably well." (Venegas, History of California, I, 82.) "The gathering of this fruit may be considered as the harvest of the native inhabitants. They can eat as much of it as they please, and with some this food agrees so well that they become corpulent during that period, and for this reason I was sometimes unable to recognize at first sight individuals otherwise perfectly familiar to me, who visited me after having fed three or four weeks on these pitahayas." (Jacob Baegert, The Aboriginal Inhabitants of the Californian Peninsula, in Smithsonian Report, 1863, 363.)

The shelled corn is ground on the metate and baked in large cakes in the ashes. Corn is also boiled with ashes, dried, and the hulls washed off, then thoroughly dried and parched with coals or over the fire. It is then made into a gruel, but is not so highly regarded as the wheat pinole.

I'savĭk. The thorns of this cactus are removed as soon as gathered, and it is eaten without further preparation.

I'tany, Atriplex sp. The heads of this saltbush are pounded up in the mortar and screened to separate the hulls. The seeds are washed, spread to dry, parched in a piece of olla, and ground on the metate. They are then ready to be eaten as pinole, or dry, in the

FIG. 3. Dried saguaro fruit.

latter case a pinch of the meal being taken alternately with a sip of water.

Ka'ĭfsa, Cicer arietinum Linn. The chick-pea is raised in small quantities and is also purchased from the traders. This is the garabanzo of Mexico. The name chicos is sometimes applied to this pea as it is to anything small, especially to small or, rather, sweet corn that is just old enough for roasting.

Kâf, Chenopodium murale. The seed is gathered early in the summer and prepared by parching and grinding, after which it may be eaten as pinole or combined with other meal.

Kâ'meûvat. After the August rains this seed is gathered, parched over coals in the parching pan, ground on the metate, and eaten as pinole.

Kan'yo, Sorghum vulgare Pers.   Sorghum is cultivated when the water supply permits.   It has been obtained recently from the whites, who raise it extensively in the Southwest.

Ki'ak.   The heads of this annual are gathered and the seeds beaten out with the kiâhâ stick used as a flail.   The seeds are moistened, parched, which makes it resemble pop corn, ground on the metate, and eaten by taking alternately pinches of meal and sips of water.

Koĭ, Prosopis velutina.   Mesquite beans[a] formed nearly if not quite the most important article of diet of the Pimas in primitive times (pl. x, *a*).   They are still extensively used, though the supply is somewhat curtailed by the live stock which feed avidly upon them.   As already stated, the crop sometimes fails, "especially in

FIG. 4. Sheds with caches on roofs.

hard times," as one of our informants naively remarked.   The mesquite harvest takes place somewhat later than that of the saguaro.   The beans are gathered and stored in the pod in cylindrical bins on the roofs of the houses or sheds (fig. 4).   While yet on the trees, the bean pods are bored by larvæ of the family Bruchidæ. [b]

---

a Analysis of mesquite beans, including the pod:

	Per cent.		Per cent.
Moisture	5. 96	Crude cellulose	32. 53
Dry matter	94. 04	Albuminoids	14. 03
Crude ash	5. 20	Nitrogen-free extract	37. 13
Crude fat	5. 12	Nutritive ratio	1: 5.8

"The amount of cellulose, or woody fiber, is very much larger in the bean, and the amount of nitrogen-free extract considerably smaller; but the albuminoids and fats compare very well indeed.   The bean pod is 4 to 8 inches in length, and grows in bunches from six to eight pods to the bunch."   Third Annual Report, 1888, Texas Agricultural Experiment Station.   Reference kindly supplied by Mr Ewell, Bureau of Chemistry, Department of Agriculture.

b "There are two species of Bruchus which are especially common in mesquite seeds in Arizona—both the common mesquite and the screw bean, namely, Bruchus prosopis Lec. and Bruchus desertorum Lec.   Occasionally other species breed in the seeds."   Dr L. O. Howard, Department of Agriculture, letter.

The beans are prepared for use by being pounded up in a mortar with a stone pestle, or, if a large quantity is required, with a large wooden one. The pods may be ground with the beans. Another method of preparation is to separate the beans from the pods, parch them by tossing them up in a pan of live coals, and reduce them to meal by grinding, whereupon they may be eaten as pinole. This has a sweetish taste and is reputed to be very nourishing.

The catkins of the mesquite are eaten without preparation by stripping from the stem between the teeth.

The white gum which exudes from the mesquite limbs is used in making candy.

The inner bark is employed as a substitute for rennet.

Ko'kitc vhûtaki, Parkinsonia microphylla (in the foothills); P. torreyana (on the mesas) (pl. x, b). The paloverde bean was formerly eaten either as gathered or after being pounded in the mortar. It was not eaten as pinole, but was sometimes mixed with mesquite meal.

Ko'mûlt. The heads are gathered and washed, sometimes twice, then boiled in an olla with a little water. Wheat flour and a seasoning of salt are added and the whole is stirred until the heads fall to pieces.

Ko'-okupaltûk. According to tradition the seeds were eaten in primitive times, but no one now knows how they were prepared. The plant is now boiled with meat as greens.

Ko'ûtcĭlt, Prosopis pubescens. Screw beans are abundant along the banks of the Gila. They are cooked in pits which are lined with arrow bushes set on end. The beans are placed in layers alternating with cocklebur leaves, the whole covered with earth and left to stand three or four days, after which they are taken out and spread to dry. They are then ready to use or store away in the arrow-bush basket bins on the house tops. They are further prepared for food by pounding up in a mortar, the fine flour then being ready to be eaten as pinole. The coarser portion is taken up in the hands with water, the juice sucked through the fingers, and the remainder rejected.

Kwa'aolt, Licium fremontii var. The red berry is boiled and eaten.

Mâ-âtatûk. This is described as resembling asparagus. The stems may be eaten raw or boiled or roasted in the ashes.

Me'la, Citrullus vulgaris Shrad. Watermelons are among the most important crops of the Pimas and are eaten during at least six months of the year.

Naf', Opuntia engelmanni. The thorns are brushed off the fruit of the prickly pear before it is gathered. It is then peeled and eaten, the seeds being thrown away. The Papagos make a sirup from the fruit (which is said to cause fever in those not accustomed to its use) and dry the fruit as they do that of the saguaro, but the Pimas make no further use of it than to eat it raw.

Nyi'âtam, Malva sp. This plant is boiled and the liquid used in making pinole in times of famine.

O'-opat, Acacia greggii. The beans of the cat's-claw (pl. vii, *b*) were eaten in primitive times, but no one of the present generation knows how they were prepared.

Ositc ʋ'w ʋtpat, Zizyphus lycioides. The black berry of this thorny bush is gathered in the basket bowls after it has been beaten down with sticks. It is eaten raw and the seeds are thrown away.

Pap'kam. The heads are tied in bunches and dried in the sun. They are then shelled, screened, the seeds parched, ground on the metate, and eaten as pinole. They are "not sweet."

Pavf(i), Phaseolus vulgaris Linn. At least one variety of the common kidney bean, pole bean, bunch bean, etc., was known to the natives before the advent of the Spaniards. Venegas states [a] that "red frixoles, or kidney beans" [Phaseolus sp.], were cultivated by the natives of lower California, and this may have been the variety known in Pimería.[b]

Pel'tûkany, Triticum sativum Lam. Wheat is the principal crop of the Pimas, and four varieties are known to them. It is ground on the metate to make the flour used in cooking the great loaves that weigh from 10 to 20 pounds. Tortillas resembling those of the Mexicans are now more commonly used than the heavy loaves of former days. A light ánd toothsome doughnut is fried in bubbling hot suet (pl. vi, *a*). One of the commonest methods of preparing wheat is to parch it, grind it on the metate, and eat it as a sort of thin gruel called hak(i) tcoï; or the wheat may be boiled before parching, in which case the product is known as pârsâɪ tcoï. Both are known to the whites by the Mexican term "pinole."

Rsat. The bulb of the wild onion is eaten. It is common on the slopes at the foot of the Estrellas.

Rso'-owût. The fine reddish seed is boiled with flour as a mush.

Rsʋr's ʋ-ʋlïk. This is used as greens with similar plants.

---

a History of California, 45.

b The entire region occupied by tribes of the Piman stock, extending over the larger part of Sonora as far northward as the Rio Gila, was known to the Spanish as Pimería. That portion between the Yaquis and the Gila was called Pimería Alta. The Papagos occupy nearly all this territory, and of late it is commonly called Papagueria. For an undetermined number of centuries the Pimas proper have occupied the middle Gila district. Their habitat differs, therefore, from that of the other tribes of the stock, and for convenience their territory will be here designated by the term Pimería.

Buschmann states in Die Pima-Sprache that "Duflot de Mofras (*exploration du territoire de l'Orégon, des Californies et de la mer vermeille* T. I., Par. 1844, p. 208) setzt die *Pimeria alta* von den Flüssen Colorado und Gila an bis zur Stadt *Hermosillo* und zum *rio de los Ures;* die *Pimeria baxa* von da an bis zum *rio del Fuerte,* welcher die Gränze von Sonora und Cinaloa bildet. Er setzt beide, zu grosse *Pimerias* gleich Ober- und Nieder-Sonora: '*La Sonore se divise en haute et basse, et prend aussi, à cause des Indiens Pimas, le nom de* Pimería alta y baja.' Arricivita (p. 396) bestimmt die *Pimeria alta* so: 'Die ganze *Pimeria alta* dehnt sich aus vom *Presidio de Ternate* bis zu den *playas de Caborca,* über 100 *leguas;* und von der Mission *S. Ignacio* von S nach N bis zum *Gila*-Flusse, wieder 100 *leguas;* ihr grösster Theil liegt unter dem 30ten Breitengrade. *Toda la Pimeria* (397) *está habitada de Indios.*'" P. 321, 322.

Sâi'tûkam iavik. The leaf of this thorny plant is eaten raw or boiled.

Si'etcu, Cucumis melo Linn. The muskmelon is extensively raised by the Pimas.

Si'vitcĭlt, Rumex hymenosepalus. The canaigre is cultivated by the whites in the Gila valley for tannin, yet it is eaten by the Pimas. The stem is roasted in the ashes or, recently, stewed with sugar. We have seen the children greedily devouring the raw roots in March. Doctor Palmer states that the roots are used to tan deerskin and also as soap.

So'-oaot, Sophia pinnata (Walt) Britton. The seeds are parched, ground, and mixed with water to form pinole. The Mexicans of Arizona use the leaves of this plant in preparing a drink. An infusion made from the leaves is also employed as a remedy for sores.

Tâki, Gosypium sp. The cotton plant is no longer raised, but from pre-Spanish days down to the last quarter of a century it was cultivated both for the fiber and the seeds. The latter were pounded up with mesquite beans in the mortar or they were sometimes parched and eaten without grinding.[a]

Tapk'. These seeds resemble those of flax in appearance. They are eaten either raw or boiled and are yet extensively used.

Tapkalt. This is one of the varieties of squash that is cultivated by the Pimas at the present time.

Tâ'ta â'nŭk, Atriplex nuttallii. The stems of this saltbush are boiled with wheat. They are cut in short lengths and used sometimes as a stuffing for roast rabbit.

Tcia, Salvia columbaria Benth. The seeds when infused in water form a pleasant mucilaginous beverage, very popular with the Pimas.

Tci'âldi. The fruit of this cactus is brought by the Papagos and traded to the Pimas. It is cooked in the same manner as Opuntia arborescens.

Tciaaolt, Echinocactus wislizeni. The pulp of the visnaga is considered valuable in lieu of water to those suffering from thirst. It is also eaten after being cut in strips and boiled all day. It is sometimes boiled with mesquite beans, a layer each in the cooking olla. It is occasionally boiled with sugar. It is quite a popular confection among the whites, who, in some places, obtain the raw material from the Papagos.

Tci'-itkwatak, Lithospermum sp. The leaves are eaten without preparation.

---

a C. D. Poston stated in 1864 that he had recently furnished the Pimas with 500 pounds of cotton seed, though he did not give any reason for doing so. It is fair to presume that the Pimas had sufficient seed from the plant that they had raised from time immemorial.

Tcil'tipĭn (Sp.).   This pepper is raised by the Papagos and brought to the Pimas.

Tco'hokia.   The leaves are gathered in spring and sometimes baked in tortillas.   In summer the seeds are gathered, ground on the metate, mixed with meal or squash, or they may be parched and ground to be eaten dry.

Tco'tcĭk â'nŭk, Suæda arborescens; S. suffrutescens.   These are added to greens or cactus fruit to give flavor.

To'a, Quercus oblongifolia.   The acorns of this oak are traded from the Papagos.   After the hulls have been removed they are parched and ground into meal.

ꞯrtam, Atriplex lentiformis.   The seed of this saltbush is cooked in pits which are lined with Suæda arborescens and the papery inner bark of the cottonwood moistened and mixed together.   The roasting requires but one night, then the seeds are taken out, dried, parched, and laid away for future use.   When eaten, it is placed in a cup and water added until a thick gruel is produced.

Vakwai'hai-ĭndûm, Solanum elæagnifolium.   The berries are put in the milk from which cheese is made to serve as a substitute for rennet.

Vak'wandam, Rumex berlandieri.   This plant is used with the cactus fruit, Opuntia arborescens, in the same manner as the saltbush, Suæda arborescens.

Vi'pĭnoĭ, Opuntia versicolor.   The fruit is sometimes eaten raw, but it is usually prepared in the same manner as Opuntia arborescens.

Dr Edward Palmer, who collected among the Pimas in 1885, obtained some nuts of the "quinine plant," Simmondsia californica Nutt., which he says are eaten either raw or parched.   Professor Thornber states that the Mexicans use the oil as a hair tonic.   He also describes an "Indian potato," Hoffmanseggia falcaria Cav., which, when roasted, tastes like the cultivated Irish potato.   However, this is a member of the pea family and not a potato.   A true Solanum is found native to Arizona, but we have not learned that the Pimas know of it.

At least three kinds of chewing gum are in use.   That most highly esteemed is called vi-ipam, "milky;" it is obtained from a plant which somewhat resembles a sweet-potato vine.   The pointed pods are gathered, their milk poured into a squash stalk and heated in the ashes, whereupon it is ready to chew.   A bush, Encelia farinosa, called *tohafs,* exudes a clear gum; and that on the stems of some of the Compositae is sometimes gathered and chewed by children.

MEDICINAL PLANTS

A'taftak. The root of the wild gourd[a] is pounded up in mortars, boiled, and the extracted juice put into the ear to cure earache. It is poured into a hollow tooth to stop aching. "It kills maggots in open sores."

Ha'tam, Sphæralcea angustifolia. The leaves are boiled and used as a remedy for diarrhea. Another informant states that the root is boiled and the liquid extracted is used as a remedy for biliousness.

Ka'kaitco v-vs, "quail plant," Heliotropium curassavicum. The upper part of the light yellowish root is dried and ground in mortars, dried again, and ground very fine upon the metate, when it is ready to be applied to sores or wounds after they have been washed.

Kâkpitäm. The leaves of this bush are boiled and the extract used as an emetic.

Kŏĭ, Prosopis velutina. The black gum of the mesquite is boiled and the dilute liquid used as a wash for sore eyes and open wounds. The inner bark of the mesquite is boiled and the liquid used as an emetic and cathartic.

Kŏĭtcĭlt, Prosopis pubescens. The bark of the root of the screw bean is pounded up in mortars, dried, and again ground into a fine powder on the metate; or it may be boiled without pounding or grinding and the liquid used as a dressing for wounds. After a few days, as the wound heals, the dry powder is substituted.

Osikâkamûk, Pluchea borealis. The bark of the arrow-bush root is separated by pounding between stones and then placed in water for a few hours to extract a liquid for washing the face and for sore eyes.

O'sitcɯwûtpat, Zizyphus lycioides. The root of this bush is pounded up in mortars and boiled, the liquid extracted being used as a remedy for sore eyes.

Pihoɪ. An evil spirit that lives in the east is called Pihoɪ. He causes certain diseases, which have their appropriate songs. One informant declared that a tree that grows near the Maricopa village on the Gila was also called pihoɪ, and from it a medicine stick is made that will cure diseases of the throat. The writer was unable either to verify or to disprove this statement.

Rsios. Two unidentified species of Bigelovia are used as a dressing for scarified wounds. The bruised leaves are applied to bleeding surfaces that have been cut with broken glass.

Rsɯkaikokŭk, Larrea mexicana. The leaves of the creosote bush (pl. IX, *a*) are boiled and the liquor is allowed to cool a little, when it is drunk as an emetic. The boiled leaves are also used as a poultice.

---

[a] In pioneer days the whites used the roots of two species of wild gourds, Cucurbita palmata and C. digitata, as a cathartic, Doctor Palmer stating that they were "very much beliked by the soldiers."

Sivitcŭlt, Rumex hymenosepalus. The root of the canaigre is dried, ground and the powder applied to sores.

So'am hi'âseikkam, "yellow flower." An infusion made from the flowers of this plant is used as a remedy for sore eyes.

Ʌrtam, Atriplex lentiformis. The root is powdered and applied to sores.

Ʌrto, Krameria parvifolia. Used in the same manner as the preceding.

Vai'ewa, Xanthium canadense. Cocklebur pulp is combined with soot as a remedy for sore eyes.

Va'vaĭsh, Houttuynia californica, called "yerba mansa" by the Mexicans. The roots are crushed and boiled. The extract is used as a tea for consumptives, according to one informant, and as an emetic according to another.

Vipûkam, Alba marginata. The root is chewed as an emetic.

Teamsters' Tea, Ephedra antisyphilitica Berland, is a native of Arizona, and is used by the Pimas in making a beverage. It is also used by both the Pimas and Mexicans as a remedy for syphilis.

A composite, Perezia wrightii, is used as a styptic.

Thamnosma montanum is said to be used as a decoction for the cure of gonorrhea by the Pimas and Apaches. (Dr Edward Palmer, manuscript.)[a]

ANIMALS USED FOR FOOD

Kâ'-âtci, or *tâsi'-ikâlt*, Tayassu angulatum sonoriense. The peccary is yet found in the larger mountain chains that were formerly reached by the hunters of Pimería, though the Gila river is about the northern limit of the range of this animal in the West. It could never have been an important article of diet, and is practically unknown to the younger generation.

Kaf, Taxidea taxus (subspecies?). The badger is occasionally seen along the Gila, but is not abundant and is no longer eaten. It is one of the animals that cause disease among men, and a badger tail is an essential part of the medicine-man's equipment.

Ka'katco, Lophortyx gambeli. The handsome topknot quail is the most abundant of the feathered inhabitants of the Gila thickets. It is tabued to the women, though no explanation for this could be discovered.

Kâ'sŏn. A "rat" was formerly eaten, but it was found impossible during my stay to get specimens for identification.[b]

---

[a] This is similar to, but not identical with, the "cordoncillo" of the Arizona Mexicans, from which an infusion is made that is used as a tonic and blood purifier. (Thornber.)

[b] Mr Fisher, of the Biological Survey, lists the following species of mice and rats for Pimería: Mus alexandrinus, introduced; Mus musculus, introduced; Mus norvegicus, introduced; Orychomys torridus; Peromyscus, 2–3 species; Sigmodon hispidus arizonæ; Reithrodontomys (sp.?); Neotoma (sp.?); Fiber zibethicus pallidus.

Kâ'vi, Castor canadensis frondator. The beaver was common along the Gila, and was esteemed highly for food.[a]

Ka'viyo, Equus caballus. The horse is seldom eaten by the Pimas. In times of famine, however, horses are sometimes used, although the more than half-starved condition of the animals suggests anything but nourishing viands.

Ko'-ovĭk, Antilocapra americana mexicana. The antelope is now unknown in Pimería, but the hunters of former centuries successfully stalked these animals upon the mesas, particularly upon the higher grassy plains to the eastward.

Ma'kûm. These unidentified worms (?) are plentiful when a rainy season insures a heavy crop of desert plants. They are gathered in large quantities, their heads pulled off, and intestines removed. The women declare that their hands swell and become sore if they come in contact with the skin of the worms. The worms are then put into cooking pots lined with branches of saltbush and boiled. The skins are braided together while yet soft and dried a day or two in the sun. The dry and brittle sticks are eaten at any time without further preparation.

Ma'vĭt, Felis hippotestes aztecus. The puma is yet abundant in the mountain ranges of Arizona, and in former times one was occasionally secured by the Pimas when in quest of other game.

Rsu'lĭk. There are at least six species of ground squirrels in this region,[b] but in the absence of specimens the writer could not learn if the Pimas distinguished among them. When water was obtainable it was poured into the burrows of these squirrels until they were driven out, whereupon they were killed with clubs or shot with arrows. They were tabued to the women under penalty of nosebleed or deficiency in flow of milk for their babies.

Si'-ĭk, Odocoileus couesi. White-tail deer are yet fairly common in the mountains and two deerskins were seen among the Pimas during the period of six months spent with them. Perhaps one in two or three years would be an excessive estimate of the number killed by the men of the Gila River reservation. The deer figures largely in their traditions and religion.

Ta'matâlt. During the winter months these birds are caught at nearly every house by means of traps. The trap commonly used is described on page 101.

---

[a] The earliest American invaders of Pimería were beaver trappers who descended the Gila early in the last century. One of the first Americans that the oldest living Pimas remember was Kâ'vi Vâ'namam, "Beaver Hat," who told the Pimas that the buildings now in ruins along the Gila and Salt rivers were destroyed by waterspouts. He lived several years among the Pimas, and was finally killed near Prescott by Apaches.

[b] Eutamias dorsalis (?), Spermophilus canescens, S. grammurus, S. harrisi, S. spilosoma macrospilotus (Oracle), S. tereticaudus (Fort Yuma).

Tâpi, Lepus arizonas.   The small cottontail is fairly common in river bottoms and on the mesa throughout the Pima country.   It is shot with arrows made with a straight point without stone or metal head.   It is included in the list of victims that result from rabbit drives in which the hares, Lepus texianus and L. alleni, are the principal desiderata.

Tcirsâny, Ovis nelsoni.   The mountain sheep has served as food when obtainable, though it has been many years since they have been abundant.[a]

Tcok tcof, Lepus texianus.   There are two species of large hares along the Gila, where they are termed "jack rabbits" by the whites, very few of whom distinguish them apart.   The Pimas, however, recognize the difference and call this species the dark or gray, and the other the white, *tcof.*

Tcu'tcult, Gallus domesticus.   During the late Spanish and the Mexican régime a small breed of fowl was introduced, probably by the Papagos, which in turn gave way to the large varieties brought by the Americans in the last half century.   Hens' eggs are eaten either fried or boiled.   One of the interpreters confided to Mrs Russell that she economized time and labor by boiling the eggs in the coffee.

To'a tcof, Lepus alleni.   These are common and utilized for food to a considerable extent.   There seems to be no preference for one species of hare over the others, but "none are so good as beef."   The stomachs of this hare and of Lepus texianus are used in making cheese.

Va'owŏk, Procyon lotor.   The raccoon is said to be used for food, though the writer did not see any of the animals or any of their skins during a stay of a year and a half in Arizona.

Vâ'prsa, Thomonys cervinus.   Gopher hunts are occasionally arranged in a manner similar to those in which the hares are driven. The animals are poked out of their retreats with sticks and without preparation thrown upon the coals to roast.

---

a "Having traversed 4 leagues, we arrived at a town, Tusonimon, which is so named from a great heap of horns, from the wild or sylvan sheep, which appears like a hill, and from the numbers that there are of the animals, they make the common subsistence of the inhabitants." (Juan Matio Mange: Diary extract translated for Schoolcraft, III, 303.)   This visit of Mange to the Pima towns was in November, 1697.   The discovery of this statement by Mange and also a letter of inquiry from Mr Hodge directed the writer's attention to the significance attaching to the horns of the mountain sheep after he had returned from his sojourn among the Pimas.   Inquiry was then made of a number of Pima correspondents and of Mr C. H. Cook, at Sacaton.   The latter ascertained from Antonio Azul, the head chief, that the horns of the mountain sheep were never brought home by hunters, which does not agree with Mange's statement.   Each man had a place set apart where he deposited them in order that they might exert no evil influence upon the winds or rains.   At times the Papagos held rain ceremonies, during which the medicine-men deposited the tails of mountain sheep together with eagle feathers at springs.   The same tribe at one time sacrificed some children in their efforts to increase the supply of water, but "instead of bringing them water this dried up all the springs."   A few mountain sheep remain in the Superstition mountains and in the other high ranges near and on the reservation.   When climbing the Sierra Estrella, in March, 1902, the writer saw a flock of five which did not manifest any such fear at the sight of man as do the mountain sheep of British Columbia and the more northern Rockies.   Indeed, the Pima chief at the foot of the mountains explained the reason for their indifference very adequately when he declared the sheep were game fit only for the Papagos, who had no fields to look after.

Vatop. There are occasional references to fish in the traditions of the Pimas and the notes of Spanish and American travelers sometimes mention them. It is certain that at times they caught large numbers of fish, but in seasons of drought the river, then as now, becoming wholly dry near the villages, could not be relied upon to furnish such a convenient supply of food. Either the long series of dry years and the absence of fish have caused the people to forget former classifications or else they never distinguished one species from another, for they now have but one name for all fresh fish. However, there were several species in the Gila and adjoining streams that were large enough for food.[a]

Wh'aĭ, Odocoileus hemionus (subspecies?). Information concerning this species was very vague and unreliable, though it seems certain that the black-tail deer was sometimes killed by the Pimas, at least before the growing power of the Apaches prevented the former from roaming through the mountains that border Pimería on the north and east.

Wo'poldo, Equus asinus.[b] The burro (donkey) is not in high repute among the Pimas, where the distances to the white settlements and between villages necessitate a more speedy animal for draft or riding purposes. Few in number, they could not be very important as an article of diet. They have been eaten in the past, but are rarely so used at present.

Snakes are not eaten, even in times of famine, and the idea of eating lizards is repudiated with scorn.

---

[a] Garcés, who traversed the Pima country in 1775, wrote: "There is found in this river no other fish than that which they call matalo'te, which is so very savory to the taste, but is troublesome on account of the many bones that it has." (On the Trail of a Spanish Pioneer, II, 142.) Jordan says: "Garcés's remarks settle the matalo'te. There are no large fish in the Gila except the two large, bony chubs called, by Baird and Girard, Gila robusta and Gila elegans. In the very mouth of the river there is also a big, rawboned sucker of the same build, called Xyrauchen cypho, the Razor-back or Hump-back Sucker. The Gila is a hump-back chub, about a foot and a half long, with a low, large mouth and a long, broad tail. It is popularly known as Bony-tail, Gila Trout, and Round-tail, and is about as poor eating as a fish can be." The Land of Sunshine, XIII, 436.

In The Fishes of the Colorado Basin, Evermann and Rutter enumerate several species that must have been accessible to the Pimas. Their names and the localities where they were collected are as follows:

Pantosteus arizonæ Gilbert. Salt river, Tempe.
Pantosteus clarkii (Baird and Girard). Gila river, Fort Thomas.
Catostomus latipinnis (Baird and Girard). Rio San Pedro and Fort Thomas.
Catostomus gila Kirsch. Fort Thomas.
Catostomus insignis Baird and Girard. Rio San Pedro and Fort Thomas.
Xyrauchen cypho (Lockington). Mouth of Gila and Fort Thomas.
Ptychocheilus lucius Girard. Various stations on the Gila. Called Gila trout by Emory in 1848.
Gila elegans Baird and Girard. Taken from several places along the Gila by collectors.
Gila robusta Baird and Girard. Also described from several Gila stations under various names.
Cyprinodon macularius Baird and Girard. "Rio Gila."
In addition to these may be included the species collected in the San Pedro and Santa Cruz rivers, which are both tributaries of the Gila above Pimería and within reach of Pima hunting parties: Leuciscus niger (Cope), Tiaroga cobitis Girard, Agosia oscula (Girard), Agosia chrysogaster Girard, and Meda fulgida Girard.

[b] It is uncertain whether the burro of the Southwest is a descendant of the Asiatic species of wild asses, Equus hernionus, E. heniihippus, and E. onager, or of the African, E. africanus and E. somaticus.

DOMESTICATION OF ANIMALS

Dogs. The only domesticated animal which there is any certainty that the Pimas possessed at the time of the discovery is the dog. The old people say that in their youth the dogs were all alike and resembled coyotes. At present there are many small mongrels, obtained principally from the Mexicans (pl. VI, c). The dogs have shared with their masters the misfortunes of the last few years. Scarcity and want has left them gaunt and weak. They formerly served a useful purpose in giving warning of the presence of enemies about the villages. There are now no enemies and little within to tempt the thief to enter and steal. Dogs are called by the word "toot," "toot," "toot," uttered rapidly in a falsetto voice, the individual at the same time holding out a morsel of food to lure the animal within reach. A dog that has been bitten by a mad dog is saved by having a cross burned on its head.

Horses. The horse may have been seen by the Pimas in the sixteenth century, but it is doubtful if they obtained this animal before the seventeenth. They have been known so long that their origin has become accounted for by myths without a shadow of historic truth in them. The only individual who ventured to dispute the commonly accepted mythical origin assured me that they came from the West. Font, who visited the Gila in 1775, stated that his party was met by 18 mounted Pimas; so that the horse was evidently in use at that time.

There were very few horses among the Pimas until the last quarter of a century. The statements of the old persons agree with the calendar records, which make it evident that there were horses enough for but a small proportion of the warriors who engaged in conflicts with the Apaches. Horses stolen in Mexico were sold to the Papagos, who in turn sold them to the Pimas at much less than their true value. As the number in Pimería increased, the thieves began to operate in both directions, selling Sonoran horses on the Gila and Piman mounts in Sonora. However, this practice has been abandoned, and the tribe has quite as many horses as are needed. They are rather undersized animals, as may be seen from the pinto pony in figure 5. As the fields now yield an insufficient supply of food for their owners, it follows that there is little grain for the horses, which grow poor and thin in winter; indeed, many die of starvation. Their principal food during that season is saltbushes.[a]

The once famous grassy plains that made the Pima villages a haven of rest for cavalry and wagon-train stock are now barren,

---

[a] Professor Thornber says that "the native saltbushes, arranged in the order of their importance, that are eaten by range stock are as follows: Woody species, Atriplex canescens, A. nuttallii, A. polycarpa, A. lentiformis, A. confertifolia. The herbaceous species that are grazed by stock are: Atriplex coronata, A. elegans, A. bracteosa. The true greasewood, Sarcobatus vermicularis, a species closely allied to the saltbushes, is also browsed to a considerable extent.

and it is not until the mesquite leaves appear in April that the horses can browse upon food sufficiently nourishing to put them in good condition. As the mesquite beans ripen, in June and July, live stock fattens rapidly. A few owners gather and store the beans for stock feed. Very few are able to buy hay or rolled barley.

Cattle.[a] Sala Hina declared that her father and his brother, two Kwahadk's, brought the first cattle to the Pimas about 1820. The Spanish missionaries throughout Papagueria brought live stock to their stations for at least two centuries before the date given, so that

FIG. 5. Men and women in modern costume, and pinto pony.

the Pimas were at least aware of the value of cattle for a long time. The custom of killing and eating the cattle at the death of their owners contributed materially toward preventing increase in Pima herds. Oxen were very scarce for half a century after their introduction, and the old men and women speak sadly of the weary waiting for their turn to use the single ox that dragged the wooden plow for perhaps a whole village. Oxen are now no longer used; with their head yokes and the wooden plows they are of the past,

---

a In 1846 Emory found that "they have but few cattle, which are used in tillage, and apparently all steers, procured from the Mexicans. Their horses and mules are not plenty, and those they possessed were priced extravagantly high." Notes, 84.

and of that period of the Pimas' past that it is best for them to forget.

Cattle are driven and "roped" with the lariat, but no conventional mode of calling them is in vogue. Like the horses, they are branded and run at large. Their range is almost unlimited in some directions, but the entire absence of water away from the river prevents them from straying. With horses, cattle formed a great attraction to the Apaches during the last century until peace was declared in 1879, and the Pimas suffered frequent losses, for some of which, it must be added, the marauders paid dearly. To guard against the thieves it was customary to corral all stock within the village at night. When it strayed away across the mesas during the day it was sought by tracking or by waiting at the water holes, and while so engaged the men had many encounters with the enemy, who were ever on the look-out for such an opportunity to attack.

Mules. A few mules are raised, but, like the horses, they are small and of little value.

Donkeys. While the burro has been used for some time, it is not a popular animal among the Pimas. It is too slow for traveling across the wide, waterless plains of Pimería and is not adapted for farm work.

Poultry. Until the recent introduction of large American breeds a small breed of poultry had been kept for several years.[a] This had been obtained from the Mexicans, from whom also the manner of calling "pul," "pul," "pul" was derived. With the new breeds came the American custom of calling "peep," "peep."

Eagles and *red-tailed hawks* were kept for their feathers. All the inhabitants of a village assisted in catching lizards and in furnishing other suitable food for the village bird. The feathers were regularly plucked for the paraphernalia of the medicine-men.

Sonora doves were and are yet confined in log-cabin cages built up of arrowwood rods.

AGRICULTURE

METHODS

IRRIGATION

The Gila river carries an unusually large amount of suspended matter when in flood. As shown by the tests made during the surveys for the dam which is intended to supply Pimería with water, it carries on an average 10.5 per cent of mud, with a maximum of 20 per cent.[b] The entire bottom land upon which the fields are located has been built of this material. It is so light that wagons cut readily into it during the dry seasons and work it into fluffy dust several

---

a "A few chickens and dogs were seen." Emory, Notes, 85.
b Water-Supply and Irrigation Papers, no. 33, p. 36.

inches in depth.   The Pimas do not practise rotation of crops, the soil being so rich from silt which is periodically deposited by the river at flood stage that the idea of exhausting it has never occurred to them.

Irrigation was practised for unknown centuries by the Hohokam, and the course of their great canals can yet be traced for miles,[a] not only along the river bottoms, but also across the mesas where the large water-worn pebbles bound together with caliche[b] or deposited lime must have required infinite labor for their construction.   At the first appearance of the Pimas it may be presumed that they used the canals already constructed by their predecessors, hence they would be dull indeed if they could not maintain irrigation systems sufficient for their needs.   The testimony of the early writers is to the effect that they possessed canals larger than they required and that the water flowed away from the fields in volume scarcely diminished from that at the head gates.   The Gila has a uniform fall of 8 feet to the mile at this place, while the canals need not have more than 2.

As the water of the Gila and Salt rivers is strongly impregnated with alkali it tends under certain conditions to deposit salts in such quantities that the land is rendered unfit for use.   The alkali rises to the surface in an efflorescence that resembles snow in appearance. From early descriptions of the country we learn that alkaline deposits were known while the tribe was yet under purely aboriginal conditions.[c]

The Pimas knew, however, how to deal with this difficulty—they flooded the tract repeatedly and in this way washed the alkali out of it.   They declare that they never abandoned a piece of ground because of it.

No very reliable estimate of the total amount of land cultivated by this people has been made.[d]   Each family cultivates from 1 to 5 acres.   With an abundance of water and the new needs of the tribe it is probable that the size of the individual holdings will rapidly increase.   The farms are rectangular, arranged with reference

---

a "The mode of canal construction employed by these pueblo builders [Hohokam] was another indication of their patience and industry.   Their canals are models for the modern farmer to imitate; yet they could have been dug in no conceivable manner save by the laborious process of hand excavation with stone or wooden implements, the earth being borne away by means of blankets, baskets, or rude litters.   Notwithstanding this, the outlines of at least a hundred and fifty miles of ancient main irrigating ditches may be readily traced, some of which meander southward from the Salt river a distance of fourteen miles."   F. W. Hodge, "Prehistoric irrigation in Arizona," American Anthropologist, VI, 324.

b For an account of this formation see P. Blake, "The caliche of southern Arizona: an example of deposition by vadose circulation," in The Genesis of Ore Deposits, 710.

c "We continued [from Casa Grande] toward the west, over sterile plains.   On all the grounds about these buildings there is not a single pasture; but appear as if they had been strewn with salt."   Mange's Diary, in Schoolcraft, III, 303.

d Garcés, writing in 1775, stated that "Todos estos pueblos hacen grandes siembras de trigo, algunas de maiz, algodon, calabazas y otras semillas, para cuyo riego tienen formadas buenas acequias, cercadas las milpas con cerco comun, y divididas las de distintos dueños, con cercos particulares."   Doc. His. Mex., 2d ser., I, 235.

to the supplying canal, and are always fenced with some care (pl. XI, *a*). Before the Pimas obtained barbed wire from the Government the fences were of willow wattling or the tops of mesquite trees and various kinds of brush. When a tract was newly brought under irrigation a committee of six men was chosen to make allotments to those who had assisted in digging the ditches. They chose the best land for themselves, which seems to have been taken as a matter of course, in a measure compensating for their trouble. The plots were from 100 to 200 "steps" (see p. 93) in width, according to the number in the family to whom they were allotted. The brush was not difficult to remove even with the primitive implements at their command; the mesquite trees were not cut down, but their lower branches were trimmed so that they did not shade the ground to any considerable extent.

The canals were dug with the digging stick and shovel (fig. 10, *a*, *b*), the former being also used to prepare the easily pulverized ground and to plant the seed. In addition to the digging stick and shovel the primitive agriculturists also used a wooden implement which served the purpose of a hoe, though it resembled a weaver's batten in appearance (fig. 10, *c*). In comparatively recent times the wooden plow (fig. 11) was added to the list of implements. From the Mexicans they also obtained a hybrid implement (fig. 10, *d*) that combined the functions of spade and hoe. At the present time the tribe is supplied with modern agricultural implements by the Government. The crops, however, are stored in much the same way that was followed in prehistoric times, in circular bins of willow, arrow bush, and wheat straw, the last having been used since the introduction of wheat.

One of the Pima villages (pl. XI, *b*) situated southwest of the Maricopa wells was too far from the river to obtain water from it and depended, as do their kinsfolk and neighbors, the Kwahadk's, already referred to, on flood irrigation. To secure the benefit of this, they cleared fields on mesa slopes, over which water from the surrounding hills might be conducted whenever there were summer rains. Around the lower sides of the diminutive fields low dikes were raised to catch and retain the water. On the slopes of the Santan hills north of the present Pima village of Santan there are several hundred acres of stony mesa that have been cleared and cultivated (pl. IV, *a*, *b*). The rocks have been gathered in rows that inclose rectangular areas of but a few square yards in extent. There are about six clumps of creosote bush inclosed in it.[a] This locality adjoins a large ancient canal and

---

[a] At various places in the Southwest the writer has seen extensive areas over which the loose bowlders that were originally thickly scattered on the surface had been gathered in rounded heaps or in rows that divided the ground into rectangles that average about 5 meters to the side. The largest of these "fields" personally inspected is north of the town of Pima, nearly 200 miles east of the Pima reservation. On a lava-strewn mesa that is too high to be irrigated and too far from the hills to be flooded

an extensive ruin of a stone pueblo. Learning that the chief had declared that these fields had been cultivated within the memory of living men, the writer sent for him, but learned on questioning that neither he nor any other Pima knew aught about them. All the fields, canals, and cleared roads over the lava hills that appear in plate XI, *c* were the work of the Hohokam.

Division of Labor

The work of clearing the fields, planting, and irrigating devolved upon the men. The women harvested the crops, carrying the products in their kiâhâs. The men thrashed the wheat—with horses after those animals were introduced. Prior to that time, and even now when the crop is small, the women beat out the grain with straight sticks. As it was thrashed, the women winnowed it in baskets and piled it on a cotton cloth, the corners of which were tied together, forming a sort of sack that was thrown upon a horse and taken by the men to the storehouse or brought in sacks on their heads by the women (fig. 6). Pumpkins and all crops except wheat were carried by the women in their kiâhâs. Considering the

Fig. 6. Burden bearer.

fact that the Pimas were constantly harassed by the Apaches, so that the men could not safely lay aside their bows during any waking moment, this distribution of labor was not discreditable to them.

there are a half dozen of these tracts. The largest is a little more than half a mile in length by nearly a quarter in width. There are no signs of human occupation on the surface other than the disposition of the stones. Five miles east of Solomonsville there is a similar field and on the Prieto plateau 40 miles northeast of the last is another among the pines. These fields are distinctly different from the terraces that one sees on the north slope of Mount Graham and elsewhere.

PRODUCTS

Possessed of the foremost American cereal, maize, at least one variety of legume, and the cotton plant, as well as species of Cucurbitaceæ and other plants, the agriculture of the Pimas was well beyond the initial stages before the arrival of the whites.[a]

CEREALS

The Pimas distinguished half a dozen varieties of maize, to which they have now added the large corn brought by the Americans. The first crop is planted in April and the second in July, the first being gathered in June and July and the second in October. When gathering corn the women lay aside the best ears for seed; they are stuck in pairs on sticks and carried in the hand. Wheat is now the principal crop, and when a wet season insures sufficient water several million pounds are raised. It is sowed in December and reaped with hand sickles in June. Of the several varieties "Sonora" and "Australian" are favorites. One called skaofkutco was raised before Kâ′mâl tkâk's father was born. Wheat is ground for the Pimas at the Government mill at Sacaton (pl. I), but a great deal of it is yet parched and ground on the metates to be made into pinole.

There have been at least half a dozen trading stores on the Gila River reservation for a number of years whose principal trade has been in wheat. The traders have naturally encouraged the growing of this cereal as much as possible and assisted in the introduction of suitable varieties. They have also profited in a legitimate way from the contracts awarded by the Government in times of famine for the support of the natives.

---

[a] " In the year 1858, the first year of the Overland Mail Line, the surplus crop of wheat was 100,000 pounds, which was purchased by the company; also a large quantity of beans called *taperis*, and a vast quantity of pumpkins, squashes, and melons. In 1859 Mr St John was sent among them as a special agent with a supply of seeds and some agricultural implements. That year they sold 250,000 pounds of wheat and a large supply of melons, pumpkins, and beans. In 1860 they sold 400,000 pounds of wheat— all the Mail Company would purchase. They had more, and furnished the Government and private teamsters all that was necessary for transportation from Fort Yuma to Tucson. Beyond this they had no market, except for about 40,000 pounds of wheat which Mr White purchased for the supply of Fort Breckenridge. In 1861 they sold to Mr White 300,000 pounds of wheat, 50,000 pounds of corn, 20,000 pounds of beans, and a large amount of dried and fresh pumpkins, which was all intended for the support of the California Column. The greater part of this crop was destroyed or given back to the Indians by the Texans under the guerrilla, Hunter, who arrived at the Pimo villages that year, robbed Mr White of his property, and took him prisoner in their flight to the Rio Grande. The Pimos sold, during the same year, 600 chickens and a large amount of other stuff, showing a gradual increase of production under the encouragement of an increased demand. In 1862 they sold to the Government over a million pounds of wheat, included in which was a portion of the previous year's crop, returned to them by the Texans. They furnished pinole, chickens, green peas, green corn, pumpkins, and melons for the entire California Column, subsisting nearly a thousand men for many months." (J. R. Browne, Adventures in the Apache Country, 110.) Browne's statements about the Pimas, though not grossly inaccurate, are not generally reliable, but as he was intimately acquainted with A. M. White, with whom he traveled from California, it is probable that the above estimates are as nearly correct as circumstances permitted.

Oats are seldom raised in that region. They are called "white tassels" by the Pimas. Barley is the universal grain feed of Arizona, and there is a ready market for the small quantity the Pimas raise.

VEGETABLES

Watermelons, muskmelons, pumpkins, and squashes are extensively cultivated. The watermelons are preserved until after the 1st of January by burying them in the sands of the river bed. The pumpkins, squashes, and muskmelons are cut in strips and dried, the best-keeping varieties being left in the storehouses until midwinter (pl. xxxv, *f*). According to tradition the first pumpkins, called rsas′katûk, were obtained from the Yumas and Maricopas.[a]

FIG. 7. Gourd canteen.

There are three species of wild gourds that are quite common along the Gila, namely: Cucurbita fœtidissima H. B. K., C. digitata Gray, and Apodanthera undulata Gray. Cultivated gourds have been known to the Pimas for a long period—how long it is impossible to say. The Papagos have a tradition that this plant was introduced by Navitco, a deity who is honored by ceremonies at intervals of eight years—or, if crops are bountiful, at the end of every four years—at Santa Rosa. The gourd is used as a canteen (fig. 7), and if it becomes cracked a rabbit skin is stretched over it which shrinks in drying and renders the vessel water-tight again. Dippers and canteens are occasionally made of gourds, but the chief use of gourds seems to be in the form of rattles (fig. 8) which contain a little

FIG. 8. Gourd rattle.

---

[a] When Garcés was among the Yumas in 1775 they were raising "countless" calabashes and melons—"*calabazas y melones*, perhaps better translated squashes and cantaloupes, or pumpkins and muskmelons. The Piman and Yuman tribes cultivated a full assortment of cucurbitaceous plants, not always easy to identify by their old Spanish names. The *sandia* was the watermelon invariably; the *melon*, usually a muskmelon, or cantaloupe; the *calabaza*, a calabash, gourd, pumpkin, or squash of some sort, including one large rough kind like our crook-neck squash. * * * Major Heintzelman says of the Yumans, p. 36 of his Report already cited [H. R. Ex. Doc. 76, 34th Cong., 3d sess., 1857]: 'They cultivate watermelons, muskmelons, pumpkins, corn, and beans. The watermelons are small and indifferent, muskmelons large, and the pumpkins good. These latter they cut and dry for winter use [they were brought to Pimería before the Maricopas came to Gila Bend].'" Note in Coues' On the Trail of a Spanish Pioneer, New York, 1900, I, 170.

gravel and are mounted on a handle. Gourds are never used as forms over which to mold pottery.

At least five varieties of beans are now cultivated. The first known, the tatcoa pavfi, "white bean," is said to have been brought in some forgotten time from the valley of the great "Red river," the Colorado. Considerable quantities are raised and the thrashing is done by horses driven in a circle on the same hard floor that is prepared for the wheat thrashing.

Not with the withering drought alone has the Gileño planter to contend, but also with the myriads of crows that are extravagantly fond of a corn diet, and with the numerous squirrels and gophers that thrive apace where protected in a measure from the coyotes, which are themselves a menace to the fields. From the birds and predatory animals the fields are guarded during the day by the boys, who amuse themselves meanwhile by a dozen games that develop skill in running, and shooting with the bows and arrows which scarcely leave their hands during their waking hours. Scarecrows, "men artificial," are used, but a fluttering rag was never as effective as a feathered shaft hurtling from a well-drawn bow. Night marauders were in olden times kept at a distance by the rings of the terrible cholla cactus, Opuntia bigelovii Engelm., that were laid up around the individual plants. Plate XII illustrates this cactus as it grows on the hills about Sacaton. It is recognized as the most effectually armed of the many cacti and is the symbol in Pima lore of impenetrability.

TRADE

STANDARDS OF VALUE

For purposes of trade or in gambling the following values were recognized: A gourd was equivalent to a basket; a metate, a small shell necklace, or the combination of a basket and a blanket and a strand of blue glass beads was equivalent to a horse; a string of blue glass beads 4 yards long was equivalent to a bag of paint; and a basket full of beans or corn to a cooking pot.

MEASURES

The principal linear measurement was the humakâ os, "one stick," equal to the distance from the center of the breast to the finger tips. The writer is inclined to regard this as a primitive Pima measurement, notwithstanding its resemblance to the yard of the invading race. This corresponds with the Aztec cenyollotli, the Cakchiquel ru vach qux, and the Maya betan.[a] It was the basis of a sort of decimal system, as follows: Ten "sticks" made one "cut" of calico, equivalent to a "load" of wheat, or about 150 pounds. Ten cuts or loads were equivalent to

---

[a] D. G. Brinton, The Lineal Measures of the Semi-civilized Nations of Mexico and Central America.

one horse in value. Two units were employed in measurement of distances. One of these is an ancient measurement which it will be of interest to apply to the Hohokam ruins of the region. It is hʉmakâ kʉirspa, "one step"—that is, one step with the same foot, equal to about 5 feet. Land is divided into plots 100 or 200 "steps" in width, according to the size of the family. Long distances were measured in terms of a day's journey on foot; thus it is said to be seven days to Zuñi. The term "step" is also applied to the English mile, but they have had as yet little opportunity to acquire a definite knowledge of the meaning of the latter term.

BARTER

For a long period prior to 1833 the Maricopas lived at Gila Bend and came at harvest time to trade with the Pimas. Soon after that time they settled beside the Pimas, living upon such intimate terms with them that barter between the tribes was of no more consequence than between two Pima villages.[a] With all other tribes they were perpetually at war, except with their Papago kinsfolk to the southward. These people live in a vast territory of cactus-covered plains, here and there interrupted by up-thrust barren peaks that, with striking outlines, form good landmarks and yet offer little to those that hunger and are athirst. The Papagos are a desert tribe, and yet so well had they mastered their all but hopeless environment that the trade which they carried on with the Pimas was by no means one-sided, as may be seen from the following list of products that were formerly brought to the Gila at the time of the June harvest. Of vegetable products there were saguaro seeds, the dried fruit and sirup; tci'aldi, a small hard cactus fruit; agave fruit in flat roasted cakes; agave sirup; rsat, an unidentified plant that grows at Santa Rosa; prickly pear sirup; wild gourd seeds; a small pepper, called tcïl'tipïn; acorns of Quercus oblongifolia; baskets of agave leaf; sleeping mats; kiâhâs and fiber to make them; maguey fiber for picket lines. They brought the dried meat of the mountain sheep, deer meat, deer tallow in small ollas, buckskins, dried beef, tallow, cheese, and cords of human hair. Cattle were formerly traded "sight unseen," but the modern "education" of the Papagos led them to exaggerate the good qualities of their stock and even to deal in "fictitious values," or cattle that the new Pima owner sought in vain to find, until finally the Pimas would consider no proposition to trade stock unless the animals were exhibited. Of mineral products they brought red and yellow ochers for face and body paint, and the buff beloved by Pima weavers. They

---

[a] The author of the Rudo Ensayo, who wrote in 1762, stated that "these very numerous nations [Opas and Maricopas] inhabit both sides for a distance of 36 leagues down the river, and at the far end of their territory there is a very abundant spring of hot water a short distance from the river to the north." This spring is now known as Ojo Caliente; it is at the southern end of the Bighorn mountains. Guitéras translation in Records of the American Catholic Historical Society, v, 129.

made religious pilgrimages to the salt lakes below the Mexican boundary to obtain the sacred salt. They lived on pinole during the journey and walked with their eyes fixed upon the trail, looking neither to the right nor to the left.

As they approached the shore of the lagoon in which the Great Spirit resided they ran at topmost speed and circled four times around the salt deposits before those who understood the proper ritual began to collect the salt. Even on the homeward journey there was magic power in the salt, and if a horse died the whole load was thrown away. As the salt gatherers approached the home village they were given a noisy welcome but were compelled to remain outside for four days, and for a long time thereafter they must abstain from certain acts that need not be detailed here. For four days those who remained at home sang for those who journeyed, and then all might eat the salt and were free to bring it to the Pimas.[a] The latter sometimes made journeys to the lake for salt, being two days on the way to Quijotoa and two days on the trail beyond.

In exchange for the objects of barter brought to them the Pimas gave wheat, which was also given the Papagos for aid in harvesting it; corn; beans; mesquite beans; mesquite meal, roasted in mud-lined pits; cotton blankets and cotton fiber. with the seed; dried squash, pumpkin, and melon; rings of willow splints and of devil's claw for baskets; besides articles of lesser consequence.

In recent years there has been some trade carried on in colored earths and salt with the once hostile Yumas and Mohaves.

From the seventeenth century the Pimas sent well-armed bands through the Apache cordon to trade at the Spanish and Mexican settlements of Sonora. The latter also sent trading parties from Tucson and other towns to barter with the Gileños. Lastly, American traders appeared about 1850, and for many years there have been half a dozen stores on the reservation. These are under bond to limit their profit to a maximum of 25 per cent, though it is supposed that this rule was never enforced until the present year. Some Pimas sometimes try to turn the tables on the traders by offering damp wheat that of course overweighs. More frequently they put a quantity of sand in the middle of the wheat sacks, which are furnished by the trader and not ordinarily emptied when the wheat is brought in. Rarely, the best wheat is put on top and an inferior quality lies concealed beneath.

---

[a] "These Papagos regularly visit a salt lake which lies near the coast and just across the line of Sonora, from which they pack large quantities of salt, and find a ready market at Tubac and Tucson. Mr. Lathrop, superintendent of the Sonora Mining Company, told me that he had bought some twenty thousand pounds annually from them." (John Walker in S. Ex. Doc. 2, 720, 36th Cong., 1st sess., 1860.) It would seem from this rather extensive traffic that the Papagos did not allow their religious scruples to interfere seriously with trade.

ARTIFACTS

The manufactures of the Pimas were few in number and simple in character. It is interesting to compare the number of implements and weapons that are of wood with those made of stone, as this is a people classed as belonging to the Stone Age. It will be noticed that the articles of stone are of little consequence in point of number as compared with those of wood, but the stone objects are of the utmost importance from a cultural standpoint. The metate admits of no wooden substitute, and without it the full food value of maize could not have been utilized nor could wheat raising have been so readily taken up as an agricultural pursuit. Without the stone ax and knife there could have been little done in wood working; architecture would have been modified; agriculture, dependent upon irrigation, would have been all but impossible. In short, these three simple implements, made by striking one stone against another, have sufficed to transform the Pimas from the slaves of a harsh environment, compelled to rend their prey with tooth and nail, into an agricultural people who adapt the environment to their needs and make some provision, however slight, for the future.

WOOD

WEAPONS

Bow. First in importance among weapons must be placed the bow and the arrow. Pima bows are simple, undecorated, and not very carefully made. Those which exhibit weakness through splitting or otherwise are bound with fresh sinew in bands which shrink around the arms at the point where reenforcement is needed. Warriors made their bows of mulberry wood [a] obtained in the Superstition and Pinal mountains. A bow that has been long used, especially in successful warfare, becomes a highly prized possession with which its owner is loath to part. The writer was so fortunate as to secure such a specimen (pl. XIII, *a*) which has the graceful compound curve of the conventional bow; it is of mulberry wood and has a neatly twisted, two-strand sinew string.[b] Hunting bows [c] (pl. XIII, *b*) are frequently made of osage orange wood, a material that is now obtainable from the whites along the Salt river. When mulberry wood was not available willow was used, and most of the hunting bows which men as well as boys continue to make for hunting hares and similar small game are of that wood. The primary type of arrow release prevails, the bow being held as in plate VII, *b*.

---

[a] "The mulberry plays an important part in the domestic economy of the Apaches; the branches are made into bows, and the small twigs are used in the fabrication of baskets." John G. Bourke, Jour. Am. Folk-Lore, III, 210.

[b] Length 1.350 m., width at grip 26 mm., thickness 18 mm.

[c] Length 1.365 m., width at grip 26 mm., thickness 22 mm.

Arrows. The arrows of the Pimas are made from the straight stem of the arrow bush. The Kwahadk's and Papagos sometimes sold arrows of yucca stem to the Gileños, but these were scarcely equal in quality to those made of wood. The hunting arrows [a] (pl. XIII, *c*) have two split feathers, two hand's breadths in length. War arrows [b] have three feathers, less than half as long and slightly

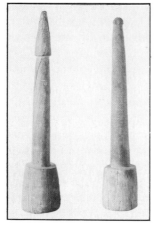

FIG. 9. War clubs.

curved. All arrow shafts are measured and cut the length from tip of forefinger to nipple of breast of the maker. Both bows and arrows are sometimes stained with the blood of the jack rabbit, and war arrows may be dyed at the ends with the cochineal which makes its home on the Opuntias. The quiver is made of wild-cat skin (pl. XIII, *d*).

War club. The club was of scarcely less importance than the bow, and it was customary for a portion of each band of warriors to fight with shield and club alone.[c]

Lance. A short sharpened stick was sometimes used by the Pimas, who adopted it from the Yumas and Maricopas after the Spaniards supplied steel heads for the weapon. The sticks were colored red with mineral paint.[d]

---

[a] There are eleven hunting arrows in the collection; length 0.785 m., sharpened to blunt points but having neither head nor foreshaft. There are 3 bands of sinew 4 cm. apart, the first at the point. The seizing at the forward end of the feathers is 5 cm. long. The feathers vary from 12 to 22 cm. in length between the seizing at ends. They project 1 cm. from the shaftment. There are 10 bands of sinew very neatly laid on to hold the feathers in place. The notches are 4 mm. deep.

[b] The single war arrow in the collection is unusually long, 0.850 m. It is stained with cochineal for a distance of 0.117 m. from the point. It carries a small obsidian point 2 cm. in length, with the sinew seizing continued from the point 3 cm. along the shaft. The feathers are 0.10 cm. long and project 7 mm. from the shaftment. The butt is stained for a distance of 5 cm.

[c] Bartlett, usually an admirable observer, failed to notice that the war club was a popular Pima weapon. He says: "The only weapon used by these tribes is the bow and arrow. The short club of the Yumas and the long lance of the Apaches I never saw among them." (Personal Narrative, II, 237.) The clubs were made of mesquite root or of ironwood, weighed about 2 pounds, and in general appearance resembled the old style potato mashers of New England kitchens. (Fig. 9.) The handle was brought to a sharp point, which was almost as effective as a dagger in a back-handed blow. The club was carried thrust point downward through the belt. One club was obtained from its owner and another found in a cache of personal property that had been made in the hills at the death of the owner. The former is 42 cm. long, the head 10 cm. long and 9 cm. in diameter; the point is 9 cm. long. A club in the National Museum, (no. 27846) that was collected some years ago at Sacaton is 0.385 m. long, 7 cm. in diameter. Doctor Palmer secured three in 1885 and believed that none remained among the Pimas. These clubs, now in the Museum, are of the following lengths: no. 76023, 48 cm.; 76024, 44 cm.; and 76025, 46 cm.

[d] The collection contains a wooden lance, made from a giant cactus rib, that was carried in sham battles near the Double buttes. It is 1.595 m. long, the larger end colored black to represent the iron head, which is represented as 0.265 m. long, 24 mm. wide, and 10 mm. thick. The handle is stained a light red.

AGRICULTURAL IMPLEMENTS

Digging stick. The earliest agricultural implement was the digging stick. It was used in planting maize and other crops, as a lever to pry out bushes when clearing the ground, as a pick when digging irrigating ditches, and in case of surprise it made an effective weapon of defense. It was made of ironwood or from the spiny tree, Zizyphus lycioides.[a] The short handle necessitated a crouching or sitting position by the operator. (Fig. 10, *a.*)

Shovel. Wooden shovels were used to throw out the earth that usually required loosening by the digging stick when constructing the irrigating canal. They were of cottonwood, in the case of the larger, lighter ones, or of mesquite. The handle and blade were in one piece, the former being very short and the latter having the natural curve of the trunk from which it came.[b] (Fig. 10, *b.*)

Hoe. Another implement of early adoption by the Pimas combined the functions of spade and hoe. It was used to loosen the soil around plants and to cut away weeds. It was made of ironwood and was thin, hard, and heavy. As it was quite short and curved but slightly it could be used only when the workman was in a kneeling or sitting position. It was sharpened along the convex curve at the wider end. The entire implement was so thin that it must

a   *b*   *c*   *d*

Fig. 10. Agricultural implements. *a*, Digging stick; *b*, shovel; *c*. hoe; *d*, dibble.

have chafed the hands. But one specimen was found on the reservation (fig. 10, *c*).[c]

Dibble. The implement described above was superseded by one obtained from the Mexicans who frequently came to trade with the Pimas. The new implement more nearly resembled the primitive digging stick than it did the flat "hoe" (fig. 10, *d*). It was furnished

[a] No genuine specimen being now obtainable, the writer had a digging stick (fig. 10, *a*) made, which measures 1.140 m. in length. It is 40 mm. in diameter, and is flattened at the lower end.

[b] The old people yet remember how the wooden shovels were made. Whether the Pimas have directly descended from the Hohokam or not, it is very probable that the former have used the same form of shovel that was used by the latter when constructing the great irrigating canals of that region. The specimen figured here (fig. 10, *b*) may therefore be accepted as a representative of the shovel that was probably the instrument that made those canals a possibility. It is 0.850 m. long; the blade is 0.276 m. long and 0.167 m. wide.

[c] It is 0.680 m. long and 0.083 m. wide; the cutting edge is 17 cm. long.

with a steel blade that was straight on one side and rounded on the other.[a]

Plow.   Of comparatively modern introduction, the wooden plow is of but passing interest in our present researches.   It is a survival of European culture that effectively influenced the Pimas for but one generation, or from 1850 to 1880, when the influx of Americans created a demand for wheat which the Pimas were able to supply in part as they could not have done without this implement.   By the end of

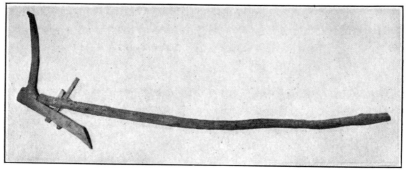

FIG. 11. Wooden plow.

that period they received steel plows.   The wooden plow was made of mesquite or ironwood with a cottonwood tongue that extended to the ox yoke.   The rear end of the tongue was beveled underneath to an edge which engaged with a transverse notch in the handle.   The bottom dragged at a considerable angle, so that the point alone came in contact with the soil.   The cutting face was usually supplied with an iron or steel covering resembling the single-shovel cultivator of the Americans.   The bottom and single handle were of one piece, the

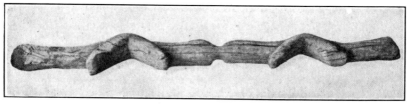

FIG. 12. Yoke.

latter being a branch that set at a convenient angle, about 70 degrees, with the trunk of the tree from which the bottom of the plow was cut (fig. 11).[b]   The tongue was held in place by a mesquite pin passing through the bottom and a slot in the butt of the tongue and tightened by two wedges which were adjusted by means of a mesquite mallet carried for the purpose.[c]

---

[a] Length, 1.090 m.; length of blade, 0.215 m. to top of socket; width, 0.115 m.

[b] Two specimens were collected; only one other was seen or heard of on the reservation.   The larger one is complete, with tongue.   It is 0.900 m. long; handle, 0.850 m., and tongue 3.490 m.

[c] A mallet in the collection measures 0.380 m. in length and 5 cm. in diameter.

Yoke. With the introduction of cattle the Pimas obtained their first draft animal. They were used principally in plowing and were fitted with yokes (fig. 12) of cottonwood or willow which were attached to the horns of the animals as in southern Europe to the present day. The yokes themselves are the best evidence that the burden upon the animals was light, for these small sticks of brittle wood would snap at the first strain if on the shoulders of an ox team with a heavy load. There are a few yokes yet to be found, though they have not been used for several years. The specimens collected are fairly well made, straight, but with sections hollowed to fit the necks of the team. [a]

HOUSEHOLD UTENSILS

Mortar. Perhaps the mortar should be placed first in importance among the utensils of this class. There are two forms, one (fig. 13, *a*) with the hole sunk in the end of the log, and which may be either sharpened at the other end and set permanently in the ground or cut flat at the opposite end so that it will stand upright and may be moved about. The other style (fig. 13, *b*) lies horizontal, with the hole in the side of the log. This is always portable. [b]

Two or three stone mortars, rounded and well shaped, were seen; they had been obtained from the ruins and were little used. At the Double buttes,

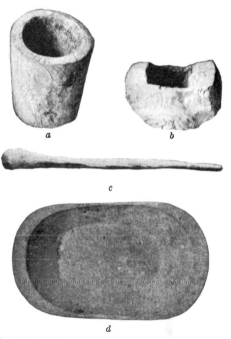

FIG. 13. *a, b,* Mortars; *c,* wooden pestle; *d,* bread tray.

near the center of the Gila River reservation, there are a few mortar cavities in the solid rock ledges. There is also one in a large bowlder which is regarded with superstitious reverence. Mortars in solid stone are not uncommon in Arizona. The writer saw a row of them at the end of a cliff ruin of eight or ten rooms in Aravaipa canyon. There are several in a rough hillock in Harshaw canyon, Patagonia mountains. The base of the conical hill at Tucson is well

---

[a] There are two specimens in the collection. The larger is 1.450 m. long; 10 cm. in diameter at the middle, with notches for necks; 30 cm. wide. The second specimen is 1.200 m. long.

[b] The mortar of the horizontal type in the collection is perhaps a trifle smaller than the average. It measures 40 cm. in length, 27 cm. in height, and 22 cm. in thickness. A heavy specimen of this type in the collection measures 37 cm. in height, 32 cm. in diameter; the cavity is 17 cm. deep.

pitted with them. They are occasionally met with almost anywhere in the eastern half of the Territory. With that portion west
of the Rio Verde the writer is unacquainted. Reference to the pages
devoted to a description of the plants that furnish food for the Pimas
will show how extensively the mortar is used in grinding seeds.

Pestle. For pounding up mesquite beans in the mortar a large
wooden pestle is sometimes used. It is simply a mesquite club with
rounded head (fig. 13, *c*).[a]

a   b   c

FIG. 14. *a*, Doughnut fork; *b*, ladle; *c*, unfinished ladle.

Bread tray. Neatly made trays of mesquite, rarely of cottonwood,
are used, and appear to be among the most prized of the household
utensils (fig. 13, *d*). They are employed for a variety of purposes besides that of mixing bread.[b] Smaller trays and plates—circular, ellip-
tical, and rectangular—are sometimes obtained from the Papagos.

[a] One specimen, the only one seen, was secured. It is 1.210 m. long and the head is 0.335 m. in
diameter.
[b] The specimen collected is 0.615 m. long, 0.355 m. wide, and 0.071 m. deep. The legs are 24 cm.
long; they are three in number and of the same piece of wood as the body of the tray. There is one
round shallow tray, no. 76051, in the National Museum that is 46 cm. in diameter.

Fork. In frying doughnuts it is necessary to have some instrument with which to remove them from the fat. A slender sharpened rod of arrowwood is used for this purpose (fig. 14, *a*).[a]

Ladle. Ladles are said to be of recent intro-duction, the Pimas having obtained them from the Papagos, who in turn had derived the art of making them from the Mexicans. They are com-monly made of mesquite, though the Papagos make them of paloverde wood. The bowls are not rounded, but are made in the shape of a flat-tened cone, as they can be more readily worked into that form with a straight-bladed knife.[b]

FIG. 15. Pottery paddle.

Pottery paddle. A paddle of cottonwood is used to shape the outer surface of pottery. It is hollowed to fit the convex surface of the vessel, and is now frequently made from a barrel stave, which has the proper curvature. The paddles are of varying sizes, according to the sizes of the vessels on which they are used, but the handles are always proportionately short.[c]

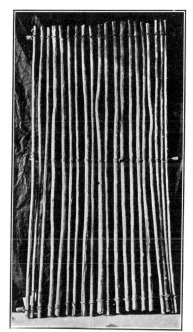

FIG. 16, *a*. Hanging shelf.

Shelves. There is a class of objects that are used indifferently for doors[d] of sheds and houses, for shelves[e] that are suspended in the arbors, and for bird traps.[f] They are usually made of large arrowbush rods, which are quite straight and of uniform diameter. The rods are tied to cross pieces, as shown in figure 16, *a*, or are held by twisted cords of hide, as in figure 16, *b*. The latter specimen was

<hr>

[a] The specimen collected is 45 cm. long.

[b] The finished specimen in the collection is rather smaller than the average (fig. 14, *b*). It is 0.394 m. long. The bowl is 94 mm. in diameter and 42 mm. deep. The unfinished specimen (fig. 14, *c*) is a large one, measuring 0.570 m. in length. The National Museum contains a specimen, no. 76050, which measures 56 cm. in length, with bowl 15 cm. in diameter.

[c] The collection contains one which is 0.268 m. long and 0.112 m. wide (fig. 15).

[d] The door (fig. 16, *b*) is 1 m. long and 0.850 m. wide. The rods are from 1 to 2 centimeters in diameter and are held by 5 hide strands, 2 at each end and 1 in the middle. The stiffening of the rawhide has warped the upper portion.

[e] The shelf (fig. 16, *a*) is 1.050 m. long and 50 cm. wide.

[f] When used as traps they are tilted at an angle of 20° or 30° from the ground and supported in that position by a short stick to which a long cord is attached. Wheat strewn under the trap lures small birds, which are caught when a jerk on the line removes the supporting stick. One of these traps was seen at nearly every house during the winter of 1901-2.

serving as a door when purchased, and the fact that a "Melicano" wanted it caused its owners great astonishment and amusement. Indeed, the Pimas manifested a lively interest in our purchases of household articles and never failed to laugh at the spectacle presented by the little wagon half buried beneath its load of unassorted objects.

FIG. 16, b. Door.

Bird cage. The cages made by the Pimas are all of the same character, whether they are made for the large eagle or for the small Sonora dove, as in the case of the specimen[a] figured (fig. 17). They are of arrowwood, laid up in log-cabin style or tied to transverse bars, as in the house doors.

Kiâhâ frame. It is to be remembered that the peculiar form of carrying basket is made possible by the use of the wooden frame. It is fully described on page 140.

Fire drill. In primitive times fire was kindled by the Pimas by means of a two-part drill (fig. 18, *a*),[b] the simplest and most widespread form of fire drill. The operator knelt upon the ends of the hearth stick and twirled the upright stick between his palms. The hearth was of saguaro wood or of any other soft wood if that were not obtainable. Tinder was not used, the flame being developed in any inflammable material as soon as the smoke began to arise from the dust accumulated at the point of the drill.

With the advent of the whites flint and steel were used to kindle fire. The men carried these, with a little

FIG. 17. Bird cage.

cotton for tinder, in leather pouches (fig. 42). Fire was preserved at each village or camp in an old stump whenever practicable.

---

[a] This specimen has an arched top and a single piece of pine board for a floor. It is 32 cm. long by 23 cm. wide and 15 cm. high.

[b] The drill hearth in the collection is 0.315 m. long and 21 mm. wide. The spindle is 68 cm. long and 9 mm. in diameter.

MISCELLANEOUS

Saguaro hook. The fruit of the giant cactus grows at so great a height[a] that it can not be reached without the aid of some long-handled implement for dislodging it. Hooks[b] are made by attaching, by means of maguey fiber, a straight piece of wood to the end of a long cactus rib. Doctor McGee has called the writer's attention to the fact that the angle at which the hook stands is of great ceremonial importance among the Papagos, but there would seem to be no significance attached to it by the Pimas, who have not been so dependent upon the cactus in the past as have their nomadic neighbors.

Tweezers. The spiny fruit of Opuntia arborescens is picked by means of willow tweezers (fig. 18, *c*). The arms are flexible and sufficiently elastic to spring back into place readily.[c]

Tree. It was formerly the custom to erect a branched post in the space before the house door, on which to hang vessels or bags containing food. Of late a few (three were seen) "tree animals" are set in the ground near the buildings to serve as seats and for the children to play upon. They are sections of mesquite trees that have each a branch perpendicular to the plane of the trunk at a point where the latter bends in the opposite direction slightly, so that when the branch is set in the ground the trunk is horizontal with the exception of the end which curves upward in a manner somewhat resembling a vaulting horse.

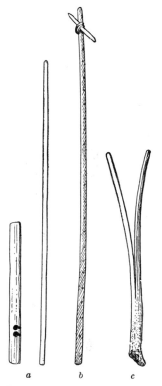

a   b   c

FIG. 18. *a*, Fire drill; *b*, saguaro hook; *c*, ha'nûm tweezers.

Cradle. The frame of the cradle is of willow, in the form of a narrow bow with from 5 to 10 cross bars (fig. 19, *a*). It closely resembles the Mohave trellis frame, but is more rudely made.[d] The frame was formerly covered with shredded willow bark to a depth of 3 or 4 inches and a bit of cotton cloth covered the whole. Now the willow bark is not so thick, and much more cloth, no longer of native make, is used. The cradle (fig. 19, *b*) is provided with a detachable

---

a See pl. IX, *a*, where the saguaro appears in flower in the background.

b The specimen illustrated in fig. 18, *b* was cut short for convenience of carrying. The handles vary in length from 2 to 5 m. The hook is 165 mm. long and 8 mm. in diameter.

c The specimen collected is 31 cm. long; natural spread of jaws, 55 mm.

d See Mason in Report National Museum, 1894, 524.

hood made of willow bark in the checker style of weaving, the surface being ornamented in geometric patterns colored black and red. Over the hood a loose piece of cloth may be thrown to protect the occupant from flies. The babies when strapped closely in the cradles are frequently carried on the heads of their mothers, who may at the

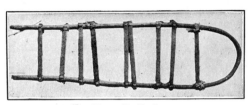

FIG. 19, a. Cradle frame.

same time have no insignificant burdens in their hands. When the children are about a year old they are carried astride the hip, unless upon a journey, when they are shifted around to the back, still astride,[a] and there supported by a shawl or large cloth bound around the waist.[b] The writer has seen women with children of 2 or 3 years on their backs, each carrying a sack of wheat on her head and lighter bundles in her hands.[c]

Paint brush. The lines of pigment with which the face was formerly ornamented were applied by means of slender bits of arrow-wood two or three inches long. The Kwahadk's were accustomed to gather the tufted ends of the arrow-bush branches and carry them southward into Papagueria to be used as paint brushes.

Calendar sticks. The Pimas keep a record of passing events by means of sticks carved with arbitrary mnemonic symbols. There are five such records in the tribe to-day—or were a year ago. The oldest of these sticks bears the history of

FIG. 19, b. Cradle.

seventy years. There were other sticks before these, but the vicissitudes of war, fire, and the peculiar burial customs of the people made away with them.[d] There are three sticks in the collection, which have been designated Gila Crossing, Blackwater, and Casa Blanca calendars,[e] from the names of the villages whence they came. The Casa Blanca stick (fig. 20, a) is of willow, peeled,

---

[a] Doctor Palmer says that as soon as a child is old enough to stand alone the mother carries it on an immense cincture of bark worn on her back. The author saw no such cinctures in use and believes that their use has been abandoned.

[b] Mason, Cradles, in Report National Museum, 1887, 184.

[c] The frame of the cradle figured is 67 cm. long by 20 cm. wide. The hood is 38 cm. high.

[d] See p. 35. They are mentioned here merely for the purpose of describing the sticks as products of the woodworker's skill.

[e] The Casa Blanca calendar is not recorded in "The Narrative," p. 38.

slightly flattened, but otherwise bearing no signs of preparation for the symbols that occupy the greater part of one side.[a] The Gila Crossing calendar (fig. 20, *b*) is a pine stick on which the record was copied several years ago from a stick yet in the same village. The record begins on the back, passes over the lower end in the figure, and extends again to the back over the upper end.[b] The Blackwater stick (fig. 20, *c*) is of saguaro wood smoothed and carved for the writer by the keeper of the record, who lost the original some years ago and who has since been using paper and pencil, but the same symbols.[c]

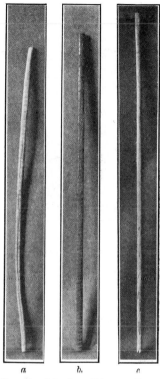

a，　　　　 b，　　　　 c

FIG. 20. Calendar sticks. *a*, From Casa Blanca; *b*, from Gila Crossing; *c*, from Blackwater.

Spurs. Wooden spurs were made from crotched limbs of mesquite of suitable size. They were attached to the foot by a deerskin thong fastened to form two loops of equal size, one passing over the instep and the other under the heel of the foot. So rare have they now become that the writer spent six months on the Gila River reservation without discovering any, and therefore hired an old man to make a pair for the collection. Soon after-

FIG. 21. Wooden spur.

wards a single old spur was found, which differs from those made to order only in having deerskin instead of maguey fiber fastenings (fig. 21).[d]

Saddle. Wooden saddletrees are sometimes made, both for riding and pack saddles. The former are covered with rawhide, shrunk on, and provided with stirrups of mesquite or willow wood. They are not common and are at best but crude imitations of the saddles made by the whites. Saddle blankets for use with them are of matted grass or maguey fiber.

---

[a] Length, 93 cm.; diameter, 16 mm.
[b] Length, 96 cm.; diameter, 18 mm.
[c] Length, 1.395 m.; diameter, 20 mm.
[d] Length, 0.152 m.; spread across fork, 9 cm.

Awl. There would seem to be no tradition of the former use of bone awls among the Pimas. They declare that awls of mesquite wood were used in making baskets before the introduction of steel. At present the points are of pieces of umbrella rib set in wooden handles of native manufacture (fig. 22, *a*).[a] It will be observed that the upper end of the handle is provided with a button, so that it may be held between the third and fourth fingers while the thumb and other fingers are engaged in the manipulation of the basket splints. Handles of round balls of creosote gum[b] are also used (fig. 22, *b*).[c]

FIG. 22. Awls. *a*, Wooden handle; *b*, gum handle.

Rope twister. This apparatus is probably of European origin. It consists of a pin or handle of hard wood, such as mesquite or willow, which is thrust through a hole near the end of another stick, which acts as a spindle whorl. The latter piece has a button at the short end, to which are attached the maguey fibers or horse hairs (fig. 23). The operator, by a slight rising and falling motion of the handle, causes the spindle to revolve rapidly, thus twisting the fibers into a cord which lengthens as he steps backward. A second person meanwhile adds fresh fibers to the other end.[d]

Â'mǐna. Among the most important of the sacred objects in the paraphernalia of the medicine-men were the â'mǐna, or medicine sticks. They are usually of arrowwood; always bound together with cotton twine of native spinning, either with or without feathers attached to each separate stick. There are six â'mǐna bundles in the collection. One was made by Kâ'mâl tkâk, to be used exclusively in the exor-

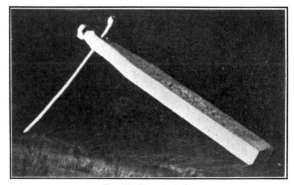

FIG. 23. Rope twister.

cism of the Tcu'nyǐm, a spirit of disease. The bundle contains four groups of sticks: Two pairs, one bundle of 4, and one of 6. All are plain, being unmarked in any way (fig. 24).[e]

[a] Length of specimen (fig. 22, *a*) 0.103 m., of which 56 mm. is handle.
[b] Deposited on the branches of the creosote bush by the minute scale insect, *Carteria larreæ.*
[c] Length, 3 cm.; diameter of handle, 24 mm.
[d] Length of pin, 0.254 m.; diameter, 8 mm.; length of spindle, 32 cm.
[e] Length, 0.167 m.; diameter, 6 mm.

The second bundle is painted green. Each stick is whittled to a blunt point at one end and has two short, downy turkey feathers attached (pl. XIV, b).[a]

The third bundle contains two sets of 4 sticks each, which were originally painted blue. They are sharpened to tapering points at one end. To each stick is tied two of the tail feathers of some small bird (pl. XIV, a).[b]

The fourth bundle contains three sets of 4 sticks each and the remains of another set which probably contained 4, though it is so old that it is in a fragmentary condition (pl. XIV, d).[c] A bundle of feathers attached by strings is bound in with the â'mĭna, each one of which also bears two feathers, all the feathers being from a red-colored bird.

The fifth bundle contains three sets of 4 sticks each, but they are so old and broken that their original length can not be determined. They also have red feathers bound to them (pl. XIV, c).

FIG. 24. Â'mĭna with reed cloud blower and attached feathers.

The sixth bundle is very small and very old and it is probable that the unusual number of sticks—5—is due to the fact that a portion of the bundle has crumbled with age (pl. XIV, e).

FIG. 25, a. Horned toad effigy.

Animal effigies. Wooden images of reptiles and the like are used in the medicine-men's efforts to cure certain diseases. Two such specimens were collected. One is intended to represent a horned toad (fig. 25, a),[d] the other a lizard (fig. 25, b).[e] They are either carelessly or clumsily made.

Mask. During his stay among the Pimas the writer heard of but two wooden masks being in their possession. One of these was collected and is here depicted in figure 26.[f] Doctor Hough called his attention to the fact

FIG. 25, b. Lizard effigy.

that it resembles those made by the Yaquis of Sonora, and it

---

[a] Length, 0.155 m.; diameter, 21 mm. The feathers are a trifle shorter than the sticks.
[b] Length, 0.136 m.; diameter, 10 mm.
[c] Length of sticks, 17 cm.; diameter, 7 mm.
[d] Length, 10 cm.; width, 42 mm.
[e] Length, 28 cm.; width, 4 cm.
[f] Length, 0.208 m.; width, 0.153 m.

is probable that the conception, if not the mask itself, was imported from the southward along with the masked Navitco ceremonies, despite the assertion of its former owner to the contrary, because it represents a higher degree of skill in woodworking

FIG. 26. Navitco mask.

than any piece of carving that the writer has seen done by a Pima. It is of cottonwood, perforated for the insertion of horsehair eyebrows, chin whisker, and two tufts on the center of each cheek, and is ornamented by an interrupted scroll and other lines unmistakably intended to be decorative. The mouth contains a half dozen pegs, giving a very realistic representation of teeth.

Wand. There are two wands or ceremonial sticks in the collection (fig. 27).[a] The longer is of greasewood, Sarcobatus vermicularis, the material prescribed for ia'kita, or ceremonial paraphernalia of this class. It is spotted with black and red paint. The shorter wand is of willow, spotted with red. Both were made to be held in the hand during ceremonies intended to bring rain, to cure disease, and for kindred purposes.

STONE

METATE

The metate is the most abundant of the stone implements of the Southwest, or, if arrow points exceed them in numbers, the former is at

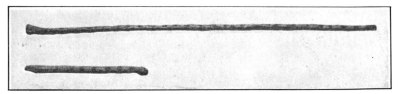

FIG. 27. Ceremonial wands.

least the most noticeable. About nearly every ruin one sees the fragments of broken metates, in some cases to the number of several score, as at the ruin near Patagonia, in the Sonoita valley, where sixty

---

[a] Length of the longer figure, 76 cm.; of the shorter, 28 cm.

metates were counted on the ground (every one had been intentionally broken), and there must have been a much larger number beneath the surface. Some of those found in the Hohokam ruins are of lava and have legs several inches in length. Most of these are hollowed out, as are those of the Hopis, whereas the metates of the Pimas are

FIG. 28. Grinding wheat on metate.

perfectly flat on the top from side to side, being slightly concave form end to end (fig. 28). They are of coarse-grained rock from the surrounding hills and never carved or provided with legs. They vary in weight from 20 to 200 pounds and are carried about the premises as needed, never being set in bins, as among the Pueblo tribes. Their grinding surface is sharpened or roughened by pecking with a stone ax, or with a similarly shaped stone if an ax is not obtainable.

MULLER

The muller is of lava or of stone similar to that of the metate itself. It is longer than that used by the Hohokam, so that the entire upper surface of the metate is worn down.

FIG. 29. Stone pestle.

It is not shaped into a rectangular bar, as is that found in the ruins. Indeed, the writer saw few that showed any evidence of having been shaped in any manner except through use.

PESTLE

The stone pestle [a] is used in every Pima household to crush the mesquite bean and other seeds in the wooden mortars. The pestle varies in size from the small stone the size of one's finger to the great

---

[a] An average-sized specimen in the collection weighs 4½ pounds; it is 253 mm. long and 76 mm. in diameter (fig. 29).

cylinder weighing 20 pounds that requires both hands to wield it. Many of these are obtained from the ruins, but some are shaped by pecking. This is not all done at once, but, a suitable stone having been selected, it is shaped little by little, day by day, as the owner has leisure for the work. This suggests that much of the stonework of primitive peoples which excites our admiration for their patience has been done in this manner, the implement being in use continually and the task of pecking it into more convenient or more pleasing shape being taken up from time to time as "knitting work."

FIG. 30. Arrowheads.

Ax

The stone axes of the Pimas were obtained from the ruins that are far more extensive than the Pima villages in the Gila and Salt River valleys. Most of these axes have each a single blade, many are double-bitted, and some are of the adz form. Others are so large and finely polished as to render plausible the supposition that they were intended for ceremonial use. All are of hard, fine-grained igneous rock called hatovĭk by the Pimas, some of whom assert that the material comes from near the Gulf of California, where they have seen it when on journeys after salt. Others declare that there is no such stone on the surface of the earth, and that all the axes we find now were made from material that was brought from the underworld when Elder Brother led the nether-world people up to conquer those then living above. However, no particular religious significance is attached to the axes, as might be expected, considering their origin. They are sold readily enough, though when a suitable ax is kept for sharpening the metate of the household it is sometimes difficult for a collector to secure it.

FIG. 31. Arrow-shaft straightener.

There is an abundance of suitable stones along the Salt river below where it breaks through the Superstition mountains, and it is probable that all the axes in the valley were obtained from that immediate locality. The few that were seen hafted were fastened with sinew in the fork of a limb of suitable size.

ARROWHEADS

A great portion of those used by the Pimas were made by the Hoho-kam. However, the Pimas always had a few arrowhead makers who worked in obsidian, shale, or flint. They produced small heads varying from 1 to 2½ cm. in length by 1 in breadth. Those represented in figure 30 are old points. The heads are stemless, sometimes having shoulders for the sinew seizing. One man was found who continues to make arrowheads, which he sells to the whites.

ARROW-SHAFT STRAIGHTENER

The Pimas had very little need for grooved stones for straightening arrows as the arrowwood is naturally as straight as could be desired. It is probable that the stones of this kind found in the ruins were used merely for polishing. The Pimas used them scarcely at all.[a]

HAMMER STONES

These are frequently seen around the ruins of Arizona, but the Pimas seem to have little use for them.

FIG. 32. Crystals from medicine basket.

FIRESTONES

Three stones, each about 15 cm. in diameter, were used to support the cooking pots over the fire. They have been largely supplanted by an iron frame obtained from the agency blacksmith. These stones were picked up when needed and little effort made to preserve them.

CRYSTALS

Crystals and curiously shaped stones of all kinds were preserved in the outfits of the medicine-men. Several such specimens were purchased and some were found in a cache among the hills (fig. 32).[b]

---

[a] A specimen (Hohokam) in the collection (fig. 31) has been shaped to represent some animal (?). It is 92 mm. long and 60 mm. wide.

[b] Compare Cushing: "In this connection it is interesting to add as of possible moment suggestively that associated with the ultra mural remains [in the Salt River valley], both house- and pyral-, were found small, peculiar concretion-stones and crystals evidently once used as personal fetiches or amulets, as is the case at Zuñi to-day." Congrès International des Américanistes, VIIme sess., 1890, 179.

MAGIC TABLETS

The collection contains two tablets which were obtained from medicine-men and half of one which was found in the cache above referred to (fig. 33, *a*, *b*, *c*). Two have ornamental borders, while

the third is quite smooth to the rounded margin; it has the figure of a horse scratched on one side and that of a man on the other.[a]

a

TURQUOISE

This stone, which is so common in some parts of the Southwest that every Indian has

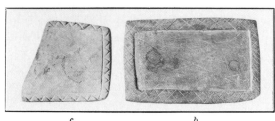

c   *b*

FIG. 33, *a*, *b*, *c*. Magic tablets.

it hanging from ears, neck, or arms, seems to be rare in Pimería. But one pair of ear pendants was seen. It was somewhat more abundant in early days. It was believed that if a man lost a turquoise the mishap was due to magic, and as a result he would be afflicted with some mysterious ailment which could be cured only by a medicine-man skilled in the cure of the "doctor's disease." He would use another piece of turquoise or a slate or a crystal, placing the stone in water and giving the latter to the patient to drink.

PIPE

A stone cylinder (fig. 34),[b] probably a pipe, was obtained from a Pima, who said that he had "found it long ago." It seems short for such a purpose, yet it is longer than a cane cylinder the writer found in actual use. The smoke is blown outward in certain

FIG. 34. Stone pipe.

ceremonies and in others drawn in. These tubes were also used by the Pimas in sucking and blowing the bodies of the sick for the purpose of expelling disease.

---

[a] The last tablet is 122 mm. long by 56 mm. wide; it is 6 mm. thick at one side and tapers to 2 mm. at the other. The largest specimen is 151 mm. long by 94 mm. wide and 10 mm. thick; the border is 10 mm. wide, marked thus: XXXX. The broken specimen is 87 mm. wide; its length can not be determined. The X pattern at the margin runs over to the surface of the reverse side.

[b] Length, 48 mm.; internal diameter, 16 mm.; maximum external diameter, 26 mm.

FIBER AND LEATHER

SADDLE

In addition to the wooden saddletrees already mentioned the Pimas made them each of two rolls of grass or straw, inclosed in blue denim or canvas and bound with a network of rawhide. A specimen[a] in the collection (pl. xv, a, b) has two such rolls fastened together with both horsehair and maguey cords. The top is covered with leather taken from two old boot legs. One stirrup is wanting; the one that remains is of native manufacture. The accompanying cinch (pl. xv, c)[b] is of horsehair neatly twisted and quite strong and serviceable. When used, it was passed over the saddle instead of being attached to it. A Pima is rarely seen riding bareback, and most have good saddles of American manufacture. Bartlett states that those who rode bareback at the time of his visit in 1850 thrust one foot under a loosely fastened surcingle.[c]

SADDLEBAG

A coarse net of maguey fiber is made to carry bulky objects upon either pack or riding saddles. The fibers are twisted into two strands, which are united to form a rope 5 mm. in diameter; with this the meshes are made about 12 cm. in length by an interlocking knot of the simplest character. The bag in the collection is about 1 m. in length (fig. 35).

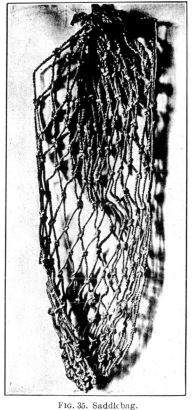

FIG. 35. Saddlebag.

HEAD RINGS

The round-bottomed water jars and many similar heavy burdens besides were borne upon the heads of the women with the aid of the rings of willow bark in the early days, and now with rings of rags wrapped with cotton cloth.[d] Of less common use are the agave-leaf rings, which should be classed as twined basketry.[e] They are

---

[a] Length, 60 cm.; diameter of rolls at the middle, 10 cm. They are thickened slightly at the ends to form pommel and cantle.

[b] Length, 75 cm.; width, 7 cm.

[c] Narrative, II, 237.

[d] The bark head ring (fig. 36, a) is 155 mm. in diameter and the opening in the center is 42 mm. in diameter.

[e] Diameter of specimen collected, 10 cm.; height, 165 mm.

folded at each margin so that a ring is made up of three thicknesses of matting. This ring is smaller than the other types and is used for lighter burdens (fig. 36, *b*). Almost any cloth (fig. 36, *c*) may be improvised into a head ring, and aprons are especially convenient for such use.

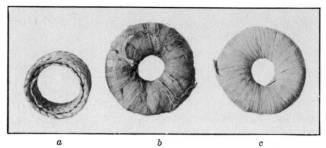

a   b   c

Fig. 36. Head rings. a, Willow bark; b, agave leaf; c, cloth.

Rope

Picket ropes of maguey fiber (figs. 37, *b* and 38) are brought by the Papagos to trade to the Pimas. They are about 10 m. long and 1 cm. in diameter, made of four 2-ply strands. They are strong, but

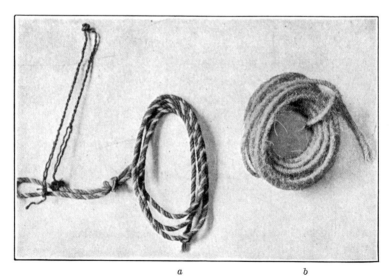

a   b

Fig. 37. a, Horsehair halter; b, maguey rope.

the harsh and coarse fiber renders them disagreeable to the touch of any but a hardened hand. The prepared fibers for rope making in this collection measure 60 cm. in length. With such material and a rope twister the process of manufacturing rope is a rapid one.

Human hair is both twisted and braided into cords for tightening kiâhâ frames. The cords are usually made of four strands of 2-ply twisted threads. They are about 5 mm. in diameter when finished.

HALTERS

Horsehair is quite popular as a material for the manufacture of halters. The halter here illustrated (fig. 37, *a*) has a loop of light cord, 45 cm. in length, to be passed over the horse's head. The rope

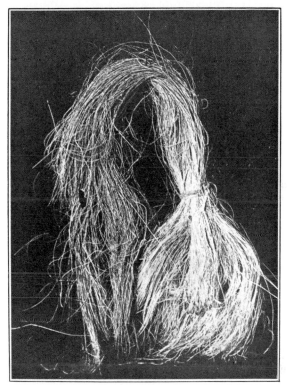

FIG. 38. Maguey fiber.

has a loop 26 cm. long that passes over the nose. The length of the rope from the knot of this loop is 3.150 m. It is of four strands of 4-ply threads, one of the strands being white.

BRIDLES

Bridles are also made of horsehair, vicious looking bits being sold by the traders for them.

FETISH

The collection contains a fetish (fig. 39, *a*) and a hair ornament made of seven wing feathers of a hawk (fig. 39, *b*) which have been joined by laying a strip of cotton cloth on the quill of each feather and binding it there with sinew, then braiding the loose ends of the strips together into a cord 15 cm. long. In this way the feathers are permanently fastened to one another and may be easily attached when it is desired to wear them as a fetish, or they may be readily attached to the hair to form a portion of the headdress.

WAR HEADDRESS

At Gila Crossing we were so fortunate as to secure a specimen of an old Pima headdress made from the hair of an Apache and the wing

feathers of three species of large raptorial birds (fig. 40). The hair is about 45 cm. long and is gathered in strands 1 cm. in thickness, which are held by two strips of cotton that are twisted or twined on each other a half turn between each pair of hair strands.[a] Viewing the headdress from the rear there are on the left four owl feathers, symbolizing keenness of vision by night; next are three hawk, then one owl, and again hawk feathers to the number of five, symbolizing keenness of vision by day; on the right are two eagle feathers, the symbol of swiftness. Thus the wearer of this headdress possessed the courage and cunning of the hated enemy, the keen sight by day and by night of

FIG. 39. *a*, Fetish; *b*, hair ornament.

the birds that have great magic power, according to Pima belief, and the swiftness as a trailer of the king of birds, which occupies a prominent place in Piman mythology.

HAIRBRUSH

Using their fingers as combs, the women become very skillful in straightening out tangled locks. They frequently smooth the hair with a brush which was formerly made of the roots of the "Sacaton grass," Sporobolus wrightii (fig. 41, *a*),[b] but as this no longer grows along the river, where the majority of the villages are situated, they now make use of maguey fiber, Agave lecheguea, Yucca paccata, etc. (fig. 41, *b*).[c]

---

[a] The general use of human hair for cords and in headdresses by the Pimas suggests Lower Californian affinities, as we are told by Venegas that the natives of that peninsula were accustomed to adorn themselves on ceremonial occasions with "a large cloak covering them from their head to their feet, and entirely composed of human hair." History of California, I, 99.

[b] Length of specimen figured. 22 cm.; diameter, 37 mm.

[c] Length of specimen figured, 17 cm.; diameter, 18 mm.

These fibers make very satisfactory brushes, but they are not so stiff as brushes made of bristles. The fibers are not set in a handle but are tied in a round bundle a little below the middle, then folded outward from the center so that the upper end or handle is round and smooth while the lower end includes all the free fiber ends. Twine is then wrapped in a coil around the upper end downward until the brush end remains just long enough to give the fibers play in passing through the hair. The wrapping may be either of fiber or of horsehair; in the latter case pleasing geometric patterns are often worked out with contrasted black and white threads. The specimen illus-

FIG. 40. War headdress.

trated in figure 41, *b* is bound with maguey fiber which has been decorated with three lines of purple dye, put on after the wrapping has been completed.

SKIN DRESSING

The use of leather in the manufacture of clothing was reduced to a minimum among the Pimas. For sandals, rawhide sufficed, and if this was not to be had there was an abundance of yucca fiber, which made a fair substitute. For the shields, with the use of which they became adept through training from childhood, rawhide was employed. So the needs which dressed leather alone could satisfy were but few, and it is probable that Gileño women did little more than enough skin dressing to keep the art alive among them. At present there are

very few who know anything about it, and this is the method which they say "long ago make it."

A skin was soaked in water for two or three days to soften it; then it was laid on an inclined log and the hair scraped off with a deer's rib. Two tanning media were used—brains and saguaro seeds. The former were kept dried into a cake with dry grass until they were needed, when they were softened in water. The seeds were available at any time, as they were always kept in store as an article of food.

The roots of the plant known as urto, Krameria parvifolia, were used to dye leather red.

FIG. 41. Hairbrushes. a, Sacaton grass roots; b, maguey fiber.

Fire Bag

Leather bags were used to carry flint and steel, and a specimen of these comparatively modern articles is shown in figure 42. It is ornamented with tin bangles and glass beads.

Tobacco Pouches

Tobacco was not recognized by the Pimas as a narcotic that would stunt the growth in youth or injuriously affect the heart as age advanced, nor yet as a solace for leisure moments. It was to them a plant of divine origin that in its death (burning) released a spirit (odor and smoke) that was wafted by the breeze to the home of the magic beings that shape man's destiny. Throughout Pimería one

FIG. 42. Fire bag.

may find sacred places where large numbers of cane cigarettes have been deposited by worshipers. It is uncertain how far this form of cigarette was in use by the Pimas. Most of those found were made by the Hohokam.[a]

To carry this sacred powder it was necessary to have something more than an ordinary receptacle, and so pouches were made of buckskin, ornamented in vivid colors with symbols of the sun and provided with rattles that tinkled with every motion of the wearer. Both in shape and in ornament they closely resemble the tobacco pouches of the Apaches. There are two specimens in the National Museum. No. 27840 (fig. 43, a) is of buckskin,[b] doubled so that the opening of the pouch on the unornamented half is covered by the fold. The margin is ornamented by a fringe of short strings of buckskin passed through holes along the edge of the pouch, most

a   b   c

FIG. 43, a, b, c. Tobacco pouches.

of them having cylinders of tin, slightly bell-shaped, arranged in pairs and pinched into place around the thongs by pounding. The front bears a conventional symbol of the sun in red and blue. There is a short loop with which to suspend the pouch from the belt or to hang it up when not in use.

Another pouch, no. 27839 (fig. 43, b, c), is of soft deerskin, with a red fringe made by parallel cuts along the edge. There are a few

---

[a] At the present time most men and some women smoke cigarettes rolled in corn husks or paper, obtained, as is much of the tobacco, from the whites. The native tobaccos are: Nicotiana trigonophylla, known as vi'opal vi'ofû, "like tobacco," gathered near Babcquivari by the Papagos and brought to the Pimas; N. bigelovii, known as pan vi'ofû, "coyote tobacco," and N. attenuata, called rsʋkai ʌu'tcâ vi'ofû, "under-the-creosote-bush tobacco." Boys learn to smoke at an early age, though the use of tobacco is not encouraged. The father's favorite saying in reply to a request for tobacco is, "I will give you some when you kill a coyote."

[b] Length, 10 cm.; width, 11 cm.; 114 bangles.

tin bangles at the bottom. The margin is ornamented inside the fringe with a herring-bone pattern burned on. One side of the pouch has a human figure and the other bears two sun symbols. These are very similar to some seen by the writer upon the walls of caves in the Chiricahui mountains, an old Apache stronghold.[a] The pouch is sewed with cotton thread and secured at the top by an American button. The cord for suspension has 4 clusters of 6 bangles each upon it.

SLING

Slings were used by Pima youths before the advent of the whites. They were of the usual elongated oval shape. The National Museum contains a sling, no. 76031, that was obtained from the Pimas half a century ago. It is of leather, probably cut from a boot leg, with strings 68.5 cm. long. The imperforate center is 18 by 7 cm. (fig. 44).

FIG. 44. SLING.

SHIELD

The fighting men were divided into two parties— those who used the bow and those who fought with club and shield. When advancing upon the enemy, the warrior crouched so that the comparatively small shield protected his entire body. He also leaped from side to side for the double purpose of presenting a more difficult target, and of bewildering the enemy and thus unsteadying their nerves through the suggestion of magic, which plays a larger part in the warfare of the American Indian than is generally known. The preparation for a war expedition is an invocation to the gods and the ceremonies during the journey are incantations for the development of magic power that shall not only render the party invincible but shall induce its magic power, on its own account, to overwhelm the magic power of the enemy. It is not the strength nor the intelligence of the Apache that they fear, nor his arrow with its sting, but his magic—a creation of their own imagination. And so the shield, with its magic symbols in brilliant colors, is kept in rapid motion not only from side to side but also revolving by the reciprocal twist of the bearer's forearm.

A long and careful search failed to disclose the presence of a single old shield among the Pimas, but there is a specimen in the National Museum, no. 27830, that was obtained several years ago (fig.45, *a*, *b*). It is a rawhide disk 49 cm. in diameter, provided with a cottonwood

---

[a] Length, 17 cm.; width, 16 cm.

handle of convenient size for grasping. The handle is slightly concave
on the side next to the shield. It is attached by means of thongs,
which pass through two holes for each end of the handle, at the center
of the disk. When not in use, it was carried by a sling strap that

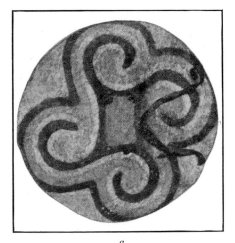 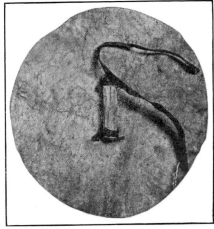

a   b

FIG. 45. a, Shield; b, reverse of shield.

passed through two holes at the border 24 cm. apart. It is ornamented by an ogee swastika in blue, red, and white.

There are also two models of Pima shields in the National Museum.
One is a small painted disk of rawhide; the other is a hoop with

a   b

FIG. 46, a, b. Models of shields.

muslin stretched over it. The former, no. 76073 (fig. 46, b), is ornamented with a cross in white, blue, red, and yellow. The latter, no.
76028 (fig. 46, a), is 225 mm. in diameter, or about one-third the full
size. The design in red and yellow is also in the form of a cross.

A similar shield decorated with swastika in red and white (fig. 47) was collected in 1887 by Mr F. W. Hodge, of the Hemenway Expedition, and by him presented to the Free Museum of the University of Pennsylvania.

SANDALS

Some protection for the feet was necessary when on journeys across the stony mesas and mountains that surround the Pima villages.

Rawhide was the most widely used material and the sandal was the form of foot gear. It was kept in place by a single thong, which passed through two holes in the front of the sandal, so as to go between the first and second and the fourth and fifth toes, then backward obliquely across the foot, so that the two parts crossed each other over the instep, down through a hole in the end of a heel plate and around behind the heel, where it was doubled back and forth two or three times before passing through the hole in the opposite end of the heel plate, and so on forward again. The heel plate passes transversely through two longitudinal slits in the heel of the sandal and is of the same hard and stiff rawhide. The doubled thongs behind the heel are usually wound with softer material to prevent chafing (fig. 48).

FIG. 47. Shield.

YOKE STRAPS

Ox yokes were bound to the horns of the animals by long strips of hide that had been roughly dressed without removing the hair. The two straps collected were the only ones seen. It is some years since they were last used for this purpose, and it is not surprising that most such straps should have been employed for other needs (fig. 49).

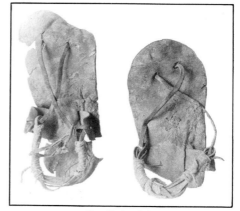

FIG. 48. Sandals.

LARIAT

The use of the lariat was, of course, learned from the whites and was developed gradually with the tardy introduction of live stock. The "rope," as it is universally known in the Southwest, is of rawhide made in a 4-ply braid, rounded by pounding when wet. The slip noose at the outer end is supplied with an ingenious loop made by folding a heavy piece of rawhide three or four times and bringing the ends together to form an oval ring. The end of the rope is passed through a longitudinal slit in one end of the ring and by a braided enlargement prevented from being pulled out again. A strip of rawhide about 1 cm. in width is rolled in the interior of the ring, and passing through a transverse cut close to one end it is continued around the outside, being itself slit where the rope enters the ring, and also pass-ing under two loops made by catching up the outer layer of hide on the ring it then passes through a transverse slit in the outer and overlapping end of the ring and is knotted. It therefore passes twice around the ring and is the only means of uniting the ends of it. When hardened the ring is large enough to permit free play of the rope through it.[a]

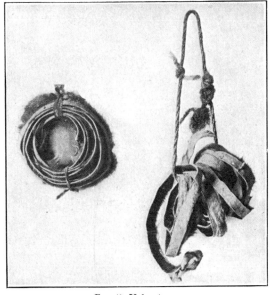

FIG. 49. Yoke straps.

HORNED TOAD EFFIGY

Among the most highly prized objects made of leather by the Pimas, found by the writer, was a life-sized effigy of a horned toad. It is of deerskin, ornamented with white beads, as shown in figure 50, *a*. It was used in the cure of the toad disease by being passed over the affected part. This act and the singing of the toad songs effected a complete cure, our informant believed. Figure 50, *b*, is a photograph of a living horned toad.

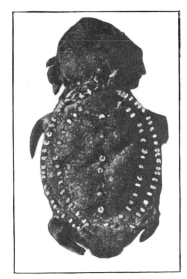

FIG. 50, *a*. Horned toad effigy, of deerskin.

[a] Length of lariat, 13.93 m.; diameter, 9 mm. Length of loop ring, 6 cm.; width, 4 cm.

POTTERY

As a tribe the Pimas are not skillful potters. Their work is

FIG. 50, *b*. Living horned toad.

decidedly inferior to that of the Kwahadk's, which in turn appears to be improving as a result of a modern demand for it. It is probable that the best potters among the Pimas are of Kwahadk' descent, or have learned the art from that tribe. A great part of the Pima ceramic ware is plain and undecorated. The cooling ollas in which water is kept about their homes are the only vessels that are generally decorated. The potters aver that the designs are copied from the Hohokam potsherds that bestrew the mesas and that the symbolism is absolutely unknown to them. Furthermore, many of the smaller decorated pieces are traded from both the Kwahadk's and the Papagos, the latter bringing them filled with cactus sirup to exchange for grain. The vessels here illustrated were made by Sala Hina (fig. 51), one of the best potters on the Gila.

MATERIAL

The common ware that is intended to be subjected to heat is generally made from clay obtained among the Skâsŏwalĭk hills, which lie on the southern border of the Gila River reservation. The material is a dry granular clay combined with quartz pebbles and feldspathic detritus. The place where it occurs looks much more like a stone quarry than like a clay pit (pl. XVI, *a*). Indeed, a

FIG. 51. Sala Hina.

great part of the mass is sharp, angular stone, which must be winnowed out by hand in the shallow baskets.

The process is well illustrated in plate XVI, *b.*[a]

Another well-known clay pit is situated on McClellen's branch, at the northeastern base of the Sacaton hills (pl. XVI, *c*), whence a whitish clay is obtained. The villages about the Casa Blanca ruin obtain clay from pits within a stone's throw of the ruin itself and from the river bottom near the village of Rso'tûk.

The tempering materials used in the clays last mentioned are sand and ground potsherds. The clay from the Skâsŏwalĭk hills is so coarse that it requires no tempering.

Red ocher is employed as a slip, which is applied to the surface of the common utensils just before the drying that precedes burning. The water coolers are usually made without this coating of ocher.

Black gum is used for decoration. This is obtained by boiling in a small earthen pot, or in a segment of a large one, mesquite chips

[a] Samples of this clay were submitted to Doctor Wiley, Chief of the Bureau of Chemistry of the Department of Agriculture, who ascertained the percentage composition of the material to be as follows:

	Per cent		Per cent
Silica, SiO_2	59. 64	Combined water, organic matter, and other volatile constituents (loss on ignition)...	4. 94
Alumina, Al_2O_3	18. 55		
Ferric oxide, Fe_2O_3	6. 72	Sulphuric acid, SO_3	. 45
Manganous oxide, MnO	Trace	Carbon dioxide, CO_2	Trace
Lime, CaO	2. 35		99. 90
Magnesia, MgO	1. 44		
Alkalies, K_2O and Na_2O	5. 81		

He also explains the general method of determination.

For industrial purposes an attempt is made to separate the proximate constituents of a clay by what is called a "rational analysis." For this purpose the clay is treated with sulphuric acid, which is supposed to dissolve the clay substance proper and leave insoluble quartz sand and sand composed of feldspar or other minerals.

In order that the composition of this clay might be compared with analyses of other clays made upon this plan, a determination was made of the matter insoluble in sulphuric acid in sample 24881, with the following results:

	Per cent
Clay substance	35. 33
Quartz sand, feldspathic detritus, etc.	64. 57
	99. 90

The sand insoluble in sulphuric acid is composed approximately as follows:

	Per cent
Feldspathic detritus, etc.	28. 57
Quartz sand	36. 00

Comparison of these results with analyses given by Langenbeck indicate that the material represented by sample 24881 resembles the clays used for the production of so-called "red ware" more than any other class of clays used in pottery manufacture by civilized peoples. The following analysis of a typical clay used for making "red ware" is quoted from Langenbeck for purposes of comparison (The Chemistry of Pottery, 1895, 60):

Total analysis		*Rational analysis*	
	Per cent		Per cent
Silica	74. 75	Clay substance	39. 12
Alumina	12. 55	Quartz	52. 54
Ferric oxide	5. 28	Feldspathic detritus	8. 55
Lime	1. 28		100. 21
Magnesia	. 85		
Alkalies	2. 27		
Combined water	3. 23		
	100. 21		

from portions of the tree on which black gum has dried into hard
scales.   After boiling, this dye is in the form of a very thin liquid
which is so pale that it is scarcely distinguishable on the dark clay,
but after the vessel has been given a slight burning the pattern
appears in deep black.

IMPLEMENTS

As the new vessel is built up the outside is struck with a paddle
(pl. XVII, b), and the inside is supported by a flat circular stone about
10 cm. in diameter.   A smaller stone is used to polish the outer
surface.   Long, smooth, finger-shaped stones are used in polishing
the necks of vessels or in places where there are sharp curves.

METHOD

The fictile ware of the Pimas is made by coiling.   The clay is first
thoroughly dried, a condition that is easily and quickly brought about
by spreading it on blankets in the sun.   It is then sifted to remove the
larger particles of stone.   It is next mixed with water and kneaded
a few minutes, formed into lumps the size of the fist, and laid aside
to "ripen" over night.   The base of the new vessel is begun by
spreading a layer of clay over the bottom of an old vessel of suitable
size and smoothing it down with the paddle until it extends out several
centimeters from the center (see pl. XVII, a, where the vessel shown
in the potter's lap has just been taken from the olla over which it
was molded).   The new bottom is allowed to dry an hour in the
sun before it is removed and the process of coiling begun.   Dipping
the fingers in water, the operator moistens the edges of the new vessel, which has dried enough to retain its shape.   Then taking one of
the prepared balls of clay she rapidly rolls it between the palms
until it is lengthened into a cylinder about 20 cm. long, which is
laid on the margin of the vessel and pinched into shape.   One or
perhaps two more rolls are laid on to complete the circuit and then
the paddle is applied with the right hand in quick taps to the outside while the circular stone is held on the inside with the left (pl.
XVII, b).   The handle of the paddle is held downward so that the transverse concavity of the instrument is adapted to the horizontal convexity of the growing vessel, which is held in the lap and the coils
applied only so fast as they dry sufficiently to cause it to hold its
shape.   For this reason it is customary for a potter to model three
or four vessels at the same time so there need be no delay by waiting
for the last layer to dry.   As each coil is finished it is placed where
the sun can shine upon it and the work progresses much faster than it
could in a less arid climate.   As soon as the vessel has been built up
a little way so there is room for the paddle to be used above the plane

of the bottom it is placed on the ground and a little loose soil is drawn up to serve as a support and in this it is turned slowly with the hands as required (pl. XVII, c). As the lower coils become dry they are smoothed with a polishing stone with strokes made from below upward; if a part has become too hard to be easily rubbed down the hand is dipped into the vessel of water that is within reach, and applied to the spot.

When the last coil has been shaped a dark red shale is ground in water until the liquid has become quite thick; this is applied to the outer surface with the hands. As the slip dries it is rubbed with the polishing stone until it becomes hard and smooth.

After drying over night the vessel is ready for burning. A very shallow pit is dug and a fire is kept in it for some time to dry the earth thoroughly, then a little dry mesquite or decayed willow wood is spread in the depression, and the vessel is laid on its side upon the wood and entirely covered with sticks laid up "log-cabin fashion." In the specimen shown in figure 52 the wood had burned away in about twenty minutes. The photograph was taken as the burning brands fell from the sides.

The final step, if the vessel is to be decorated, is to apply the black mesquite pigment with a sharpened stick (pl. XVII, d), made from Baccharis glutenosa, which has a large pithy center. The vessel is again subjected to heat for a few minutes until the decoration has assumed a deep black color, when it is finished.

FINISHED PRODUCTS

Water reservoirs or coolers (fig. 53, a, b) are the largest and finest pieces of fictile ware made by the Pimas and Papagos. The latter carry on a thriving trade with the whites by supplying each house with one or more of these big round-bottomed pots, which are so porous that the evaporation from the outside measurably cools the water within. Although the term "olla" is applied to all Indian pottery in the Southwest, the word generally refers to this particular class of vessels. One will be found set in a three-forked post under the arbor at every Pima home.[a] An olla was secured which had been hidden away among the rocks in the hills for many years (fig. 54). It is among the smallest of those used for water coolers, and may well serve here to illustrate the minimum size and also a variation in decoration.[b]

Ollas with angular profile are not uncommon (fig. 55).

Cooking pots (pl. XVIII, a) are more numerous than the water

---

[a] The larger specimen (fig. 53, b) collected is 0.387 m. high, 0.275 m. in diameter at the top, and 1.161 m. in its maximum circumference. The decoration is derived from the Hohokam pottery of the Casa Blanca district.

[b] Height, 0.330 m.; diameter at top, 0.175 m.; maximum circumference, 0.950 m.

coolers. Every kitchen contains several; some of them broken in halves or smaller fragments, yet retained for use in parching wheat or corn over the fire, or for other purposes. They are undecorated and not carefully smoothed and polished "because they would be slippery to handle when they became wet." [a]

FIG. 52. The burning.

Bean pots are made with handles as represented in pl. XVIII, *b*. They form a distinct type unlike any other aboriginal ware known to the writer.[b]

Canteens were formerly made of pottery, but they have been

[a] The specimen shown in pl. XVIII, *a*, is 0.285 m. high, 0.255 m. in diameter at the top, 0.950 m. in maximum circumference.

[b] Pl. XVIII, *b*, represents one of these vessels, which is 0.159 m. high, 0.195 m. in diameter at the top, 0.748 m. in maximum circumference.

superseded by the cheap and scarcely less fragile metal ones of American manufacture. They were globular in form, and not provided with projections or loops for the attachment of straps. In fact, they were intended to be carried in the woman's kiâhâ; men on the warpath or traveling far from water must learn to endure thirst, but the women when compelled to go far for wood or cactus fruit were accustomed to carry water in these canteens. The vessels were sometimes broken, and Sala Hina told us of such an experience in which she nearly perished of thirst before she reached the river, though she had gone but a few miles from home. Canteens were decorated in a variety of patterns, including human figures.[a]

What may be termed a parching pan (pl. xix, a) is made for roasting grains preparatory to grinding them for pinole. It is a large oval shallow dish with margin extended at ends for handles.[b]

a   b

FIG. 53, a, b. Water coolers.

A tortilla baking plate (pl. xix, b) is sometimes seen. It is nothing more than a slightly concave undecorated disk.[c]

Cups were seldom made of clay; dippers of gourd or bowls of basketry were lighter and less perishable. It is probable that most of the few cups of Indian manufacture now to be found among the Pimas were obtained from the Kwahadk's or the Papagos. They are so highly polished as to appear to be glazed and are usually decorated with geometric designs to which no meaning can be ascribed by their makers.[d]

---

a There are three specimens in the collection. Pl. xviii, c is 0.195 m. high, 0.600 m. in circumference, with an opening at the top 31 mm. in diameter. Pl. xviii, d is 0.135 m. high, 0.365 m. in circumference, and has an opening 29 mm. in diameter. Pl. xviii, e is a double-necked canteen.

b Represents a pan that is 0.445 m. long, 0.354 m. wide, 0.117 m. high.

c The collection contains one of these plates, which is 0.350 m. in diameter and stands 63 mm. high.

d Pl. xix, e, represents a cup which was made by the Kwahadk's and traded to the Pimas. It is 84 mm. high and 84 mm. in diameter.

Plates (pl. XIX, *c*, *f*) are now obtained from the Kwahadk‘s, but it is doubtful if the latter made them before the advent of the whites. They are polished and decorated in a manner similar to the cups.[a]

Fanciful figures of a variety of shapes are made by the Kwahadk‘s in

imitation of American crockery, and the like, and are traded to the Pimas, who sometimes sell to gratify the desires of tourists for souvenirs, the seller being as ignorant of the fact that the buyer wishes to get specimens of Pima handiwork as the latter is of the fact that the ware is packed on the heads of women from the villages of another tribe 30 to 50 miles to the southward.

Two specimens (pl. XIX, *d*) were obtained from a Pima woman at Casa Blanca, who had

FIG. 54. Olla found hidden in the hills.

"made them to sell," which have not the characteristic polish and the decoration of Kwahadk‘ ware. They are of interest because they show the Pima method of treatment of the human figure in clay modeling, and also the manner in which the face was painted. The larger effigy[b] has light brown lines on the body, both front and back, which represent a necklace, belt, skirt (perhaps), and what would seem to be the V-shaped opening at the neck of an upper garment. The face is painted in vertical stripes of red and blue, as was the custom with this tribe a few years ago. The front hair is represented on the forehead by prominent ridges.

The smaller effigy[c] has fewer lines on the face, and the body is undecorated.

FIG. 55. Olla with whitish designs on red ground.

From the ruins pottery spoons or ladles are sometimes taken which have apparently acquired magic import from the character of their source. These spoons are used in feeding the sick, and for no other

---

[a] The larger specimen figured is 264 mm. in diameter and 73 mm. high. The smaller is 212 mm. in diameter and 43 mm. high.

[b] Height, 212 mm.

[c] Height, 20 cm.

purpose, so far as the writer is aware. The collection contains one very old spoon of Pima manufacture,[a] which is practically an elongated bowl (pl. xx, *a*). Another specimen[b] was made for us to illustrate the type, which, though rare, is well recognized (pl. xx, *b*). The collection contains also a bowl (pl. xx, *c*), two coiled bowls (pl. xx, *d*), and two decorated bowls (pl. xx, *e*).

Pottery was mended with gum from the creosote bush, Larrea mexicana (pl. IX, *a*). This bush grows abundantly on the driest plains of the Gila watershed, but its leaves are so bitter that it is not touched by stock, however extreme may be their hunger.

BASKETRY

The art of basket making is practised in nearly every Pima home. The more skillful basket makers produce wares that are useful, durable, and handsome. The work, which is done by the women, requires much time and patience. Owing to the poverty of the tribe since the river water has been taken from them, some women have been induced to begin the manufacture of baskets without having received the necessary training in girlhood and without any pride in the finished product, as it is possible to dispose of them at once at a fair price, no matter how wretchedly bad they may be.

Fig. 56. Willow tree.

MATERIALS

There are three materials which surpass all others in importance, and quite a number that play a minor part. First of all should be named the willow, Salix nigra (fig. 56), twigs of which are gathered in March just before the leaves appear. The Yavapais who now live at old Fort McDowell use the willow for the white part of the outside of baskets and for the inner coil as well; but the Pimas employ the willow for the weft only. The twigs are about 50 cm. in

---

[a] Length, 115 mm.; width, 74 mm.; depth, 25 mm.
[b] Length, 130 mm.; width, 25 mm.; depth, 30 mm.

length.   The bark is removed by catching it at the middle of the
twig in the teeth and raising it far enough to insert the thumbs of
both hands between the bark and the wood, and then running the
thumbs outward to the ends of the twig.   Two such movements

a   b   c
Fig. 57. *a*, Willow splints; *b*, martynia; *c*, cottonwood.

suffice to strip the twig, which is then split into three or four strips
at the smaller end with the teeth and the splitting carried to the other
end of the twig by careful manipulation with both hands, so that the

Fig. 58. Bundles of martynia pods.

strips may be as even as possible.   These strips are kept in coils,
which are from 10 to 15 cm. in diameter (fig. 57, *a*).   Willow bark is
also used in basketry, both alone (cradle shields) and in conjunction
with other materials (grain baskets).

The stems of the cat-tail, Typha angustifolia Linn., are used as foundation in the common baskets. They are gathered in July when green, and are split and dried. The stalks curl inward along the split surface while drying, so that they have the appearance of round stems with a mere line running along one side to show where they were split. These stalks are from 1 to 2 m. long and are kept in bundles, sometimes 25 cm. in diameter, but usually much less.

The pods of the devil's claw, Martynia fragrans Lindl., furnish the third material necessary for the ordinary basket. The supply of wild plants is not large enough, and a few martynia seeds are planted each year by the basket makers. These are gathered in the autumn at any time after the plant has dried. They are made into bundles (fig. 58) for storing or for barter by tying a few hooks together and then pushing other hooks down into the center and allowing the pods to curve over one another. Each half of a pod is provided with one of these long recurved hooks, from 15 to 20 cm. in length (fig. 59). They are black on the surface, and hence desired for the purpose of contrasting with the white willow to form the designs. Their central portion is pithy, but the outside is very tough and woody. To prepare for use, the devil's claw is soaked over night and then buried in moist

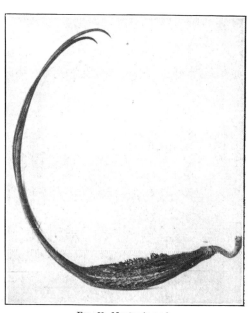

FIG. 59. Martynia pod.

earth for a day or more. It is then dug out, usually by a party of women, who make a "bee" of it, and the outer fiber of each claw is removed by breaking the hooked end and holding it in the teeth while the split fiber is pulled off with the fingers. Figure 60 shows such a party stripping the fibers, which appear in a coil at the knees of the second figure from the right. In the foreground is a heap of stripped pods. A small board in front of each woman is to lay the splint on when thinning and shaping it. Instead of soaking and burying the devil's claw, some have begun to hasten the process by pouring hot water over it and proceeding at once to strip off the fiber. The strips are kept in coils (fig. 57, *b*) similar to those of willow. They are valued somewhat more highly than the willow splints, and hence a higher price is sometimes demanded for baskets in which a large amount of devil's claw is used.

Leaves of the agave are sometimes used, but baskets of this material are obtained chiefly from the Papagos. Wood from the slender branches of cottonwood is sometimes used to take the place of willow, but it is less durable and soon becomes yellow. It is prepared in the same manner and kept in the same sort of coils as the willow (fig. 57, c).

Wheat straw is extensively used in the manufacture of the jar-shaped grain baskets. It is of modern introduction, and has not fully supplanted the ancient style of grain bin.

Fig. 60. Stripping martynia.

The arrow bush (Pluchea borealis) was the principal material employed in the construction of storage bins or baskets. It is everywhere abundant along the river, and is one of the few shrubs of Pimería that is not armed with thorns, its slender, graceful stalks being easily manipulated (pl. XXI, a).

Reeds, Phragmitis communis, were formerly common along the Gila, but continuous seasons of drought caused them to disappear. Sleeping mats were made from them, but such mats are now rarely seen, agave leaf being used instead.

Plate XXI, c illustrates the crucifixion thorn, Holocantha emoryi, surrounded by saltbushes.

IMPLEMENTS

The only implements used in the manufacture of the common baskets are awls and knives. The awl was formerly of bone or mesquite wood. Now it is of steel with a wooden or gum handle (fig. 22, *a*, *b*). Common case knives or light butcher knives, well sharpened, are used to trim the strips of willow at the time of use.

METHOD

The ordinary baskets are made by the process known as coiling. The center is of devil's claw, which is generally started as a coil, but is sometimes made by the process called checker weaving for a few centimeters before beginning the coil. The half stalks of the cat-tail are again split before being used and about a dozen of these splints are taken to form a foundation. The other two materials, willow and devil's-claw splints, are kept in water at the time of use to render them flexible. One end of each splint is held in the teeth while the knife is rapidly scraped along the rough side and while the edges are trimmed smooth and made parallel. Upon this part of the operation depends much of the evenness and fineness of the finished basket. The details of the work do not differ from those of coiled basketry everywhere, which have been so fully and entertainingly described by Professor Mason. The margin was left with the splint wrapped smoothly around it until a few years ago when "some man," supposed to have been a Papago,"told them to braid it;" the tops of baskets are therefore usually finished by passing a single devil's-claw splint in and out and backward and forward over the margin, to which it gives a braided appearance. When the weaving is completed the ends of the splints project on the exterior surface, making it very rough. It is also soiled and stained from having been lying about during the intervals when it was not in the maker's hands for the weeks or months that have elapsed since it was begun. By means of a knife the longer and tougher ends are cut away, while the others are broken and the stains are removed by thoroughly rubbing the surface with leaves and twigs of the saltbushes, Atriplex lentiformis, A. canescens, A. polycarpa, etc.

BASKET BOWLS

This term may be accepted in lieu of a better one, for the tray- or bowl-shaped baskets, which are shallow and have their sides sloping at a low angle from the horizontal. They range from a perfectly flat disk to a bowl with rounded bottom having a depth of 20 cm.

The designs upon these old-style baskets are often very pleasing and even remarkably good. When questioned as to the meaning of the elements of these patterns, the basket makers invariably replied: "I don't know; the old women make them in this way. They copied the patterns long ago from the Hohokam pottery." While these statements are true in the main, some of the elements will be seen to be of wide distribution and some are peculiar to the Pacific coast. There are three common designs: Those embodying the fret, the equal-armed cross, and the spiral. Nearly all that do not represent these directly are more or less evident modifications of them. The fret, which the Pimas probably with truth called the oldest motive, leads almost directly into the swastika and suavastika pattern, as shown in the illustrations. The flower design based upon the cross is apparently the same as that on the necks of water jars made by the Hohokam, and such vessels are similarly decorated to the present day by both Pimas and Papagos. On the pottery the design is laid upon a convex surface, while in the baskets it is worked upon the interior, or concave, side. The elements of the design are, first, a series of four radiating arms of black separating the petal-like areas which are usually in the shape of spherical triangles. The second element is a series of encircling lines that lie parallel to the radiating bars and follow their outline entirely around the basket, having also rectangular enlargements where they change direction to cross the ends of the bars or to follow along their sides. It is just such a design as might easily originate in pottery decoration where a complete line may be traced continuously, but it is not one that can be easily explained if it is assumed that it originated in basketry, especially when it is remembered that these people prepare no pattern whatever beforehand, but develop the designs upon the baskets as previously conceived in the mind.

The volute, or whorl, is a common motive in primitive art, and is especially frequent in Southwestern basketry. As the angular weaving necessitates irregularities in the lines of curvature, they are not infrequently modified by terrace-like enlargements. Terraces are used in combination with nearly all the other elements known to the basket maker.

It will be observed that the decoration of Pima baskets is in black on a white ground for the most part, yet the proportions vary greatly. Brown, and more rarely some other color, may be seen in perhaps one basket in a thousand. Occasionally a basket is made with a dozen or more blue glass beads fastened on the border at equal intervals by weft splints passing through them. Rarely, work or trinket baskets are made to sell that have open spaces in their sides.

DESCRIPTION OF PLATES

The fret is a common motive in Pima basketry. In the small—and usually badly made—baskets it is commonly single and of uniform width. In the first of our series (pl. XXII, a) it appears as a double line with five folds. Had there been but four the effect of the whole would have suggested the swastika. The large basket, *b*, has three parallel lines, a larger number of folds, and an unusually large center of unrelieved black. Baskets *c*, *d*, and *e* exhibit slight modifications of the fret, in *c* the parts of the inner circle being four in number and in *e* five. The design in *f* is a fret of four folds, and the fret is the principal motive also in some of the upright baskets shown in plates xxix and xxx. Basket *g* shows an equal-armed cross in white and a series of four broken lines that pass, in the form of a whorl, from near the center to the margin after each taking one and a half turns around the basket. Basket *h* combines the fret and whorl, there being seven radiating lines that reach the margin after half a turn each.

In plate xxiii, *a*, is shown a rare form—a flat disk, ornamented with a whorl of six broken lines, an intermediate form between the fret and the whorl. In *b* there is an unusual treatment of the dark center, elsewhere invariably a solid disk of black. It looks as if the maker had changed the design after starting the six rather irregular bars of black from the center. In *c* the six radiating lines advance toward the periphery by the interpolation of an independent motive that will be seen later in upright shapes. Baskets *d* and *e* are ornamented with five pairs of whorled lines that contain squares of black, which may also be regarded as an independent motive. In *f* the number 5 again reappears and also the simple motive of *c*, but this time in white on a black ground. This is called by some the "coyote track." It is well shown in plates xxix and xxx.

Plate xxiv, *a*, illustrates a combination of the broken whorled lines of the preceding plate with a pattern obtained by the children at school in an early stage of their instruction in drawing. At the margin is the diamond pattern that has the effect of netting. In *b*, although the lines do not radiate from the center, they have something of the whorled effect, and they unite with the fret of the preceding illustrations a new element—the terrace—which is so common on the ancient pottery of Arizona. The parts are in five, there being two reduplications of the unit in the outer row to one in the inner. In *c* the parts are again in six. The central portion is difficult to analyze, but the outer repeats the terrace, together with a fret that by its breadth of line at the center suggests the form of the cross known as the swastika. Basket *d* has the fret combined with the terrace, being similar to the first basket in the last figure. The parts of the design in this plate are in four, five, and six.

Plate xxv, *a*, depicts a form of equal-armed cross that we shall later see passes into another type of design that is complicated, yet pleasing, namely, the flower pattern. Baskets with the design shown in *a* are quite common. In *b* the attenuated arms may be likened to the limbs of some giant spider. They will be seen to be nearly the reverse of the white arms of the design in basket *c*. Basket *d* represents a variant that was seen in a few shallow baskets and which occasionally appears in the upright forms, as in plate XXX, *j*. It resembles a gigantic pictograph upon an ancient altar near Sacaton, the largest pictograph the writer has seen in Arizona. Baskets *e* and *f*, and also *a, b*, and *c*, plate XXVI, contain designs that are perhaps the most abundant

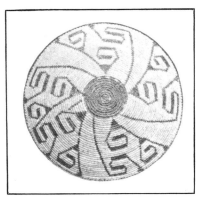

FIG. 61. Basket with scroll decoration.

to be found in Pima basketry. The patterns are whorled frets with many modifications. The decorative effect is enhanced by the addition of the triangular element, to which the same name, mo'ûmvĭtcka, "triangle," is applied as to the terrace. It is seen to be an independent element completed by an extended hook. In plate XXVI, *a, c*, the triangle at the margin is relieved with white, but in *b* it appears in its more common form. In plate XXV, *f*, the mode of origin of the triangle is seen in the terminal enlargement of a segment of the terrace. The triangle gives color balance to the whole, as in *b*, and also fills space due to the elements of the main figure being carried as a whole nearly straight to form an equal-armed figure on a spherical surface. These designs are usually in fours, though sometimes in threes and fives. Figure 61 includes two designs with dissimilar elements which adapt equally well rectangular designs to a hemispherical surface. The design, while clumsily made and unsymmetrical, is yet pleasing by the at least partial harmony of design and form. The motive in this design will be recognized by students of Californian basketry. The basket shown in figure 62 is a rarely beautiful one, having simplicity of design pleasing by its rhythm or repetition and colors well proportioned.

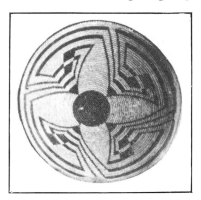

FIG. 62. Basket with scroll-feet decoration.

Plate XXVII contains several examples of good baskets. The second has many triangles, those along the margin suggesting a mode of origin of what is known as the "top-knot" design. The outer band on this basket has the appearance of having been added as an afterthought, but such was not the case, as the device is not uncommon and occurs in the unusually fine basket shown in *c*. The latter is the largest basket in the collection, yet it is so well proportioned, notwithstanding the reduction of the number of repetitions to three, that an artistic design is produced. The warp coils grow successively narrower from the center, thus making the walls thin and flexible. Figures d and e contain modifications of the equal-armed cross, with an apparently new element in d, which is shown in e to be a derivation of the triangle. These two baskets are examples of one of the oldest designs. It is also seen in the upright basket, plate XXXII, c. The white in f suggests the rattlesnake rattle design.

Plate XXVIII introduces a new design which the Pimas call si'sitcut-cufĭk, "very much figured" or "complicated." Analysis shows c and d to be much simpler than they appear at first sight. The elements in d are an equal-armed cross and parallel lines around it, with enlargements wherever they change direction. The effect of the whole is suggestive of a flower with four petals. In a the petals appear largely in white. This flower design is said to be of recent origin. Sala Hina, who is perhaps 70 years of age, declares that it was unknown in her girlhood days.

Plates XXIX, XXX, XXXI, and XXXII include a series of baskets from photographs representing basket collections in Sacaton. Many have the upright waste-paper basket form, and are recent. Nearly all the Pima baskets made during the winter of 1901-2 were of these shapes. Many are decorated with simple motives that depend for their effect upon repetition. A notable feature of the ornament is the introduction of badly executed human figures. Certain traders urged the basket makers to put as many human and animal figures as possible on the baskets. Truly we need a society for the protection of American art. The most successful of these designs seen by the writer is the Gila monster shown in plate XXX, n. However, it is but a sorry substitute for the old-time simple motives. These baskets serve also to illustrate the varied treatment of the geometric elements met with in the shallow baskets as applied to the convex surfaces of the upright forms.

In conclusion, it is believed to be advisable to add the names of the elements of the designs which the Pima basket makers regard as distinct. But two in the list refer to natural objects, namely, numbers 3 and 7 below. It is worthy of note that the continued inquiries of visitors have aroused the interest of the natives to such a degree that they have begun to devise plausible interpretations to symbols the meaning of which is absolutely unknown to them.

1. Atc'uta, the black center of all baskets.
2. Ka'kiopĭns, "crossed lines" (pl. XXII).
3. Kâm'ketcĭt, "turtle," applied to a square design (pl. XXII).
4. Mav'spĭtchita, "locked together," the interrupted fret (pl. XXVI, e).
5. Mo'ûmvĭtcka, "triangular," all triangles and terraces.

6. O'pûmusult, "parallel lines doubled on themselves" (pl. XXIII).

7. Pan ikâ'kĭta, "coyote tracks" (pl. XXIX).

8. Sâ'-âĭ, "figured," plain design with radiating black bars (pl. XXVIII, e).

9. Si'hitalduwutcĭm, "spiral," whorled or spiral designs (pl. XXIII).

10. Si'sitcutcufĭk, "very much figured," the flower pattern (pl. XXVIII).

11. Stoa, "white," having a few narrow lines.

12. Sûp'epûtcĭm kakaitoa, "striped with black and white," a general term for designs in alternating black and white lines.

13. Ta'sita, "set" or "prearranged," the swastika and suavastika.

14. Tco'ho-otcĭlt, "crooked lines," the fret.

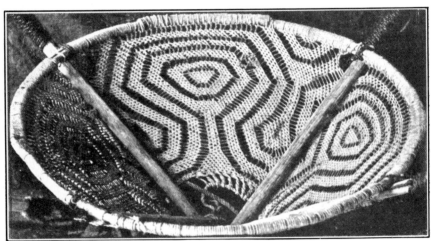

FIG. 63. Kiâhâ.

KIÂHÂ

In the Golden Age of Pimería all burdens were borne by the women, either upon their heads with the aid of the head ring or upon their backs with the unique contrivance which they call kiâhâ (fig. 63), a name that it may be well to retain for the purpose of precise description, as the term "carrying basket" suggests the conical receptacle of other tribes, which is an entirely different affair. The kiâhâ, though unwieldy in appearance, is very light and strong, and heavy loads of wood and other bulky articles may be piled upon the framework, as may be seen in the series of pictures (pl. XXXIV a, b, c, d), which illustrate the manner in which the kiâhâ is loaded while set on the ground with the two long front frame sticks and a separate helping stick (fig. 64), forming a tripod. After loading the kiâhâ, the old dame is seen in b rising to her feet with the aid of the helping stick. Had she had to carry a baby in its cradle she would have placed it in a horizontal position on the top of the heap of mesquite wood; as it was, her load weighed nearly 100 pounds, yet she knelt down, engaged her head under the carrying strap, and struggled to her feet without assistance (c). The method of unloading is shown in d, where, by bending forward, the entire burden is thrown off clear of the head. Figure 65 illustrates the manner in which a kiâhâ net is mended.

As the kiâhâ is distinctively a woman's utensil, so is it closely associated with her life history. The young girls of 8 or 10 begin to use small kiâhâs made especially for them or that have been cut down from old ones. They learn the methods of loading so that the burden may be stable and of proper bulk, they acquire the necessary nerve and muscle coordinations that enable them in later years to lift loads weighing more than do they themselves, they become inured to the fatigue of long journeys, and they learn to preserve their kiâhâs with care from rain. The maiden must have long and gaily-spotted frame sticks at the front of her kiâhâ, which are wound with long hair cords. She uses a helping stick that is ornamented with a long deerskin fringe pendent from the binding at the crotched end (fig. 64). As she walks along with the sharpened end of the stick thrust into the load the fringe hangs above and forward of her head, swinging at every step or fluttering with every breeze. It is indeed a conspicuous object, and it is not surprising that it should have caught the attention of every passing traveler, whose illustrations of it are uniformly bad.[a]

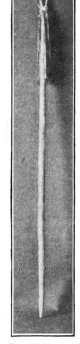

Fig. 64. Helping stick.

As the age of the owner advances she becomes careless of the appearance of her kiâhâ, the spots on the frame are less frequently renewed, the cordage grows short and worn, and the foresticks of the frame are cut down in length. However, her burdens do not diminish, and the woman here photographed, though her age exceeds the scriptural allotment, is yet able to carry more than 100 pounds at a load.

The kiâhâ is of entirely different materials from the ordinary Pima baskets. Wood is used for the four frame sticks, two at the front and two at the rear. Saguaro ribs are invariably used for the purpose, as they are very light, symmetrical, straight, and sufficiently strong. The hoop is a double band of willow.

---

[a] "They are highly prized by their owners, as they are very useful to them, and are made with much labor. For the only specimen I could obtain I was obliged to give goods to the value of $10." Bartlett, Personal Narrative, II, 236.

Agave leaf serves for the front matting or apron that rests against the back.   Between the front and the frame a roll of bark or cloth is usually placed to prevent chafing.   The headband is of the same material as the apron.   It is really a circular band that is flattened out and doubled across the forehead.

Human hair is used to attach the hoop to the frame sticks.   It is of 2-ply 4-strand cord, which is made fast to the hoop and, after drawing the hoop as high as possible to tighten the net, wound from 10 to 50 times around the frame sticks.

The maguey, Tasylirioni wheeleri, furnishes the fiber for the net (fig. 38).   Yucca elata is also a valuable fiber plant and it is probable that the Papagos obtain netting material from Agave heteracantha.   The first two of these plants are found on the higher hills

Fig. 65. Mending kiâhâ net.

and mountains of Pimería, whence they are gathered by parties who go especially for them.   Pits are dug and fires are built in them as the maguey is gathered.   After the fire has died down it is cleared out and the pits are lined with small stones.   The maguey is spread on these, covered with earth, and allowed to roast over night.   After it has been removed from the pit the pulp of the roasted plants is scraped away with a deer's scapula, leaving the fibers a foot or two in length.   These are dried, and when they are long a roll 6 inches in diameter will be sufficient for a kiâhâ net.   Such a roll of fiber is easily transported, and is a recognized article for barter between Pimas and Papagos.   The spinning of kiâhâ thread is a social event, and the women gather for the purpose and gossip merrily as they twist the 2-ply twine, which is rolled into balls that may also be bartered or kept for some time before being made into the nets of conventional pattern (fig. 63).[a]

After the net has been bound to the hoop by a spirally wound cord that completely covers the latter, it is colored with red and blue dyes in such a manner as to emphasize the outlines of the pattern.

Maguey fiber, or horsehair, may be used for the cord which extends from the headband to the frame. It is about 8 mm. in diameter. When of maguey, it is often so well made as to pass readily for machine-made cordage until we examine it closely.[b]

FIG. 66. Storage baskets.

STORAGE BASKETS

The use of large baskets made especially for storing grain and other supplies was widespread in America. They were and are yet of the highest utility to the Pimas, who have raised an abundance of corn and later of wheat to supply all their own needs and more. Two types prevail: A circular bin of arrow bush covered with bushes and earth (fig. 66), and a globular basket of wheat straw built up by coiling (fig. 67).

---

[a] For detail of the weaving see Mason's Origins of Primitive Culture, 251; also Report National Museum, 1894, 471, where Professor Mason makes the statement that the kiâhâ net, worked in what is "commonly called the buttonhole or half-hitch stitch, finds its most northern extension among the Piman stock. Nowhere in the Pueblo tribes is it found, according to the collections in the U. S. National Museum. But south of the Piman it occurs in Central America, in Latin South America as far south as Tierra del Fuego, where it will be found to be the only attempt at textiles." This is another link in the chain of evidence that separates the Pimas from the Hohokam and other Pueblo peoples.

[b] The collection contains an old woman's kiâhâ, the foresticks of which are 1.340 m. long and 3 cm. in diameter at the butt. The shorter sticks are 70 cm. long. The hoop is 65 cm. in diameter. The apron is 58 cm. long by 28 cm. wide. The headband is 35 cm. long and 8 cm. wide. The accompanying helping stick is 1.90 m. long and 22 mm. in diameter; the notch is 6 cm. long and 35 cm. wide at the opening.

The former type is furnished with a bottom of willow branches. The sides are built up by twisting rolls of arrow bush with the butts thrust into the coil beneath to bind the whole together.[a] This type is used for storing mesquite beans on the tops of the houses or sheds (fig. 4). They are also built on the ground in groups, which are inclosed by a low fence to protect them from stock. They are made before the harvest begins, and as the coils are large and there is no close work required a large bin may be built up in half a day.

The straw baskets have their coils fastened with strips of willow bark about 5 mm. in width. The stitches pass through the upper margin of the last coil and are about 20 mm. apart. The coils are from 1 to 2 cm. in diameter. The baskets are from one-half to 1½

Fig. 67. Small storage basket, showing weave.

meters in height. They are covered by a circular disk of the same material or, more frequently, by a section of the bottom of an old worn-out basket.

In making these baskets two rolls are carried around at once, but as they are made with some care it takes much longer than to make a bin of arrow bushes. The baskets are made after the harvest, when the straw is available.

---

[a] The remains of a basket of this type were found by the writer in June, 1901, when examining the two large cliff-houses about 4 miles south of the Salt river, opposite the mouth of the Tonto. Bandelier gives the ground plan of these structures in Papers of Archeol. Inst., Am. ser., IV, pt. II, 426. This would suggest relationship with the Pueblo cliff-dwellers (assuming that the place had not been occupied recently by Apaches or other invaders), were it not for the fact that this type of bins, as well as the arbors on which they are built, prevails among the southern California tribes.

MINOR TYPES

Rectangular trinket baskets (fig. 68, *a*) are made of agave leaves, but nearly all are obtained from the Papagos, as the Pima women seldom make them. They are deeper than broad, somewhat enlarged at the bottom, and are provided with lids.[a] They are of the twined style of weaving. At a distance of 1 cm. from the interior margin of the lid the warp splints (so termed for the sake of clearness in description—they are exactly like the weft) are cut and the ends show on the inside of the lid. The weft is continued to the margin, turned back on itself at right angles to form what looks like a separate ring around the lid; at a height of 5 or 6 cm. it is again folded in and the ends of the splints are cut about 1 cm. from the last fold, so as to be concealed from view.

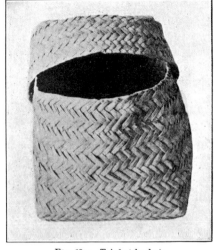

FIG. 68, *a*. Trinket basket.

"Medicine" baskets (fig. 68, *b*) are of the same material and style of weaving as the trinket baskets. They have a characteristic shape—long, square cornered, with rounded margin. They are made in two nearly equal parts, one of which slips over the other as a lid.[b]

FIG. 68. *b*. Medicine basket.

Food bowls of remarkably fine workmanship and graceful shape were carried by warriors on the warpath. They were used to mix

---

[a] The collection contains a specimen of average size, which measures 19 cm. in height, 17 by 18 cm. at the base, and 16 cm. square at the top.

[b] The collection contains one very old medicine basket which is 29 cm. long, 10 cm. wide, and 9 cm. deep.

pinole in and also served as drinking cups. They were light and indestructible. They are no longer made and but two were seen on the reservation.

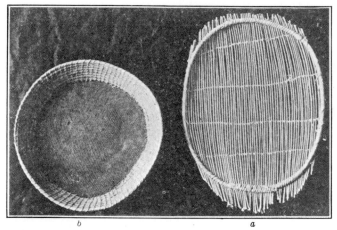

b   a

FIG. 69. *a*, Old sieve; *b*, modern sieve.

Head rings of agave leaf (fig. 36, *b*) are occasionally seen, but they are supposed to have been adopted from the Papagos (see p. 113).

FIG. 70. Sleeping mat.

Oval sieves were made of willow rods, and were very useful in cleaning seeds, and in separating juice from pulp in a variety of plants (fig. 69, *a*). They have been supplanted by a wire sieve [a] made by building a coiled basket rim around a piece of wire netting that has a mesh of 1 mm. (fig. 69, *b*).[b]

Bird traps, house doors, shelves, bird cages, and the like verge upon basketry, but these have all been described in connection with other objects of wood.

The hoods of cradles (described on p. 103) must be included in the list of articles of basketry in use by this people. They are of willow bark cut into strips about 5 mm. wide and woven in the simplest checker style. They are light and flexible, and thus better adapted for their purpose than if made of willow and devil's-claw splints. At the bottom of this hood or shield the strips are gathered into two wrapped bundles, which slip into place on each side of the first transverse bar beneath the baby's head The convexity of the rolls prevents the hood from slipping past the bar and the weight upon them insures stability, while at the same time the hood may be readily detached.

FIG. 71. Detail of sleeping mat.

SLEEPING MATS

Mats were formerly made by the Pimas of the cane, Phragmitis communis, that grew in abundance along the Gila until the water supply became too scant for the maintenance of this plant. They are now made of agave leaves by the Papagos, who barter them to the Pimas (fig. 70). They are woven in a diagonal pattern, each splint passing under three others before appearing again, and the wrong side being rough.[c] The splints are softened by soaking at the time of weaving and become somewhat stiff when dried. The warp and woof are alike,

[a] Twenty-six cm. in diameter at the top and 22 at the bottom. There are 7 coils in the rim, making it 4 cm. deep.

[b] The willow sieve in the collection was made on request by Sala Hina, as there are now none of the old style to be found. It is 32 cm. long, the ends of the rods projecting 3 cm. beyond the hoop to form a sort of handle. The hoop is 26 cm. wide. There are 4 cross-twisted strands to hold the rods in place. The willow rods are 2 mm. apart and 2 mm. in diameter.

[c] Fig. 71 shows the detail of this, with the ends of the splints that have been doubled back, showing at *a, a, a*. Thus the warp splints continue as such to the margin and double back to *a* as weft. The under or what may be called weft splints, similarly treated, appear in the figure at *b, b, b*. The length of the mat collected is 2.100 m.; width, 1.480 m.

and extend in a direction oblique to the sides of the mat. At a distance of about 7 cm. from the margin of both sides and ends the warp and weft splints are woven separately to form a double border, which is held together by single splints occurring at intervals of about 15 cm.

TEXTILES

SPINNING

The Pimas no longer spin and weave; the art is dying with the passing of the older generation. It was with difficulty that enough raw

FIG. 72. Model of loom

cotton of Pima raising was secured to make the beginning of a piece of cloth on the small model loom shown in figure 72. This loom was made by the writer's old friend Kâ'mâl tkâk, who, though an adept in weaving, could not spin and had to engage a woman to do that portion of the work. She removed the seeds by first spreading out the cotton and beating it with a switch.

Kâ'mâl tkâk succeeded in finishing the spinning (see spindle, fig. 73) before the writer had an opportunity to witness the process. However, it has been well described by others.[a]

---

[a] Lieutenant Emory thus describes the manner in which it was done in 1846: "A woman was seated on the ground under the shade of the cotton sheds [arbors on which the cotton was spread to dry]. Her left leg was tucked under her seat and her foot turned sole upwards. Between her big toe and

Fortunately, Doctor Palmer obtained in 1885 a complete loom with sample balls of cotton thread (fig. 74) from the Pimas. The warp is smoothly and evenly spun into a thread about 1 mm. in diameter. The woof threads are softer and are about 3 mm. in diameter; the ball (Museum no. 76012) is 61 cm. in circumference.

Sinew from the back and legs of deer was made into thread and was used in tying cradle bars, shield handles, arrows, kiâhâ frames, and even tattooing needles.

An unidentified species of grass, called â'kivĭk by the Pimas, is said to have been spun into thread in ancient times. According to the myth, it supplied the son of Corn Woman with material for his bowstring. When there is sufficient rain, this grass grows on the Mo'hatûk hills, north of Gila Crossing.

WEAVING

The art of weaving was not highly developed among the Pimas, yet the few simple fabrics of cotton which they produced sufficed to satisfy their needs for clothing and adornment.[a] Unlike their neighbors, they have all but abandoned the art of weaving; at no time in their history have they advanced as far as the Pueblo tribes. Where they learned the art or if they developed it themselves we may not know. We can only hazard the guess that they had the ingenuity to imitate the fabrics which the Hohokam left behind or which the Pimas actually saw them using.

FIG. 73. Spindle.

Early accounts of the Pimas [b] contain references to their fields of

the next was a spindle about 18 inches long, with a single fly of four or six inches. Ever and anon she gave it a twist in a dexterous manner, and at its end was drawn a coarse cotton thread." (Notes, 85.)

[a] " The implements used by these tribes for spinning and weaving are of the most primitive character. A slender stick about 2 feet long passing through a block of wood, which serves to keep up the momentum imparted to it, constitutes the spindle. One end of this rests on a wooden cup inserted between the toes and the other is held and twirled by the fingers of the right hand, while the left hand is occupied in drawing out the thread from a supply of cotton which is coiled on the left arm in loose rolls." (Bartlett, Personal Narrative, II, 225.)

The spindle collected is of arrowwood, the cross bar is of cactus rib. Length, 730 mm.; diameter, 7 mm.; length of bar, 175 mm.; width, 31 mm. (Fig. 73.)

[a] " I suppose that all are provided with cotton blankets; but, owing to the almost incessant heat of the day, they seldom wear them," writes Bartlett (Personal Narrative, II, 229); but in fact there were many poor Pimas who had no blankets and in winter they must have been miserable, indeed, despite the mildness of the climate. Those who were unable to weave but were well to do obtained blankets by bartering corn, beans, and other produce, or horses at the rate of one horse for two blankets.

[b] Bartlett describes the Pima method of weaving as follows: " In weaving, the warp is attached to two sticks, and stretched upon the ground by means of stakes. Each alternate thread of the warp is passed round a piece of cane, which, being lifted, opens a passage for the shuttle in the manner of a sley. The operator sits in the fashion of a tailor, and, raising the sley with one hand, with the other passes the shuttle, which is simply a pointed stick with the thread wound upon it, between the threads of the warp. The work is beaten up after the passage of each thread by the use of a sharp smooth-edged instrument made of hard wood. The operation of course progresses slowly, and from the length of time consumed in spinning and weaving they set a high price upon their blankets, asking for them ten or twelve dollars in money, or a new woolen blanket of equal size. The weaving is generally done by the old men." (Personal Narrative, II, 225.)

cotton, which was picked and spread on the roofs of their arbors to dry in the pod.   When dried and separated from the pods it was stored in large ollas, where, if covered, it would keep for an indefinite period in that dry climate.   Usually, however, it was stored until winter, when there was time for the women to spin it into threads and for the men to weave it[a] into squares of cloth which served as robes for protecting the body by day and as blankets by night, girdles for the waist, and similar but smaller bands for the head.   In later times it is said that bolts of cloth of considerable length were woven to be bartered with adjoining tribes, but this would seem not to have been in accordance with primitive custom.

Accounts of the Pimas that were written in the seventeenth and eighteenth centuries contain references to the use of wool as well as native cotton, but very little information is obtainable concerning the

FIG. 74. Cotton balls, native spinning.

use of wool, and there was not a single sheep on the reservation at the time of the writer's visit.

No dyes were used except a dark buff ocher[b] bartered from the Papagos, into which the cotton was dipped.   No mordant was used and the resulting color was neither brilliant nor permanent.   However, it was applied only to the selvage thread.   Bayeta was unraveled to obtain scarlet thread for belts after the inauguration of trade relations with the Mexicans.

Sewing was unknown, and holes were patched by weaving in a new piece.

Implements and methods.   The loom was simpler than that used by the surrounding tribes and was spread horizontally instead of being set upright.   Four stakes were first driven firmly in the ground out-

---

[a] It is of interest to note that this division of labor differs from that of the Hopis and the Zuñis.
[b] A sample of the mineral used was found upon analysis to contain 30.52 per cent ferric oxide.

lining a rectangular space the exact size of the projected fabric. A deep layer of clean white sand from the river bed was spread between the stakes to prevent the under surface of the fabric from becoming soiled. The end or yarn beams were of saguaro ribs of suitable size, held in place across the end stakes by cords which were stretched taut at the sides. The beams were about 6 inches from the ground, thus permitting the warp to pass freely around them as it was wound over one and under the other in a continuous thread. A heavy double binding thread, usually dyed buff, was passed through the loops at the ends of the warp and was given a half turn as each loop was caught up. The yarn beams were then removed, leaving a lease rod of arrowwood in place of one of them. The binding thread was next bound to the yarn beams by a heavy thread wound in a spiral from end to end. The warp could then be stretched in place by again putting the beams outside the stakes and pulling the side cords taut. The heald rod was also of arrowwood put in place by passing a loop from a thread that had been slipped through the open shed from the right under each lower warp thread and pushing the rod through the loop from the left.

The weaver sat upon his haunches on the ground or on the cloth when it was finished too far for him to reach from the end. He lowered the lease rod beyond the heddle and gathered the upper threads in front of the heddle on a slender sharpened rod, which enabled him to lift them high enough to pass the shuttle through. The shuttle was an arrowwood stick to one end of which the weft thread was tied and then passed to the other in a slightly spiral direction; there it was wound twice around and then passed back; thus it was wound from end to end of the shuttle until the latter carried many yards of thread. After the shuttle was passed through the shed the thread was struck home with a flat batten of mesquite wood. If the warp threads were irregular, they were adjusted with a short peg which took the place of the comb used by the other tribes that weave in the Southwest.[a] Two heavy selvage threads lay at the side of the warp, and as the shuttle was passed through the shed it was brought between them and they were given a half turn to engage the woof thread before it passed back in the other shed which was opened by raising the heddle.

The width of the cloth was not well maintained, as there was a strong tendency for it to become narrower, but by the aid of a stretcher or temple this was partially overcome. The temple had two longitudinal grooves separated by a distance equal to the width of the cloth. In each groove was placed a section of willow or arrowwood stem an inch in length, bound with a heavy thread around the stretcher. The outer end of the short stick was sharpened so that it might be pushed

---

[a] Length of the specimen collected, 11 cm. It is shown in fig. 72 at the margin of the finished cloth, where it was pushed under a few threads to hold it in position for photographing.

through the cloth under the selvage, thus rendering the temple readily adjustable.[a]

The collection contains one old headband[b] or belt (fig. 75, a), which its owner had laid away wrapped around his long hair which he had been induced to cut off. It is woven from tightly twisted cotton yarn, the colors being black, white, green, and yellow, arranged in a zigzag pattern, as shown in the figure. The reverse side is without pattern and not intended to be seen. Another headband[c] (fig. 75, b) was made

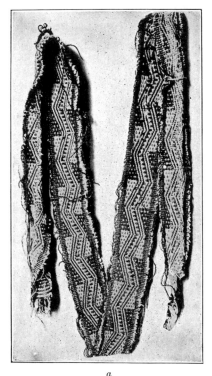 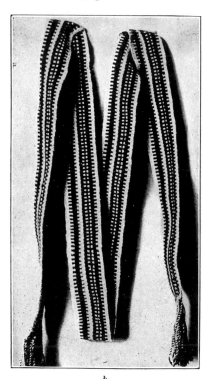

a   b

FIG. 75. a, Old belt headband; b, new belt headband.

to order and is of a much simpler design and style of weaving. The colors are black, white, and red.

There are two belts or headbands in the National Museum that were collected by Bartlett in 1850. One of these, no. 178911, is a

---

[a] Doctor Palmer collected a Pima loom in 1885, which is now in the National Museum, no. 76008. The beams are of cactus wood, 1.410 m. long, 6 cm. in diameter. The heddle is of arrowwood, the same length as the beams, and is 8 mm. in diameter. The blanket, which is about half finished, is 57 cm. wide and 1.100 m. long. The selvage is not dyed, but there is a red weft thread 29 cm. from the end and a second one near it which passes across the middle third of the cloth. The batten is 91 cm. long, 25 mm. wide, and the shuttle 92 cm. The cloth is smoothly and evenly woven, having 8 warp and 11 woof threads to the inch.

[b] Length, 1.900 m.; width, 65 mm.

[c] Length, 2.270 m.; width, 57 mm.

fine specimen of double weaving.[a]   It is of tightly twisted cotton
thread in dark blue, red, yellow, and white.   The fringe threads are
braided together so that two colors are united in each strand.

The other belt, no. 178910, is also double, and woven in dark blue,
light blue, buff, red, and white.[b]

The abandonment of the art of weaving these simple fabrics with
their tasteful patterns is unfortunate.   Their loss is relieved by no
compensatory improvement in other directions.[c]

ARCHITECTURE

In their natural state the Pimas built dwellings of four different
types besides a storehouse.   First in importance is the round, flat-
roofed ki, which resembles an overturned wash basin in shape.
Notwithstanding the fact that some have declared that the Piman
ki suggests the pueblo style of architecture and should therefore be
admitted as evidence of relationship between the Hohokam and
Pimas, the author must confess that he has been unable to detect
the remotest resemblance to the pueblo type.   On the contrary,
analogies may be found with the dwellings of tribes much farther
distant from Pimería.   The ki is built by the men, who gather in
parties of ten or fifteen for the purpose—a custom which affords
another instance of a different division of labor from that in vogue
among the Pueblos, as with them the house building is the work of
women.[d]   Though the Pimas have had an example of pueblo structure at their very doors ever since they have inhabited the Gila
valley, in the noble Casa Grande, the walls of which yet rise 30 feet
above the plain, and have seen the adobe buildings of the Spaniards
and Mexicans for three hundred and fifty years, nevertheless they
have continued to construct houses of the simplest type that are but
little better than temporary shelters.   The first Piman adobe house
was built by the head chief, Antonio Azul, twenty two years ago,
and since that time the people have made very commendable progress.   Some villages—such, for example, as Blackwater—now contain
few dwellings that are not of adobe.   However, there are others,
such as Skâ′kâïk, that retain the old-time ki.   As an inducement
toward progress, the Indian Department or its authorized agent has
stipulated that a man must cut off his long hair and build an adobe
house before he may receive a wagon from the Government.   The

---

[a] Length, 2 m.; width, 6 cm.; length of fringe, 15 cm.

[b] Length, 2.03 m.; width, 65 mm.   The fringe is 20 cm. in length and neatly braided.

[c] Fröbel, who visited the Pimas half a century ago, says of their weaving, "Man würde sich aber irren
wenn man glaubte, dass diese Künste durch die Bekehrung zum Christenthum befördert worden seien.
Im Gegentheile sind sie dadurch in Verfall gerathen, denn bei den heidnischen Pimas findet man die-
selben in einem höheren Grade von Vollkommenheit." Aus Amerika, II, 440.

[d] It is worthy of note that the southern California Coahuilla [Kawia] similarly differ from other
American Indians.   In that tribe, also, the houses (jacals) are built by the men.   See D. P. Barrows in American Anthropologist, n. s., 1901, III, 755.

old custom of destroying the buildings at the death of their owners has practically disappeared, but its retarding influence upon architectural development continued throughout the aboriginal period.

Usually but one family occupies a single dwelling, though sometimes two and even three related families live together. If there are two, their sleeping mats are placed on each side of the entrance, so that in sleeping the heads may be toward the east, the door being on that side in order that the inmates may rise early to greet the Day god as he appears over the distant summits of the Sierra Tortilla. A more practical motive for placing the doors on the east side is to avoid the southwest winds which blow in the afternoon during nearly the entire year and which are especially strong during the month of March. The wind usually begins to blow at about 10 in the morning and increases to a velocity of 10 miles an hour by mid-afternoon, after which it decreases until midnight.

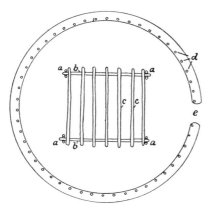

FIG. 76. Diagram of house. Scale: 1 inch = 10 feet.

TYPES

The general plan of the house is shown in the accompanying diagram (fig. 76). The central supporting framework is usually entirely of cottonwood, though other timber is sometimes used. The lighter framework shown in plate XXXV, a, is of willow, on which is laid the arrowwood, cattail reeds, wheat straw, cornstalks, or similar material that supports the outer layer of earth.

The roof is supported by four crotched posts set in the ground 3 or 4 m. apart, with two heavy beams in the crotches.[a] Lighter cross poles are laid on the last, completing the central framework. Light willow poles are set half a meter in the ground around the periphery of the circle, their tops are bent in to lap over the central roof poles, and horizontal stays are lashed to them with willow bark. The frame is then ready for the covering of brush or straw. Although earth is heaped upon the roof to a depth of 15 or 20 cm. it does not render it entirely waterproof. When finished the ki is very strong and capable of withstanding heavy gales or supporting the weight of the people who may gather on the roof during festivals.

---

[a] " For the larger dwellings nine are used—three on each side and one in the center." Bartlett, Personal Narrative, II, 233.

Lieutenant Emory estimated the size of the ki at from 25 to 50 feet in diameter,[a] which is much too high. From 10 to 25 feet would have been much nearer the true diameter. The average dimensions are as follows:

	Meters
Circumference	18.59
Interior diameter	5.48
Interior height	1.72
Distance between main supporting posts	2.28–2.43
Distance between posts and walls	.91–1.60
Diameter of rafters	.08
Distance between rafters	.30
Distance between horizontal ribs	.30
Distance between arched willow ribs	.20
Height of door	.81
Width of door	.61

The absence of a smoke hole is noteworthy, as it is almost universally present in primitive dwellings. Its absence can not be explained by the fact that the mildness of the climate permits the Pimas to spend most of their time in the open air and build their fires outside, because in winter fires are maintained within to such an extent that the roofs become loaded with masses of soot. It would seem probable that the roofs were not provided with openings in order that the houses might be as little open to the attack of the Apaches as possible were it not for the fact that the Cocopas and others living southwest of the Pimas build huts similarly devoid of smoke vents, which suggests that the Pimas have come from that quarter where the torrid heat renders indoor fires unnecessary at any season. The doorways were low and narrow for the same reason (60 by 90 cm. in size). They were closed by pieces of old blankets (pl. xxxv, b), by slats woven together with rawhide, or by loose sticks of wood (pl. xxxv, e, f).

In each village a low rectangular council house afforded a meeting place for the men and at times the women also of the community. Rev. C. H. Cook informs the writer that he has addressed an audience of as many as 80 persons in one of these houses, all bending low to avoid the smoke. The last council house was destroyed at Pé-eptcĭlt in January, 1902.

Another form of dwelling place was the woman's menstrual lodge, which was a mere shelter of branches to afford protection from the sun.

The fourth type of dwelling is the arbor, or, as some of the early writers termed it, "the bower." It is a cottonwood framework supported by crotched posts, roofed with arrowwood and earth, affording a shade from the sun, from which protection is desirable during

---

[a] Notes, p. 85.

the greater part of the year.   The roof furnishes a convenient place
for drying squashes, melons, fruit, and, in the old days, cotton,
where the dogs and poultry can not disturb them.   Under its shade
the olla of drinking water is set in a crotched post or is suspended
from above by a maguey fiber net.   Here two parallel ropes may be
hung and a cloth folded back and forth upon itself across them, thus
forming an impromptu hammock in which to swing the baby.   Here
the metate and mortar are usually seen, and here the women sit and
weave baskets or perform such other labor as may be done at home.
It is the living room throughout the day the year around, and now
that the fear of Apaches has gone it is becoming the sleeping place
as well.   From a hygienic point of view it is a great pity that the
Pimas are learning to build adobes, for the tendency is for them
to live indoors and to abandon the healthful arbors, every inch of
whose floors is purified by a burning sun that throws its sterilizing
rays well under the arbor during the morning and afternoon.   Tuberculosis is present in nearly every family, and it is difficult, if not
impossible, for the agency physician to induce those stricken with
it to remain out of doors; they invariably confine themselves within
the bacilli-laden dwellings.   The arbor is kept well swept and clean,
as is the entire yard about the house, so that a more healthful habitation could not be devised.   Occasionally one or more sides of it
may be inclosed with arrowwood through which the cool breezes
readily find their way.

Beside each dwelling will be found a rectangular storehouse built
with a framework of about the same shape and size as the arbor,
but with walls of upright okatilla trunks or cactus ribs.   The large
bush, Baccharis glutenosa, is often used for this purpose.   It is seen
in its natural state in plate xxi, b; also surrounding the unit figure
in plate xxxvi and forming the walls of the storehouse in plate
xxxv, f.   Plate ix, b, illustrates the okatilla, Fouquiera splendens,
as it grows on the mesas within 2 miles of Sacaton.   Each stem is
crowned with a brilliant spray of scarlet flowers.   Plate xxxv, d,
shows the framework of a storehouse at the right and the finished
wall of arrow bush in the center.   Plate xxxv, e, is a complete storehouse with arrowwood bins for mesquite beans on the roof.   Sometimes mud or adobe is added to the walls, which renders the structure
equivalent to the Mexican jacal.   The most noticeable feature is the
door, made by piling up a great heap of unwieldy logs before the
opening.

While not to be dignified by the name of house or dwelling, the
Pima kitchen is an extremely practical affair, as will be realized by
anyone who attempts to cook on an open fire exposed to storms.
Plates vi, b, and xxxvi show the manner of arranging these wind-
breaks, for they are nothing more.   In exposed situations the sand

in time accumulates in a drift of sufficient height to require a change of location. Not all families have such a kitchen, and there is reason to believe that it has been adopted from neighboring tribes in recent years.

CLOTHING

The description of Pima clothing need not be long. Throughout fully three-fourths of the year clothing for protection is quite unnecessary in that region, and that worn in winter was of the simplest character. The history of Pima clothing may be divided into four periods, namely: The first, in which natural products, little modified, were employed; the second, in which native textiles were introduced; the third, in which more or less remote imitations of Mexican costumes were in vogue; and the present period, when very plain and serviceable clothing is purchased from the whites.

MATERIALS AND TYPES

In primitive times the men wore breech-cloths (pl. XXXVII, a, b) and the women kilts that fell to the knee, both made of the soft and flexible inner bark of the willow, which is used by some among the Colorado River tribes to the present day. During the brief season when the temperature approached the freezing point at night the men wore deerskin shirts, and when abroad upon stony trails encased their feet in red-dyed moccasins, also of deerskin. For protection at home both sexes wore rawhide sandals, which appear to Caucasian eyes all too scant protection for the feet where nature arms most species, animate or inanimate alike, with tooth and claw.[a]

After the adoption of the art of weaving, the cotton blanket was worn in winter, and in summer also by the women, who girded it, doubled, around their waists with maguey cords, neatly woven belts, or merely tucked one edge within the other. When the winds from the sacred caves blew cold upon their shoulders they were shielded by the outer fold of blanket, which was drawn up around the neck; at least by all save the widow, who dared not raise the blanket above the armpits during the period of mourning. Plate XXXVI illustrates the mode of wearing this garment. As the blanket hung to the knees it might be converted by the men into baggy trousers by looping a cord from the girdle behind down between the legs and drawing it up in front. Some there were too poor or too strongly beset by the passion for gambling long to retain the single fabric that served for clothing by day and bedding by night, and they were compelled to resort to the bark garments of the ancients. Another material avail-

---

[a] As an example of this tendency of desert plants to clothe themselves with armor, mention may be appropriately made of the crucifixion thorn, Holocantha emoryi, as it grows abundantly upon the mesas between the Gila villages and the Salt River Pima settlement, 30 miles northward. It becomes a small leafless tree that is a tangle of thorny spikes, each a hand's breadth in length (pl. XXI, c).

able for winter blankets was rabbit skins, which were cut in strips and braided together in the manner customary among so many American tribes.

During the Spanish and Mexican régime the sombrero found favor, and even yet the steeple crown of this head gear may occasionally be seen. The women adopted a sleeveless chemise, which they wear to some extent to-day; it is shown in plate xxxviii, b, though usually no longer worn by a woman so young. A few women also follow the Mexican fashion of covering their heads with improvised mantillas—usually towels or aprons—as shown in figure 5, where the costumes of a group of both sexes are well shown. This view was taken at the agency, and as they were unaware of the author's presence with the camera, which was kept concealed, the posing was perfectly natural. When the summer heat begins to be felt the older men strip to the breechcloth, as shown in plate xxxvii, a, b, when they are about their homes.

ESTHETIC ARTS

Personal Decoration

The Pimas of to-day are rapidly adopting the personal adornments of their civilized neighbors. With the exception of the manner of treating the hair, the old methods of enhancing personal beauty have been almost entirely abandoned. Judging from the statements made by the old people, this art could never have reached the development among the Pimas that it did among the Pueblos. Their status recalls that of the Yuman tribes on the great river to the westward.

Pride of person manifested itself among the men in the care of the hair and the elaboration of the designs painted upon the skin. Feathers and beads were also worn in abundance. When through uncleanly habits a man became too filthy his associates said "skulof," "He smells like an old man." But the whole tribe has a characteristic odor that is easily detected by the nasal organs of the whites; even the school children who are regularly bathed and well clothed exhibit this characteristic.

HAIR

Men wore their hair long (see pl. xliii, c); that of the old chief Tiahiatam reached to his heels when he stood upright, but usually the hair fell about to the waist. At the age of 20 the young men began to braid or twist their hair into skeins, which retained the hairs shed—and other things besides—a marvelously convenient abiding place for microbes. It was the fashion to wear the skeins cut squarely across at the bottom, and they did not scruple to piece out their shorter locks with hair from the tails of their horses. Sometimes, indeed, they even added the hair of their women, who trimmed their hair in mourning for lost relatives. The skeins were from 1 to 2 cm. in diameter; the hair of one old man, purchased from him, is 1.1 m. long; one of the skeins has been broken in the middle and tied in a hard knot. Such flowing locks could not, of course, be worn unconfined at all times; they were usually wound around the head and inclosed beneath a headband or by a cord of variegated colors (pl. XLIII, *a;* see also fig. 75). The earlocks that are the pride of so many tribes were sometimes braided by the Pimas and ornaments of shell, bone, and, later, tin and scarlet cloth, were tied to them. The front hair was cut squarely across the forehead.

The eyelashes and eyebrows were not tampered with, but the scanty beard was plucked out with tweezers. The hair of children was formerly "cut" with a burning brand whenever it reached their shoulders, in order that it might grow more abundantly. The portion cut off was mixed with mud and plastered on the head again for a few hours that it might improve the growth of the new hair. It was an evil omen if the child should chance to touch the hair just cut from his head, for was it not a sign that he would steal the sacred salt?

Women wore their hair long, but not twisted into skeins as was that of the men, and, furthermore, they were accustomed to cut it in mourning to a much greater extent than the men, so that it never attained extreme length. When at work it was twisted up on the head in a temporary coil that was confined by any convenient cord or bit of cloth. Unless engaged in vigorous exercise, as grinding with the metate, the older women allowed their hair to hang loose (pl. XXXVIII, *a*, XLVI, *c*). The front hair was trimmed to fall just clear of the eyes, as in same plate, *b*. Incidentally, it thus protected the eyes from the sun, though it is questionable how far the originators of the fashion were conscious of this useful purpose. Above all else the hair was the pride of Pima women; twice at least each day it was brushed until it shone in smooth, ebony waves that were ever luxuriantly abundant. "Every once in a while," or about once a week, the hair was treated to a mud bath made by mixing black river mud with mesquite gum and allowing the plaster to remain over night (pl. XXXVIII, *c*). Sometimes the gum was diluted with warm water and applied as a wash before the mud was laid on. The mud killed the vermin and cleansed the hair as does soap. The gum is believed to darken the hair and prevent it from growing gray. The Pimas declare that when widows mourn for four years without washing their hair it becomes a rusty red from being burned by the sun. The method of cleaning the hair above described is still practised, even by the younger generation.

NAILS

Finger nails were bitten off when they reached a troublesome length. The nails of the toes received little attention, and in old persons to-day they are seen of inordinate length, curled over the ends of the toes.

FIG. 77. Paint bags. *a*, Deerskin; *b*, cloth.

TEETH

Many brown teeth were seen, but no satisfactory information was obtained as to the cause. All agreed that the red berry of Licium fremontii would temporarily blacken the teeth, but as the Kwahadk's and Papagos, who do not eat this berry, have the darkened teeth, some other cause must be sought. Rumex berlandieri, Rumex hymenosepalus, and a thorny weed called by the Pimas *sâitûkam iavak* are also said to blacken the teeth. Charcoal was used to clean the teeth before the advent of the whites, and the practice is still continued.

PAINTING

In bags of deerskin or cloth (fig. 77, *a*, *b*) bright-hued ochers and other minerals were kept with which to paint the face and body.[a] Baby Pima had his face painted immediately after birth with red ocher mixed with his mother's milk "to improve his skin." Thereafter the paint was mixed with grease or the grease was applied to the skin first and the paint was added. In cold weather the grease and color were applied to prevent chapping and even for the sake of warmth. Usually the

---

[a] Upon the four samples of face paint that were collected at Sacaton and submitted for analysis the following report was received: "It was found that with the exception of traces of manganese in 24884 and 24887 the color of these substances is due to varying amounts of iron as modified by the presence of and combination with other substances which by themselves possess practically no coloring power.

"The percentages of iron (calculated as ferric oxide) found in these samples are as follows:

No 24883	6. 13	No. 24885	13. 87
No. 24884	1. 28	No. 24887	9. 62

face alone was painted, but during festivals and on other special occasions the entire body was painted. On dress occasions the lines on the face were made much narrower, and instead of being applied with the hands the color was laid on with a splinter or twig of arrow-wood 2 mm. wide by 80 mm. long. Both men and women painted their bodies and both used the same colors on their faces, but in different proportions. The men used more black and were especially careful to intensify the tattoo marks. The women also emphasized the tattooing, and there were black lines, therefore, under the eyes of both sexes, showing that the permanent embellishment was regarded as especially significant.

The designs were simple vertical and transverse lines, as shown in plate xxxviii, *d.* The paint was not often washed off, but additional lines were added as the design became effaced. Each person painted his own face and used an olla of water as a mirror. The men painted the hair of the frontal region either white or red in preparing for a dance, and never both colors at the same time. The women painted their hair in spots and bands of white.

Besides the yellow ocher obtained from the Skâsŏwalĭk hills (pl. xvi, *a*), the yellow pollen of the cat-tail, Typha angustifolia Linn., was used. Red was obtained from the Mohaves, and in recent years from the Yumas. From the latter also was bartered the bluish black specular iron ore that glistened on the warrior's cheeks. Red and white were brought by the Papagos from out of the vast desert to the southward, the mineral resources of which are yet scarcely known to the invading race. Lastly, diamond dyes were used to some extent, but their day was short, for now no Pima paints at all. Indeed, it was with difficulty that two persons could be hired to paint their faces that the writer might photograph them.

If in the pristine period of Pimerían history the lines upon the rich brown skins were meant to symbolize the thought or fancy of the artists, no knowledge of the fact has survived the vicissitudes of war and strife through the centuries. To-day they are meaningless and to-morrow will have been forgotten.

TATTOOING

A few lines were tattooed on the faces of both men and women. Thorns and charcoal were used in the operation. The thorns were from the outer borders of the prickly-pear cactus; from two to four were tied together with loosely twisted native cotton fiber to enlarge the lower portion to a convenient size for grasping, while the upper end was neatly bound with sinew. The charcoal, from either willow or mesquite wood, was pulverized and kept in balls 2 or 3 cm. in diameter (fig. 78).

Both men and women did the work, but the female artist was preferred, as "she was more careful." Their fees were small and uncertain, as the operation was not one calculated to expand the heart of the victim and induce him to pay generously. The lines were drawn on the face first in dry charcoal, then some of the powdered charcoal was mixed with water, and the thorns were dipped into this and pricked into the skin along the outlines. As the operation progressed the face was frequently washed to see if the color was being well pricked in. Two operations were necessary, though it sometimes took more; one operation occupied an entire day. For four days thereafter the face remained swollen, and throughout that period the wound was rubbed with charcoal daily. At the end of that time a wash of squash seeds macerated in water was applied. Sometimes the lips were slow in healing and the individual was compelled to subsist upon pinole, as the swollen lips and chin forbade partaking of solid food; during this time the squash applications were continued.

a   b   c
Fig. 78. Tattooing outfit. a, Mesquite charcoal; b, willow charcoal; c, needles.

The men were tattooed along the margin of the lower eyelid and in a horizontal line across the temples. Tattooing was also carried across the forehead, where the pattern varied from a wavy transverse line to short zigzag vertical lines in a band that was nearly straight from side to side. Occasionally a band was also tattooed around the wrist.

The women had the line under the lids, as did the men; but instead of the lines upon the forehead they had two vertical lines on each side of the chin, which extended from the lip to the inferior margin of the jaw and were united by a broad bar of tattooing, which included the whole outer third of the mucous membrane of the lip on either side.

The tattooing was done between the ages of 15 and 20; not, it would seem, at the time of puberty, but at any time convenient to the individual and the operator. Oftentimes a bride and groom were tattooed just after marriage. All the older Pimas are tattooed, but the young people are escaping this disfigurement. As in the case of painting, the practice of the art is passing away and the meaning of the designs is unknown. The Pimas aver that the lines prevent wrinkles; thus fortified they "retain their youth." The purely apocryphal theory that the women about to be married have their lower eyelids tattooed, that they may thereafter "look at no man except their husband," is untenable, as we shall see when we come to study their marriage customs.

ORNAMENTS

Both sexes, but especially the men, wore strands of beads suspended from their ear lobes and necks. The beads and gorgets were of disks cut from seashells, stone, more or less wrought, bone carved and decorated, small deer bones without other manipulation than drilling, and turquoise, which was usually rubbed into flat rectangular pendants. Upon the arms of the women and on the right arm of the men were bracelets of similar materials. The men wore on the left arm a soft coyote skin wrist guard or one of rawhide for the bowstring. Large beads of blue Venetian glass were brought by the earliest Spanish missionaries, and are now to be found scattered about the sacred places of the Pimas.

"A very brave man" pierced the septum of his nose and wore therein a skewer of neatly polished bone, or else suspended from it a bit of turquoise or a shell. Two men yet living in the Santan village have pierced noses, though they long ago abandoned the practice of wearing anything in them. Indeed, all the old-time ornaments have been abandoned, and the Pimas exhibit a marked contrast to the bead-covered Navahos and other tribesmen.

The men ornamented their long rope-like locks with the soft breast feathers of the eagle, turkey, or other large bird. The war headdresses were of eagle, hawk, and owl wing feathers. We secured one that contained the hair of an Apache warrior in addition to the feathers (fig. 40).

FIG. 79. Runner's hair ornament.

Contestants in the relay and distance races wore an ornament in their hair that suggests those of the Yumas, which in turn resemble the "eyes" of the Huichols.[a]

The women twined in their hair coronets of sunflowers or of corn husks, in recent years colored red or blue by boiling with calico.

ORNAMENTATION

We have seen that the Pimas, by means of paint, tattooing, and ornaments, had developed the art of personal decoration to a considerable extent. When we examine their implements and weapons it soon becomes evident that their taste for ornamentation was more rudimentary. Indeed, their desire for embellishment seldom reached expression in carving; it was confined chiefly to painting, as in the case of shields, or to the smooth finish given to their bows. Paint-

---

[a] Such an ornament was made for the writer's collection by Sika'tcu of arrowwood with four hooks of devils' claw attached to it with sinew. The hooks are arranged in the same plane and curved downward as shown in figure 79. The upper pair are wound with blue strings terminating with buff at the tips. Total length, 237 mm.; spread of hooks, 170 mm.

ing upon shields, cradle hoods, kiâhâs, and tobacco pouches was of a crude sort and manifestly inferior to that upon the person. The moderately smooth finish given to all weapons, to trays, ladles, pottery paddles, fire-drills, awls, pestles, axes, basketry, and some pottery was of course based upon utilitarian motives, though the gratification of esthetic needs must have been subsidiary thereto and concomitantly developed. That the desire for embellishment was less consciously felt is evident from the fact that the other articles made by the Pimas that may be equally effective, when smoothness and symmetry are lacking are coarse and rough. The metate, for example, is unhewn and angular except upon the grinding surface and presents a striking contrast to the symmetrical metates of the Hohokam. Not only do the Pimas not give a pleasing finish to all artifacts, but they exhibit so dull an esthetic sense in their treatment of the beautiful polished axes that they find about the ruins that we are moved alike by pity and indignation. There are tons of stones within easy reach of the villages suitable for roughening the grinding surfaces of metates, yet the Pimas take the axes that are almost perfect in symmetry and polish and batter them into shapeless masses for the purpose. To the writer this affords an argument stronger than all the surmises of the early Spanish writers to the contrary that the Pimas are not the descendants of the Hohokam. Furthermore, the poverty of design and the absence of symbolism are a very strong indication of relationship with the California tribes rather than with the Pueblos.

One of the most striking examples of the poverty of esthetic resource among the Pimas is seen in their textiles. The wonderful possibilities of this art were almost unknown. True, after the whites brought bayeta to them their weavers produced a very creditable belt by closely copying the ornamentation from the Hohokam relics and from their southern congeners. But the principal pieces, the blankets, the weaving of which kept the art of making textile fabrics alive, were ornamented with nothing more elaborate than a dingy border of doubled selvage threads. After the red thread was imported we find scant trace of it in the blankets. However, we must credit the Pimas with the rudimentary esthetic sense that found expression in the smoothness and evenness of weaving in these plain white blankets.

The arts of basketry and pottery making do not furnish much evidence of a well-developed esthetic sense in the Pimas. The former art is recent and borrowed; at best it is in a mediocre state. If the baskets of the Pimas are compared with those of the Yavapais (pl. XXXIII, a, b, c, d), who have also begun to use similar motives very recently, we see that the latter tribe manifests superior taste. The Yavapai baskets were the only ones at the Fort McDowell camps at the time of the writer's visit, so that they were certainly not selected specimens, whereas the Pima baskets, and particularly the upright forms, which the writer did not collect himself, were better than the average Pima product. The Yavapai baskets command just double the price in the open market that is paid for Pima baskets of equal size. The principle of rhythm is well understood by the Pima basket makers, as the illustrations show. Both the simple elements, such as the so-called coyote tracks, or plain triangles, and the more complex, such as the flower pattern, or the scroll fret, are frequently repeated. But the principle of symmetry is not so well developed and it is rare that a basket exhibits it. The specimen in figure 62 shows that its maker possessed this faculty.

It is rare that the descent of pottery making from basketry is reversed, but among the Pimas this is true to some extent; that is, the basketry designs are in part copied from the pottery of the Hohokam. In part they were adopted from the Maricopas. The pottery designs likewise are copied, so that the credit due to the Pima decorators is reduced to a minimum. Their wares are mostly unornamented, as we have seen, and the decorations that are used are applied with indifferent taste. Though they have abundant examples of fictile ware scattered over their fields, much of which is embellished by indented coils, they seem never to have conceived the idea of utilizing this simple though effective form of ornamentation. The pottery illustrated in this memoir is rather better than the average Pima ware. The Kwahadk' pottery, while superior to the Piman, is yet lacking in symmetry. It is pleasing by reason of the rich brown color and the polish that almost equals a glaze, but the ornamentation is crude and vastly inferior to that of the ancient Hohokam.

We can not explain the inferiority of Piman ornamentation by saying that the Pimas had degenerated because they were harried by the Apaches and Yumas until they had no energy or inclination left for indulging their esthetic tastes, for this is not true. They whipped the Yumas until the latter were ready to accept peace upon any terms, as appears from the calendar records, which are well authenticated by white testimony. They kept the Apaches in wholesome fear of their clubs and arrows and made frequent raids into the enemy's territory. They never hesitated to attack the Apaches in equal numbers and fight hand to hand. In short, they were not the degenerates that some have considered them, an error that the records of Pima scouts accompanying the United States army in Apache campaigns would do much to dispel.[a] Their backwardness

---

[a] Early accounts of the Pimas uniformly testify to their ability to fight their enemies. They "have ever been numerous and brave," wrote Garcés a century and a quarter ago (Schoolcraft, III, 299), and in 1859 Mowry declared, "The Pimas and Apaches wage hereditary and fierce war, in which the Pimas are generally the victors." Arizona and Sonora, third edition, p. 30.

can not be explained by their environment, because the same surroundings produced the superior culture of the Hohokam, which there is no reason to believe was not indigenous. It may be surmised that the Pimas would have accomplished more in recent years in the art of ornamentation if they had adopted the curved knife that has become so widespread among other American Indians since the advent of the whites. A full discussion of the factors that have influenced their culture would better be deferred until after an examination of the evidence furnished by social organization (which through the absence of totemism has not directly influenced their art), by history, and by religion.

MUSICAL INSTRUMENTS

The Pimas have four kinds of musical instruments—the flute or flageolet, the basket drum, the scraping stick, and the rattle, the last having many forms. They say that the first two instruments were adopted from the Maricopas within a century or two. If this be true Pima attainments in instrumental music must have been of a very modest character indeed. There are few flutes to be found and the drum is never heard except in ceremonies which are themselves becoming increasingly rare. The gourd rattle is the commonest form of the last class of instruments.

a   b   c

FIG. 80. Flutes.

FLUTE

The Pima or Maricopa flute is of cane cut of such a length that it includes two entire sections and about 4 cm. of each of the two adjoining. It therefore contains three diaphragms, of which the two end ones are perforated, while the middle one is so arranged that the air may pass over its edge from one section into the other. This is done by burning a hole through the shell of the cane on each side of the diaphragm and joining them by a furrow. With such an opening in the upper section the instrument can not be played unless a piece of bark or similar material be wrapped over all but the lower portion of the furrow to direct the air into the lower section. The forefinger of the left hand is usually employed as a stop if no permanent wrapping directs the current of air so that it may impinge upon the sharp margin of the opening into

the second section.[a]   As there are but three finger holes the range
of notes is not great and they are very low and plaintive.

These instruments are usually ornamented with geometric designs
having no symbolic significance at the present time among the Pimas.
A bit of cloth or ribbon is sometimes attached to the middle of the flute,
as in specimen *c*, figure 80.[b]

DRUM

Any shallow basket of sufficient size, such as are in common use
in every household for containing grain or prepared food, may be
transformed into a drum by simply turning it bottom up and beating
it with the hands.   In accompanying
certain songs it is struck with a stick
in rapid glancing blows.

SCRAPING STICK

The notched or scraping stick is in
very general use to carry the rhythm
during the singing of ceremonial songs.
When one end of the stick is laid on
an overturned basket and another
stick or a deer's scapula is drawn
quickly over the notches the resulting sound from this compound instrument of percussion may be compared
with that of the snare drum.   However, it is usually held in the hand and
rasped with a small stick kept for
the purpose.   So important are these

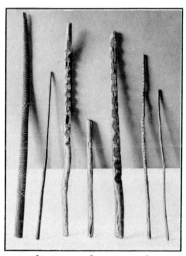

a   b   c   d   e   f   g
Fig. 81. Scraping sticks.

instruments in Pima rain ceremonies that they are usually spoken of
as "rain sticks."

There are four scraping sticks in the collection.   One of these
(fig. 81, *a*), is smoothly cut, tapering, and evidently very old.   The
wood has not been identified, though it resembles ironwood.   There
are six small notches at the side of the handle, possibly fulfilling
some mnemonic purpose.   At the base of the series of notches is a
broad X; there is another at the middle, and evidences of a third
appear at the tip, which is broken away.   There are 36 deep transverse

---

[a] "The principle of its construction is believed to be different from any known among other tribes or
nations.   These instruments are common with the Coco-Maricopas, and Yumas or Cuchuans, and
among the tribes on the Colorado.   Young men serenade their female friends with them."   Whipple,
Pac. R. R. Rep., II, 52.

[b] Length of flute *a* (fig. 80), 364 mm.; diameter, 22 mm.; *b*, length, 518 mm.; diameter, 23 mm.; *c*, length,
512 mm.; diameter, 22 mm.   Flute *c* has an old pale yellow necktie tied around the middle as an ornament and to direct the air past the diaphragm.

notches on the lower part and 49 on the upper.[a] This stick was used for the cure of the piholt disease (p. 265) and was probably obtained from the Yaquis. The other three sticks (c, e, f) are much rougher and are undoubtedly of Pima make. The two large ones (c, e) have deep notches, which are few in number.[b]

RATTLES

The gourd rattle is used in most Pima ceremonies. It is made by fitting a wooden handle to a gourd in which gravel have been placed.

The handle passes through the center and, reduced in diameter, projects slightly from the larger end, as shown in figure 82,[c] which also illustrates the distribution of the perforations, which are said to be for the purpose of "letting the sound out." It will be observed that the sacred number 4 is represented by the principal lines of holes extending longitudinally. About a dozen specimens were seen and none were decorated in any way except in the arrangement of the perforations; the handles were invariably rudely made.

A disk rattle that has been used in the Navitco ceremonies was secured at the village of Pe'-eptcïlt. It is not a Pima instrument, but whether Papago or Yaqui the writer can not say. It contains two sets of four tin disks loosely held by wires passing through a wooden handle. The sound emitted resembles that of tambourine rattles (fig. 83).[d]

FIG. 82. Gourd rattle.

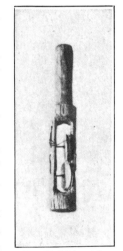

FIG. 83. Disk rattle.

From the same individual who used the disk rattle the writer obtained a rattle that had been used as a belt during the Navitco ceremonies. It is made of successive layers of canvas, red cotton cloth, oilcloth, and an old braided hatband, to which are attached by leather strings 21 brass cartridge shells (fig. 84).

There are two sets of cocoon rattles in the collection that were worn on the calves of the legs in certain ceremonies. The cocoons were

[a] Length, 675 mm.; width, 25 mm.; thickness, 15 mm. The accompanying stick (b) used to scrape with is 494 mm. long.

[b] Scraping stick (fig. 81, c), is 630 mm. long, 19 mm. in diameter, and has 11 notches; e is 625 mm. long, 26 mm. in diameter, with 12 notches; f is 555 mm. long, 11 mm. in diameter, and is provided with 35 shallow notches.

[c] Length, 332 mm.; diameter, 90 mm.; diameter of handle, 25 mm.

[d] Length, 247 mm.; diameter, 36 mm.; diameter of disks, 40 mm.

obtained from the Papagos or Yaquis of Sonora. They are of a species of bombycid moth; their outer coverings have been removed,[a] and a few gravel have then been sewed in each cocoon. There are

FIG. 84. Belt rattle.

70 pairs of cocoons in one strand and 66 in the other (fig. 85). The rustling sound given out by this number of rattles is not unlike the warning of the rattlesnake.[b]

FIG. 85. Cocoon rattle.

At the village of Sacaton Flats at least one turtle-shell rattle is still used in the treatment of the "turtle disease," although no specimen of such rattle was seen.

---

[a] "The Huichols use the cocoons of Attacus orizaba for necklaces." Lumholtz, Symbolism of the Huichol Indians, 189.

[b] Each cocoon now measures 30 mm. in length by 25 mm. in breadth. The entire strands are 1.900 m. long.

Hoof rattles, usually of dewclaws, were of universal distribution among the American Indians and were common among the Pimas, though none are to be found at the present day. Bartlett figures such a rattle in his Personal Narrative (II, 223).

DANCING

Dancing was frequently indulged in by both sexes and was accompanied by song, together with instrumental music furnished by the basket drum and the rattle. The dancers stood in a circle with arms extended across the shoulders of those adjoining. This position did not permit much freedom, and movements were confined to stamping the feet and bending the body. When food was plentiful dances might occur at any time. Their number increased and their moral character sadly deteriorated as the men relaxed their vigilance after peace was made with the Apaches. The energy formerly expended on the warpath was then wasted in debauchery. The dances began in the morning and lasted all day. Both men and women came with freshly painted faces and bodies, the women with their hair neatly dressed. Each woman brought a contribution of food in the form of mesquite dumplings, corn and wheat pinole or tortillas, meat, and the like. Throughout the day a few at a time stopped to eat, so that the dancing and the feasting both proceeded without interruption. For an account of the war dances, see page 205; puberty dance, page 182.

FESTIVALS

Of course all festivals partook somewhat of the nature of sacred ceremonies, but when this element was at a minimum, as in the saguaro harvest festival, its description may properly appear here with the arts of pleasure. These festivals were of annual occurrence, except during the occasional seasons when the fruit failed. The leading feature of these gatherings was the preparation and drinking of navait or saguaro liquor, and they became drunken orgies in which, since the introduction of knives and firearms, men were sometimes killed. The Government has prohibited "tizwin drunks," as they are called by the whites, though they are still surreptitiously held.

The sirup of the saguaro fruit is boiled for two days in the preparation of the liquor, and in the meantime the people gather and dance in the plaza nearest to the spot where the large ollas are simmering. During the final carousal all the men and some of the women become intoxicated. Through the influence of the missionaries, the native police under the agent's orders, and the actively exerted influence of the more intelligent men in the tribe, the custom is dying out. The subchief, Kâemâ-â (pl. II, c), at Gila Crossing has been a zealous advocate of temperance for a number of years, and it is not unlikely that the folly of such debaucheries was apparent to some members of the Pima community during preceding generations before outside influences were brought to bear upon them. Indeed, some measure of prudence was enforced by the fact that the Apaches were hovering upon the outskirts of the villages watching for an opportunity to attack when the warriors were incapacitated for resistance.

The "Name song" is a social device that accomplishes the ends of organized charity, together with those of the ordinary festival. If a village suffers from a scarcity of food, it visits one where the crops have been plentiful and shares in the bountiful harvest in the following manner: The visitors camp outside the village and come in during the evening to learn the names of the residents and to arrange these names in the song, which provides places for two names in each stanza. There are seventy stanzas in the song, and if there are more than twice that number of visitors it may be repeated and other names substituted. Each visitor assumes the name of a resident of the village as a seal of fellowship and for the purpose of contributing to the pleasure of the festivities of the morrow, when the strangers come into the village to sing. As the song is sung and a name is called the wife or daughter of the person of that name runs with some light object, and the wife or daughter of the person who has assumed the name for the day pursues the other woman to take it away from her. If she is unable to catch her, some of the other visiting women aid in capturing the runner, and she leads her captors to where "the value of her husband's name," in the form of corn, wheat, beans, or other foodstuffs, is ready to be presented to the visitor.

When there are many participants in the ceremony nearly the entire day may be consumed in its performance. When some of the resident villagers are destitute, only the names of those who have plentiful crops are used. The visitors give nothing but their services as singers, and they receive very substantial rewards. Etiquette requires that the visit be returned within a reasonable time—late the same season or during the following year. However, when the nomadic Papagos come to give the Pimas entertainment the visit can so seldom be returned that the gifts are more of the nature of exchanges by barter, with the advantages in favor of the Papagos. The Pimas always received the Papagos cordially, though rarely returning their visits—so rarely that in the last fifty years the Pimas have sung the name song but twice in Papagueria, the two visits being to Suijotoa.

ATHLETIC SPORTS

The men received thorough training in speed and endurance in running during their raids into the Apache country, but they had few sports that tended toward physical improvement except the foot races. Sometimes a woman ran in a contest against a man, she throwing a double ball by means of a long stick, while he kept a kicking ball before him.   But the women seldom ran in foot races, though their active outdoor life, engaged in the various tasks that fell to them, kept them in fit condition.   However, they had an athletic game which corresponded in a measure to the races of the men and developed skill in running.   This game was played as follows:

ÂLDÛ

Two of the swiftest runners among the women acted as leaders and chose alternately from the players until all were selected in two groups.   Two goals were fixed about 400 yards apart, one side saying, "To the trail is where we can beat you," while the other party declared, "To that mesquite is where we can beat you."   Two lines were formed about 25 yards apart, and the ball was put in play by

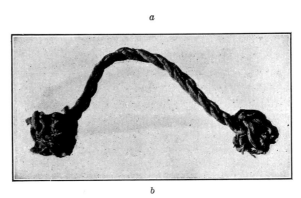

a

b

FIG. 86. *a*, Alder stick; *b*, double ball.

being tossed up and started toward the opponent's goal.   It was thrown with sticks until some one drove it beyond the goal and won the game.[a]   To touch the ball with the hands debarred the person from further play.   This game was abandoned about 1885.

KICKING-BALL RACES

These races were frequently intertribal, and in their contests with the Papagos the Pimas nearly always won.   The use of these balls in foot races is very widespread in the Southwest, and even yet we hear of races taking place that exceed 20 miles in length.

The kicking ball, when of wood, resembles a croquet ball in size, but it is usually covered with a coating of creosote gum.   These balls

---

[a] The stick in the collection is of willow, 1.230 m. long, with a maximum diameter of 18 mm.   The balls are in pairs, 15 cm. apart, connected by a 4-strand 2-ply leather thong, the balls being mere knotty enlargements of the thong (fig. 86, *a*, *b*).

are made of mesquite or paloverde wood (fig. 87, *a, b*). Stone balls about 6 cm. in diameter are also used, covered with the same black gum (fig. 88, *a, b*).

Each contestant kicks one of these balls before him, doing it so skillfully that his progress is scarcely delayed; indeed, the Pimas declare that they can run faster with than without the balls, which in a sense is true. Perhaps the occurrence of the stone balls in the ruins gave rise to the idea that they possessed magic power to "carry" the runner along, for all things pertaining to the Hohokam have come to have more or less supernatural significance. Two youths will sometimes run long distances together, first one and then the other

a 　　　　　　 *b*

FIG. 87. Kicking balls. *a*, Wood covered with gum; *b*, without covering.

kicking the ball, so that it is almost constantly in the air. The custom of using these balls is rapidly disappearing, as, it is to be regretted, are the other athletic games of the Pimas.

RELAY RACES

At various points in Arizona the writer has found what appear to have been ancient race tracks situated near the ruins of buildings. One of these was seen on the south bank of the Babacomari, 3 miles above the site of old Fort Wallen. It is 5 m. wide and 275 m. long. It is leveled by cutting down in places and the rather numerous bowlders of the mesa are cleared away. In the Sonoita valley, 2 miles east of Patagonia, there is a small ruin with what may have been a race track. It is 6 m. wide and 180 m. long. At the northern end stands a square stone 37 cm. above the surface. These will serve as examples of the tracks used by the Sobaipuris, a tribe belonging to the Piman stock. The dimensions are about the same as those of the tracks that the writer has seen the Jicarilla Apaches using in New Mexico. The tracks prepared by the Pimas opposite Sacaton Flats and at Casa Blanca are much longer.

a 　　　　　　 *b*

FIG. 88. Kicking balls. *a*, Stone covered with gum; *b*, without covering.

The relay races of the Pimas did not differ materially from those among the Pueblo tribes of the Rio Grande or the Apaches and others of the Southwest. When a village wished to race with a neighboring one they sent a messenger to convey the information that in four or five days, according to the decision of their council, they wished to test their fortunes in a relay race, and that in the meantime they were singing the bluebird (or, as the case might be, the humming-bird) songs and dancing in preparation.   Both had the same time to practise and the time was short; in this preparation the young men ran in groups of four or five.   There were 40 or 50 runners in each village, and he who proved to be the swiftest was recognized as the leader who should run first in the final contest.   It was not necessary that each village should enter exactly the same number of men in the race; a man might run any number of times that his endurance permitted. When the final race began each village stationed half its runners at each end of the track; then a crier called three times for the leaders, and as the last call, which was long drawn out, closed the starter shouted "Tâ'wai!" and they were off on the first relay.   Markers stood at the side of the track and held willow sticks with rags attached as marks of the position of the opposing sides.   Sometimes a race was ended by one party admitting that it was tired out, but it usually was decided when the winners were so far ahead that their runner met the other at the center where the markers also met.

The women encouraged their friends with shouts in concert that were emitted from the throat and ended in a trill from the tongue. At the close of the race the winning village shouted continuously for some time; after which the visitors would go home, as there was no accompanying feast.

SWIMMING

Mention is made in the calendar records of parties of Pimas or Maricopas being engaged in swimming and diving to catch fish with their naked hands, and Mr Cook assures the writer that he has seen them do both.

GAMES

The Pimas were deeply imbued with the passion for gambling, and many games were played for the gratification of that desire.   The old games are now practically abandoned and those who have the means and the desire to gamble employ a deck of filthy Mexican cards. Beads, paint, blankets, and any and all personal or family property were wagered.   The women were quite as fond of gaming as the men, and staked their blankets when all else was lost, making shift to get along with a smaller piece of cloth in lieu of a skirt.   When everything was gone the loser might win some stipulated article from her opponent if she could beat her in a foot race.   A woman might gamble away the family sleeping mat, the metate, in fact any household property, although she hesitated to wager the drinking gourd, probably owing to the fear of provoking Navitco, the deity who gave the gourd to man.

In common with other American Indians the Pima knew naught of "luck" or "chance." He felt himself aided or opposed by supernatural beings, whose assistance he sought by gifts of beads and other sacrifices deposited on altars in the recesses of the hills, which will be described later. A favorite place of prayer for gamblers was the ceremonial hill northeast of Casa Blanca, near the center of Pimería. The following games were played by the men:

KIⁿTS

Under the name of "ghing-skoot" this game has been described as played by the Papagos.[a] The Pima name of the game is kiⁿts, of the sticks kiⁿtskŭt. Four sticks are used in playing. The set collected (fig. 89)[b] is of giant cactus wood. The sticks are not named "old man," "old woman," etc., as among the Papagos, but are designated as follows:

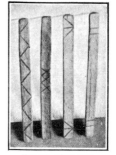

> No. 1—Ki-ik, "four."
> No. 2—Tco-otp', "six."
> No. 3—Si-ĭkâ, meaning of word unknown to informants.
> No. 4—Kiⁿts, meaning also unknown.

The players sit about 10 feet apart and put the sticks in play by striking from below with a flat stone held in the left hand. The sticks are held nearly vertical, but are inclined a little forward so

FIG. 89. Kiⁿtskŭt.

that they will fall in the center of the space between the players, who rake them back with a long stick after each throw.

The count is similar to that described for the Papago game, if we substitute the Pima names for the pieces, as follows:

> 2 backs and 2 faces count 2.
> 1 back and 3 faces count 3.
> Ki-ĭk facing up and others down count 4.
> All faces up count 5.
> Tco-otp' facing up and others down count 6.
> All faces down count 10.
> Si-ĭkâ facing up and others down count 14.
> Kiⁿts facing up and others down count 15.

The counts are kept upon a rectangle marked upon the ground usually approximating 12 by 8 feet, having 10 holes or pockets, counting the corners each time, along each side. At two alternate corners are 2 quadrants called ki, "houses," of 5 holes each, not

[a] Culin in Report National Museum, 1896, 738. His description is from notes and material collected by McGee.

[b] Length, 222 mm.; width, 17 mm.; thickness, 7 mm.; hemispherical in section; not colored on either side.

counting the corner holes, called ut῾pa, "doors."[a] The stick used by each player or side to mark its throw is called rsâika, "slave" or "horse." When a player is "coming home" and his count carries his "slave" only to the last hole of his house it is said to be "in the fire" and remains "burnt" until he throws a number less than 14 or 15.

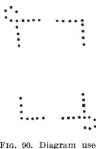

The corner hole of the rectangle is called tcolût, "hip;" the second, tco-olrsân, "near the corner;" the third, rsa-akĭt, "middle;" the fourth, ko'kĕtam, "above the end;" the fifth, ko-ok, "last;" the first hole of the house, tco'-oletam, "above the hip;" the second, ki-ĭk vak῾ utra, "four-hole end;" the third, vai-ĭk vak῾ utra, "three-hole end;" the fourth, sap῾k῾ utra, "right end" or "place;" the fifth, tai-ĭ utra, "fire end" or "in the fire." (See diagram, fig. 90.)

Fig. 90. Diagram used in kiⁿts.

HAEYO

This game affords considerable amusement for the spectators as well as the participants. Four men provide themselves with moderately large stones, hayakŭt, which they throw between two holes set about 50 feet apart. All stand at one hole and try successively to throw into the other. If but one succeeds in throwing into the hole he and his partner are carried on the backs of their opponents across to the opposite goal. If both partners throw into the hole, they are carried across and returned to the first hole, the "horses" who carry them attempting to imitate the gallop of the horse.

VÂPÛTAI

A guessing game in which a number of players act as assistants to two leaders. A small bean[b] is used by the Papagos and a ball of black mesquite gum by the Pimas. It is placed in one of four joints of reed. The reeds are then filled with sand, all being concealed under a blanket, and the opponents guess which reed contains the ball.

a   b   c   d

Fig. 91. Canes used in vâpûtai.

The reeds are called vâpûtakŭt (vâpûtai, lay), "laying implements" (fig. 91).[c] Reed a, called kuli, "old man," has 17 longitudinal rows of 8 spots each; reed b, âks, "old woman," is unmarked; reed c,

---

[a] Culin in Report National Museum, 1896, p. 739.
[b] Obtained from Sonora from the tree called paowĭ by the Pimas and chilicoti by the Mexicans.
[c] The collection contains one set of reeds which are 27 cm. long and 22 mm. in diameter.

hota stcok, "middle black," has 6 longitudinal rows; reed *d*, ma-atcoʌolt, has 5 rows around the open end.

One hundred grains of corn are placed between the players in a hole, from which they are taken as won and placed in a hole in front of each player. When a player wins all the corn, he puts up a stick in the sand. The number of sticks may be from 1 to 10, as determined beforehand. Each player cancels one of his opponent's sticks when he wins one himself.

Two players confine their attention to the guessing; one on each side fills the reeds; one on each side watches the counting. Four men, one at each corner, hold the blanket, under which the filling is done, and sometimes offer suggestions to the leaders. The "old people," the plain

FIG. 92. Diagram used in vâputta.

reeds, and the marked reeds, are kept together and the "young people" are used by the opponents. When the two pairs are filled with sand and a bean or ball is concealed in each pair, the blanket is dropped and the reeds are laid in the center, each filler handing his pair over to the side of his opponent. If A guesses wrong and B right, four grains of corn are forfeited to the winner. If neither guesses right, they exchange reeds and begin again. If both guess right, there is no count. When one guesses right, he takes the four reeds and places his ball in one and the opponent then decides which pair it is in by laying one reed across the other in the pair which he thinks does not contain it. Then he pours out the sand of first one then the other. If he has guessed right, he does not score, but continues the play by filling and offering to his opponent. If he guesses wrong, the opponent scores 4 and 6 additional if the ball is in the under reed, 10 if it is in the upper.

FIG. 93. Pottery disks.

Cheating is done in various ways, but there is reason to believe that this practice has arisen since the Pimas have come in contact with the whites.

VÂPUTTA

Any number of players may participate, but they are under two leaders who are selected by toss. Each draws up his men in line so that they face their opponents (fig. 92). A goal about 50 yards distant is marked out and the game begins. A small object, usually a circular piece of pottery, one of those so common about the ruins of the Southwest (fig. 93), is carried around behind the line by a leader and placed in the hands of one of his men. The opposite leader guesses which man holds the object. If he guesses wrong, the man at the end of the line in which the object is held who stands farthest from the goal runs and jumps over the upheld leg of the man at the opposite end of his own line. This moves the winning line the width of one man and the length of a jump toward the goal. If the first guess is correct, the object is passed to him and there is no jumping until a guess fails.[a]

The boys play several simple games which develop skill in shooting the arrow or in running In the former class may be included the following game:

VATÂMɅMɅLĬTC HɅKOɅOLIWIA

The players stand in a circle while a boy runs around outside, dragging at the end of a string a bundle of rags. When the play begins each boy deposits an arrow in a heap and the one who transfixes the bundle as it flies past is entitled to the pile of arrows. At the end the best marksman may have nearly all the arrows. The same runner continues throughout the game and receives a few arrows as compensation for his services.

PAPAIETCITAKŬT

The name of this game signifies "cooking place." Several boys play in the game. A rag ball the size of one's fist is tossed up and the one nearest where it falls tries to throw it against another, using a slightly curved stick called henyusika. The one hit has to stand with his head down to protect his face while the others throw the ball at him. After all throw, the game begins anew.

OKMAITCĔKĔ

A bundle of grass, called woliwikke, is tied with willow bark so that it is about 125 mm. long and 50 mm. in diameter. The player tosses the bundle upward with his left hand while holding the bow in his right, ready to shoot the bundle before it can strike the earth.

When the bundle is thrown forward instead of upward it is called tcomält maitcĕkĕ, "to shoot the bundle low."

NAOF TOWE KɅKRSA

The title given above signifies "prickly-pear standing opposite." There are usually four players, though sometimes two engage in this shooting game. Prickly-pear leaves are set up opposite each other at a distance of about 30 yards. The game is to pierce the

---

[a] The object is called rsâika, "slave." It is 40 or 50 mm. in diameter, is pitted in the center "to prevent cheating," and may be of either pottery or stone.

leaf with an arrow, and when four are playing the two partners share equally the winnings or losses. Arrows, bows, and such similar property as these ragged urchins possess are wagered. A bow is considered worth from 10 to 20 arrows, according to quality.

KꞂORSA

Either two or four may play. The game consists in shooting an arrow so that it will lie on the ground at a distance of about 100 feet and then shooting two more arrows with the intention of casting them across the first.

KWAĬTUSĬWĬKŬT

The children sometimes amuse themselves by tossing into the air corncobs in which from one to three feathers have been stuck. They do not shoot arrows at them.

There are three games in addition to the athletic game of âldû which were played exclusively by the women.

MEKŮT TOAKŬT

Two women play this game. Five stones that have been carefully selected from rounded pebbles 3 to 4 cm. in diameter (fig. 94) are used. The first player calls one of these "my stone" and tosses it into the air, keeping her eyes fixed upon it while she snatches up one of the other four

FIG. 94. Gaming stones.

stones before the first falls. After all are picked up in this way she begins again and picks up two at a time, then three and one, then all at once. If she proceeds thus far without mistake she wins the game. The next game is more difficult. The named stone is tossed up as before, but those remaining are shoved under an arch formed by the thumb and middle finger with the first finger crossed over the middle one. The stones are pushed under the arch in the same order as in the first game. In the one-plus-three combination the player selects one stone which she calls her opponent's and says she will not pick that one up first.

KÂ-ÂMĬSAKŬT

This stave game is played with eight sticks in two sets of four each, which are colored black on the rounded side in one set and on the flat side in the other, the opposite side being stained red (fig. 95). Two play, each using her own set of sticks, but exchanging them alternately, so that first one set is in use and then the other. They are held loosely in the right hand and are thrown from the end of the metate or any other convenient stone. If all fall red side up one point is scored by a mark in the sand. If all are black two are counted. Winning four points completes the game.[a]

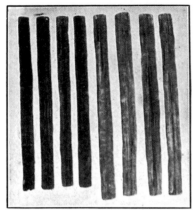

FIG. 95. Staves used in game of kâ-âmĭsakŭt.

TCⱭLIKIWĬKŬT

This is the Gileño form of the widespread dart-and-ring game. It is not exclusively a woman's game, but was sometimes played by them. The younger generation knows nothing about it. The apparatus consists of a series of rings cut from cultivated gourds (fig. 96). They vary in diameter from 3 to 12 cm., and are strung on a 2-ply maguey fiber cord 50 cm. long. They are kept from slipping off at one end by a rectangular piece of gourd a little larger than the opening in the smallest ring, which is at that end. At the other end of the string is fastened a stick 20 cm. long, the outer end of which is sharp-

FIG. 96. Dart-and-ring game.

ened. The game is to toss the rings up by a swing and, while holding the butt of the stick, thrust the dart through as many of them as possible. If the thrower fails she hands the apparatus to her opponent, but she continues throwing as long as she scores, and counts the number of rings that are caught on the dart. In the specimen collected

---

[a] This is similar to the game described in Report National Museum, 1896, 742.

there are 14 rings, but only a few may be caught at a single throw.
A certain number of marks, 2, 3, or 4, agreed upon in advance, constitute the game. These marks are made upon a diagram laid out in
the sand in the form of a whorl (fig. 97). The scoring
commences in the center, called the tcᴜnni ki, "council
house," and runs out to the last hole, called hoholdega
ki, "menstrual house," which is on the west side of the
diagram; then the score returns to the center before
the player is entitled to one point toward game.
If the player who is behind throws a number that
brings her counter to the same hole as that of her opponent she
"kills" the latter and sends back her counter to the beginning point,
but this is not done if she passes her opponent's position.

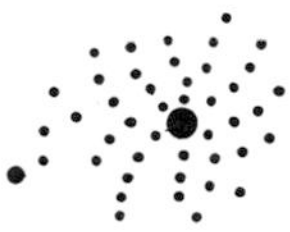

Fig. 97. Diagram used in tcᴜliki-wĭkŭt.

Two specimens were obtained at Sacaton which were probably
used in games by the Hohokam, illustrations of which are here presented for the benefit of those engaged in special researches concerning gaming devices.

CUP STONE

Fig. 98. Cup stone.

One of these objects is a cup-shaped stone of lava
which was obtained from a Pima who had found it
in one of the Gila Valley ruins west of the Casa
Grande (fig. 98). Doctor Fewkes has called the
writer's attention to the fact that it resembles the
wooden cups used by the Hopis in a game not unlike the European "shell game."[a]

RING STONE

A few rings of porous lava have been found about
the ruins which have been called "head rings"
because of their resemblance to the ordinary head
rings of cloth or bark in common use among the Pimas
(fig. 99). However, as most of them are too small
and the material is extremely unsuited for such a purpose it is
much more probable that they were employed in some game with
which the present race is unacquainted.[b]

Fig. 99. Ring stone.

---

[a] It is 96 mm. long, 53 mm. in diameter, with cavity 26 mm. in diameter and 42 m.m. in depth.

[b] Diameter of ring, 115 mm.; internal diameter, 45 mm.; thickness, 55 mm.

SOCIOLOGY

FAMILY ORGANIZATION

RELATIONS BEFORE MARRIAGE

Accurate information concerning the relations between the sexes before marriage can only be obtained from the oldest persons among the Pimas, as the moral atmosphere has been heavily clouded since the advent of the Americans and since the peril from the Apaches has ceased to exist. With all their surplus energies expended in warfare, the young men formerly lived exemplary lives as compared with the youths of the last generation, who would chase and even lasso any girl that they could catch. Nevertheless, the conditions were never as bad as among the Yumas of that period.[a] Before the Pimas came in contact with "civilization" chastity was the rule among the young women, who were taught by compelling precept, though ever witnessing the demoralizing example of free and easy divorce.

PUBERTY DANCE

A girl reached the age of puberty at 11 or 12, sometimes as early as 10. The acquirement by a young woman of the (to them) wholly mysterious functional characteristics of the age of puberty rendered her an object of concern and distrust to the elders. When the fact was discovered her mother selected some favorite woman friend, not a relative, in whose charge she placed the girl for a period of four days. During this time the preceptress taught her how to perform such household tasks as she may not already have learned; also the principles of industry, honesty, chastity, and the like. They cooked their meals and ate together apart from their families. When not otherwise engaged the girl occupied her time in making a basket which must be given as a present to the elder woman. She talked little; if she wished to scratch her head she used a stick—to use the fingers at this critical period would cause lice. She dared not blow the fire or her teeth would come out.

There was "danger" in the girl that must be breathed out by songs ere she, the members of her family, and the community as a whole were exempt from the hazard of the lightning stroke and other perils. Woe to the girl who concealed her condition, for the medicineman's magic would enable him to discover the culprit and should accident befall he would ascribe it to her. As a matter of fact, however, some girls avoided the "coming-out" ceremonies as long as possible and when the parents were poor no dance was held. When the parents had a sufficient supply of food on hand to entertain with becoming hospitality they invited friends and neighbors to participate

---

[a] Compare Rusling, The Great West and the Pacific Coast, 361.

in a dance that occupied four nights.   The father and mother did not dance, but they took care to select the best girls to dance with their daughter "for their good influence."   The men and women formed two lines facing each other on the hardened and well-swept plaza outside the house; their arms were extended to embrace those adjoining, and the blankets were stretched along the line to cover as many as they would reach over instead of being wrapped around each individual.   The lines advanced and retreated rhythmically while the puberty songs were sung.   These songs were in sets that were retained in the memories of certain persons and the set for the night was generally determined by the chance that brought the first leader to the spot when all was ready to begin.   It was an exhausting dance, as there was no stopping for rest or food during the night.   In the morning all returned to their homes to spend the day in sleep.

During the menstrual period all women were secluded for four days, during which they lived in the bushes near the village, making little shelters to shade them from the sun and occupying their time in making baskets.   They lived on pinole, which was brought each morning and left at a short distance from their camp.   Sometimes there were several together.   They always bathed in the river before returning to their homes.

MARRIAGE

The youth of Pimería marry "early and often."   In the majority of cases the choice is made by the girl who seeks to avoid an alliance with a lazy man.   A handsome fellow is of course desired, but when she "knows in her heart" that he is the right man even the homely youth is chosen.   As to what is the ideal of physical beauty, questioning naturally elicited only general information.   For example, he must be tall and strong; dark, because he will not wrinkle as soon as the lighter colored; he must not be too fat.   The woman must not be fat nor yet thin; "she must have good hair and a good face."   The writer's informant volunteered information that a stranger might distinguish between the married and the unmarried women by the fact that the latter kept their hair in much better condition than the former.   No peculiar style of hair dressing such as that in vogue among the Hopis serves to distinguish the unmarried girls (see pl. XLVII); with the change of state they simply "let themselves go" in a very human way, though even at the worst their hair receives probably more attention than that of the vast majority of their white sisters.

When a youth selects a bride he visits her home in company with a young married friend who pleads his cause while he sits in the background.   After several nights of wooing by proxy, if his cause is favored he remains and is accepted as a husband without further ceremony.   For four days they remain at her home and on the evening of the fourth day they go to the home of his parents. At dawn the next morning the mother-in-law gives the bride a large basket of wheat to grind on the metate. She is expected to have completed the grinding by sunrise. In the quaint language of the interpreter we were informed that "if she ran away and left part of it unground it was a sign that she would not be a very good wife. When she finished her work she went quietly into the house and sat talking with those around her until she got acquainted with her new home." The groom presented the bride with a new blanket and his parents gave her presents, but there was no idea of purchase and no gifts were made to the bride's parents.

Occasionally a man possessed such a character that no woman would marry him, and more rarely a woman would remain unmarried. There is one such at Casa Blanca and one at Blackwater at the present time, the latter being regarded as possessed of supernatural powers because of her spinsterhood.

A rejected suitor might appeal to the medicine-man for assistance. If he stole a hair from her head and the medicine-man buried it the girl would die. How like the folklore of the Caucasian is this bit of superstition that savors more of vengeance than of love. But that the divine passion does take strong hold upon the Pimas there can be no doubt, as disappointed hopes have been known to lead to suicide.

Polygamy was practised to some extent, but the division of labor was such that no great economic advantage resulted. There were seldom more than two or three wives, though a chief's son in recent years had six. The plural wives lived in separate houses, the husband spending most of his time with the first. When a youth married he brought his wife to the home of his parents if there was room for them; if not, a house was built near by and the families ate together.

It was the custom for a widower to wed the sister of his deceased wife. "Supposing that she does not like the man and does not wish to marry him?" the writer inquired. Whereupon the answer was given with an air of superior wisdom, "She always wants to." Uncles and nieces are not permitted to marry and cousins do not marry "out of respect of the parents for each other." The most careful search failed to discover any trace of groups within the tribe between which marriage was prohibited.

DURATION OF UNION

Separation was lightly regarded and easily effected. The woman usually took the initiative, by either going to the home of her parents or going away with another man. Sometimes such remarks as "Rainbow Leaves is trying to get Sand Cloud's husband away from her," "Dawn Tinkle has changed husbands," were heard. Notwithstanding the natural independence of the women, they made an effort to retain the affection of worthy husbands, and even resorted to suicide when deserted. Moreover, the desirability of lasting unions was recognized by some, as, for example, by the father of wise old Sala Hina. "Work well at home," he told her, "Go not to others for the morsel they must needs in hospitality bestow, and then when you serve faithfully your husband he will provide well for you. If the husband you choose proves to be lazy do not desert him; work in the field with him; help and encourage him."

CHILDREN

Further evidence in support of the fact that the Pimas were not a degenerate race at the time of the introduction of the white man's whisky and diseases is found in the size of their families. As many as twelve children have been known in a single family, and twins are received with general rejoicing. Every inhabitant of the village brings gifts and the mother feels assured that she will henceforth be a fortunate woman. Male children were preferred, because "they would grow up to fight Apaches." With the consent of the parents deformed infants were taken by the midwife, who watched them until they died of exposure and want of nourishment. So strong was the feeling of the Pimas against the abnormal that they tried in recent years to kill a grown man who had six toes.

Tribal pride is sufficiently strong to induce the Pimas to destroy infants of American or Mexican fathers in the same manner as those which are deformed. The writer learned of but two persons who had escaped such a fate. Inquiries concerning albinos met with the reply that "there never were any." Probably such a child would share the same fate as that accorded any other exhibiting abnormal characteristics.

A pregnant woman was not allowed to eat anything that an animal had touched. For example, if a gopher had cut a vine on which a melon was ripening, she might not eat the fruit; or, if the mice nibbled at a basket of wheat she might not eat of the tortillas made therefrom. She dared not go where Apaches had been killed, or the baby would die. If her husband killed a rattlesnake at that time, her child's stomach would swell and it would die soon after birth. She must not eat liver or her child would be disfigured by birthmarks.

During confinement the husband absented himself from the home and women friends attended the patient, who sat over a hole in the floor in which a cloth had been spread. The placenta was buried in a hole and covered with ashes. The mother bathed in the river immediately after delivery, and until the umbilicus of the child was healed she dared not eat salt. At times much pain was suffered, and some died in labor, in which case, if the child lived, it was taken in charge by the maternal grandmother.

Babies were nursed until the next child was born. Sometimes a mother nursed a child until it was 6 or 7 years old and if she became pregnant in the meantime she induced abortion by pressure upon the abdomen. The unborn was sacrificed because it was believed to be prejudicial to the welfare of the nursing child, which the mother loved the more "because she could see it." Illegitimate children were aborted at three or four months. One case of abortion at seven months was reported, but it was done with the aid of the medicine-man. These operations were usually successful, but in a small percentage of cases they caused the death of the woman.

No attempt was made by any of the Pimas to explain the cause of sterility.

The tribe has been large enough to prevent ill effects from close inbreeding, and there has been a constant addition of foreign blood. Sala Hina (fig. 51), who is perhaps 65 or 70 years old, recalled the names of three Apache women who had been married by Pimas. One of these had "many children." She had also known two Maricopa men married to Pima women and two Pimas married to Maricopa women. How lasting these unions had been she was unable to say. There is a Hare-eater from Sonora and a Yaqui who have married Pima women at one of the upper villages. Intermarriage with the desert-dwelling Kwahadk's has been fairly common. The father of Sala Hina was a Kwahadkʿ and prominent in Piman history as the man who brought the first cattle to the tribe. The few Kwahadkʿ women among the villages make the peculiar pottery that is characteristic of their tribe, and which should not be confounded with that of the Pimas. Detecting a slight dialectic difference in the speech of one of the temporary interpreters the author learned upon inquiry that his mother had been a Kwahadkʿ. Another interpreter said that his people called him "mixed," which is not surprising, as in his veins flowed the blood of Pimas, Maricopas, Papagos, and Apaches, peoples of three distinct linguistic stocks. The greatest influx of foreign blood has been from the related Papago tribe whose caravans annually made their appearance at the harvest season. Some Papago families have always lived with the Pimas, at one time forming an outpost on the north by maintaining a village on the Salt river.

In the past there was also some intermarriage with the Sobaipuris, and there is both traditional and historical evidence of the final amalgamation of the remnants of that tribe with the Pimas. Some were captured by the Apaches, as shown by Bourke in his researches upon the clans of that tribe. "The Apaches have also among them

Tze-kinne, or Stone-house people, descendants of the cliff-dwelling Sobaypuris, whom they drove out of Aravypa Cañon and forced to flee to the Pimas for refuge about a century ago." [a]

CEREMONY OF PURIFICATION

As soon as a child began to creep about it was taken by the parents some afternoon to the medicine-man in order that the rite of purification might be administered and the child's future be rendered free from harmful magic influences. Putting a sacred pebble and an owl feather into a seashell containing water, the medicine-man waved an eagle feather (fig. 100) about, while the parents and the child drank the water and ate some white ashes or a little mud. This simple ceremony was sufficient to thwart the malice of all evil demons; lightning would not strike the child, and the possibility of accidents of all kinds was thus precluded. As a further precaution the mother must not eat salt for four days thereafter.

FIG. 100. Eagle feather aspergills.

This appears at first glance to be a modification of the Christian rite of baptism. Further investigation seems to show that it is similar to that and also to a purely aboriginal ceremony that in the opinion of the writer was practised before the advent of the friars. The Pimas declare that their "medicine-men got it up themselves." Cushing found "that the Zuñi of to-day are as eager as were their forefathers for baptism and for baptismal names additional to their own But it must be remembered," he continues, "that baptism—the purification of the head by sprinkling or of the face by washing with medicine water—was a very old institution with this people even before the Spaniards found them."[b] He also ascribes the readiness of various other tribes to receive baptism to the existence of their own similar custom. This readiness is otherwise difficult to account for, as the zeal, and, at times, lack of judgment, of the priests led them to baptize as many of the Indians as they were able to con-

a Capt. John G. Bourke, Journal of American Folk-Lore, IX, 114.
b Cushing in Thirteenth Annual Report of the Bureau of Ethnology, 335.

trol for the purpose; this procedure must have caused trouble very soon had the ceremony been wholly unknown to the natives.[a]

BAPTISM

Before a child is a year old it is named by friends of the parents in the following manner: The friends, or godparents, accompanied by other visitors, come for four successive mornings and seat themselves just before sunrise on the ground before the house in which the child lives.   First one and then another of the company holds the child for a moment, but if it is a boy the kŏmpalt, godfather, repeats a ceremonial speech, passes his hands across the limbs of the infant and holds it aloft to receive the first rays of the rising sun; then he bestows upon the boy the name by which he shall be known throughout life—though nicknames are common and often supplant the baptismal name to some extent.   If it is a girl, the kâmûlt, godmother, delivers the speech and gives the name.   Beads .were formerly held up to receive the first rays of sunlight, and were then placed about the child's neck.   Gifts of clothing, food, baskets, and the like were also made by the godparents, who "think as much of the child afterwards as its own father and mother," said one of our informants.   The parents in their turn reciprocate by naming the children of the couple that acts as godparents to their own.[b]

The names assumed by the men during later life are very frequently derived from the sexual organs, particularly those of the female, but such names are never bestowed at the time of baptism.   Any unusual event or physical peculiarity may impose a name upon an individual. For example, a man who worked several weeks for the missionary was so well fed that he began to lay on flesh.   Ever afterwards he was known as Preacher's Fat.   One is known as Uvaatuka, Spread Leg, from his peculiar gait.

From the age of 10 until about the time of marriage neither boys nor girls are allowed to speak their own names.   The penalty is bad luck in losing arrows in the case of the boys, in losing the rsa'lĭka, or kiâhâ stick in the case of the girls.   The name of a deceased person is not used; he is alluded to as the brother of So-and-so.   The word or words in the name, however, are not dropped from the language.

---

[a]Whipple, Ewbank, and Turner in the Pacific Railroad Reports, III, 35, mention the occurrence of the custom of baptism among the Cherokees when the infants are 3 days old.   "They believe that without this rite the child can not live.   They have a custom of sacrifices and burnt offerings."

[b]"Cada niño tiene un *peri*. que es una especie de padrino, que convidan sus padres.   Este, despues de haberle hecho un largo discurso al recien nacido sobre las obligaciones propias de su sexo, le va tentando por todo el cuerpo, estirándole los brazos y piernas, y luego le impone un apellido ó nombre de su lengua, no significativo.   Despues de la ceremonia, el peri y ɥl niño se reputan en lo civil como una misma persona, y tienen con sus respectivos parientes la misma relacion.   Lo mismo hacen las mugeres en su proporcion con las niñas."   Alegre, Historia de la Compañía de Jesus en Nueva-España, II, 217.

NAMES

The names of the Pimas proved so interesting to the present investigator that a number of examples were recorded, as follows:

Names of men

Rainbow
Rainbow-Bow
Stick-Rainbow
Cloud-Rainbow
Bear-Rainbow
Apache-Back
Sand-Arms
Cloud-Thundering
Cloud-Heart
Ant's-Cry
Moon-Fragment
Big-Moon
Scared-Eagle
Tail-Shed
Fog
Shining-Star
Coyote-Footprint
Coyote-Shed
Coyote-Dust
Coyote-Lightning
Coyote-Skin
Coyote-Flower
Coyote-Running-Races
Coyote-Runner
Coyote-Howl
Coyote's-Quiver
Bear
Bear's-Body
Bear's-Paws

Bird-Eyes
Black-Wheat
Frozen-Beans
Bean-Barter
Greasy-Eagle
Big-Eagle
Evening-Murmuring
Evening-Come
Closing-Twilight
Light-Shines
Wind-Milky-Way
Wind-Bow
Speaking-Bow
Evening-Hands
Running-Wind
Evening-Roaring
Soft-Feathers-Morning
Sun-Sparks
Eagle-Sparks
Hawk-Bow
Milky-Way-Bow
Sun-Bow
Foam-Bow
Sticking-Feathers
Hawk-Shield
Telling-Shooting
Raven
Brown-Eagle
Coyote's-Hair

Squash-Stem
Shields-in-Line
Eagle-Head
Light-Bird-Down
Shield-Light
Rat-Skin
Rattlesnake-Rattle
Thin-Leather
Hide-Bucket
Bad-Bow
Running-Noise
Red-Corn
Scorpion's-Stomach
Drum-Stomach
Hawk - Beginning-To-Lay-
　Eggs
Shining-Nose
Coyote
Centiped
Centiped's-Rattle
Beaver's-Mouth
Ducks
Birds-Feather
Bird Sharp
Cliff-Rainbow
Many-Shields
Round-Frog
Shining-Back

Names of women

Cloud-Flower
Cloud-Peak
Cloud-Curve
Flowers
Sun-Flower
Flowers-Flying
Flowers-Running
Sun's-Rays
Sun-Flying
Morning-Rays
Morning-Running
Morning-Clouds
Morning-Waving-Hands
Bluish
Singing-Rattle
Pleasing-Mirage
Snowflakes
Water-Fern-Leaves
Foam-Rolling
Ancient-House-Shining
Ancient-House-Drops
Ancient-House-Sparks
Rainbow-Dispelled
Rainbow-Leaves
Leaves-Flying
Bows-Spotted
Water-Fern-Tops
Song-Flower

Morning-Disappearing
Morning-Beating
Clouds-Passing
Darkness-Passing
Darkness-Loosened
Morning-Loosened
Morning-Kneading
Willow
Sing-Tinkle
Bird-Down-Flowers
Bird-Down-Sprinkle
Rainbow-Water-Grass
Cloud-Tinkle
Gray-Leaves
Morning-Dew
Big-Leaves
Sunflower
Night-Wind
Dawn-Tinkle
West-End
Spring-Leaves
Morning-Water-Grass
Morning-Leaves
Sun-Leaves
Bow-End
Morning-Trail
West-Sprinkle
Quivering-Heat-Waves

Foam-Tinkle
Morning-End
Morning-Tossing-Up
Morning-Shadow
Cloud-Rolling
Water-Grass-Growing
Night-Twinkle
Many-Leaves
Sand-Cloud
Night-Flower
First-Flower
Red-Flower
Yellow-Flower
Singing-Noise
Two-Flowers
Basket-Leaves
They-Come
Sun-Mirage
Mirage-End
Salty
Raw
Soft
Alone
Crooked-Knife
Dew-Woman
Butterfly

EDUCATION

In addition to the education that every Pima child received by the method of imitation and apprenticeship, careful oral instruction in moral, religious, and other matters was also given by the elders. While yet quite young the Pima lad was taken up in his father's arms at daybreak and held there while he was told something of the mysteries of the great Sun god that nearly every morning in the year rises bright and free from clouds above the Sierra Tortilla. As he grew too big to be held in arms he had to sit up very straight and pay strict attention while his father or guardian lectured to him on the proper conduct of a Pima warrior and citizen; or, in other words, soldier and gentleman. If he was not fully awake and paid indifferent heed to what was told him, the father's stiffened middle finger would suddenly strike the side of his nose, bringing his face around until he looked straight into his father's eyes. (See pl. XLII, c, XLV, XLVI.)

He learned that he must be ever alert and ready with bow and arrows to repel the attacks of Apaches. Day by day this lesson was taught by precept and example until it became the strongest instinct of the youth to be ready and watchful. He was taught to go on scout duty in the morning or to look after the live stock before he partook of his morning meal. It was well for him to accustom himself to cold food and to that which remained after the family had satisfied their hunger, for it was only by practising abstemiousness that he could hope to be fit for the long war trail into the barren Apache stronghold. "If you are wounded in battle," said the father, "don't make a great outcry about it like a child. Pull out the arrow and slip away; or, if hard stricken, die with a silent throat. Go on the war trail with a small blanket. It is light and protection enough for one aided by the magicians. Inure yourself to the cold while yet a boy. Fight not at all with your comrades; preserve your strength for the combat with the Apaches. Then, if brave, will come to you high honor. Be unselfish or you will not be welcome at the fire of the friendly. The selfish man is lonely and his untended fire dies. Keep your peace when a foolish man addresses the people. Join not in his imprudent councilings. Above all, talk not foolishly yourself. Bathe in the cold water of the early morning, that you may be prepared for the purification ceremony after killing an enemy."

Thus the lad was taught fortitude, courage, forbearance, unselfishness, industry—qualities that might well be adapted to the changed conditions and incorporated in the system of instruction of the white man's "Indian schools." As time went on he learned that if he profited by the advice given him he would become a desirable party for some soft-voiced home keeper, and with his marriage his education ceased.

As a hunter he made his debut by giving away all the first deer that he killed. Afterwards he took his choice of the meat before sharing with his fellows.

Every youth when about 20 years old was told the ancient traditions, or Hâ-âk Aga, Story of Hâ-âk. For four days and four nights he remained with the keeper of the legends, who was usually a man selected as tribal historian because of possessing a good memory. During that period he was not allowed to eat salt. This and similar tabus with reference to salt may have been due to contact with the Papagos or to survival from the period when the Pimas lived by the sea.

The advice given Sala Hina by her father may be taken as an example of the kind of instruction given the girls. Sala's mother was careless and indifferent, so that the responsibility of her training fell upon the father, as often happens. "Stay at home with your mother," he told her. "Watch and help her handle the cooking pots, the mortar, and metate, that you may know how to prepare the seeds of Pimería. Keep the fire alive and have wood ever ready. See that the drinking olla is never empty. If you do these things well, you will not gad about after you are married and leave your hearth vacant so that your husband may come home to find the fire out or to put it out to your discomfiture; for it is the office of man to kindle the fire but the part of woman to keep it burning."

As in the case cited, one parent may neglect the training of the children. It rarely happens that both are wholly indifferent. They are inclined to punish the children more than do the members of any other tribe with which I am acquainted. The youngsters are seldom whipped, but they may be scolded, slapped, or shaken for their misdemeanors until they become 10 or 12 years old. If a girl stumbles and breaks an olla when going for water, her elders take some of the broken pieces and scratch her naked arm. The girls begin to assist in the cooking at 7 or 8 and at 9 or 10 they begin to make baskets. Some are lazy and are allowed to idle away their time, never making more than the single basket required during their puberty ceremonies.

The younger girls make very realistic rag dolls, which they carry through the drama of life with as great seriousness and "make-believe" as their white sisters. The writer once came upon them when they had twenty or more figures variously posed around them as spectators of the burial of a whole family, with accompanying destruction of ("make-believe") property. In addition to "funerals," they had parties for which they ground wheat for pinole, though an adult observer would have said that they were grinding up weed seed. The "dishes" were molded with mud on their little brown elbows and were ready for use after scarcely more than a minute's drying in the sun. One form of mischievous activity was to play hide-and-seek in the wheat fields, but such a game was brief and apt to be attended with unpleasant consequences. In the evenings they played "puberty dances" or listened to the wonderful tales of prowess of their elders or of the adventures of the mythic animals of ancient Pimería. The boys practise day after day, year after year, until it is not surprising that they become such accurate shots with the bow. Woe to the birds and squirrels that cross their path. Unlike the pueblo lads, they are not prohibited from killing the rattlesnake, but they must not use the same arrow again. If the rattles are desired for ornament, they must be taken from a living snake. We have seen them teasing a Gila monster, but this and the horned toad are exempt from their arrows. Fish offered a splendid target for them when there was any water in the river and any fish were to be seen. There was no parental prohibition against destroying birds' nests, though the warning "If you touch quail eggs you will go blind" served most effectually to protect one species at least. The owl was not so much a bird of evil as of mystery and death, and its feathers were sought for their magic potency in medicine and other ceremonies. If a lad shot one, he had to pluck the feathers from the bird before it died or the magic power of the plumes was lost. Besides the bow and arrows the Pima youngsters possessed the sling of rawhide, which, by the usual process of evolution, came to be made in later years of boot leg. From the scanty Mexican population with which they came in contact they learned to use stilts, but none were seen in use during the writer's stay among them. As they grew older they were cautioned not to eat from an olla, else when they had to run away from superior numbers of Apaches the olla would get between their legs and obstruct their movements.

OLD PERSONS AND THEIR TREATMENT

Favored by the mildness of the climate, the lot of the aged among the Pimas was less unenviable than among most of the other Indian tribes. As they were a sedentary people, the custom of abandoning the aged on the march could not prevail. As a matter of fact, the old and helpless were not killed by the active members of the community, though they were sometimes neglected until they starved to death and sometimes they set fire to their houses to commit suicide. The heartlessness of youth sometimes manifested itself in such acts as throwing stones at aged persons, merely "to see them act like children."

One case observed may be mentioned—that of an old man at Sacaton dragging out a miserable existence. Totally blind and scarcely able to walk, he lived in a brush shelter about 8 feet square that contained a little straw and the single blanket that served to cover him. When he ventured abroad into the world the limits of his journeys were prescribed by the length of the rope which was attached by one end to his doorpost. His food was cooked by some of his adult grandchildren who occupied a house near at hand. His time was spent absolutely alone in the shelter, which was as devoid of utensils or furnishings as any dog kennel. And yet, with a pride that is death-less in the human soul, he boasted of the time when he was a man among men and overcame the ferocious Apaches on the latter's own ground.

VIEWS CONCERNING DEATH

The usual primitive views of death—that it was not a natural event, but a result of magic influences brought to bear by enemies, human or superhuman—prevailed among the Pimas. In the legends the first death that occurred in the history of the human race is attributed to the venom of Soft Child, the rattlesnake, who was given the power of death to protect himself from unmerited abuse by man. The legends also indicate a disposition to view the Destroyer philosophically, inasmuch as the predecessors of the present race are regarded with commiseration on account of their becoming so crowded because of none dying to give place to the oncoming generation.

Again and again the information was elicited that those who died during the day were killed by the Sun, while those who died during the hours of darkness were killed by Night. This the author inter-prets to mean that the prayers that were regularly addressed to Sun and Night were for preservation, and that death resulted from some lapse or inattention on the part of these two deities. This agrees with the equally emphatic statements that "death is always due to magic, to animals, or to neglect of the ceremonies or tabus."

MODE OF BURIAL

At the moment of death the friends of the dying flee from them as if to avoid the magic that may not be satisfied with one victim. The near relatives cover the face of the corpse and bind the body in a bundle, with the legs drawn up. Before the Pimas obtained horses the body was borne to the grave on a litter. With primitive tools the graves were not dug as deep as at the present time, and to this burial in shallow graves is attributed the cause for covering the graves with the timbers of the sheds or storehouses of the deceased (see pl. XXXIX, *a, b, c*). Now a round hole is dug to a depth of 5 or 6 feet, then a small chamber is scooped out on the west side, in which the body is extended, with the head to the south. Billets of wood are then placed so as to lean against the roof over the body, so that in filling the grave no earth falls upon it. Medicine-men are buried in a sit-ting position, and in several instances have been buried in isolated places which have acquired special sacredness.

The dead are never cremated, as they are by the adjoining tribes on the west.   There is an apparent exception to this rule in the occasional cremation practised while on the warpath.   The writer is unable to account for this, unless it be due either to the influence of the Maricopas or to a survival pointing toward western affinities of the Piman stock.   So far as ascertained, no disinterment for removal had ever been made by the Pimas.   They never buried beneath the floors, as did the Hohokam.

FUNERAL RITES

Water and pinole are placed on the grave for the use of the soul in the other world, not on the journey thither, as that takes but a

FIG. 101. Funeral cache south of Casa Blanca.

moment's time.   In order that the soul may betake itself to the proper abiding place and not disturb the survivors, the latter are accustomed to say at the grave, "We put you here.   Go to your home in the East.   Do not come back."   Ghosts are uncanny things to have about and are liable to touch sleeping persons, this meaning that the one touched must accompany the visitor back to the land of shades.

When a householder died his ki was formerly burned—an excellent hygienic precaution, but detrimental to the development of architecture.   The other structures about the premises were either burned or piled on the grave.   Personal property was similarly destroyed, and if there was any live stock, it was killed and eaten by anyone who chanced to be on hand, though the immediate relatives never partook of such food.[a]   When a husband was so fortunate as to possess two blankets, his widow sometimes kept one of them. The name of the deceased was not mentioned thereafter, and all things possible were done to obliterate his memory from the minds of the survivors except that the rites of mourning were practised for some time.

The death of a pauper who had nothing to leave at the grave released a vexed soul to wander about until some one in charity placed an offering on the grave. Sometimes the paraphernalia of a medicine-man, when it was not handed down to a successor in the family, was concealed in an olla in the hills instead of being destroyed. More rarely these caches were made of the property of ordinary men. Figure 101 shows such a cache, which was found in a rugged granite hill about 4 miles south of Casa Blanca. The olla was covered with a bowl, and as neither was broken it was perfectly water-tight. Among the contents of the cache (pl. XL) were a number of crystals and concretions, a neatly carved stone rattlesnake, three seashells for use in medicine, and a war club. The last was too large to be placed in the olla, and, being exposed outside, it was somewhat gnawed by rodents.

MOURNING

In mourning for near relatives the men cut their hair so that it does not fall below the middle of the back. The women cut theirs to the level of the ear lobes for husband, child, etc., and an aged widow cropped her hair close to the head "because she felt the worst." In all cases the cut hair was buried in the sand of the river bed; if it were burned it would cause headache and death. And yet when blankets were destroyed at the death of their owner they were burned.

Very few widows mourned for the full period of four years. During that time they were compelled to remain at home, to refrain from washing their hair, and to cry aloud the name of the deceased every morning at daybreak. They were allowed to bring their blankets up around under the armpits, but not over the shoulders, even in the coldest weather. When the chemise was adopted, as the blankets went out of use, it was customary to revert to the blankets during the period of mourning.

SOCIAL ORGANIZATION

OFFICERS

The Pimas are governed by a head chief and by a chief for each village. These men are assisted by village councils, which do not, the author believes, appoint any representatives to the tribal coun-

---

[a] Compare Bourke, "When a Mohave dies, there is a feast made of some of his horses and other edibles; but none of his clansmen will eat of it." Journal of American Folk-Lore, II, 184.

cils. The office of head chief is not hereditary, though the present
incumbent succeeded his father. He is elected by the village chiefs.

The present head chief is Antonio Azul (pl. ii, a), known among his
people as Uva-a′tûka, Spread Leg, from a peculiarity in his gait;
also as Ma′vĭt Ka′wutam, Puma Shield, and by other names less ele-
gant. The calendar records are silent upon this, and as to the date
of his accession, reference to it in contemporary literature has been
seen. He became chief before 1864, as Poston mentions in his report
as special commissioner in that year that Antonio had just had his
commission revoked for bad conduct.[a]

Antonio's father had been the preceding head chief. He was known
as Culo Azul, also as Ti′ahiatam, Urine. His predecessor was Rsân′talĭ
Vi′akam, who was killed by Apaches before Kâmâl tkâk, who is probably 75 years old, was born. His predecessor was named O′sĭvf,
Joseph. No recollection of any earlier chief remains. In the Rudo
Ensayo Tavanimó is named as the chief about the year 1757,[b] and
it is possible that he was the predecessor of O′sĭvf.

The decrees of the councils are announced from a house top by
the village crier, who is selected because of possessing the loudest and
clearest voice. There are sometimes two of these officials in a village.

In each village there was also a "ceremony talker," or master of
ceremonies, whose duty it was to arrange and control the details of
the festivals and general ceremonies not especially provided for by
the religious fraternities.

At the command of each council was a messenger who might be
sent to summon those required by that body.

Any man of acknowledged courage might, with the approval of
his fraternity (the information obtained at this point was somewhat vague—perhaps "neighbors" or "the community" is the better
term), organize a war party. He was then called Tcʊnyĭm or
Tcʊ′yĭnyĭm, Smoker, or War Speaker. His name and authority ended
upon returning from the campaign.

It is important to note that the tribe acted as a unit against the
Apaches. With their compact territory and well-developed agriculture they might well have easily developed yet further their
division of labor and established a warrior class. Then, with their
increasing numbers under the stimulus of material well-being, they
might have easily extended their power. No neighboring tribes
except the Apaches and Papagos surpassed them in numbers; the
former were without resources, the latter were related and friendly.
The advantages of confederation had been learned from more than
half a century's experience with the Maricopas, a tribe of alien speech
and blood.

---

a See Report of Commissioner of Indian Affairs 1864, 153, 1865.
b Records American Catholic Historical Society. v, 129.

GENTES

Descent is traced in the male line and there are five groups that may be called gentes, though they exert no influence upon marriage laws nor do they manifest any evidences of organization so far as ascertained. The names of these groups have lost all meaning. They are called Â'kol, A'pap, A'pŭkĭ, Ma'-am, and Va'-af.

The first three are known as the Vulture or Red People, the last two as the Coyote or White People. However, they are spoken of as the Sûwû'kĭ O'himal and Sto'am O'himal, or Red Ants and White Ants.[a] In the Pima creation myth presented in full in this memoir reference is made to black ants, tcotcĭk tâtâny, and to the termite, hiapĭtc, but no connection is supposed to exist between them and the o'himal.

The Red People are said to have been in possession of the country when Elder Brother brought the White People from the nether world and conquered them as described on page 226. There were more than two gentes of the White People, but Coyote laughed too soon at them and the earth closed before the others got through. The author suspects that this division signifies that the tribe was formed by the junction of two peoples, the only trace of the original groups being the names and the maintenance of the laws of vengeance.

SLAVES

The slaves taken by the Pimas were chiefly from the ranks of the Apaches or their allies.[b] Though war was waged for many years against the Yumas it was not of a character to enable them to capture many Yuma children. When captured, Apache children were not killed; they were soon forwarded to Tucson, Altar, or Guaymas and sold to the Spaniards or Mexicans. These captives were well treated, but their origin was never forgotten and the fear and suspicion of the tribe found expression at times in the decrees of the medicine-men that certain misfortunes were caused by the presence of the aliens. Somewhat rarely the girls were married into the tribe and an appreciable amount of foreign blood was introduced in this way which doubtless had its effect upon the vigor of the race.

SOCIAL MORALS

It would be a more agreeable task to write of the morality of primitive Pimas than of that which developed as a result of contact with Spaniards and Americans. To the honesty and virtue of the tribe a

---

[a] The same divisions exist among the Papagos, and José Lewis, the Papago who interpreted for Professor McGee, submitted specimens of the ant as examples of the insect referred to as "o'himal."

[b] "Que los Cocomaricopas apressan los muchachos Nijoras (que todos son gentiles) y los venden por esclavos á los mas, y estos á los Españoles, que los compran en cortas cantidades." Villa-Señor, y Sanchez, Theatro Americano, 1748, pt. 2, I, 396.

score of writers have testified, leading to the belief that moral standards in Pimería at least equaled if they did not resemble our own. Life and property were secure. By their industry they had mastered the difficulties of their environment. The relations of the sexes and the division of labor had been adjusted in a manner creditable to them.[a]

The law of vengeance operated to prevent homicide. "Speak not foolishly," said the elders; "do not quarrel and kill your neighbor, for that leads to retaliation." Thus the youth were instructed and the abhorrence of bloodshed grew deep and lasting. Within the tribe there was but one exception to this—to kill the convicted sorcerer was meritorious.

No odium attached to the crime of suicide. The body was buried in the usual manner and the property was similarly divided or destroyed. Several instances of self-destruction were ascertained. A blind old man had shot himself and a young man had ended his career because his father would not let him sell some piece of personal property. Another man had shot himself because his wife had deserted him and their family of small children. A woman had starved herself and baby in the hills of the desert because her husband had left her.

The crime of arson was unknown, though dwellings were frequently burned by accident.

Adultery was punished by turning the woman away from the home. Sometimes the husband shot the horse of the offending man and "then he felt all right."

Prostitution with its train of diseases has not depleted the numbers of the Pimas as it has the population of so many surrounding tribes. Loose women are said by the old people to have been rare in the old days. Independent testimony of the whites accords with this. "They are exceedingly jealous of their females; and their chastity, as far as outside barbarians are concerned, remains, with a few exceptions, unimpeachable." [b] One informant assured the writer's party that the infant daughter of a prostitute by an unknown father was always destroyed lest she "grow up to be as bad as her mother."

---

[a] "The Indians, although they were crowding about our tents, and everything was exposed to them, made no effort to steal anything." Captain Johnston, Journal, 600.

" Um das Bild dieses indianischen Volksstammes zu vervollständigen, muss ich nur noch hinzufügen dass derselbe mit seinen friedlichen und liebenswürdigen Eigenschaften eine unbestrittene Tapferkeit verbindet, die selbst dem wilden Apachen Hochachtung einflösst. Ich glaube nicht dass sich bei irgend einem anderen noch erhaltenen Stamme der Charakter der amerikanischen Urbevölkerung auf eine vortheilhaftere Weise darstellt." Julius Fröbel, Aus Amerika, II, 448, 449.

Emory found them "surpassing many of the Christian nations in agriculture, little behind them in the useful arts, and immeasurably before them in honesty and virtue."

" The heathen Indians received us with jubilee, giving of their provision to the soldiers, and we counted two hundred persons, who were gentle and affable." Mange's Diary, from an extract translated by Buckingham Smith in Schoolcraft's Indian Tribes, III, 303.

" These Gila Pimas are gentle and comely." Ibid., 301, from Diary of Pedro Font.

[b] C. D. Poston, in report as special Indian commissioner, in Report of Commissioner of Indian Affairs 1864, 152, 1865.

Theft became a common crime with the increasing vagabondage arising from deprivation due to the whites. An extensive system of horse and cattle stealing grew up, whereby the Papagos stole in Sonora and sold to the Pimas, and the latter stole from one another and sold to the Papagos, who bought or stole to sell again in Mexico.

During the worst period of their demoralization they stole wheat from each other and sold it to buy whisky. It is to be remembered that by far the greater part of the tribe disapproved of such deeds, and the few that engaged in such enterprises had not the support of public opinion, which even in an Indian village is an autocratic power.

Thus intoxication was always regarded as reprehensible, though a distinction was made between the persons guilty of drinking the white man's whisky and those who followed the immemorial custom of getting drunk on native-brewed liquors during the saguaro harvest.

Laziness was condemned, and boys and girls were taught to spin and delve—how well may be judged from the fact that the tribe produced a large surplus crop year after year during the early period of American occupancy of the region and at the same time fought back the Apaches and aided the soldiers materially, while the Americans and Mexicans with all their soldiers and outside resources were driven into the shelter of the forts.

Cleanliness is learned by imitation. The floors of the houses are kept free of such objects as can be picked up with the hands and the yards are swept with bundles of arrow bushes or mesquite branches. Bathing was a daily practice.

Public opinion strongly condemned lying. Stinginess could not be more abhorred. The chiefs, especially, were expected to bestow liberally all gifts within their control. The present chief has had a canny sense of thrift and possesses a large bank account, which renders him much less popular than he might otherwise be.

FORMULAS OF POLITENESS

No conventional words of greeting were in use before the introduction of the Spanish and American forms. Tciârs tam wu′sahaĭn, "the god sends his regards," were the closing words of any speech. Hâ′iku-ult, "good-bye," was the usual response of the listeners. Sometimes in finishing a story the narrator exclaimed atoa′tûk, "anus," at which those present said the word expressing the degree of their relationship to the speaker, or if they were not related they said na′wotc, "friend." The same expressions are used in accepting a gift.

Hand shaking was unknown until introduced by the whites, though it is now universally practised.[a] It is said that the custom of kissing

---

[a] "Antonio and his son had tipped fingers and grunted in token of joy," wrote J. R. Browne, in describing the meeting of the chief and his son after a long separation. Adventures in the Apache Country, 84.

was confined to mothers and infants. Accurate information of the primitive custom can not now be obtained. Formerly, when long-separated friends met they expressed their joy in tears. The terms expressing their degrees of relationship or simply "friend" were sometimes used.

Guests were offered pinole upon arrival if it were not near meal-time. Pinole was easily prepared without cooking and stayed hunger. At meals guests were helped to food in a dish apart from the common bowl out of which the family ate.

INTERTRIBAL RELATIONS

ALLIANCES

The relations of the Pimas to their neighbors had a profound influence upon their social organization and general cultural development. They held possession of the best agricultural lands in their section of the Southwest, and were compelled to fight for the privilege. Their alliance with the Maricopas entailed a long and sanguinary struggle with the Yumas, which resulted in what Bancroft has termed "the almost total annihilation" of the latter tribe. From the Maricopas they received, however, efficient aid against their principal enemy, the Apaches. Thus the Pimas learned the advantages of confederation, and there is reason to believe that their culture, based on a thrifty system of agriculture, in time might have surpassed that of the Hohokam. The Yavapais were sometimes hostile, but do not appear to have been very formidable opponents.[a] In the Annals there are references to a few tribes of minor importance that it is almost impossible to identify from their Pima names, but they were always allied with either the Yumas or the Apaches. Aside from the Maricopas, the tribes friendly to the Pimas were their congeners, the Papagos and Kwahadk's and the Sobaipuris of the Santa Cruz and San Pedro valleys.

WARFARE

RAIDS

A better understanding of the division of labor prevailing among these people may be had by studying the conditions imposed upon them by the presence of the aggressive Apaches. The men may be forgiven for allowing the women to perform certain tasks in the cultivation of the crops that are usually considered the portion of the stronger sex when it is learned that this plan was necessary in order to maintain pickets constantly for long periods, and that an armed guard was the sole guaranty of safety to the villages. Every three

---

[a] Garcés relates in his Diary that the "Yabipais Tejua," [Yavapais] have "in some way remained enemies of the Pimas and Cocomaricopas Gileños." Coues', On the Trail of a Spanish Pioneer, II, 449.

or four days small parties of five or ten would come to steal live stock or to kill any individual that might have gone some little distance from the villages. Larger war parties came once or twice a month, though longer periods sometimes elapsed without a visit from the Apaches. Chief Antonio declares that the Apaches formerly lived farther away from the Pimas, and hence their raids were less frequent than they were during the middle portion of the last century. At all events the activity of the enemy became sufficient to cause the abandonment of the outlying villages east of the present agency of Sacaton and the concentration of the tribe into seven villages upon the Gila plain. On stormy winter nights, when the noise of the elements might afford cover for the approach of the enemy, sentinels were posted about the camps. These men were accustomed to build little shelters of brush and leave smoldering fires in them, then conceal themselves in the darkness near by and watch for marauders that might attempt to steal toward the light. In this way the main trails were guarded, and the coyote-like curs at the houses afforded additional security from surprise. They supposed that the Apaches always guarded their own camps.

When a chief "felt in his heart" that he would like to avenge his people for some particularly flagrant outrage, or that he desired the honors that reward the successful warrior, he went from settlement to settlement making an appeal for followers by repeating conventional speeches of magic character. The arrangements for the campaign were speedily made. The preparation of the roasted meal for pinole required much less time than the ceremonies necessary to secure the requisite amount of magic power to insure victory. The extra supplies of food were carried, before the introduction of the horse, by one or more women. These women were chosen from those who had recently lost kinsmen in battle and they were invariably accompanied by a male relative. At night the party was surrounded by pickets, who came in to report at intervals. During the evening a set speech was repeated by a man whose office it was to keep appropriate speeches in memory. These were arranged in order, as "first night," "second night," etc., and were "adapted" for the occasion, though based upon the supposed speeches of the gods at the time of the creation. The valor of the party was roused by the recital of deeds performed, but the primary object was to compel the attention of supernatural beings and secure magic power that would not only enable them to overcome but would also attack the magic power of the enemy. Then, of course, if the magic power of the enemy were defeated, the Pimas could easily overpower the Apaches.[a] After the speech the warriors sang the magic war songs, a'-atän nyuĭ, while the

<hr>

[a] "The Pimas, though not an aggressive, are a brave and warlike race. They are the dread of the Apache, who always avoids them." Sylvester Mowry in S. Ex. Doc. 11, pt. 1, 587, 35th Cong., 1st sess., 1858.

makai, or magician, swung an owl feather over them.   At the close of
the songs he foretold the number of the enemy that would be killed.
Thus they fared forth, carrying a little roasted meal and a small but
shapely basket bowl from which to eat it, provided with a little
tobacco for the ceremonial smokes that wafted their individual
prayers to the Sun god.   A portion of each band was armed with
bows and arrows; the former of the elastic mulberry wood from the
same mountains in which the enemy found refuge, the latter of the
straight-stemmed arrow bush, whose tufted tips waved in billowy
masses on the Pimerían lowlands.   When a comrade fell in battle his
bow was broken and his arrow shafts were snapped and left upon the
spot.   Oftentimes the body of a man killed in battle was burned,
though this method of disposal of the body was never employed at
the villages.   It may have been a survival from the time when the
Pimas lived on the Colorado or it may have been recently adopted
from the Maricopas, who habitually cremate their dead.   On the
homeward journey no fires were allowed for cooking or warmth, though
with due precautions they might be built on the outward trail.
Another portion of the war party was provided with circular shields
of rawhide and short but heavy clubs of mesquite and ironwood.
Their appeal to the God of War was expressed by the sun symbols
that decorated the shields, and the latter were kept swiftly rotating
upon the supple forearms of their bearers as the advance was made
for hand-to-hand conflict.   The frequent use of the figure, "like predatory animals or birds of prey," in the ceremonial speeches imbued
all with the spirit of agility and fierceness that manifested itself in the
leaps from side to side and the speed of their onward rush.   Crouching low, springing quickly with whirling shield that concealed the
body, in feather headdress and battle colors, they must have presented a terrifying spectacle.[a]   Their courage can not be questioned,
and in some conflicts, of which there is independent white testimony,
they killed several hundred warriors.   But these were rare occasions,
and their raids usually terminated with the loss of a man or two and
the destruction of an Apache camp, with perhaps a half dozen of the
enemy killed and a child taken prisoner.

The head chief, Antonio Azul, thus described to the author the
circumstances of his first campaign: With 30 friendly Apaches from
the San Xavier settlement, 200 Papagos, and about 500 Pimas he
went up the Gila a distance of about 50 miles and encountered the
enemy in the rough country around Riverside.   The Apaches tied
the bushes together to prevent the mounted warriors from getting

---

[a] "In battle the Indians are not quiet for a moment, but, with constantly bended knees, leap rapidly
from side to side, waving their shield and its long streamers, for the purpose of dazzling the eyes of
their adversaries.   Apaches are said to oil their joints before going to battle, in order to make them
supple."   Whipple, Ewbank, and Turner. Report upon the Indian Tribes, in Pacific Railroad Reports,
III, 30.

through, so that the Pimas fought on foot. Without the advantage of surprise the ardor of the latter soon cooled, and being of divided opinion as to the advisability of pursuit, they permitted the enemy to escape with a loss of but 6. Then this by no means inconsiderable body of warriors marched bravely home again. Further accounts of more sanguinary struggles are given in The Narrative, in the present paper, page 38.

Three Pima women known to Sika'ʻtcu went out on the mesa to gather cactus fruit. Another woman was asked to accompany them, but at first she refused to go because she had had a bad dream. After the others had started she set out to follow them and ran into a trap set for them at the hills south of the villages. The four captives were forced to walk naked before their enemies. Two were soon killed by the wayside. That night two Apaches were detailed to watch the other two women. These men relaxed their vigilance toward morning, whereupon the captives gathered all the bows and arrows of the party and threw them over the cliff. They also tried to strangle their captors and partially succeeded. They then made their escape. One of these brave women is yet living.

It was customary for the Pimas to attack the Apaches at night or at the earliest dawn. This required careful scouting during the preceding day in order to locate the position of the enemy, who were always at least equally alert and wary, without betraying their own presence.

On one of their raids toward the east a war party came upon a young Apache and his wife in the Sierra Tortilla. The man escaped, but the woman, named Hitalu'ĭ, was captured and brought to the villages, where she was questioned through Lâ'lâlĭ, an Apache woman who had been captured in childhood. The chief asked about the attack that had recently been made upon a party of Pimas at Ta-a'tû-kam. She replied, "I shall tell you the truth about that. I shall never take my life to my people again. I am here to my death." She was soon led to the open ground east of the Double buttes, where a death dance was held with the captive in the center of a group of old women, for it was not dangerous for them to touch the Apache. Outside the old women the other members of the community danced until at length the victim was killed by an old man who stepped upon her throat. The body was tied to a pole in an upright position and left as a warning to Apache prowlers.

These raids were not infrequent, but they could hope to reap no better reward for their efforts than revenge for past injuries, whereas the Apaches were spurred on to constantly renewed attacks for the sake of the plunder that they might secure. Thus the feral pauper preyed upon the sedentary toiler, but paid dearly in blood for his occasional prize of grain or live stock. The effect upon the two tribes of so strenuous a life was beginning to manifest itself in an interesting manner at the time of the intervention of the Americans. The Spaniards and Mexicans had shown their utter incapacity to cope with the Apaches, and their presence in Sonora was rather an aid to the enemy than otherwise. The Pimas were compelled to fight their own battles. In doing so they learned the advantage of concentrating their fields. They perfected a system of attack, appointed runners for bringing in assistance, and organized a fairly satisfactory method of defense. They never used smoke signals except to announce the victory of an incoming war party. They kept themselves constantly in fit condition by their campaigns, and even engaged in sham battles for the practice. These have been held within the last decade at the lower villages on the reservation. Their daily duties were ordered with reference to the possibility of attack. Their arts were modified by the perpetual menace. Their myths were developed and their religion tinged by the same stress. In short, the Pimas were building up a war cult that in time might have led them from the lethargic state in which the natural environment tended to fix them.

LUSTRATION

There was no law among the Pimas observed with greater strictness than that which required purification[a] and expiation for the deed that was at the same time the most lauded—the killing of an enemy. For sixteen days the warrior fasted in seclusion and observed meanwhile a number of tabus. This long period of retirement immediately after a battle greatly diminished the value of the Pimas as scouts and allies for the United States troops operating against the Apaches. The bravery of the Pimas was praised by all army officers having any experience with them, but Captain Bourke and others have complained of their unreliability, due solely to their rigid observance of this religious law.

Attended by an old man, the warrior who had to expiate the crime of blood guilt retired to the groves along the river bottom at some distance from the villages or wandered about the adjoining hills. During the period of sixteen days he was not allowed to touch his head with his fingers or his hair would turn white. If he touched his face it would become wrinkled. He kept a stick to scratch his head with, and at the end of every four days this stick was buried at the root and

---

[a] "All savages have to undergo certain ceremonies of lustration after returning from the war-path where any of the enemy have been killed. With the Apaches these are baths in the sweat-lodge, accompanied with singing and other rites. With the Pimas and Maricopas these ceremonies are more elaborate, and necessitate a seclusion from the rest of the tribe for many days, fasting, bathing, and singing. The Apache 'bunches' all his religious duties at these times, and defers his bathing until he gets home, but the Pima and Maricopa are more punctilious, and resort to the rites of religion the moment a single one, either of their own numbers or of the enemy, has been laid low." John G. Bourke, On the Border with Crook, New York, 1891, 203.

on the west side of a cat's claw tree and a new stick was made of greasewood, arrow bush, or any other convenient shrub. He then bathed in the river, no matter how cold the temperature. The feast of victory which his friends were observing in the meantime at the villages lasted eight days. At the end of that time, or when his period of retirement was half completed, the warrior might go to his home to get a fetish made from the hair of the Apache whom he had killed. The hair was wrapped in eagle down and tied with a cotton string and kept in a long medicine basket. He drank no water for the first two days and fasted for the first four. After that time he was supplied with pinole by his attendant, who also instructed him as to his future conduct, telling him that he must henceforth stand back until all others were served when partaking of food and drink. If he was a married man his wife was not allowed to eat salt during his retirement, else she would suffer from the owl disease which causes stiff limbs. The explanation offered for the observance of this law of lustration is that if it is not obeyed the warrior's limbs will become stiffened or paralyzed.

Dance in Celebration of Victory

Upon the return of a victorious war party the emotions of those who had remained at home in anxious waiting and those who had returned rejoicing were given vent in vigorous shouting and dancing. It is interesting to observe that the abandonment of these occasions was not wholly approved by the leaders, as is shown by the invariable formula that closed every war speech that was delivered while the party was on the campaign: "You may think this over, my relatives. The taking of life brings serious thoughts of the waste; the celebration of victory may become unpleasantly riotous." Throughout the ceremonies the women of the tribe play a prominent part, particularly in mourning for relatives if any have fallen victims to the attacks of the Apaches.

The dance was held on the low rounded hill near the Double buttes (see pl. XLI, a), or on a hill near the railway siding called Sacaton, or upon some alkali flat which the deposits of the rainy season leave as level and the sun bakes nearly as hard as a floor. Sometimes the dance was held on any open ground about the villages. Four basket drums were beaten in the center, while either four or ten singers formed a close circle around them. Within a larger circle numerous appointed dancers stamped and swayed their bodies, moving ever in a sinistral circuit. Sometimes the crowd danced within the circle of selected dancers, in which case they danced as individuals without holding hands; but usually they remained outside the circle. Outside the circle of spectators twenty men and two or more young women, according to the number of female relatives of those killed in battle kept running.   In addition to these forty horsemen also circled from left to right about the whole gathering.

SOPHIOLOGY

MYTHS

The traditions of the Pimas are kept by those who show special aptitude in remembering them and who gradually become recognized as the tribal historians.   To them the boys are regularly sent that they may listen for four nights to the narrative of how the world was made and peopled; whence the Pimas came and how they struggled with demons, monsters, and savage enemies.   These tales are not usually told in the presence of the women, and consequently they know only imperfect fragments of them.

The myths are not related in the summer because of the fear of being bitten by rattlesnakes, which of course hibernate.   No information was obtainable that the Pimas believe that the snakes then carry venom, nor why the snakes should bite those who disregard the tabu. The Pimas do not hesitate to kill rattlesnakes except in certain cases.

TCⱭ-ÛNNYIKITA,[a] THE CREATION MYTH

In the beginning there was nothing where now are earth, sun, moon, stars, and all that we see.   Ages long the darkness was gathering, until it formed a great mass in which developed the spirit of Earth Doctor, who, like the fluffy wisp of cotton that floats upon the wind, drifted to and fro without support or place to fix himself.   Conscious of his power, he determined to try to build an abiding place, so he took from his breast a little dust and flattened it into a cake. Then he thought within himself, "Come forth, some kind of plant," and there appeared the creosote bush.   Placing this in front of him, he saw it turn over as soon as his grasp upon it relaxed.   Advancing toward it, he again set it upright, and again it fell.   A third and yet a fourth time he placed it, and then it remained standing.   When the flat dust cake was still he danced upon it, singing:

> Earth Magician shapes this world.
>   Behold what he can do!
> Round and smooth he molds it.
>   Behold what he can do!
>
> Earth Magician makes the mountains.
>   Heed what he has to say!
> He it is that makes the mesas.
>   Heed what he has to say.

---

[a] "Smoke talk," from tcu-utc, smoke, and nyiâk, talk.   This myth is also called Hâ-âk Akita, " Hâ-âk Telling."

> Earth Magician shapes this world;
>> Earth Magician makes its mountains;
> Makes all larger, larger, larger.
> Into the earth the magician glances;
>> Into its mountains he may see.

Next Earth Doctor created some black insects, tcotcĭk tâtâny, which made black gum on the creosote bush. Then he made hiapitc, the termite,[a] which worked upon and increased the small beginning until it grew to the proportions of our present earth. As he sang and danced the wonderful world developed, and then he made a sky to cover it, that was shaped like the round house of the Pimas. But the earth shook and stretched so that it was unfit for habitation. So Earth Doctor made a gray spider, which he commanded to spin a web around the unconnected edges of earth and sky. When this was done the earth grew firm and solid.

All that we now see upon the land—water, mountains, trees, grass, and weeds—was made, and then he made a dish, poured water into it, and the water became ice. Taking this block of ice he threw it toward the north, where it fell at the place where earth and sky forever meet. At once the ice shone forth as the brilliant disk we now know as the sun. For a certain distance the sun rose into the sky and then fell back again. Earth Doctor took it and threw it toward the west, where earth and sky are sewn together, and again it rose and slid back into the ground. And in the south it behaved in a similar manner, but when he threw it to the east it rose higher and higher, until it reached the zenith, and then went on to sink in the west, and thus it has continued to do until this day. As the evening glow grew dim the darkness fell in inky blackness. So Earth Doctor poured more water into the dish and it became ice, and he sang:

> I have made the sun!
> I have made the sun!
> Hurling it high
>> In the four directions.
> To the east I threw it
>> To run its appointed course.

Then to the north he threw the ice until it dropped at the edge where the earth and sky are woven together. It became the shining circle which we call the moon. The moon rose in the sky, but soon fell back as the sun had done, so he threw it to the west, and then to the south, and finally to the east before it rose and pursued its course across the sky as it does to the present time.

---

[a] Termes flavipes Koll. It was formerly believed that if anyone ate food prepared from grain that was contained in anything upon which this insect lived that person's teeth would fall out.

Then he sang:

> I have made the moon!
> I have made the moon!
> Hurling it high
> In the four directions.
> To the east I threw it
> To run its appointed course.

Earth Doctor saw that while the moon was yet above the horizon there was sufficient light, but when it disappeared the darkness was intense, so he took some of the water in his mouth and blew it into the sky in a spray, which formed the stars, but the night was still dark. Then he took his magic crystal and, after breaking it, threw it also into the sky to form the larger stars, so the darkness was less intense. Then he sang:

> I have made the stars!
> I have made the stars!
> Above the earth I threw them.
> All things above I've made
> And placed them to illumine.

Next he took his walking stick, and placing ashes on the end he drew it across the sky to form the milky way.

When the earth was thus prepared for habitation, Earth Doctor created all manner of birds and creeping things. Next he formed images of clay, which he commanded to become animate human beings, and they obeyed him. For a time they increased and over-spread the earth until it became so populous that food became scarce and there was not sufficient water to supply their needs. Of sickness and death they knew nothing, and their numbers grew apace. Hungering, they began to kill one another and to eat human flesh. Earth Doctor pitied them in their extremity, but could devise no plan for relieving their distress, except to destroy all, and this he at length felt forced to do.

Earth Doctor said: "I shall unite earth and sky; the earth shall be as a female and the sky as a male, and from their union shall be born one who will be a helper to me. Let the sun be joined with the moon, also even as man is wedded to woman, and their offspring shall be a helper to me." Then he caught the hook of his staff into the sky and pulled it down, crushing to death the people and all other living things. Thrusting his stick through the earth, Earth Doctor went through the hole and came out alone on the other side. He called upon the sun and moon to come forth from the wreck of world and sky, and they obeyed him. But there was no sky for them to travel through, no stars nor milky way, so he created all these anew. Then he called for the offspring of earth and sky, but there was no response. Then he created a race of men, as he had done before; these were the Rsâsanatc.

Out in the west beneath the toahafs bush the moon gave birth to Coyote and then went down. Coyote grew apace, and when large and strong he came to the land where lived the Pima nation.

After a time the earth gave birth to one who was afterwards known as Itany and later as Siuuhû, Elder Brother. He came to Earth Doctor and spoke roughly to him, and Earth Doctor trembled before his power. The people increased in numbers, but Elder Brother shortened their lives, and they did not overrun the earth as they had done before. But this did not satisfy Elder Brother, who announced to Earth Doctor that he would destroy the latter's people, and this is how he accomplished the second destruction of the world:

Elder Brother created a handsome youth, whom he directed to go among the Pimas, where he should wed whomsoever he wished.

He must live with her until his first child was born, then leave her and go to another, and so on until his purpose was accomplished. His first wife gave birth to a child four months after marriage and conception. The youth then went and took a second wife, to whom a child was born in less time than the first. The period was yet shorter in the case of the third wife, and with her successors it grew shorter still, until at last the child was born from the young man at the time of the marriage. This was the child that caused the flood which destroyed the people and fulfilled the plans of Elder Brother. Several years were necessary to accomplish these things, and during this time the people were amazed and frightened at the signs of Elder Brother's power and at the deeds of his agent. At the time of the commencement of these strange events Elder Brother began to make a jar or olla of some substance, either bush or gum. When this should be finished the flood would come. How? This is the way in which it came: The handsome young man, whom Elder Brother sent about among the people to marry and beget children in so short a period of time, came at last to the home of Vakolo Makai, South Doctor, who lived somewhere in the south, and who had power similar to that of Elder Brother. South Doctor was noted for his knowledge of all things and his skill in reading signs. He declared that he would put an end to Elder Brother's schemes. One day South Doctor asked his beautiful young daughter why she cried all the time. She replied that she was afraid of the handsome young man who went about marrying the young women and begetting sons and daughters. Her father told her that it was her duty to marry the young man in order that a divine plan might be accomplished. But she continued crying, so her father told her to fetch some of the topmost thorns of a cholla cactus. When she had obeyed him he placed the thorns upon her, telling her not to be afraid of the young man, but that when he came she should take good care of his bow, arrows, shield, war club, spear, or any other weapon he might bring. At this the maiden dried her tears and awaited with pleasure the bridegroom's coming. When he came she took his bow and arrows and carefully put them in a safe place. After exchanging good wishes for health and happiness, they went to the dwelling prepared for them. Soon the screams of a child aroused old South Doctor and his wife, who came running, desirous of seeing their grandchild. The old woman took up the babe and tried to present it to her daughter, but she refused to accept it, saying, "I am not the mother. He gave birth to the child. Give it to him." So the young man took the child away and returned to Elder Brother, but as he was very much ashamed of himself, he did not bring the baby, but left it by the wayside. Elder Brother knew what was happening, for he was finishing his olla. As the youth approached he asked, "How does it happen that you come alone and do not bring the young child that is born of you? Go bring it hither, and we will take care of it. We have been outwitted and our plan defeated, but that is the best we can do." The young man went after the child, the screams of which shook the earth and could be heard for a great distance. Earth Doctor then called his people together and told them there would be a great flood. After describing the calamity that would befall them, he sang:

> Weep, my unfortunate people!
> All this you will see take place.
> Weep, my unfortunate people!
> For the waters will overwhelm the land.
> Weep, my unhappy relatives!
> You will learn all.
> Weep, my unfortunate relatives!
> You will learn all.
> The waters will overwhelm the mountains.

He thrust his staff into the ground, and with it bored a hole quite through to the other side of the earth. Some of the people went into the hole, while others appealed to Elder Brother. Their appeals were not heeded, but Coyote asked his assistance, and he was told to find a big log and sit upon it. This would carry him safely on the surface of the water along with the driftwood. Elder Brother got into his olla and closed the opening by which he entered, singing in the meantime:

> Black house! Black house! Hold me safely in;
> Black house! Black house! Hold me safely in,
> As I journey to and fro, to and fro.

As he was borne along by the flood he sang:

> Running water, running water, herein resounding,
> As on the clouds I am carried to the sky.
> Running water, running water, herein roaring,
> As on the clouds I am carried to the sky.

When he finally emerged from the olla he sang:

> Here I come forth! Here I come forth!
> With magic powers I emerge.
> Here I come forth! Here I come forth!
> With magic powers I emerge.
>
> I stand alone! Alone!
> Who will accompany me?
> My staff and my crystal
> They shall bide with me.

The young man went to the place where he had left the child and found that its tears were welling up in a great torrent that cut a gorge before it. He bent over the child to take it up, but at that moment they both became birds and flew above the earth over which the floods were spreading. It is said that five birds in all were saved from all those that had been previously known. These were Kolivĭtcûkam' Hikĭvĭk (flicker), Vĭpisimal, Kisŏpĭ, and Nyuĭ (vulture). They clung by their beaks to the sky to keep themselves above the waters, but the tail of the flicker was washed by the waves, and that is why it is stiff to this day. Finally, as they were threatened with destruction, the god Vikârskam took pity on them and gave them power to make "nests of down" from their own breasts which floated on the surface of the waters and so enabled them to survive the flood. If anyone harms the little Vĭpisimal to this day the flood may come again. Accidental injuries to the bird must be atoned for; if it be killed, its tail feathers must be kept for a time to avert disaster; if it is found lying dead, it must be buried and appropriate gifts must be placed upon its grave.

When the child had been taken from them, South Doctor called the people to him and announced that a flood was coming to destroy the earth and all things thereon. Then he sang:

> The waters dissolve the land.
> The waters dissolve the land.
> The mighty magician tests his strength.
> The waters dissolve the mountain.
> The waters dissolve the mountain.
> Nasi foresees what is coming.

Some of the people came to him and were saved from the flood by passing through to the other side of the earth by means of the hole which he had made with his cane. He told the others to go with him to Earth Doctor and hear what he might say to them. Earth Doctor told them that they were too late in coming, that he had already sent all that he could save to the other side of the earth. However, there was yet hope for them if they would climb to the summit of the Crooked mountain. He gave power to South Doctor and directed him to aid the people to the extent of his ability, so the

latter conducted the people to the top of the Crooked mountain,
and as they went away Earth Doctor sang:

> Haiya! Haiya! Flood! Flood! Hai-iya!
> See the doom awaiting them!
> Haiya! Haiya! Flood! Flood! Hai-iya!
> Here are my doomed people before me.

As the flood rose toward the top of the mountain, South Doctor
sang a song which caused the mountain itself to rise higher and
ever higher above the waters which raced toward them as if on the
level plain. These are the words that lifted the mountain upward:

> On the Crooked mountain I am standing,
> Trying to disperse the waters.
> On the Crooked mountain I am standing,
> Trying to disperse the waters.

When he ceased singing he traced a line around the mountain and
this marked the limit of the flood for a time, but it soon rose again
and threatened to overflow the summit. Again South Doctor sang:

> On the Crooked mountain top I'm standing,
> Trying to disperse the waters.
> On the Crooked mountain top I'm standing,
> Trying to disperse the waters.

Four times he sang and raised the mountain above the rising waters
and then declared that he could do so no more, for his power was
exhausted. He could do but one more thing for them, and holding
his magic crystal in his left hand he sang:

> Powerless! Powerless!
> Powerless is my magic crystal!
> Powerless! Powerless!
> I shall become as stone.

Then he smote with his right hand and the thunder peal rang in all
directions. He threw his staff into the water and it cracked with a
loud noise. Turning, he saw a dog near him, and this animal he
sent to see how high the tide had risen. The dog turned toward the
people and said, "It is very near the top." When the anxious
watchers heard the voice they were transfixed in stone; and there
to this day we see them as they were gathered in groups, some of the
men talking, some of the women cooking, and some crying.[a]

---

[a] Pedro Font has given the following version of this myth in his Diary, pages 23 to 24a of original
manuscript: "He further said that after the old man, there came to that land a man called El Bebedor
(the Drinker), who became incensed with the people dwelling there and sent so much water that it
covered all the land. He then set out for a mountain ridge, which may be seen from that place, called
the Ridge of Foam, whither he brought with him a little dog and a coyote. This ridge is called the
Ridge of Foam, because at its summit, which ends gradually and. accessible after the fashion of the edge
of a bastion, may be descried near the very top a white crest like a cliff, which follows horizontally
along the ridge for a good space. The Indians say that this is a mark of the foam of the waters which
reached that height. The Bebedor remained above and left the dog below, so that he might warn him
when the waters reached that height. When the waters rose to the crest of foam, the beast warned
the Bebedor (for in those days animals could speak) and the latter raised him up from below. A few

Coyote was carried southward by the drifting log to the place where all the driftwood of the flood was collected. To this day the place is referred to as Driftwood mountain, though its exact location is not known. Coyote came out of the drift after the water had fallen.

Earth Doctor escaped destruction by inclosing himself in his reed staff, which floated upon the surface of the water. We do not know what adventures befell him, but suppose that his staff came to rest somewhere in the east, as he is next heard from in that quarter.

Elder Brother was rolled along on the ground under the waters in his olla and finally came to rest beyond Sonoita, near the mouth of the Colorado river. The olla, now called Black mountain, may be seen there to this day. It is black because the gum from which the vessel was made was of that color. After the waters disappeared Elder Brother came out and went about until he had visited nearly all parts of the land. At length he met Coyote and Earth Doctor. Each claimed to have been the first to appear after the flood, but finally Elder Brother was admitted to have been the first, and he became the ruler of the world, and is accepted as such by many to this day. Elder Brother on becoming the chief ruler told his subordinates to search for the center of the land, which is known as hĭk, navel. He sent Earth Doctor to the east and Coyote to the west. The latter returned first, and a long time afterwards Earth Doctor came in. They all went some distance east and again the messengers were sent out—Coyote east and Earth Doctor west. This time Earth Doctor returned first, so they all journeyed yet farther east before sending out the messengers. Coyote was sent west this time and again returned first. Then all moved east a little farther, and

days later the Bebedor sent the Humming-bird (Sheparosas) and the coyote to bring him mud, and when it was brought he made from it various men, some of whom turned out good and others bad. These men spread over the land up and down the river. Not long afterwards he sent some of his men to see if those who dwelt up the stream could speak. They set forth and shortly returned, saying that although they spoke, they could not understand what they said. At this the Bebedor was greatly incensed, namely, that those men should speak without having received his permission. Thereupon he sent other men downstream to look after those who were there. They returned, saying that they had been well received and that the people there spoke another language, which, however, they had been able to understand. Then the Bebedor told them that the men who dwelt downstream were the good men, who extended as far as the Opas, with whom they were friendly; and that the others who dwelt upstream were the bad men and were the Apaches, their enemies. The Bebedor once grew wrathful with the people and slew many of them, converting them into Saguaros in that land. The Saguaros is a green trunk, aqueous, of fair height, of uniform circumference, and perfectly straight from its base to its top, with rows of thick thorns which extend along its whole length and usually with two or three branches of the same shape which look like arms. Once again did the Bebedor become wrathful against men and caused the sun to descend to burn them. Thus they were on the point of being destroyed when the men entreated him earnestly not to burn them. Then the Bebedor said he should not now burn them, and ordered the sun to ascend once more, but not to such a distance as before, saying that he left it lower down in order that he might burn them with it if they should again anger him. For this reason it is so hot in that land during the summer. At this point he added that he knew other stories which he could not relate because the time did not permit, and he agreed to relate them to us another day. But inasmuch as we made some fun of his stories, which he told quite seriously, we could not afterwards persuade him to tell us anything else; for he kept saying that he knew no more. All this story I have related in the phraseology you have doubtless noticed in order better to adapt it to the fashion in which the Indians explain it."

from that point both returned at the same time, so they knew they were at the middle of the land.

This is the song that Elder Brother sang when they reached the middle:

> Here I have come to the center of the earth;
>> Here I have come to the center of the earth.
> I see the central mountain;
>> I see the central mountain.

He then bent down and scratched his head. The lice that dropped became ants, which dried up that particular spot in a very short time, for the earth had been everywhere wet and muddy. Then they all sat down to create the various animals that had lived before the flood. Elder Brother sat facing the west, for, said he, "I came out upon the earth in the west and I am going to face that way." Coyote sat facing the south, for "I came out in the south and I am to face that way." Earth Doctor seated himself facing the east, for, said he, "I came out in the east and I am going to face that way." Each agreed not to look at what the others were making nor to tell what he was doing until all was finished, and then all that they had made should be showed at once. A moment later Elder Brother said he was ready and asked the others to show what they had made. So Coyote and Earth Doctor brought their work before him. Coyote had made all the web-footed animals, snakes, and birds. Earth Doctor had made creatures resembling human beings, but they were deformed—some having but one leg, others immense ears, some with imperforate bodies, others with flames of fire in their knees.[a]

Elder Brother told Coyote to throw the animals which he had created into the water. He told Earth Doctor to place his creatures in the west. Both obeyed. After throwing his beings into the west Earth Doctor sank into the earth, but while his body was yet halfway down Elder Brother jumped and tried to grasp it. He was not successful, and Earth Doctor disappeared. Elder Brother in trying to hold Earth Doctor got his hands covered with dirt and blood, like those of a man killing an animal. He shook his hands and the blood sprinkled over all the earth. That is what causes all kinds of sickness among us now, for the diseases were scattered over the land and in the water.

Elder Brother and Coyote were left in possession of the land. After the images which the former had made had been kept for four days, one of the Apache group (they were divided into equal groups) came to life and said, "It's very cold," and began to sway its body back and forth. Earth Doctor said, "Oh, I didn't think you would be the first to awake!" and he was so angry he took all the Apaches

---

[a] There is no generic name for these monsters. Earth Doctor is supposed to have created them thus in order that they might not become rivals to his underworld people for the possession of the earth.

up in his hand and threw them over the mountain.   That made them angry, and that is why they have always been so fierce.

These were the Indian people of which there were four tribes: The Wä-akï Âp,[a] the Apaches, the Maricopas, and, lastly, the Pimas, though they were given superior qualities—such as a knowledge of the seasons, the power to bring down rain from the sky, the ability to cure sickness, and the like.

These people occupied this country from that time forward and multiplied in numbers.   The Yumas and Maricopas were at first united, but the Maricopas left the Yumas and joined the Pimas, finally settling in the Salt River valley, where they formed permanent settlements.   They tried to build canals, but were not successful, on account of the hard rocks and soil.

The Maricopas asked Elder Brother for advice or assistance.   He caused the ground to become soft for a while, but it hardened again, and upon being appealed to a second time he said he could do no more for them, but told them to go and see Toa′koă-atam Âks, White-eater-old-woman, Elder Brother's sister, who also had great power.   She finished all the work in a single night, but Elder Brother refused to do anything more for the people.   From that time on he began to do mischief, such as marrying the young women and then deserting them for others.   The people began to be jealous of him and planned to destroy him.

For a time after the creation of the four tribes of men and the animals they were confined in a great house together.   Rattlesnake was there, and was known as Mä′ik Sol′atc, Soft Child.   The people liked to hear him rattle, and little rest or peace could he obtain because of their continual prodding and scratching.   Unable to endure it longer, he went at last to Elder Brother to ask help of him.   Elder Brother took pity upon him and pulled a hair from his own lip to cut in short pieces to serve as teeth for Soft Child.   "Now," said he, "if anyone bothers you again, bite him."   In the evening Tâ-âpi, Rabbit, came to Soft Child as he sat at the door and scratched him as he had so often done before.   Soft Child raised his head and bit his tormentor as Elder Brother had instructed him to do.   Feeling the bite, Rabbit scratched Soft Child again, and again was bitten; then he ran about telling that Soft Child was angry and had bitten him twice. Again he went to him and again he was bitten twice.   During the night his body swelled and the fever came upon him.   All through the dark hours he suffered and throughout the next day; often he called to those around him to prepare a place that might give him rest.   No bed that they could make brought any ease to his stricken frame.   He asked for sea sand that he might lie upon it and cool his

---

[a] " Go in Ap."   An unknown tribe that is believed by the Pimas to have lived somewhere in the northwest, perhaps the Hualapis [Walapai.]

fevered body. Coyote was sent to the sea to fetch the cooling sand, but it gave no relief. Rabbit asked for a shade of bushes that the cooling breeze might blow beneath them upon him, but this, too, failed to help him. The traveling shade likewise brought no relief. His agony increased until death came to give him peace.

For this first loss of life the people blamed Elder Brother, because he had given Soft Child the teeth that made him a menace to all who approached him. The disposal of Rabbit's body formed a serious problem to the tribes, for they feared the interference of Coyote. Said one, "If we bury him Coyote will surely dig him out." "If we hide him," said another, "Coyote will surely find him." "If we put him in a tree," said a third, "Coyote will surely climb up." Finally the Maricopas proposed that he be burned, and in order to get Coyote out of the way during the ceremony he was sent to Sun to get some fire, for he always kept the flame lighted in his house.[a]

As soon as Coyote had gone the people called upon Tcu-utak(ĭ) Moʌaɩt, Blue Fly, to help them, and this is how the first fire drill was made. Taking a stick like an arrow, he twirled it to and fro between his hands, the lower end resting in a socket at the margin of a flat stick that lay upon the ground. Soon smoke ascended, and the first fire began to glow. Gathering fuel, they proceeded to burn the corpse.

When Coyote left them he was suspicious of their intentions, and said to himself, "I think they have some purpose in sending me away." So he looked back frequently as he went along, and soon saw the smoke ascending. With excited heart he turned and ran back as fast as he could go. When he made his appearance the people formed a circle and tried to shut him away from the burning body. "Let me see my brother! Let me see with one eye!" he cried as he rolled upon the ground. No one would listen to him, so he ran round and round the circle seeking an opening. There was a weak spot in the cordon where two short men were standing, and he jumped over their heads, bit out the heart of the burning body, and ran away with it. The people pursued, but Coyote outstripped them. South of the Sierra Estrella Coyote stopped and laid the heart upon the an bush, but the people came up and he fled again. To this day that halting place is called Anûkam Tcukwoanyĭk, Place of the

---

[a] "When Matyavela died, Mustam-ho, by his direction, started in to cremate him. The Coyote wanted to eat the corpse. At that time there was no fire on earth. The Blue Fly put a star in the sky; 'Go over there and get me some of that fire,' he said to the Coyote. The Coyote was fooled, and scampered off to bring in the star. He didn't know that the Blue Fly had learned the art of rubbing sticks together and making fire. While he was gone the Blue Fly made a big fire and Matyavela was burnt up.

"The Coyote happened to look back; he saw the blaze, and knew that something was up. He came back on the full run. All the animals were present at the funeral; they saw the Coyote returning, and formed a ring round the fire to keep him away from the corpse.

"The Coyote ran round the ring until he came to the Badger, who was very short. The Coyote jumped over him, seized the heart of Matyavela, which was the only part not burnt up, and made off with it. He burnt his mouth in doing this, and it's black to this day." John G. Bourke, Notes on the Cosmogony and Theogony of the Mohave Indians of the Rio Colorado, Arizona, Journal of American Folk-Lore, II, 188.

Uprooted An Bush. Near Kihâtoakʿ he stopped again upon a mountain to eat the heart, but he saw that it was covered with ashes, so he shook it and the ashes fell and covered the mountain, so that it is white to this day, and is called Gray mountain. Again the people overtook Coyote, and he ran northward across the Gila, where he ate the heart, and as he did so the grease fell upon every stone of the mountain, which accounts for its appearance and the name it bears to this day—Mo'hatûk, Greasy mountain. From that place Coyote ran to live in the sea in the south.

Now the tribes of men began to learn how they should provide for themselves, how they might gather food, hunt, and till the soil. Mavit, Puma, and Ȓsu-u-û, Wolf, joined their fortures and went hunting together. One day Wolf said, "I wonder where is our brother, Coyote; suppose I call him." So he took the kidney of a deer and roasted it and the wind carried the appetizing odor toward the south. When Coyote smelled it he said, "Surely, these are my brothers, who wish me to return." So he ran to the place where Puma and Wolf were living. When he reached them he was in great distress, for when he ate food it fell from him as wheat falls from the broken sack. Finally, Puma and Wolf stitched his skin until it retained the food he ate. Then they all went in search of wives. Coyote found a woman and called to the others, who came to see her. She became the wife of Puma, but Coyote said he would take her home. On the way he fell and pretended to be in great pain. The woman was frightened and knew not what to do. Coyote said, "I shall not get well unless you strip off my clothing and your own and carry me on your back for a few yards. That is the way my brothers treated me when I was in this condition before." So she obeyed and made their clothing into a bundle, which she carried on her head, as is the Pima custom. Coyotem humeris sustulit, sed cum paucos modo passus ingressa esset, "Siste! Siste!" exclamavit Coyote, "Doleo; paulum me dimitte." Ubi quod poposcit fecerat, copulare potuit. Mulierem turpiter dum domum iebant Coyote egit. This was the cause of much trouble, for she belonged to a tribe that had great magic power. They tried to induce her to return, but she would not. Furthermore, Puma refused to restore her to her friends. Then the Ȓsarsûkatc Â-âtam,[a] magicians, revenged themselves by driving the deer, the antelope, and every animal that is swift of foot and soft of fur and useful to human kind into a cave in the Aloam or Yellow mountain, which lies south of the present Pimería and northeast of Baboquivari. This deprived the tribes of men of their chief support, and messengers were sent to see if some means could not be found by which the imprisoned animals could be liberated. One by one these agents failed to

---

[a] The mirage that distorts the early morning landscape in Pimería is called rsarsûkatc, and it is believed that it is the spirits of the ancient magicians returned to earth.

accomplish the task assigned to them.   Year after year they returned
without success.   At last Coyote was sent to liberate the inhabitants
of the cave, who exclaimed as they saw him coming, "Now, we have
a visitor who will do us harm."   They thought to appease his appe-
tite by offering a piece of meat in the hope that he would eat it and go
away.   When Coyote had roasted the meat in the fire and looked
about him, he saw the gate of the cave and this is what happened:
"Where shall I put this meat?   It is hot.   Where shall I put it?   It is
hot," he said, and then ran straight to the door of the cave.   Before
the occupants could recover from their alarm he threw open the door
and out swarmed the deer and other game animals as pour forth the
bees from a newly opened hive.

Coyote ran for his life and the people pursued him, but he escaped
and went to live in the water in the west.

When A-anhitŭpakĭ Si'vanʸ, Feather-breathing Si'vanʸ, was a boy
he was mischievous and troubled his grandmother.   He went to the
cave of the Winds and saw the bow.   He made one like it and showed
it to his fellows, but they handled it and so took away its power.   He
made several bows, but the people ruined them by looking at them
or handling them.   At last they ceased troubling him and he was able
to kill rabbits and give them away.

Seeing that he was a good shot, the people told him to take his stand
at the two hills and close the gap.   He went as directed, but instead
of shooting the deer as they were driven past he paid no attention to
them, but occupied himself in building a fence of brush from one hill
to the other.

Again they told him to perch in a tree above a game trail and watch
for anything that might pass under him.   He did so and saw the game
running, but did not shoot.

A third time they drove the animals toward him and instructed him
to shoot the pregnant ones, as they would be fat.   He took his place
and shot a pregnant woman instead of a doe.

The fourth time they told him to shoot an old one (meaning a deer
with large antlers), and he killed an old man.

Then he showed that he had magic power, for he was able to go out
and bring in deer without taking days of time like other hunters.   He
built a house (Va'-aki, now one of the ruins of Salt river), married, and
settled down.   Väntre was a thief, gambler, liar, and profligate who
came to the house of A-anhitŭpakĭ Si'vanʸ, who, knowing his character, did not wish to see him.   Väntre brought four reeds filled with
tobacco, lighted one, and smoked it.   A-anhitŭpakĭ Si'vanʸ would
not speak to him and Väntre finally went away.   This happened three
nights, but not a word was spoken until the fourth night, when
A-anhitŭpakĭ told Väntre he would be his friend if Väntre would stop
lying, stealing, and the like.   He would make the sticks called

ki^{n}tcs, and with them Väntre might win if he wished to gamble. He placed such magic power in the markings on the sticks that no one could win from Väntre. Elder Brother recognized the power in the sticks and told the people that they were powerless to win from Väntre. Elder Brother told the man at whose house Väntre gambled that if he would let his son and daughter work for him (Elder Brother), he would arrange it so that Väntre could not win from others. The man agreed. Elder Brother sent the son to a roosting place of large birds to get feathers. The boy brought the feathers to the house. The girl was told to singe the feathers, grind them into a powder, and mix them with some pinole.

The next day Väntre came to the same place to gamble. Elder Brother said to the young woman, "Go to the pool with your kiâhâ and ollas. Take the pinole and make it ready when Väntre goes there." She followed Elder Brother's directions and went to get the water. Väntre said to the man with whom he had been playing on previous days, "I am going to the pool to get a drink of water before we begin playing." The others told him to go into the house to get the drink, but he went off, saying that he wished to see the young woman. When he came to her he said he wanted her for his wife, but she replied that she would not make any promises unless he drank her pinole. So Väntre was glad to take the drink. The first swallow seemed sour or bitter, but he took a second, a third, and a fourth drink. The moment he took the fourth drink feathers began to appear upon his body; these grew out at once and he became a large eagle. The young woman took her basket, returned to the village, and told what had happened. The people then took their bows and arrows, went to the pool, and there found the eagle sitting on the bank. They surrounded him, but he flew away and found refuge in the mountains, whence he came from time to time to carry away men and women to his hiding place. As their numbers decreased the people cried out for help to Elder Brother, who said he would kill the eagle after four days. He told the people to watch a sharp-pointed mountain after his departure and if a cloud appeared at the left of the peak they would know that he had been killed; if the cloud appeared at the right they would know that he had done some great thing. Eagle was so large and strong that when he sat on the mountain top it broke beneath his weight. It used to be all flat and smooth, but it was his sitting on it that made the peaks and rough places. When arrows were shot at him he caught them in his hand. (This must be a true story, for there is a picture of him with the arrows in his hand, on the dollar. So the Americans must have known about him.)

When Eagle was away Earth Doctor climbed the cliffs to his house, singing as he ascended:

> Up the cliff, steep and smooth,
>> Up the cliff, steep and smooth,
> Up the cliff, steep and smooth,
>> Climbs Elder Brother.
> With his shining power,
>> Up the cliff, steep and smooth,
> Up the cliff, steep and smooth,
>> He climbs, step by step.

He then carried on the following conversation with Eagle's wife:
"Can this baby talk?"

"No; he doesn't say very much and doesn't seem to know anything; he's too small."

"Does Eagle ever sleep in the daytime?"

"No, not very often; but sometimes, if I sit down with him and scratch his head, he will go to sleep."

"Do that next time I come."

At that moment Eagle was again heard approaching with a roar that shook the mountain like a tree in the wind. He brought four living men, whom he threw from a distance upon the rock, where they lay groaning for a time before breathing their last. Eagle asked his wife if anybody had been there and she said no one was about. He declared that he smelled some one, but finally concluded that he had been mistaken. After he had eaten he lay down, and as she sang the following song and rubbed his head he quickly went to sleep:

> Haya yakahai yahai mo! Haya yakahai mo!
> I am sleepy, I am sleepy.
> Haya yakahai yahai mo! I am sleepy.

When Eagle returned, the baby tried to tell him what had happened, and his father inquired, "What made him say that? He never talked that way before; besides, I smell somebody. Some one must have been here."

"No, nobody; we have been here alone."

Then in the form of a fly Earth Doctor concealed himself among the dead bodies that were corded up like wood and sang:

> Himovali! Die fly! Himovali! Die fly!
> I shall sleep! I shall sleep!
> Himovali! Let die! I am drowsy.
> I will sleep! Buzz-z!

When he had gone to sleep she began to whistle. He awoke and said:

"What made you whistle like that?"

"Oh, nothing; I was just playing with the baby; that's all."

So he went to sleep again and again she whistled; he awoke again and asked:

"Why did you whistle?"

"Oh, I was just playing with the baby."

So the third time he went sound asleep, and she whistled softly, but he did not awake. Then she whistled louder and Elder Brother came out and resumed his natural form. He beat the head of Eagle until it was flat. He cut Eagle's throat and that of his son, sprinkled their blood upon the dead bodies, whereon they all regained their lives. He asked them where they belonged, and on finding where each lived he sent him home. When he came to the last bodies he found that they spoke a different tongue, so he sent them to a distant land, where they practised their peculiar customs. The Pimas suppose that these were the whites, who became white from lying under the others until decayed.[a]

Elder Brother then went home and told the people how to conduct themselves when they had killed an enemy, such, for example, as the Apaches. On his return he found the people singing and dancing. He arranged four periods, and each period contained four days. So to this day the man who kills an Apache must live sixteen days in the woods and subsist upon pinole.

While these events were occurring here the people about Baboquivari wished to have Elder Brother come to them.

At the time when Elder Brother transformed Väntre into an eagle strange things happened to the people of Casa Grande. There is a game called tâkal played by the women. One day the women were playing tâkal, and among them was the daughter of Si'al Tcu'-utak Si'van[y]. Suddenly a strange little green lizard dropped in front of her while she was standing among the other women. The earth about the spot became like the green part of the rainbow. They dug there and found some green stones (stcu'-uttŭk hâ'tai'), which became very useful for necklaces and ear pendants.

There were people living at some tanks on the east side of the mountains (Ta'-atûkam) north of Picacho, and among them was a man named Tarsnamkam, Meet the Sun. He saw the beautiful stones used at Casa Grande and wished to get some of them; but how was

---

[a] "Mr J. D. Walker, an old resident of the vicinity of Casa Grande, who has been to me personally an excellent friend and valuable informant, told me this tale:

"'The Gila Pimas claim to have been created on the banks of the river. After residing there for some time a great flood came that destroyed the tribe, with the exception of one man, called Ci-ho. He was of small stature and became the ancestor of the present Pimas. The tribe, beginning to grow in numbers, built the villages now in ruins and also spread to the north bank of the river. But there appeared a monstrous eagle, which, occasionally assuming the shape of an old woman, visited the pueblos and stole women and children, carrying them to his abode in an inaccessible cliff. On one occasion the eagle seized a girl with the intention of making of her his wife. Ci-ho thereupon went to the cliff, but found it impossible to climb. The girl, who was still alive, shouted down to him the way of making the ascent. When the eagle came back Ci-ho slew him with a sword, and thus liberated his people from the scourge.'" A. F. Bandelier, Papers Archeol. Inst., ser. IV, pt. II, 462–463.

he to do it? He made a fine green bird, stcʊ-ʊtûk o'-ofĭk, parrot, and sent it to Casa Grande, telling it to swallow all the green stones it could find about the houses. The parrot went to Casa Grande and was found one day by the daughter of Si'al Tcʊ'-ʊtak Si'vanʸ. The bird was kept several days, but it would not eat, so it was turned loose. It went about until it found a piece of turquoise, which it swallowed. The daughter of Si'al Tcʊ'-ʊtak Si'vanʸ saw this and told her father, who directed her to give the bird all the turquoises she could find in the house. The people gathered to see the bird that ate stones, but as soon as it had eaten until it was full to the mouth it flew away. Tarsnamkam was glad to see it come safely home. The parrot vomited the stones, which its owner gave to the people to use, and there were plenty for all. Si'al Tcʊ'-ʊtak Si'vanʸ was angry when he learned that the bird had been sent to steal all his turquoises. He sent the rain for four periods, or sixteen days, to destroy Tarsnamkam, but the latter also possessed magic power and was not injured. At the end of the sixteen days Tarsnamkam sent a man with a fine football (rso'nyikĭvol), directing him to give it to Si'al Tcʊ'-ʊtak Si'vanʸ's daughter, whose name was Pia Kŏnĭkam Of'(i). The messenger went near the woman's house as she was at work and kicked the ball so that it rolled close to her. She took it up and hid it under her dress and told the man there had been no ball there when he came up to inquire about it. He declared that it stopped close by her, but she again said no, she had seen no football. The man went off, but the young woman called to him to come and get his football. When he came back she searched for the ball, but it was not to be found. It had gone into her womb and become a child. When this child was born it was a strange-looking creature. The people wanted to destroy it, but the mother said it was her child and she wished to care for it.

The people wished to destroy the child, because it had long claws instead of fingers and toes; its teeth were long and sharp, like those of a dog. They gave it the name of Hâ-âk, meaning something dreadful or ferocious. This female child grew to maturity in three or four years' time. She ate anything she could get her hands on, either raw or cooked food. The people tried to kill her, because she killed and ate their children. She went to the mountain Ta'-atûkam and lived there for a while in a cave. Then she went to Baboquivari for a time and then to Poso Verde, where she was killed by Elder Brother. As Elder Brother and the people were preparing to overcome the magic power of Hâ-âk they sang together:

> Dazzling power has Elder Brother,
> Mastering the winds with song.
> Swiftly now we come together,
> Singing to gain control.

Kovakova, kovakova,
   Kovakova, kovakova.
Singing on the summit
   Of great Mo′hatûk mountain,
Anayokuna, anayokuna, hayokuna.
Sacred pipe of Tcu-unarsat,
   Sleep-inducing sacred pipe,
Anayokuna, anayokuna, hayokuna.
   Hâ-âk flees from her pursuers,
But her spring and mortar stay.
   Throw a great stone!
Throw a great stone! [a]
   The blue owl is brightest,
Throw a great stone!
   The blue owl is brightest,
Throw a great stone.

When he killed Hâ-âk a great feast was made, just as when Eagle was killed, and to this day the cave remains there where Hâ-âk was killed, and 2 or 3 miles distant is a stone inclosure, Hâ-âk moakkût, Place where Hâ-âk was killed. The people formerly placed offerings within the inclosure to bring them good luck.

Another version of the same story states that Vaktcuktcĭthâp, the mosquito hawk, wished to marry the virgin at Casa Blanca, who had many suitors. He went to the Sun, who gave him a many-colored ball, which he took to the woman Pia Kŏnĭkam Of′(i). When near her he kicked it as the Pimas do the kicking ball, so that it rolled near her. She placed it in the fold of her blanket and became pregnant.

After Hâ-âk was killed the people were invited to come and partake of the feast which had been cooked there. One old woman and her two grandsons were not invited to come. When the feast was over she told her grandsons to go and see if they could find any of Hâ-âk's blood, and if so to bring it to her. After the boys had brought the few drops of blood which they found among the rocks she put it into a dish and told them to look at it after four days. When they did so they found two eggs in the dish. On reporting this to their grandmother she told them to look again after four more days. When they looked they saw two little birds, at which their grandmother told them to look again at the end of four days. When they came to look they found two very beautiful birds. After four days the people came and tried to destroy the grandmother and the boys in order to get the birds. The old woman told her grandsons that after another four days the people would come and take their birds away. So they must take them at night to a distant land and set them free there. She said that when they returned they would find her dead, as the people would have killed her.

---

[a] The stone referred to is the one thrown against the cave walls by Hâ-âk when she was entrapped. In proof of the story we may see the stone there to the present day.

After the people had killed Hâ-âk they followed the tracks of the boys, who had gone toward the east with their parrots. The pursuers raised a cloud of dust as they went along, which betrayed their presence on the trail to the boys, who exclaimed, "What shall we do!" At length they set free the parrots, which flew up into the mountains, where they concealed themselves in the forest. Following their example, the boys hastened to the same place, where they successfully eluded the pursuers. After the people had abandoned the search the boys went back to their former home and found that their grandmother had been killed. She had left directions which they carried out. They gave the body proper burial in the sand. At the end of four-day periods she had told them to visit her grave until they saw a plant growing out of it; four days after it appeared they were to gather the leaves, and in time they would learn what was to be done with them. The boys obeyed her commands and obtained tobacco, which they learned to use through the instruction of Elder Brother.

After killing Hâ-âk Elder Brother made his home at Baboquivari for some time. Hearing of the fact that the boys were living alone at their old home, he visited them. He inquired about their welfare and seemed to be disposed to befriend them. Finding the tobacco leaves, he inquired if they had been used yet, and was assured that they had not been. Elder Brother then revealed the purpose for which the leaves had been intended. "These are to be rolled in corn husks and smoked," said he; "I will give you, also, earth flowers[a] to mix with the tobacco when you smoke if you desire to gain the favor of the women." He showed them how to collect the bark of the tree which induces sleep.[b] "Make this into a powder," said he, "and when you wish to overpower anyone just shake this before them." Then Elder Brother left the youths, who followed his instructions and found the love philter and the sleeping powder to be irresistible. But the people were incensed at their use of the charms and finally killed them.

Elder Brother continued to live in the cave at Baboquivari for some time. He went about the country from village to village seeking to do mischief. He sang the song of the menstrual period and accompanied it by reviling the family of the young girls. At last the people could endure his pranks no longer and drove him away. He went to Mo'hatûk mountain, north of the Gila, and the people there gathered to destroy him.

Elder Brother went into his house and the people came and clubbed him to death. They pounded his head until it was flat, then dragged

---

[a] *Tcuwut hiâsik*, a whitish lichen gathered by the Pimas and kept in little bags or in hollow reeds 3 or 4 inches long.

[b] *Kâ'sitakŭt* (" to make sleep "), said by the Papagos to stand on a mountain about 40 miles southwest of Poso Verde. So powerful is it supposed to be that those who go to gather the bark are overcome with sleep if they do not hasten when cutting it.

him into the woods and left him there. The news was spread about the country that he was dead, but the next day he reappeared among the people. They were afraid, but gathered together and killed him again. After carrying him to the woods they cut his flesh and scattered the pieces, pounded his bones into powder and cast it to the winds, but the next day at the same hour he was about among them again. Again they killed him, and this time his body was burned to ashes. Yet he was among them the next day as before. Then a great council was called and they discussed plans for getting rid of Elder Brother. Some declared that if they did not kill him the fourth time they would never kill him. So they called on Vulture, who had been saved with Elder Brother at the time of the flood, thinking that he must have magic power or he would not have survived the flood.

Vulture was a man who transformed himself into a bird with his own magic power and had gone through the openings in the sky and thus saved himself from destruction during the flood. After he came down from the sky he wandered about the country and finally built a va'-akĭ, magic house, the ruins of which yet remain, south of where Phoenix now stands, between the Gila and Salt rivers.

Vulture was living in this va'-akĭ when the people came to him with their complaints concerning Elder Brother. They asked if he could do anything to help them. Vulture said he had never used his magic power, but he would test it. He asked the people to come to his va'-akĭ and he would make the trial in their presence.

After the people had gathered in the house and the doors had been closed he brought on darkness with his magic power while it was yet daytime. The darkness was so heavy that the people could see nothing. A beam of light arose which grew stronger and stronger until during the second night of their sojourn in the house it became as brilliant as sunlight. There were four colors, four threads of light, that extended upward until they reached the sun. Vulture then ascended each thread in turn, telling the people that he must have magic power or he could not have done so. He told the people that in four days Elder Brother would fall dead. On the fourth night he reached the sun and remained there. All the people who were in the va'-akĭ saw these miracles performed.

Vulture told the sun to spit on the house of Elder Brother,[a] on the four pools of water at the va'-akĭ where Elder Brother kept his magic power, on his dwelling places so that heat might fall upon him and smother him. The sun did as he requested. Toward the end of the four days Elder Brother acted like a lunatic. The heat became so intense that the cool fountains became boiling water and he was finally suffocated.

---

[a] Said by Thin Leather to be in the Estrella mountains. Antonio thinks it is in Baboquivari mountain.

After his death his skeleton was exposed for a long time, until one day some boys were playing near where it lay. They heard a strange noise like thunder that shook the earth, though there were no clouds in the sky. The boys saw that Elder Brother was regaining life and power. He sat up and rocked back and forth like a drunken person. The boys ran and told their story to the people, who were perplexed and alarmed. They gathered together, bringing all their weapons, and finally surrounded Elder Brother, who was by this time in full possession of his power. As the people came about him with their bows and arrows in hand he began to sink down into the earth, and in spite of their outcry he disappeared before their eyes.

Elder Brother sank through the earth and found the people that Earth Doctor had assisted to reach that side in order to escape the flood. Elder Brother told the people there of his ill treatment and asked them to come through and fight with him and to take the land away from the Indians. After four months' preparation they set out upon their journey, first singing the following song:

> We go; we go; we go; we go.
> Happy, we leave our homes.
> We go; happily we go.
> We run; we run; we run; we run.
> Happy, we leave our land.
> With pleasure hence we hasten.

Elder Brother told Gopher (Tcu′ohŏ) to bore a hole for the people to come through. Gopher made a hole through the earth like a winding stair.

Coyote learned that these people were coming out in our country and he went about looking for the place of their emergence. He finally discovered them coming through like ants from their hills. Elder Brother told Coyote not to go near them until all had come forth. Coyote did not heed the caution, but went and looked down the hole and laughed, which caused the opening to close. Five gentes[a] had come out, and it is supposed that those that were shut in belonged to yet other gentes. Upon their emergence Elder Brother and his followers danced and sang as follows:

> Together we emerge with our rattles;
> Together we emerge with our rattles,
>   Bright-hued feathers in our headdresses.
>
> With our nyñnyĭrsa we went down;
> With our nyñnyĭrsa we went down,
>   Wearing Yokʋ feathers in our headdresses.
>
> This is the White Land, we arrive singing,
>   Headdresses waving in the breeze.
> We have come! We have come!
>   The land trembles with our dancing and singing.

---

[a] See p. 197.

> On these Black mountains all are singing,
>   Headdresses waving, headdresses waving.
> We all rejoice!   We all rejoice!
>   Singing, dancing, the mountains trembling.

About half of these people came out and followed Elder Brother's leadership until they had killed all his enemies and captured young and old that did not resist.

Elder Brother's greatest enemies were the people living in the large pueblos, the ruins of which yet remain scattered about the Gila and Salt river valleys. He and his supporters approached one of the easternmost of these pueblos on the Gila, which is now known as Casa Grande, singing:

> Yonder stands the doomed habitation.
>   About the pueblo runs its frightened chieftain
> In yellow garment with hand-print decoration.

They attacked and defeated the forces of Morning-Blue Si'van^y, and then moved about 18 miles northwestward to Santan, where they sang:

> In their house of adobe they are staying;
>   Their chief with magic power fears me.
> In their house of adobe we see their chief.

The chief of this extensive pueblo was Kia-atak Si'van^y. His forces were defeated and his pueblo overrun by Elder Brother's warriors, who next moved to the villages about 4 miles west of Santan, where they sang:

> Some will truly see;
> Some will truly see;
> Will see their house
> Behind the okatilla stockade.

The chief of this place was called Tcuf Baowo Si'van^y, and after he had been overcome the conquerors moved across the Gila toward the pueblo of Sweetwater, singing as they approached:

> There is the land of many beads.
>   There is the land of many beads.
> Some one comes forth.
>   He knows what will befall him.

The leader, Ta'-a Si'van^y, was easily defeated, whereon the victors moved upon the pueblo of Casa Blanca, singing:

> It will be difficult,
>   It will be difficult,
> To capture this pueblo
>   With its magic power.

They then attacked Tco'tcûk Tâ'tai Si'van^y, who was the most powerful of all the chiefs who ventured to oppose them.

He knew that they would defeat him, yet he struggled bravely to save his people and at the last to save himself. He first took some soot from his chimney, powdered it in the palm of his hand, blew it into the air, and darkness immediately fell so dense that Elder Brother's warriors could see nothing. Tco'tcŭk Tâ'tai Si'vanʸ then threw down his dwelling and made his way through the midst of his enemies. But the god of darkness dispelled the night and the escaping leader was seen in the distance. Elder Brother's warriors succeeded in getting ahead of him and were about to surround and kill him when he wiped the tears from his eyes and blew the drops among the men about him. This produced a mirage which concealed him from view. But the god of the mirage caused the veil to lift and again he was seen fleeing in the distance. Again Tco'tcŭk Tâ'tai Si'vanʸ was headed and in danger; but this time he took out his reed cigarette and blew puffs of smoke, which settled down upon his pursuers like a heavy fog through which he continued his flight. The god of the fog drove it into the sky and he was seen escaping. He now realized that he had but one more chance for his life. When the fog had formed clouds in the sky he took his belt and threw it upward and climbed up and laid himself against the clouds as a rainbow. It was impossible for the god of the rainbow unaided to bring him down; he made several unsuccessful attempts before he hit upon the expedient of making some spiders which he sent after the rainbow. They formed a web over the bow and brought it to the earth and destruction.

Elder Brother's warriors were so astonished at the prowess of Tco'tcŭk Tâ'tai Si'vanʸ that they thought he must have a strange heart, so they cut it open to see and, sure enough, they found within it a round green stone about the size of a bullet. The stone is kept to this day in a medicine basket which they captured with his grandson. Before he had undertaken his flight he had told the boy, Kâ'kânyĭp, to go with his basket and hide under a bush; after the grandfather should be killed the lad should come, touch him, and swallow the odor of the body and he would acquire the power of the Si'vanʸ. But a warrior named S hohany discovered the little Kâ'kânyĭp and after a time sold him to the Papago chief, Kâk Si'sivĕlĭkĭ, Two-Whirlwinds. The box is yet kept by the Papagos living 30 miles south of Gila Bend. If it is disturbed a severe storm is produced and cold weather prevails in Pima Land.

After capturing the pueblo at Sweetwater and destroying its chief the invaders moved against Vulture's pueblo, 6 miles west of where they fought the last battle.

They then sang:

> Child of the Raven! Child of the Raven!
> You of the dazzling power.
> See my magic power shining like the mirage.

Elder Brother told his army to capture Vulture alive. "How can we identify him? We do not know him," said they. Elder Brother told them to capture the warrior with white leggings; they were the distinguishing mark of Vulture. They obeyed and brought the defeated leader to Elder Brother, who scalped him; this accounts for the naked head of the vulture of to-day.

Moving on to Gila Crossing, Elder Brother and his party sang:

> I am the magician who with the sacred pipe
> Of Tcu-unarsat increase my magic power.
> I am the magician of the downy feathers.
>   With the soothing sacred pipe
> I bring sleep upon my enemy.

In the battle which ensued Tcu-unarsat Si'van^y was defeated, whereon the victors proceeded to Mesa; and before the pueblo of A'-an Hi'tûpakĭ Si'van^y they sang:

> The small Blue Eagle alights;
>   The small Blue Eagle alights,
> After emerging from the middle of the land.
>   To and fro he moves before me
> As my staff already has foretold.

After capturing this pueblo the conquerors moved against the Vĭ'-ĭki-ial Ma'kaɪ Sĭ'van^y near Tempe, singing:

> Look for him!   Look for him!
>   Poor distracted enemy; take him!
> Poor fear-stricken enemy; take him!

They then proceeded westward against other pueblos, which they destroyed, and afterwards returned to take possession of the Gila valley.

While the war raged along the Gila some of the inhabitants of the Salt River pueblos sought safety in flight toward the Colorado. They descended that stream to the Gulf of California, the east coast of which they followed for some distance, then turned eastward and finally northeastward, where they settled, and their descendants are the Rio Grande pueblo tribes of to-day.

Kâ'kânyĭp married Kold Ha-akam, the daughter of Kâk Si'sivĕlĭkĭ, and lived with his father-in-law in the Salt River valley near where Phoenix now stands. There his wife became pregnant and would eat nothing but green plants and game found in the mountains. So one day Kâ'kânyĭp went to the mountains to search for provisions for his wife. He killed a deer which it took him some time to dress. In the meantime the Apaches surrounded him. He fought bravely, but they succeeded in killing him. His father-in-law awaited his coming during the evening and through the night; then he called the people together and told them that his son-in-law had disappeared. All searched until his body was found. This they burned to ashes before

returning to their homes. After this event the people moved southward as far as Santa Rosa. There Kâ′kânyĭp's′son was born. He
was named Pat′ A′-anᴜkam, and under his mother's care became a
brave and noted man. While yet a boy he one day accompanied the
people on a hunting expedition. Some of the hunters asked him many
questions to learn if his mother thought about marrying them. He
told his mother about these inquiries, which caused her to weep bit-
terly. She told him how his father had been killed. After hearing
this sad story he went into the council house and told the people that
he wished to see the springs and other places where the Apaches
obtained drinking water, and also to see the trails they used. His
further adventures are related in the texts, page 353.

COYOTE

At the time of the destruction of the earth, Coyote was saved in the
manner already described, and he again appeared at the emergence of
the underworld Pimas that Elder Brother brought up to fight his own
battles. Then it was that Coyote looked down the opening to see the
humans struggling upward like a long line of ants ascending a tree, and
the sight provoked him to laughter, an act that caused the earth to
close up and prevent many people from reaching Pima Land. After
that Coyote disappeared again. Now we are to hear the story of his
subsequent life.

Coyote wandered about alone somewhere in the West after we last
heard of him, until one day he made two other coyotes from his image,
which he saw reflected from the water; one he called the elder brother
or Sandy Coyote, and the other younger brother or Yellow Coyote.
He told each to fetch a log. When they brought the logs he told them
to embark upon the sea and seek for land beyond it. They followed
his directions and sailed for days and nights across the water, the
younger always behind the other. One day the elder said:

"Younger brother, why are you always behind? Why don't you
come faster?"

"My log will not go any faster, that is why I am not with you,"
replied Yellow Coyote.

"How are you traveling, with your eyes wide open or with them
closed?"

"My eyes are closed," answered Yellow Coyote.

"Oh, that is why you are so slow. Look up and open your eyes and
your log will travel fast."

Yellow Coyote opened his eyes, but when he looked upon the water
the wind blew the foam into his face and blinded him. "I am blind,"
he cried.

Sandy Coyote stopped and tried to restore his sight, but without
success, finally concluding that they had better return to their father

Coyote for assistance. After they had returned to land and Coyote had restored the sight of Yellow Coyote the two brothers went to dwell in the land lying between the Pima country and the Mohave territory, near the mouth of the Grand Canyon. There they built a house with the doorway toward the east, as is the Pima custom. When it was finished Sandy Coyote said, "Go in and take your choice of sides. You need only half the house, and I will take the other half."

Yellow Coyote said, "You take your choice and I will take what is left."

And so they continued telling each other to go in and take the first choice until the house grew old and fell down. They built a second house, and again their dispute lasted until it fell. The same result was reached with the third house, but when the fourth was built the elder brother went in and chose the south side of the house, leaving the north side for the younger.

When they went to gather the screw bean the elder brother took the beans on the south side of the trees and the younger brother took those on the north side. One day the elder said to the younger, "How do the beans taste on that side of the tree."

"They are very good," replied the younger, but when they returned home in the evening he was taken sick.

"It is caused by the beans you ate," said Sandy Coyote. "The beans on the north side are not ripened by the sun as are those on the south side. To-morrow you shall see the difference." And so the next day they went again and found the screw beans sweeter on the south side of the trees.

Every evening they sat and split sticks with which to build bins, log cabin fashion, for the screw beans that they gathered. One day the elder brother said, "Let us play some kind of a game and bet our screw beans, and then we will not sleep too soon." So they made some ki^{n}tskût.[a] The younger lost all his screw beans that night and the next day the elder said, "We will not go for beans to-day." So that day the younger went hungry, and for many days thereafter, for the game of ki^{n}ts continued until the beans were rotten and not fit to eat. Then they wagered their arrows and other property. Sandy Coyote won the arrows, bow, sinew, and feathers belonging to Yellow Coyote and then went out and brought in all the large and fierce animals, but Yellow Coyote without a weapon could get nothing but the small creatures which were of little use to him.

In these straits Yellow Coyote sought the aid of Finish, who lived in the West. "I need your help, for I am losing a great deal," said he. Finish accompanied Yellow Coyote to the latter's home. When they reached the house Yellow Coyote went in first, but when the stranger tried to enter he was caught by sticks and held fast in the doorway.

---

a See p. 175.

He saw that the house was divided into two parts before him; even
the fireplace was divided, and no one said a word to indicate which
side he should enter. For a long time he was silent. Then he said:
"What kind of people are you that you do not speak to me? It is
the custom to ask a stranger 'Where are you from?' or, if they come
at night, 'Where were you when the sun went down?' Why are you
not thus courteous? Am I a thief, a murderer, or a ghost that makes
you speechless with fright?"

After the stranger had spoken, Mountain Lion got up, took his
tobacco, rolled and lighted a cigarette.

"Ha, you are here also," said the stranger, "and have said nothing
to me." But Mountain Lion put away his tobacco without offering
any to the other, who exclaimed: "Do you think I have no tobacco?
Don't you see that I am caught here in the door because I have so
much tobacco in my bundle that it will not go through?" Then
Yellow Coyote invited him to come to the south side of the house.

For many nights they played different games, but Yellow Coyote
continued to lose at all of them. At last he told Finish that he had
hit upon a game that he believed they could win with. So he called
Tco'kokoi, or Black Beetle, and told him that they wanted him to
run a football race with Vap'kai-ĭki, Duck. When Black Beetle
heard that the south division of the house wanted him to run a race
he said, "While you people were planning for this I had a dream. I
dreamed that I had in my right hand a green ball, which I threw or
kicked with my right foot toward the east. After I had kicked four
times I reached the place where the sun comes up. When I turned
around the darkness came behind me, but I kicked the ball four
times and reached the place where the sun goes down, and the darkness did not catch me."

All his party were glad to hear of Black Beetle's dream, saying that
it was a sign of good luck. So the next day Yellow Coyote said to
his brother, "We will draw a line here for the starting place. If
your man kicks his ball back over this line first he will be the winner
and if my man kicks his ball first over the line I shall be the winner."
They agreed that whoever won should have the privilege of marrying
at the end of four days.

Duck and Black Beetle started off and ran for miles, and after a
long time the latter came in, kicking his ball first over the line,
thus winning the race for Yellow Coyote. At the end of the four
days Sandy Coyote acted in bad faith, for he went away in the evening
and toward midnight returned with a wife whom he had taken among
the Va-aki Â-âp, who lived northwest of the Coyote home. Her name
was Itany Of'ĭ.[a] Yellow Coyote said, "I am going to build a fire
and see what kind of looking woman my elder brother's wife is."

---

[a] Itany is the name given a saltbush, Atriplex sp., the seed of which is eaten by the Pimas.

But the fire would not burn, and he got angry, exclaiming, "What shall I do? Here is that dirty syphilitic woman. I know her. I have passed her house many times, and I never thought she was to be my brother's wife. When she came in I smelled her breath, and the odor filled the house. What a lunatic my brother is to bring such a woman into the house." Then he covered the embers of the smoldering fire and laid down to sleep.

After four days Yellow Coyote went away in the evening toward the southeast and came home with a wife at midnight. She belonged to the people living on the Gila river supposed to be the ancestors of the Pimas, and her name was Ho-ony Of'ĭ,[a] Corn Woman. When they entered the house Sandy Coyote said, "I am going to build a fire and see what kind of looking woman my younger brother's wife is." But the fire would not burn, and he became angry, exclaiming, "What shall I do? Here is that dirty syphilitic woman. I know her. I have passed her house many times, and I never thought she was to be my brother's wife. When she came in I smelled her breath, and the odor filled the house. What a lunatic my brother is to bring such a woman into the house." Then he covered the embers of the fire and lay down to sleep.

After a time they began to play kiⁿts again, and Yellow Coyote lost as before. . After he had lost all his property he wagered his body and soul, which Sandy Coyote won. Then the latter killed him and ate his flesh. Yellow Coyote's wife was pregnant at that time and later gave birth to a boy. When this boy was about nine years old he went out one day and met Sandy Coyote, who was bringing in a deer on his shoulders. A piece of the deer fat fell, and the boy picked it up, concealing it in his armpit. Sandy Coyote asked him if he had seen anything of the fat, but the boy said he had not. Sandy Coyote searched him and found the fat, which vexed him so that he thought to treat the lad as he had his father. "Let us play kiⁿts together," said he. The boy told his mother about it, and she cautioned him not to gamble, as that was the cause of his father's death. For fear that he might do so she took him that night away toward the east. It was raining, but she carried fire with her in a small olla. She took up her residence in the Superstition mountains, where they lived upon herbs and grass seed. One day while the mother was away gathering seed the boy killed a bird with his little bow and arrows. When she returned he declared that he had killed a bird, but she would not believe that he had done it. But they buried the bird in the ashes and ate it. After that the boy killed many birds, rats, cottontails, and large hares. From time to time his mother made larger arrows and a heavier bow for him. One day he came running to his mother asking for a yet larger bow that he might kill a mule deer. She told

---

[a] There is a conflict of opinion as to which of these two women was married by Sandy Coyote.

him that only a grown man and not even he single handed could kill a mule deer. But he insisted, saying that he could kill it. So she made the large bow, and he went away with it. When he reached the place where the deer was and was creeping close upon it a soft whistle reached his ear. He looked around and saw Mountain Lion coming toward him. When Mountain Lion came up he said, "Wait here and I will kill the deer for you." He was as good as his word and brought the deer and also gave the boy his bow, arrows, quiver, and clothing, at the same time telling him not to let his mother know who had killed the deer, but to tell her that a man had given him the other things. The mother went with the boy and tried to find a track, but she could find nothing. After that the boy killed plenty of deer. One day he shot a deer which escaped with an arrow in him.

One day as Vulture was returning to his home near Maricopa he saw a dead deer with a strange arrow in it. He took both deer's meat and arrow home with him and showed it to the people who gathered according to their custom about him. He asked whose arrow it was, but no one could tell him. Sandy Coyote was in the company and recognized the arrow, but was too much ashamed to speak. Then Vulture said, "I think I know the arrow. I have heard of a boy living in the west who was ill treated, so that he and his mother were driven away to the mountains. I think they must have found a home somewhere in this country, for this is his arrow."

Sandy Coyote admitted that it was his son's [nephew's] arrow. "Give it to me, and I will some day go there and give it to him," he said. The next day Sandy Coyote searched for and found his brother's widow and her son. When he reached their house he went in and saw them eating a dish of meat. "Here, take your arrow," said he. "You shot a deer, which carried it away and your father's brother found it, brought it to his home, and inquired whose it was. At last they said it was yours, so I bring it to you." The boy said nothing, but took the arrow and put it away. After the boy and his mother were through eating they put away the remaining food without a word.

Sandy Coyote turned to leave, making an attempt to whistle to show his indifference to the coldness manifested toward him, but he only succeeded in shedding tears. "What is the matter with you that you cry so?" said the boy; "when I was younger and lived with you, you never gave me meat, but I did not cry."

A long time after that the woman said to her son, "I am going home to my own people, where I may get something to bring to you, and then you may go and play ki^{n}ts with Sandy Coyote, who killed your father; I think you are clever enough to beat him now." For many days he waited for his mother to return, and at last he went

after her. On the way he saw two attractive girls approaching him.
Turning aside, he lay down beside the trail and began to sing a
pleasing song just after the girls had passed him. Surprised at hearing a voice behind them, they looked back to see whence it came,
but could find no one. They saw nothing except a dead body that
was well advanced with decay. When they started on they heard
the singing again, but when they renewed the search they could find
no living person. The younger said, "It must be this decaying
corpse that is singing."

"Let us go," said the elder; but the younger refused, saying, "I
am going to take that dead body, for I can see it winking." So she
took it to her home and left it while she went to gather grass seed.
Soon the younger girl wanted to return to the house.

"You want to go back to that putrid corpse," said the elder;
"you crazy thing!"

"Well, I am going; and if you are going to stay here, stay as long
as you like." So the younger woman got ready to go home, but the
other also got ready and accompanied her. When they reached the
house the younger went in and found a handsome young man, to
whom she went without a word. The elder girl called her several
times, asking her to come and help cook some food. At last the
elder girl came and discovered the young man, and she also came to
him. But the younger said, "You scolded me for bringing him here;
now you may go out and leave him to me."

Finally the young man said, "Go out, both of you, and cook something for me to eat; I am hungry." So they both went to do as he
wished. The next day the husband of the two young women came
home, and was very angry at finding the young man there.

"Put up one of your wives," said he, "and we will have a game."

The young man said, "I have nothing to wager." But the husband replied, "Put up one of your wives." Then the young man
said, "You must put up your shirt." And it was the turn of the
husband to reply, "I have no shirt."

"Yes, you have."

"No, this is my skin," he answered, scratching his breast until
the blood came.

"It is not your skin; it is your shirt. If you do not believe me,
I will take it off you and then I shall win the wager from you." "I
agree," said the other. So the young man took the husband of the
women up by the hands and shook him, and he dropped dead out of
his skin.

At this time the young man's mother came, and they took the two
young women with them to their home. Soon he went to play ki[n]ts

with Sandy Coyote, taking with him beads, deerskins, and other things to wager. As he journeyed he sang:

> Vasohona, vasohona, âikinynamuginu yângai ku-ulĭ.
> Vasohona-a, vasohona.
> Over there, over there, you pay me my father old.
> Over there, over there.

As he went along he took some white stones, which he made to resemble white birds' eggs. These he put in a little nest which he made. When he reached his uncle's house he told Sandy Coyote that he had come to play kints with him. They got ready to play and put up their wagers, but the young man said, "It is about time the birds laid their eggs."

"No," said Sandy Coyote, "it will be two or three months from now before they begin to build their nests."

"As I came along I saw that the dove had already laid her eggs."

"No; you are lying to me."

Then the young man said, "Well, if I go and bring those eggs to you and show you that I was telling the truth I shall win our wager, if I do not bring them you shall win." So the young man went out and brought the eggs. After the wager had been paid they prepared for another game and another wager was laid. When they were ready the young man cut his toe nail and threw it into the west, where it hung, looking like the rim of the new moon.

"Look at the moon there in the west," said he.

"No; we are having a full moon now," said Sandy Coyote, "it is in the east; you are lying to me. How could the full moon be in the west in the evening?"

"Well, suppose you look. If you find any moon you shall pay me the wager, and if you do not then I shall pay you." So Sandy Coyote looked and saw the supposed moon and came back and said, "You win."

Again and again they played and again and again the young man won.

When they were ready to play kints Sandy Coyote said, "Sit there; it is your father's place."

But the young man answered, "No; I shall sit here and you may sit there. If you wish me to sit there you must carry me there. If you can carry me there you will win all we have wagered this game; if you can not, then I shall win."

So Sandy Coyote thought he could do it easily, and took hold of the young man to carry him to the other side, but he found the man so heavy that he could not move him. So Sandy Coyote lost again, and was compelled to admit that he had lost all that he had. The young man said he would like to have Sandy Coyote wager himself, if he had nothing else, and the other agreed to this.

When they were ready to throw the ki^{n}ts the young man said, "Your cane is looking at me very sharply; I would like to have it turned the other way."

Sandy Coyote replied, "No one can move it in any way. I can not, nor can you."

"Well, suppose I pull it out and turn it the other way, then I shall win the wager; and if I can not, then you shall win."

The other agreed; so he got up and moved the cane around as he wished, thus winning the final wager. Then the young man grasped Sandy Coyote by the hair and shook him until he dropped down dead. Taking all that he had won, the young man went home.

After a time his mother said she would like to go to where her people were living. After some preparation they started on their journey. At the end of the first day they camped. During the night the mother turned herself into a gray spider. The second day they went on again and camped in the evening. That night the elder wife turned herself into a black spider. At the end of the next day's journey they camped again, and that night the remaining wife turned herself into a yellow spider. The young man was left alone the next day, but he hoped to reach his mother's people, and so journeyed on until nightfall, when he camped. During the night he turned himself into a rough black lizard.

Even to this day Coyote is known as the wise one. It is dangerous to kill or harm him, for he will avenge himself by stealing or doing worse mischief. He knows well the house of the one who tries to injure him, no matter where the deed may have been performed. And yet he is not always unfriendly, for if he is heard to cry out as if jumping it is a warning that the Apaches are near and danger menaces.

ANOTHER VERSION OF THE CREATION MYTH[a]

before the earth was made nothing but darkness. It has been found only wind blows came rolling from one place to another, nothing but wind. at the time there was a man in the darkness alone. and has told that this man was wandering from point to point.

This has been for quite awhile. and no pleace for to rest on. So the man feel himself and know that he was a man by himself. and more of he found a push called (Shiquia) [b] and after he found this, and he call (Shiquia)

And also he made the earth. and so he call himself a God. now at the

---

[a] It seems worth while to present here the version of the cosmogonical myth which was written for the author by a young Pima who had learned to write English during the term of several years which he spent at a Government school. It illustrates the confusion existing in the minds of the younger generation; to some extent, also, the order of words in the Pima sentence, as well as the difficulties that must speedily beset the ethnological investigator as soon as the older people shall have gone.

[b] Rsukoi.

time this darkness was still on yet. so the first he made water. when
he had done this work, he took the water and throught up in Heaven.
which means stars. also he made the moon and mialk-way. to give
more light. he also made the sun. which is greater then what he made.
now in those day's there. at a ceatan day. He sitted himself to made
a first man out of a very hard mud. and there was another man name
(Sis Hia.) and (Gia- (via mack)

These two men begain too make all kinds of living creaters. and when
these two men made men out of hard mud the pleaced at a house to
see what will be, in a day or two.

now when these men pleaced at.   they want a little way to
see what will be done with they work. so the haerd sone one speacking
in that house. but could not understand. next there was another one
speacking in our Lounger and Sie Hia) said that he understand that
will be great wares to all nathion, not very long after this poeple at
Mesa trying to make a ditch. so they gather one day saking each other
of way to get water.

And one of these pearty said that there was man name Cea-gens who
knows much about ditch, so the send for, when this Cea-vens) came
to there camp. and told them that the must make a spath out of a
tree call (Oie a came) so they work on for quite a while.

while the working this man Cea-ven went away for some reason,
while he way. these poeple at mesa had a great trouble anong them-
self.

there where begain they war.

so they call a day, which these poeple to make Bows and arrows.
Sho-jiak,[a] (Caveid) [b]

and so these poeple start way down near Florince and then come to
Casa great Rounen, and so on to Casa Planco.

A mowan who's name (Stoke qui tham) his two son's one of them
name (Parhane) another (Par-lrad)

one day when the were at home. thire mother told about an eagle of
there owne. and one day these boy's wanted to go and see what there
mother been told them.   So the start for there Eagle.

when the were at the plaece. the youngest said to his brother. that
he may try first. to clime up for the birds. he tryd But could not
make. then the oldest one. got them. and bring them down. the
youngest brother took the oldest bird. and there begain to quirral
about these two birds, the oldest said to his brother that he might
have the youngest becouse he was the youngest.

and the oldest might have the oldest too.   But the youngest would
not let his oldest bird go. becouse he was the first one that he took.
and would not let his brother give what he got first.

---

a Club.   b Shield.

CHILDREN OF CLOUD

[Told by Inasa]

When the Hohokam dwelt on the Gila and tilled their farms about the Great Temple that we call Casa Grande there was chagrin among the young men of that people, for the prettiest woman would not receive their attentions. She would accept no man as her husband, but Cloud came out of the east and saw her and determined to marry her. The maiden was a skillful mat maker, and one day she fell asleep when fatigued at her labor. Then Cloud sailed through the skies above and one large rain drop fell upon her; immediately twin boys were born.[a]

Now all the men of the pueblo claimed to be the father of these children. After enduring their clamors for a long time the woman told her people to gather in a council circle. When they had come she placed the children within the circle and said, "If they go to anyone it will prove that he is their father." The babies crawled about within the circle but climbed the knees of no one of them. And so it was that the woman silenced them, saying, "I wish to hear no one of you say, 'these are my children,' for they are not."

When the boys had reached the age of 10 they noticed that their comrades had fathers and they inquired of their mother, "Who can we call father? Who can we run to as he returns from the hunt and from war and call to as do our playmates?"

And the mother answered: "In the morning look toward the east and you will see white Cloud standing vertically, towering heavenward; he is your father."[b]

"Can we visit our father?" they inquired.

"If you wish to see him, my children, you may go, but you must journey without stopping. You will first reach Wind, who is your father's elder brother, and behind him you will find your father."

They traveled for four days and came to the home of Wind. "Are you our father?" they inquired.

"No; I am your uncle. Your father lives in the next house; go on to him." They went to Cloud, but he drove them back, saying: "Go to your uncle and he will tell you something." Again the uncle sent them to the father, and four times they were turned away from the home of each before their father would acknowledge them.

---

[a] Bourke mentions this myth in his notes upon the Mohaves: "This Earth is a woman; the Sky is a man. The Earth was sterile and barren and nothing grew upon it; but by conjunction with the Sky (here he repeated almost the very same myth that the Apaches and Pimas have to the effect that the Earth was asleep and a drop of rain fell upon her, causing conception) two gods were born in the west, thousands of miles away from here." Journal of American Folk-Lore, II, 178.

[b] Among the Navahos Sun is the father of the twins who grow to manhood in four days and then set out to find their parent. See Washington Matthews, The Navajo Mythology, in American Antiquarian, V, 216, 1883.

"Show me that you are my children," said he; "if you are, you can do as I do." Then the younger sent the chain lightning with its noisy peal across the sky. The older sent the heat lightning with its distant diapason tones. "You are my children," exclaimed Cloud, "you have power like unto mine." As a further test he placed them in a house near by where a flood of rain had drowned the inmates. "If they are mortals," thought he, "they will be drowned like the others." Unharmed by the waters about them, the children demonstrated their power to survive, and Cloud then took them to his home, where they remained a long time.

When they longed to see their mother again, Cloud made a bow and some arrows different from any that they had ever known and gave to them. He told them that he would watch over them as they journeyed, and admonished them against speaking to anyone that they might meet on the way. As the boys were traveling toward the westward, they saw Raven coming toward them, but they remembered their father's injunction against speaking and turned aside so as not to meet him. They also turned aside to escape meeting Roadrunner, Hawk, and Eagle. Eagle said: "Let's scare those children." So he swooped down over their heads, causing the boys to cry from fright. "Oh, we just wanted to tease you, that's all; we don't mean to do you any harm," said Eagle.

Thus they journeyed on until they met Coyote. They tried to turn aside in order to avoid him, but he ran around and put himself in their way. Cloud saw their predicament and sent down thunder and lightning, and the boys by their magic power added to the bolts that flashed before the eyes of Coyote until he turned and fled.

It was on the mountain top that the boys were halted by Coyote, and one stood on each side of the trail at the moment when they were transformed into the largest mescal that was ever known. The place was near Tucson.

This is the reason why mescal yet grows on the mountains and why the thunder and lightning go from place to place—because the children did. This is why it rains when we go to gather mescal.[a]

---

[a] A similar version of this myth was related to Lieutenant Emory by the interpreter of the Chief Juan Antonio Llunas. This man said: "That in bygone days a woman of surpassing beauty resided in a green spot in the mountains near the place where we were encamped. All the men admired and paid court to her. She received the tributes of their devotion—grain, skins, etc.—but gave no love or other favor in return. Her virtue and her determination to remain unmarried were equally firm. There came a drouth which threatened the world with famine. In their distress the people applied to her, and she gave corn from her stock, and the supply seemed to be endless. Her goodness was unbounded. One day as she was lying asleep with her body exposed a drop of rain fell on her stomach, which produced conception. A son was the issue, who was the founder of a new race which built all these houses."

When he was asked if he believed the story he replied: "No; but most of the Pimos do. We know, in truth, nothing of their origin. It is all enveloped in mystery." W. H. Emory, Notes of a Military Reconnoissance, S. Ex. Doc. 41, 83, 30th Cong., first sess., 1848.

SKULL AND HIS MAGIC

Once there was a pretty girl who was unwilling to marry anyone. All the young men brought presents of game to her parents, but none found favor in the eyes of the critical maiden. At last to the surprise of neighbors and kinsmen she chose for her husband one who was a man by night and a skull by day. Then all laughed at the marriage, saying, "One man in this valley has a bone for a son-in-law."

One morning the crier of the village made this proclamation: "To-day we hunt deer in the mountains to the northward!" Skull went ahead of the party and hid in a defile in the mountains. When the hunters came driving the game before them the deer all fell dead at the sight of gruesome Skull; so the people had an abundance of venison without the trouble of trailing and killing. Thus it was that Skull rose in their regard and ridicule was no longer heaped upon him.

The next day had been appointed for the foot race in which the runners would kick the ball. Skull entered as one of the contestants, though his neighbors laughed and said: "How can one ball manage another?" But when he reached the goal a winner the last voice of contumely was silenced.

ORIGIN OF THE HORSE

Two brothers who lived apart from their kinsfolk were skillful deer hunters. Day by day they followed the deer and antelope, and when their chase was successful they carried the game home on their shoulders. This was heavy work, and at last the elder in the goodness of his heart took pity on his younger brother, saying: "You must help me to carry out my plans and I shall become transformed into something that will be useful to you. Shoot an arrow through my body from front to back and another from side to side; cut me transversely into four pieces and throw them into the water. In four days you may come back and see what has happened."

When the younger man, sorrowing and wondering, had obeyed he returned to find four strange animals which we now call horses, two males and two females, colored black, white, bay, and yellow or "buckskin." He was not frightened, for his brother had given him warning, and he had provided himself with a rope, which he tied around the neck of one of the horses, took a half hitch in its mouth, and rode it home, driving the others.

Thereafter horses multiplied in Pimería and in time all were provided with mounts, though had it not been for the sacrifice of the good brother we should never have had any.

26 ETH—08——18

Another version

At the time when the Rsârsûkatc Â-âtam confined the game animals in the cave at Aloam mountain[a] our people were living between Casa Grande and Tucson. Among them were two unhappy brothers, one blind and the other lame. One day as the elder was lamenting, crying, "Why am I lame?" and the other was saying, "Why am I blind?" they suddenly heard a peal of thunder and a voice said, "Take care! Take care!" At this they were frightened, and the younger opened his eyes to see and the elder sprang to his feet and walked.

Then they went to hunt for game, but the Rsârsûkatc Â-âtam had cleared the ranges of every living thing that could supply the Pimas with food, so that the brothers wandered over mountain and mesa without success until they were gaunt with hunger. Then the elder told his brother that he would die for the latter's sake and that after a time the younger brother should return to see what had been the result of his sacrifice. When the young man returned he found two horses, a male and a female.

NURSERY TALES

THE FIVE LITTLE ORPHANS AND THEIR AUNT

Five little Indians (not Pimas) were once left orphans because their parents had been killed by Apaches, and they got their aunt (their mother's younger sister) to come and live with them. She had no man, and it was very hard for her to take care of them. One day the children all went away to hunt, and they were met by five little rabbits (cottontails) in the mountains. The oldest of the rabbits came running to the children and crying, "Don't shoot me; I have something to tell you." So the children stood still and the rabbit said, "The Apaches have come to your place and burned down all the houses; you had better go home now." But the children surrounded the rabbit and killed it with an arrow and took it home.

When they reached home, they saw their aunt lying outside the ki in the shade, and something bloody near her. The oldest boy said, "Just look what auntie has been doing! She's been eating our paint and poisoned herself." But it was blood they saw coming out of her mouth, for the Apaches had come and killed her. When they came closer, they saw that a bunch of her hair had been cut off, and she looked so unnatural in death that they thought it was somebody else, and that their aunt had gone away. They had never seen a dead person before. So they said, "Let us dig a big hole and make a fire all day long and put hot stones in it, for she has gone to the mountains to

---

[a] Twenty-five miles southwest of Tucson.

get some mescal." So they did, and waited all day long till sunset, when she usually came, but she did not come. Then they said, "She has gone far and has a heavy load and is waiting for us to come and help her; let us go." But the oldest boy said, "No, she will come anyway, she always does, even if she has a heavy load." So they waited till night, and gave her up, and went into the house to sleep; but they kept their sandals on, as the Pimas always did, so they could start off quickly if there were danger.

In their sleep they heard her coming in her sandals, groaning and murmuring, so they all got up and went outdoors. They heard her go and look into the fire pit, and then come and stand in their midst. One said, "I think it is a ghost;" so they turned to the right and ran around the ki, and she followed them around and around. Finally they all went inside, still pursued, and the children stood on each side of the door and turned into stone. And the woman went away.

COYOTE AND THE QUAILS

Once Coyote was sleeping very soundly and a great number of quails came along and cut pieces of fat meat out of him; then they went on. Just as they were cooking the meat Coyote overtook them and said, "Oh, where did you get that nice fat meat? Give me some." They gave him some, and after he had eaten all he wanted he went on. When he had gone a little way, the quails called after him, "Coyote, you ate your own meat."

"What did you say?"

"Oh, nothing; we heard something calling behind the mountains."

Presently they called again, "Coyote, you ate your own meat."

"What?"

"Oh, nothing; we heard somebody pounding his grinding stone."

So Coyote went on; but finally he felt his loss, and then he knew what the quails meant. So he said he would eat them up, and turned around after them. The quails flew above ground, and Coyote ran under them. Finally the quails got tired, but Coyote did not, for he was angry and did not feel fatigue.

By and by they came to a hole, and one of the smartest quails picked a cholla cactus branch and pushed it into the hole, and they all ran in after it. Coyote dug out the hole, and when he came to the first quail he said, "Was it you that told me I ate my own meat?" "No," said the quail, so he let him go, and he flew away. The next one he asked the same question and received the same reply, and let him go; and so on till the last quail was gone, and he came to the cactus branch. This was so covered with feathers that it looked like a quail, and the Coyote asked it the same question. There was no answer, and Coyote said, "I know it was you, because you do not answer." So he bit into it very hard and it killed him.

THE WOMAN AND COYOTE

Once the river rose very high and spread over the land. An Indian woman was going along with tortillas in a basket on her head, and she waded in the water up to her waist.

Coyote was afraid of the water, so he was up in a cottonwood tree. When he saw the woman he said, "Oh, come to this tree and give me some of those nice tortillas."

"No," said the woman, "I can not give them to you; they are for somebody else."

"If you do not come here I will shoot you," said Coyote, for he was supposed to have a bow. So she came to the tree and said, "You must come down and get them, for I can not climb trees." Coyote came down as far as he dared, but he was afraid of the water. Then the woman said, "Just see how shallow it is, only up to my ankles." But she was standing on a big stump. Coyote looked and thought it was shallow, so he jumped down and was drowned. And the woman went on.

THE PIMA BOY AND THE APACHES

An old woman once lived with her grandson. The boy's father had been killed by the Apaches and his mother taken captive. They had treated the woman very badly and burned her arms with hot ashes and coals and made big scars. The boy had heard these stories about his mother.

The boy and the old woman had a very hard time getting along, and he used to go where certain persons were grinding corn and brush a few grains as they fell from the metate into his blanket and carry them home and the grandmother would make soup of them, and that was the way they lived. But by and by these people went away and when the boy went to get some corn there was none there and he had nothing to take home. The grandmother scolded him and told him to go back; and when he refused she whipped him. Then he said, "I know where my mother is, and I am going to her." The old woman said, "No, you must not; the Apaches will kill you." But he said, "I am going; my mother will not let them harm me." So he went. His grandmother trailed him to the mountains, and finally from the very highest peak she saw him going along toward the camp. She also saw his mother, her daughter-in-law, out alone gathering seeds. She recognized her at a distance by the shining of her scars. The old woman ran after the boy, but when she caught up with him he stepped aside and turned into a saguaro. Then after she had turned around and gone back he resumed his form and went on to his mother.

When she saw him she cried out, "Don't come near me, the Apaches will kill you; you know what they did to me, and they will kill you."

"What can I do?" he said, "What do the Apaches like?"

"They like little doves."

"Then I will turn into a little dove."

He did this and she carried him home in her basket. The Apaches asked, "What is that?" and she replied, "The young of a dove; so I brought it home." But when the Apaches left the room they could hear her talking to it, and when they came in she would be still. They could not understand the words but knew she was speaking her own language, so they said, "This thing belongs to her tribe. Let us kill it."

So they went in and the chief took it in one hand and smashed it hard with the other and the pieces came through between his fingers. These pieces then flew up out of the smoke hole and turned into a flock of hawks, and they fell upon the Apaches and beat them all to death with their wings.

Then they turned back into the boy again and he and his mother started home. But when they reached the place where the grandmother had turned back they could go no farther. They turned into saguaros, one on each side of the road.

THE BIRDS AND THE FLOOD

When the waters covered all the earth two birds were hanging onto the sky with their beaks. The larger was gray with a long tail and beak; the smaller was the tiny bird that builds its nest like an olla, with only a very small opening to get in. The larger one cried and cried, but the other just held on tight and said, "Don't cry. You see that I'm littler than you, but I'm very brave. I don't give up so easily as you do. I trust in God; He will take care of those in danger if they trust in Him." [a]

DEATH OF COYOTE

After the waters had gone down Elder Brother said to Coyote, "Don't touch that black bug, and do not eat the mesquite beans; it is dangerous to harm anything that came safe through the flood." So Coyote went on, but presently he came to the bug, and he stopped and ate it up. Then he went on to the mesquite beans and looked at them and said, "I will just taste one, and that will be all." But he stood there and ate and ate till they were all gone. And the beans swelled up in his stomach and killed him.

THE BLUEBIRD AND COYOTE

The bluebird was once a very ugly color. But there was a lake where no river flowed in or out, and the bird bathed in this four times every morning for four mornings. Every morning it sang:

> Ga'to setcu'anon ima rsoñga.
> Gunañursa,
> Wus'sikâ sivany tcutcunoña.

---

[a] This sentence is clearly inspired by Christian teachings.

(There's a blue water, it lies there.
I went in,
I am all blue.)

On the fourth morning it shed all its feathers and came out in its bare skin, but on the fifth morning it came out with blue feathers.

All this while Coyote had been watching the bird; he wanted to jump in and get it, but was afraid of the water. But on that morning he said, "How is this all your ugly color has come out of you, and now you are all blue and gay and beautiful? You are more beautiful than anything that flies in the air. I want to be blue, too." Coyote was at that time a bright green. "I only went in four times," said the bird; and it taught Coyote the song, and he went in four times, and the fifth time he came out as blue as the little bird.

That made him feel very proud, because he turned into a blue coyote. He was so proud that as he walked along he looked about on every side to see if anyone was noticing how fine and blue he was. He looked to see if his shadow was blue, too, and so he was not watching the road, and presently he ran into a stump so hard that it threw him down in the dirt and he became dust-colored all over. And to this day all coyotes are the color of dirt.

THE BOY AND THE BEAST

Once an old woman lived with her daughter, son-in-law, and grandson. They were following the trail of the Apaches. Whenever a Pima sees the track of an Apache he draws a ring around it with a stick, and then he can catch him sooner. But at night while they were asleep the Apaches came and grasped the man and woman by the hair and shook them out of their skins as one would shake corn out of a sack, and the old woman and the boy were left alone. They had to live on berries, but in one place a strange beast, big enough to swallow people, camped by the bushes. The grandmother told the boy not to go there, but he disobeyed her; he took some very sharp stones in his hands and went. As he came near the animal began to breathe and the boy just went inside of him and was swallowed all up. But with his sharp stones he cut the intestines of the beast so that he died. When the grandmother came to hunt for the boy he came out to meet her and said, "I have killed the animal."

"Oh, no; such a little boy as you are to kill such a dangerous beast!"

"But I was inside of him; just look at the stones I cut him with."

Then she went up softly and saw the holes and believed. And after that they moved down among the berries and had all they wanted to eat.

THE THIRSTY QUAILS

A quail had more than 20 children and with them she wandered over the whole country in search of water and could not find it. It was very hot and they were all crying, "Where can we get some water? Where can we get some water?" but for a long time they could find none. At last, away in the north, under a mesquite tree, they saw a pond of water, but it was very muddy and not fit to drink. But they had been wandering so many days and were so tired that they stopped in the shade, and by and by they went down one by one and drank the water, although it was so bad. But when they had all had enough it made them sick and they died.

THE NAUGHTY GRANDCHILDREN

An old woman had two bright grandchildren. She ground wheat and corn every morning to make porridge for them. One day as she put the olla on the fire outside the house, she told the children not to fight for fear they would upset the water. But they soon began quarreling, for they did not mind as well as they should, and so spilled the water, and the grandmother had to whip them. They became angry and said they were going away. She tried to make them understand why she had to whip them, but they would not listen and ran away. She ran after them, but could not catch up. She heard them whistling and followed the sound from place to place, until finally the oldest boy said, "I will turn into a saguaro, so I shall last forever, and bear fruit every summer." And the younger said, "Well, I will turn into a palo verde and stand there forever. These mountains are so bare and have nothing on them but rocks, so I will make them green." The old woman heard the cactus whistling and recognized the voice of her grandson; so she went up to it and tried to take it into her arms, and the thorns killed her.

And that is how the saguaro and palo verde came to be.

Abstracts of Myths

THE CREATION MYTH

Out of primeval darkness spirit of Earth Doctor developed. He first created creosote bush from dust. Next created black ants and termites; these caused the world to develop and Earth Doctor created the sky. Then made gray spider and commanded it to spin web connecting edges of earth and sky. Threw blocks of ice into the sky for sun and moon and spray of water for stars; large stars made from magic crystal, and milky way by walking stick dipped in ashes. All living things then created and human beings from images of clay. Earth became overpopulated, as there was no death yet,

so Earth Doctor pulled the sky down on the earth and crushed everything to death. But he came through a hole to the other side and
made a new creation. After a time Elder Brother, a rival to Earth
Doctor, arose and threatened to destroy the people again. This
accomplished, through the child of Elder Brother's agent and South
Doctor's daughter, who was the last of the youth's many wives.
Child was abandoned and its tears caused a flood that overwhelmed
the earth. Elder Brother was saved in his olla, Coyote on a log,
father and child by turning into birds, Earth Doctor by hiding in his
staff, and some people by going into a hole in the earth made by Earth
Doctor.

After the flood Elder Brother was the ruler and Earth Doctor and
Coyote his subordinates. When they found the middle of the land
they all took part in a new creation. First death caused by Rattlesnake biting Rabbit. Burning corpse stolen by Coyote; afterwards
he abused the woman and in retaliation the magicians concealed all
the useful animals in a cave; these released by Coyote.

Väntre supplied with magic gambling sticks by Feather-breathing
Si'van^y. Elder Brother interfered and caused Väntre to be turned
into an eagle. Eagle lived on mountain and preyed on the people
until killed by Elder Brother.

Tarsnamkam sent his parrot to steal turquoises at Casa Grande;
sent football to daughter of Si'van^y there; child born from this
became the monster Hâ-âk, who killed and ate children until destroyed
by Elder Brother. Tobacco plant grew from grave of old woman
who had stolen Hâ-âk's blood.

Elder Brother fell into disfavor with the people, who killed him
several times, but he always came to life again, until the magic power
of Vulture was invoked, who killed him through the agency of the
sun. Came to life once more, but sank through a hole to the underworld, where the survivors of the flood lived. Some of these came
above under his leadership and conquered the people there.

COYOTE

After closing up by his laughter the hole through which the underworld people were coming up, Coyote wandered to the west, and one day
made two other coyotes from his image in the water, Sandy Coyote
and Yellow Coyote. They sailed on logs across the water, but Yellow
became blind and they turned back and went to live near the Grand
Canyon. Gambled with each other and Sandy won; Yellow assisted
by Finish, who causes Duck and Black Beetle to run a race, in which
latter won for Yellow. Sandy finally won Yellow's body and soul
and killed him. Death finally avenged by his son, who won from
Sandy by stratagem.

CHILDREN OF CLOUD

Twin boys immediate result of marriage of Cloud and the beautiful mat maker, who had refused all suitors. Boys grow up, inquire for father, sent to the east to find him. Meet Wind, their uncle, and Cloud, their father. Tested by rain, thunder, and lightning, and accepted. After long visit start for home; encounter Raven, Hawk, Eagle, and Coyote; stand on each side of trail to avoid latter and are transformed into mescal.

SKULL AND HIS MAGIC

Man by night and Skull by day, he married maiden who had refused other suitors. Successful hunter because deer fell dead at sight of him. Winner in football race, thus silencing all ridicule.

ORIGIN OF THE HORSE

Two brothers burdened with heavy game. One conceives plan of relief and asks other to help him. Latter cuts body of former into four pieces and throws them into a lake; in four days returns and finds four horses.

ABSTRACTS OF NURSERY TALES

THE FIVE LITTLE ORPHANS AND THEIR AUNT

Parents killed by Apaches and unmarried aunt supported children. While hunting one day warned by cottontail rabbit that Apaches had been at their house. On return find aunt dead, but never having seen a corpse did not recognize her. With mescal kept fire against her return; at night frightened and pursued by her ghost until all turned to stone.

COYOTE AND THE QUAILS

Quails cut pieces of fat from Coyote as he slept; he awakened and overtook them in camp; asked for refreshment and was given of his own flesh; starting on he was taunted about it by the quails. Turned to pursue them and almost ran them down when they ran into a hole, the foremost carrying a cholla stem. Coyote asked each in turn if she were guilty; on denial, let them go; finally asked cholla, and receiving no reply, bit it hard and it killed him.

THE WOMAN AND COYOTE

Coyote in cottonwood tree asked woman wading in river to give him some of her tortillas; she refused, but on being threatened went up to tree and told him to jump down, as the water was shallow; but she was standing on a stump; when he jumped he was drowned in the deep water.

THE PIMA CAPTIVE AND HER SON

Boy whose mother captured by Apaches lived with his grand-mother. Quarreled with her and started to find his mother. Reaching her he turned into a dove, and she carried him home; Apaches heard her talking in her language to it, so the chief crushed it in his hand; pieces flew up through the smoke hole and turned into flock of hawks, who beat the Apaches to death. Mother and son started home, but turned into saguaros on the way.

COYOTE AND THE BLUEBIRD

Bird became blue by bathing in lake. Taught Coyote how, and he became blue, too. So proud that he gazed at himself as he went along and ran into a stump, fell into the dust, and became gray, as he is to-day.

THE BOY AND THE BEAST

Parents killed by Apaches and boy lived with grandmother. Frightened from berry bushes by terrible beast. Boy took some sharp stones and approached the beast, who swallowed him; cut his way out with the stones and thus killed the beast.

THE NAUGHTY GRANDCHILDREN

Quarreled with grandmother and ran away; when pursued the boy turned into a saguaro and the girl into a palo verde. Old woman grasped the cactus and it killed her.

RELIGION

DEITIES

The Pimas are far less given than their pueblo neighbors to the outward show of religion, such as is seen in the varied and frequent ceremonies of the Hopis and Zuñis. On the contrary, they appear to have no other than an occasional "rain dance," the navitco (see p. 326), and other ceremonies for the cure of disease. So far as could be ascertained in a comparatively brief sojourn among them their religion comprised a belief in the supernatural or magic power of animals, and especially in the omnipotence of the Sun. When in mourning, sick, or in need, the Pima addressed his prayers to the Sun in the morning: Tars! Oek i'up sǐnhâ-ǐkuǐ-ǐtûk iup ǐn'yǐmak kuv'kutûki! "Sun! Kindly help me through the day!" Or at nightfall his petition was raised: Stcoho'komam! Oek iup sǐnhâ'ǐkuǐ-ǐtûk iup ǐnyǐmak kukutûki! "Darkness! Kindly help me through the night!" The following form of supplication was often employed: Tars! Pa'pûtitcû sǐnhâ'ǐ-iku[ldi], contracted from Tars! Pa'pût itcok'si sǐnhâ'ǐkuǐt, "Sun! There, have mercy on me." When weary upon a journey, the

Sun was appealed to, and the first whiff of cigarette smoke was puffed toward him. The disk was not regarded as the "shield" or "head-dress," but as the veritable person of the god. He moves unceasingly around the flat earth, going beneath the western rim and passing across below to rise in the east.

It is Sun that, by means of magic power, kills those who die during the day. It is Night who kills those who die during the hours of darkness. Moon is Sun's wife, but she is not accredited with the power that is given to Darkness. Coyote is the child of Sun and Moon, and figures largely in the myths. His character, by its buffoonery and trickery, much resembles that of the culture heroes of some other tribes.

At the present time two deities are recognized, Tcu'wut Makai, Earth Magician (medicine-man or doctor), and Si'ûû, Elder Brother. They live in the east, dividing the control of the universe between them. The former governs the winds, the rains, etc.; sometimes he is called Tciors, Dios [Spanish]. Their names are pronounced when a person sneezes, or, he may simply exclaim "pity me," referring tacitly to one or the other of these two deities. There is a puzzling mingling of the old and the new in the myths, though it seems probable that the greater part of them have been of ancient origin with recent adaptation of Earth Doctor and Elder Brother from the Christian religion. Among the Pimas themselves opinion is divided as to whether the myths have been largely adopted from the Papagos.

At the solstitial point in the northeast lives Tcopiny Makai, Sinking Magician, who also has a "house" in the northwest. In the southeast lives Vakolif Makai, South Magician, who also occupies the corresponding point in the southwest. Along the Sun's path are the houses of the four minor gods:

Wupuki Makai, Lightning Magician, is the southernmost, and when the Sun is in his neighborhood we have lightning that is not accompanied by thunder.

Toahïm Makai, Thunder Magician, causes the thunders that are heard during the second month.

Huwult Makai, Wind Magician, produces the strong winds that blow so continuously in the spring.

Tâtrsaki Makai, Foam Magician, causes the river to rise and bear foam upon its waves in the month succeeding the month of wind.

It is difficult to determine the exact position of Coyote in the Pima pantheon, though he is classed with the leading deities in the myths, and his modern but degenerate descendants are regarded as very wise.

When a coyote comes by moonlight and sees the shadow of a chicken he can pounce upon the shadow and so bring down the bird within reach. He has been known to steal a baby from between its

sleeping parents, an informant declared. Considering the manner
in which the moon is supposed to have originated, it is strange that
it should contain the figure of a coyote. No explanation of this
belief was found.

The stars are living beings: Morning Star is the daughter of a
magician; her name is Su'mas Ho'-o, Visible Star. Polaris is the Not-
walking Star, but is otherwise not distinguished from his fellows.
Possibly this term has been adopted since the advent of the whites.
Once a mule with a pack load of flour was going along in the sky,
but he was fractious and not gentle, as is the horse. He bucked off
the load of flour, which was spilled all along the trail. A part of it
was eaten by Coyote, but some remains to form the Milky Way.

THE SOUL AND ITS DESTINY

The soul is in the center of the breast. It makes us breathe, but
it is not the breath. It is not known just what it is like, whether
it is white or any other color.

The views of the Pimas concerning the destiny of the soul varied
considerably. Some declared that at death the soul passed into
the body of an owl. Should an owl happen to be hooting at the time
of a death, it was believed that it was waiting for the soul. Referring
to the diet of the owl, dying persons sometimes said, "I am going
to eat rats." Owl feathers were always given to a dying person.
They were kept in a long rectangular box or basket of maguey leaf.
If the family had no owl feathers at hand, they sent to the medicine-
man, who always kept them. If possible, the feathers were taken
from a living bird when collected; the owl might then be set free
or killed. If the short downy feathers of the owl fell upon a person,
he would go blind. Even to-day the educated young people are
very chary about entering an abandoned building tenanted by an
owl.[a]

By some it is said that after death souls go to the land of the
dead in the east.[b] All souls go to Si'alĭk Rsân, Morning Base, or

[a] "Having been asked what information they possessed of their ancestors (*antepasados*), they told
me about the same things as (*lo mismo poco mas ó menos que*) the (Pimas [Maricopas?]) Gileños said
to the señor comandante, and Padre Font put in his diary, concerning the deluge and creation; and
added, that their origin was from near the sea in which an old woman created their progenitors; that
this old woman is still somewhere (*quien sabe en donde*), and that she it is who sends the corals that
come out of the sea; that when they die their ghost (*corazon*) goes to live toward the western sea;
that some, after they die, live like owls (*tecolótes*; and finally they said that they themselves do not
understand such things well, and that those who know it all are those who live in the sierra over
there beyond the Rio Colorado." Garcés' Diary in Coues, On the Trail of a Spanish Pioneer, I, 122.
"After death Mohaves become spirits; then they die again and become a kind of an owl; a second
time they turn into a different kind of an owl, and a third time into still another; fourthly, they become
water beetles; after that they turn into air.
" If anything is left of their bodies, the arms, the muscles of the upper arms become one kind of an
owl, and the heart another." J. G. Bourke, Journal of American Folk-Lore, II, 181.
[b] Compare the Navaho belief, as recorded by Matthews: "For is it not from the west that the snow
comes in the winter, the warm thawing breezes in the spring, and the soft rains in the summer to nour-

place where the sun rises. The East Land is separated from the
land of the living by the chasm called Tcu′wʊt Hi′ketany, Earth
Crack. When one of the writer's interpreters had gone to school at
Hampton, Va., her associates said that she had gone to the abode of
spirits. All is rejoicing and gladness in that other world. There
they will feast and dance, consequently when one dies his best clothing must be put on and his hair must be dressed with care, as is the
custom in preparing for an earthly ceremony. No idea of spiritual
reward or punishment for conduct in this life exists.

Again, the souls of the dead are supposed to hang about and perform unpleasant pranks with the living. They are liable to present
themselves before the living if they catch the right person alone at
night. The ghost never speaks at such times, nor may any but
medicine-men speak to them. If one be made sick by thus seeing
a ghost, he must have the medicine-man go to the grave of the
offending soul and tell it to be quiet, "and they always do as they
are bid." Old Kisatc, of Santan, thought that the soul continued
to reside in the body as that was "its house." During his youth
he had accompanied a medicine-man and a few friends to the grave
of a man who had been killed near Picacho, about 40 miles southeast of Sacaton. The medicine-man addressed the grave in a long
speech, in which he expressed the sorrow and regret of the relatives
and friends that the corpse should thus be buried so far from home.
Kisatc avers that the spirit within the grave replied to the speech by
saying that he did not stay there all the time, but that he occasionally went over to hang about the villages, and that he felt unhappy
in the state in which he found himself. Of course the medicine-men
claim to be in communication with the spirits of the departed as well
as with supernatural beings capable of imparting magic power.

DREAMS

Dreams are variously regarded as the result of evil doing, as a
natural and normal means of communication with the spirit world,
and as being caused by Darkness or Night. During the dream the
soul wanders away and passes through adventures as in the waking
hours. The young men never slept in the council ki for fear of bad
dreams.

To dream of the dead causes sickness in the dreamer and if he
dream of the dead for several nights in succession he will die. Dreams
are not consulted for information concerning future action except in

---

ish the corn in the valleys and the grass on the hills? Therefore it is that when we are in need we
pray to Estsanaltehi, the Goddess of the Sunset Land.

"But first man and first woman were angry because they were banished to the east, and before
they left they swore undying hatred and enmity to our people. And for this reason all evils come
from the east—smallpox and other diseases, war, and the white intruder." The Navajo Mythology,
in American Antiquarian, v, 224, 1883.

the case of the would-be medicine-man who may be called to his profession by means of persistent dreams. Since Night may cause one to dream as he wishes it is fair to presume that it is that god who oversees the destinies of the medicine-men.

Many years ago Kisatc, in either a swoon or trance, believed that he went far away to a place where a stranger gave him a magnificent bow and a set of beautiful arrows. On regaining consciousness he asked for the things that had been given him while he was away and became quite indignant when they assured him that he had not been out of their sight. To this day he believes that they deceived him.

SACRED PLACES

Hâhâtesumiehĭn or Hâhâtai s'maihĭsk, Stones Strike, is a large block of lava located in the eastern Santan hills (see pl. XLI, b). The largest pictograph ever seen by the writer in the Southwest is cut upon it and 2 or 3 tons of small angular stones foreign to the locality are piled before it. There are also many pictographs on the bowlders round about. This was probably a Hohokam shrine, though it is regarded with reverence by the Pimas, who still place offerings of beads, bits of cloth, and twigs of the creosote bush at the foot of the large pictograph. There is a tradition that a young man was lying asleep upon the flat rock and was seen by two young women who were passing along the opposite hillside. They tried to awaken him by tossing the pebbles which are yet to be seen. Pima maids thus awaken their lovers to the present day.

Hâ-âk Vâ-âk, Hâ-âk Lying, is a crude outline of a human figure situated about 5 miles north of Sacaton. It was made by scraping aside the small stones with which the mesa is there thickly strewn to form furrows about 50 cm. wide (fig. 102). The body furrow is 35 m. long and has a small heap of stones at the head, another at a distance of 11 m. from the first, and another at the junction of body and legs. The latter are 11 m. long and 1 m. apart. The arms curve outward from the head and terminate in small pyramids. In all the piles of stone, which have a temporary and modern appearance, are glass beads and rags, together with fresh creosote branches, showing that the place is yet visited. The beads are very old and much weathered. Beside the large figure is a smaller one that is 4.5 m. long, the body being 2.7. Hâ-âk is supposed to have slept one night at this place before reaching Hâ-âk Tcia Hâk, a cave in the Ta-atûkam mountains, where she remained for some time.

I'aksk', Place of Sacrifice, is a heap of stones on a knoll near Blackwater where it is probable that a Hohokam or Pima medicine-man has been buried.

Pat'anĭkäm, Place of the Bad One, is the name of a grave at Gila Crossing. It seems probable that the grave of some Hohokam medicine-man has been taken for that of the son of Kâkanyp.

There is another similarly inclosed but unnamed grave at Gila Crossing, also one between Sweetwater and Casa Blanca, and there are three at Blackwater. Such inclosures are called o'namûksk, meaning unknown. Beads are to be found strewn about all of them.

Ma'vĭt Vâ-âk, Puma Lying, or Tci'apatak, Place of the Mortar, is a heap of small stones (pl. XLI, c) between the Double buttes, 10 miles west of Sacaton. Stones are there piled over a shallow mortar in which beads have been placed and partly broken. Bunches of fresh creosote branches were mingled with the decaying fragments of arrow shafts at the time of the writer's visit, showing that while the shrine

FIG. 102. Hâ-âk altar.

is yet resorted to it is of considerable antiquity, for wood does not decay rapidly in that climate.

Evil spirits dwell in the Picacho and Estrella mountains, but this belief may be presumed to be an inheritance from the Apache period. The writer has not learned of any shrines being located in those ranges.

It is said that in the Santa Rosa mountains there was once a tightly covered medicine basket which was kept on a mountain top by a Papago medicine-man who carried offerings to it. All others were forbidden to touch it; but someone found it and when he lifted the cover all the winds of heaven rushed forth and blew away all the people thereabout.

Near the summit of one of the lava-formed Santan hills is a small cave in which the Hohokam placed sacrifices. A number of articles were discovered there a quarter of a century ago and sent to some eastern museum. Since that time the Pimas deposited the body of a child and some other things in the cave, which were secured by an Arizona collector in 1901. The cave is known as Va'rsa Vâ'-âk, Basket Lying, because it contained a basket such as the Pimas use for their medicine paraphernalia. It was discovered by two Pima warriors, who were serving their sixteen-day period of lustration for having killed Apaches. The basket contained sinew from the legs of deer, and sticks, which the finders assumed to be for the same purpose as those with which they were scratching their own heads at the time.

When a medicine-man dies his paraphernalia, if not transmitted to his descendants, may be placed in an olla and hidden under a heap of stones in the hills. He may also sacrifice a part of his stock in a similar way during his lifetime. The property of warriors is sometimes similarly cached.

Such places were formerly respected by the tribe, but they are now robbed with impunity to get "relics" to sell. A man at Pe-e'pûtciltk' informed the author's interpreter, José Lewis, of the location of one of these caches in the low hills south of Casa Blanca. We found that a number of concretions, crystals, shells, a bird carved from stone, and a war club had been deposited in an olla with a bowl turned over it, rendering it water-tight. The whole had been hidden under a heap of stones at the summit of a spur of the hill about 4 miles from the villages.

MEDICINE-MEN

There are three classes of medicine-men among the Pimas. Those who treat disease by pretended magic are known as Si'atcokam, Examining Physicians. As many women as men belong to this order, to which entrance is gained chiefly through heredity. This is the most powerful class in the community, though its members pay for their privileges at imminent risk. How great this risk is may be seen from the calendar records, page 38. The Si'atcokam were more numerous than the other classes. Those who have power over the crops, the weather, and the wars are called Makai, Magicians. Only one or two women were ever admitted to this order among the Pimas. There were usually about five Makai in each village. These two classes were the true rulers of the tribe, as their influence was much greater than that of the chiefs. Their combined strength was for years turned against the missionary, Rev. C. H. Cook, but their influence is now fast waning and several medicine-men have become avowed Christians. From these converts information was obtained that in all probability could not have otherwise been secured.

Yet another class of persons, including both men and women, and few in number, might be termed medicine-men. They are called Hai'-itcottam, Something given to drink. They are not highly esteemed, however skilled they may become in the use of roots and simple remedies, yet they are the true physicians of the Pimas. It may be that among the many empiric remedies which they employ some will be found to possess true therapeutic qualities.

The traditional history of the tribe tells of many families of medicine-men, and the profession was very generally handed down from father to son. Those receiving magic power in this manner were somewhat more highly regarded than others. A second method by which a person might secure power was by what might be termed a process of natural selection; anyone who recovered from a rattlesnake bite on the hand or near the heart might become a medicine-man or medicine-woman. A third method was by dreams and trances. Kisatc said that during his youth he had dreamed every night that he was visited by some one who endowed him with magic power. Under the influence of these dreams he decided to become a medicine-man, but as soon as he began to practise the dreams ceased. These dreams are not sought by fasting or other unusual conditions, nor does the person to whom they come seclude himself from his fellows.

Several informants declared that "any man who received instruction from a medicine-man and learned to do some little tricks could become a medicine-man." The process of acquiring power was called va'ikita, "getting power" (literally, "pouring in olla"). The novice was tested, either alone or along with one or more fellow-aspirants, by the medicine-man, who had the youth kneel before him on all fours, and then threw four sticks, each about 8 inches long, at him. If the novice fell to the ground during the throwing he was "shot" with the power and could then take the next degree. This was administered by the instructor, who "coughed up" tcu'tcaka (word of unknown meaning), white balls the size of mistletoe berries, and rubbed them "into" the breast of the novice. Another informant said that the novice swallowed the balls. Four or five balls were thus administered, though the "power began to work" in some cases where only one or two balls were used. One informant thought that the medicine-man had a sort of "nest of power" wherein the balls developed as in the ovary of a hen. No matter how many were given off the supply continued undiminished.

Sometimes the doctor wished to teach the youth, in which case the latter paid nothing for his instruction.[a] But the usual fee was a

---

[a] "The Indians of the nation of Loretto had schools, whereby these professors instructed their youths in the above opinions, and some other needless puerilities: but recommended to them as truths of great importance. In order to this, their pupils attended them to caves or solitary places, at a distance

horse, "a piece of calico," or the like.   Throughout the period of his initiation the novice was not permitted to go near a woman's menstrual lodge nor might he allow anyone to know that he was learning; that implied that he should not practise until the end of the novitiate period, usually two years, sometimes four.   When at length he began to practise his success depended on his ability to develop dreams and visions.

While the Si'atcokam can induct any young man into the mysteries of the order, that man's son can not inherit his father's profession.

LEGERDEMAIN

The Makai were intrusted with the important duty of securing supernatural aid to insure good crops.   One method of procedure was to gather the people in the large lodge and have some one bring in an olla filled with earth.   This the Makai stirred with a willow stick and placed before a clear fire, where it stood all night while rain songs were being sung.   At dawn the olla was emptied and was found to contain wheat instead of earth.   Four grains were given to each one present, to be buried at the corners of the fields or the four grains together at the center.

For a consideration the Makai would go to a wheat field and perform rites which he assured the owner would result in a heavy yield of wheat.   After rolling and smoking a cigarette at each corner of the field, he would go to the center of it and bury a stick (â'mĭna) 3 or 4 inches long.

To cause an abundance of melons and squashes, the Makai entered the field and took from his mouth—or, as his followers supposed, from the store of magic power in his body—a small melon or squash. The object was partially covered with hardened mud, symbolic of the productive earth.   The rite was performed at a time when no melons or squashes had yet appeared, and it is supposed that he obtained the "magic" melon by stripping the outer leaves from the growing end of young vines.   This was buried at the root of a growing plant to insure a prolific yield.

Again, the germination and growth of wheat were sometimes imitated by concealing several grains of wheat in the hair and shaking them down upon the soil.   Then by a dextrous manipulation of a previously prepared series of young wheat shoots the growth was represented up to the point where a stalk 2 feet in length was

---

from the woods: and there they taught them to form certain figures on tablets, and when perfect in these, they were taught others, as children in our schools are taught to write. . . . But their most usual device was to hold up in their hands some little tablets of wood made with great labour, for want of iron tools of mesquite, or another hard wood called Una de Gato, on which were painted some grotesque figures, affirmed to be the true copy of the table, which the visiting spirit left with them at his departure to heaven: and these figures were the same which the Loretto professors [medicine-men] taught the boys at their private academy."   Venegas, History of California, I, 98, 100.

slipped from the long coils of hair at the operator's shoulders and shown to the awe-stricken spectators as a fully developed plant.

A favorite trick was to have young men chew mesquite leaves, which on being ejected from the mouth were seen to be wheat or corn.

During the rain ceremonies, when the Makai were at the height of their glory, one of their most impressive acts was to pour dry earth out of a reed until it was half empty and then it would be seen that the remainder was filled with water. "Then it rained right away." If the Makai put one of the magic slates in a cup of water at the time the rain songs were being sung and also dug a shallow trench to show the rivulets how they should cut their way, it would rain in four days.

Another device of the Makai was to conceal reeds filled with water and then while standing on a house top to direct the singers to stand in a close circle around below him. Exhibiting a handful of eagle down or eagle tail feathers and throwing dust on them to show how dry they were, he would then sweep his hand about and scatter water over the spectators and singers, apparently from feathers but in reality from the reeds.

During the season when rain is especially needed any one may petition for it by means of the small gray fly that has a large head. Rubbing soot from the roof or chimney in the fly's eyes the person must say, "Go quickly, little fly, tell your grandmother to send the rain."

Some Si'atcokam arouse the wonder and admiration of their fellows by placing hot coals in their mouths (where they hold them between the teeth), or by holding them in their hands (taking care to have a thin layer of ash or mud beneath them).

When the exigencies of the case demand it, the Si'atcokam sink small pointed pieces of wood, an inch in length and flat at the larger end, into the flesh of their patients. The bits of wood are "twisted back and forth between the thumb and forefinger as one would twist a thread until the wood disappears." The great grandmother of Jacob L. Roberts, a young man of Apache-Maricopa and Pima-Kwahadk' lineage, thus treated him during a temporary attack of sickness in his infancy. She sank two pieces of creosote bush into his breast and predicted that he would not be ill as would other children. She also said that she would die within the year—and she did. Strange to say, Jacob also escaped the epidemic diseases that afflicted his playmates.

The Si'atcokam prize certain crystals very highly and claim to obtain them in the following manner: The person possessing the necessary power may be going along in some quiet place when all of a sudden a man will be seen approaching. The stranger never reaches him but will be seen to disappear; then if the Si'atcokam searches about the spot where the man was last seen, he will find a transparent crystal, hâ'tai tân'tam, stone white, which contains a spirit that will aid him in all his subsequent undertakings and which will desert the stone at the death of the holder.[a]

The Si'atcokam treats a wounded man by sucking the evil from the wound. He shows a strand of green that resembles a roll of water plants about 8 inches long. The wounded man sucks this crosswise four times and the Si'atcokam pretends to swallow it. "This insures complete recovery."

Cause and Treatment of Disease

The Si'atcokam carries his tcaekut or staff in hand when called to treat the sick. He begins by singing the "cure songs" or causing them to be sung for the purpose of aiding him in correctly diagnosing the case. Then he puffs out cigarette smoke over the body of the patient in order that he may "see" the disease. Most common ailments are attributed to certain definite causes and the diagnosis is easy. When he is well paid for his services he may sing more than one night before announcing the name of the disease. If he is too hasty he may "see" the bear when it is really the deer that is causing trouble. However, he can not sing more than four nights; then, if he fails, he must call in a fellow-practitioner. The case of Sala Hina is an interesting and instructive one and will illustrate very adequately these peculiar methods. Several years ago Sala carelessly ate some weed which poisoned her and she had barely strength enough to reach home. As close relatives are not allowed to treat a patient, a neighboring medicine-man was called in. Her husband rolled a cigarette for the learned doctor, who smoked it, but however skillfully he spread the smoke cloud over the groaning patient he could not "see" the cause of the trouble. Then another Si'atcokam was called in and a cigarette was rolled for him and he peered through the veil sufficiently to see "something." But he could not tell just what it was and advised sending for another medicine-man who was a specialist in intangible shapes. Sala was suffering the greatest agony in the meantime. If she moved she "felt full of pins inside." Those about her expected her to die at any moment. Number three at length arrived and smoked his cigarette, blowing the smoke across the patient from a distance to dispel the unusually heavy darkness. He said he must have his gourd rattle and magic feathers brought before he could see clearly. Meanwhile the husband had brought in a fourth medicine-man. Number four then smoked a cigarette and pro-

---

[a] "Small rock crystals, supposed to be produced by the shamans, are thought to be dead or even living—a kind of astral bodies of the Theosophists. Such a rock crystal is called tevali (plural tevali'r) or 'grandfather'—the same name as is given to the majority of the gods. But it may, however, represent any person or relative, in accordance with the directions of the shaman." Lumholtz, Symbolism of the Huichol Indians, 63.

nounced the verdict of death.   Poor Sala had been compelled to lie
quiet to avoid the torture from the "pins" but her mind was active
and she understood every word that was said in her presence.   Determined to do what they could, the last two arrivals set to work singing.
Number three sang four songs, followed by four more songs from
number four.   Then number three sang four more, and so they
alternated all night.   Toward morning they put ashes into a cup of
water, sweeping eagle feathers across the dish meanwhile.   They
then announced that they would get the evil out soon.   Number
four sprayed water from his mouth over the patient and declared
that he had found her to be suffering from the presence of the horn
of a horned toad in her heart.   Falling on his knees beside her he
sucked with all his might until he had removed the offending object.
As it flew into his mouth it gagged him and he hastened to withdraw
it.   Calling for a piece of cotton he put the hot and burning horn
into it and told the brother of the patient to throw it into the river.
Then the two Si'atcokam sang twice and later in the day sang twice
through their set of four songs for the horned toad.   This faithful
treatment brought about a recovery.

Sala's brother fell ill of some throat disease over which the doctors
sang, sucked, and smoked for a month before he died.

It will be seen from the cases described that the songs play an
important part in the treatment, and they are sung with endless
repetitions.   After the cause of the affliction has been decided upon
the songs of that animal or object are sung.   An image or a part of
the animal or object is pressed upon or waved over the part affected
and then the farce of sucking out the evil is gone through.   Juan
Thomas informed the writer that he had frequently concealed under
his thumb nail the objects which he pretended to suck from his
patients.

Sometimes ashes are rubbed upon the skin of the sick person.   No
matter what the disease may be, the ashes are administered with light
rubbing.   No explanation could be given for this treatment.   For
any disease, also, pledgets of cotton might be burned on the skin, and
as these were half an inch in diameter and two or three might be
burned in one place, the effect must have been very painful.

The female Si'atcokam never treated children; they confined their
labors to the treatment of abdominal troubles not necessarily peculiar
to sex.   They treated men for abdominal difficulties and men treated
women for all diseases.

Payment is promised to the Si'atcokam when they are called in.   It
may be a horse, cow, some wheat, a basket, or similar property.   If
he contracts to sing three nights and to receive a horse in payment,
he will not receive the horse if the patient dies after he has sung two

nights, but will receive some compensation. The death of the patient does not annul the obligation under any circumstances.

In addition to the animals, birds, and reptiles that cause disease, the variety of human ailments and the fertility of the native's imagination necessitated the invention of yet other causes. These were sometimes superhuman, but only too often the tribe merely descended to the level of the African savage, and accused some medicine-man of the crime of causing disease. There would seem to be some reason in this if the medicine-man who had the case in hand were the one accused, but that was not the custom; it was a rival practitioner who bore the onus and frequently paid the penalty with his life, as may be seen from the accompanying annals. It would seem that every epidemic of any extent that ever afflicted the Pimas caused an almost wholesale destruction of medicine-men. In individual cases of malice on the part of the medicine-man the treatment is to sing the medicine song and afterwards to place four magic stones in a cup of water, taking out one at a time and holding it under the nose of the patient, that he may inhale its power; then he must drink the water.

If a person believes that a medicine-man has brought sickness upon his household he calls in another doctor to find the charm. The one consulted takes four assistants and searches day and night until some object is found which they can safely assume was hidden in the vicinity by the malicious medicine-man. When found the object must not be touched, for fear of death, but the mere discovery renders it harmless to the person against whom it was aimed.

Sometimes the medicine-man causes sickness by "shooting" charcoal, made from the burned body of an enemy, into some one who does not notice it at the time, but whose body burns in consequence. If it is sucked out before it is entirely consumed the charcoal loses its power and the patient recovers.

The badger causes a severe throat disease, which, however, is considered to be of rare occurrence. The remedy is to sing the badger song (p. 321) and to press the tail of the badger on the patient's neck.

The bear causes swellings upon the body, headache, and fever. The remedy is to sing the bear songs, of which there are several (p. 318); the singing is sometimes continued throughout the entire day. No part of the animal is used in the treatment. The bear is friendly to the Pimas. If a man meets one he must say, "I'm red," and then the bear will not touch him, though he is free to kill the animal.

The black-tailed deer causes diseases of the throat and lungs. The remedy is to sing the deer song (p. 317) and to press the tail of the deer on the affected part.

The coyote causes sickness in children; some believing that he brings on the dysentery when the mother eats melons before the birth of the child, others thinking that he causes rash and blisters on the baby's tongue. The remedy is to sing the coyote song (p. 316) and swing the tail of the coyote over the child.

The dog, a very near relative of the coyote in Pimería, also causes trouble for the children. When a child a month or two old is fretful and sleepless the medicine-man is pretty certain to diagnose the case as "dog disease." He does not treat it in any manner, but some one who knows the dog song (p. 315) is called in to sing, and as he sings he sways a stick that has some of a dog's vibrissæ tied to it, to and fro over the child.

The gopher causes stomach trouble, particularly in children. The remedy is to sing the gopher song (p. 319) and to press moistened earth from a gopher hill upon the affected part. At Gila Crossing were obtained two small deerskin bags containing tufts of eagle's down and two or three twigs that had been cut by a gopher. These were to be pressed upon the stomach of the child.

The jack rabbit causes open sores. The remedy is to sing the rabbit song (p. 314), and during the singing to swing over the patient the tail of the hare to which the animal's vibrissæ have been tied.

The mouse, kʋwakawâpâkam, causes constipation in children. This is cured by singing the mouse song (p. 314), and pressing the tail of the mouse on the abdomen. If no prepared tail is available a dead mouse is used.

The ground squirrel of the mesas causes nosebleed.

There are but four birds that cause disease. There appears to have been no conscious classification in the minds of the Pimas in attributing certain afflictions to the birds. These diseases are all of a different nature, and are similar to those assigned to mammals and reptiles.

The eagle causes hemorrhage. The remedy is to sing the eagle song (p. 289) and to pass the down of the eagle over the part.

The eagle is also blamed for the lice that find refuge in the hair of the Pimas. The remedy is to blow cigarette smoke over the head.

The hawk causes hemorrhage in grown persons only. The disease is cured by singing the hawk song and passing the wing feathers of the bird over the patient. If one touches a hawk he must be secluded for four days.

The owl throws people into trances and fits. They are restored by having the owl song (p. 311) sung while six owl feathers mounted on a stick are swung over them. The cry of the small owl, kokovol(t), in the night is a bad sign. When the large owl utters a sound resembling human speech sickness may be expected.

The vulture or turkey buzzard causes sores, especially syphilis, and sore eyes on the baby if the parent eat a dead animal just before the child is born. The remedy is to sing the buzzard song and pass the wing feathers of the buzzard over the child.

A Gila monster if killed by the father just before the birth of a child causes the baby's body to become red and feverish. The remedy is to sing the Gila monster song (p. 307). Such a disease must be of rare occurrence and no other treatment is prescribed.

The horned toad causes rheumatism and hunchback. The remedy is to sing the horned toad song (p. 307), and press an image of the creature upon the patient (fig. 25, a). If one accidentally steps on a horned toad he must tie a red string around its neck and let it go, saying, "nyu u-ut hok," my blood eat. This is to cause the subtle toad to eat the bad blood that may cause disease in the person.

The large lizard, tcosokalt, is responsible for a fever in children, the most prominent symptom of which is the whitening of the skin. If any one who knows the lizard song (p. 308) is available he comes and presses an image of a lizard (fig. 25, b) on the child as he sings; if not, a lizard is killed and fat from its body is rubbed upon the child.

The rattlesnake causes kidney and stomach troubles in children. These are cured by singing the rattlesnake song (p. 309) and pressing the parts affected with an image in wood or stone of the rattlesnake.

The bite of the rattlesnake is cured by sucking the wound every morning for four days. Others suck it one or two days, and also ligature the limb with horsehair, or draw a circle around it with charcoal to define the limit of the swelling. The Papagos and Mexicans use the plant Euphorbia marginata to poultice snake bites, and it is possible that some Pimas use it also, though the writer was unable to find anyone who knew of its being so used.

While the rattlesnake is dreaded and under circumstances previously mentioned is regarded as possessing magic power, he occupies a far less important place in Pima thought than in that of the Hopis. It is said to be unlucky to come upon two rattlesnakes, one soon after the other, when engaged in searching for anything. If a child puts its foot through an olla head ring that is commonly left lying about the premises, the mother warns him that the rattlesnake will bite him. The same fate is threatened if he puts his foot into the mortar in which the mesquite beans and other articles of food are ground. The rattlesnake is accredited with wisdom that directs it to the place where the best mesquite beans are to be had, though why such a locality has any attractions for it was not explained.

The turtle causes large sores on the body or cripples the legs. The treatment is to sing the turtle song (p. 306) and shake a rattle over the patient. The rattle is made by killing a river turtle and placing the body in an ant-hill until the ants have thoroughly cleaned out the shell, which is then mounted on a handle, and some gravel put into it.

A butterfly with striped wings causes internal pains. The treatment consists in singing the butterfly song (p. 295) and pressing the body of the patient with four or five images of the butterfly cut from deerskin.

The worm, kămmâlt, when found dead and dried is ground up in the mortar and the powder used to cure sores around the baby's mouth.

One's teeth will fall out if he eats food over which some caterpillars have crawled.

The nausea of pregnancy is caused by unfaithfulness on the part of the woman. It is cured by singing the proper songs and striking two sticks a foot long over the patient afterwards.

The remolinos, or whirlwinds, that are so common in Pimería, cause pains in the legs, but not swellings. The remedy is to sing the wind song (p. 324) and to rub the limbs with the black gum of the okatilla, Fouquiera splendens.

The sun may cause disease for which there would seem to be no special song. However, a small colored image of the sun with feather rays attached is used by the medicine-man.

A captured Apache child might cause lameness in some member of the family by whom he was kept. It was cured by some one who had killed an Apache singing over the patient. Then the child must be sold to the Mexicans or Americans. It was also supposed that the touch of an Apache woman might cause paralysis.

Piholt was once a man, but is now an evil spirit living in the east, and causing a disease which has its songs.

The Nyavolt, an evil spirit, may induce a horse to throw his rider and injure him. The patient is cured by singing the Nyavolt song (p. 329) and swinging a pair of crossed sticks over the injured part.

A certain disease of the throat is called wheita, and the same name is given to a stick made from mesquite root, which is thrust down the patient's throat four times and then passed four times over the heart to cure him.

Tcŭnyĭm is an evil spirit that causes sickness in children. The most characteristic symptom is fretfulness. The Tcŭnyĭm song is sung and the child's body is pressed with a strand of hair taken in war from an Apache's head. The hair is cleaned and washed by some old person, then the ends are glued together with the gum of the creosote bush before it is ready to use. Â'mĭna sticks tied with bluebird and redbird feathers are also used.

Kâ'mâl tkâk (pl. XLIV, b), who was accustomed to assist the doctors, states that this name is applied to a disease of the throat which causes the victim to lose flesh. The treatment consists in placing â'mĭna in an olla of water to soak while the doctor or his assistant blows through a tube, called the tcŭnyĭm cigarette, upon the forehead, chin, breast, and stomach of the patient. The tube has a bunch of feathers attached called a-an kiatûta, and these are next swept in quick passes downward over the body. The â′mĭna are then taken and sucked four times by the patient, after which the end of the bundle is pressed against the patient's body, then laid flat upon his breast and rubbed. Finally, the assistant repeats the speech of Siu-u at the time when that deity restored himself to life, at the same time making passes toward the patient.

Magic influence exerted by evilly disposed persons, especially medicine-men, may cause a particular ailment, called "doctor's disease," in the cure of which the slate tablets found in the ruins are believed to be most efficacious. The information was given that no marking was made on the slates; they were simply placed in a vessel of water and the patient drank the water.

Sometimes the sickness of a child was believed to be due to the fact that some person desired to take it away from its parents. If they went to the covetous one and accused him of the crime the child immediately recovered.

Navitco (fig. 26) is an evil spirit adopted from the Papagos. His home is in the mountain called Papak, Frog.[a] This spirit causes the knees to swell and the eyes to become inflamed. It may safely be inferred that this disease has been a common one, as it is the practice to treat several at one time in a somewhat more elaborate ceremonial than is usual in the treatment of other diseases. One medicine-man personates Navitco, another known as Kâkspakam accompanies him; both are masked. At a signal from Navitco, given by throwing corn meal on the baskets, 15 or 20 persons appointed for the purpose sing the Navitco song (p. 326), accompanied by the notched sticks, after which Navitco goes to each patient and pats him with eagle feathers until he has presumably drawn out all disease. He then throws away the feathers. He is followed by Kâkspakam, who seats himself before each patient to give him an opportunity to touch the mask and then the swollen knees. When the singers have finished, they rub the notched sticks over their own bodies to prevent contagion. All concerned in the ceremony must not eat salt for four days thereafter.

The Navitco medicine-men also claim to possess the power to bring rain.

The treatment of a child afflicted with dysentery mingles the new order with the old in an interesting manner, combining Christian baptism with pagan sun worship and magic medical practice.

A man and his wife who are close friends of the parents come early in the morning and wash the baby. If it is a boy, it is taken up at sun-

---

[a] Santa Catalinas, north of Tucson; altitude, 10,000 feet.

rise by the man, who breathes upon a cross and holds it toward the sun four times.   If it is a girl, it is taken by the woman, who breathes upon a medal and holds the object toward the sun four times.   Whichever object is used is next passed in the form of the cross over the face and again over the body of the infant by both the man and the woman. Each then holds the child four times in his or her arms before handing it to the parents.   A name is given the child by the godfather and godmother.   No child except one thus ill or another in the same family of a naming age at the time is ever christened thus.   The godparents must give the child some wheat or corn each year until it grows up, and the parents give a basket each year in return.

Even horses may become sick through the evil influence of malicious medicine-men, who, it is said, "shoot" live coals into them— coals that have been taken from an Apache fire.   The remedy is of a similar magic character.   A reputable medicine-man is called in, who diagnoses the case and decides from what direction the coal was "shot."   He does not sing, but after smoking a cigarette and blowing puffs of smoke about the premises and upon the horse he determines the place to suck out the coal from the distressed animal.   When he gets the coal into his mouth he makes a pretense of being burned by it and immediately fills his mouth with water, after which he casts out the coal.

The transparent trick of sucking a hair from the body is resorted to in veterinary practice in a manner similar to that pursued when treating human ailments.

PREVALENT DISEASES [a]

Consumption is the most frequent and fatal disease, due to poverty of diet and contagion.   The Pimas do not attempt to prevent infection.   Their former treatment was a diet of mountain turtle and sun-dried beef.

Dysentery is common in summer because of the peculiar habit, by no means confined to the Pimas, of eating unripe melons.

Impetigo contagiosa is the worst skin disease, and is principally confined to the children.

Children are intentionally exposed to smallpox and measles, that they may have the diseases in lighter form.   Smallpox was regarded as an evil spirit of which they did not dare to show fear.   They said "I like Smallpox," thinking that he would be thus placated.   At one time they attempted inoculation from persons that had light attacks, but the experiment resulted in many deaths.   From 1870 until the Government sent a physician to the agency, the missionary, Rev. C. H.

---

[a] From 1892 until 1895 Dr A. E. Marden held the position of agency physician at Sacaton and from 1900 until the time of the writer's visit to the Pimas in 1902 continued his practice as missionary physician among the Pimas.   The writer is indebted to him for the greater portion of the information relating to the degree of prevalence of disease.

Cook, supplied the Pimas with vaccine. They retained some of their old dread of the demon and continued to place the bandages with which the arm had been dressed upon a certain mesquite tree, not daring to burn them for fear of offending. Smallpox has usually been brought to the Pimas by the Papagos from Mexico. Measles appears every three or four years, but does not seem to be any more fatal than among the whites, though it is more likely to be followed by consumption.

Rheumatism of the chronic articular type is fairly common and is treated like many other pains by scarifying the part affected with bits of broken glass.

There are a few cases of acquired syphilis among the Pimas and a few due to hereditary taint, but they are fairly free from the disease, considering their habits, and are much more exempt from it than their allies, the Maricopas.

Diarrhea was supposed to be due to touching ripe wheat in the fields, and it was considered necessary for a medicine-man to walk about in the standing grain and blow the danger away with smoke.

Bleeding wounds were bandaged; burns were plastered with wet mud; broken limbs were set with skill and inclosed in light and strong splints made of reeds.

Melancholia sometimes afflicts "a man who has killed Apaches" so that he wanders about without clothing and refuses to talk. No treatment is attempted, and the victim dies of neglect.

Massage is a common form of treatment of almost any disease and of itself is enough to endanger the patient, for it sometimes happens that the operator administers a vigorous pommeling to the abdomen.

Table of diseases

Rare	Occasional	Common
Acne	Asthma	Bronchitis
Epilepsy	Cataract	Caries
Dementia	Eczema	Conjunctivitis
Lupus	Favus	Consumption
Melancholia	Heart disease	Diarrhea
Typhoid	Neuralgia	Dysentery
	Pleurisy	Impetigo contagiosa
	Scabies	Measles
	Smallpox	Pneumonia
	Syphilis	Rheumatism
	Urticaria	Toothache

LINGUISTICS

VOCABULARIES

There are four short vocabularies of the Pima language in manuscript in the possession of the Bureau of American Ethnology:

The first is published in Schoolcraft, volume III, page 461, and forms the basis of the English-Pima vocabulary published in Die Pima-Sprache by Buschmann in 1857 (p. 367). Doctor Parry employed a Maricopa interpreter. Buschmann's vocabulary also includes words obtained by Doctor Coulter, which were published by Gallatin in Transactions of the American Ethnological Society, volume II, page 129, and by Scouler in the Journal of the Royal Geographical Society of London, volume XI, page 248. Buschmann further drew from Pfefferkorn's Beschreibung der Landschaft Sonora, volume II, passim; three words from Mühlenfordt's Schilderung der Republik Mejico, volume II, page 225; and words from the Lord's Prayer in Pima as given by Hervas in Saggio Practico Delle Lingue (p. 124–125). There are 182 words, in all, in Buschmann's list. Fewer than half the 53 pages of his paper are devoted to the language of the Pimas.

Lieutenant Whipple obtained a vocabulary of 67 Pima words, which was published in his Report upon the Indian Tribes, Pacific Railroad Reports, volume III (pt. III, p. 94).

In the Journal of the Royal Geographical Society for 1841, page 248, there is a Pima vocabulary of 38 words that was collected by a Doctor Coulter; where, it is not stated. The orthography is not explained.

In his Opuscula, page 351, R. G. Latham has published a vocabulary of 27 words, stating neither from whom it was derived nor where it was written. In his Natural History of the Varieties of Man, Latham devotes three pages to quotations from Lieutenant Emory descriptive of the "Pimos."

As examples of the orthography and extent of these vocabularies, two are republished below.

Vocabularies

English	Coulter	Latham	English	Coulter	Latham
Man	tiuot	huth	Salt	ŏnă	
Woman	ūbă	hahri	Light	tai	
Indian		huup	Day	tashimĕt	
Boy	āndī		Night	stuükum	
Chief	capit		Cold	scapit	
Father	niook		Hot	stōn	
Mother	intui		Stone	jōtē	
Body	nionh		Mountain	tóăk	
Head	nemŏh	mouk	White	stoxa	
Hair		ptmuk	House	nihki	
Ear	nāānk	ptnahauk	Door	pūālīt	
Nose		tahnk	Bow	ñikāt	
Mouth		chinits	Arrow	napot	
Tongue		neuen	I		ahan
Tooth		ptahan	He		yeutah
Beard		chinyo	One		yumako
Hand	noh	mahahtk	Two		kuak
Foot		tetaght	Three		vaik
Heart	īpŏtŭk		Four		kiik
Sky		ptchuwik	Five		puitas
Sun	tash	tahs	Nine	humukt	
Moon	maskat	mahsa	Ten	huistemăm	
Star		non	Eleven	māātŏ	
Snow		chiah	Twelve	kóóhk	
Fire		tahi	Brave	tiout	
Water	shōñtik	suntik	Bad	mūmkō	
Sea	kakatchck		Good	skukit	
River	ākĕmŭli		Great	vŏhŏvākuitch	
Lake	vō				

SONGS

CLASSIFICATION

During a stay of seven months among the Pimas not a single native song was ever heard from a man, woman, or child. This is in striking contrast with the writer's experience among most other tribes that have not been longer in contact with the whites. Not half a dozen individuals can be found in the upper villages who know any considerable number of the old songs. And yet the number of these songs is very great and most of them are by no means unpleasing even to a Caucasian ear. The songs are in series that are known to different individuals. Thus, the songs sung at the puberty dances are in series that are started by the first singer to arrive upon the scene in the evening. If another singer arrives first during the next evening the series of songs for the night is changed; though all belong to the general class of "menstrual songs." Sometimes a festival is inaugurated because of the accidental presence of some one who knows a group, as the "Bluebird songs" or the "Swallow songs." Examples of all the principal groups of songs are here recorded. They include:

Archaic songs; included in the cosmogonical myth; they are known as "Emergence songs," and contain a few words of a meaning unknown, owing either to age or to borrowing.

Festal songs; including "Circling," "Basket beating," "Middle run," "Name," etc.

Game songs; these are short, not numerous, and often borrowed.

Hunting songs; there are a few songs that appear to have once been used in the ceremonial preparations for hunting, but which are now employed in the magical treatment of disease.

Medicine songs; this is the largest class; every conceivable ailment has its appointed song, ascribed to some animal or natural phenomenon or even supernatural agency. Many of these are from the Papagos.

Puberty songs; some are especially for this ceremony, though any festal songs may be sung at this time.

Rain songs; these contain interesting references to deities not elsewhere mentioned. So far as known, their source has not yet been ascertained.

War songs; these were numerous and of great importance in the ceremonies.

ARCHAIC SONGS

[Told by Kâ'mâl tkâk, Thin Leather]

CREATION SONGS BY EARTH DOCTOR

THE CREATION OF THE EARTH

I

Tcuwutu Makai tcuwutu natâ miakukâ nyuïta hasïtco-onyï!
Earth   Magician,   earth   make   come,   see   what you intend!

(Repeat)

*Sikâlamû natâ miakukâ nyuïta hasïtco-onyï! (D. C. to *)
Round   make   come,   see   what you intend!

†Tcuwutu Makai tâʌakû natâ miakukâ, nyuïta hasiyaña!
Earth   Magician mountain make   come,   see   what you tell!

Tapïnyïmû natâ miakukâ, nyuïta hasiyaña! (D. C. to †)
Smooth   make   come,   see   what you tell!

II

Tcuwutu Makai tcuwutu natâ; Tcuwutu Makai tcuwutu natâ, himlo,
Earth   Doctor   earth   make;   Earth   Magician   earth   make. going,

himlo, himlo, himutco-o. (Repeat)
going,   going,   going (causal).

*Tcuwutu Makai tâv'a ku natâ; Tcuwutu Makai tâvakû
Earth   Doctor mountain kind of make;   Earth   Doctor   mountain

natâ, himlo, himlo, himlo, himutco-o. (D. C. to *)
make,   going,   going,   going,   going.

III

Tcuwutu tapa sihaitconyoka-ana:
Earth   open   magician

Tâvañgû tapa sitco mamatcu-u.
Mountain   open magic powers knows.

Translation

Earth Magician shapes this world.
  Behold what he can do!
Round and smooth he molds it.
  Behold what he can do!
Earth Magician makes the mountains.
  Heed what he has to say!
He it is that makes the mesas.
  Heed what he has to say.
Earth Magician shapes this world;
  Earth Magician makes its mountains;
Makes all larger, larger, larger.
  Into the earth the Magician glances;
Into its mountains he may see.

IV

THE CREATION OF THE SUN

Vanyĭñgi Tarsaiwʊ natâkahĭ; vanyĭñgi Tarsai natâkahĭ, hiyanyi
  I am   Sun   made;   I am   Sun   made;   here me

tamai ya-ahai pʊnanaitco-o.   (Repeat)
above   both   directions throw.

*Si-ĭyaldĭ takĭo wopahimû kahowʊ taitcʊnyʊkû sapâva mʊnʊna-a.
East   direction   throw   there   rise running   right running back.

(D. C. to *)

Translation

I have made the Sun!
I have made the Sun!
Hurling it high
In the four directions.
To the East I threw it
To run its appointed course.

V

THE CREATION OF THE MOON

Vanyĭñgi Marsatû natâkahĭ; vanyĭñgi Marsatû natâkahĭ; hiyanyi
  I am   Moon   make;   I am   Moon   make;   here me

tamai ya-ahai pʊnanaitco-o.   (Repeat)
above   both   directions throw.

*Si-ĭyaldĭ takĭŏ wopahimʊ kahowa tcʊrsanyʊkʊ sapâva himʊna-a.
East   direction   throw   there   came up   correct   come.

(D. C. to *\

Translatión

I have made the Moon!
I have made the Moon!
Hurling it high
In the four directions.
To the East I threw it
To run its appointed course.

VI

THE CREATION OF THE STARS

Vanyĭñgi Yo-ohowʊ natâ; vanyĭñgi Yo-ohowʊ natâ, tamaiwʊ nañgĭta
  I am   Stars   make;   I am   Stars   make,   above   throw

tcʊwʊtʊ mamasi-i.   (Repeat)
earth   light.

*Vanyĭñgi wʊs aitco natâ tamaiwʊ nañgĭta tcʊfhʊtʊ tânâli-i.
 I am   all   things   make   above   throw   land   shines.

(D. C. to *)

Translation

I have made the Stars!
I have made the Stars!
Above the earth I threw them.
All things above I've made
And placed them to illumine.

FLOOD SONGS BY EARTH DOCTOR

THE WARNING OF THE FLOOD

Haya, rsâ-âhĭñgʋ nyhʋ-ʋmatcita tcomuñgâ wʋ-ʋwʋsi nyʋĭnahi-imʋ;
Weep,   pitiable   me people   you will   all   see happen;

haya,   rsâ-âhĭñgʋ nyhʋ-ʋmatcita tcomʋñgâ wʋ-ʋwʋsi nyʋĭnahi-imʋ.
weep,   pitiable   me people   you will   all   see happen.

Kosi'na rso-otaki kosina tcʋtcʋwuʇʋ vamohai-i.   (Repeat)
That   water   that   land   dissolve.

* Haya, rsâ-âhĭñgʋ nyha-atconyi tcomuñgâ wʋ-ʋwʋsi mamatcʋ-ʋ;
Weep,   pitiable   my relatives   you will   all   learning;

haya,   rsâ-âhiñgʋ nyha-atconyi tcomʋñgâ wʋ-ʋwʋsi mamatcʋ-ʋ.
weep,   pitiable   my relatives   you will   all   learning.

Kosina rso-otaki kosina tâtâvakʋ vamohai-i.   (Repeat to *)
That   water   that   mountain   dissolve.

Translation

Weep my unfortunate people!
All this you will see take place.
Weep my unfortunate people!
For the waters will cover the land.
Weep my unhappy relatives!
You will learn all.
Weep my unhappy relatives!
You will learn all.
The waters will cover the mountains.

THE PEOPLE CLIMBING SUPERSTITION MOUNTAIN

Haiya! haiya! vina, vina, hai-iya!   Pʋnha rsâhika tconyihi-i,
Aha!   Aha!   Flood, flood, Aha!   Remember pitiable   making.

haiya! haiya! vına, vina, hai-iya!   Pʋnha rsâhika tconyihi-i.   Hamai
Aha!   Aha!   Flood, flood,   Aha!   Remember pitiable   making.   Here

pa-apaitcomhi nyhʋ-ʋmatcita rsâhika himʋna-a.   (Repeat)
before me   me people   pitiable   going.

Translation

Haiya! Haiya! Flood! Flood! Hai-iya!
See the doom awaiting them!
Haiya! Haiya! Flood! Flood! Hai-iya!
Here are my doomed people before me.

FLOOD SONGS BY SOUTH DOCTOR

ON SUPERSTITION MOUNTAIN BEFORE THE FLOOD

Rsonañgi tcuwuɹu vamohai-i ; rsonañgi nyuwutu vamohai-i,
Water   land   dissolve ;   water   land   dissolve,

kundañgu   makaiva   sihaitco-o   rsonañgi   nanakâ   tconyihi-imu.
in   magician   powerful   water   experimenting   making.

Rsonañgi tâvaku vamohai-i ; rsonañgi tâvaku vamohai-i, kundañgu
Water   mountain   dissolve;   water   mountain   dissolve,   in

Nasiavâ sitco-omai-i rsonañgi nanakâ wowoi-hi-mu. (Repeat)
Nasi   understand   water   experimenting   toward-going.

Kakânda ku tâtâvañgu ta-atama nanyolĭnaka rso-otaki yomahi-
Crooked   kind   of mountain   top   I stay   water   disperse.

imu. (Repeat)

Ta-atama nayolĭnaka rso-otaki yomahi-imu. (Repeat)
Top   I stay   water   disperse.

Translation

The waters dissolve the land !
The waters dissolve the land !
The mighty magician tests his strength.
The waters dissolve the mountains !
The waters dissolve the mountains !
Nasi foresees what is coming.

On Crooked mountain I am standing,
Trying to disperse the waters.
On Crooked mountain I am standing,
Trying to disperse the waters.

BEFORE THE PEOPLE TURNED TO STONE ON SUPERSTITION MOUNTAIN

Sihaitcohâ! Sihaitcohâ! Nyhânaka wuwuma sihaitcohâ! Wuwuma
Powerless!   Powerless!   My magic   crystal with   powerless!   With

siamhu nyhâtaitco. (Repeat)
right   petrify.

And again he sang before they became petrified:

Translation

Powerless ! Powerless !
Powerless is my magic crystal.
Powerless ! Powerless !
I shall become as stone.

FLOOD SONGS BY ELDER BROTHER

IN HIS OLLA BEFORE THE FLOOD

I

Tcokoi vavahaki! tcokoi vavahaki! Ku-unɹa nyi yolina. Kuɹa nyi
Black   house!   black   house!   In   I   hold.   In   I

yolĭnha-a wu-umatci yahai nyimitco-o. (Repeat)
stay   with   to and fro   I go.

Translation

Black house! Black house! Hold me safely in;
Black house! Black house! Hold me safely in,
As I journey to and fro, to and fro.

II

THE FLOOD

Rsotaki mᴜtᴜ-ᴜ! rsotaki mᴜtᴜka! Muɹava pᴜtanyû, tamaiᴧᴜkatcima
Water   running!   water   running!   In   sounding,   top laying

tcuvaki parsa pa-anyhimitco.
cloud   near by   on there I borne.

Rsotaki mᴜtᴜ-ᴜ! rsotaki mᴜtᴜka! Muɹava rsarsavai, tamaiᴧᴜkatcima
Water   running!   water   running!   In   roaring,   top laying

hononyi parsa pa-anyhimitco.   (Repeat)
evening   near by   on there I borne.

Translation

Running water! Running water! Herein resounding,
As on the clouds I am carried to the sky.
Running water! Running water! Herein roaring,
As on the clouds I am carried to the sky.

III

COMING FROM HIS OLLA AFTER THE FLOOD

Hianyai worsᴜnyᴜ; hianyai worsᴜnyᴜ-ᴜ, sihai nyoka hiayai
Here I   came out;   here I   came out,   magician   here I

worsᴜnyᴜ sihai tcoka-a. Hianyai worsᴜnyᴜ; Hianyai worsᴜnyᴜ-ᴜ,
came out   magician.   Here I   came out;   Here I   came out,

sitco matcᴜ hianyai worsᴜnyᴜ sitco matcᴜ-ᴜ.
magical powers   here I   came out   magical powers.

Hianyai worsᴜnyᴜ-ᴜ sihai nyoka; hianyai worsᴜnyᴜ sihai tcoka-a.
Here I   came out   magician;   here I   came out   magician.

Hianyai worsᴜnyᴜ-ᴜ sitco matcû hianyai worsᴜnyᴜ sitco matcᴜ-ᴜ.
Here I   came out   magical know   here I   came out   magical know.

(Repeat)

Tânyo wᴜmû; tanyo wᴜma kᴜkiᴧa. Sᴜndai wᴜmû, sᴜndai wᴜmû
Who I   with;   who I   with   stand.   Who   with,   who   with

tahiwa.
sit.

Itañgu nyo-osihaka wᴜma kᴜkiwa. Itañgu nyâ-âtahaka wᴜmû
This my cane   with   stand.   This   my crystal   with

tahiwa.   (Repeat)
sit.

Translation

Here I come forth! Here I come forth!
With magic powers I emerge.
Here I come forth! Here I come forth!
With magic powers I emerge.

I stand alone! Alone!
Who will accompany me?
My staff and my crystal
They shall bide with me.

POST-FLOOD SONGS BY ELDER BROTHER

AT THE CENTRAL PART OF THE EARTH

Kaʈʊ nyʊtva worsa hikû nyʊwʊndû vanyʊina; katʊ nyʊtva worsa
There   I   came   navel   land   I see;   there   I   came
hikû nyʊwʊndû vanyʊina.   (Repeat)
navel   land   I see.

* Kaʈʊ nyʊtva worsa hikû navañgû vanyʊina; katʊ nyʊtva worsa
There   I   came   navel   mountain   I see;   there   I   came
hikû navañgu vanyʊina.   (Repeat to *)
navel   mountain   I see.

Translation

Here I have come to the center of the earth;
Here I have come to the center of the earth.
I see the central mountain;
I see the central mountain.

CLIMBING THE CLIFFS TO ATTACK EAGLE

Kand vavai tapĭnymû, kand vavai tapĭnymû.   Kand vavai tapĭnymû,
Up steep bank   smooth,   up steep bank   smooth.   Up steep bank   smooth
kand vavai tapĭnymû.   Vâpăt tcotcoa kâĭnatca himʊna.   (Repeat)
up   bank   smooth.   Points   stick   after   going.
Kand vavai napĭnymû, kand vavai napĭnymû, vâpăt tcotcoa kâĭnatca
Up   stone   smooth;   up   stone   smooth,   points   stick   after
himʊna.   (Repeat)
going.
Tanyĭ tâhai I-itâĭ, tanyĭ tâhai I-itâĭ,
I am   white   Elder   I am   white   Elder
           Brother,   Brother.
Tanyĭ tâhai Litâĭ, tanyĭ tâhai Litâĭ.
I am   white   Elder   I am   white   Elder
           Brother,   Brother.
Va-asĭf tcotcoa kâĭnaka himʊna.   (Repeat) (Repeat both lines
Leafless   stick   after   walking.
twice)

Translation

Up the cliff, steep and smooth,
Up the cliff, steep and smooth,
Up the cliff, steep and smooth,
Climbs Elder Brother
With his shining power.
Up the cliff, steep and smooth,
Up the cliff, steep and smooth,
He climbs step by step.

ELDER BROTHER AS A FLY

Song sung by Elder Brother as he concealed himself in the form of a fly

Himovali movali moko, himovali movali moko. Hivanytâ sikâsiimo,
 (?)   fly   die,   (?)   fly   die.   I will   sleep,
hivanytâ sikâsiimo. (Repeat)
 I will   sleep.
Himovali moko, hivanytâ sikâsiimo, hivanytâ sikâsiimo. (Repeat)
 (?)   die,   I will   sleep,   I will   sleep.
Tcinyny.
 Buzz-z.

Translation

Himovali! Die fly! Himovali! Die fly!
I shall sleep! I shall sleep!
Himovali! Let die! I am drowsy.
I will sleep! Buzz-z.

Song sung by the Eagle's wife to put him to sleep

Haya yakahai yahai mo, haya yakahai mo, hovanytâ sikâsiimo,
 (?)   (?)   (?)   (?)   (?)   (?)   (?),   I   sleep.
hovanytâ sikâsiimo. Haya yakahai mo, hovanytâ sikâsiimo, hovanytâ
 I   sleep.   (?)   (?)   (?),   I   sleep,   I
sikâsiimo. (Repeat)
 sleep.

Translation

Haya yakahai yahai mo! Haya yakahai mo!
I am sleepy, I am sleepy.
Haya yakahai yahai mo! I am sleepy.

DESTRUCTION OF HÂ-ÂK

As they prepare to destroy the female monster, Hâ-âk, Elder Brother and the people sing together

I

Tâ-ânɯnâma   Lɪtâĭ   hɑwɯli   voponak   nyɯhûna.   Amɯnyɯtâ
 Dazzling power Elder Brother winds   tie   singing.   Then sing
mɯlivak   wɯ-ɯmany   voponak   nyɯ-ɯhûna'.
 came swiftly   together   tie,   singing.

II

Kovakovɐ,   kovakovɐ,   kovakovɐ,   kovakovɐ.   Iyali   Moahanañ-
 (?)   (?)   (?)   (?)   Great   Mo'hatûk[a]
inamnyɯ-ɯna.   Kovakovɐ,   kovakovɐ.
 top singing.   (?)   (?)

Translation

Dazzling power has Elder Brother,
Mastering the winds with song.
Swiftly now we come together,
Singing to secure control.

Kovakovɐ, kovakovɐ,
Kovakovɐ, kovakovɐ.
Singing on the summit
Of great Mo'hatûk mountain.

---

[a] Mo'hatûk, Greasy mountain, between the Gila and Salt rivers near their confluence. It is supposed to be the home of Elder Brother.

III

Anayokûna,   anayokûna,   hayokûna.   Tcu-unarsat‘,[a]   yâvatcukǐ;
　　(?)　　　　　　(?)　　　　　　(?)　　　　　　　(?)　　　　　　cigarette:
kâsinakon   yâvatcuki.   Anayokûna,   anayokûna,   hayokûna.
sleep-inducing   cigarette.   　(?)　　　　　　(?)　　　　　　(?)

IV

Ala wus mo'-omok tâtâvaka tci'pia mi'ak âvaɟiaña mi'ak ât'cupaña.
This   all   sharps   mountains   moving   near   their well   near   having mortar

V

Vaɟ   wutama   vopahimû.   Vaɟ wutama   vopahimû.   Vaɟ wutama
Steep bank   on   throw.   (Repeat)
vopahimû.
Tcutcunoñi   ko'kovoli   sis'vûnûka-a.   Vaɟ wutama vopahimû.
Blue (or green)   owl   having brightest.   Steep bank   under throw.
Vaɟ wutama   vopahimû.
(Repeat)

Translation

Anayokûna, anayokûna, hayokûna.
　Sacred pipe of Tcu-unarsat‘,
Sleep-inducing sacred pipe.
　Anayokûna, anayokûna, hayokûna.

Hâ-âk flees from her pursuers.
　But her spring and mortar stay.
Throw a great stone!
　Throw a great stone!

The blue owl is brightest,
　Throw a great stone!
The blue owl is brightest.
　Throw a great stone.

Songs sung by Elder Brother and his followers in the Nether World

IN THE NETHER WORLD

I

Vatcikǐa himu: vatcikia himu;   vatcikia himu;   vatcikia himu.
We   go;   we   go;   we   go;   we   go.
Huk âsinyu apu ka'na.   Hita tuvavakǐ ahiya wunañitâ.   Vatcikǐa
That   me   pleases (?).   This   home   here   we leave.   we
himu; vatcikǐa himu; huk âsinyu apu ka'na.
go;   we   go;   that   me   pleases   (?)

Translation

We go, we go, we go, we go,
　Happy we leave our homes.
We go happily we go.

---

[a] Tcu-unarsat' is the name of a former Pueblo chief who lived near Mo'hatûk mountain.

II

Vatci'ki mʊtdʊ; vatciki mʊtdʊ. Vatciki mʊtdʊ; vatciki mʊtdʊ.
We   run;   we   run.   We   run;   we   run.
Vatciki mʊnʊ; vatciki mʊnʊ. Hʊkâsinyâmʊ kana. Hita tʊyâitaka
We   run;   we   run.   That me pleases   (?).   This   our country
hiya. Vavoyŏk vatciki mʊnʊ. Hʊkâsinyâmʊ kana.
here.   To leave   we   hasten.   That me pleases   (?).

Translation

We run, we run, we run, we run.
Happy we leave our land;
With pleasure hence we hasten.

On Emergence from the Nether World

On their emergence upon the surface of the earth the Nether-world
people danced together and with Elder Brother sang the following:

Itâvany nyi rsavikŭt dawʊwʊm aworsanyʊ.   (D. C.)
We thing   our   rattle   with   together.
Inʊ yatdâ mʊmai gĭñgĭñ vâikŭ.
This parrot   tails   waving   (?).

Itâvany nyi nyññyĭrsa awʊwʊm anyopinyʊ.   (D. C.)
We thing   our   (?)   with   we went down.
Ĭn a yokʊ mamai iyĭñyĭñ vâikû.
This (?)   tails   waving   (?).

Kʊsi tâhai tcʊtcʊwʊta(r) tamai tcitciviaka nyʊhʊnatci.
Kind of white   countries   on   come   singing.
Vâpânama hʊwʊtda-a.   Kotca wʊs tcitciviaka.   (D. C.)
Head-dresses   moving.   We   all   come.
Nyʊhʊnatci tconanyʊka tcʊtcʊwʊtda tcʊnâ nyʊ-ʊ-ʊ.
Singing   dancing   lands   shakes   (?)

Kʊsi tcokwe tâtâvakʊ tamaitʻ a-ahʊka nyʊhʊnatci sisivâta
Kind   of black   mountains   on   all come   singing   head-dresses
moñʊva-a
waving.
Kotca wʊs sita-ahʊka; kotca wʊs sita-ahʊta.
We   all   cherished;   we   all   cherished.
Nyʊhʊnatci, tconayʊka, tâtâvakʊ kâvânyʊ-ʊ.
Singing,   dancing,   mountains   rumbling.

Translation

Together we emerge with our rattles;
Together we emerge with our rattles,
Bright-hued feathers in our head-dresses.
With our nyññyĭrsa we went down;
With our nyññyĭrsa we went down,
Wearing Yokʊ feathers in our head-dresses.
This is the white land; we arrive singing,
Head-dresses waving in the breeze.
We have come! We have come!
The land trembles with our dancing and singing.
On these black mountains all are singing,
Head-dresses waving, head-dresses waving.
We all rejoice! We all rejoice!
Singing, dancing, the mountains trembling.

Songs of Elder Brother and his underworld supporters as they approached Casa Grande

I

Kan(d)ukai moki va-aki   ku-uka   amâ va-aki   ta-amai   sivany
Yonder   dead habitation   standing.   There habitation at that place he runs
mumuda-a', Sâ-âhamu maopanû kama iko-osi-i-i.[a]
about,   Yellow   hands   having   fabric.

Translation

Yonder stands the doomed habitation.
About the pueblo runs its frightened chieftain
In yellow garment with hand print decoration.

On Approaching Pueblos

As the underworld people approached Santan

Pipinû havavahaki kutda hamo-olina, pipinû havavahaki.
Mud   their house   in   they stay,   mud   their house.
Kutda maka hitcu, kotdena sinyu-upuitâka kutda ahamo-olina.
In   one hav- see,   he was   me   afraid   in   they stay.
   ing power
Pipinu   havavahaki   kutda   maka   hitcu.
Mud   their house   in   one hav- see.
                  ing power

Translation

In their house of adobe they are staying;
Their chief with magic power fears me.
In their house of adobe we see their chief.

As they approached the village below Santan

Amukâ vu-uhânyui-ita; amukâ vu-uhânyuita-a; hamânyui-i-i'.
Some will truly see;   some will   truly see;   some will see.
Kuhiyu hukiva mu-ulihâku rsâ-ânuka puva-aki nyui-i'.
That   old   okatilla   fence   their house   see.

Translation

Some will truly see,
Some will truly see,
Will see their house
Behind the okatilla stockade.

As they approached Sweetwater

Katdu kanyuvu-untdai sikâmumâli; katdu katcuvu-utdai
There   land   plenty beads; there   earth
sikâmumâli. Ku-u nanyutâ-â wo-orsai-i'. (Repeat from beginning)
plenty beads. The somebody come out.
        place

Hamiva yuna-a nutâ-â-i' wo-orsai-i' ku nyi-inuita-a Kutânâli-i.
There   place   somebody   came out his   soul   shines.
(Repeat)

Translation

There is the land of many beads,
There is the land of many beads.
Some one comes forth;
He knows what will befall him.

---

[a] Iko-osi-i-i' is for iks, meaning almost any textile fabric.

As they approached Casa Blanca

Kʋisi	kavʋhʋka;	kʋisi	kawʋhʋkʋ,	vavahaki	kʋtda	makahi
Very	difficult:	very	difficult,	house	there	magic power

tcʋ-ʋ'.
see.

Translation

It will be difficult,
It will be difficult,
To capture this pueblo
With its magic power.

As they approached Vulture's home

Hava'nyĭ	yali	nyanga,	Hava'nyĭ	yali	nya-aka,	tânâlikû	nanavai-i.
Raven	child	saying,	Raven	child	me call,	brightness	glitter.

(D. C.)

*Hiyanyi	yamʋkâ	nyuita	tânâlikû	konyonyoï.	(D. C. to *)
Here me	there	see	brightness	mirage.	

Above Gila Crossing

Nanyiki	va-aho	mʋkai	hiyanyĭ	worsanyʋk	himʋna	Tcʋnarsan
I am	?	magician	here me	arose.	went	Tcʋnasat

yâvatcʋkĭ	yoahana	hʋkatcĭ	nâmaiina	siamʋ	kokomaiᴧoaki-i.
cigarette	holding	with	my enemy	correct	incantation.

Nanyiki	vi-ikiho	mʋkai	hiyanyi	worsanyʋk	himʋna	kâsikʋn
I am	soft feather	magician	here me	arose	went	sedative

yâvatcʋkĭ	yoahana	hʋkatcĭ	nâmaiina	siâmû	kâkanasi-i.
cigarette	holding	with	my enemy	right	make sleep.

Hiyanyi	worsanyʋk	himʋna	Tcʋnarsan	vâvatcʋkĭ	yoahana
Here me	arose	went	Tcʋnasat	cigarette	holding

hʋkatcĭ	nâmaiina	siâmʋ	kokomaiᴧoaki-i.	Hiyanyi	worsanyʋk	himʋna
with	my enemy	correct	incantation.	Here me	arose	went

kasikʋn	âvwatcʋkĭ	yoahana	hʋkatcĭ	namaiina	siâmʋ	kâkâ-âsi-i.
sedative	cigarette	holding	with	my enemy	correct	make sleep.

At Mesa

Halisi	tcʋ-ʋnâki	pahaka	pahivwoa.	Halisi	tcʋ-ʋnâki	pahañgʋ
Small	blue	eagle	puts tail on.	Small	blue	eagle

pahivwoa	tcʋvwʋna	s-ʋtpava	worsanʋ-ʋ.	(D. C.)
put tail on	land	middle	came out.	

Hiyanyi	paiitcomi	yahaiiᴧa	kukivwa	tâvanyi	yosiañga	hʋkio
Here me	before me	to and fro	stand	it was	my cane	already

simamatcʋ-ʋ.
know.

Between Tempe and Phoenix

Hamʋkâ	vanyʋitahimʋ	hamanyʋ	tâtahivwoaka	nyuitahimʋ
Some will	you look for	there me	sit	you look for

hamʋka	nyʋinahɪ.	(D. C.)
you will	you look for.	

Rsâhikʋ	nâpahʋi	tʋnâtaku-ʋ	hamʋka	pʋmʋihi-i.
Pitiable	enemy	crazy	you will	take.

Rsâhikʋ	nâpahʋi	tʋnavamo-o	hamʋka	pʋmʋihi-i.
Pitiable	enemy	drunken	you will	take.

FESTAL SONGS

Ꞁ-ᴀʟᴀ Vâᴘâĭ Nʏɑĭ, Mɪᴅᴅʟᴇ Rᴜɴ Sᴏɴɢ

[By Ki-iwa, Bitten]

I

Makai kik(i) nyᴜitcota. * Makai kik(i) nyᴜitcota itany tânᴜlikany
Magician houses singing to. Magician houses singing to this my shining
rsᴜrsᴜ꜀ tcotcoa kony am nyᴜi tco. (Repeat. Then repeat twice
my straight stand I there singing to.
from *)

II

Tcᴜtcᴜpavfi yohovfi wᴜpᴜñgᴜ vâĭfimna; * tcᴜtcᴜpavfi yohovfi
Prostitute women first came running: prostitute women
wᴜpᴜñgᴜ vâĭfimûna, tcᴜtcᴜtâñgĭ yiâsiñga yokatc. Vâĭfimûna
first came running, blue flowers holding. Came running,
siyaliñgᴜ tatañgĭo vavanyiñañgi tconyopitci nyᴜnyâkimᴜ. (Repeat
east direction filing slow talking.
stanza; then repeat twice from *)
(At the beginning of this stanza the appointed singers appear in two
files, men and women apart)

III

Vanyĭñgi nyonyᴜ꜀a himᴜhᴜna; * vanyĭñgi nyonyᴜ꜀a himᴜhᴜna
I am crooked going; I am crooked going
honᴜnyñgᴜ. Ʌᴜhᴜʌᴜiva himᴜkaĭ kikiyânû kahatc mañgᴜvak
west. Toward going to rainbows with swing the arms
gamonya himᴜhᴜna. (Repeat same as above)
there I going.

Translation

Singing to the gods in supplication;
   Singing to the gods in supplication,
Thus my magic power is uplifted.
   My power is uplifted as I sing.

Prostitutes hither running come;
   Prostitutes hither running come,
Holding blue flowers as they run.
   Talking in whispers they file along.

Along the crooked trail I'm going,
   Along the crooked trail going west.
To the land of rainbows I'm going,
   Swinging my arms as I journey on

IV

Tânânâma sialĭk varsatca imuna; * tânânâma sialĭk varsatca imukuk
Shining   morning   up there   come;   shining   morning   up there   come

nyaihimuna yoipikot. Aimuna marsata imuna tarsaiʌa tcursatcimu
me reaching   pleiades.   Come   moon   come   sun   appear

sisiʌâɬ yovaya puihimuna. (Repeat stanza; then repeat twice from *)
rises   high   lifting.

V

Huvatcondu vâĭfimuna * momoi yohofi; vâĭfimuna tcuvañgi mâmâtâk;
Bluebird   came running   many   women;   came running   clouds   heads carrying;

vâĭfimuna wusat mâmunama tcuʌahañgi yongunyi nak vat vâñgu
came running   all   there top of   heads clouds   shaking   it   that   shaking

nyihina-a. (Repeat as above)
us.

VI

Aɽiwus kâmañgi tâkunad makai * tarsai; wopondak marsat yalihimuna
Kind of   gray   spider   magician   sun;   tie   moon   roll

hamukai kukiwoak yopam hyaimûkam. ɽnyuina tcunâñgi tciâĭkond
there   stand   turn   go.   See   green   cane

katc yovaya puihimuna-a. (Repeat as above)
with   raising   higher.

Translation

The bright dawn appears in the heavens;
    The bright dawn appears in the heavens,
And the paling pleiades grow dim.
    The moon is lost in the rising sun.

With the women Bluebird came running;
    With the women Bluebird came running;
All came carrying clouds on their heads,
    And these were seen shaking as they danced.

See there the Gray Spider magician;
    See there the Gray Spider magician
Who ties the Sun while the Moon rolls on.
    Turn back, the green staff raising higher.

TCɒTCꞀKA NYꞀĬ, NAME SONG

[By Vĭrsak Vâĭ-ĭ, Hawk Flying]

There are seventy stanzas in this song. Two names are called in each, a name being inserted in place of the words here in brackets. The song may begin with any stanza, but the name of the place where the dance is held must be inserted as the first name: thus, in the stanza below, the name of the village would be substituted for "Ma-akahi."

I

Halakoit namanꞹ vapaka worsanyꞹk mâhâĭnama tcꞹᴧꞹli. (Repeat)
(?)   top reeds arose   placing increase in
                       height.

Hitaᴧꞹ (Ma-akahi) moa-akatc yâhakaha hꞹkatcâĭ pawꞹsika kopatc
This [   ] kills with painted with it all over hair
maitcꞹ-ꞹ.
knock down.

Hitavꞹ Hivayomi pꞹkatc yâhakaha hꞹkatcâĭ pawꞹsika katâtc
This [ ] catch painted with it all over bow
maitcꞹ-ꞹ. (Repeat)
knock down.

II

Halakoĭt, ma-akahi wꞹma worsahi; halakoit (ma-akahi) wꞹma
(?)   magician with came up; (?)   magician with
worsamꞹ.
came up.

Hꞹkaitcꞹᴧꞹ Ma-akahi kopatc maitcꞹ-ꞹ; hꞹkaitcꞹᴧꞹ Hivayomi
That long [ ] hair knock down; that long [ ]
katâtc maitcꞹ-ꞹ.
bow knock down.

Translation

The ceremonial reeds are lifted;
 The ceremonial reeds are lifted.
Ma-akahi has killed an Apache,
 And we meet together here in war paint
To collect hair trophies with their power.
 Hivayomi has taken a captive,
And the magic of his bow dies with him.

Ma-akahi has come to our festa;
 Ma-akahi has come to our festa.
Ma-akahi ties the enemy's hair;
 Hivayomi kills the enemy's bow.

III

Siyal wutcâka huma-akahi yâhandak maitcu-u.
East   under   magician   colored   knock down.

Honony wutcâka humaakahi va-apaku yâhandak maitcu-u.
West   under   magician   reed   colored   knock down.

Ma-akahi sapâʌuhu nyâ-âku ko-opatc maitcu-u; Hivayomi sapâʌuhu
[   ]   correct   talk   hair   knock down; [   ]   correct

tcohi ka-atâtc maitcu-u.
do   bow   knock down.

IV

Imovali kâvâhaikĭ, kâvâhaikĭ, kaivaya, mokovaya tamâhi, (Repeat)
Near to   rumbling,   rumbling,   passing,   waving   top go,

tamâmhu.
top go.

Hitavu Ma-akahi pahañgu ʌupuhâva kavandaimu na-aka worsahi;
This   [   ]   eagle   like   shield   grasp   arose;

hitava Hivayomi virsañga vupuhava rsânvitcuki muka worsamu.
this   [   ]   hawk   like   club   grasping   arose.

V

Kamonya imuka nyuwunda nyuitahi sikuñga kop maitcu-u.
There   going   land   looking   good   hair   knock down.

Komonyi munduku navañga nyuitamhu sikuñgu, katâ maitcu-u.
There   run   mountain   seeing run   good,   bow   knock down.

Ma-akahi wumatc nyuitahi sikuñga kop maitcu-u; Hivayomi
[   ]   with   looking   good   hair   knock down; [   ]

wumatc nyuitahi sikuñgu katâ maitcu-u.
with   seeing   good   bow   knock down.

Translation

On this side the East Land the magician
   The sacred colored object has knocked down.
On this side the West Land the magician
   The sacred colored reed has overthrown.
Ma-akahi wisely talks, tying hair;
   Hivayomi wisely acts, killing bow.

The scout hears with trembling the sounds of night;
   The scout hears with trembling the sounds of night.
Ma-akahi eagle-like grasps his shield;
   Hivayomi hawk-like comes with his club.

Well-seeming is the land to the warrior
   As he goes to collect an enemy's hair;
And its mountains, as he kills the bow.
   Ma-akahi sees clearly as he ties the hair;
   Hivayomi sees clearly as he kills the bow.

VI

Kakâtak　tamai　pahañgʋ　naiwo-orsa,　Yakimʋli　tamai　virsangû
Crooked　　top　　eagle　　arose,　　　river　　top　　hawk
naiwo-orsa.
arose.

Hitavʋ　Ma-akahi　pahañgʋ　wʋmʋ　nyâhâkʋkaʌʋ　handa　tañgu
This　　[　　]　　eagle　　with　　talk　　　shield　grasp
kaworsahi.
arise and go.

Hitavʋ　Hivayomi　virsañga　wʋmʋ　nyâhâka　rsânyi-itcʋki　pʋhʋka
This　　[　　]　　hawk　　with　　talk　　club　　grasp arise
worsamʋ.
and run.

VII

Tcʋnâkima　kopanya　ikitcʋ　iya　vawoʌapa.
Blue　　　hair　　cut　here　brought.

Sivakimu　katânyi　mʋhʋka　iya　vawovapa.
Full-leaved　bow　catch　here　broughtɛ

Ma-akahi　moaka　hi-iya　vʋ-ʋnâñgiñga　vovapa;　Hivayomi　mipʋhi
[　　]　　kill　here　　dizzy　　brought;　[　　]　catch
hi-iya　vʋnavamoñgi　vovapa.
here　　drunk　　brought.

VIII

Gamonya　imʋna;　gamonya　imʋna;　gamonya　imʋhʋna.
There I　going;　there I　going;　there I　go.

Gamonyi　mʋnʋna;　gamonyi　mʋnʋna;　gamonyi　mʋnʋhʋna.
There I　run;　there I　run;　there I　run.

Itavʋ　Ma-akahi　paha　yonanda　hak　tânlimʋna;　hitava　Hivayoma
This　[　　]　eagle　arrow feathers　that　shining;　this　[　　]
virsaka　yomanda　hak　nyʋnyʋvâĭkʋ.
hawk　arrow feathers　that　air waves.

Translation

From the Superstition mountain rose the Eagle;
　From the sluggish-moving Gila rose the Hawk.
Ma-akahi talked with the Eagle, then
　Arose, grasped his shield, and went his way.
Hivayomi talked with the Hawk and then
　Arose, grasped his club, and journeyed forth.

With hair trophies our courage is renewed.
　Many of the enemy's bows we've captured.
Ma-akahi bravely endures fasting;
　Hivayomi bravely endures all thirst.

There I am going; there I am going.
　There I am running; there I am running.
Ma-akahi's eagle-feathered arrows!
　Hivayomi's strong hawk-feathered arrows!

IX

HaliΔuta   sihuñi   na-anakâ   kainamʊ nyâkna yoviva sipʊhimo
Brother   older   incoherent   sounds   talk   woman   take
kaiyavʊ nyâkna hatcyahami.
here   talk   accomplish.

HaliΔuta   sihuñi   na-anakâ   kainama   nyʊhʊna yaliva sipʊhimo
Brother   older   incoherent   sounds   sing   child   take
kaiyava nyʊhʊna hatcyahami.
here   sing   accomplish.

Itavʊ Ma-akahi na-anakâ kainamʊ nyâkna yoviva sipʊhimo kaiyavʊ
This   [   ]   incoherent sounds   talk   woman   take   here
nyâkna hatcyahami.
talk   accomplish.

Itavʊ Hivayomi na-anakâ kainama nyʊhʊna yaliva sipʊhimo
This   [   ]   incoherent   sounds   sing   child   take
kaiyava nyʊhʊna hatcyahami.
here   sing   accomplish.

X

Hi-i-i yoliva hi-iyoliva ya viyoli-iva hi; (Repeat) mhʊ.
(?)   (?)   (?)   (?)   (?)   go;   run.
HihitaΔʊ Ma-akahi ipoitatc tcʊtânyu hi-i-iyoliva yaviyoli-ivahi.
This   [   ]   hard   beating   (?)   (?)
Hihitava Hivayomi hʊɲa tatc kâvânyʊ hi-i-iyoliva yaviyoli-ivamhʊ.
This   [   ]   mind   (?) rattling   (?)   (?)

XI

Panʊmand katcokatc vihili hana vili   vawʊ-ʊpâ vatcohiña.
Coyote cub there it is   (?)   on   (?)   like   appearance.
(Repeat)
Hʊkaitcʊfʊ Ma-akahi pahaka wʊ-ʊpâ vatcohiña; hʊkai tcʊfʊ
That long   [   ]   eagle   like   appearance;   that   long
Hivayomi virsaka wʊ-ʊpâ vatcohiña.
[   ]   hawk   like   appearance.

Translation

Elder Brother mumbling caught the woman;
Elder Brother crooning caught the child.
Ma-ahaki mumbling takes the woman;
Hivayomi crooning takes the child.

Hi-i-i yoliva! Hi yoliva!
Hi-i-i ya viyoli-iva mhʊ!
Ma-ahaki's heart trembles on the war path;
Hivayomi's soul shivers with its fear.

There's the Coyote cub, Coyote cub!
There's the Coyote cub, Coyote cub!
Ma-ahaki resembles the Eagle;
Hivayomi resembles the Hawk.

XII

Yavahimʋ yavahimʋ yavahi. (Repeat)
Yavahimʋ yavahi.
Yavahimʋ yavahimʋ yavamhʋ. (Repeat)
Yavahimʋ yavamhu.

Nañʋ sʋkʋ Ma-akai taiwonyʋk kavandai paimitco yavahimʋ
I guess that   [   ]   arose   running   shield   (?)
yavahimʋ   yavahimʋ   yavahi,   nañʋ   sʋka   Hivayomi   taiwonyʋk
   (?)   (?)   (?)   I guess that   [   ]   arose
rsânyitcʋki mʋlitco, yavahimʋ yavamhʋ.
   club   make run,   (?)   (?)

Translation

Yavahimʋ, yavahimʋ, yavahi!
Yavahimʋ, yavahimʋ, yavahi!
Ma-akahi rose and ran with his shield;
Hivayomi rose and ran with his club.

CIRCLING SONGS[a]

PA-AK NYɴĭ, EAGLE SONG

[Composed by Vârsâ Âkam, Rat-Back. Told by Ki-iwa]

Accompanied by dancing and the beating of baskets. The dancers move in a circle made up of men and women alternately. "It looks bad for two men to be together."

I

Tarsaiĭ gamai yononyimʋta kʋn(d)a mânanahiwoakai tamaikû
  Sun   there   go down   in   sit   there
pahaka nyʋnyuĭ kop iyʋ rsǎnawoitco. (Repeat)
 Eagle   songs   you here commence.
Makai ki tava worsanyhʋ kamo nyi paitci tcʋwʋᴊʋ katcimhʋ.
Magician house arises   before me in front land   lays.
Tamaikʋ pahaka nyʋnyui kop iyʋ rsǎnawoitco. (Repeat)
 There   Eagle   songs   you here commence.

Translation

As the Sun sinks to the westward
We begin singing the eagle songs.
The home of the magician rises,
Standing before me in the land.
We begin singing the eagle songs.

---

[a] Sikâlhĭm Nyʋ̆ĭ; called also Basket-beating songs, Hoa Rsârsûna.

II

Yâi kapi worsa, yâi kapi worsa; Hatcuwuɟu Makai, yâi kapi
Now order arises, now order arises; he Earth Doctor, now order

worsa (Repeat)
arises.

Yai kapi worsa, hinâvat awutcâ tcut nyunyui tcoma worsana
Now order arises, hidden below from songs there arise

tcuwuɟu yâïnukamâ tcoatcoaiï. (Repeat)
land after planted.

III

Tcuwuɟu sapânyiki nyuï, tcuwuɟu sapânyiki nyuï, siyalïñgû
Land right I see, land right I see, east

tañgïo tcuɟ Itâï yahaɟ tcuwuɟu sapânyiki nyui. (Repeat)
direction from Elder child land right I see.
Brother

Tcuwuɟu sapânyiki nyuï siyalïñgû tañgïo tcut Itâï yahaɟ tcuwuɟu
Land right I see, east direction from Elder child land
Brother

sapânyiki nyuï. (Repeat)
right I see.

IV

Tâvañgû mai-ï, tâvañgû mai-ï; honoñyikû tañgïo tcuɟ, Toakoatam
Mountain win, mountain win; west direction from, White-Eater

havivihi tavukû mai-ï. (Repeat)
she remained mountain win.

Tâvañgû mai-ï, honoñyikû tañgïo tcuɟ, Toakoatam havivihi
Mountain win, west direction from, White-Eater she remained

tavukû mai-ï. (Repeat)
mountain win.

Translation

Earth Magician now comes hither;
Earth Magician now comes hither.
From the depths the songs are rising,
And by him are here established.

As now the land is prosperous ;
As now the land is prosperous
Elder Brother comes from the East;
He comes here as a child might,
The land prospers with his coming.

It was in the western mountains
That White-Eater Woman dwelt.
It was in the western mountains
That White-Eater Woman dwelt.

V

Hononyĭ ikamoisi iwʊgiom kʊna ka-ayofika hawʊs anyivia
West   there   reddish in   there bird   they all came

hanânyi wʊñga nyĭ.
there   around me.

Pahaka hanyʊnyâkĭ ivaʌuna hiyanyi imapai imaʌoaka anyʊĭna,
Eagle   his voice   stretched here I to you to touch   to see,

haiya ha aiya haya haya ha-a! Hamʊkâ nyʊĭta. (Repeat)
haiya (?) (?)   (?)   (?)   (?)   You   see.

Hiya nyi imapai imavoaka anyʊĭna, haiya ha aiya haya haya ha-a!
Here   I to you   to touch   see,   (?) (?) (?)   (?)   (?)   (?)

Hamʊkâ nyʊĭta. (Repeat)
You   see.

Translation

The evening glows red in the West,
    And the birds here gather about me.
Now I hear the screams of the Eagle.
Haiya ha aiya haya haya ha-a!
Now I meet and see you. Haiya ha!

HOA RSASÛNA NYꞁĬ BASKET-BEATING SONG

[By Virsak Vâi-ĭ]

I

Kanʊ vavai k̓okoana iyaimʊ. (Repeat)
Yonder cliff   end   roll.

Vavaki yʊwʊlimʊ. (Repeat)
Steep house windy.

Hitʊ ma-akahi yʊwʊlikatci opamana vitana, kanʊ vavai kokoana
This   magician   windy with   turn back wind borne, yonder cliff   end

iyaimʊ.
roll.

Vavaki yʊwʊlimʊ. (Repeat)
Steep house windy.

II

Siyaꞁ tânʊndûka mʊhʊka mʊꞁʊna ꞩikoꞁi kamhovatcokahi yahana
Morning   dawn   far   running younger brother preceding   feathers

rsoliñgahimʊ. (Repeat)
throwing.

Translation

Roll from cliff end to cliff end,
    Roll, Winds, from the steep house walls.
Thus the growing excitement
    Gathers like the winds that blow
From the house of Wind Magician.

In the East, my younger brothers,
    We are preceded by the bearers
Of the sacred eagle feathers.
    In the East, my younger brothers,
We are preceded by the bearers
    Of the sacred eagle feathers.

III

Pahakʊ yâitañga mʊtânyunʊ.   (Repeat)
 Eagle   field   thud.

Sahapâ kainama   mʊtânyimʊ tcorsaʃi pʊmʊnaikmʊ-ʊ.   (Repeat;
 Agreeable sounding   thud   rolling   thunder.

then sing all twice)

Translation

In the distant land of Eagle,
In the distant land of Eagle
Sounds the harmonious rolling
Of reverberating thunder.

KIKITÂVAL NYꟗI, SWALLOW SONG

[By Ki-iwa]

A song for fiestas that is accompanied by dancing.

I

Kikitâvalĭ yofĭñgû hiyany wʊwʊma nyʊnyuĭ ivamâ rsârsânûtco
 Swallow   birds   here   with me   songs   more   commence

hiyamy wʊwʊma nyʊhʊta-a.   (Repeat)
 here   with me   singing.

Rsâĭngama so-ofĭ yʊmapĭm olĭna-a hiyany wʊwʊma nyʊhʊta-a.
 Poor   women   together   stay   here   with me   singing.

(Repeat)

II

Vavaisa ñĭñĭtâvalĭ nam kʊka-a, vavaisa ñĭñĭtâvalĭ nam kʊka-a;
 Rocks   swallows   meet standing,   rocks   swallows   meet standing;

kʊʃamâ nyovapa-a, kʊʃamâ nyovapa-a, hanâny wʊwʊkany tcʊtâñĭa
 there   me brought,   there   me brought,   there me around   blue

kikihyâtû wovakĭmhû.   (Repeat)
 rainbows   appeared.

Vavaisa ñĭñĭtâvalĭ nam kʊka-a kʊʃamâ nyovapa-a hanâny wʊwʊkany
 Rocks   swallows   meet standing   there   me brought   there me around

tcʊtâñgĭa kikihyâʃû wovakĭmhʊ.   (Repeat)
 blue   rainbows   appeared.

Translation

Now the Swallow begins his singing;
Now the Swallow begins his singing.
And the women who are with me,
The poor women commence to sing.

The Swallows met in the standing cliffs;
The Swallows met in the standing cliffs.
And the rainbows arched above me,
There the blue rainbow arches met.

III

Tcotcoka kiñitâʌa‖d hiatâvâĭʌᴜka, hiatâvâĭʌᴜka monyĭ vanyimuʇa
Black   swallows   (they) here run-   (they) here run-   took   leading me
                                    ning came,   ning came

kamᴜ kâĭ-ĭny vanyimuʇa.   (Repeat)
there   me   brought me.

Hiatâvâĭʌᴜkahi kamᴜ kâĭ-ĭny vanyimuʇa kamᴜ kâĭ-ĭny vanyimuʇa.
Here running came   there   me   leading me   there   me   leading me.

(Repeat)

IV

Haiya! Rsâĭñga tcuʌᴜñgĭ pi yᴜnañgita-a kahosiyalĭ ʌᴜpᴜtcâhâ
Alas!   Poor   clouds   not   discoverable far in the east under

tâʌanga itcᴜ-uʇaa hamᴜ katcᴜ konya-am himᴜlivᴜka-a.   (Repeat)
mountain   in   there   lay   I there   arrived running.

Tcuʌᴜñgi pi yᴜnañgita-a kaho siyalĭ ʌᴜpᴜtcâhâ tâʌanga itcᴜ-ᴜta-a
Clouds   not   discoverable far in the east under   mountain   in there

hamᴜ katcᴜ konya-am himᴜliʌᴜka-a.   (Repeat)
lay   I there   arrived running.

V

Vatciki hyoata pᴜngâ hihivaka nyᴜhᴜna, vatciki yoa tapᴜngâ
We are   basket scraping   singing,   we are   basket

hihivaka nyᴜhᴜna; hodony muʇa vahamᴜtânyᴜ konyᴜñgᴜ kaitcoñga
scraping   singing;   evening in   thud   I am   listening

hitanyi yahana kokana tcᴜfa kianû rsaitcoñga.   (Repeat)
this my   feathers ·   tips   clouds   there   hanging.

Vatciki hyoata pᴜngâ hihivaka nyᴜhᴜna; hodony muʇa vahamᴜtânyᴜ
We are   basket   scraping   singing: evening   in   thud

konyᴜñgᴜ kaitcoñga hitanyi yahana kokana tcᴜfa kianû rsaitcoñga.
I am   listening   this my   feathers   tips   clouds   there   hanging.

(Repeat)

Translation

The Black Swallows running hither;
   The Black Swallows running hither,
Running hither came to lead me,
   Lead me there, lead me there.

Haiya! Far in the distant east
   Lie the clouds hidden under the mountain.
Far in the east direction
   To the hidden clouds come running.

We are beating the basket drums;
   We are beating the basket drums.
I am singing, I am listening;
   From my feathers clouds are shaking.

VI

Vanyʋ tânânadʋñgû kamʋdûkai vapamoɩ(d) rsorsonakĭ; namha
I am   dizzy   run   bog   water;   there

nanyinyiviha kuɟa uk mâkâfaɟ nyʋta-a vapaaka ñgiñgi rsa-aka ihya
I came   in there tadpole   singing   reeds   bark   girdle   here

vanyʋta.   (Repeat)
singing.

Vapamoɩ(d) rsorsonaki namha nanyinyiviha kuɟa uk mâkâfaɟ nyʋta-a
Bog   water   there   I came   in there tadpole   singing

vapa-aka ñgiñgi rsa-aka ihya vanyʋta.   (Repeat)
reeds   bark   girdle   here   singing.

VII

Hodony kânyʋnyʋʌʋnd katcʋ tamai sitcʋnâ-âki vañgitcʋd yâĭmʋɟa
Evening   land   lay   top   very blue   dragon fly   going

rsona-aki nanamai, ʌʋañgihya hʋnyʋl mamai kany rsotañgi tcoakana.
water   top,   hanging   his   tail   with   water   stick in.

(Repeat)

Kony hya-ama nyinyiviha kanyʋita hʋnyʋl mamai kany rsonañgi
I   there   came   see   his   tail   with   water

tcoakana yanakʋʌi rsamhonyʋ.
stick in   flapping   rustling.

VIII

Himonyi mʋnʋ-ʋna, himonyi mʋnʋ-ʋna; tcokañgia sisikimʋ,
There   I run,   there   I run;   darkness   rattling,

tcokañgia sisikimʋ-ʋ, tciavoɩd hyâsinga kony hʋnga sifânatcama
darkness   rattling,   visnaga   flowers   I   that   wear in hair

nyʋimʋlhimʋ.   (Repeat)
singing place going to.

Himonyi mʋnʋ-ʋna, tcokañgia sisikimʋ, tcokañgia sisikimʋ-ʋ,
There   I run,   darkness   rattling,   darkness   rattling,

tciavoɩd hyasiñga kony hʋnga sifânatcama nyʋimʋlhimʋ.   (Repeat)
visnaga   flowers   I   that   wear in hair   singing place going to.

Translation

I ran into the swamp confused;
   There I heard the Tadpoles singing.
I ran into the swamp confused,
   Where the bark-clothed Tadpoles sang.

In the West the Dragonfly wanders,
   Skimming the surfaces of the pools,
Touching only with his tail.   He skims
   With flapping and rustling wings.

Thence I run as the darkness gathers,
   Wearing cactus flowers in my hair.
Thence I run as the darkness gathers,
   In fluttering darkness to the singing place.

IX

Sikâla imṵta vanyi kinyonyoi vawṵpâ nyiwoata-a, hai-iya!
Round going   I   vulture   like   I make,   haiya!

Tamaiʌṵ katcimṵ parsâ vanyolina kanyṵita-a itâvanya ipṵinanga
Top   laying   near by   to I stay   see   this   breath

tcṵtcṵnâñgṵ-ṵ. (Repeat)
blue.

Tamaivṵ katcimṵ parsâ vanyolina kanyṵita-a itâvanya ipṵinañga
Top   laying   near by   to I stay   see   this   breath

tcṵtcṵnâñgṵ-ṵ. (Repeat)
blue.

X

ʌṵngihomi nakamṵla, ʌṵngihomi nakamṵla; hiâʌat nyṵihṵnda
Reddish   bat,   reddish   bat;   here   song end

ʌâkamṵnanahakimṵ pahañga viviñgi hṵkanyĭ sivânatconaha ʌâkamṵ-
rejoices   eagle   down   that I   put in head dress   re-

nanahakimṵ pawoĭ yâsi-imṵ.
joices   pawoi (tree) flower.

Translation

I am circling like the Vulture,
Staying, flying near the blue.
I am circling like the Vulture,
Breathing, flying near the blue.

Now the Reddish Bat rejoices
In the songs which we are singing;
He rejoices in the eagle down
With which we ornament our headdress.

Hâhâkima'i Nyḷĭ, Butterfly Song

[By Virsak Vâi-ĭ]

I

Yâkimaḷi nyṵnyṵi rsânatco, yâkimaḷi nyṵnyṵi rsanatco; *vatâ
Butterfly   song   commence,   butterfly   song   commence;   they

tcotconakṵ yahaipṵ vapaki(f)wa komoinanyi yovaiya pṵmṵhimṵ-ṵ.
dance   either side   to and fro   smoke   raise   higher.

(Repeat all; then repeat four times from *)

II

Yâkimaḷ yofiñu, yâkimaḷi yofiñu, *mohomoi nyṵhiʌṵ rsânatco
Butterfly   bird,   butterfly   bird,   many   song   commence

wṵhṵwṵi nyi nṵdṵna kita rsârsânûk komṵhi. (Repeat all;
toward   I   run   house   close to   dust.

then repeat twice from*)

Translation

The Butterfly song we now commence;
The Butterfly song we now commence,
Dancing on sides to and fro
Until the dust arises.

The Butterfly Bird, the Butterfly Bird
Commences to sing his many songs.
I run to where the dust arises,
Close to the walls of the house.

III

Vanyiki   yumotci   nyunyuiʌu   rsânatco.   (Repeat)
I am   now   song   commence.

*Konyami   kakayâk   wuhuʌui   nyi   mudukai   konyka   wumaika
I there   heard   toward   me   run   I that   with

wumanyi   rsânawoitco.   (Repeat all; then repeat twice from *)
with him   commence.

IV

Yonofañgu   yahaka   mohofi   *yakanyhi   wuwumu   rsânawoitco,
Cat-tail   leaf   woman   here me   with   commence,

hinhovat   wuganya   himihimu   iakoñga   nyi   iovaha   hayany
in there   round   going   here   my   taking   here

imamarsâku   mawoihimuna-a.   (Repeat all; then repeat twice from *)
my breast   touch.

V

Mâtcipand   unâvañgu   moi   tcuʌañgi   katci   wuma   nyuna.
Ma-atcpat   mountain   toward   cloud   lay   with   singing.
(Repeat)

*Kâmundak Unâvañgu piâ kiaya tcuʌañgi katci wumâ nyuhuna-a.
Kâ'matûk   mountain   not have   cloud   lay   with   singing.
(Repeat all; then repeat twice from *.   Sing four times)

VI

Mokalĭ   nâvañgu   kuhuka,   mokalĭ   tâvañgu   kuhuka;   * yaifiñgia
Dead   mountain   standing,   dead   mountain   standing;   hurry

imukama   tciviyaka   nyuitana   sikolĭ   kâkiwonda   yuwuhulitc
run   arrive   see   younger brother   I guess   wind his

an   avaiyu   ñgagaiva   munduhuna-a.   (Repeat as above)
there   pass   across   run.

Translation

I commence the song, I commence the song.
   I heard the singing as I ran;
I heard the singing as I ran.
   I join in with the singing.

The Cat-tail Woman commences singing;
   The Cat-tail Woman commences singing.
I join the circling dancers,
   Striking my breast and singing.

I sail in the clouds to Table mountain;
   I sail in the clouds to Table mountain,
And I sing with Kâ'matûk mountain
   Upon which there are no clouds.

Hurry to the Dead Standing mountain;
   Hurry to the Dead Standing mountain.
See there, my Younger Brother,
   How the winds there run their course.

VII

Mâyaɹ　　Nâvañgu,　　　Mâyaɹ　　Nâvañgu,　　* hanâvanyi　　wutcoma
Ma-ayal　　mountain,　　　Ma-ayal　　mountain,　　　yonder　　　before

tcuwuɹ　unakiomainu　hamâvaki　yundañga　yohof(ĭ)　yuhumuna-a.
land　　　strip　　　　house　　　in　　　woman　　　laughing.

(Repeat as above)

VIII

Kakândaku　Nâvañgu　yalikâpa　nyuna.　(Repeat)
Kakotuk　　mountain　down hill　singing.

* Tâtârsaki　ñgingikoatci　muɹiva　kuuwusi　tcunangi　rsonañgitco-o.
Foam　　　head band　came running　kind that　blue　　water.

(Repeat as above)

Translation

> At the clearing of Ma-ayal mountain;
> At the clearing of Ma-ayal mountain,
> Before the house of the Magician,
> There stands the woman laughing.
>
> Here on the slopes of Crooked mountain;
> Here on the slopes of Crooked mountain,
> Around whose crest the foam remains,
> We have run for blue water.

GAME SONGS

Tâkaʻɪ(d) Nyɒĭ, Tâkal Song [a]

[By Vɪrsak Vâɪ-ĭ]

I

Tâkalimhu, tâkalimhu, * tâïta wiva yuwuli mulitco-o.　(Repeat all;
Takalimhu,　　takalimhu,　our field toward　wind　make run.

then repeat twice from *)

Translation

> Takalimhu, takalimhu,
> The wind helps us with our ala
> When we play the game of takal(d).
> Takalimhu, takalimhu,
> The wind helps us with our ala
> When we play the game of takal(d).
> The wind helps us with our ala
> When we play the game of takal(d).
> The wind helps us with our ala
> When we play the game of takal(d).

---

[a] This song is sung in the evening, and during the next day the women play the game called Tâkaɹ(d).

II

Hʊwʊli mʊlitcona, * huwuli mʊlitcona hʊkanyki tâkalimʊ wʊsi
Wind,   make it run,   wind   make it run   that I with   takal(d)   all

kʊkʊhʊva-a. (Repeat as above)
win.

Translation

Wind, swiftly make our ala run
That I may win at takal(d).
Wind, swiftly make our ala run
That I may win at takal(d),
That I may win at takal(d),
That I may win at takal(d).

WOITCOTA OR RSÂNYKI NYɒĭ, FOOTBALL SONG ᵃ

[By Virsak Vâi-ĭ]

I

Momoi yânama humiaki nyiâkimʊ. (Repeat) *Konyʊ simâ
Many   people   together   talking.   That I   there

kʊkiwak yosi kawonakʊ naitcona kitâvalĭ yofĩñgʊ nyapâyanʊñgʊ
stand   stick   ball   throw   swallow   bird   me   flapping

vimʊ. (Repeat all; then repeat twice from *)
(?)

II

Tcokoikamʊ tânâvañgʊ *kamova hondonyiñgʊ parsâva kʊkimʊta
Black   mountain   far   west   this side   stand

samʊkâ wʊwʊĭ pamʊmʊlimʊ tarsai yʊnda nyoka wʊñgany naipimʊ.
toward   run   sun   in   middle   round   run.

(Repeat as above)

III

Tawot yatamʊ *komûs siny wʊnata-akʊ vany mʊlitco kamova
Who   man   you   me   with   me   run   there

tcokama nyʊitaimʊ hinavany nyoñgi ta nʊmamangʊvi yʊkaimʊ
goal   looking   there me   in front   of   waving the hands his shadow?

(Repeat as above)

Translation

Many people have gathered together,
I am ready to start in the race,
And the Swallow with beating wings
Cools me in readiness for the word.

Far in the west stands the Black mountain
Around which our racers ran at noon.
Who is this man running with me,
The shadow of whose hands I see?

ᵃ Sung the evening before the day of the foot race.

VÂPÛTAI NYɑĬ, LAY SONG [a]

[By Virsak Vâĭ-ĭ]

I

Yandʋndo itcaya, yandʋndo itcaya.   (Sing three times)

II

Yandʋndo iya-andʋndo.   (Sing three times)
Hoho kaviyo fʋnd, ama aimivakavi yo fund; ova, ova, yo wiyanhi hila atcovayo nimiya no kiyaho.   Hoho kaviyo fʋnd ama, âĭniva kaviyo fʋnd.   (Repeated until the opponents guess where the sticks are)

A-AL HATCITCIVITAK NYɑĬ, CHILDREN PLAY SONG

[By Sika'tcu, Dry]

ʌuk'imûlolo tak vaiwana.   (Repeat indefinitely)
The children clasp hands and dance and sing this song. They are divided into two parties, one leader saying â'nûmatcĭt and the other kĭl'siyâ.

HUNTING SONGS

KÂTɑTÂPĬ NYɑĬ, DATURA SONG [b]

[By Virsak Vâĭ-ĭ]

I

Tâhaiva siyalĭ kʋkĭm, *tâhaiva siyalĭ kʋkĭm; kʋta nyi worsanyûk
White   morning   stand,   white   morning   stand;   in   I   arose
hi-ĭm.   (Repeat from *)
go.

Tcʋtâñgĭ yondany kʋñgʋsĭm, *tcʋtâñgĭ yondany kʋñgʋsĭn; kʋta nyi
Blue   evening   falls,   blue   evening   falls;   in   I
worsanyûk hi-ĭm.   (Repeat from *)
arose   go.

Translation

At the time of the White Dawn;
At the time of the White Dawn,
I arose and went away.
At Blue Nightfall I went away.

---

[a] Derived from another tribe, but from which is not known. The meaning of the words is not known to the Pimas.

[b] This and the Pihol song are sung to bring success when setting out on a deer hunt. This song is principally depended upon in cases of sickness where the characteristic symptoms are vomiting and dizziness.

II

Kâtʊndamiᵃ ya-ahañgʊ, *kâtʊndami ya-ahañgʊ; konyitcoma
Thornapple leaves, thornapple leaves; I that

hoñgiyâk nânɉahangʊ rsakalĭ mʊmʊlihimʊ. (Repeat all; then repeat
eat dizzy stagger run.

from *)

Kâtʊndami yâsĭñgʊ, * kâtʊndami yâsĭñgʊ; tcoma hiyâkʊ navahamo
Thornapple flowers, thornapple flowers; that drink drunk

rsakalĭ mʊmʊlihimʊ. (Repeat from *)
stagger run.

III

Kakatâ kʊviholi yânamʊ nyâïta-a, * hiyavâ nyiahʊ vatâny, mʊmoak
Bows great remaining man following, here overtook he me, killed

inyi, wopa hitany yahañga hikomiaka rsolĭñga-a. (Repeat from *)
me, left this my horns cut off throw away.

Vapakâ kʊviholi yânamʊ nyâïta-a, * hiyavâ nyiahʊ vatâny,
Reeds great remaining man following, here overtook he me,

mʊmoak inyi, wopa hitany nânhavia hikomiaka rsolĭñga-a. (Repeat
killed me, left this my feet cut off throw away.

from *)

IV

Momovali nâtakimʊ, * momovali nâtakimʊ, kaɉoho miawaka hamâ
Fly crazy, fly crazy, there drop there

yanaki taimhʊ-ʊ. (Repeat from *)
flap.

* Yâkimalĭ navakâhi, yâkimalĭ navakâhi, kaɉoho miawaka hamâ tapai
Butterfly drunk, Butterfly drunk, there drop there open

kimʊ-ʊ. (Repeat from *)
and shut wings.

Translation

I ate the thornapple leaves
And the leaves made me dizzy.
I drank thornapple flowers
And the drink made me stagger.

The hunter, Bow-remaining,
He overtook and killed me,
Cut and threw my horns away.
The hunter, Reed-remaining,
He overtook and killed me,
Cut and threw my feet away.

Now the flies become crazy
And they drop with flapping wings.
The drunken butterflies sit
With opening and shutting wings.

ᵃ A native thornapple, Datura meteloides D. C. It is popularly believed that if one eat an undi-
vided root it will render him temporarily insane, but if the root be divided or branching it is
innocuous. There is a tradition that a man at Blackwater ate of the root and directed that he be
locked in an empty house until the effects should wear off. He was locked in at noon and toward
evening he was seen running through the thickets toward the river a couple of miles distant. He
recovered his senses when in the middle of a thorny thicket of mesquites. His limbs were scratched
and bruised, yet he had been unconscious of any injury until the moment of recovering his wits.

PIHOT NYꞏĬ, PIHOL SONG

[By Virsak Vȧĭ-ĭ]

I

Yali	tcovu	makai	tcokak	ut	muꞌutatc	yoai	tcokak	yoapa,
Younger	hare	magician	blackness	in	running	black-tailed deer	meat	bring

sialĭm	antâ	yoapa,	sialĭm	antâ	yoapa-a.	Yali	kaꞈu	makai	tcokak	ut
morning	I will	bring,	morning	I will	bring.	Younger badger magician		blackness		in

muꞌutatc	yoai	tatat	yoapa,	sialĭm	antâ	yoaka,	sialĭm	antâ	yoapa-a.
running	black-tailed deer	feet	bring,	morning	I will	bring,	morning	I will	bring.

(Repeat four times)

II

Nany	pia	hyᴜwᴜlĭk,	nany	pia	yᴜwᴜlĭk,	nany	pia	hayᴜwᴜli-ika-a.
Had I	no	wind,	had I	no	wind,	had I	no	wind.

Nany	pia	hatcᴜʌakĭk,	nany	pia	tcᴜvakĭk,	nany	hatcᴜva	ki-ika-a.
Had I	no	clouds,	had I	no	clouds.	had I		no clouds.

Kahova	siyalĭ	wᴜtca	sâhama	IkoꞮ	kᴜkatc	yamhâ	nyᴜ	vaita,	nany	pia
Distant	east	under	yellow	(?)	standing	there	me	calling,	had I	no

yᴜwᴜlĭk,	nany	pia	hayᴜwᴜli-ika-a.	Kamhova	hondony	wᴜtca	sâhama
wind,	had I	no	wind.	There	west	under	yellow

IkoꞮ	kᴜkatc	yamhâ	nyᴜ	vaita,	nany	pia	yᴜwᴜlĭk,	nany	pia
(?)	standing	there	me	calling,	had I	no	wind,	had I	no

hayᴜwᴜli-ika-a.	Kamhova	hondony	wᴜtcâ	sâhama	IkoꞮ	kᴜkatc
wind.	There	west	under	yellow	(?)	standing

yamhâ	nyᴜ	vaita,	nany	pai	tcᴜwᴜkĭk,	nany	pia	hatcᴜwᴜki-ika-a.
there	me	calling,	had I	no	clouds,	had I	no	clouds.

Translation

Young Hare Magician running
Brings black-tailed deer venison.
And young Badger Magician
Brings the feet of black-tailed deer.

Had I neither winds or clouds?
In the east the Yellow Ikol,
In the west the Yellow Ikol
Called me.   I had no winds or clouds.

MEDICINE SONGS

Toatcita Nyɔ̆ĭ, Cure Song[a]

[By Juan Thomas]

I

Hodony ʌungiomima kâĭhowa nyopinyima, hodony ʌungiomima
  Evening   red   not yet   sink,   evening   red
kâĭhowa nyopinyima; * kony suña yuna tcomu nahivaka nyuina
  not yet   sink;   me   I   in   there   sit   see
itanyi rsâvikŏna sikâɾ munukai muɟa sisĭnyi hikimu.
  my   gourd   round   run   in   rattling hikimu.

Hodony ʌungiomima kâĭhowa nyopinyima, hodony ʌungiomima
kâĭhowa ·nyopinyima; ** kony suña yuna tcomu nahivaka nyuina
itanyi matcuowina sikâɾ munukai muɟa pupunai hikimu. (Repeat
             feathers   rumbling
to *)

Kony suña yuna tcomu nahivaka nyuina itanyi rsâvikŏna sikâɾ
  I   I   in   there   sit   see   this my   gourd   (?)
munukai muɟa sisinyi, hikimu. (Sing from **)
  (?)   (?)   (?)   (?)
Kony suña yuna tcomu nahivaka nyuina itanyi matcuowina sikâɾ
  (?)   (?)   (?)   (?)   (?)   (?)   (?)   feathers
munukai muɟa pupunai hikimu. (Repeat all four times)

II

Kus sitcoña muʌany vâññnyi taĭma. (Repeat)
  Kind of all   night   he me shaking.
Kaho makai kiyundavam nyoapaimu kus sitcoña muʌany vâññnyi
  Up   there   magician's house me brought kind of all   night   he me
                 in there
taĭma. (Repeat second line; then repeat all four times)
shaking.

Translation

The evening glow yet lingers;
  The evening glow yet lingers,
And I sit with my gourd rattle
  Engaged in the sacred chant.
As I wave the eagle feathers
  We hear the magic sounding.

Puissant Night is shaking me
  Just as he did at the time
When I was taken up in spirit
  To the great Magician's house.

---

[a] This song was sung by a Blackwater medicine-man when making his diagnosis of a case. In this connection read the history of Sala Hina's treatment when poisoned (p. 260).

III

Alisi yoa-amʊ vavatcosĭ hʊtcʊ̢ ya-ana yopanaka yʊkatc vanyi
Kind of yellow wren himself feathers pull out with it make me

tcʊpaftcona *hiyanyi mâmâtamʊ maʌʊrsapaiĭmʊ tcʊwʊnda wʊsikâ
prostitute here my head clasp hands land all over

mʊmʊhʊlimʊ. (Repeat; then repeat twice from*; repeat all four
run.

times)

IV

Alisi tcʊtcʊnañĭ kâlâkamʊ * tcʊwʊnda loñitan(ʊ) tcʊtâñi yʊwʊlhʊla
Kind of blue kakakamu land edge blue wind

vâĭrsapaiĭmʊ tâta yʊwʊlhʊla vipiahimʊ vatâĭ hʊʌʊndak tcʊnyʊwʊna
lying on white wind left make wind land

kopânyima. (Repeat as above)
dust.

V

Mamʊrsanû tânâli kia nyʊ̢a viñĭ kʊkionyût. *Amʊkâ valnyʊihita
Moons shine here me in here stand. You men will see

nalo-oʝi tcʊtañi vapʊkanyi kohona varsoi mʊk nyi nanamʊ. (Repeat
women blue reed me blow far distant me meet.

as above)

VI

Haiya! Haiya! Rsâvikohot man sisikimʊ. (Repeat)
Haiya! Haiya! Gourd there rattling.

Konyʊ wʊwʊiʌa himûk am nyʊita himan vâĭtcokimʊ rsâvikohot
That I toward go there see laying gourd

man sisikimʊ. (Repeat; then repeat all four times)
there rattling.

Translation

Yellow Bird placed his feathers
 Where they fell on the head of the woman;
Making of her a harlot who ran about
 With her hands clasped before her.

Bluebird drifted at the edge of the world,
 Drifted along upon the blue wind.
White Wind went down from his dwelling
 And raised dust upon the earth.

The moonshine abides in me;
 And soon you men and women will see
The reed that I now am blowing
 Bring the Moon down to meet me.

Haiya! The gourd is rattling;
 Haiya! The gourd is rattling.
When I go to see it there
 I surely find it rattling.

VII

Kotc yυmoiva loɿony taimυ, kotc yυmoiva loɿony taimυ; ha
We now evening taimu, we now evening taimu; our
rsυrsυpinyimυ * kυsυ tâta mâhâmama kiñi tâvalĭ matcυwoena ñĭngi
younger brothers kind of white headed swallow (bird) wing feathers four
kaya pυtânyinaha kiya loɿony taiĭmυ. (Repeat; then repeat twice
there rattling here evening taiĭmυ.
from *. Sing all four times)

VIII

Litâĭ Makai * vapaka likotcυkυ kamo nyi paitcomi vopa
Elder Brother reed magician cut yonder me before in front throw
kυirsapaiĭmυ kυnɿak tcυʌañĭ kaitañima. (Repeat from *. Sing all
step on in clouds sounding.
four times)

IX

Alisi kâkâmaki Wυmυkalĭ * vâviki s'oam aiitco tconyitcokimυ
Kind of gray Coyote he is yellow something making
p'mυmυs hυk vamät an kiwonatcoña. (Repeat all; then repeat twice
meddler that snake there belt.
from *)

X

Aliwυsi tcυtâñi papat lohoȷi namkâk varso nyi nanamûk kamhony
Kind of blue frog woman meet there me meet somewhere
pυĭtcokimυ * kaho sialiñυ. Marsâ sυtâta tcυʌakia pâĭtcotco hamυñυ
carry me yonder east. Front white clouds there stand there
yâĭnυka pâiny pυĭ tcokimυ. (Repeat all; then repeat twice from *)
after me carry me.

Translation

It is evening, it is evening.
And four times at evening
Calls the white-headed Swallow
As he plucks out his feathers.

Elder Brother cuts his reed,
Yonder before me now he throws it,
Stepping upon it so that the
Clouds loudly repeat the sound.

Gray Coyote is a dirty meddler,
He wears a belt of snake skin.
Gray Coyote is a dirty meddler,
He wears a belt of snake skin.

Blue Frog-woman met and carried me
To the cloud land in the East.
Blue Frog-woman met and carried me
To where the clouds are standing.

XI

Kokakĭ momovĭny tcʋfʋhʋlimʋ * kʋnɟa kʋs kâmaki Wʋmʋkalĭ,
Wood   triangle   rising   in kind of gray   Coyote,

naiwonyima ʋyânʋ kaiʌʋ matcʋowina hʋkanyâĭ nyi tânâlhitaimʋ.
arose   at one side of the back wing feathers   with it   me   shine.

XII

Yâĭnʋpanʋ tâtâvaña * kʋɟaña Litâĭ tcʋnyʋwʋnda tcopolitaiimʋ
Dead field   mountain   in   Elder   land   rectangular
                              Brother

kŏnyʋ huñʋ yʋnda mâvavaka nyʋina konyʋ huñu nyʋita-ımʋ.
I in   that   in   enter   there see   I in that   saw.

XIII

Alwʋs yoa-am vavatcosĭ * kahamova mʋhʋmʋkâ tcʋtcâkamʋ
Kind of yellow   wren   yonder   distant   caves

tâtâvañu woeka pʋnyĭ pʋĭtcokimʋ kamodanyi mamaitcomhi
mountain toward there me   carry me   before me   close to

pâkʋnyĭm tcʋkahima.
thump   so far.

XIV

Alwʋsʋ kâkâmañi Taɟrai wotʋ makai kamhʋ mamaɟatc piohokimʋ
Kind of   gray   Road-runner he magician he   young his   hungry

tcom rsoakimonha * hia tâtaiwonyk tcʋtcʋwʋna tcʋtcʋmâka
then   cry   here   arose   lands   everywhere

mʋmʋhʋlima alʌâpâyolĭ mʋmoahak kʋʌarsatc kahĭ yan mâtâĭ
running   millipeds   killed   approaching across there carry

tcoña.
on back.

Translation

Gray Coyote stood in the forest,
   From his shoulders he plucked feathers
That gave me shining power,
   Plucked wing feathers bearing power.

I entered Yâĭnʋpanʋ mountain
   And saw Elder Brother's land
Marked off with its square corners,
   Marked as in a rectangle.

Yellow Bird carries me to the caves,
   To the distant caves of the mountain.
And we hear the sound of his footsteps
   As he moves upon his way.

Gray Road-runner, the magician,
   As his young cried out with hunger,
Ran about engaged in killing
   Millipeds that he carried home.

XV

Alwʊsʊ	tcotcok	kâmkitcʊma	*tcokañi	ñiopondak	varsatc
Kind of	black	turtle	darkness	made a belt	toward

vâĭtcokimʊ	am	kai	panyʊmʊnda	tcokaki	yoñu	nyitaimu.
laying	there	make	shake	darkness	shaking	nyitaimu.

XVI

Icʊpaf	yohofi	naiwonyk	*anâvany	wʊwʊkany	mʊmʊhʊlimʊ	yâvany
Harlot	woman	arose and run	around me	me	ran	here me

pamarsâĭpʊ	mamakʊʌa.
breast	beat the air.

XVII

Âiñâ	smamatcʊn	rsʊrsʊpĭnyĭ	*inañʊ	tarsai	kaho	toconyihima
Hurry	know	younger brothers	around	sun	up there	come up

yâĭñâ	smamatcʊn	rsʊrsʊpĭnyĭ	kâsikâyany	mamaka	himʊ.
hurry	know	my younger brothers	drowsiness	gave	himu.

Translation

The Black Turtle now approaches us,
    Wearing and shaking his belt of night.
The Black Turtle now approaches us,
    Wearing and shaking his belt of night.

The harlot arose and ran about,
    Beating her breast and the air.
The harlot arose and ran about,
    Beating her breast and the air.

Understand, my younger brothers,
    That it is the Sun that gives me
The trance vision that I see.
    The Sun gives magic power.

KÂMKʌTCʌT NYʌĬ, TURTLE SONG

[By Virsak Vâĭ-ĭ]

Sivany	lahai,	sivany	lahai,	sivany	lahai,	sivany	lahai.	(Repeat)
Chief	told,	chief	told,	chief	told,	chief	told.	

Kʊwʊsi	kʊhʊñga	siyali	worsa	kʊndañgʊ	pahaka	wʊwʊmia	nyʊkai,
Kind of good	morning	rise	at the same time	eagle	with		sang,

sivany	lahai,	sivany	lahai.	Kʊwʊsi	kʊhʊñga	hondony	tcopi	kʊndañga
chief	told,	chief	told.	Kind of good	evening	sank	at the same time	

virsaka	wʊwʊmia	nyʊkai,	sivany	lahai,	sivany	lahai.	(Repeat four
hawk	with	sang,	chief	told,	˙ chief	told.	times)

Translation

Tell their leader, tell their leader;
    With their leader sings the Eagle
When the morning dawn is here;
    Hawk sings with him at even.

Kâmkʊtcʊt, kâmkʊtcʊt, papt vatcĭvĭ varso hʊtcʊɩ rsotk ʊt vatcĭvĭ,
Turtle, turtle, where swim there pond water in swim

kosta, kosta, kosta, kosta, kosta, kosta. (Repeat four times)
(?) (?) (?) (?) (?) (?)

Translation

Turtle, Turtle, where are you?
Where is the pond in which you swim?
Kosta, kosta, kosta, kosta,
Where is the water you swim in?

Tcɑmamaikĭ Nyɑĭ, Horned Toad Song

[By Virsak Vâĭ-ĭ]

I

Siyalikâ nyʊnyʊwʊta vasitʊ mâhâĭtama tcohiñga. (Repeat)
East direction land pleasant looks.

*Konyʊka wʊhʊwʊĭva himʊkâ nyʊita vasitʊ mâhâĭtama tcohiñga.
I that toward go see pleasant looks.

(Repeat as above)

II

Hondonyikâ nyʊnyʊwʊtʊ vasita mʊpʊitama tcohiñga. (Repeat)
West direction land very fearful looks.

*Samʊkâ wʊhʊwʊĭva mʊndʊ ka nyʊita vasita mʊpʊitama tcoiñga.
There toward run see very fearful looks.

(Repeat as above)

Translation

The East Land seems very pleasant.
I go toward it and I see
How pleasant it seems to be.
I go toward the Pleasant Land.

West Land is most terrible.
I go toward it and I see
How terrible the Land is.
I go toward the fearful Land.

Tciatakĭ Nyɑĭ, Gila Monster Song

[By Sʊtatk(i), Prepare]

I

Rsâĭngali tcʊpafi yohof, *kâĭhova yon(d)onyima nyi moitakʊ
Pitiable prostitute woman, not yet evening me soul

yâhâsimʊ kahova nyâĭnaka tcʊpafia nyi moitakʊ yâhâsimʊ.
flower up after prostitute me heart flower.

(Repeat; then repeat from*. Sing all four times)

Translation

Pitiable harlot though I am,
My heart glows with the singing
While the evening yet is young.
My heart glows with the singing.

II

Ya-aɪ vavaitcotcom hanâvany ʌuñganyi ñgâñgâkĭ nyʊkai *hami
That   stone standing   there   around   two   sing   there
tamai tcokañgi hʊwʊn(d)aku noahimʊ kâinaku yahai yanañgʊhʊʌa.
top   black   wind   roaring   after back and forth flutter.

(Repeat as above)

III

Ya-aɪ tâhai Ñgiwolĭk, *hami tamai sʊtcʊnañgĭ mamahat nyʊ-ʊhʊna
That white Ñgiwolik,   there top   green   frog   singing
kʊsʊ tcuñañgi tcʊvakĭ kahatc momoi nyʊhʊna. (Repeat as above)
kind of blue   clouds   lay   many   singing.

Translation

Where the two stones were standing,
  Black Wind roared in fearful blasts,
Driving the birds before him
  Fluttering back and forth.

On the summit of white Ñgiwolik
  There the green frogs are singing.
Lying near the blue storm clouds
  There many frogs are singing.

Tcoso-okaɪ Nyɒĭ, Black Lizard Song

[By Ha-ata, Finished Olla]

I

Makai ki wʊpʊkʊ nyʊĭtco, *makai ki wʊpʊkʊ nyʊĭtco, sikoɪ tarsai
Magician house first   sing to,   magician house first   sing to,   round sun
tcʊrsʊnyĭng tarsai sisvân hʊwʊwʊm haimhʊna-a. (Repeat; then
arose   sun   rays   with   go.
repeat from*. Sing all four times)

II

Tcʊtcʊpavi yohofi kaka wondʊ ʌâĭfimʊna, *tcʊtcʊpavi yohofi
Prostitute   women   group come running,   prostitute   women
kakawondʊ ʌâĭfimuna, tcʊtcʊpavi ʌâĭfʊnʊna hikimoli yâsika
group   come running, prostitute   come running (a plant)   flower
ñgĭñgikoatci ʌâĭfimʊna-a. (Repeat as above)
crowns   come running.

Translation

We first sing at the Magician's;
  We first sing at the Magician's,
The round disk of the Sun arose,
  Accompanied with its rays.

Harlots came running in a group;
  Harlots came running in a group.
Harlots came with hikimoli,
  Flower crowns upon their heads.

III

Hali wʋsʋ tcotcok tcosokalĭ *Hitâĭ mulkon kâĭnak tâta tcʋʌahañgi
That   kind of   black   lizard   Elder of running following white   clouds
                                    Brother trail

nyʋyâpa nânâvitc âĭnak kʋhʋwʋs tâtam rsorsoñgimʋ. (Repeat as
came out   arms   following kind of   white   pools.
above)

IV

Yali vaʌʋñgam navañgʋ *tamai tcokaki yondʋnyihimʋ, wʋkanyi
That   stony   mountain   top   darkness   go down,   round

minyʋmʋ tataip yoakoñgimʋ. (Repeat as above)
going   backward   scatter.

V

Hali wʋsʋ ʌʋpʋñgiom vapamandʋ tâkʋnândʋ vinyina tcoikatc
That   kind of   reddish   snakes   spider   string   like

yondʋnyʋ̆, kamovingi yondonyikâ vaʌana tâkûnândʋ vinyina tcoika
came down   west   direction   stretched spider   string   like
there,

yahai   pʋvaopana-a.
opposite sides   stretching.

Translation

Black Lizard found the trail where
Elder Brother had been running,
And he came out from the clouds
With water upon his arms.

Darkness settles on the summit
Of the great Stony mountain.
There circling round it settles
On the great Stony mountain.

The ruddy beams like spider threads
Across the sky came streaming.
The reddish snakes like spider's web
To the opposite side came flaming.

KÂKÂĬ NYʌĬ, RATTLESNAKE SONG

[By Ki-iwa]

I

Yalova yondonaa kanyʋhʋta, *yalova yondonaa kanyʋhʋta;
Early   evening   I sing,   early   evening   I sing;

kamodanyĭ mamatcomĭ nyʋnyʋĭ ʌʋmamatâkaimʋ konyhʋñga
ahead of me   in front   songs   open   I that

wʋhʋʌʋma momoiva nyʋhʋ-ʋna. (Repeat from beginning; then
with   many   singing.

repeat twice from *)

Translation

In the early evening,
In the early evening
We begin to sing many songs;
And I join in singing many.

II

Kâmᴜndakᴜ nânâvaka worsanyimᴜ, *hamalĭ mamarsâka likorsapĭ
Kâ′matûk   mountain   came forth,   there   near   low clouds

nyᴜyâpakimᴜ-ᴜ.   Kâmᴜndakᴜ nânâvakᴜ miapitaimᴜ kokongama
came out.   Kâ′matûk   mountain   closer   top

nyᴜyâpakimᴜ.   (Repeat as above)
came out.

III

Tâwondᴜ yâhânama iyatcom ᴜmasĭ, *tâwondᴜ yâhânama iyatcom
Who   man   here   appear,   who   man   here

ᴜmasi?   Konyi tcoma yañgamᴜ kâkâĭva yᴜlina piâviki yᴜngai
appear?   I   there   horned   snake   think   not   him

wonda tciyatcomᴜ mamasimᴜ?   (Repeat as above)
here   appear?

IV

Tcotcokᴜ yâkimaʃĭ nyᴜ-ᴜna, tcotcokᴜ yâkimaʃĭ nyᴜ-ᴜna; *va-aki
Black   butterflies   sing,   black   butterflies   sing;   ruins

rsârsânanᴜ yâ-ana ko-onyᴜñgᴜ marsâvikĭ nyo-onyi yahimᴜ-ᴜna.
below   marked   I that   front   passing   going.

(Repeat as above)

Translation

It was near Kâ′matûk mountain
That this Rattlesnake came forth;
And he saw the low clouds lying
Near the summit of the mountain.

Who is this, who is this?
Is it not Horned Rattlesnake?
Is it not Horned Rattlesnake
Who now appears before us?

The Butterflies are singing;
The Butterflies are singing,
As I go past the foundations
Below, of the ancient house.

Tcokot Nɥɹĭ, Owl Song

[By Virsak Vâĭ-ĭ]

I

Yahalĭ Kâmʊndak nânâvangʊ, * moiva hondoniñga kongana
Large   Kâ′matûk   mountain,   many   evenings   summit
ʌʊpʊngiohomi kony huñga wʊwʊĭ nyʊinʊndʊk imʊkai, momoi
reddish   I   that   toward   to sing   going,   many
nyʊnyʊi wʊwʊsi namûkimʊ.   (Repeat from beginning; then repeat
songs   all   meet.
twice from *)

II

Tcokot yâ-âtama mʊʊmʊka nyʊhʊna kony kaitcongatci wʊwʊiny
Owl   man   far   singing   I   hearing   toward
haimiʊhʊna.   * Momoi yo-ofĭ mâmâtama tcʊpafinga-a amifâĭʌʊkʊ
going back and   Many   women   top   prostitute   there come
forth.
kayʊhinʊi kainakimʊ-ʊ.   (Repeat as above)
running   sounding.
laughing

III

Tcokot yofiñgʊ kokowoɩ(d) yâ-âtama tcoma sinyĭ wʊpâviñgi
Owl   bird   small owl   man   try   me   like
tcohikamʊ ya-ahana kony yʊdanyi amʊʌʊlhângi taimʊ hano
class   feathers   I   with   to make   wind   there
kokoñganû kâkâmaiwakimu.   (Repeat as above)
points   ashy.

IV

ʌʊñgihomi rsonañgi *tcomʊngâsi mamangia nyi-itcoho-ona;
Reddish   water   you   slowly   me make drink;
pianyiñgi papaki navahamo kam siyalika wohoirsakal
not I   slowly   drunk   there   east   toward
himʊmʊɩhimʊ-ʊ.   (Repeat as above)
wobble run.

Translation

Toward great Kâ′matûk mountain
I go to join the singing,
During the glow of evening.
I meet all the singers there.

Owl is singing in the distance,
I hear him moving back and forth.
Many harlots came here running;
Here came running and came laughing.

Small Owl resembles Tcokot;
The winds rise from Owl's feathers.
With their ashy tips he starts them.
Small Owl is like the Large Owl.

Owl makes me drink the reddish water;
Rapidly intoxicated
I try to walk straight toward the east,
And find my footsteps staggering.

Kakaitco Nyⁿǐ, Quail Song

[By Sutatki]

I

Kâkâmañgi kakaitcovû kakawoɹa miyanyita.   ʌumungali mulivak
    Gray   quails   bunched   grouping.   Coyote   came running
tatai panyuinahimu.   (Repeat four times)
above   looking.

II

Tcutcunañgi kakaitcova kakawoɹû vâïʌukai, ʌumungali nyuinâkû
    Blue   quails   bunched ran   together,   Coyote   saw
kakai vanyuïnahimu-u.   (Repeat four times)
sidewise   looking.

Translation

The Gray quails were bunched together,
Coyote ran to look upon them.
The Blue quails were bunched together;
Coyote looked sidewise at them.

Tatai Nyⁿǐ, Roadrunner Song

[By A-an Tâɹrsaki, Feathers Foam]

I

Tatai,   Tatai, sivâlik mâ-âka, Tatai,   Tatai, sivâlik mâ-âka
Roadrunner, Roadrunner, bushy   head, Roadrunner, Roadrunner, bushy   head
kita ʌungañy rsursulu, poi! poi! poi! (Repeat four times)
house   round   always,   poi! poi! poi!

II

Tatun(d)ai, Tatun(da)i piwopûsâ; Tatun(d)ai, Tatun(d)ai, piwopûsâ,
Roadrunners,   Roadrunners unattended; Roadrunners,   Roadrunners, unattended,
masika hohotcut utciawa.   (Repeat four times)
morning   lizards   he devours.

Translation

Roadrunner with the bushy head
Is always crying, poi! poi!
As he runs around the house.
Poi! poi! poi! around the house.

Here is the lonely Roadrunner;
Here is the lonely Roadrunner.
He eats lizards in the morning;
He eats solitary lizards.

III

Alisi ʌʊpʊñgi wopʊikam ꞯtan(d)ai, alisi ʌʊpʊñgi wopʊikam
Kind of   reddish   eyed that   Roadrunner,   reddish   eyed that
ꞯtan(d)ai hinañgʊ yakawânda tcʊñga tcoviny! tcoviny! Alisi
Roadrunner   about   mistletoe   see   (imitative)   Kind of
ʌʊpʊñgi wopʊikam ꞯtan(d)ai. (Repeat four times)
reddish   eyed that   Roadrunner.

IV

Konyi kamo yañgitâka mʊmʊlihimʊ, konyi kamo yañgitâka
  I   there   hide   had running,   I   there   hide
mʊmʊlihimʊ kâmañgi tcosokaꞁi moakai vâkatc ki-ima ho-o. (Repeat
had running   gray   lizard   kill   stomach   fat   eat.
four times)

V

Kaꞁo tcʊof koi kʊka kcñganû kiâhâsi haopaꞁ mat taꞁ tcoi-ika
Over yonder long mesquite stand   tops   basket   hawk   young talon   like
koñganû kiâhâsi. (Repeat four times)
  tops   basket.

VI

Konyi ngamo rsâhika mʊmʊlihimʊ ama aitcovasi nyâïkʊita ama
  I   there   pitiable   had running   there something   lucky   there
aitcovasi nyâïkʊita hiyâ vany mosi yʊn(d)a siviahawa. (Repeat four
something   lucky   here   my   vulva   in   put penis.
times)

VII

Moi yâ-âtama, moi yâ-âtamaka; siʌʊñgivia, siʌʊñgivia mâ-âtama
Many   people,   many   people;   red penis,   crown
ikitanyi hiyami nyʊm(d)a rsotaki vitciwanyʊ. (Repeat four times)
  cut   from   there   water   whirlpool.

Translation

Here is the red-eyed Roadrunner;
  Here is the red-eyed Roadrunner,
Who runs about the mistletoe.
  This is the red-eyed Roadrunner.

I run and hide! I run and hide!
  Now I kill the Gray Lizard
And I eat his fat body.
  I run and hide! I run and hide.

Over yonder in the mesquite
  Stands the Hawk's nest with its branches
Which rise like kiâhâ frame sticks,
  Over yonder in the mesquite.

(Translation of sixth and seventh stanzas omitted)

NAHAKIÂ NYƆĬ, MOUSE SONG

[By Virsak Vâɪ-ɪ]

I

Halapita nyʊitamokam ofĭñga *hihyâvat tatamaiva limʊnatcĭ hyana
Something   inaccessible   bird   here   top   walking   feathers
kʊviny kainhikimʊ am tgai kʊkiᴧakai tatai mâmâtcʊka tconyopiny
wave   sounding   there you   stand   up   head   slow
kaihama.   (Repeat; then repeat twice from *)
listen.

II

Vanyĭñgĭ rsâhĭngʊ hyatâta vinâkâ tcʊnyʊwʊtʊ rsârsânʊ vamhoĭkimʊ
I am   pitiable   here we   flooded   land   bases   caving in
haya-ava hanyĭ sʊpʊnyʊ, kamova siyalĭkâ naifonyima haya-ava hanyĭ
cry   see   afraid,   there   before east   came out   cry   see
sʊpʊnyʊ kamova hondonyĭkâ naifonyima hayava hanyĭ sʊpʊnyʊ.
afraid   there   west direction   came out   cry   see   afraid.
(Repeat)

Translation

Wings of birds invisible
Are now fluttering above you.
You stand with face uplifted
And quietly listen there.

Our land was unfortunate;
The floods came rolling westward,
Then they came flowing eastward,
And I cried out much afraid.

TOCFÛ NYƆĬ, HARE SONG

[By Virsak Vâɪ-ɪ]

I

Rsʊrsʊ[tcotanyʊk nyʊhʊta, * rsʊrsʊ[tcotanyʊk nyʊhʊta; hiya nyi
Straight   danced   singing,   straight   danced   singing;   here   me
tamai yʊwʊli mʊtâkĭmʊ-ʊ.   (Repeat all; then repeat twice from*)
top   wind   roaring.

II

Kakai tcotanyʊk nyʊhʊta, *kakai tcotanyʊk nyʊhʊta; hiya nyi
Horizontal   danced   singing,   horizontal   danced   singing;   here   me
tamai tcʊvañgi mʊtâkimʊ-ʊ.   (Repeat as above)
top   clouds   roaring.

Translation

Hare is jumping and singing;
Hare is jumping and singing,
While the wind is roaring,
While the wind is roaring.

Hare is dancing and singing;
Hare is dancing and singing,
While the clouds are roaring,
While the clouds are roaring.

III

Tcokondû ya-ana vamʊtâm sesivânatco, * tcokondû yana vamʊtâm
  Owl   feathers   flop   headdress,   owl   feathers   flop

sesivânatco; mʊmʊkâ tcʊnyʊwʊta tanʊmanʊ kakatâ namʊkimʊ.
  headdress;   far   country   top   bow   made.

(Repeat as above)

IV

Kâkamaki Nahakiâ *hondonyi simamatcima kʊhʊnda mâtaiwonyʊkai
  Gray   Mouse   evening   very know   in   came out running

tcokangiñga ipoiwa.   (Repeat as above)
  darkness   breath.

V

Vatâ masi, vatâ masi, siâmʊ, tâny kokopaimʊ; *vatâ masi,
 I guess morning, I guess morning, right I shut;   I guess morning,

vatâ masi, siâmʊ tâny kokopaimʊ; vatâ masi, vatâ masi, siâmʊ
 I guess morning, right I shut; I guess morning, I guess morning, right

tâny kokopaimʊ-ʊ.   (Repeat as above)
 I shut.

Translation

With headdress of owl feathers·
With headdress of owl feathers,
He comes to my far country;
He comes bringing hence his bow.

The Gray Mouse came at nightfall;
The Gray Mouse came at nightfall,
Came running in the darkness;
Came breathing in the darkness.

I am shut in at day dawn;
I am shut in at day dawn,
All night I am free to run
But am shut in at day dawn.

Kâks Nyɑ̆ĭ, Dog Song [a]

[By Virsak Vâĭ-ĭ]

I

Hodony kâ nyʊnyʊĭ rsârsân, *katcĭm tangĭŏ tcʊt yʊwʊhʊ[(t)
 Evening at songs commence, laying direction from wind

mʊndʊkai vatâ mʊmʊĭnama mʊndʊkai vatâ yongĭnyʊ tcopina wʊfʊĭ
 running was terrible running was shaking north toward

nyi pahiva viyohon(d)a.
 me tail wind blew over.

Translation

The songs commence at nightfall,
And the winds blow toward the north.
The winds are blowing strongly,
Blowing my tail toward the north.

[a] Sung rapidly while the side of a basket is beaten to carry the rhythm.

II

Yâkimalĭ yahanû, *yâkimalĭ yahanû; hiyâ vany nanamana kopalĭ
Butterfly   wings,   butterfly   wings;   here   I   above   face
ñguñgursu hama hukâ nyuina nyi ipoĭna sivahamâ tcoĭnga-a. (Repeat
down fall   there you   see   me   soul   more   appearance.
all; then repeat twice from *)

III

Yahalĭ gâñgâs simuliwuka, rsâiñgalĭ gâñgâs muliwuka, vapukialĭ
Small   dogs   came running,   pitiable   dogs   came running,   riders
mâĭnaka wovakimu haluhumimâkainangu-u.
after   came up   laughing sounding.

Translation

Butterfly wings are falling;
Butterfly wings are falling,
Falling upon and harming;
My suffering is greater.

See the small dogs come running;
See the poor dogs come running.
See the horsemen coming after;
See the horsemen coming laughing.

PAN NYNĬ, COYOTE SONG

[By Virsak Vâĭ-ĭ]

I

Panai kukiwaka nyunyuĭ rsârsânutcona-a. (Repeat) *Tcovañga
Coyote   stands   songs   commence.   Girl at puberty
mohofĭ yâĭkapĭ worsanyimu Panai nyunyuĭ vaʌunahimu. (Repeat
woman   hurry   came   Coyote   songs   stretching.
all; then repeat twice from *)

II

Pahañgu yahanû, *Pahañgu yahanû komus huku vany vânam
Eagle   feathers,   Eagle   feathers you that that my   hat
hatcona-a, komus huku vany vânam hatcona-a vahamâ tcoĭkama, nyi
made,   you that that my   hat   made   more   looks,   me
imoitakû vahamâ tcoiñga.
heart   more   looks.

Translation

Coyote commences singing;
Coyote commences singing.
The young woman hurries forth
To hear the Coyote songs.

A hat of eagle feathers;
A hat of eagle feathers,
A headdress was made for me
That made my heart grow stronger.

III

Sikálĭ rsonʊkama, *sikalĭ rsonʊkama; kʊ_ʇañgʊ Panai sitcʊnakimʊ
Around　　water,　　around　　water;　　there in　Coyote　　blue

mamasina konyʊñga wʊwʊi vâpâĭmʊna.　(Repeat as above)
dyed　　I in　　toward　run.

Translation

Coyote ran around it;
Coyote ran around it,
Ran into the blue water,
Changed the color of his hair.

Hoai Nyɲĭ, Black-Tailed Deer Song

[By Ki-ĭwa]

I

Vavaki yʊwʊʇa, vavaki yʊwʊʇa; * konyʊka wʊtcâma yʊkahimʊna,
Ruins　　windy,　　ruins　　windy;　　I that　　under　　put in the shade of

wʊtcâma　yʊkahimʊna;　kʊñgʊ　nyahañga　yʊwʊʇʊna,　kʊnyʊ
under　　put in the shade of;　　large　　horns　　windy,　　that

nahanaka yʊwʊdʊna.　(Repeat; then repeat twice from *)
my ears　windy.

II

Hamâ　mʊʇa　nyoñgitcʊ, hamâ　mʊʇa　nyoñgitcʊ; kʊngamâtcomʊ
Over there　run　shaking,　over there　run　shaking;　　ahead

vâpâĭmʊhʊ *kaho nyâĭnak kañgatâ tâtânʊlihi kaiya mʊkâ nyaĭhinʊna.
run many　up　after　bows　shining　here　far　me reach.

(Repeat as above)

Translation

Down from the houses of magic;
Down from the houses of magic,
Blow the winds and from my antlers,
And my ears they stronger gather.

Over there I ran trembling;
Over there I ran trembling,
For bows and arrows pursued me.
Many bows were on my trail.

III

Tâwonʇu kaviyo, tâwonʇu kaviyo; hiya mʊkâva pʊny namʊkimʊna
What   horse,   what   horse;   here   far   in   meet me

hami nyâĭna, hami nyâĭna,   siyonyoena,   siyonyoena; rsahavasi
there   after,   there   after,   trying to catch up,   trying to catch up;   how

inamangia himʊ kʊnyĭ yaĭhimʊna. (Repeat)
slowly   going   I   reaching.

*Ho-o koakam kaviyo hiya mʊkâva pʊny namʊkimʊna hami
Star   forehead   horse   here   far   me   meeting me   there

nyâĭna, hami nyâĭna,   siyonyoena,   siyonyoena; rsahavasi
after,   there   after,   trying to catch up,   trying to catch up;   how

mamañgia himʊ kʊnyĭyaihimʊna. (Repeat from *)
slowly   going   reaching me.

IV

Atcĭmtcia pâkaĭtcʊna, yatcĭmtcia pâkaĭtcʊna. (Repeat)
We here   sit,   we here   sit.

Siyalĭkâ vavanyima nyʊnyʊĭ kotcʊngʊ wʊs am yanga, yatcĭmtcia
East direction   there   songs   we are   all   there   sing,   we here

pâkaĭtcʊna. Hondonyikâ vavanyima nyʊnyʊĭ kotcʊngʊ wʊs am
sit.   West direction   there   songs   we are   all   there

yanga, yatcĭmtcia pâkaĭtcʊna.
sing,   we here   sit.

Translation

What horse is trying to catch me?
What horse is trying to catch me?
The horse with the star forehead
Now slowly gains upon me.

We are sitting here together;
We are sitting here together,
Singing the song of the east,
Singing the song of the west.

TCOTOM NYʌĬ, BEAR SONG[a]

[By Virsak Vâĭ-ĭ]

I

Nanyi wonda tcotcoka tcodohom, *hiyâvany tamai kakayʊ vaopa
Was I   black   bear,   here me   top   across   stretched

sikâdaka himʊ kamhâ nyʊĭta yanakʊvia sima hanyʊ-ʊ. (Repeat all;
around   going   there   see   waving   dew   falling.

then repeat twice from *)

Translation

I am the Black Bear. Around me
You see the light clouds extending.
I am the Black Bear. Around me
You see the light dew falling.

---

[a] Sometimes used as a rain song.

II

Haliwusi ʌuñgihomi rsotañgi *konyama ihyokʊ; kamo nya imʊhai
Kind of   reddish   water   I there   drink;   there I   going

nyʊʇa vamomokimʊ vany tgisʊmʊhʊnyʊ-ʊ. (Repeat as above)
me in   dead   I   afraid.

III

Nyʊnyʊĭʌʊ rsârsâna; *wʊwʊĭ nya himʊna hany nya sikoli nyʊnyʊĭ
Songs   commence;   toward I   going   cry I younger songs
                                                  brother

simamatcimʊ-ʊ.   (Repeat as above)
know.

Translation

I drink the reddish liquor
Which kills the spirit in me.
I drink the reddish liquor
Which kills the spirit in me.

Now the singing has commenced,
Now the singing has commenced.
I go with my younger brother;
I know the songs we're singing.

TCᴀFHÂ NYᴀĬ, GOPHER SONG

[By Sʊtatki]

I

Hon(d)ony siʌupuñgiomi kony âinatca ihimʊna-a; itanyimoina
Evening   reddish   I   after   go;   this my many

ʌupʊñgiomi ivasi yâsimʊna-a wʊwʊĭ nyokai ʌapañganyi nyʊwʊn(d)ʊ
reddish   makes flowers   toward go   holes   land

yaihimʊna.   (Repeat four times)
reaching.

II

Pahangʊ matcʊwʊĭna ngĭngĭkâva yʊwʊn(d)a, pahangʊ matcʊwʊĭna
Eagle's   wing feathers four   windy,   eagle's   wing feathers

ngĭngĭkâva yʊwʊn(d)a; yakâvany woa kâviki nyʊina tânâlĭñga
four   windy;   here me turn to   see   shining

nyimoĭ kayʊkayâmĭna. (Repeat four times)
soul   crossed.

Translation

In the reddish glow of nightfall,
In the reddish glow of nightfall
I return to my burrow,
About which the flowers bloom.

With the four eagle feathers,
With the four eagle feathers
I stir the air. When I turn
My magic power is crossed.

V

Tcʋwʋn(d)a mʋihimʋ, tcʋwʋn(d)a mʋihimʋ; konyika yʋɟa tcoma
Land　　　 burning,　　　 land　　　 burning;　　　 I　　in　 there

worsanyĭmʋ, konyʋ yʋɟa hapânyʋnâhʋngʋ hanâvany ᴧʋnganyitc(ĭ)
rise go,　　　 I　　 in　 there I looking　　around me　　 behind me

nyʋinâhâñgʋ hanavata vʋnganyĭ tcʋwʋn(d)a kakavitc tcama
looking　　　 many　　　 around　　 land　　　 narrow　 there

tcʋnâkimʋ. (Repeat eight times)
green.

VI

Vanyʋ pĭnyi mamatcʋka vamâ nyiwahana, *vanyʋ pĭnyi
I　　 not　 know surely　 more　 I make,　　　 I　　 not

mamatcʋka vamâ nyiwahana; kʋsi tcʋpafi kama anyitaka
know surely　 more　 I make;　 very　 prostitute　 hold　 feel

siâmanyi mamʋkaha kony hʋnga imoitaka tcama yon(d)onyiñga
right　　 give　　　 I　 that　 take in　　 there　 west

wʋwʋĭ tcʋtcʋmâ. (Repeat; then repeat from *. Sing all four
toward　 reached.

times)

VII

Vikamʋ Ñakân(d)ak nyoñinanʋ movinyama yʋkaimʋna *vikamʋ,
Remaining Crooked mountain　 me before　 pointed　　 shadow　　 remaining,

Ñgakân(d)akʋ nyoñinanʋ ñañakâli yʋkaimʋna kʋɟaña nyʋnyʋi
Crooked mountain,　 me before　 curved　 shadow　　 in　　 songs

ᴧʋkaivâ nakimʋ rsâĭkala nyimoitañga tcʋpafi tcona. (Repeat; then
sound　 pitiable　 my heart　 prostitute.　 (?)

repeat from *. Sing four times)

VIII

Kakaitcoᴧʋ yahala hon(d)onyĭnga vʋngioma makû natâĭmhʋ
Quails　 small　　 evening　　　 glow　　 arrive　 make

hapâvĭñĭ nyonyopitci nyʋnyʋkamʋ tcokañgiñgʋ tangiomakai
there　　 slowly　　　 fly　　　　 darkness　　　 stripped

mâmânamʋ tañitâĭmʋ. (Repeat eight times)
crown　　 throw on.

Translation

The land is parched and burning,
　The land is parched and burning.
Going and looking about me
　I see a narrow strip of green.

Yet I do not know surely,
　Yet I do not know surely.
The harlot is here among us.
　I go away toward the west.

The shadow of Crooked mountain,
　The curved and pointed shadow.
'Twas there that I heard the singing;
　Heard the songs that harmed my heart.

The light glow of evening;
　The light glow of evening
Comes as the quails fly slowly,
　And it settles on the young.

Wehâm Nyɔĭ, Lightning Song

[By Sʊtatki]

I

Weyâma himʊnatcia himʊnania kaiyam kaiyany, sikolĭ, mʊmʊkâ
　Wĕham　　　went　　　going　　　listen　　here,　　younger　far
　　　　　　　　　　　　　　　　　　　　　　　　　　brother
yohosi mumoahi [tataka sitana-a].　(Sing four times, alternating the
　tree　　kill　　　half　　split.
last two words with the one preceding)

II

Rsâĭ kanya sikolĭ kamo nyimʊitcoka, kamo nyimʊitcoka, hanâ nyi
Pitiable　I　younger there　me carry,　there　me carry,　there　me
　　　　　　brother
wʊwʊñgatcĭ tânâvañga tcotcĭm parsâ nyoʌana.　(Repeat four times)
　around　　　mountain　　stand　near by there carry.

III

ʌʊpʊñgiomi　vapamand　tcomaiya　weyâmi,　tcomaiya　weyâmi,
　Reddish　　　snakes　tries to make　lightning,　tries to make　lightning,
kahova yosi tapa kʊkiwopa pivanyi nakâka.　(Repeat four times)
there up　tree　on　stand　　not I　do.

IV

Rsâĭ　　kanya　　sikolĭ　tcokañgi　noahimtconakia　vâpâhimʊ　vanyʊ
Pitiable　I　younger　darkness　roaring going　running　I
　　　　　　brother
pina-akâk tamai ʌʊkahatcimu parsâpʊ katawa.　(Repeat four times)
　not do　　top　sky　near by　shoot.

Translation

See the destructive lightning
　Going to kill the distant tree.
It is going, my younger brother,
　To split the distant tree.

Around the mountain I carry
　My poor younger brother;
Carry him around the mountain
　And then I stand before it.

The lightning like reddish snakes
　Tries to lash and shiver the trees.
The lightning tries to strike them,
　But it fails and they yet stand.

(Translation of fourth stanza omitted)

HꞯwɑꞮꞆD Nyɑĭ, Wɪɴᴅ Sᴏɴɢ

[By Ha-ata]

I

YuwuꞮdĭ nyuhuma, *hiyawu rsânahatco, kamo danyimamaitcoma
  Wind   sing,   here   commence,   there   my in front

tcunyuwuta nyonyoahañgu-u. (Repeat all; then repeat twice from *)
  land   stretching.

II

Yuwuhuld ki-iki mumunaiku, *yuwuhuld ki-iki mumunaiku;
  Wind   house   thunder,   wind   house   thunder;

konyi kamho imuna tcuwunꞏa tcutcumâka mumunaiku-u. (Repeat
  I   there   going   land   covered   thunder.

as above)

III

Himo tâtâvaka yuwuhuꞏa, *himo tâtâvaka yuwuhuꞏa, himo
  There   mountain   windy,   there   mountain   windy,   there

tâvâvaka yuwuhuꞏa; wusikâ simaihâñgindañgu tciya muliva-a.
  mountain   windy,   all over   centipeds   here came running.

(Repeat as above)

IV

Tcotcok vapamanda huwuling *tcotcok vapamanda huwuling;
  Black   snake   wind,   black   snake   wind;

ñgai hiyata nyuiyuta muliva kuñgata nyuiyut pimihivi. (Repeat
  that   here   song in came running that song   in tie   around.

as above)

Translation

Wind now commences to sing;
  Wind now commences to sing.
The land stretches before me,
  Before me stretches away.

Wind's house now is thundering;
  Wind's house now is thundering.
I go roaring o'er the land,
  The land covered with thunder.

Over the windy mountains;
  Over the windy mountains,
Came the myriad-legged wind;
  The wind came running hither.

The Black Snake Wind came to me;
  The Black Snake Wind came to me,
Came and wrapped itself about,
  Came here running with its song.

V

Vanyi naiwonyĭm　*vasipi　mᴜhᴜk　naiwonyᴜka　mi-ịtco　vanyitâ
I am　　came out　　cup of water　hold　　came swiftly　　make　　drink I

nânakᴜ naiwonyᴜka sisikâlĭ imᴜndᴜhᴜna-a.　(Repeat as above)
crazy　came swiftly　round　　running.

VI

Tâta yanami ivakimᴜ, tâta yanami ivakimᴜ; kᴜnda nyi mᴜlivᴜkaĭ
White　cactus　leaves,　white　cactus　leaves;　in　I　came running

rsâĭñgᴜ mᴜmᴜlihi-i.　(Repeat as above)
poor　running.

Translation

Swiftly with a cup of water
I came running to make you drink.
I make you drink the water
And turn dizzily around.

Among the white cactus leaves;
Among the white cactus leaves,
I came running to that place;
I came running to that place.

Kokpᴜ Nyɑĭ, Fetish Song[a]

[By Virsak Vɑɪ-ĭ]

I

Kokopᴜ nyᴜnyᴜi rsârsân,　*kokopᴜ nyᴜnyᴜi gando viñgi rsârsân;
Fetish　song　commence,　fetish　song　there　commence;

woivanya imᴜna piâvat matcimakâ rsârsân, tcokañgi mᴜɹa sigi
toward　going　not　know　commence,　night　in　very

konyimᴜna-a.　(Repeat all; then repeat twice from *.　Sing four times)
noisy

II

Kokopᴜ nyᴜnyᴜi tcotcoahimᴜ,　*kokopᴜ, nyᴜnyᴜi tcotcoahimᴜ;
Fetish　song　stood,　fetish　song　stood;

kaiyâk wᴜwᴜi vâpâ himᴜɹa sitcᴜpafinga-a.　(Repeat as above)
heard　toward　run　going　crazy.

Translation

We commence the fetish song;
We commence the fetish song.
It is difficult but I try;
The night grows very noisy.

The fetish song arises;
The fetish song arises.
To it the crazed women run;
To it the crazed women run.

---

[a] Apache hair with the down of birds is placed in a medicine basket where a spirit "developes" that is helpful if food is set out each night for him to eat. If he is neglected he may cause disease, whereupon this song is sung.

III

Rsâĭganywâna, rsâĭganywâna; wᴜsikâĭny nañgioma, rsâĭganywâna,
Poor me,   poor me;   all over me   stripping,   poor me,

wᴜsikâĭny nañgioma knyᴜhᴜna-a.   (Repeat as above)
all over me   stripping   singing.

IV

Tcokañgi nyᴜimᴜꞁhimᴜ, tcokañgi nyᴜimᴜꞁhimᴜ; Sivât Tânâfañgᴜ
Night   sing going,   night   sing going;   Sievat   mountain

wᴜwᴜi vanyᴜimᴜlhimᴜ konyhᴜngᴜ wᴜwᴜi tcomᴜ vapahimᴜ.   (Repeat
toward   lead me   I that   toward   there   running.

as above)

Translation

Pity me! Oh pity me!
And strip away my disease.
Now strip away my disease;
Clear it away by singing.

I'm going to the singing;
I'm going to the singing.
It is leading to the mountain,
Running to Sievat mountain.

Navitco Nyɑĭ, Navitco Song

[By Virsak Vâĭ-ĭ]

I

Tcotcᴜlĭk viahâka tcᴜtcᴜlᴜk miaʌa tcᴜtcᴜlᴜk miaʌa.
Fowl   bean   sounds   drop   sounds   drop.

II

Kat vavaiworsᴜnyᴜ, kat vavaiworsᴜnyᴜ; sami worsᴜnyihimᴜ
There   stone wall arose,   there   stone wall arose;   there   arose

sahapâ kainama kohai, sami worsᴜnyᴜ, sami worsᴜnyihimᴜ.   (Sing
pleasing   sound   burn open,   there   arose,   there   arose.

once and dance)

Translation

The chicken beans are rattling,
They are rattling as they fall.
The chicken beans are rattling,
They are rattling as they fall.

And the stone wall arose there,
And the stone wall arose there.
When the gourd seed was planted
It made its way through to grow.

Makai Nyñĭ, Magician Song

[By Virsak Vấĭ-ĭ]

I

Kʊsi tâhai vasialikuĭ vavahaki kʊnɉa nyʊtâ tciviha-a.   (Repeat)
Kind of white   morning   ruins   in   I   come.

* Hamanyʊtâ tcivihakʊ nyipoinakʊ sisivaɉʊ tânâli-i.   (Repeat twice
There I   came   my heart   flame   shine.

from *; then repeat all twice)

II

Yahanʊ vapakosi tatamanhʊ ihihamʊ vâyonyʊ-ʊ.   (Repeat)
Feathers mat-like   topmost   business singing.

* Tamai kʊkʊkimhʊ nyipoinakʊ sisivâɉʊ tânâli-i.   (Repeat as above)
There go slowly   my heart   flame   shine.

III

HaliʌUta sihʊñgia wowosaikʊ tcʊtcʊwʊtʊ, tamhaiʌU imʊkai hʊñga
That our older brother first came out   lands,   topmost   go   that
                  to walk

tâsi vahomâ hiyava tcohinyʊ-ʊ.   (Repeat)
very more   here   looks.

* Tcʊtcʊwʊta tamhaiva himʊkai tânâlika nyimoitangʊ hiyaʌU
Land   topmost   go   shining   my heart   here

vamhonyʊ-ʊ.   (Repeat as above)
more.

IV

Tcʊwʊnɉʊ makahi * tcʊwʊnɉʊ makahi; wʊmatci papamo wʊwʊmia
Land   magician,   land   magician; with   angry   with

himʊkai vavakia sihainyiñgi tco-o.   (Repeat as above)
go   ruins   wasted   make.

Translation

At early dawn I entered,
  Entered in the white light of day.
And my heart flamed with power
  As I entered the magic house.

In the lofty feather house
  His magic is increasing,
And he moves very slowly
  With the power in his heart.

Elder Brother first came forth;
  Elder Brother first came forth,
And with his shining power
  Governed over all the land.

Earth Magician became angry;
  Earth Magician became angry,
And with his magic power
  He destroyed all the houses.

V

Sitcokai   vamaɳatco,   * sitcokai   vamaɳatco,   hυkanyi   vavaki
Black   snake made,   black   snake made,   with I   ruins
wopona-a.   (Repeat as above)
tie.

VI

Sitahai vamaɳatco * hυkatci vavaki wopona-a.
White   snake made   with it   ruins   tie.
Kosinanυmυinaka worsanyυ.   (Repeat as above)
That fears me   go out.

Translation

With a Black Snake I tie them;
With a Black Snake I tie them,
The houses with a Black Snake,
The houses with a Black Snake.

With a White Snake I tie them;
With a White Snake I tie them,
The houses with a White Snake,
The houses with a White Snake.

VIKITA NYɴĬ, DOWN SONG [a]

[By Virsak Vâĭ-ĭ]

I

Moadañgi tamai monoi tcυvañgi tcotco.   (Repeat)
Mo'hatûk   top   many   clouds   stand.
Moandañgi tamai momoi ikomυ worsa.   (Repeat)
Mo'hatûk   top   many   fog   arose.
Hami tamai tcotco hoho.
There   top   stand.

II

Hiatât   vinâk   sivai   yυwuɳa. * Hiatât   vinâk   sivai   yυwuɳa; momoi
Here we   flood   bitter   wind.   Here we   flood   bitter   wind;   many
gañgatâ   nyυitco, momoi gañgatâ   nyυitco hoho.   (Repeat all; then
bows   singing to, many   bows   singing to.
repeat twice from*)

Translation

On the top of Mo'hatûk
There are many clouds standing.
On the top of Mo'hatûk
Many fog clouds are rising.

The bitter wind blows on us;
The bitter wind blows on us,
As we sing with many bows.

---

[a] Vipinyĭm Hanyuĭ, North People song. In the treatment of some swellings upon the body the vipinyĭm songs are sung by a number of men, who at the same time perform a simple ceremony intended to assist in the cure of the patient. Retiring to a structure temporarily erected from poles and sleeping mats, the participants, not necessarily medicine-men, make a number of images of animals and edible plants, which they take, one at a time, to the patient, and allow him to touch. After he has touched the object carried by each man in the party of singers they retire to get a second supply. This is repeated a number of times until the cure is supposed to have been completed.

III

Nanyi	wot	navitcho	komsap	naka	tamaikatcĭm	mâkahap
I	am	Navitco	you	talk	about laying	through put head

mᴜlitcota	navitcho	kahatc	mᴜlitco	hoho.	(Repeat as above)
run	Navitco	like	run.		

IV

Yo-osa ikomiakahi, * yo-osa ikomiakahi, yo-osa ikomiakahi rusᴜrsᴜ[
Sticks   cut,   sticks   cut,   sticks   cut   straight

tcotamhᴜ. (Repeat as above, dancing)

Translation

Though I am a Navitco,
I hear you talk about me.
I thrust my head through the sky
And with it I run away.

Cut sticks, cut sticks, cut sticks straight.

NYAVOLT NYɑĭ, DEMON SONG

[By Virsak Vâĭ-ĭ]

1

Kâmᴜndak nâvañga kᴜnda kamomoi nyᴜnyᴜi kaihima, * Kâmᴜndak
Kâ′matûk   mountain   in   many   songs listen,   Kâ′matûk

nâvañga kᴜnda kamomoi nyᴜnyᴜi kaihima; kᴜnda nyi mᴜliʌakᴜ
mountain · in   many   songs   listen;   in   I came running

yakaimᴜ mᴜdaʌᴜ rsarsavaikᴜ. (Repeat all; then repeat twice from *.
sang   within   echoed.

Sing four times)

II

Hodonyisi miamᴜnda mᴜrsârsâna, *hodonyisi miamᴜnda mᴜrsârsâna;
Evening   close to   foundations,   evening   close to   foundations;

kᴜnda   kanyᴜnyawo[d   anyᴜyapaka   hiya   avâĭvaka   nyimoina
in   demons   appeared   here   came running   my soul

kunangiomahimᴜ. (Repeat as above)
stripped.

Translation

Singing at Kâ′matûk mountain;
Singing at Kâ′matûk mountain,
I listen to their singing;
I come running to sing with them.

Evening now is falling;
Evening now is falling,
And demons appeared running
To strip and expose my soul.

III

Tcʊvai Tânâvañga mʊna nyʊnyʊ kaimʊ, * Tcʊvai Tânâvañga mʊna
Tcuva   Toak mountain   in   hole,   Tcuva   Toak mountain   in

nyʊnyʊ; kaimʊkʊnda nyʊnyʊkaimʊ, kʊnda nyhivaka nyʊta, kʊnda
hole;   in   hole in   in   I enter   see,   in

kanyʊnyawoɪ(d) aimohiva.   (Repeat as above)
demons   breath out.

IV

Nyʊnyawoɪ(d)   iyahala,   * hiya   vâïʌʊkahi, huʌʊsyasingam   nyʊ
Demons   boys,   here   came running,   many flowers   me

rsa-akima kʊkimʊ kamo mʊmʊkâ kaʌʊka tcʊnyʊɟʊnda huku namanha
grasp   standing there   far   hard   land   that   top

nyoʌapimʊ nyimoitañgu yovaiya puihimʊ.   (Repeat as above)
bring me   to my heart   lift   higher.

Translation

In a Santa Rita cave;
In a Santa Rita cave,
As I entered in the cave,
I saw the breath of demons.

Here demon boys came running;
Here demon boys came running,
Grasping my hair they carried me,
Brought me to a distant land.

WOAKA NYꞂǏ, PUBERTY SONG

[By Virsak Vâï-ɪ]

I

Âika   piworsanymhʊ,   âika   piworsanymhʊ; * hʊkia   tovatcoma
Hurry   come out,   hurry   come out;   already   became

yondohonyʊ katcokañi rsarsavaikimʊ.   (Repeat; then repeat from *.
go down   that night   echoing.

Sing all four times)

II

Tcovak mohof(i), * tcovak mohof(i); kâsiñgʊ pivayʊ rsʊmatcona
Virgin   woman,   virgin   woman;   sleepy   not   indifferent

hamʊkai nyʊnarsʊna-a hamʊkai, nyʊnarsʊna-a tcokañgĭk yâïtaimʊ.
there   wake   there,   wake   night   think about.

(Repeat all; then repeat from *)

Translation

Come hurry forth, hurry forth.
Already the echoing sounds
Of darkness are heard around.

The Virgin is not sleepy,
She is wakeful through the night.

III

Harsany yâmainañgu, * harsany yamainañgu; kadomia woissimu
Giant   cactus broken,   giant   cactus broken;   there   piled

kudañgu nahana miawoitañgu wuvutcimu yovaiya mumuhuk
in there   feathers   drop   laying   raise   higher

Mâtcipant yaihi. (Repeat as above)
Ma-atcpat   close to.

IV

Hali puñgu kâvânyuk vany puitcokimu itali yoof(i) kakayaku
Small   that   rumbling   I   carrying   this   woman   heard

vapikâkârsâ itany tâtaɹan kokokana hotc hairsa, hairsa.
they not sleep   this   on feet   there points   nail   broke,   broke.

V

Tcokañgi mamahanga woisi, tcokañgi mamahañga woisi; konyi
Night   branch   thrown   night   branch   thrown   I
     down,   down,

suka wutcâ miñgi worsa, konyisuka wutcâ miñgi worsa nyahanu
in   under   there   gone past,   I in   under   there   gone past   my feathers

maikomia.
cut off.

Translation

The Saguaro lies there broken;
    And my fallen feathers rise
O'er the top of Table mountain.

The boy stirred the rumbling stones;
    The woman heard and could not sleep.
And my toe nails are broken.

The branches of darkness fell,
    Cutting my feathers as I passed.

RAIN SONGS

HOAHIHIĊF

[By KÁ′MÁl tkÁk]

I

Hi-ihiyanaiho-o; *Nyunyuĭ rsânatcona, hanyunyui rsânatcona;
(?)   Song   commence,   our song   commence;

havatumâhâinamû rsânatcota, hitciya yahina-a. (Repeat from *)
pleasing   commence,   (?)   (?)

Hañgunñgunda onyŏĭ nyuitcota, vatumâhâinamû rsânatcota, hitciya
Large   corn   singing to,   pleasing   commence,   (?)

yahina-a. Hiya-ala onyŏĭ nyuitcota; vatumâhâinamu rsânatcota;
(?)   Small   corn   singing to;   pleasing   commence;

hitciya yahina-a.
(?)   (?)

Translat on

Hi-ihiya naiho-o! Let us begin our song,
    Let us begin, rejoicing. Hitciya yahina-a.
Let us begin our song, let us begin, rejoicing,
    Singing of the large corn. Hitciya yahina-a.
Singing of the small corn. Hitciya yahina-a.

II

Hi-ihiyanaiho-o, tcunoñi hŏnonyĭña kusimû kûdavat iañgûta
    (?)   blue   evening   drops   in there ceremonial sticks

nyuĭtco, yahaiva monananka ñiñivâi kuna-a, hitciya yahina.
sing to,   all around   tassels   waving   there,   (?)   (?)

Tâhaiva sia-aliña kukiva kudavat iañgûta nyuĭtco, yahaiva
White   dawn   rises   there   ceremonial sticks sing to,   all around

monanaka ñiñivâĭ kuna-a, hitciya yahina-a. Tcutâñi hononyĭña
tassels   waving   there,   (?)   (?)   Blue   evening

kusimû kudavat iañgûta nyuĭtco, yo-onyŏĭ mondanaka ñiñivâi
drops   in there ceremonial sticks sing to,   corn   tassels   waving

kuna-a, hitciya yahina. Tâhaĭva sia-aliña kukiva kudavat iañgûta
there   (?)   (?)   White   dawn   rises   there ceremonial sticks

nyuĭtco, ya-ali yahaka ñiñivâi kuna-a, hitciya yahina-a.
sing to,   squash   leaves   waving   there,   (?)   (?)

III *a*

Hi-ihiyanaiho-o, *tcuwuna mumunai, tcuwuna mumunai; vatciki
    (?)   earth   rumbling,   earth   rumbling;   we are

yoa iwuna; tcuwuna mumunai; wusikâ $\genfrac{}{}{0pt}{}{1}{2}$ { noahi hitciya yahina-a.
                                    nyoko-o

basket sounding   earth   rumbling; everywhere $\genfrac{}{}{0pt}{}{1}{2}$ { humming (?)   (?)
                                        raining

(Repeat from *; then repeat all)

Translation

Hi-ihiya naiho-o! The darkness of evening
   Falls as we sing before the sacred âmĭna.
About us on all sides corn tassels are waving.
   Hitciya yahina! The white light of day dawn
Yet finds us singing, while corn tassels are waving.
   Hitciya yahina-a! The darkness of evening
Falls as we sing before the sacred âmĭna.
   About us on all sides corn tassels are waving.
Hitciya yahina! The white light of day dawn
   Yet finds us singing, while the squash leaves are waving.

Hi-iya naiho-o! The earth is rumbling
   From the beating of our basket drums.
The earth is rumbling from the beating
   Of our basket drums, everywhere humming.
Earth is rumbling, everywhere raining.

----

a Song not accompanied with dancing.

IV

Hi-ihiyanaiho-o,　*Pahangᴜ　matcᴜvwena　yopanha,　sia-aliñgû
　(?)　　　　　　　Eagle　　last wing feathers　pull out,　　east
tañĭo　vayolinha　guñguña　tᴜwangimᴜta-a,　hitciya yahina-a.　Pahanga
direction　point out　large　　clouds there,　　(?)　　　(?)　　　Eagle
vĭñgĭñga　yopanha,　hononyñgu　tañĭo　vayolinha;　ya-ala ikomainûka-a,
soft feathers　pull out,　　west　direction　point out;　small　clouds there,
hitciya　yahina.　(Repeat from *)　Hamo　vakĭ　wᴜtco　vanoahimᴜ
　(?)　　　(?)　　　　　　　　　　There　house　below　rumbling
guñguña　onyoĭmᴜta-a,　hitciya　yahina-a.　　Hamo　vakĭ　wᴜtco
large　　corn there,　　(?)　　　(?)　　　　There　house　below
vanyokonha,　ya-ala　onyoĭmᴜta-a,　hitciya　yahina.
raining,　　small　　corn there,　　(?)　　　(?)

Translation

Hi-ihiya naiho-o! Pluck out the feathers
　From the wing of the Eagle and turn them
Toward the east where lie the large clouds.
　Hitciya yahina-a! Pluck out the soft down
From the breast of the Eagle and turn it
　Toward the west where sail the small clouds.
Hitciya yahina! Beneath the abode
　Of the rain gods it is thundering;
Large corn is there. Hitciya yahina!
　Beneath the abode of the rain gods
It is raining; small corn is there.

Ho-ONYI Nᴠnĭ, CORN SONG[a]

[By Kâ'mâl tkâk]

I

Hi-i-lo-o ya-a-a.　Tâ-âma wᴜs sinyᴜĭna yali kak aonyoĭ vworsanyᴜ
　(?)　　(?)　　　Who　all　seeing　that　two　corn　standing
tâ-âma wᴜs sinyᴜĭna siko-oholĭ, hi-ilo-o ya-a-a.　Tâ-âma wᴜs sinyᴜĭna
who　all　seeing　younger brother,　(?)　　(?)　　　Who　all　seeing
yalĭ kâk alĭ worsanyᴜ; tâ-âma wᴜs sinyᴜĭna siko-oholĭ, hi-ilo-o ya-a-a.
that two squash standing;　who　all　seeing　younger brother,　(?)　　(?)
Ta-atûkam hᴜtanma onyoĭ vworsanyᴜ, tâ-âma wᴜs sinyᴜĭna siko-oholĭ,
Ta-atûkam　that　top corn　standing,　who　all　seeing　younger brother,
hi-ilo-o ya-a-a.　Ta-atûkam hᴜta-ama ali vworsanyᴜ tâ-âma wᴜs
　(?)　　(?)　　Ta-atûkam　that top　squash　standing　who　all
sinyᴜĭna, siko-oholi, hi-ilo-o ya-a-a.　(Ended by singing hi-ilo-o
seeing　younger brother,　(?)　　(?)
woihᴠ)

Translation

Hi-ilo-o ya-a-a! He who sees everything
　Sees the two stalks of corn standing;
He's my younger brother. Hi-ilo-o ya-a-a!
　He who sees everything, sees the two squashes;
He's my younger brother. Hi-ilo-o ya-a-a!
　On the summit of Ta-atûkam sees the corn standing;
He's my younger brother. Hi-ilo-o ya-a-a!
　On the summit of Ta-atûkam sees the squash standing;
He's my younger brother. Hi-ilo-o woiha!

---

[a] The first songs ever sung to bring rain. Ho-onyĭ was the name of the Corn god who left the Pimas for many years and then returned to live at the mountain north of Picacho, Ta-atûkam, whence he sang as above.

II

Hi-ilo-o ya-a-a. Ta-atûkam hʊ tânâvañgʊ tatamana tcʊvwakĭ
  (?)   (?)   Ta-atûkam   that   mountain   topmost   clouds
rsaika-a amâñʊs sikai-ĭtamʊ toahimʊ, hi-ilo-o ya-a-a. Ta-atûkam hʊ
suspended there makes very loud rumbling,   (?)   (?)   Ta-atûkam   that
tânâvangû tatamana hikom hʊ rsaika-a, amâñʊs sikai-ĭtama tcokona,
mountain   top above clouds   that suspended, there makes very loud   raining,
hi-ilo-o ya-a-a. Tcʊ-ʊnañgi hʊvwatcona tcʊwaki yokanyĭ sanâvwʊ
  (?)   (?)   Blue   bluebird   clouds   holding   there
rsaika-a amâñʊs sikaĭtamʊ toahimʊ, hi-ilo-o ya-a-a. Sâ-â-ham[a] hʊ
suspended there makes very loud rumbling,   (?)   (?)   Yellow   that
vanyokoña hikom ha yokanyĭ sanâvwʊ rsaĭka-a, amâñʊs sikaitama
bird   clouds that holding   there   suspended, there makes very loud
tcokona, hi-ilo-o ya-a-a.
raining,   (?)   (?)

III

Hi-ilo-o ya-a-a. I-itâi vahimo'ĭna hʊwʊndʊka kahoñʊ; Ta-atûkam
  (?)   (?)   Elder Brother breathe out   wind   over there;   Ta-atûkam
hʊ ta-ama tcʊwakĭ vo-orsa vasitʊmâhâĭtamʊ toahimʊ, hi-ilo ya-a-a.
that above clouds   very pleasant to appear rumbling,   (?)   (?)
I-itâi vahimoĭna hʊwʊndʊka kahoñu; Ta-atûkam hʊ ta-amʊ hikomʊ
Elder Brother breathe out wind   over there; Ta-atûkam that above   clouds
rsaika vasitʊmâhâĭtama tcokona, hi-ilo-o ya-a-a. Hami yʊna, sami
suspended pleasant appear raining,   (?)   (?)   There   in,   there
yʊtda, hamanyĭ yolihina kanyʊ-ʊ vasitʊmâhâĭta-amʊ toahimʊ, hi-ilo-o
in,   there me stay   sing   very pleasant appears rumbling,   (?)
ya-a-a. Hami yʊna, sami yʊtda, hamanyi yolihina kanyʊ-ʊ vasitʊ-
  (?)   There   in,   there in,   there me   stay   sing   **pleasant**
mahaita-ama tcokona, hi-ilo-o ya-a-a. (hi-ilo-o woihʋ)
to hear again raining,   (?)   (?)

Translation

Hi-ilo-o ya-a-a! Over Ta-atûkam
Rise the clouds with their loud thundering.
Hi-ilo-o ya-a-a! Over Ta-atûkam
Rise the clouds with their loud raining.
Hi-ilo-o ya-a-a! The Bluebird is holding
In his talons the clouds that are thundering.
Hi-ilo-o ya-a-a! Yellowbird is holding
In his talons the clouds that are raining.

Hi-ilo-o ya-a-a! See Elder Brother
Breathe out the winds that over Ta-atûkam
Drive the clouds with their loud thundering.
Hi-ilo-o ya-a-a! See Elder Brother
Breathe out the winds that over Ta-atûkam
The welcome storm clouds are suspending.
Hi-ilo-o ya-a-a! In the great rain clouds
Let me sing my song of rejoicing.

---

[a] Sâ-â-ham from Sâ-am, is a Sonora Papago word.

WAR SONGS

Rsɑᵀ Nyɑĭ, Straight Song [a]

[By Virsak Vâĭ-ĭ]

I

Hihi　tcotcok　âiyañgama　nyunyuwunda　tama　numulva　aihivaihi
That　　black　　sandy　　　　land　　　　　top　came running　(?)

vutañguvi.　(Repeat)
(?)

Tama　numulva　aihivaihi　vutañguvi.　　(Repeat)
Top　came running　(?)　　　　(?)

II

Hihi　himtco　himtco,　himtco,　vitco　tañguvi　himtco,　vitco　tañguvi.
That　shove　shove,　　shove,　　(?)　　(?)　　　shove,　　(?)　　(?)

(Repeat)

Liho liho li　yawoine　sikyo　yawoine　sikyo　apiatama　sikyo　tañguvi
(?)　(?)　(?)　(?)　　　(?)　　(?)　　(?)　you also　　(?)　　(?)

apiatama　sikyo　tañguvi.　　(Repeat)
(?)　　　(?)　　(?)

III

Hana　okolrsanihi　maoli　kiyan　tañguyi.　　(Repeat)
On　　　(?)　　　　(?)　　(?)　　(?)

Tâkiwoḻa　nyihâli　moakahi　hopama　uḻkâna　sitana　mâĭkana　rsene
That was　　slave　　killed　skin empty　strip off　stretch　soften　　(?)

rsolihiye　tañguvi.　　(Repeat)
(?)　　　(?)

Translation

Over that black sandy land,
Over the top came running,
Over the top came running.
The Apache slave was killed
And his hide tanned for leather.

---

[a] Sung on returning victorious from war. The singers dance and shake gourd rattles. This is believed to be a very old song original with the Pimas.

Wolutâ Nyñĭ, Tie Song[a]

[By Virsak Vâ̆l-ĭ]

I

Tânâhâli vavanyimhʊ yanama hiyava tcimyivia hiyava nyinyivia
Shining　　　row　　　　man　　　here　　　came　　　here　　　came
kanyhʊina tcokangikʊ yatâny yahatcimʊ.　(Repeat four times)
see　　　　darkness　here me　collected.

II

Panai yahaɹi kavahanda kikitaka kʊnda tcomʊ narsawopimʊ vanyʊ
Coyote　young　　shield　　house　　in　　there　　sat　　　I am
iñgi sâhâi mʊndatcoma ihinaha kimʊ.　(Repeat four times)
like　in there　　shouting.

III

Panai yahaɹi tcokañgĭ yawolima vʊvʊikanyi vanyi mʊlimʊ kʊda
Coyote　young　darkness　　tied　　toward me　leading　me　　in
mânyoapa hanâva nyi wʊkañgi yavatcʊkia kiñgi kahimʊna.　(Repeat
brought me　there　me　around　cigarettes　four　departures.
four times)

Mâhyal nâvañga kʊka tamai virsakʊ vanyi ʌʊmʊkai mʊnda tcoma
Mahyal　mountain standing　top　hawk　here me　with　　in　　there
pʊtâhâkimʊ.　(Repeat four times)
flop.

Translation

Here the warrior, Shining-row,
　　Came and saw the night around me.
Young Coyote made a shield house
　　And he sat in it shouting,
And that was pleasing to me.
　　Young Coyote tied the darkness;
The cigarettes were passed around,
　　Four times when he led me there.
The Hawk on Mahyal mountain[b]
　　Stood with me beating his wings.

---

[a] Sung on return from an Apache campaign at the time when the hair of the enemy is tied by the aged companion appointed for each successful warrior.

[b] Mahyal is the Pima name of the mountains about Silver King.

MÂ-ÂT'K' NYɒĬ, SCALP SONG[a]

[By Virsak Vâĭ-ĭ]

I

Siyaliñgû tangio yâtamû taiwonyʊ, *sivaliñgû tangio yâtamû
East   direction   man   arose,   east   direction   man

taiwonyʊ; kʊhʊwʊsi yâsĭkamû nyâvatcʊki vany nanamʊ komâ
arose;   kind of   flowers   cigarettes   I   meet   there

hâkomâ hanyʊ. (Repeat all; then repeat twice from *)
smoking.

II

Navamokʊ nyaka, navamokʊ nyakatci, ñgamova mʊkâ mʊndʊhʊna.
Drunk   false said,   drunk   me about said,   there   far   running.

(Repeat)

  * Rsâĭñgal anyimoinañga wʊwʊmʊ navamo Kakândakʊ nânhâvañgʊ
Pitiful   my soul   with   drunk   Crooked   mountain

yaihimʊ. (Repeat twice from *)
moving toward.

III

Kamo nya himʊna, *kamo nya himʊna; kʊsi ʌʊñgiomi nâvaita
There   I   go,   there   I   go;   kind of reddish   liquor

nyitcona pia nyiki navamok rsakalâĭ mʊmʊhʊlimʊ. (Repeat twice
I caused   not   me   drunk   stagger   run.
to drink

from *)

IV

Yâhândʊ kavinyĭk, *yâhândʊ kavinyĭk; kʊnda ĭgalĭ nyohonyoiʌʊ
Sandy   hill,   sandy   hill;   in   kind of   vulture

taiwonyʊk hanâ vany wʊkany tcʊwʊt ɉamʊ tânâhâlĭ. (Repeat all;
come out   there my   around   land   on   shining.
running

then repeat twice from *)

Translation

There arose in the East Land
  One whom I met there smoking
Flowerlike cigarettes.

Running dazed and falsely speaking
  Pitiable and faint-hearted
I feel at Crooked mountain.

There I'm going, there I'm going.
  I have to drink the liquor
That makes me stagger as I run.

Vulture arose from Sandy hill
  Shining upon the land around.

---

[a] Accompanied by dancing.

V

Kâkâmaki tâkʊtât makaiñga tcʊ, * kâkâmaki tâkʊtât makaiñga
Gray   spider   magician   find,   gray   spider   magician

tcʊ; kʊsi tcopolima kihâta makai nyahañga, haiya, hiya, hiyaka himʊ.
find; kind of squarely like a kiâhâ magiciam   he said,   (?)   (?)   (?)   (?)

(Repeat as above)

VI

Kahova hinakimʊ * kahova hinakimʊ; yatciʌu tâvañga wʊtcâva
Up there   shouting,   up there   shouting;   Atci   hill   under

hinakimʊ yâtam hawʊs am rsâĭkâ ʌʊkaitcʊna.   (Repeat as above)
shouting   people   all   there   poor   said.

Translation

The Gray Spider magician
He made a square kiâhâ.
He is indeed a magician.

They are shouting, they are shouting,
Around the hill of Atci.
The poor people there are shouting
As the news of battle comes.

Koʇ(d)û Ha-akam Nyɑĭ, (?) Olla Song [a]

[By Sika'tcu]

I

Patamahimʊ, patamahimʊ, vapi yâĭjima tciviahimʊ nañgʊsi
Where going,   where going,   not   quick   come   I guess

yʊkiyʊpai mokonama mʊhiʌʊpâ kama hyova kʊkimʊ. Haya
already somewhere   die   fire like   there   distant   stand.   (?)

mailo mane. (Repeat ad lib.)
(?)   (?)

II

Namʊ tâny yavany hitconakĭ yo-osĭ kokapʊ vany naki-hiya.
You   do me   raven   to make   tree   top   me   hang.

(Repeat ad lib.)

III

Kanŏñgalĭ vavai tânʊn(d)âma yovi napʊthiñgi rsaitc unda
Far down   rocks   shining   woman   you   grass   in

yañgitâka mʊndʊkai samʊ tamai pahañgʊ namʊkʊ kakʊvihimʊ.
hide   run   there   top   eagle   meet   whipping.

(Repeat ad lib.)

Translation

Now where is he, where is he,
That he has not already come?
Yes, I fear that he has been killed.

You hung the Raven trophies
On a pole and danced around them.

Amid the rocks of the mountain
The women tried to hide themselves;
But the men ran and killed them.

---

[a] When the Pimas were victorious the women sang these songs at the moment of hearing the
first news from the runners that came in advance of the war party.

Speeches

Set speeches which recited portions of the cosmogonical myth were a feature of many ceremonies and were especially important in the preparation for war. They were slightly adapted for each occasion but their general content remained the same. Highly figurative language is used and in consequence it is extremely difficult to obtain even an approximately correct translation. The free translation offered is the result of many discussions with the older men.

In the ten speeches here given reference is made to the following deities, magicians, etc.:

Elder Brother.	Black, Blue, Red, and	White, Blue, Black, and
Earth Doctor.	White Measuring	Yellow Dragonfly.
South Doctor.	Worm.	Yellow Spider.
Vulture.	Lightning Magician.	Down Roll.
Talking Tree.	Thunder Magician.	Yellow Raven.
Sun.	Wind Magician,	Bluebird.
Gray Gopher.	Foam Magician.	Yellow Bird.
Black, Blue, and White	Sinking Magician.	Mountain.
Mocking-bird.	Vakolif Magician.	Mocking Bird.
Kuvĭk.	Vikârskam.	Blue Coyote.
Gray Spider.	Nasia.	Black Kangaroo Mouse.
Blue Gopher.	Old Woman Magician.	Owl.

ELDER BROTHER AS HE RESTORED HIMSELF TO LIFE

You people desired to capture Elder Brother so that you might destroy him. You secured the assistance of Vulture, who made a miniature earth; you saw him at his home engaged in this work. He shaped the mountains, defined the water courses, placed the trees, and in four days completed his task. Mounting the zigzag ladders of his house [a] he flew forth and circled about until he saw Elder Brother. Vulture saw the blue flames issuing from Elder Brother's heart and knew that he was invulnerable. In his turn Elder Brother knew that Vulture wished to kill him and had made the miniature earth for that purpose.

Komtâva   Sis   Makai   spadâ   âlitûk   tatcoa.   Ĭt   tcuwuɬ
You were   Elder Brother magician   ill   plan   desired. This land

tcukĭtc   âĭtkʿ si-ĭmâĭtatcotkʿ   am   sʿap   tcu-umâ-â.   Ĭt   tâ-âta-ak
placed by followed very many plans there right   covered.   This mountains
him

tcotcoatc âĭtkʿ si-ĭmâĭtatcotkʿ   am   sʿap   ko-okiʿ.   Ĭt   rsârsânûkaṁ
handiwork followed very many plans there right   tips.   This springs

rsorsokĭ   tâtoatc âĭtkʿ si-ĭmâĭtcotkʿ   am   sʿap   tcu-umâ-â.   Ĭt   os
water   placed   followed very many plans there right   covered.   This this tree

ku-ursatc âĭtkʿ si-ĭmâĭtatcotkʿ am sʿap ko-okiʿ.   Am ki-ĭkʿhâ tcux
put   followed very many plans there right   tips.   There four times bounce

himĭtcotkʿ am tcoĭkâ kopal hutculwoĭtc.   Ka-am katckahimĭtc am
pushed   there elsewhere turned   down slide.   There   remains   there

---

Elder Brother, as he regained consciousness, rose on hands and feet and swayed unsteadily from side to side. He thought of the world about him and it seemed but a barren waste around him; as he recovered from his bewilderment he saw the true condition of things.

Looking about him he saw a river toward the west along which grew arrow bushes. From these he cut four magic sticks; placing his hand on these he blew cigarette smoke over them, whereupon magic power shone forth from between his fingers. He was much pleased with this and laughed softly to himself. He rubbed his magic bag of buckskin four times with each of the four sticks and then put them in and tied it. He then arose and stamped down all mortal magicians and even ground his own house into the earth. He stamped upon the orator, the warrior, the industrious, and the provident woman, and crushed them down. Then he sank beneath the surface of the earth. He reappeared in the east and made from the point of

---

utcukĭta. Ka̧si-ĭtatakrskᶜ ivam(pi) am uvwukatc inyunhâk tcum
it life.   With his hands   raised there around   look   he

nyuĭ âvapĭ hukam haĭtco kanhastcoĭk.   Ĭt wuskᶜ ap tcum
saw   not   them   thing   fami//ar.   This all that   he

umatcĭamahimûk piunakâ.   Ĭm ho̧ĭnyĭk woĭ ʌâtuvâ kus tcutakĭᶜ
it ponder   fails.   In   west   toward lay kind of blue

uʌamatûta hokĭt am woĭhyamûk am puĭ vatak os.   Am ki-ĭk
snake   beside there went to there catch wet tree. There four

hĭkomĭak am uwutcâ toak am sikommo.   Kotak tânâlĭkatc am
cut   there under placed there conjure.   That   rays   there

maorsatûkĭt siwoʌak towe katcĭm tcuwu̧ tam am kokoʌa.   Towe
between the   fingers opposite fixed country on there reach. Opposite

katcĭm tcuwu̧ maskâ oltᶜ; towe tcotcĭm tâ-âta-ak ʌupukĭomĭtkᶜ
fixed   country clear remains; opposite fixed mountains   reddish

tcotcoa.   Tak hap tcoĭkam tcom nyuĭtok am uta tcorsal ihuhumĭâ.
made and   That this thing   he   saw   there in murmur   laugh.
erected.

Ĭm ho̧ĭnyĭk takĭŏ tcut ihimĭtc kus tcok ukâ-âmhaĭʌakĭta. Huk
In   west   direction from pushed kind of black   his haze.   That

hukatc itakĭhonûk uta pimaskâ iolĭnûk sa-apĭ itâ-âtan.   Ĭm katcĭm
with   strip   in invisible hold   manner made.   In laying

takĭŏ ihimĭtc kus ta-atᶜkĭᶜ ukâ-âmhaĭwakĭta huk hukatc isita-akĭhonûk
direction pushed kind of blue   his haze   that with   strip thoroughly

uta pimaskâ iolĭnûk sa-ap itâ-âtan.
in   invisible stay hold manner made.

Ĭm sialĭk takĭŏ tcut ihimĭtc kus tântâm ukâhaĭʌakita huk hukutc
In   east   direction from pushed kind of white   his haze   that with

sitakĭhonûk uta pimaskâ iolĭnûk sa-ap itâtan.   Ĭt tutamu tcut ihotony
strip   in invisible hold   manner made.   This above from down

kus tcutakĭ ukâ-âmhaĭʌakĭta huk hukûtc sita-akĭhonûk uta pimaskâ
kind of blue   his haze   that with   strip   in invisible

iolĭnûk sa-ap itâtan.   Ĭm ho̧ĭnyĭk takĭŏ tcut himĭtc kus tcoak
hold   manner made.   In   sunset direction from pushed kind of black

uʌamatûtak huk hukûtc isiʌotkᶜ natâ.   Ĭm katcĭm takĭŏ tcut
his snake   that with it   tie   finish.   In laying direction from

ihimĭtc kus ta-atᶜkĭᶜ uʌamatûtak huk hukûtc isivotkᶜ natâ.   Ĭm
pushed   kind of blue   his snake   that with it   tie   finish.   In

sialĭk takĭŏ tcut ihimĭtc kus tântân uʌamatutakᶜ huk hukûtc
east   direction from pushed kind of white   his snake   that with

emergence a transparent trail to the place where he had gone down. About the base of his mountains the water began to seep forth; entering, he came out with spirit refreshed. Taking all waters, even those covered with water plants, he dipped his hands in and made downward passes. Touching the large trees he made downward sweeps with his hands. Going to the place where he had killed Eagle he sat down looking like a ghost. A voice from the darkness asked, "Why are you here?" He answered that notwithstanding all that he had done for them the people hated him. Renewing his power four times in the east at the place where the sun rises, he blew his hot breath upon the people, which like a weight held them where they

---

isivotkᶜ nᴀtâ. Ĭt tʊtamʊ tcʊt ihotĭny kʊs tcʊ-ʊtaki ʊᴧamatatûk
tie   finish.   This   above   from   down   kind of   blue   his snake

hʊk hʊkûtc isivotkᶜ nᴀtâ. Am ivorsanyuk am siûkʊĭrs. Âva
that   with   tie   finish.   There   arose   there   stamp on.   It was

hʊpai taha kʊs makaitᶜkam â-âtam kotak am sikʊĭhitcony ata-am
where   sitting   having powers of magician   people   that   there   stamp down   then

pai-ĭtc siûkʊĭrs. Âva hʊpai taha kʊs nyiâkam â-âtam kotak am
further   stamp on.   It was   where   sitting   kind of   orator   man   that   there

sikʊĭhitcony ata-am pai-ĭtc si-ikʊĭrs. Âva hʊpai taha kʊs siakam
stamp down   then   further   stamp on.   Then   where   sitting   kind of   brave

â-âtam tak am sikʊĭhitcony, âvawot iwʊs taam siûkʊĭrs. Âva hʊpai
man   that   there   stamp down,   it was   last   then   stamp down.   Then   where

tahakʊ ofᶜĭ stcopoihitûkam kʊ ofᶜĭ stcotcûkitûkam kot hʊk
sitting   kind of   woman energetic   gathers   kind of   woman stored   that   that

hawʊnatkᶜ am sikʊĭhitconyĭtkᶜ am tco-opiᶜ. Am kâmalm miarspahinûk
together   there   stamp down   there   sank.   There   thin   cover with earth

sialĭk takĭŏ mâ-âkanyĭk am tcʊt kʊs tântâm ʊᴧâkĭta ĭtcʊ. Kʊs
east   direction   eruption   there   from   kind of   white   his trail   put up.   Kind of

kʊ-ʊkʊ-ʊĭtam tâ-âta-ak tcotcoatc ʊrsârsân ap vapa-aᴧany. Hʊk wʊsk
large   mountains   made and erected   its bases   there   seeping.   That   all

ʊta vapᶜkiᶜhĭtc hʊkʊtc hʊk ʊipûtak ivaosĭtahĭm. Rsârsânûkam
in   enters and returns   with   that   his soul   moisten.   Springs

rsorsokĭ tâtoatc haakĭa nanûkâtcoĭkam mămâthăt katcpᶜ ʊi-ĭntc
water   placed   many   various   water plants   with it   covered

wʊo(f)ʊtck hʊk wʊsk ʊt mawopĭtc hʊkʊtc hʊk ʊi-ipʊtak ivaosĭtahĭm.
lays   that   all   in   dips   with   that   his soul   wet.

Kʊs kʊ-ʊkʊtam o-os tcotcoatckᶜ hʊk wʊsk ap mawopĭtc hʊkatc
Kind of   large   trees   made and erected   that   all   there   dipped   with

hʊk ʊipʊtak ivaosĭtahĭm. ᴧataᴧa tcʊmâ-â hʊkʊ Pa-ak ʊmoa-akŭt
that   his soul   wet.   Therefore   cover   at   Eagle   he kill

woĭtcotkᶜ pitcĭmûk woĭtcotkᶜ napatoᴧak vi-ĭtckŭt tcoĭk tcivĭa. Hastco
straight to   go around   straight to   sitting   (?)   resembles   came.   What

pŭhimʊtkᶜ tcivĭak vi-ĭtckŭt tcoikᶜtcᶜ tcivĭa. Hi-ĭks, nanypĭm akĭt
grasp   came   (?)   resemblance   came.   Yes,   I thus   told

spathâlĭtk tatcoa tcʊwʊ̣ Ĭtcʊkĭ hʊmata tarsa. Ta-am sialĭk woa
think evil   desires   country   for me placed   human   set.   There   east   toward

ki-ĭk aprsârs, ᴧataᴧa tcʊ-ʊmâ-â taᴊs tcʊtcrsatckŭt ki-ĭk ap (m)âĭtam
four   renewals,   therefore   reached   sun   place of coming up   four   there   groups

kâvâtltkᶜ ki-ĭk ap (m)âĭtam tcʊtany. Âvaᴧût kʊĭrspakutatc wʊs kâs
hollow   four   there   groups   thud.   It was   stepping place   all   over

huwʊlhâkĭtak wʊs kâs tcʊᴧakitak tcŭm pipapakᶜĭ hʊk ʊta ap
windy   all   over   cloudy   not   slowly   that   in   there

were. He accompanied the Sun on his journey, traveling along the south border of the trail where there was a fringe of beads, feathers, strings of down, and flowers.[a] He jerked the string holding these so that they fell and made the magicians jump. In the north he saw a trail bordered like the one in the south and overturned it.

On his journey along the Sun's orbit Elder Brother came to Talking Tree. "Why do you come like a ghost?" asked Tree. He replied, "Notwithstanding all I have done for the people they hate me." Tree broke one of its middle branches and cut a notch around it to form a war club and gave it to him. Then Tree broke a branch on the south side and made a bundle of ceremonial sticks from it for him. He saw a trail toward the south and another toward the north bordered with shells, feathers, down, and flowers, which he overturned.

---

takuïrspan ʋtco kotak ʋta ap siʋkuïrs. Âvawot takrspakŭtatc wʋs
enough   result   that   in there stamp.   It was   place for hand his   all

kâs huvʋhâkĭtak wʋs kâs tcuʌakĭtak tcompipapak'ï huk ʋta apta
over windy   all   over cloudy   if not slowly   that   in   there

takrspam ʋtco kotak ʋta ap si-ĭtakrs. Am iʌorsanyĭk koiwoa
may put the hand   that   in there put his hand. There   arose   about to
result   throw down

i-ipoïʌoak koïwoa itak'tc'kowa paitcok koïwoa i-ipoiwoa koiwa
breath   about to   shoved   further   about to   breath   about to
throw down   throw down   throw down

itakk'tc'kowa. Am pai-ĭtcok koïwa i-ipoïwoak koïwa itakk'tc' koïwa
shoved.   There   further   about to   breath   about to   shoved   about to
throw down   throw down   throw down.

Âvawot iwʋrs ta-am i-ipoïwoak koïwa itakk'tc'kowa. Âvawot ʋta
It was   final   there   breath   about to   shoved.   It was   in
throw down

katcĭm vâkĭtatc kotak iâ'ï katcĭm takĭŏ vâkĭtatc wʋs kâs payokatak
main   route   that   follow laying direction   route   all   over   necklace

wʋs kâs nahakiâtak a-an kiatŭta hokĭtûk vi-ĭk kiatŭta hokĭtûk os
all   over   earrings   feathers string   side   down   string   edge   tree

hiktc'ka hiasĭtastc hokĭtûk kak sivantc koʌatc sikopal woihĭm.
short piece flower stuck   edge   that   drags   jerks   face down   thrown.
on artificial

Nanûk'ï âĭt takĭŏ vâkĭtatc wʋs kâs payokatak wʋs kâs nahakiâtak
North   field direction   route   all   over   necklaces   all   over   earrings

a-an kiatŭta hokitak vi-ĭk kiatŭta hokĭtuk os hikutc'ka hiâsitastc'
feathers strings   edge   down   strings   edge   tree   short piece flowers stuck on
artificial flowers

hokĭtûk kak sihopanytc.
edge   that   uproot.

Sitcuxhĭm tcotahĭm. Kahʋpai taha kʋs makaĭt'kam â-âtam
Jumping high   continue.   Where   set   kind of   having powers of   man
magician.

kak am sitcʋxhĭm tcotahĭm. ʌatava tcʋ-ʋmââ kʋ nyiakʋtam os.
that there jumping high   continue.   Therefore   reach   kind of   Talking   Tree.

Woïtcotk' pitcĭmûk' woïtcotk' napatoʌak viïtckŭt tcoïk'tc' tcivĭa.
Straight to   go around   straight to   sitting   (?)   resembles   came.

Hastco pŭihĭmutk' tcivĭak viïtckŭt tcoïk'tc' tcivĭa. Hi-ĭks, nanypĭm
What   grasp   came   (?)   resembles   came.   Yes,   I thus told

akĭt spathâlĭtk' tatcŏa tcuwuɟ ĭtcukĭ hʋmata tarsa. P'ata kaĭtam
think evil   desires   country for me   human   set.   So   noise
placed

Arriving at the drinking place of the Sun he knelt down in the tracks made by the Sun to drink, and saw a dark-blue stone. [a] He left there the arrow-bush ceremonial sticks containing his enemies' power, but retained in his grasp the sticks cut from Talking Tree. Toward the south were strewn necklaces, earrings, feathers, strings of down, and flowers, all of which he jerked and threw face down. Toward the north he threw down the same objects, and as they struck the earth they caused the magicians to jump. Reaching the place where the sun sets he slid down four times before he reached the place where Earth Doctor lived.

"Why do you come looking like a ghost?" asked the god. "Notwithstanding all that I have done for them the people hate me," he answered. By Earth Doctor's order the wind from the west caught him up and carried him far to the east, then brought him back and threw him violently down. . . . The south wind carried him to

tcʊtcʊa	aʌawŏt	ʊta	kʊkam	vaʊokatc	tak	siâm	kioʌltʿkatkʿ	ap	isi
said	it was	in	standing	stalk	that	right	cut around	there	more

kâmʊrspĭtcʿ	avawot	kâsĭvoltatc	tak	ap	vanytcʿkʿ	kʊ	sialĭk
carry on the rump	it was	chrysalis	that	there	pluck	kind of	east

ʌʊkĭomĭlĭkatc	wʊs	ka	itakĭhonûk	ʌʊnatkʿ	ap	isi	kamʊrspĭtcʿ	âvawot
dawn	all over	strip		with it	there more	carry on the rump	it was

ulʊtatcʿ	kas	siâm	tcokŭt	matsĭk	akʿtcʿ	korsâ	ĭpʿ	takĭtcony	vi-ĭkam
skin	how	proper	owl	hook	call	nape	persist	shove	remainder

ap	isi	kakâmhaĭtckatat.	Ĭm	mot	katcĭm	takĭŏ	mamhakatc
there more		cut cheek hair.	In this direction	laying	direction		branch

tak	ap	molinûk	siâm	âmĭna	vʊpatkʿ	sikapĭtckatkʿ	rsak.	Âvawot
that	there	break	right	ceremonial	like sticks	bound	hold.	It was

ʊta	katcĭm	vâkĭtatc	kotak	iâĭ	katcĭm	takĭŏ	vâkĭtatc	wʊs	kas
in	laying	route	that	follow	laying	direction	route	all	over

payokatak	wʊs	kas	nahakĭâtak	a-an	kina-atʊta	hokĭtuk	vi-ĭk	kiatûta
necklaces	all	over	earrings	feathers	strings	edge	down	strings

hokĭtûk	os	hikʊtcʿka	hiasĭtastc	hokĭtuk	kak	sivantcʿkoʌatc	sikopal
edge	tree	cut	stuck up artificial flow	edge	that	pull by jerking	face down

woĭhĭm.	Nanûkĭ	âĭt	takĭŏ	ʌakitatc	wʊs	kas	payokatak	wʊs	kas
lay.	North	field	direction	route	all	over	necklaces	all	over

nahakĭâtak	a-an	kiatʊta	hokĭtuk	vi-ĭk	kiatûta	hokĭtuk	os	hikĭtcʿka
earrings	feathers	strings	edge	down	strings	edge	tree	short cut

hiasĭtastcʿ	hokĭtûk	kak	sihopanytcʿ	sitcʊxhĭm	tcotahĭm.	Ka hʊpai
stuck up artificial flow	edge	that	uproot	jumping high	continue.	Where where

taha	kʊs	nyâkam	â-âtam	kak	am	sitcʊxhĭm	tcotahĭm.	ʌataʌa
setting	kind of	talking	man	that	there	jumping high	continue.	Therefore

tcʊ-ʊmâ-â	kʊ	tars	i-ĭkŭt	rsotakĭʿ	kaot	tan	woĭkotatc	wʊs	kas
reach	kind of	sun	drinking place	water	that was knee	place for kneeling	all	over

hʊwʊlhakĭtak	wʊs	kas	tcʊʌakĭtak.	Tcʊm	pipapakĭ	hʊk	ʊta apta
windy	all	over	cloudy.	Not	slowly	that	in there

tân	woĭm	ʊtco	tak	ʊta	ap	sitânwoa.	Kaot takrspakotatc	wus	kas
up knee not put	result	that	in	there	stamp knee.	That was	hand hold	all	over

hʊʌʊlhâkĭtak	wʊs	kas	tcʊʌakĭtak.	Tcʊm	pipapakĭʿ	hʊk	ʊta apta
windy	all	over	cloudy.	Not	slowly	that	in higher

takrspam	ʊtco	tak	ʊta	ap	si-ĭtakrs.	Am	i-ĭtcomalkatkʿ	am i.
may place hand	result	that	in	there	put hand.	There	he stooped	there drink.

---

[a] Square, rough edged; causes consumption if one finds it and does not properly care for it.

the north; the east wind carried him to the west; the wind from the
zenith carried him to the sky; all returned to throw him violently down.
From his cigarette containing two kinds of roots Earth Doctor blew
smoke upon the breast of Elder Brother, whereupon green leaves
sprang forth and he gained consciousness. Earth Doctor cleared the
ground for a council and then picked up Elder Brother as he would
have taken up a child and put him in his house.

Earth Doctor sent Gray Gopher up through the earth to emerge in
the east by the white water where lay the eagle tail. He came out by
the black water where lay the raven feathers. He came out by the

---

Am tcᴜm nyᴜĭ kᴜk ᴜta am kᴜk stcᴜ-ᴜtakĭ hâtaĭ tapĭnya. Kot
There he saw that in there stand blue stone smooth. That

hᴜk wᴜtcâ am maorsk am takĭthâ hᴜk Â-âps̒ kam ᴜamĭna.
that under there thrust in there relinquish that enemies' power short sticks.

Nyĭâkŭtam os ᴜamĭna viak hᴜk rsa-ak iâĭ. Âʌawot ᴜta katcĭm
Talking tree short sticks left that grasp he followed. It was in laying

vâkĭtatc kotak iâĭ katcĭm takĭŏ vâkĭtatc wᴜs kas payokatak wᴜs
trail that he follow laying direction trail all over necklaces all

kas nahakiâtak a-an kia-atᴜta hokĭtak vi-ĭk kiatᴜta hokĭtvk os
over earrings feathers strings sides down strings edge tree

hiktc̒ka hiâsĭtastc̒ hokĭtvk kak sivanĭtckovatc sikopaɪ woĭhĭm.
short sticks artificial edge that jerks face down thrown.

Na-ankĭ âĭt takĭŏ vâkĭtatc̒ wᴜs kas payokatak wᴜs kas nahakĭâtak
North field direction trail all over necklaces all over earrings

a-an kiatᴜta hokĭtvk vi-ĭk kiatᴜta hokĭtvk os hik̒tcka hiâsĭtastc̒
feathers strings edge down strings edge tree short cut artificial

hokĭtvk kak sihopanytc̒ sitcᴜxhĭm tcotahĭm. Kahᴜpaĭ taha kᴜs
edge that uproot jumping high going. Where sitting kind of

siakam â-âtam kak am sitcᴜxhĭm tcotahĭm. ʌataʌa tcᴜ-ᴜmâ-â
brave man that there jumping high going. Therefore reach

kᴜ taɪs hotokot ki-ĭk ap mâĭtam sᴜtapĭonytc katc kotak âĭtk̒
kind of sun every other four there groups smooth lay that followed
evening

ki-ĭkhâ itapĭonyĭk ĭmho tᴜʌutca s̒papaki tcᴜ kᴜ sis makaĭ.
four times slides there us under slowly discover kind of older brother
magician.

Woitcotk̒ pitcĭmk̒ woitcotk̒ napatoʌak vi-ĭtckŭt tcoi-ĭk̒tc̒ tcivĭa.
Straight to go around straight to sit flat (?) resembles came.

Hastco pŭĭhimût̒k̒ tcivĭa, hastco pŭĭhĭmût̒k̒ tcivĭa, hastco pŭĭhĭmŭt̒k̒
What do you wish to get come, what do you wish to get come, what do you wish to get

tcivĭa, hastco pŭĭhĭmŭt̒k̒ tcivĭak vi-ĭtckŭt tcoĭk̒tc̒ tcivĭa. Hi-ĭks,
come, what do you wish to get came (?) resembles came. Yes,

nanypĭm akĭt spathâlĭtk̒ tatcoa tcᴜvᴜɪ nytcᴜkĭ hᴜmata tarsa p̒ata
I thus told think evil desires land for me placed people set he said

kaĭtam tcᴜtcu. Ata-im hoɪinyĭk takĭŏ tcᴜt âĭtktcᴜt tcivĭa.
noise said. Far in west direction from after came.

Ĭm sialĭk woĭ tcᴜxhĭmtcotk̒ sialĭk parsâĭnâtkĭtk̒ opam tarsowa ĭm
In east toward jumping high east turn back near home set in

katcĭm takĭŏtcŭt âĭtktcᴜt tcivĭa. Na-ankĭ âĭt woĭ tcᴜxhĭmtcotk̒
laying direction from follow came. North field toward jumping high

na-ankĭ âĭt parsâĭpâtkĭtk̒ opam tarswoa. Ĭm sialĭk takĭŏtcᴜt
north field turn back near home set. In east direction

âĭtk̒tcᴜt tcivĭa. Hoɪinyĭk woĭ tcᴜxhĭmtcotk̒ hoɪinyĭk parsâĭnâtkĭtk̒
follow came. West toward jumping high west turned back near

opam tarswoa. Ĭt tamᴜtcut âĭtktcᴜt tcivĭa. Tam atcĭm woĭ
home set. Here above follow came. Top sky toward

blue water where lay the bluebird's feathers. He came out by the
yellow water where lay the hawk feathers. He found so many people
that he feared they could not be conquered. But he gnawed the magic
power of their leader until he weakened it. Then he returned to the
council in the nether world, where his power as a magician was recognized, and he was placed on a mat with Elder Brother.

The people were now ready to do whatever Elder Brother desired of
them and, like fierce predatory animals or raptorial birds, they poured
out of the underworld and fell upon the inhabitants of the upper
world, whom they conquered without difficulty. The victors swept

---

tcʋxhĭmtcotk tam atcĭm parsâinâtkĭtkᶜ opam tarswoa haapatavâĭtâ-âta.
bounding   top sky   turned back near   home set   done.

An wʋkatc hʋk tcʋwʋɬ itakĭŏmk hastcoprs alĭ wʋpâtkᶜ ikâmûk hʋk
There around   that land   stripped resembles young make like hold that

ʋta am tarswoa. Kawot kʋ kâkâĭ tax aɟĭtcĭkĭtcᵃ pawoĭs tax aɟĭtcĭkĭtc
in there set.   That was kind of ghost root cigarette his pawois root cigarette his

kotak ap parsâ i-ïpûĭhʋɪʌoa kota siâm ʋiʌakitat kavaot kʋs kâmakĭ
that there near   he puffed   that right   left   it was kind of gray

tcʋfha rsâikatc kotak ap imûk rsârsoâ. Kota am tcopĭnyk am sialĭk
gopher pet   that there my cry.   That there sank   there east

takĭŏ mâ-âkanûk am kʋs tântâm rso-otakiᶜ tcʋ. Kʋ Pa-ak pahĭwoa
direction pop out there kind of white   water discov- Kind of Eagle   tail
                                                 ered.

katc am simaĭrsk tcʋ. Am pai-ĭtc tcopĭnyĭk am mâ-âkanyĭk am kʋs
lay there covered placed. There further sank   there pop out there kind of

tcok rso-otakiᶜ tcʋ. Kʋ haʌany a-an katc ʋʋaĭrsk am tcʋ. Am
black water   discov- Kind of raven feathers lay covered there placed. There
               ered.

pai-ĭtc tcopĭnyk am mâ-âkanyk am kʋs tcʋ-ʋtakĭ rsotakĭ tcʋ.
further   sank   there   pop out there kind of blue   water   discov-
                                                                  ered.

Hʋʌatcot a-an katc naĭrsk am tcʋ. Am pai-ĭtc tcopĭnyk am
Bluebird feathers lay covered there placed. There further sank   there

mâ-âkanyk am kʋɢ ɢoam rso-otakĭ tcʋ. Kʋ ʌatcokok a-an katc
pop out   there kind of yellow water discov- Kind of hawk feathers lay
                                       ered.

maĭrsk am tcʋ. Am tcopĭnyk am mâ-âkanyk am ikoatcĭtkᶜ am
covered there placed. There sank   there pop out   there look around there

tcʋm nyʋĭ. Ĭt ʌâkʋta katcĭm pipapakĭ hastco katc tcoitcĭm tcoi-ĭk.
he saw.   This trail laying   not slowly what lay manner   thing.

Âvak tcom sitaĭrstc takatkᶜ ʋ-ʋlĭt hʋk makai. Kota am wʋkatc
They   firmly seated think   that   magician. That there around

katcĭm na-ankâ tcoi-ĭtckatc sisârspâl ki-ĭkomĭa. Pʋk am opam
laying all   belongings   short   bite off. Took there home

tcopĭᶜ. Ki-ĭk ap mâ-âkanyk makaĭ na-ata tcʋ-ʋmûk hokĭt an takĭtâ.
sank.   Four there pop out   magician fire covered beside   release.

Sᶜmakai-ĭtakam â-âtam vaksĭtkᶜ tam tarswoa. Tak ʋta hʋk isi
Powerful magician man   placed for on set.   There in   that ready

kʋĭrsk kʋkĭʌak nyʋĭ ʌiapâkʋ-ʋlĭka tcʋwʋɬâ mʋtʋtam ʋʌʋpâkiᶜ o-ofĭk
stamped stood   me   sons   land   running   like   birds

ᵃ Aɟĭtcĭkĭtc from Papago.

the property and everything relating to the conquered from the face of the earth.

Consider the magic power which abode with me and which is at your service.

---

ta-atam ᴜᴧᴜpâkitkᶜ nyᴜĭnyk tam ap ᴜiaᴧak ap piatco tatkĭtcotkᶜ ap
flying   like   fly   on   there   seize   there   nothing   wrestle   there
sᴜtapam pᴜĭ. Am ᴧᴜkûtc katcĭm nananûka tcoĭtckatc si-ĭnasĭk
smooth   catch. There   around   laying   all   belongings   gather
sᶜpapakĭᶜ kaᴧolkatkᶜ sᶜpapakĭᶜ hahâk inyᴜ woa.
slowly   bundled   slowly   revolve   me   throw down.

Hapkᴠk hᴜmŭs ᴜhitkᶜ tatcoa âᴧaot kᴜs kᴜ-ᴜk toakak konta ap pᴜk
You   may   think   desire   it was   kind of good   life   I took there took
antaᴧaĭoapa.
brought.

Explanation

When rain is desired one of the leading men who understands the ceremony will notify the medicine-men, the orator or reciter, and the singer. These agree upon beginning the ceremony at the end of four days. On the third day they send one or more men as criers to announce to the people of the adjoining villages that the ceremony will be held on the morrow.

When all have assembled in the evening the leader calls out the names one by one of the medicine-men, who take their position behind the fire, facing toward the east. Then the names of those who will sing are called. The leading singer sits behind the medicine-men and his assistants place themselves on either side of him and around the fire. Then the orator is named and takes his place with the medicine-men. When the leader announces that it is time for the ceremony to begin, the orator recites the following:

Translation

Is it in this condition that we are sitting here, understanding the advice of our forefathers? There is an unknown house in which lies the magic brand; toward this we point the ceremonial cigarette and smoke, thus acquiring an insight that shall enable us to speak wisely.

When the earth was new it was shaking and rough.[b] As you know, Black Mocking Bird lives in the west. I had considered my relation-

---

Nâ	Hums	hapa	tcoĭk˙	kotcs	hʊk	utû	tathaktc˙	haps	ma-atc
Not	like	this	condition	that	for	in	sitting in	therefore	understand

haĭtco	a–ak.	Kâvawot	qetai˙	ki,	hʊk	uta	amkatc˙[c]	hʊk[d]	kotck˙
thing	counsel.	It was	(?)	house,	for	in	lays		brand

vi–itûk.	Oatcĭkĭ˙	tân	hʊk	woĭ	amʊkʊk	kotc	hʊkap	hâwâktc	hap
remnant.	Cigarette	knee	that	one	standing	that	which	inhaling	there_ fore

samatc	haĭtco	ak.	Kota	tcʊwʊꜣ	hʊmoĭ	ʊtcʊ	amʊta	hâĭntc	katc
know	thing	counsel.	Then	earth	new	was	made in	moving	lay

amʊta	tcŏtcoaktc˙	katc.	Âva	ĭm	hoꜣĭnyĭk	takĭŏ	kʊs	tcok
in	inserted and projecting	lay.	As you know	toward	west	direction	kind of	black

rso-ok	kontak	hap	tcoĭkam	mamatcʊk	ap	ĭmûk[e]	rsârsoa	kotap
mocking bird	I had	therefore	that class visible	guessing		my	weep	because

---

[a] The so-called Tcʊtc kita, make rain.

[b] It shook because it was wet and spongy at that time, "like the wet bank of the river."

[c] Am = a prefix denoting certainty.

[d] Connective inserted for euphony.

[e] Ĭmûk = "My (brother or other relative)," a form of entreaty.

ship to him and guessed what should be the right manner in which to
address him. Because of my entreaty he was disposed to be friendly
toward me.

Yes, Black Mocking Bird, if your plans for controlling the earth
have failed, go far hence and leave the black wind and the black clouds
behind you. Your people will henceforth entreat your assistance
from a distance.

When the land was new I knew of a Blue Mocking Bird in the
south, and I called on him also for help, and he came. He gave commands to control the hills, mountains, trees, everything. But still
the earth continued shaking.

Yes, Blue Mocking Bird, if your plans have failed, go hence and

---

sǐnyhâĭ-ikuǐ-itam utatkᶜ amĭtcût tcivǐa. Ha-akǐa haĭtco ua-aka ǐt
friendly   felt   from   came.   Many   things his counsel this

tcuwuɹ tcumûk vaopanûk tcuwuɹ tcovitûk ap kuorspahimûk ap
land   everywhere stretched land hills on touching on

tâta-ak kokok ap kukuorspahimûk o-os kokok ap kukuorspahimûk
mountain tops on touched   trees tops on touched

natâ.   Âvak hukutc tcûmsi katcĭkâk ak hap tcumtco. Âva
finish. Then with   covering remain fixed deter- he made it has As you
                                              mining since failed. know

amuta hâĭntc katc amuta tcotcoaktc katc. Ahu-u, kus tcok rso-ok
in   moving lay   in   inserted and lay. Yes, kind of black mocking
                            projecting

vatcǐm piam utcon hukûm tcoĭtcĭk kop varsatcᵃ iolĭnhǐ kus tcoĭtcĭk
may   try   your   plan   you   farther stay kind of black

uhuwulĭk kus tcoĭtcĭk utcuwakîk kâmĭsɹhi ap kukiovan.
your wind kind of black your clouds carried behind there stand.

Hûk hum humata hupaĭ tcukakᵇ apamuk mimhi rsâsoakan kop
That your people some time   future my   entreaty you

pimaskâ vai-iwumkan pᶜata tcu-uk va-arsatc iol(t). Im ka-atcĭmᶜ
unseen   will help,   he   said   near   stay.   This laying

takĭŏ kus tatkᶜ rso-ok kontak hap tcoĭkam mamutcĭk ap imûk
direc- kind blue mocking I was there- I know guessing to my
tion   of   bird   fore

rsârsoa tap sǐnyhâĭ-ikuǐ-itam utatkᶜ amtcut tcivǐa. Ha-akia haĭtco
weep   conse- friendly   felt   from   come.   Many   things
       quently

ua-aka ǐt tcuwuɹ tcu-umk vaopanûk tcuwuɹ tcovitk ap
his advice this land   covering stretched land   hiĺ! to

kuowurspahimuk ap tâ-ata-ak ko'kok ap kukuowurspahimûk o-so
touching   on mountain tops on touched   trees

ap kukuowurspahimûk na-atâ. Âvak hukutc tcomsi katckâk
on touched   finish. Then with that for the remain
                                              purpose

a-ak hap tcumtco. Âva amuta hâĭntc katc amuta tcotcoaktcᶜ
fixed deter- he made it has As you in moving lay in inserted and
      mining since failed. know   projecting

katc. Ahu-u, kus tatkᶜ rso-ok vatcum piam utcon hukum tcoĭtcĭk
lay.   Yes, kind of blue mocking bird your may try your plan

kop varsatc iolĭnhǐ kus tatkᶜ uhuwulĭk kus tatkᶜ utcuwakĭk
farther stay kind of blue your wind kind of blue your clouds

ᵃ Kop varsatc, "farther," when any one is moving toward an object near at hand; "near" when
speaking of an object close by if no one is approaching or seeking it.

ᵇ From Papago.

ᶜ Speaker here points to the quarter about which he is speaking.

leave the blue wind and blue clouds behind you.　Your people will henceforth entreat your assistance from a distance.

Then I knew the White Mocking Bird in the east, and I called on him for help, and he came, bringing commands that would control the hills, mountains, trees, everything.　But the earth continued shaking.

Yes, White Mocking Bird, if your plans for controlling the earth have failed, go hence and leave the white winds and the white clouds behind you.　Your people will henceforth entreat your assistance from a distance.

Then, above me enveloped in darkness lived the magician Kuvĭk, on whom I called for help.　He came in a friendly spirit, with commands that would control the hills, mountains, trees, everything. The earth became much quieter, but still moved somewhat.

---

kamĭrshĭ ap kukĭovan.　Huk hum huma-ata hupai tcukak apamuuk
carried　there　stand.　That　your　people　some　time　future
behind

mimhi rsâsoakan kop pimaskâ vaiwumkan p⸰atatcu-ûk varsatc iol(t).
my　entreaty　you　unseen　will help　he said　farther　stay.

Ĭm sialĭk takĭŏ kus tântâm rso-ok kontak hap tcoĭkam mamutcûk
This　east　direction kind of　white　mocking　I was determin-　I know　guessing
　　　　　　　　　　　　bird　ing

apimûk rsâsoa tap⸰ sănyhâĭ-ikuĭ-itam utatk⸰ am tcut tcivĭa.　Ha-akĭa
to my　weep　he　friendly　felt　from　come.　Many

haĭtco ua-aka ĭt tcuwuɭ tcumk vaopanûk tcuwuɭ tcovitûk ap
things　his advice this　land　covering　stretched　land　hill　there

kuowurspahĭmûk tâ-âtak kokok kukuorspahĭmûk o-os kokok ap
touching　mountains　tops　touched　trees　tops　there

kukuorspahĭmûk na-atâ.　Âvak hukatc tcŏmsi katckâk a-ak
touched　finish.　Then　with　for the purpose remain　fixed

hap tcumtco.　Âva amuta hâĭntc katc amuta tcotcoaktc
deter-　he made it has　As you　in　moving　lay　in　inserted and
mining　since failed.　know　　　　　　　　　　　　　projecting

katc.　Ahu-u, vatcĭm piam utcon hukûm tcoĭtcĭk kop varsatc iolĭnhĭ
lay.　Yes,　　　may　try　your　plant　you　farther　stay

kus tâta uhuwulĭk kus tâta utcuwukĭk kamĭrshĭ ap kukĭovan.
kind　white　your wind　kind of white　your clouds　carried　there　stand.
of　　　　　　　　　　　　　　　　　　　behind

Huk hum humata hupai tcukak apa mu-uk mimhi rsârsoakan
That　your　people　some　time　from　far　my　entreaty

kop pimaskâ vaĭ-iwumkan.　Âva![a] Iat tam huk stcohokam
your　unseen　assistance.　As you know! Here　above　that　darkness

kusikâlk⸰tc⸰ ka-atc⸰.　Âva! Uta siâmp uolĭntc huk Kuvik kârskam
enveloping　there. As you know! In　right　held　that　Vi-ik　nest

ma-akai.　Kontak hap tcoĭkam mamutcĭk ap imûk rsârsoa.　Kotap
magician.　I was　that　kind of　guessing　to　my　weep.　Because

sănghâĭ-ikuĭ-itam utatk⸰ ha-akĭa haĭtco ua-aka rsa-akû⸰ amtcut
friendly　felt　many　things　his advice　grasping　from

tcivĭa.　Ha-akĭa haĭtco ua-aka it tcuwuɭ tcumûk vaopanûk tcuwuɭ
come.　Many　things　his advice this　land　covering　stretched　land

tcovĭtk ap kuorspahimûk tâtak kokok ap kukuorspahimûk o-os
hill　to　touching　mountain　tops　to　touched　trees

kokok ap kukuorspahimuk na-atâk ata hukatc am hu-us tâtâlĭm
tops　to　touched　finish　fly　with that from　little　quiet

utcu.　Am ha-as ihikâva amuta hâĭntc katc amuta tcotcoak⸰tc⸰ katc⸰.
remain.　From　brief　time　in　moving there　in　inserted and　lay.
　　　　　　　　　　　　　　　　　　　　　　　projecting

---

a Âva means "as you know," but is here an interjection.

Then, there was a Gray Spider in the west.[a] I called on him for
assistance. He was friendly to me and came in answer to my appeal.
He took bundles of sticks, which he placed in the edges of the land
and sewed them firmly together. He pulled the black corner at the
west, where stands the house of the Rain god of the west. He firmly
enveloped the earth with his black power. He pulled the blue corner
at the south, where stands the house of the Rain god of the south.
He firmly enveloped the earth with his blue power. He pulled the
white corner at the east, where stands the house of the Rain god of the
east. He firmly enveloped the earth with his white power, and with
that the earth became quieter.

Im hoɉinyĭk takĭŏ kᴜs kâmaki tâktât.   Kontak hap tcoikam
In   sunset   direction kind of gray   spider.   I was   that   class

mamûtcik ap imûk rsârsoa.   Kotap sĭnyhâĭ-ikᴜĭ-itam utâtkᶜ o-os
guessing to my   weep.   Because   friendly   felt   trees

uhikĭaka rsa-ak amtcᴜt tcivĭa. It tcᴜwuɉ hohokitak sikoapitkᶜ
bundles of grasping from come. This land   edges   firmly sewed
sticks   together

natâ. Ĭm hoɉinyĭk woĭ ivanyonûk am kᴜs tcok mawatatûkᶜ kᴜs
finish. In   sunset toward pull   from kind of black four corners of kind
                                                  the earth tied of
                                                  with something

tcok va-akĭ katc am si maitcoyitûkᶜ kᴜs tcotcĭkᶜkᶜ omû katc
black house with from firmly envelope kind of black two-feathered lay
                                                              arrow

am si kᴜowᴜrs. Im ka-atckᶜ woĭ ivanyunak am kᴜs tatkᶜ
from very hold down. In laying toward   pull   from kind of blue

mawatatûkᶜ kᴜs tatkᶜ va-akĭ katc am si maitconytkᶜ kᴜs
four corners of kind of blue house lay from firmly envelope kind of
the earth tied
with something

tatkᶜ omû katc am si kᴜowᴜrs. Im sialĭk woĭ ivanyonûk
blue two-feathered lay from firmly hold down. In east toward pull
     arrow

am kᴜs tântâm mawatatûkᶜ kᴜs tântâm va-akĭ katc am si
from kind of white four corners of kind of white house lay from firmly
                the earth tied
                with something

maitcoyĭtûk kᴜs tâta omᴜ katc am si kᴜowᴜrs. Hᴜk
envelope kind of white two-feathered lay from firmly hold down. That
                    arrow

ata hᴜkûtc amahava tâtâlĭm ᴜtcu. Im hoɉinyĭk takĭŏ kᴜs tcok
was with it make   quiet remain. In   sunset   direction kind of black

âtcᴜvĭk. Kontak hap tcoikam mamatcᴜk ap imûk rsârsoa.
measuring I was   that   class   guessing to my   weep.
worm.

Kotapᶜ sinyhâĭ-ikᴜĭ-itam ᴜtatkᶜ amtcᴜt ki-ĭkhâ iᴜtcovitkatkᶜ am
Because   friendly   felt   from   four times raises up   from

rsâ-ârspâl uâ-âminûk am siâm ᴜtcᴜtântatkᶜ unatâ. Im ka-atcĭm
short   broken from right itself on posts finish. In   laying

takĭŏ kᴜs tatkᶜ âtcᴜvĭk kontak hap tcoĭkam mamûtcĭk ap
direction kind of blue measuring worm I was that   class   guessing to

imûk rsârsoa.
my   weep.

Then, in the west there was a Black Measuring Worm that was
friendly to me and came in answer to my entreaty. He came in four
strides and in short broken lengths stood up as crotched posts. In
the south there was a Blue Measuring Worm that was friendly to me
and came in answer to my entreaty. He came in four strides and in
short broken lengths formed the joists to lie upon the posts. In the
east there was a White Measuring Worm that was friendly to me and
he came in four strides in answer to my entreaty. He in short broken
lengths covered the joists with a layer of small poles. In the north
there was a Reddish Measuring Worm that was friendly to me and
came in four strides in answer to my entreaty. He in short broken
lengths covered the other parts in a curved outer layer, thus finishing
the framework.

Then, in the west there was a Blue Gopher who came with plenty
of brush which he placed layer above layer around the house, covering it as with thin clouds. Around the house were four gopher hills
with which he covered it with earth in a thin, even layer, as snow

---

Kotap' sĭnyhâĭ-ikʋĭ-itam ʋtatûk amtcʋt ki-ĭkha iʋtcovitakatûk
Because   friendly   felt   from four times raise up

am rsârspâl ŭâminûk am siâmp kakai-ĭ ʋvâopa. Ĭm sialĭk takĭŏ kʋs
from short   broken from right level it laying. In east direction kind of

tântâm âtcʋvĭk kontak hap tcoĭkam mamtcĭk ap imûk rsârsoa. Kotap
white measuring worm I was that class guessing to my weep. Because

sĭnyhâĭ-ikʋĭ-itam ʋtatʋk amtcʋt ki-ĭkha iʋtcovitakatʋk am rsârspâl
friendly   felt   from four times he it raise up from short

ʋaminûk am siâmp rsʋ-ursʋrl ʋvaopaᶜ. Im nanûkᶜ âitû takĭŏ kʋs
it broken from right straight it laying. In north field direction kind of

wʋkĭŭm âctʋvĭk kŏntak hap tcoĭkam mamtcĭk ap imûk rsârsoa. Kotap
reddish measuring worm I was that class guessing to my weep. Because

sĭnyhâĭ-ikʋĭ-itam ʋtatkᶜ amtcʋt ki-ĭkhâ iʋtcovitakatûk am rsârspal
friendly   he felt from four times he it raised from short

ʋâminûk am siâmp ʋkikĭâtatkᶜ ʋnatâ. Ĭm katcĭm takĭŏ kʋs tatkᶜ
it broken from right curve themselves finish. In laying direction kind of blue

tcʋfhâ kontak hap tcoĭkam mamtcʋk ap imûk rsârsoa. Kotap
gopher I was that class guessing to my weep. Because

sĭnyhâĭ-ikʋĭ-itam ʋtatkᶜ ha-akĭa rsaĭ ʋmoa-atak amtcʋt tcivĭa. Hʋk
friendly   felt   many grass killed   from   came. That

itcʋwʋlĭtkᶜ hʋkûtc ap isirsa-itcitkᶜ natâ. Kʋs kʋk kâmalt
he raised with that to he thoroughly covered finish. Kind of good thin

tcʋwakita ak hap tco. An wʋkatcĭk tʋcwʋɳ ki-ĭk ap mo-oat.
clouds   make and has failed. There behind land four to gopher hills.

Huk ihimĭtcotûk hʋkʋtc ap isihiarsk natâ.
That pushed   with that to he covered dirt finish.

Kʋs kʋk kʋfainta ak hap tco. An wʋkûtcĭk tcʋwʋɳ itakĭomûk
Kind of good set make and has failed. There around dirt clean

hastcopspᶜ alĭ mʋwʋpâtĭkitûk ĭm kamûk ĭt ʋta ĭmʋ tarsowa.
what thing young your likeness in hold this in here place.

Siwât mʋhʋtam ko-otckᶜ ipʋk ĭmʋ wʋtcantcʋ. Oatcĭkᶜ tân hʋk
Flame light   brand he took here lower place. Cigarette knee that

woĭ am kʋĭ. Tak ap ko-orsk vamʋsk am sialĭk woĭ si-ipʋeva.
toward from stand. That to stick smoke from east toward puff.

Ta-am kʋs tâtam ʋtcotcua himûk sialĭk sʋpapûk tcʋmâ. Kʋs tâta
Then kind of white stand went east slowly reached. Kind of white

covers the ground.   Looking around the earth I selected one to take me up like a little boy and place me in the house.   He placed a brand of fire down before me and a cigarette also.   Lighting the cigarette he puffed smoke toward the east in a great white arch.   The shadow of the arch crept across the earth beneath.   A grassy carpet covers the earth.   Scattering seed, he caused the corn with the large stalk, large leaf, full tassel, good ears to grow and ripen.   Then he took it and stored it away.   As the sun's rays extend to the plants, so our thoughts reached out to the time when we would enjoy the life-giving corn.   With gladness we cooked and ate the corn and, free from hunger and want, were happy.   Your worthy sons and daughters, knowing nothing of the starvation periods, have been happy.   The old men and the old women will have their lives prolonged yet day after day by the possession of corn.

People must unite in desiring rain.   If it rains their land shall be as a garden, and they will not be as poor as they have been.

---

kikihât	uvaopanûk	sialĭk	sĭpapûk	tcumââ.	Wutcâ	tcuwuɹ
rainbows	stretched	east	slowly	reached.	Below	land

sᶜahamasma	ukahimûk	sialĭk	supapûk	tcumâa.	Wutcâ	tcuwuɹ
beautiful	shadow goes	east	slowly	reached.	Below	land

sᶜahamasama	mamûthâtᶜtkᶜ	utcu.	Huk	tam	wors	hukunanûkâ
beautiful	branched	placed.	That	on	grow	that different

tcoĭkam	mukaiitûta.	Kursavatkᶜ	vaok	tatany	hahak	skuk	motatûk
sort	your seeds.	Very large	stalk	wide	leaf	good	tassel

hiâsĭk	hikûm	pimokam	kai-ĭktcᶜ	paĭ.	Ta-am	amutco	ta-am	siâm
flowers	those	undying	grains	ripe.	Then	was made	then	good

hasitcok	puk kantcu.	Kaot taɹs	sisĭwutakᶜtcᶜ	huk	uta	ap	kokokuva.
intend	take placed.	It was sun	rays	that	in	to	had ended.

Kotak	wunatûk	am	hasĭtcok	pa-ak	wutcum	kupi	haskam	haĭtco
That was	together	from	intend	swallow	happy	nothing	not noticing	thing

tatam.	Kus	kuk	mu	viapoku-ulĭka,	skuk	mu	tcuhiaka	wum
feeling.	Kind of	good	your	sons,	good	your	daughters	with

kupi	haskam	haĭtco	tatam.	Kota	humakâ	vi-ĭkam	kulĭmhâkam
nothing	not noticing	thing	feeling.	That	one	remnant	old man

âkᶜ	ap	tcinyĭvak	wutcûm	kâ-âk	hoɹony	uwue	nviatcᶜ	kamvampᶜ
old woman	to	put mouth against	inanimate	two	evenings	opposite	give sight	forward

panymût.	Hapûkhums	âulĭtkᶜ	tatcoak	humok	âithĭ	hap	masĭn
crawling.	Perhaps will	think	desire	now	think	determining	venture

hukûtᶜ	tcuwutīka	kotc	huk	nyuitan	natc	apahâp,	rsâsaĭkam
that	land our	we	that	try	our right	thing	discouraged

tᶜtatᶜkan.
ourselves feel.

Because I was a boy I did not understand these things. When any-one was preparing food I stood with folded arms. They gave me food so hot that it burned me. I went with a hunting party. They killed a little bird and gave it to me. I thought it was good to eat, so I carried it home to my mother and threw it down before her. When she saw it she turned her back upon it and began to cry. She turned and told me about my father's death. I grieved in my heart and after a time went to consult a man of authority, to whom a boy should not have had the temerity to go. He listened to my story, approved of my plans, and told me to come at a time which he appointed. Then the people would accompany me to the enemy's country that I might see it. When we had gone to an appointed camping place we encamped and I slept well. The next day we continued to the camping place

---

Konyŏ	vawŏɹaps	alĭkʿtcʿ	ithap	tcoĭkam	pimatc.	Hastco
Because	I was	young	this	kind	not know.	What thing

hatconyĭ	woĭ	kukĭtc	nyʊ	vâ-âk	kâmûtc.	Koma	hastco	stânyĭk
cooked	toward	standing	my	stomach	hold.	You	what	hot

nyʊma	konta	nyʊ	papaĭtcĭtûk	ho.	Hastco	alâ-âĭtamʊlt	ka-atc	kont
me give	I was	me	burned	eat.	What	hunting	place	I

hʊk	âitkʿ	iwors.	Komʊta	hastco	kutivĭtc	mat	moak	nyʊ
that	after	go.	You	what	kutivitc	young	kill	me

tcultsp.	Konyak	skʊk	hastco	mokĭk	akʿtcʿ	kahap	tcŏntcŏkʿtcʿ
carry at hip.	I was	good	what	shoot and kill	telling	from	bringing

ipʊk	an	nyʊ	âkĭtak	wʊtcâ	iwoa	kota-amtcʊm	nyʊitâk
fetch	there	me	mother	under	to blame for knocking down	then	she saw

kamko-okam	itanewaʿ	ha-akĭa	ʊkokoi	matâ.	Kota	hʊpaĭ	tcʊkak
turned back	sat	many	her cry	open.	That	sometime	then

am	kookĭtûk	ipʊk	in	nyʊ	wʊtcâ	iwoa	ithap	tcoĭkam
there	ended	fetch	in	me	under	to blame for knocking down	this	kind

haĭtco	has	ʊtcokʿtcĭm.	Kota	it	imho	nyʊ	ʊta	kukĭva	kontak	pʊk
anything	making	accident.	That	this	there	me	in	stand	I was	hold

iwors.	Â-âtam	hʊpaĭ	ta	wotatcʊm	kuhas	ʊlata	kont	hʊk	pihas
rise.	People	where	sit	important	kind of	regard	I	that	no

ʊlitak	hʊk	woĭ	ivapûkʿkĭ.	Ithap	tcoĭkam	nyʊ	tatcoĭ	ipʊk
think	that	toward	pass through.	This	kind	me	plans	fetch

an	wʊtcâ	iwoa.	Kotaps	nyʊ	hâĭ-kʊĭ-itam	ʊtatûk	an	pʊĭk
there	under	to blame for knocking down.	He was	me	friendly	felt	there	grasp

haĭtco	nyĭʊ	aka.	Am	tcotcoĭ	hʊk	sialĭ	kontak	am	sihasiɹrsolkahĭm
thing	me	advice.	There	appoint	that	mornings	I was	there	clear away with something

kot	am	himûk	am	ʊai	kont	hʊk	pʊk	iwors.	Himʊk	hʊpai
that	there	going	there	reach	I was	that	grasp	rise.	Going	some

agreed upon and there I slept well. The next day we reached the land
of the Apaches, where I was afraid. I kept my body protected with
my shield and carried my club in hand. I could not rest for fear.
Then I remembered how my mother had told me what my feelings
would be in the enemy's country. She told me that the birds would
sing differently, all nature would be strange; but she did not tell me all.
This is the feeling that one experiences. The next day I reached the
Apache mountain, where I felt like a drunken person from fear. I lost
faith in my bow. I was frightened at sight of an old reed arrow of
the Apaches. Then as I sat below the mountain I swayed from side
to side looking for the enemy. Again I remembered what my mother
had told me of the perils among the enemy. The next day I arose and
went to the springs of the Apaches, where I saw a gourd drinking cup,
with which I cleared away the surface of the water and drank. Thinking that perhaps my father had been brought to that place by the
Apaches, I was alarmed and feared that I must already be in danger,
because I had drunk the water belonging to the enemy. The next day

tɔuwuɟ matcolĭtûk hʊk tam hoɟĭnyĭk woak sʿaptahatam kâĭ. Kota
land   appointed   that over evening overthrow right feeling sleep.   That

massĭ kont worsanyĭk himûk hʊpaĭ tɔuwuɟ matcolĭtûk hʊk tam
morning I was   went   going   some   land   appointed   that over

hoɟĭnyĭk woak sʿaptahatam kâi.   Kota masĭ kont worsanyĭk
evening   overthrow right feeling sleep.   That morning I was   went

himûk ap aĭ Â-âp tɔuwʊtaka hʊk nâtakĭk katc siʊkafwkatcʿ
going there reach Apache land   that madness lay   difficult

ka·atc.   Hâkĭʿ sikâlkʿ katc ʊmaĭrstcʿ katc, os rsâpalk katc
there.   Hide   round   lay   covered   lay, stick short   lay

siʊmaĭrstc katc.   Âva-am a-aĭ nyʊ iaɟ. Konya hap ĭntatam.
very covered lay.   And there sway me rolling. I was with feelings.

Ahʊ-ʊ, ĭt âksᵃ hap a-aktcʿ hap kaitcʿ hʊk nyʊ âkĭtak panya ĭntatam.
Yes,   this is what was meant as said that me mother I was feelings.

Kota masĭ kont himûk ap aĭ Â-âp tŏaka kok hʊk naʌamûtak
That morning I   went there reach Apache mountain it   that   drunkenness

katc siûkakavitc katc tcotc.   Kat molĭnyĭk va-apkʿ takrsûnyĭk
lay very resembling lay small mountain Bow broken   reed   strip
                       peaks stand.

katc siʊtcutânytc tcotc.   Kŏt hʊk wʊtcâ ap nyʊ tarsûvak
lay very strengthen standing.   It   that under there me sat

âʌa-am a-ai nyʊ iaɟ. Konya hap ĭnta'tam, ahʊ-ʊ, ĭt âks
and then swaying me rolling. I was with feelings, yes, this is

hap a-aktcʿ hap kai-ĭtc hʊk nyʊ âkĭtûk panyʊ ĭntatam. Kota masĭ
what was meant as said that me mother I was feelings.   That morning

kont worsanyĭk himûk ap aĭ Â-âp rsotakĭ. Âvawoɟ nyʊ mâ-â
I was   rose   going there reach Apache water.   It was me hair

hĭkĭvanyĭkʿtcʿ hʊkatcʿpʿ ʊmairstcʿ katc kʊs kʊk mamathoɟ ʌpâɟak
cut out roughly   that with   covers   lay kind of good water plants like

hʊk hokit ap katc hʊk nyʊ kârsova haĭnyĭk. Kŏnta hʊk ipûk
that beside to there lay that me skull   broken.   I was that   take

hʊkûtc kamikʊfĭtckʊʌa am vasipûk ap i.   Anya hastco
with it   knock down   there take there drink. I was something

anhotcʊm rsapʊpʊ. Kota masĭ kont worsanyĭk himûk ap aĭ
trying   to grasp.   That morning I was   rose   going there reach

―――

ᵃ Ĭt âks refers to something held in the hand or discovered to be true.

we reached a black water, where I smelled traces of the Apaches, who had washed off their paint in this water. I cried when I thought of the camp fires whose ashes now drifted to and fro on the winds. Around that spot my imagination revolved four times, like the wind twisting around an object. Wandering about I again remembered what my mother tried to tell me. This is what one feels in the land of the Apaches.

My friend Coyote went toward the east to spy upon the enemy. I relied upon him for information and assistance and put away my imaginary fears. He looked carefully about and returned to tell me that he had found the Apache fires. Then our party, with the courage of fierce predatory animals and raptorial birds, ran toward the enemy. Nothing could stop us and we swept them away with scarcely any resistance. We killed all and gathered up their property to return. My trail was down a steep declivity and I reached home, slackening speed only four times during the march.

Â-âp rsotaki.   Kawot nʊ woĭhĭâ tcokolĭtakᶜtcᶜ hʊkatcp ʊmairstc,
Apache water.   That was my face black paint   at once   covered,

wʊskâ sᶜmataĭmakĭ hʊk hokĭt ap katc hʊk nʊ kârsova haĭnyĭk.
all over ashes resemble that beside to there, lay that me skull   broken.

Kʊs kʊk kâʌaᴊk hao wʊpâᴊak kont hʊk am pʊk hʊkatckam
Kind of good hollow cup like I was that there take   with it

ikʊfwĭtckuʌa am vasĭpkᶜ ap i.   Âva saso-ofw(u).   Map kʊ-ʊk
it knock   there take there drink. And smell.   Close to standing

hʊk hâtaĭ ap wʊtcâ hʊk tcʊwuᴊ sva-avanyĭtc katc. Âvawoᴊ nʊ
that stone there under that earth wet lay.   It was me

â-âktc hap tcoi-ĭk, an ʌʊkatc hʊk nʊ huwʊlĭk ki-ĭkhâ siûĭtâp
tears as   it is there around that me wind four times twisting

konya hʊk parsâ aptcĭm nʊ hadrsap ka-am a-aĭ himĭn naᴊkĭt.
I was that front of there me stick to was swaying going to and fro.

Konya hap intatam; ahʊ-ʊ, ĭt âks hap akᶜtcᶜ hap kaĭtc hʊk nʊ âkĭtak
I was with feelings; yes, this is what was meant as said that me mother

panya ĭntatam. Kaĭm sialĭk takĭŏ kus kâmakĭtᶜ ʊwʊmakalt
I was feelings. Far away east direction kind of gray our friend

kʊtpkᶜ Â-âp sᶜkakĭkam kont ap imûk rsârsoa kotap sĭnyhâĭ-ikuĭ-itam
able Apache trailer I was there my cry   he was friendly

ʊtatûk ametcût wʊpûk tcivĭa. Ami ʊtcʊwʊlitkᶜ am tcʊ Â-âp
felt   from   first came.   There he raised himself there saw Apache

nanta worsanyĭk wʊkûtc pitcĭmitahimûk tcoĭkam nyʊnarsûnahimûk
fires rose   around around going   appearance me look carefully

opam tcivĭak nʊ akĭt. Tcʊwuᴊâ mʊtʊtam o-ofĭk ta-atam ʊwʊpâkĭk
turn around came me tell. Ground on running birds fly it like

hʊk nʊ viapâkʊ-ʊlakak nyʊnyĭk tam ap ʊiava ap piatco
that me sons   jump   on there alight on there nothing

tatûkitcotûkᶜ ap sûtapam puĭ. Wʊkʊtc katcĭm nanûkatcoitcikatc
easily capture there sweep clean catch. Around home   occupations

si-ĭnasĭk sûpapakĭ kawolkatkᶜ pʊk opam ha-ahâk inyûoa. Kotak
all gathered slowly packed grasp turn around me around. With that

nʊ vâkĭta skoĭvâtam utcʊ kont hʊk âitûk ki-ĭk aprsorsûk
me trail   steep false appearance I was that followed four incantations

ap nʊ tcʊwutĭka tam oapa. Hʊkûtc am simaĭsk tcʊ hʊk
there me country on brought. With it there entirely left that
                                                           covered

The news of victory which I brought caused my people to rejoice
with singing and dancing.   There was a magician's house, enveloped
in white winds and white clouds, into which we went to perform our
ceremonies.   The captives excited the children, who ran about bewil-
dered.

You may think this over, my relatives.   The taking of life brings
serious thoughts of the waste; the celebration of victory may become
unpleasantly riotous.

---

nyʊ tcʊwʊtĭka.   Âvawoɹ   makai   ki,   stâta   huwʊlĭkûtc   si-ĭpistc
me   country.   It was that magician house, white   wind with entirely around

tâta   tcʊvak katc si-ĭmaĭtconĭtc kʊ-ʊk.   Kŏnt hʊk ʊta am va-akiᶜ
to put clouds lay entirely envelope stand.   I was   that   in there get into

Â-âp alĭ nyʊ pʊi,   kot hʊk ʊta am   rsârsoa.   Kŏt hʊk â-âkûtc
Apache young me captive, it   that in   there   cry.   It   that   tears

stcʊhʊtûkĭm sûka-akâl hihimûk skʊ-ʊk nyʊ viapâpʊ-ʊlĭka ap kuĭ,
       blue   curves   going   good   me   sons   there drop,

skʊ-ʊk nyʊ tcʊĭhĭyaka ap kui.   Sᶜha-ap hapûk hʊmrsâ ʊlĭtkᶜ
 good   me   daughters   there drop.   That way   you   you will   think

tatcoa, na-ankâ tcoĭkam nyʊ imikiᶜ kotc hʊmo hap paɹûma tâ-atan
 want   various   things   me   relatives   we   now   that   lazy   make

hʊk pat rsâĭka natc apohâp takaĭhâkim kaĭtc.
that despised slave   we   right think   disturbance   said.

Yes, my poor brothers-in-law; this land was covered with herbage.
The mountains were covered with clouds. The sunlight was not bright
and the darkness was not dense. All was rolling before our eyes. It
was thought that the time had come for considering these things in
council, my brothers. Then wood was gathered and a fire kindled,
the flames of which burst forth, reaching to the sky and causing a
portion of the earth to fold over, disclosing the under side, where a
reddish mountain stood. After these things had happened the enterprise was decided upon.

Then my breast was tightened and my loins girded; my hunger was
appeased; sandals with strings were made for my feet; my canteen

Ahu-u,	rsâĭk	tahatam	nyu	kikiû.	Kâva	humo	ĭt	Aakta	katcĭm
Yes,	sad	feelings	me	brothers-in-law.	It was	how	this thing	spread laying on the ground	to sit upon

ha-akĭa	a-anûkatc	umaĭrstcaĭp	tcom	katc.	Tam	tâta-ak	tcotcoatc
many	feathers	with he covered	it	lay.	On	mountain	his standing

ha-akia	suvikitak	tca-ip	tcom	tcotc.	Tam	tataf	tcom	ihivathĭk
many	lets down	with	it	stands.	On	sun	it	came but

pitânûlĭktc ihi.	Tam	tcohokomolĭtatc	tcom	i-ia	vathĭk	piukûtaktc i-ia.
ray not shone came.	On	darkness his	it	came but he rolling		no darkness came rolling.

Tâva	ĭt	hapa	utco	moĭ	manûkâ	tcoĭkan	nyi-ĭmĭl(ĭ).	Âvaoɟ	hutcul	nyâ-â
It was	this	was happened	many	different		class	my relatives.	It was	alone	me

vakomakĭtak	kŏnta	inasĭk	am	siâ-âm	nai-ĭ.	Kota	am	u-uɟa	sitoahimûk
bones old	I was	gathered	there	right	kindle fire.	It was	there	within	rumbling.

am	sisiAâɟ	muk	tamatcĭm	supapak(ĭ)	maxanûk	skoiAâɟam	i-inairs.[b]
there	flames	burning	sky	slowly	open	hollow	fold.

Tuwoĭ	katcĭm	tcuwuɟ	maskâ	oɟ(t)	tuwoĭ	tcotcĭm	tâta-ak	wupkiomĭtk
Opposite	laying	land	to cause to bring to view	hold	opposite	standing	mountain	make red

tcotcoa	ĭtak	haptcoĭkam	tcom	nyuĭ.	Kotava	ĭt	hapa	utco	moĭ	nanûkâ
stands	I	that class	then	saw.	It was	this	was	hap-pened	many	kind

tcoĭkam	nyimĭk(ĭ).	Âvaoɟ	hutcuɟ	nyânâ-âm	kontak	ap	isitcutk	ap
sort	my relatives.	It was	alone	my ribs	I was	there	very saw	there

ipûtat.	Âvaoɟ	hutcuɟ	nyhihi	kŏnta	ivanyonûk	hukatc	sĭs	iâm	hoɟa
make heart.	It was	alone	my bowels	I was	stretch	with	very proper	across

nywo.	Kaoɟ	hutcuɟ	nyhahap	kŏnta	hastco	sku-uk	hok(ĭ)	ak	pa-ak
tied.	It was	alone	my intestines	I was	what	good food	intend	swallowed

---

[a] This speech is believed to be based upon an adventure in which a Pima gambled with the
Apaches and lost all his property. Overcome by the passion for gambling, he wagered the life of
his brother and lost. The striking figures of speech indicate the speaker's greed.

[b] Here *s* = a mere hissing.

was made ready. I went about the country, from mountain to village, beneath the sheds and trees, offering all an opportunity to join me. Returning home I thought I saw my brother when I was in a trance. I tried to grasp him and my arms embraced nothing but myself. I somehow caught in my palm what I thought to be his power; turning this over I found it to be but a creation of my imagination, and again I was disappointed. I was unkempt and rough, and my tears moistened the land.

The plan occurred to me to ask Nasia, the old woman magician, for aid. Thinking that I saw her I ran toward the eastward and finally reached her. I said "Yes, you who make the bow of the Apache like a kiâhâ and crush his arrowheads, you who paint triangles and curves on the kiâhâ bottoms with the arrow foreshafts of the Apache dipped

---

ĭp skâvât.　Âvaoɟ hʊtcʊ⎰ nymâ-âtkᶜ ʊlʊtak kŏntak nymâ-â hopûtak
then full.　It was　alone　my head　skin　I was　my hair　loose

ap isĭ kai kia-ataɟk siâm isitcʊka.　Âvaoɟ hʊtcʊ⎰ nykârsʊva kŏnt
there very make sandal string right　put up.　It was　alone　my skull　I was

hʊtcʊ⎰ nyʊ-ût ap vaĭkĭtkᶜ i ĭk sʊnavaman nyiâk.　Iworsanyĭk
alone　me blood there　put in　drink　intoxicated　talk.　Arose

tcʊtcʊwʊɟ tcotcovĭtkᶜ âĭtkᶜ ikʊxiamhĭ mamtaip iawĭs kŏntʊk âĭtk
lands　hills　after　slowly go　ashes　thrown　I was　after

ikʊxiamhĭ.　O-oȿ ʊ-ʊktak ʊta ikʊxiamhĭmûk tcom nyʊ matciamahimûkᶜ
slowly go.　Trees　shadows　in　slowly go　then　my　considering

pinakâ.　Tcʊwʊɟ sʊtapkᶜ tam kopa⎰ hʊtcʊ⎰woa, kota ĭt kʊ himûtam
unsuccessful.　Land　smooth　on face down　slide　it was　this　kind of

tʊtamai tcʊkak amtcʊt koewoa ihʊtcʊ⎰woak nyparsâ kʊ kiowoa.
going our above came　there　from　down slide　my breast　stand.

Kŏnta an tcom kâmûk antaprs ʊtcʊ⎰ nykâm.　Hasĭtcok pʊk nymatkᶜ
I was about try embrace　I was　alone me embrace.　Somehow take my palm

ʊta woak a-ai wopak tcom tcʊtcʊkak âva hapta nyʊĭt hâkĭm tcoĭ-ĭk
in throw all throw then　examine　it was sight of disagreeable sort

kʊs kʊ-ʊkʊny rsâiktak.　Woĭhya stcoktak mâ-â sikĭvânyk.　Ahʊ-ʊ,
kind of good　sorrow.　Face　dirty　head　rough.　Yes,

kônyûks anytcôm sirsâĭktak taktcĭtkᶜ nyʊlĭt.　Piam haĭ-ĭtco iâ-âksûn
guess me then　much misery　embrace　thought.　But　here　something

tampᶜ ʊolĭntcᶜ kʊs kʊ-ʊk rsâiktaktc amtcʊt â-âkatc kokoiʌa sisĭʌaɟ
are on　being held kind of good　misery　from　tears　down　trembled

ihohotktc wʊtcâ tcʊwʊɟ va-akanûk tcʊ.　Kâva ĭt hapot tcoĭ-ĭkam
descending under　land　damp　place.　It was this thing　class

mʊntatcoĭ kônta ipʊx mʊk sisiaatkᶜ parsâ woa kʊ Nasia âks makai.
my plan　it was took　far　east　front of throw kind of Nasia old woman magician.

Kŏntak hap tcoĭ-ĭkan mamtcʊk hʊk woĭ stcʊkam taĭ-ĭwonyk ap
I was that class　guessing　that toward dark　sat　there

sʊpapak(ĭ) tcʊmâ-â.　Anya hap kaiitam wʊmatc nyiâk.　Ahʊ-ʊ,
slowly　covers.　I was　that　loud　with　talk.　Yes,

kopava apĭm olĭntc.　Â-âp kat sᶜiâm vapûkaɟ wʊpâkĭt.　Â-âp
you　there　hold.　Apache bow right reed　artificial likeness.　Apache

o-o kop kaikʊirsontc sᶜiâm isiâmmakĭɟat.　Â-âp vât kopʊk.　A-âp
arrow you　crushed　right　put back on.　Apache his at take.　Apache

ʊ-ʊt katc sᶜahamasma mo-omovĭtc â-âhântc hʊkatc hʊk ʊkiâhâ
blood with　beautiful　triangles　painting　with　that　his kiâhâ

sĭsʊvinam kʊo(f)ʊrsp.　Â-âp ʊ-ʊtkatc sᶜahamasma ka-akâ⎰ iâ-âhânû(k)
very hard　more weight.　Apache blood with　well look　curved　painted

in his blood, you who twist the hair of the Apache and tie your kiâhâ with it." Thus I addressed her and she gave me a bundle of power which I grasped under my arm and ran with it to my home.

I thought of Vikârskam and prayed for his aid. When I finally reached him I said, "Yes, your house is built of Apache bows and bound with their arrows; you use his bowstrings and sinew to tie these withes. You use Apache headdresses and moccasins to cover your house. Within it you have square piles of Apache hair. At the corners of the piles cigarettes give off wreaths of smoke, resembling white, black, glittering, purple and yellow blossoms." Thus I spake and he gave me power which I carried away beneath my arm.

I thought of South Doctor and finally prayed to him. I said to him, "Yes, you who can make the Apache bow as harmless as a rainbow, his arrows like the white tasseled grass, his arrow shafts like soft down,

---

ukiâhâ.	Â-âp	kop	kŏp	s'âkrsp	imulutcotc	hukatc	sîs	iâ-âmp	ipuphu.
his kiâhâ.	Apache hair	you	left	make run	with	very	right		tighten.

S'ha-ap	anya	ikaĭtam	wumatc	nyiâk	kota	hastco	sku-ukam	ak	sĭs
Way	I	noise	with	talk	it was	what	good	said	very

kavitcĭm	nyhukrsp(ĭ)	ĭtak	siskavitcĭm	hukrsk	am	tai-ĭwors.	Ap
narrow	me hugged	I that	very narrow	hugged	there go out	running.	There

kuĭrsk	tcux	iahapunytco.	Âva	ĭt	tam	kus	tcohokom	sikâlktc	katc.
stepped	bound	here approach.	It was this	on	kind of	darkness		round	lay.

Âva	uta	s'iâ-âmp	uolĭntc	ku	vidârskam	makai.	Kŏntak	hap
It was	in	right	being held	kind of	down nest	magician.	I was	that

tcoĭ-ĭkam	supapaki	tcumâ-â.	Anya	hap	kai-itam	wumatc	nyiâk.
class	slowly	correct.	I	that	loud a	with	talk.

Ahu-u,	kopava	apĭm	olĭntc.	Â-âp	kat	s'iâ-âm	sikikiâ.	Â-âp	o-o	katc
Yes,	you	there	hold.	Apache bow	right	bend too much.		Apache arrow		lay

kaisipirsp.	Â-âp	kia-aɹak	Â-âp	tatakatc	sîs	vinam	woɹ.	Â-âp
across bind.	Apache	bowstring	Apache	sinew	his	tighten	knot.	Apache

vanam	Â-âp	taɹârsakatc	simai-ĭtcontc	kux.	Huk	uɹak	Â-âp	kops
headdress	Apache	sandals	with cover	stand.	That	in	Apache	hair

tcotcopolĭmp	ia-aks.	Tcotcpolĭɹ	ap	tcotc	â-âvaptck(ĭ)	tatantc	hutcuɹ
squarely	piles.	Made corners	there	stands	cigarettes	knees	alone

kodrsantc	ku	nanûkâ	masma	uhiasĭtahĭm.	Stâtam	uhiasĭtahĭm
smoking	kind of	different	colors	blossoms.	White	blossoms

stcotckom	uhiâsĭtahĭm	sunanafkĭm	uhiâsĭtahĭm	supitumukĭm
black	blossoms	glittering	blossoms	dirty

uhiâsĭtahĭm	s'oa-ama	uhiâsĭtahĭm.	S'ha-ap	anyaĭ	kaiitam	wumatc
blossoms	yellow	blossoms.	Way	I	noise	with

nyiâk.	Kŏta	hastco	sku-ukam	ak	sĭskavĭtcĭm	nyhukrsp(ĭ)	kŏntûk
talk.	It was	what	good	tell	very narrow	me hugged	I was

sĭskavĭtcĭm	hukrsk'	am	tai-ĭwonyûk	kaiĭrsp	ĭnataki.	In	ku	Vakolo
very narrow	hugged	there go out	running	straddle	came.	In	kind of	South

Makai	kŏntak	hap	tcoĭ-ĭkam	supakak(ĭ)	tcumâ-âk	anya	hap	kai-itam
Doctor	I was	that	class	slowly	covered	I	that	loud

wumatc	nyiâk.	Ahu-u,	kopaʌa	apĭm	olĭny.	Â-âp	kat	kopa	kus
with	talk.	Yes,	you	there	hold.	Apache bow		you kind of

ku-uk	kiâhâɹ	wupâkĭt.	Â-âp	o-o	kopa	kus	stâta	moɹatkam	wupâkĭt.
good	rainbow	liken.	Apache arrow	you	kind of	white	tassel	liken.

Â-âp	vât	kopa	kus	ku-uk	vik(ĭ)	wupâkĭt.	Â-âp	ors	kopaprs	pĭt
Apache arrow-shaft	you	kind of	good	down	liken.		Apache arrow-head	you make	mud

---

a In this manner or in this wise, what was said or how the voice is modulated.

his arrowheads like thin dry mud, his arrow poison like water fern
upon the pools, his hair like rain clouds."

Thus I spake, and he gave me power which I grasped under my arm
and journeyed westward with four slackenings of speed. The home
magician gave me a seat of honor. The cigarette smoked, and I took
it and, drawing in a cloud of smoke, I prayed to Old Woman Magician,
saying, "Yes, you make the Apache bow like a game ring; you crush
his arrow shafts and make headbands of them; you split his arrow
foreshafts, color them with Apache blood and make game sticks of
them; his arrowheads you make like pottery paddles; you make a
girdle of Apache hair." Thus I spake and he gave me his power,
which I caught under my arm and ran home, with four slackenings of
speed. The home magician gave me a seat of honor. The cigarette
smoked, and I took it and, drawing in a cloud of smoke, breathed it
forth in the direction of the enemy. The power grew and shone on

kâmaɪk wʊpâkĭt.   Â-âp hinatc kopaprs kʊs kʊ-ʊk mamathâɪ wʊpâkĭt.
thin   liken.   Apache arrow you make kind of good water plant liken.
                      poison

A-âp kop kopa siâ-âm vi-ĭtcwoɪ wʊpâkĭt.   Sʻha-ap anyaĭ kai-itam
Apache hair you right   (?)   liken.   Way   ĭ   loud

wʊmatc nyiâk kota hastco skʊ-ʊkam ak siskavĭtcĭm nyhʊkrsp(ĭ)
with   talk it was what   good   told very narrow   me hugged

kŏntak sĭskavĭtcĭm hukrsk am taĭwonyûk am hotĭnyĭk woĭ ki-ĭkap
I was   narrow   hugged there go out run- there west toward four
                                     ning

rsârs kʊ Aks Makai supapak(ĭ) tcʊmâ-âk anya hap kai-itam wʊmatc
renew- kind Old Magician slowly   covered ĭ   that loud   with
als   of Woman

nyiâk. Ahʊ-ʊ, kopova apĭm olĭny. Â-âp kat sʻiâ-âm haxoatc s iâ-âm
talk.   Yes,   you there hold. Apache bow right make a ring right
mʊlĭtcĭtakŭtʻ wʊpâkĭt. Â-âp o-o kop ki-ĭrsonytc ʊkoawʊtcâ sikikoat.
runner   liken.   Apache arrow you crush   his forehead very circle.
                                                    below

Â-âp vât kop taprsatc Â-âp ʊ-ʊtkatc paprsâ iwʊpʊkântc sʻiâ-âm
Apache arrow you split Apache ʊ-blood with in front of redden right
foreshaft

kâ-âmhairsakot wʊpâkĭt. Â-âp ors kopa kʊs kʊ-ʊk ha-atakŏt
a game   like.   Apache arrow you head kind of good instrument used
                                                          for pottery paddle

wʊpâkĭt. Â-âp kop kopa sʻiâ-âm isikisa-a. Sʻha-ap nyaĭ kai-iam
liken.   Apache hair you right   bark girdle.   Way   ĭ   loud

wʊmatc nyiâk. Kaoɪ ʊwʊ-ʊwʊe kokokam kŏta pinyhoʌĭtct
with   talk. It was facing   points it was not me prevent

sĭskavĭtcĭm nyhʊkrsp(ĭ) kŏntak sĭskavĭtcĭm hʊkrsk am tai-ĭwonyuk
very narrow me hugged   I was very narrow hugged there go out running

am wʊtcom ki-ĭk ap rsârsk makai nata tcʊmûk hokĭt an takûtâ.
there to   four there renewals magician fire covered edges there release.

Smakaitkam â-âtam sivaksitkʻ tam tarsʊwoa. Avaoɪ makai oatckʻ
Expert Magician people place prepared on sitting. It was magician cigarette
                   with something
                   spread to sit on

tântc hʊtcʊɪ koɪrsanyĭtc kʊk. Kŏntak ap sihâʌâk am nyâpûtak
knee alone   smoking   stand. I was there inhale there my enemy
woĭ siʌostanûk taihiwoa. Kŏta am kʊs tâtam ʊtcotcoahĭmûk ap
toward puffed   sat.   It was there kind of white   erected there

and on until it slowly disclosed the enemy. The Pima magician
desired that the earth move, the trees take on their leaves, the land
be softened and improved, that all be straightened and made correct.
The place was one where food was increased and they were gathered
about it. Their springs were made larger and they were gathered
about them. Their game was gathered together. Some of the enemy
were in the west and they said, "We know that harm may come to
us if we go to that place, but we will not heed our own misgivings."
They started on their journey and camped on the way. In the morning they arose and continued, reaching their friends' camp during the
day, where they saluted them. In the distant east were other enemies
who heard that their friends were gathering. When they heard of it
they said, "We know that harm may come of it if we go to that place,

---

sʋpapak(ĭ) tcʋmâ-âk nyuâpûta. Tcʋwuɹ hokĭt ap sikaɹ ihi os ap
slowly   covered   me enemy.   Land   edge there around came tree there

kʋ-ʋkam shahaktcotkᶜ wʋtcâ tcʋwuɹ mâikatkᶜ sᵃptahatcotkᶜ
stand   select a tree with under land   softened satisfied
        many leaves

rsʋlʋtcotkᶜ woĭtcotkᶜ ivantckʋwoak hʋk tam ap taktâ.   Âvak
straight   toward   jerked   that on there release. It was

hastco kai-ikam matcŏm sĭstaɹanyĭm katc ʋ-ʋlĭt kŏnt hʋk tanɹ ap
what plants with seed considered very wide lay thought I was on there

sihʋmap ioɹ. Rsârsânûkam rsorsokia tcum sĭstatanyĭm wʋtckᶜ ʋ-ʋlĭt
together hold. Springs   waters   then very wide   lay   he thought

kŏnt hʋk tam ap sihʋmap ioɹ. Hastco âimʋtʋtam matcŏm
I was that on there together hold. What   walking considered

sĭstatanyĭm âimʋlĭk ʋ-ʋlit kŏnt hʋk tam ap sihʋmap ioɹ. Kŏta am
very wide   haunts thought I was that on there together hold. It was there

tcŏm ka hotĭnyĭk takĭŏ takam kʋs mas sʋnyâpûta. ꟼmokikatc ot
then here west toward sitting kind of kindly appearance His dead he
                                                           me enemy.

pĭk ʋ-ʋlĭttamtc am tcŏm kaiâk pi-ĭnakâk worsanyk himûk hʋpai
like he thought there then heard impossible arose   go   somewhere

tcʋwuɹ matcolĭtkᶜ tam kʋrsk kâĭ. Imasĭ kot worsanûĭk himûk tataf
land considered on fall sleep. Next he arose   go   sun
       carefully   morning

hʋpai tcok tciviak skai-ĭtamp ʋimû. Âva kamʋk sialiĭtk ap uolĭntc
somewhere there arrive very loud   (?).   It was distant east there being
                                                                   held

kʋs mas sʋnyâpûta. ꟼmokikatc ot pĭk ʋ-ʋlĭttamtc am tcŏm kaiâk
kind friendly appearance His dead he like it he thought there then heard
of   me enemy.

pi-ĭnakâk worsanyĭk himûk hʋpai tcʋwuɹ matcolĭtkᶜ tam kursk kâi.
impossible arose   go   somewhere land considered on fall sleep.
                                          carefully

Imasĭ kŏt worsanyĭk himûk tataf hʋpai tcok tciviak skai-ĭtamp ʋimû.
Next he arose   went sun some- where came very loud   (?).
morning   where

Âvaoɹ kʋ tâhâkiho koĭ-ĭrsâm kʋtars sisi(f)takatc no-omovĭtc pʋm
It was kind of cochineal dye kind of sun headdress triangles he
                               rays

â-âĭ kak sivantckʋwomtc hʋkatc sisiâmp ʋtcʋtcʋhitc katc. Kota
figured that jerked   with   right   it covered   lay. It was

ʋta hʋx isikuĭrsk kʋxiwoak nyʋ viapa kʋ-ʋlʋka. Tcʋwuɹû
in already firmly stepped stand me boy reared.   Land

mʋtʋtam, o-ofĭk ta-atam ʋwʋpâkĭtkᶜ nyʋnyĭk tam ap ʋiwoak ap
running birds flying liken   fly   on there alighted there

but we must go." They started on their journey and camped once
before arriving and saluting their friends. They took sun's rays and
painted triangles on their blankets.

While this was happening among them my young men were preparing to fight. They rushed upon them like flying birds and swept them
from the earth. Starting out upon my trail I reached the first water,
whence I sent my swiftest young men to carry the message of victory
to the old people at home. Before the Magician's door the earth was
swept, and there my young men and women danced with headdresses
and flowers on their heads. The wind arose and, cutting off these
ornaments, carried them to the sky and hung them there. The rain
fell upon the high places, the clouds enveloped the mountains, the
torrents descended upon the springs and fell upon the trees.

You may think this over, my relatives. The taking of life brings
serious thoughts of the waste; the celebration of victory may become
unpleasantly riotous.

---

pia-atco tatkitcotk⁦ ⁩ ap sʊtapam pʊĭ. Tait nyʊ vâkĭta skoeʌâ̧am
nothing   wrestle   there smooth take. That this me trail hollowed

ʊtcʊ kŏntûk âĭtk⁦ ⁩ am ki-ĭkap rsârs. Hokĭtkâ rsotakĭ tam si
laid I was after there four renewals. Edge water on very

hʊmapt ol(d). Amtcʊt mamtcʊk am tcotcoaa kʊs stco-otcoaatcmakam
one make. There from guess there stand kind of swiftest

nyʊ vipiâpka. Kŏta ki-ĭkap rsârsk mʊlifkai-ĭ kai-ĭtc kʊlivi-ĭkam
me boy. It was four times renewals came running notify old man remain

âks vi-ĭkam. Âva am makai kitcĭk amʊk tcʊwʊ̧ tcoĭ-ĭstc katc.
old woman remain. It was there magician door there land powdered lay.

Kotak tam mʊmʊtak tcitcivi kʊs kʊ-ʊk nyʊ viapâkʊ-ʊlka kʊs
It was on run play kind of good me boy reared kind of

kʊ-ʊk nyʊ tcʊhyaka wʊm mawârsk tam mʊmʊtak tcitcivi. Kʊs
good me daughter with clasping hands on run play. Kind of

kʊ-ʊk nyʊ viapâkʊ-ʊlka kʊs kʊ-ʊk paihiwoatc si̧tat kʊs kʊ-ʊk
good me boy reared kind of good tail touch kind of good

nyʊ tcʊnhyaka kʊs kʊ-ʊk tâ̧rsak(ĭ) ʊkoa wʊtca kikoatk⁦ ⁩ wʊm
me daughter kind of good foam her forehead under crown with

mawarsk tam mʊmʊtak tcitcivi. Kŏtak hʊwʊ̧katc am sivanyʊkumiak
clasp hands on run play. It was his wind there broken

tamatcĭm parsâ pia-atcokam an haha̧rs. Amtcʊt ko-okoewa si-ĭsiʌâ̧
spy near by nothing there sticks. There from down flames

ihohotk⁦ ⁩ kʊvipkam sisiatcotcokam tcʊtcʊwʊ̧ tco-otcovĭtk⁦ ⁩ tam am
descended surviving powerful magicians lands hills on there

kokokoa. Amtcʊt ko-okoewa si-ĭsiʌâ̧ ihohotk⁦ ⁩ kʊvipkam
touches. There from down flames descended surviving

sisiatcotcokam tâta-ak kokok ap rsarsai-ĭwa. Amtcʊt ko-okoewa
powerful magicians mountains peaks there hang. There from down

si-ĭsiʌât ihohotk⁦ ⁩ kʊvipkam sisiatcotcokam rsârsânûkam rsorsok(ĭ)
flames descended surviving powerful magicians springs waters

vʊfʊtcĭm tam kokokoa. Amtcʊt ko-okoewa si-ĭsiʌâ̧ ihohotk
laying on touched. There from down flames descended

kʊvipkam sisiatcotcokam o-os kokok ap rsarsai-ĭwa. S⁦ ⁩ha-ap hap
surviving powerful magician trees tops there hang. Way that

hʊmsâ ʊlĭtk⁦ ⁩ tatcoa nanûkâ tcoi-ĭkam inyi-ĭmĭk(ĭ) kotc hʊmo hap
you think plan different sorts my relatives we now that

pa̧ma tâta hʊk pa̧ rsâĭka natc apâhâpta kaihâkĭm kaĭtc.
lazy make that bad slave way right noise said.

We have come thus far, my brothers. We have already laid our plans. With magic power the trail is made easy, bordered with flowers, grass, and trees. The enemy saw the apparent bounty of nature and assembled, laughing, to gather the seeds and plants. It was the power of the distant magician which made the enemy enjoy his fancied prosperity. In the center of our council ground the fire burned and, lighting a cigarette, I puffed smoke toward the east. Slowly a vision arose before me, a white cane before a whitish house. I grasped the cane and thrust it into the corner of the house and there came forth a kind of white water. Afterward there came forth a kind of white dragon flies, which circled about four times before they sank. In the south stood a blue house with a blue cane before it. Thrusting

---

Iat täva tcʋtcka nanûkâ tcoĭ-ĭkam nyi-ĭmik(ĭ). Hʋk(ĭ) attavaĭ natâk
Here we came various classes my relatives. Already we finished

hai-ĭtcot aka. Hʋk(ĭ) isĭvakĭtkᶜ tcʋ. Konta ĭm sia-lĭk takĭŏ kʋs tâtam
something tell. Already planned trail placed. I was in east direction kind of shining

hiasĭtkᶜ am nyʋ ʌâkĭta hokĭt am takĭtâ. Kota am nyʋ ʌâkĭta âĭtk
artificial there my trail edge there dropped. I was there my trail after
flower

kʋ nanûkâ masma ʋhiasĭtahĭmûk ap katcĭm tcʋwʋɹʋ sʋpapaki tcʋmâ-â.
kind different appearance like a wave there laying land slowly cover.
of flowers came

Kot ap katcĭm tcʋwʋɹʋ kʋnanûkâ masma hiâ. Ap kʋkam os
That there laying land kind of various full-blown flowers. There standing tree
kinds

kʋnanankâ tcoi-ĭkam hiâ. Kota am tcʋm nyʋĭ kʋny âpûtak hastco
various classes full-blown flowers. I was there then see my enemy what

skʋ-ukam ʋɹ(d)ĭtkᶜ am ʋta tcorsal ihʋhʋmihâ.ᵃ Kaot mʋk mamakai
good thought there in slowly he laughed. It was far magicians

tadrsa pamûtaktcᶜ sᶜhʋ apai ʋtcoktcᶜ. Âva ĭm tcʋwʋɹ sᶜʋtafĭtcotcᶜ
placed unite correct result. It was in land mark center

kʋtânɹam hâtai tʋnata katc. Hʋk woĭ am kʋkʋk oatck(ĭ) tantc hʋtcʋɹ
kind of white stone our fire lay. That toward there standing cigarette knee itself

koɹrsantc kʋk kontak ap sihâvâk am sia-alĭk woĭ si-ĭphʋewoa. Kota
smokes stand I was there inhale there east toward exhale. I was

am kʋs tâtam ʋtcotcoahĭmûk sialĭk sʋpapak(ĭ) tcʋmâ-â. Âva apa kʋk
there kind of white stand east slowly cover. It was there stand

kʋtânɹâm va-akĭtcʋk parsa ap kʋx kʋtânɹam tciâĭkot. Kontak ipûk
whitish house before there stand whitish cane. I was grasp

hʋkatc ap itcoɹkᶜ ap sitcoa-akat. Kota ap nyʋiâpă kʋs tâta rsotak(ĭ).
with there made there stick. I was there came out kind of white water.
corner

Hʋk âĭtkᶜ ap nyʋĭapa kʋs tâta vaktcʋtcʋɹhâpĭ. Am ki-ĭkhâ si-ĭskat
That after there came out kind of white dragon flies. There four times around

hihimûk am koavĭt tcotcp(ĭ). Ĭm katcĭm takĭŏ kʋs tatk(ĭ) va-akĭ kʋx
going there down sink. In laying direction kind of blue house stand

---

ᵃ A "half laugh; more than a smile and less than a hearty laugh."

the cane into a corner there came out a blue water and then blue
dragon flies, which flew about four times and then went back. In the
west stood a black house with a black cane before it. This I thrust
into a corner and there came forth a black water followed by black
dragon flies, which flew around four times and then sank down. In
the north stood a yellow house with a yellow cane before it, which I
took and thrust into the corner. There came forth yellow water followed by yellow dragon flies, which circled about four times and then
sank down.

On the mountain tops was a yellow spider magician, upon whom I
called for help. He went to the enemy, darkened their hearts, tied
their hands and their bows, and made them grow weak as women.
Then he pushed us on to destroy the enemy. We rushed upon the

---

tcuk parsâ ap kux kᴜs tatk(ĭ) tciâĭkot. Kontak ipᴜk hᴜkatc ap
in   front   stand kind of blue   cane.   I was   grasp   with there

itcolkᶜ ap sitcoa-akat. Kota ap nyᴜiâpa kᴜs tatk(ĭ) rsotakᶜ kᴜk âĭtkᶜ
made there stick.   I was there came out kind of blue water   that after
corner

ap nyᴜiâpa kᴜs tatk(ĭ) vaktcᴜtcᴜɹhâp(ĭ). Am ki-ĭkhâ si-ĭskâl hihimûk
there came out kind of blue   dragon flies.   There four times around   going

am koavĭt tcotcp(ĭ). Ĭm hoɹĭnyĭk takĭŏ kᴜs tcok va-akĭ kᴜk tcuk
there down sink.   In sunset direction kind of black house stands in

parsâ-âp kux kᴜs tcok tciâĭkot. Kontak ipᴜk hᴜkatc ap itcoɹkᶜ ap
front of there stands kind of black cane.   I was   grasp with there made there
                                                                        corner

sitcoa-akat. Kota ap nyᴜiâpa kᴜs tcotckᶜ rsotakᶜ kᴜk âĭtkᶜ ap nyᴜiâpă
stick.   I was there came out kind of black water that after there came out

kᴜs tcotckᶜ vaktcᴜtcᴜɹhâpĭ. Am ki-ĭkhâ si-ĭskâl hihimûk am koavĭt
kind of black   dragon flies.   There four times around   going   there down

tcotcp(ĭ). Ĭm nanûk(ĭ) âĭt takĭŏ kᴜs oam va-akĭ kux tcuk parsâ-âp
sink.   In north field direction kind of yellow house stands   front

kux kᴜs oam tciâĭkot. Kontak ipᴜk hᴜkatc ap itcoɹkᶜ ap sitcoa-akat.
stands kind of yellow cane.   I was grasp with   there made there stick.
                                                                 corner

Kota ap nyᴜiâpa kᴜs oa-am rsotakᶜ kᴜk âĭtkᶜ ap nyᴜiâpa kᴜs oa-am
I was there came out kind of yellow water   that after there came out kind of yellow

vaktcᴜtcᴜɹhâp(ĭ). Am ki-ĭkhâ si-ĭskâl hihimûk am koavĭt tcotck(ĭ).
dragon flies.   There four times around   going   there down   sink.

Âvak âtûk ap ᴜolĭntcᶜ kᴜs oam tâkûtât makai. Kontak hap tcoi-ĭkam
It was near there being held kind of yellow spider magician. I was   that   class of

mamûtcᴜk ap imûk rsârsoa tap sĭnyhâĭ-ikᴜĭ-itam ᴜtatkᶜ amtcᴜt ki-ĭkhâ
guess   there address cry he   friendly   felt   from four times

skawoɹ tahiwoak ap sᴜpapak(ĭ) tcᴜma-a kᴜny â-âpûta. Hux ipimaskâ
crouch set   there slowly   cover   my enemies. Already not visible

ipûtatc kakhai wopotkᶜ nânâvĭtc kakhai wopotkᶜ kat kiattatc kakhai
his   soul crossed tied his hands crossed tied bow string crossed

wopotkᶜ ataprs hastco pat ʌᴜpâtk ap woa. Hᴜk âĭtkᶜ inyoĭhai kont
tied   he made what bad like there throw. That after me push I was

hᴜk âĭtkᶜ ita-ak ap kᴜrsk ap pia-atco tatkitcotkᶜ ap sᴜtapam pᴜi.
that after jumped there fall there nothing wrestle there smooth take.

An wᴜkatc katcĭm nanûkâ tcoi-ĭtckatc si-inasĭk sᴜpapak kaʌoɹkatkᶜ
About around laying various belongings gathered slowly grouped

Apaches and killed them without difficulty. With gladness in my heart I gathered the evidences of my victory and turned toward home.

You may think this over, my relatives. The taking of life brings serious thoughts of the waste; the celebration of victory may become unpleasantly riotous.

---

puk opam ha-ahâkinyûwoak nytcuwuɹuka tam oa-apa.   Huk hukatc
take homeward   face turned   my land   on   brought.   That   with

am simai-ĭrsk tcuk nytcuwuɹuka. S῾ha-ap hap humsâ ulĭtk῾ tatcoa
there covered   placed   my land.   That way that   you   thought desired

kotc humo hap padma tâtanûk pat rsâika natc apahâpta kai-ihâkĭm
we   now   that   lazy   made bad slave way   right   noise

kai-itc.
said.

We have come thus far, my brothers. I prayed to the Ocean, to the distant Magicians, and to Down Roll[a] to grant me power. Sun extended his power to me as a descending trail along which the various villages gathered with greetings to each other. A gray headdress was placed upon me. A blue haze enveloped and concealed me as in a garment; in this I was borne along.

I called upon Yellow Raven, who came gladly to my aid. Four times he with crackling gashed the land. Drawing blood from the enemy he sprinkled it in drops upon the land.

On the mountain top was Yellow Spider Magician upon whom I

Iat	tava	tcʋtcka	nanûkâ	tcoi-ĭkam	nɥi-imĭk(ĭ).	Konya	vaprs
Here	we	came	various	classes	my relatives.	I was	there

matai-ĭtc	ʋta	kopaɩ	katc	mʋk	vavanɥĭm	imĭtc	rṣoak.	Mʋk	mamakai
ashes	in face down lay lying	far	extending	my	cry.			Far	magicians

tadrsa	pamûtak	imĭtc	rsoak.	Vik	Iaɩ(d)	Makai	imĭtc	rsoak.	Tâva
placed	unite	my	cry.	Down	Roll	Magician	my	cry.	It was

kʋ	vi-ĭtckŭt	itcʋrsatck͑	ʋʌâkĭta	skoeʌâɟam	itcʋ.	Kotʋk	âĭtk͑	am
kind of	deer	ascend	his trail	down	placed.	He then	after	there

ʋiatcʋk	tcʋwʋɟâ	mʋtʋtamûk	skai-itamp	ʋim.[b]	Paĭtcp͑	ʋiatcʋk	o-ofĭk
grouped	land	running	loud	naming.	Further	grouped	birds

ta-atamûk͑	skai-itamp	ʋĭm.	Am	paĭtcp	ʋiatcʋk	tcʋwʋɟâ	mʋtʋtamûk
flying	loud	naming.	There	further	grouped	land	running

skai-itamp	ʋim.	Paĭtcp͑	ʋiatcʋk	o-ofĭk	ta-atamûk͑	skai-ĭtamp	ʋĭm.
loud	naming.	Further	grouped	birds	flying	loud	naming.

Vatai-ip	uptcʋrsatck͑	kʋs	kâmak(ĭ)	usiʌʋta	ihodonyĭtk	hʋkatc
They were	rising	kind of	gray	head dress	bring down	with

sikopaɩ	pʋnɥ	atc.	Vatai-ip	uptcʋrsatck͑	kʋs	tcʋtak(ĭ)	ʋkâmhaiʌakĭta
face down myself throw	put around neck.	They were	rising	kind of	blue	hazy	

ihodonyĭtk	ʋta	pimaskâ	myolĭnûk	ĭnɥû	pʋpʋhĭ.	Âva	ĭt	tam	kʋs
bring down	in	invisible	me held	me	carry.	It was this	top kind of		

oam	haʌanta	kontak	hap	tcoĭ-ĭkam	mamûtcʋk	ap	imûk	rsârsoa	kotap
yellow raven	magic	I was	that	sort of	guess	there	naming	cry	it was

sĭnɥhâĭ-ikuĭ-itam	ʋtatk͑	ki-ĭkhâ	am	ʋta	sikâkâfk	ihodonykʋk
he me friendly	felt	four times	there	in	crackling	bring down

tcʋwʋɟ	an	katcĭm	kakhai	sikʋofdrs.	Hʋmatckam	ap	âĭmʋtʋtam
land	about	laying	crossed	gashed.	People	there	moving

hʋk	ipimaskâ	ʋ-ʋɟ	itcʋrsutctk͑	hâhâtai	tatʋɟam	s͑ahamasûma
that	invisible	blood	bring up	stones	setting	fine appearance

isipanymat.	Hʋk	âtûk͑	ap	ʋolintc	kʋs	oam	tâkûtât	makai.	Kontak
fall in drops.	That	side of there	he stays	kind of		Yellow	Spider	Magician.	I was

[a] Living in the ruin at Tempe.

[b] Imĭtc, past tense; ʋim, present. Both convey the meaning of addressing by naming speaker's relationship and person addressed.

called for help. He went to the enemy, darkened their hearts, tied their hands and their bows, made them grow weak as women. Then he pushed us on to destroy the enemy. We rushed upon the Apaches and killed them without difficulty. With gladness in my heart I gathered the evidences of my victory and turned toward home. There I left my firebrands, and I left my knife that the enemy should know that destruction was impending. The sharp stone was left there with which to cut his hair. The land thundered, the darkness trembled, the mountain roared, the trees waved; it was difficult for me to remain under such conditions. One of the enemy came running to that place. He slept a part of the night; but at length fled in terror with a light to seek a hiding place in the rocks.

In the evening Blue Bird sang, because he was glad. Shaking his feathers he transformed the land into a habitable world again, as smooth as the moss under the bushes. In the evening Yellow Bird in the gladness of his heart sang, shaking his yellow feathers.[a] Mountain

---

hap	tcoĭ-ĭkam	mamûcuk	ap	imûk	rsârsoa	tap	sĭnyhâĭ-ikuĭ-itam
that	sort of	guess	there	naming	cry	he	me friendly

utatkᶜ	amtcut	ki-ĭkhâ	skaʌoɪ	tahiwoak	ap	supapak(ĭ)	tcumâ-â	kuny
felt	from	four times	crouch	set	there	slowly	arrive	my

â-apûta.	Hul	ipimaskâ	iputatc	kakhai	wopotkᶜ	nânâvĭtc	kakhai
enemy.	Already	invisible	soul	crossed	tied	hands his	crossed

wopotk	kat	kiatûtatc	kakhai	wopotkᶜ	ataprs	hastco	pat	ʌupâtk	ap
tied	bow	string	crossed	tied	he made	what	had	like	there

woa.	Huk	âĭtkᶜ	inyoĭhai	kont	huk	âĭtkᶜ	ita-ak	ap	kursk	ap
throw.	That	after	me push	I was	that	after	fly	there	fall	there

pia-atco	tatkitcotk	ap	sutapam	puĭ.	An	wukatc	katcĭm	nanûkâ
nothing	wrestle	there	clean	catch.	About	around	laying	different

tcoi-ĭtckatc	si-ĭnasĭk	supapak	kaʌoɪkatkᶜ	puk	opam	ha-ahâk	ĭnyuwoa.
occupations	gathered	slowly	grouped	catch	turn	face	me home.

Huk	tam	ap	takutâx	nyu	kotck(ĭ)	vi-ĭtak,	tafkoan	smo-okŭk	tam
That	top	there	release	my	brand	remaining,	flint	sharp	on

ap	takûtâk	hukatcûk	ukikiat	hoɪaʌâkihâk	ak	hap	tco.	Hukatcûk
there	release	with	abandoned	disturb	told	that	made.	With

ukop	hixiʌânhâk	ak	hap	tcok	huk	tam	ap	takûtâ.	Kotak	hukatcûk
hair	cut roughly	told	that	made	that	on	there	release.	It was	with it

tcuwuɪ	am	uta	sipuputkᶜ	utcu.	Stcohokmom	am	uta	sikikifk
land	there	in	roar	lay.	Darkness	there	in	tremble

utcu.	Tâta-ak	tcotcĭm	am	uta	sirsarsafk	utcotcoa	o-os	tcotcĭm
lay.	Mountains	stand	there	in	echoed	stands	trees	standing

am	uta	simokuofk	utcotcoa-akuk	tam	pita	hodontam	utco.	Kota
there	in	waved	somebody placed in a standing position	on	not	camping place	make.	It was

humakâ	vi-ĭkam	nyuâpûta	hupaitcut	mutatc	huk	tam	kursk	tcum
one	remaining	me enemy	wherefrom	running	that	on	fall	then

kârsk	hu-us	tcohok	uta	pi-inakak	kotkᶜ	hastcoi-ĭkam	kaʌaɪkᶜ	ap
sleep	night part of	night	in	can not stand	fire	what sort of	hollow	there

itcum	vakiamhĭ.	Kota	hodonûk	huʌatcot	makai	s'hux	utatkᶜ	kox.
he	enter.	It was	evening	Blue Bird	Magician	glad	filled	sing.

Kus	tcuhutak(ĭ)	uwâpâ	ikik(ĭ).	Kotak	hukatcûk	tcûwuɪ	s'ahamasma
Kind of	blue	his feathers	shake.	It was	with it	land	fine appearance

---

[a] The yellow flowers that color the mountains.

tucked these feathers under his belt to improve his appearance. In the evening glad Mocking Bird[a] sang and shook his white feathers which made white the earth.[b]

You may think this over, my relatives. The taking of life brings serious thoughts of the waste; the celebration of victory may become unpleasantly riotous.

---

mamathâtk⁣ʿ utcu.   Kota hodonûk vatcokok makai sʿhux utatkʿ kox
water plants   lay.   It was evening Yellowish Magician glad felt sing

kus oa-am uwapâ ikiki.   Kotak huxatcûk tâta-ak tcotcĭm sʿahamasma
kind of yellow his feathers shake.   It was with it mountain stand fine appearance

sʿoa-am hihifurspatakûtc tcotc.   Kota hodonûk rsok makai sʿhux
yellow   tuck under   stand.   It was evening Mocking Bird Magician glad

utatkʿ kox kus tata uwâpâ ikiki.   Kotak huxatcûk tcuwuɳ wuskâ
felt sing kind of white his feathers shake.   It was with it land all over

tânâtkʿ utcu.   Sʿha-ap hap humsâ ulĭtkʿ tatcoa kotc humo hap paɳma
white   lay.   Way that you thought desire way now that lazy

tâtanûk pat rsâika natc apahâpta kaihâkĭm kai-ĭtc.
made bad slave way proper noise set.

---

a People.   b With sunshine.

We have come thus far, my brothers. I went from village to village, telling you to be ready. You came to our village and ate our humble fare and drank from our ollas. As the blue shadows of evening began to fall we gathered in a circle and neglected our usual duties. The next day at nightfall we again gathered and repeated the ceremonies of the first evening.

To-night our medicine-man shall render the darkness yellow and gray, so that we may become invisible to our enemies. He examines his equipment, his shield and club, his sandal strings and the netting of his gourd canteen are tightened, his headdress is moistened and shaped, his black paint is renewed that he may be properly painted

---

Iat͏ͨ	tava	tcʊtcka	nanûkâ	tcoï-ĭkam	nyimĭkĭ.	S͏ͨha-ap	ant,	hʊms,
Here	place	we	various	classes	relatives.	That	I,	yes,

itâta,	os	nyʊ	molʊna	wʊsk	ap	iwoetahĭ	ka-am	smatc͏ͨ	âit	himûk	am
do	tree	me	broken	all	there	distribute	there	know	after	going	there

ʊtcʊmâ-âk	himûk	am	ʊtcʊmâ-â.	Kota	hʊpaitcʊt	muɹʊtam	nyimĭkĭ
arrive	going	there	arrive.	It was	where from	running	relatives

atavaĭ	tcivĭa.	Âvaprskam	katc	hʊk	hastcony	pat	hohokĭ	katc
had	came.	He was	that	lay	what my	bad	food	lay

ʊkʊkosĭt.	Rsotakĭ	nyʊ	vasĭpĭtc	ĭp	ʊvavĭnyĭt.	Kota	imasĭ,	kota
he eats.	Water	me	take	with	he quenched.	It was	morning,	it was

itany	ipʊm	hʊtcʊlʊwa	kʊs	tcʊtakĭ	nyhoɹĭnyĭk	kʊs	tcʊtakĭ	nyhakoata
now	you	slide	kind of	blue	me evening	kind of	blue	me ring

kontak	hap	tcoï-ĭkam	takʊtâk͏ͨ	hʊk	ʊta	am	s͏ͨiâm	vakĭtk͏ͨ	tarsʊwa.
with that	that	sort of	release	that	in	there	right	enter	placed.

Kota	imasĭ	kota	itany	ipûm	hʊtcʊlʊwa	kʊs	tcʊtakĭ	nyhoɹĭnyĭk
It was	morning	it was	now	you	slide	kind of	blue	evening

kʊs	tcʊtakĭ	nyhaxoata	kontak	hap	tcoï-ĭkam	takʊtâk͏ͨ	hʊk	ʊta	am
kind of	blue	me ring	with it	that	sort of	release	that	in	there

s͏ͨiâm	vakĭtk͏ͨ	tarsʊwa.	Kota-ama	pi-ipʊk	nyʊnyâ	konta	iworsanyĭk
right	enter	placed.	It was the	in	breathless	silent	I was arose

tcʊwʊɹ	tciakâsĭk	sikʊĭrsk	kʊkiwa.	Kota	ama	makai	tcokakĭ	ikʊĭ
land	rock shelter	stepped	stood.	It was then		magician	darkness	fell

ʊhokĭt	an	oama	ʊhokĭt	an	m'ata[a]	tak͏ͨ	si-ivantckʊwak͏ͨ	hʊkatc	sĭs
side by side	there yellow	side by side	there	ashy	that	jerk		with	very

iâ-âmp	maĭ-ĭrsk	tcʊ.	Anya	hʊk	wʊkatc	am	taktc͏ͨ	amhʊnyʊwă.
good	covered	placed.	I was	that	around	there	sitting	preparing.

Nyʊ	kaʌat	masĭt	ors	rsâpatk͏ͨ	nyʊ	wʊntahĭm.	Nyʊ	kaĭkĭa
Me	shield	renew	stick	short	me	together.	Me	sandal

sivinukutcot	nyʊ	vakâ	sisûvinam	pihiwûk.	Nyʊ	sivʊta	sihiavtck͏ͨ
strings tighten	me	gourd	tightening	envelope.	Me	headdress	soften

woehyâ	nytcokolĭtc	ap	ʊta	ip	sĭntatak,	hʊk	wʊkatc	amûtaktc͏ͨ
face	me black paint	there	in	with	spread,	that	around	sitting

---

[a] A guttural expulsion of breath follows *m'*.

for the last journey if he should take it. He extends his hands toward
the four cardinal points that he may foretell the result of the expedition. We went into the enemy's country and our scout saw the animals running, which the Apaches have started, and he trails them until
he comes upon the Apaches warming themselves about their fire.

The scout upon the back trail reports no enemy in sight. The scout
in the direction of the enemy, the scout at the west, and the scout at
the north report and again return to their posts. From the south the
animals come and I have wondered what is happening there. All is
silent in that quarter; the land, the mountain, the beasts, the trees
are quiet.

The scout from the north reports that he has discovered an old man
and a young one. The scout said, "I went out and took my stand in
an advantageous position where I could see in all directions. From

---

haĭtcok	malĭk	kaihyam.	Kota	sia-alĭk	takĭŏ	tcut	kᴜrsk	avaipᴜng
something		listen.	It was	east	direction from	fall		he was

akĭt.	Ĭm	kᴜrsotak(ĭ)	worsᴜtak	takĭŏ	tcut	hastco	vâpâkam	ᴜkâk̂ûta
telling.	In	much water	origin	direction from		what	hairy	killing

hĭmûk	itcᴜtcĭtk	ĭn	pᴜm	iaʌa.	Ahᴜ-ᴜkrs,	apa	katc	apâĭtc	nyiatc
going	ascended	here	them	fell.	Yes,	there	lay	after	looking

nyᴜi-ĭtanûk	ap	âithivaĭ	ᴜmamasĭtam	s‘ha-apavaĭ	ᴜtcoktcinûk
saw	there	after follow	appears and dis-appears, moving rapidly	that manner	he made

tcoĭ-ĭtckatc	p‘any	avai-ikaĭtc	mokiak‘tc‘	kᴜl	katc	pᴜny	hokatcĭt.	Ĭm
property	I	thus tell	sitting	big	lay	me	warming.	In

rsᴜlĭtcotk‘	ta-ak	ĭn	kᴜrsk	âvaĭ-ĭpᴜny	akĭt.	Ĭm	kᴜ	vâk	worsûtak
straightened	fly	in	fall	he me	told.	In	kind of	trail	appeared

takĭŏ	tcᴜt	ta-ak	ĭm	kᴜrsk	âvaĭ-ĭpᴜny	akĭt.	Ahᴜ-ᴜkrs,	apa	katc	ap
direction	from	fly	in	fall	he me	told.	Yes,	there	lay	there

âĭtc	nyiatc	nyᴜĭ-ĭtank	ap	âĭthĭvaĭ	ᴜmamasitam	sha-apâvaĭ	ᴜtcoktcĭnûk
after looking	seeing	there	after	appear	that manner	he does	

tcoĭ-ĭtckatc	pany	avaĭ-ĭkaitc	mokiaktc‘	kᴜlkatc	pᴜny	hokatc.	Ĭm
property	I	manner tell	sitting	big lay	me	warming.	In

hoᴣĭnyĭk	takĭŏ	tcᴜt	ta-ak	ĭm	kᴜrsk	âvai	ipᴜny	akĭt.	Ĭm	kᴜ	Pa-ak
west	direction from	fly	in	fall	he	me	told.	In	kind of	Eagle	

kârs	takĭŏ	tcᴜt	ta-ak	ĭm	kᴜrsk	âvaĭ-ĭpᴜny	akĭt.	Ahᴜ-ᴜkrs,	apa	katc
nest	direction from	fly	in	fall	he me	told.	Yes,	there	lay	

ap	âĭtc	nyiatc	nyᴜĭ-ĭtank	ap	âĭthivaĭ	ᴜmamasĭtam	s‘haapâvai
there	after	looking	seeing	there	follow	appear and disappear, moving rapidly	that way

ᴜtcoktcĭnûk	tcoĭ-ĭtckatc	pa-any	avaĭ-ĭkaitc	mokĭaktc	kᴜlkatc	pᴜny
he does	property	I	told	sitting	big lay	me

hokatcĭt.	Ĭm	kᴜ	rsotakĭ	worsûtak	takĭŏ	tcᴜt	ta-ak	ĭm	kᴜrsk	âvai
warming.	In	kind of	water	origin	direction from	fly	in	fall	he	

ĭpᴜny	akĭt,	p‘any	avaĭ-ĭkaĭtc	kos	has	ᴜtco.	Tcᴜwᴜꜣ	tâtâlĭm	katc	os
me	told,	I	said	how	what	do.	Land	stationary	lay	tree

tâtâlĭm	kᴜx	tâ-âta-ak	tâtâlĭm	tcotc	hastco	vâpâkam	tâtâlĭm	â-âimᴜlĭk.
stationary, stand	mountain	stationary	stand	what	with hair	stationary	undisturbed.	

Ahᴜ-ᴜkrs,	hap	a-atcok‘tc‘	kahĭm	hiap	kᴜkiwahai	s‘ha-akok	iᴜwoan
Yes,	there	stay	direction	stand	turn and look	some one	

pâvaĭ-ĭ	ᴜtcoktcĭnk	tcoĭ-ĭtckatc	p‘any	avaĭ-ĭkaitc	mokĭaktc	kᴜlkatc	pᴜny
manner	he stays	belongings lay	I	said	sitting	big lay	me

hokatcĭt.	Ĭm	kᴜ	Pa-ak	kârs	takĭŏ	tcᴜt	ta-ak	ĭm	kᴜrsk	avaĭ-ĭpᴜny
warming.	In	kind of	Eagle	nest	direction from	fly	in	fall	he me	

the west something told me that there were an Apache and his nephew
there who killed some game and carried it home, to return at once for
more." "Yes," I said, "like foolish children, they wish to die with
their daughters, sons, and valuable property." From the east a scout
came to tell me that in the brulés the tracks of the Apaches show
plainly. "Yes, like foolish children, they wish to die with their
daughters, sons, and valuable possessions."

Now a man with the strength and agility of the wildcat crept upon
them from that side. And one with the sinuous silence of the gray
snake glided upon them from the other side. Another crept up
behind the shelter of the trees. Render yourselves invisible upon the
gray earth! Crawl through the arroyos, advance slowly. I select a
patient aide, telling him what he shall do. He called loudly to another

---

akĭt.   Ahʋ-ʋkrs, hapa-atcoktcʿ kahĭm hiap kʋkiwahaĭ sʿha-akok iʋwoan
told.   Yes,   there   stay   direction stand turn   and look some one

pȧvaĭ ʋtcoktcĭnûk tcoĭ-ĭtckatc pa-any avaĭ ĭkaĭtc mokĭaktc kʋlkatc
manner   he stays belongings lay   I   said sitting big lay

pʋny hokatcĭt.   Aik wʋsk ap kakaitcĭtkʿ hʋmiap ʋolʋnan kony am
me   warming.   Now all   there   notify   gather   crowd   I   there

iworsʋnyhi haĭ-ĭtcova am tcotan pʿany avaĭ-ĭkaitc mokiaktc kʋlkatc
arose   something   understand I   manner   sitting   big lay

pʋny hokatcĭt.   Kotava vȧhȧ wʋsk ap kakaĭtc kotavaĭ-ĭ hʋmiap ʋoɪ.
me   warming.   It was   true all there notify there were gather crowd.

Konta iworsanyĭk tcʋwʋɹ tciȧkȧsĭk sikʋĭrsk kʋkiwa.   Ĭm hotĭnyĭk woĭ
I was   arose   land   rock shelter stepped stand.   In sunset toward

sʿhovĭtam mawak sialĭk woĭ sʿhovĭtam mawak rsʋlĭtcotk sʿhovĭtam mawa.
selfish   reach for east toward selfish reach for straight selfish reach for.

Kota ĭm hoɹĭnyĭk takĭŏ tcʋt ta-ak ĭm kʋrsk âvaĭ-ĭpʋny akĭt.   Â-âp hʋk
It was in sunset direction from fly in fall he me   told.   Apache that

ʋtcotcoɹ wʋmʋk ʋmoa-a hʋmo ĭm ĭmât kâkhâ ataĭ imât.   Ahʋhʋ a-alva
her nephew with   game now in carry twice they carry.   Yes,   children

naɹa ʋki apɜt oa apaĭm ʋovitak sʋʌʋmam ʋalĭtak sʋʌʋmam skʋ-ʋk
crazy his house there fetch daughter coax   his son   coax   good

hastco ʋtcoĭ-ĭtak sʋʌʋmam.   Ĭm sialĭk takĭŏ tcʋt ta-ak ĭm kʋrsk avaĭ-ĭ
what   his things   coax.   In east direction from fly in fall he

pʋny akĭt.   Ĭn kʋs vâpâik tamûk vâpâk mʋĭ-ĭpa-atoa hastco
me   told.   In kind top   top   top   trails many appeared what

pʋĭhyamkotatc sʌʋtcitckamaĭp ʋmasĭt.   Ahʋhʋ, a-alʌa nâta ʋki apɜt
gathered places   fresh   appears.   Yes,   children crazy his house there

oa-apaim ʋofitak sʋʌʋmam ʋalitak sʋʌʋmam skʋ-ʋk hastco ʋtcoĭ-ĭtak
bring   his daughter coax his son   coax   good   what things

sʋʌʋmam.   Kota-ama hʋmakâ vi-ikam nyʋ viapâkʋ-ʋlʋka ta-ama
coax.   It was   then one   remainder me son   then

kʋofhâ stcoviatkam tcok(ût).   Hʋmakâ hâtai mâ-âtcotkʿ kaipanyĭm.
wild cat sly assume   flesh).   One   stone head   came crawling.

Ata-ama hʋmakâ vi-ĭkam nyʋ viapâkʋ-ʋlʋka ta-ama shâmakĭ vamat
And then one   remainder me son   then   gray snake assume

tcokût.   Hʋmakâ osʋkatc mâ-âtcotkʿ kaipanyĭm.   Ata-ama hʋmakâ
flesh.   One   tree   his head   came crawling.   And then   one

vi-ĭkam nyʋ viapâkʋ-ʋlʋka ta-ama skâmakĭ tcʋwʋɹ tcokût.   Hʋmakâ
remaining me son   and then gray   ground assume flesh.   One

vi-ĭrsany mâ-âtcotkʿ kaipanyĭm.   Kŏnyak âĭtc ipkukhĭm.   Awaoɹ sĭstco
small arroyo head   came crawling.   I was   after advancing slowly.   It was very

to accompany him to see what shall happen. He reached a gap in the mountain and peeped through. Calling to his companion he told him to look and see what is before them. There they saw a fire built by a stump and an old Apache cracking bones. A boy was shouting and a girl was laughing. When he heard this he sent his companion to tell us to hide and remain hidden until he gave the call of the road runner. We heard the messenger coming and thought it was the Apaches, so that we caught up our belongings. Our leader said that some of our friends must have shown themselves, which would cause the Apaches to take the alarm and to depart. As we listened the sun went down and the messenger arrived. He told us to hide and our

papkĭkam nyimikĭ kontak mamutcuk am kuĭk âʌa uwumkam akĭt.
  patient   my relatives   I was   guessing   there appoint and his companion   told

Âĭk rsasĭkotc vâphai hai-ĭtco va-amtctan pʻata kai-ĭtam tcutcu.   Atava
Hurry   then we   run something   understand   he   loud   said.   Then

vâhâ vâpk toa-akatc rsa-a[kʻ am spa-apak(i) ikoatcĭtk uʌumkam akĭt.
true   run mountain like his gap there   slowly   peeped   his companion told.

Âĭk miak i-iolĭn kony am ĭnytcu ʌulĭthĭ haitco va-amtctan pata kaitam
Hurry here   hold   I   there raised   something   understand just as   loud

tcutcu. Tava vâhâ miak i-ĭo[(t). Ta-am i-itcuʌu[itkʻ tcum nyuĭ kota
  said.   That   true here   hold.   And then he raised   there   saw then

humakâ orsân ap atavaĭ ĭnaĭ. Huk u[ak â-âp kuli sʻap kaitam a-a
  one stump there   built fire.   That   in Apache old right sound bones

rsânv sku-uk viapâĭ sʻap kai-ĭtam rsava[hinukʻ sku-uk tcuhya
pounding good boy   right sound adult condition shout   good   girl

sʻap kai-ĭtam rsava[tcutcĭak, kotaam tcum kayâk uʌumkam akĭt.
right sound adult condition laugh,   then   there heard his companion told.

Kamai opam kuksĭmhai hupaĭt imik(i) tcu-ukhi akitank hupai
There homeward fall at intervals where   relatives   found   told   where

hastcoĭ-ĭkam kâʌâ[kʻ ap itcom u-ustân. Kony hapa tcoi-ĭkahĭm
somewhere   hollow there   try u. hid.   I   here   was like

hiwukatc pitcimĭthai tcuwu[tcumihiakhaĭ hu-us tcohok uta
around lay going around   earth   covered   little   dark   in

hastcoĭ-kam kâvâ[ĭk ap haprs itcom humu kakan. Kotava vâhâ opam
what kind   hollow there will   you   look.   He then true homeward

kuksimûk woitcok tcorsa[tcovĭnyhĭm. Kota katho nyu wukatcûk
fall at intervals straight slowly chortling.   Then   there   me   behind

hastco pat koa-aki tatuku varsai tatuku.
what   bad firewood wrestle   grass wrestle.

Rsam piatcu-ûk hai-ĭtco kai-iham na-aks hupaiva utcukĭ hukt
Silent   nothing something   listen   might   where   showed   our

imik(ĭ) tuwoi tcorsal tcovĭnyhĭm pʻata kai-itam tcutcu. Kotaʌa vâhâ
relatives to us   slowly   chortle   not loud kept saying.   Then   true

rsam piatcu-ûk hai-ĭtco kai-iham kotak tataf vaprs kam tcôm kuvĭtp
silent   nothing something   listen   that   sun westward glance

kotak uta vai-ĭ tcivĭa. Haspkʻ umakĭtan nanûkâ nyimĭk(ĭ) na-anysapa
then   in here   came.   Undecided   told   various relatives I guess right

tcivĭa. Kotrs hapa tcoi-ĭkaihĭmhai hupai hastcoi-ĭkam kâvâlĭk ap
came.   Perhaps we   in same condition   where   what kind   hollow there

itcôm tu-ustăn pʻata kai-itam tcutcu. Kava vâhâ hastcoi-ĭkam
try   hide   not   loud kept saying. It was true   what kind

kâvâ[ĭk ap isiatuvintc tai-ihĭm. Ka-am hap tcoi-ĭkahimtcʻ worsanyĭk
hollow there retreat   sitting.   There there was in that condition arose

wukatc pitcĭmĭtahĭmûk tcoi-ĭkam nyunarsûnahimûk hu-ustcohok uta
around   going around   kind   examine   in the night   into

scout would come for us during the night. We went and concealed ourselves in a cave. The scout came for us and we mistook him for the Apaches and wrestled with the grass and stones in our efforts to conceal ourselves. Our leader said we must be quiet and listen, for it was our friend that was coming. He said he came carefully so as not to give the alarm, but that there were no rocks or trees about the camp of the Apache, so the medicine-men must cause darkness with a yellow and gray edge that will render the warriors invisible.

The medicine-man threw his spell upon the enemy and they slept. The Apache dreamed, and when he awakened he thought it was true that his younger brother and his uncles had been killed. Again he dreamed, and when he awakened he thought, "Did I eat food that I never saw? Did I drink water that I never saw? Things that I never saw have I used for clothing?" When he thought of these things he was frightened and tried to hide himself.

I sent the men with shield and club in two parties in the east and west direction to meet at the camp of the Apaches. Some went straight with me. There, gathered about a stump, are the Apaches. When

---

tυwoe rsamonyĭm. Kota katho nyυ wυkatcûk hastco pat koa-ak(ĭ)
us   making noise.   It was behind me at that place what bad firewood

tatυkû varsai tatυkû. Rsam piatcυ-ûk hai-ĭtcυ kai-iham na-aks
wrestle grass wrestle. Silent nothing said something listen might

hυpaiʌa υtcυkĭ hυkt imik(ĭ) tυwoe rsamonyĭm p'ata kai-itam
where showed our relatives us straight making noise not loud

tcυtcυ. Kotava vâhâ rsam piatcυ-ûk hai-ĭtco kai-iham kotak υta
kept saying. It was true silent nothing said something listen that in

vaĭ tcivĭa. Haspk υmakĭtan nanûkâ nyimik(ĭ) na-amysapa tcivĭa.
here came. Undecided told various relatives guess right came.

Pia-âva wυkatc hâtai ta pia-âva wυkatc os kυ-υk p'ata kai-itam
Not good around stone sitting not good around tree stand not loud

tcυtcυ. Kota-ama makai tcokak(ĭ) ĭkυĭ, υhokĭt an oama υhokĭt
kept saying. And the magician darkness fall, side by side there yellow side by side

an mata. Kotak ivantc(υ)kovak hυkatc sĭsiâmp maĭrsk tcυ. Kotak
there ashy. That jerked with very right covered placed. That

υta am kυrs karsk am pajâtp υtcυtckihĭm. Hυ-υs tcohok υta am
in there fall sleep there perhaps of himself dreampt. Some night in there
                                    bad

ĭnyiak hap utatam rsat υtco tâva hυkiaĭ puĭkûn siυ-υhûkĭ
waked that felt himself how do it was long ago catch him older brother

nydrsυpĭtc hûntata nyhaki vat hĭk tcivĭa. Kυpĭny nyυita
younger brother mother's father's I guess he came. Nothing seen
          younger brother younger brother

hυmatckam vant hĭk rsakĭt ai-ĭmυ. Kυpĭny nyυita hastco hohokĭ
people guess got in among going. Nothing seen what food

vant hĭk ho. Kυpĭny nyυita rsotak(i) vasip(ĭ) vant hĭk i. Kυpĭny
guess ate. Nothing seen water take guess drink. Nothing

nyυita hastco tcoi-ĭtak vant hĭk tcoi-ĭt't'. Hap ata-atatk'
seen what property guess own. That he thought

amahavapk' mok katc. Awaoɬ kaof(w)k takakam kŏnt am υta taf
there then died lay. It was hard rooted I there in split

tapanûk sia-alĭk takĭo pitcimĭtk' hotĭnyĭk takĭŏ pitcimitk' s'iâmp
in half east direction go around sunset direction carry around right

υnam. Kontak hastco pat wυm rsυlitcut ita. Apai-ĭ hυmakâ
meet. I was what bad with straightened jump. Up there one

our men heard of this from a messenger they sprang upon the enemy. We killed one who slipped upon the grass and fell down hill and another who stumbled upon a branch. We cleaned up everything about the Apache camp. Animals and birds alone remained to prey upon the dead.

I turned back and my trail was downward. I reached home after slackening speed four times. When at the first drinking place I sent four of my sons to give notice of our approach. They told the old men and the old women at the villages and they rose and cleaned their faces and brushed their hair smooth. Then I came bringing the evidences of my victory. My land rejoiced with me and the mountain donned its headdress, the trees took on gladness. We notified our relatives to the east, west, and south, that we might rejoice together.

You may think this over, my relatives. The taking of life brings serious thoughts of the waste; the celebration of victory may become unpleasantly riotous.

orsân	ap	p'ata	kai-itam	tcutcu.	Kontak	âĭtkʿ	ita-ak	ap	kᴜrsk
stump	there	not	loud	kept saying.	I was	after	jumped	put against foot	

ap	pia-atco	tatûkĭtcotkʿ	ap	sᴜtapam	puĭ.	Kaoɂ	ᴜtcĭnykatc	stco
there	nothing	wrestle	there	smooth	catch.	It was	his mouth with	expert

moa-atkamtcʿ	ap	ki-ĭrsk	ap	itcᴜʌaĭm.	Kaoɂ	ᴜhotckatc	stco
killing	there	bite	there	drag.	It was	his nails with	expert

moa-atkamtcʿ	ap	hokrskʿan	itcᴜʌaĭm.	An	wᴜkatc	katcĭm	nanûkâ
killing	grasp	there	drag.	There	around	laying	various

tcoi-ĭtc(ĭ)	katc	sinasĭk	sᴜpapak	kaʌoɂ(d)	katk	pᴜkᴜ	opam	ha-ahok
powdered ground	lay	gathered	slowly	group		took	homeward	face

inyᴜwa.	Kota	it	nyᴜ	wâkĭta	skoiwaɂam	ᴜtcᴜ.	Kontak	âĭtkʿ	ap
I.	That	this	me	trail	steep incline	placed.	I was	after	there

ki-ĭkap	rsârs.	Kaoɂ	rsotakiᴜ	nyi-ĭkŏttcʿ	kanvarsan	pᴜkᴜkrsa	kont
four	renewals.	It was	water	drinking place	near by	fall	I was

hᴜk	ᴜta	am	kᴜrsk	am	i.	Kaoɂ	kᴜs	tcootcoa-atcmakam	hᴜnyᴜ
that	in	there	fall	there	drink.	It was	kind of	swiftest	my

vipiâpka	kont	hamam	tcᴜk	am	hatcotcoa-a.	Kota	ki-ĭkap	rsarsk
youths	I was	had	found	there	appointed.	That	four	renewals

mᴜlifkai	ikai-ĭtc	kᴜlĭ	vi-ĭkam	âks	vi-ĭkam.	Kota	kat	si-ĭtatakrsk
center	running to	old	remainder	female	remainder.	That	there	put hands

ivamĭk	ᴜwoĭhia	mawoak	kamiᴜtakoa	ᴜhakvâtûtak	ᴜta	mawoak	kam
arose	his face	touch	rub off his mistletoe	like head	in	put hand	brush

kaniᴜtap	ka.	Konyak	âĭtckʿ	kᴜs	s'aptahatkam	nyᴜ	moa-a	oa-atc
smooth.	I was	after	kind of	good feelings	me	killing	holding

antavai-ĭ	oa-apa.	Hᴜk	hᴜkatc	am	simai-ĭrsk	tcᴜk	nytcᴜwᴜɂûka
then	brought.	That	with	there	covered	placed	my land

nytâta-aka	isisisʌᴜtatc	os	nyᴜ	kᴜ-ᴜrsa	isitaktcotk	isikok(ĭ).
my mountain	very headdress	tree	my	planted	grasp	put on top.

Hotĭnyĭk	takĭŏ	takam	tᴜimĭk(ĭ)	kaitanûk	sᴜmatchait	imᴜtan
Sunset	direction	sitting	our relatives	notify	inform	address

katcĭm	takĭŏ	takam	tᴜimĭk(i)	kaitanûk	sᴜmatchait	imᴜtan	sia-alĭk
laying	direction	sitting	our relatives	notify	inform	address	east

takĭŏ	takam	tᴜimĭk(ĭ)	kaitanûk	sᴜmatchait	imûtan.	S'ha-ap
direction	sitting	our relatives	notify	inform	address.	That way

hapûk	hᴜmsâ	ᴜlĭtk	tatcoa	kotc	hᴜmo	hap	patmatâtan	hᴜk	pat
that	you	think	desires	for	now	that	lazy make	that	bad

rsûika	natc	apahâpta	kaihâkĭm	kai-ĭtc.
slave	guess	on which	noise	said.

We have come thus far, my brothers. The land about us is truly
our own. On my way hither I have slackened speed but four times.
The trail led to the white reed, with which I made four passes downward, but there were four layers of earth and I could not reach them
all. I made four passes upward, but there were four layers of sky
and I could not reach them all. I stood in the center of the world and
looked about me. To the westward extended the black trail as far as
the base of the black reed. I made four passes downward and four
passes upward as before. Again I returned and stood in the middle of

Ia-ataʌa tcu-ʋtcka nanûkâ tcoi-ĭkam nyi-ĭmĭk(ĭ). Kâvaot nyʋ
We have / come / various / classes / relatives. / It was / me

tcʋwʋtûka kontak kʋĭrsk ĭm kʋkiʌak ĭm aai nyʋnhâk tcʋm nyʋĭ.
land / that / stepped on in / stood / in / looking around / then / saw.

Ĭm sialĭk woi kʋs toa han(y) tcʋkrsantalĭk katc kont hʋk âĭtkʿ
In / east / toward kind of white / my / drawn line / lay / I / that / after

am ki-ĭk pʿtcʋkak ap tcʋ-ʋmâ-âk tcʋm nyʋĭk ap rsânt ap kʋk
there / four / coming / there / covered / then / saw / there / base / there / stand

kʋs toaha vapkʿ. Kont ap rsânt ap mawoak ĭm koavĭt itakĭŏ
kind of / white / reed. / I was / there / base / there / reach / in / down / strip

kaĭt tcʋwʋɬ ki-ĭk ap ʋtam katc kak am pia-is kontak am
this / land / four / there on top of another / lay / this / there / not rich / I was / there

pihʋkaitcotkʿ am tcʋx itakĭŏ kaĭt tamkatcĭm ki-ĭk ap ʋtam katc
mistaken / there / bound / strip / this / above laying / four / there / on top of another / lay

kak am pia-is kontak am pihʋkaitcotkʿ am opam hap intcok ĭm
this / there / not rich / I was / there / mistaken / there / homeward / that / went as before / in

tcʋwʋɬ sʿʋtaf kʋkiwoa. Am a-ai nyʋnhâk tcʋm nyʋĭk ĭm hoɹinyĭk
land / center / stand. / There look in various directions / then / saw / in / west

woi kʋs tcok nyʋ tcokrsantalĭk katc. Kont hʋk âĭtk am
toward / kind of black / my / drawn line / lay. / I was / that / after / there

ki-ĭk pʿtcʋkak ap tcʋ-ʋmâ-âk tcʋm nyʋĭk ap rsânt ap kʋk
four / going there / there / covered / then / saw / there / base / there / stand

kʋs tcok vapkʿ. Kont ap rsânt ap mawoak ĭm koavĭt itakĭŏ
kind of / black / reed. / I was / there / base / there / reach / in / down / strip

kaĭt tcʋwʋɬ ki-ĭk ap ʋtam katc kak am pia-is kontak am
this / land / four / there on top of another / lay / this / there / not rich / I was / there

pihʋkaitcotkʿ am tcʋxitakĭŏ kait tamkatcĭm ki-ĭk ap ʋtam katc
mistaken / there / bound strip / this / above laying / four / there on top of another / lay

kak am pia-is kontak am pihʋkaitcotkʿ am opam hap intcok
this / there / not rich / I was / there / mistaken / there / homeward / that / went as before

ĭm tcʋwʋɬ sʿʋtaf kʋkiwoa. Am a-ai nyʋnhâk tcʋm nyʋĭk
in / land / center / stand. / There / in various directions looking / then / saw

375

the earth. Looking about me I saw in the south[a] the Sea god, to whom I loudly cried for swiftness, dreams, visions, magic bow and arrows, immunity from cold, thirst, and hunger, and accuracy of aim. These favors he gave me tied in a bundle and I bore them away to my home. In the north were the four living streams[b] stretching in a line, behind which sat the Apache magician. His camp fire shone out upon a reddish reed, which I went and easily pulled out, though I thought I could not. With this reed I scattered the fire, destroyed his food and water. I did this because I feared him, yet when I had finished I was not satisfied. I returned to my home and stood in the center of the land. Again I looked around me and saw in the heavens Talking Tree.

---

avarsan hʊt vâta katc kont hʊk woĭ iahap nyʊ tcotcohimûk
there then   that laid lay I was that toward here me   coming

ap sʊpapak(ĭ) tcʊʊmâ-â. Anya-am sĭsk ai-itam imʊtc rsoak. Kota
there slowly   covered.   I was   very loud address cry.   This

pĭnyʊ hovĭtc kʊ nanûkâ tcoi-ĭkam ʊkʊofkʊtalĭk skʊ-ʊk tcʊ-ʊtcĭk(ĭ)
not me unselfish kind of various things   his strength   good   dreams

tânalĭm haĭtco nyʊita. S'apûkam kat kia-atkam sʊlʊ ta-atam vapk
visible something saw.   Good   bow   string   straight   fly   reed

tcoi-ĭta. Hʊoʌastalĭk kostalĭk piohokĭstalĭk tcoatcmatalĭk sulĭwĭ
smooth.   Inured to cold inured to   inured to hunger   swift   accurate
                        thirst   of aim

talĭk. Hakĭa katcĭm nankoaa tcoi-ĭtcĭk pĭnyʊhovitcĭtc' sĭskavĭtcĭm
held.   Many   laying   various   occupations   unselfish   very narrow

hʊntak(ĭ). Kontak sĭskavĭtcĭm tak opam ha-ahâk ĭnyʊ woa. Kaĭm
held.   I was   very narrow   hold home- face   me toward. In this
                                        ward   direction

nanûk(ĭ) âĭt woĭ kʊ vipʊkam rsorsok(ĭ) ki-ĭk apmâĭtam wʊʌʊftc
north   field toward kind of remainders   waters   four successive   stay

konyak kakhai am sikʊkshĭm. Kainot wʊkatc katcĭmtc hʊk
I was   across   there falling.   In this   around lay   stay   that

wʊkatcûk makai am ta. Ha-as siʌât mʊhʊtam nata. An wʊkatcĭk
around about magician there sitting. Large flames   light fire. About   around

stcohokmom sitânâttc' katc, hʊk hokĭt am am katcĭk' s'wukiom
darkness   shone   lay that edge   there there staid   reddish

rsotakitc' hʊk ʊtca am kʊ-ʊk hʊk kʊs swʊkiom vapk. Am
water   that in there stand that kind of reddish   reed. There

pihʊpai miacʊt hastcokatc tatcoi-ĭtcĭm tcoĭ-ĭk. Kontak hʊk(ĭ)
nowhere   near   something   powerless   condition. I was   that

sĭspathâk ʊlĭtk hʊk imʊlivitahĭmk antaprssʊpʊtam antcʊm
very determined thought that dodging toward I   feared   there I

pʊk antaprskam hop(û). Antak hʊkatc hʊk makai nata am a-ai
grasp I   did   pulled out. Then   with   that magician fire there both

sikantat. Skâʌâkam hastco hohokĭtc ap iawoĭtc. Kʊs vavĭnyĭkam
directions Cloying   what   plenty of there thrown   Kind of quenching
scattered.   food   away.

rsotakĭ vasĭpĭtc ap sivasĭpowĭtc. Antak am (p)rstcʊm hʊkaiitcotk
water   take a drink there empty.   Then   there make   that resemble
      in a cup for some one
      who is absent

tatcoa, kaowoɿ pihʊkai-ĭ. Kont opam hapĭntcok ĭm tcʊwuɿ
plan,   it was   not that.   I was homeward just as before in   land

s'utaf kʊkivoak am a-ai nyʊnhâk tcʊm nyuĭ. Ava ittamatcĭm
center   stand   there both directions   then   saw. It was this above
                        looking

---

[a] Vata Katc.   [b] Vipûkam.

Branches extended in the four directions; that toward the west held the black wind, which came down upon me and, taking me by the hair in his grasp, carried me to the margin of the earth where he left me. This he did to render me hardy and brave. The branch toward the south bore the hurricane, which grasped and bore me to the edge of the world. He did this that I might become brave. The east branch bore the white wind, which came slowly down and grasped my head and swung me to the margin of the earth. He did this that I might become brave. The straight branch bore the licking wind, which grasped, swung, and slowly carried me to the edge of the earth. This he did to inure me to hardship. Now I thought that all was done, but it was not.

I returned to my home and stood in the middle of the land. Looking about I again saw above me Talking Tree, bearing on its western

parsâ kʊk hʊnyiâktam os. Am a-ai sʿnânâlĭtc kʊk. Ĭm hotĭnyĭk
near　tʰat　kind talking　tree.　There both　directions　stand.　In　sunset
　　　under

woĭ ĭmamahaktc hʊk tam am kʊk kʊs tcok hʊoʌʊ̣(d). Amtcʊt
toward　branch　that　on　there stand kind of black　wind.　There from

a-akrsp ihodonyĭk iany mâ-âtam nyʊ rsak tamatcĭm parsâ ki-ĭk ap
down　went down　overhead　me　grasp　above　near below four there

sinyʊvitotkʿ amtcʊt sʊpapak(ĭ) ĭnyʊ hodontahĭmûk tcʊwʊ̣ hohokĭt ap
me swing　therefrom　slowly　me　down　land　edges　there

a-ai sĭnyʊ kʊkioliktc. Âvapihaskam haitco tathâk nyʊaktc ap nyʊ tco.
both　me　fix at edges.　It was nothing　what　feel　me told there me　do.
directions

Âva ĭm katckʿwoĭ ĭmamahaktcʿ hʊk tam am kʊk hʊk kʊsiofhʊwʊ̣(d).
It was in ocean toward　branch　that　top there stand that kind of bitter wind.

Amtcʊt a-akrsp ihodonyĭk iany mâ-âtam nyʊ rsak tamatcĭm parsâ
Therefrom　down　went down　here　head top　me　grasp　sky　near

ki-ĭkap sĭnyʊ vitotkʿ am tcʊt sʊpapak(ĭ) imyʊ hodontahĭmûk tcʊwʊ̣
four times　me　swing there from　slowly　me　lowered　land

hohokĭt ap a-ai sĭnyʊ kʊkioliktc. Âva pihaskam haitco tathâk nyʊ
edges　there both　me　standing.　It was　nothing　thing　feel　me
directions

aktcʿ ap nyʊ tco. Ĭm sialĭk woĭ ĭmamahaktcʿ hʊk tam am kʊk hʊk
told there me　do.　In　east toward　branch　that　on　there stand that

kʊs toahʊwʊld. Amtcʊt a-akrsp ihodonyĭk iany mâ-âtam nyʊ rsak
kind of white wind.　Therefrom　down　went down　here　head top　me　grasp

tamatcĭm parsâ ki-ĭkap sĭnyʊ vitotkʿ amtcʊt sʊpapaki inyʊ
sky　near　four times　me　swing　from　slowly　me

hodontahĭmûk tcʊwʊ̣ hohokit ap a-ai sĭnyʊ kʊkioliktcʿ. Âvapihaskam
lowered　land　edges there both　me　stand.　It was　nothing
directions

haitco tathâk nyʊ aktcʿ ap nyʊtco. Sʊld kʊkam tam am kʊk kʊ
thing　feel　me　told there　me do.　Straight standing　on　there stand kind of

vinyom hʊwʊld. Amtcʊt a-akrsp ihodonyĭk iany mâ-âtam nyʊ rsak
licking　wind.　Therefrom　down　lowered　here　head top　me　grasp

tamatcĭm parsâ ki-ĭkap sĭnyʊ vitotkʿ amtcʊt sʊpapak(ĭ) ĭnyʊ
sky　near　four times　me　swing　from　slowly　me

hodontahĭmûk tcʊwʊ̣ hohokĭt ap a-ai sinyʊ kʊkioliktcʿ. Âva
lowered　land　edges　there both　me　stand.　It was
directions

pihaskam haitco tathâk nyʊ aktcʿ ap nyʊ tco. Hap atavaĭnytco.
nothing　thing　feel　me　told there　me　do.　There　finished tests.

branch the black lightning. This came in a thunderbolt, which split the earth and made a furrow toward the north as far as the Apaches. This caused the spirit of our youth to be strengthened. In a vision the location of the enemy was disclosed. The south branch bore the blue lightning, which descended to split the trees in all directions, rendering visible our enemies. In the east the white lightning descended to split and scatter the mountain in all directions, rendering visible the enemy. The straight stem bore the blue lightning, which descended in a bolt, splitting the sky in two parts and disclosing the plan of the Apaches. After receiving these powers I was pushed toward the enemy. I rushed upon the Apaches and killed them without difficulty. With

---

Kontak amʊrsptcʊm hʊkai-ĭtcotkᶜ tᶜtcoa kaoɹ pihʊkaĭ-ĭ. Kont opam
I was   there then   that thing (or that) desires it was   not that.   I was home-
    ward

hapĭnytco. Ĭm tcʊwʊɹ sᶜutaf kʊkĭwoak am a-ai nyʊnhâk tcʊm nyʊĭ.
just as before. In land center stand there both looking then saw.
    directions

Konta tamatcĭm woĭ inyiak tcʊm myʊĭ. Âva ĭt tamatcĭm parsâ kʊk
I was sky toward look then saw. It was this sky near stand
hʊk kʊ myiâktam ostc am a-ai sʊnânâldtcᶜ kʊk. Ĭm hoɹĭnyĭk woĭ
that kind of talking tree there both branches stand. In sunset toward
    directions

ĭnaldkᶜ apta kʊs tcok woehâm. Am ʊɹa sikâponyĭk ihodonyk amt
branch there kind of black lightning. There in explosion descended there
sitting

ʊɹa sikʊkioʍoak hʊk tcʊwʊɹ am kavĭtc sihioftanûk tʊwoe katcĭm
in stand firm that land there narrow furrowed us opposite laying

tcʊwʊɹ tam am kokowoĭtc. Hʊk âĭtkᶜ hʊk viapâĭ ipûtak am
land on there points reach. That after that youth soul there
sitânâlĭtkᶜ aptco. Aptarsâ prsoɹ(d) hʊk nyʊ âpûtak hʊki atava nyʊ
visible that do. Disclose throw that my enemy that   me

woitatkᶜ haptco. Ĭm katckᶜ woĭ ĭnaldkᶜ apta kʊs tatk(ĭ) woehâm. Am
for me made. In ocean toward branch there kind of blue lightning. There
    sitting

ʊta sikâpânyk ihodonyĭk o-os aptcotcĭm am ʊta sitafʊtrsk am a-ai
in explosion descended trees standing there in split there both
sĭnyʊntc. Aptarsâ prsoɹ(d) hʊk nyʊ âpûtak hʊk(ĭ) atava nyʊ woetatkᶜ
directions Disclosed through that my enemy that   me for me
throw.

haptco. Ĭm sialĭk woi ĭnaldkᶜ apta kʊs toaha woehâm. Am ʊta
made. In east toward branch there kind of white lightning. There in
    sitting

sikâpânyk ihodonyĭk tâ-âta-ak tcotcĭm am ʊta sikamtrsk am a-ai
explosion descended mountain standing there in split there both
    directions

sinyʊntc. Aptarsâ prsoɹ(d) hʊk nyʊ âpûtak hʊk(ĭ) atava nyʊ
thrown. Disclosed through that my enemy that   me
woetatkᶜ haptco. Sʊɹ(d) kʊkamt apta kʊs stcʊtak(ĭ) woehâm. Am
for me made. Straight standing sitting kind of blue lightning. There
    there

ʊta sikapanyĭk ihodonyĭk hʊk tʊtamatcĭm am ʊta sikâmûtanûk ap a-ai
in explosion descended that our sky there in split there both
    directions

sitarswoa. Aptarsâ prsoɹ(d) hʊk nyʊ âpûtak hʊk(ĭ) atava nyʊ
fly apart. Disclosed through that my enemy that   me
woetatkᶜ haptco. Hʊk âĭtkᶜ inyoĭ-ĭhai. Kont hʊk âĭtkᶜ ita-ak ap
for me made. That after me pushed. I was that after jumped there

gladness in my heart I gathered the evidences of my victory and turned toward home.

You may think this over, my relatives. The taking of life brings serious thoughts of the waste; the celebration of victory may become unpleasantly riotous.

---

kursk ap pia-atco tatkĭtcotk ap sutapam puĭ. An wukatc katcĭm
fell there nothing   wrestle   there smooth take. About around laying

nankâtcoĭ-ĭ tcikatc simasĭk supapak(ĭ) kawoɹkatk puk opam ha-ahâk
various   belongings gathered   slowly   grouped   grasp home- around
        lay   ward

ĭmyu woa. Hapûk humsâ ulĭtk tatcoa nankâ tcoĭ-ĭkam nyu imĭk(ĭ)
me toward.   You   now   thought desire   various   sorts   me   relatives

kotc humo hap patmatâtan huk pat rsâĭka natc apâ-âpta kaihakĭm
we now   that   lazy make   that bad slave   us   right   discord

kai-itcĭtan.
said.

We have come thus far, my brothers. The evening has come when I complete my preparations for attacking the enemy. I have made them dislike their bows and arrows and made their magicians drowsy. Their wives and children are reproved and rejected. May they fall out among themselves. May they be unable to eat or drink. The time approaches when they shall die.

After the sun arose we left camp and went to the Sand Hills,[a] where we halted and held a council of war. Morning came quickly and again we went on. I brought my young men together to kill rabbits, rats,

---

Iat tava tcᴜtcka nanûkâ tcoi-ĭkam nyi-ĭmĭk(i). Tâva hoɹĭnyĭk ikᴜĭ
Here we came various classes my relatives. It was evening fall

kᴜny hᴜk ᴜta moĭ-ĭ nanûkâ tcoi-ĭtcĭk tam maĭ-ĭ tcᴜxitahĭm kᴜny
I that in many different sorts on there placed for I

â-âpûta. Katatc sᶜâhatatctahĭm vapatckatc sᶜâhâtatctahĭm kâkâĭɹû-
enemy. Bow his cause to dislike reed his cause to dislike be-

tahĭmûk kâsĭtahĭmûk sᶜha-ap itâta. Kota hoɹĭnyĭk ikᴜĭ kᴜny hᴜk ᴜta
witch make sleepy proper make. It was evening fall I that in

moĭ-ĭ nanûkâ tcoi-ĭtcĭk tam maĭ-ĭ tcᴜxitahĭm kᴜny â-âpᴜta. Ofitatc
many different sorts on there placed for I enemy. Woman desire for

wᴜmatc vâĭmûtatc s âhâtatctahĭmûk alitatc kamkĭmtatc sᶜâhâtatctahĭm
gather to lay with desire make dislike child his desire to embrace causes to dislike

kâkâĭɹûtahĭmûk kâsĭtahimûk sᶜha-ap itâta. Kota hoɹĭnyĭk ikᴜĭ kᴜny
bewitch make sleepy proper make. It was evening fall I

hᴜk ᴜta moĭ-ĭ nanûkâ tcoi-ĭtcĭk tam maĭ-ĭ tcᴜxitahĭm kᴜny â-âpᴜta.
that in many different sorts on there placed for my enemy.

Wupa tcoi-ĭkam wᴜmatc âĭmᴜlᴜkatc wᴜmatc nyiakĭmtatc sᶜâhâta-
Fellow-man sort of with accompany with address make

tctahĭm kâkâĭtᴜtahĭmûk kâsĭtahĭmûk sᶜha-ap itâta. Kota hotĭnyĭk
dislike bewitch make sleepy proper make. It was evening

ikᴜĭ kᴜny hᴜk ᴜta moĭ-ĭ nanûkâ tcoi-ĭtcĭk tam maĭ-ĭ tcᴜxitahĭm kᴜny
fall I that in many different sorts on there placed for my

â-âputa. Hastco hohokĭmtatc rsotak(ĭ) vasĭpĭtc i-imtatc sᶜâhâtatctahĭm
enemy. What eating desire for water drink drinking make dislike desire for

kâkâĭtᴜtahĭmûk kâsĭtahimûk sᶜha-ap itâta. Ava ĭt kᴜhimûtam sᶜhâtû-
bewitch make sleepy proper make. It was this kind of going

kaĭ-ĭp ᴜnâɹahitcai-ĭp kamo-o. Kontavai-ĭ ipᴜĭ siʌâɹ mᴜhᴜtam nyᴜ
hurry bend afternoon. I was catch flames burning my

kotak rsotakĭ nyᴜ vasip(ĭ). Varsun alhia tam atava ᴜtcᴜ siatcokam
stick water me drink. Yonder small sea on they lay magical sand

nyᴜ tcokakita kontûk tairsk tahiwoa. Am wᴜtcom tatcoĭp sᴜtatkĭm
my darkness I was press sitting. There before me thinking adjusting

---

[a] Sand Hills in the Reservoir, a Hohokam reservoir a few miles north of the Double buttes.

and quails.   About noon we moved on to Salt river and camped again in the evening.   We had too much food and ate it half cooked.   Next morning we journeyed on.   I went swiftly along the dry water courses, where stands the cat's claw.   I went past the rocks to camp at the ironwood trees in the evening and ate the left-over food half raw again.   Continuing, I appointed a place of meeting and the day passed. Gathering my young men I told them to grasp their weapons and run forward.   Crossing a small canyon they proceeded, killing deer and antelope, beyond the red hill.   Knowing the location of the small springs, they went to the low mountain.   Others I told to grasp their weapons and run in a westerly direction.   They ran through bushes and met those who ran in a line along the dry water courses until they

---

kʊsĭm.   Kota sʿhâtkai nyʊ masĭtatc kontavaĭ ipʊĭ sıʌâɹ mʊhʊtam nyʊ
difficulties.   It was   hurry   me early morning I was   take flames burning   me

kotak.   Kamaintalâ ipʊpʊhimûk varsun tcʊtckikŭt am antaʌa tcʊ.
brand.   Before me soon   carried   yonder   replace   there I was placed

Kota prstcʊm sikâl mʊk tataf kotavai hʊmap ioɹt kʊny vipiâpka
It was   then   round running sun   I was   come together I   youths

kʊnya am ha-akĭt.   Kota ap ikʊkʊkʊk alnaktcʿ âĭmʊtʊtam alkikʿtcʿ
I was there   told.   It was there   striking   little ear   moving   little house

takam ala-antcta-atam tarspi ha-apam tâta.   Varsan kʊ mʊtatam tam
sitting   small feathers   way   perform.   Yonder kind of running   top

ataʌa ʊtcʊ siatcokam ntataɹka kontûk taĭrsk taihiwoa.   Ha-akĭa nyʊ-
they   place   magician   my sun   I was   press   sitting.   Many   my

moaa tâyak pʌ wʊtcom itatcoĭp sʊtatkĭm kʊsĭm.   Âva ĭt kʊhimʊtam
killing   raw before swallow thinking   adjusting difficult.   It was this kind of going

sʿhâtkai-ĭp ʊnâdahĭtciap kamo-o.   Kontavaĭ ipʊĭ sıʌâɹ mʊhʊtam nyʊ
quickly   curved   afternoon.   I was   grasp flames   burning   my

kotak rsotakĭ nyʊ vasip(ĭ).   Vâ-ârsany mʊlĭnûk hohokĭt an alsopatkam
brand   water me   drink.   Dry washes   junction   edges about cat's claw

vâ-âtkak konyʊk âĭtcʿ pinatâĭ hap tcoĭ-ĭtcĭk.   Alhâtai kʊx piak
dry wash   I was   after unfinished there condition at the Small stone go around
                                           time of going. standing

antaʌa pĭtc.   Alhâĭtkam tcotckʿ ap atava ʊtcʊ siatcokam ntcokakita
I was go around.   Small iron tree standing there they placed   magician   my darkness

kontûk taĭrsk tahiwoa.   Ha akĭa nyʊ moa-a tâyak pʌ wʊtcom tatcoip
I was   press   sitting.   Many   me killing   raw swallow before thinking

sʊtatkĭm kʊsĭm.   Kota sʿhâtkai nyʊ masĭtatc kontavai ipʊĭ sıʌât
adjusting difficult.   It was   quickly   me early morning   I was   grasp flame

mʊhʊtam nyʊ kotak(ĭ).   Kamaint ala ipʊpʊhĭmûk varsʊny tcʊtckikŭt
burning   my   brand.   Before I soon   carry   yonder   ceremonial
                                                                   ground

am antava tcʊ.   Kota prstcom sikâl mʊk tataf kotavai-ĭ hʊmap iold
there I was placed.   It was   make   round run   sun   it was   unite

kʊny vipiapka konya am ha-akĭt.   Kota am rsarsk taitcĭtkʿ ipûm
my   youths   I was there   told.   It was there grasp   ran up   you

athai.   Aɹ(d) rsarsûkĭk kakhaip ʊkâkûtahimûk al ʌʊk Kamaɹk
run after.   Small   canyons   crossed   they killing   small red   thin

Taxtcoiᵃ ĭm iava.   Ald rsotak(ĭ) worsʊtak amtcʊt takitâk takĭtâk aɹ(d)
end of   in   fall.   Small water   came   therefrom release   release small

hâtai kʊx ap haahok i-iwoa hʊk wʊpʊkatc.   Konyak vi-ĭkam akĭtûk
stone standing there face   home   that   first.   I was   remainder   told

kʊny vipiâpka kota am rsarsk hodon takĭŏ ipûm athai.   Aɹ(d)
my   youths   it was there grasp   sunset direction you run   after.   Small

---

ᵃ Camel Back mountain, near Scottsdale.

reached the place where many yuccas stood. They proceeded in two
lines, with a narrow interval between them. Unacquainted with the
country they went forward, finding deer and antelope, which they
killed. Camping on the summit of the small mountain they ate their
venison half raw. There they made preparations for continuing, as the
time fled swiftly on. Taking up my possessions and a supply of venison for the next day I went forward to camp at the small Gravelly
Water. I renewed preparations when I halted at nightfall. Morning
came quickly and I went on. During the next day I addressed my
young men, telling them to go and kill mountain sheep. They went
on to the spring under the kâm tree, where they camped and continued
their preparations for war. Morning came quickly and I conjured the

---

rsarsai-ĭkam âĭtkᶜ ᴜrsarsaittahimûk aɪ(d) vaptâpat kitcĭk an ĭm iaʌa.
grassy   after   penetrate   small   shade   door   about in   fall.
                                     abandoned

Aɪ(d) vâ-ârsany mᴜlinûk amtcᴜt takĭtâk takĭtâk aɪ(d) otûkoa taʅhak
Small   dry washes   junction   therefrom   release   release   small   yucca   setting

ap hahok i-iwoa hᴜk wᴜpᴜkatc. Ata ha-asp rsapalt nyᴜ vi-ĭ konta
there   face   home   that   first.   It was small   narrow   me   remain-   I was
                                                                         der

iwors hastco pat wᴜm. Hap horsp al(d) tcotcoi-ĭkam sitatakhĭm
arose   what   bad   with.   That   way   small   appearance   handle

ᴜtarspi matckᶜ tatkû tcotck paphaikam nyᴜ viptckot tâta vâpkam nyᴜ
I not   know   wrestle   black   tails   me   deer   white   bellies   me

viptckot ntarspĭ ha-apam tâta. Varsatc al(d) vapûk tam ataʌa ᴜtcᴜ
deer   I not   way   make.   Up there   small   reed   top   they   stay

siatcokam ᴜtataʅka ĭtᴜk tairsk tahiwoa. Ha-akĭa nyᴜ moa-a tâyak pa
magician   my sun   I   press   sitting.   Many   my   killing   raw

wᴜtcom tatcoĭp sᴜtatkĭm kᴜsĭm. Âva ĭt kᴜhimûtam sʿhâtkaĭ-ĭp
swallow   thinking   adjusting   difficulties.   It was this   kind going   hurry
before

ᴜnâdahitcaiĭp kamo-o. Kontavai ipᴜĭ siʌâʅ mᴜhᴜtam nyᴜ kotak
bend   afternoon.   I was   grasp   flame   burning   my   brand

rsotak(ĭ) nyᴜ vasĭp(ĭ). Konyarsp koewoa sihᴜtcᴜʅwoehĭm. Aɪ(d)
water   my   drink.   I was   step down   slide.   Small

â-âtûkam rsotakĭ tam atava ᴜtcᴜ siatcokam ĭtcokakĭta ĭtᴜk tairsk
gravelly   water   top   they   placed   magician   my darkness   I   press

tahiwoa. Am wᴜtcom tatcoĭp sᴜtatkĭm kᴜsĭm. Kota sʿhâtkai-ĭ
sitting.   There   before   thinking   fixing   difficulties.   It was   quickly

nymasĭtatc kontavaiĭ ipᴜĭ siʌâʅ mᴜhᴜtam nyᴜ kotak(ĭ). Kamaint ala
me early morn-   I was   grasp flame   burning   my   brand.   Before I   soon
ing

ipᴜpᴜhimûk varsᴜny tcᴜtckikŭt am antava tcᴜ. Kota prstcom sikâʅ
carry   yonder   ceremonial place   there   I was   placed.   It was   made   round

mûk tataf kotavaiĭ hᴜmap ioɪ kᴜny vipiâpka kᴜnya am ha-akĭt.
run   sun   it was   come   together   I   youths   I was   there   told.

Kotaprs am skavitcĭm nyᴜ pia-aɪ ĭtarspi matckᶜ tatkᶜ rsᴜm mâmam
It was   there   narrow   me   surround   I not   know   wrestle kind   heads

tᴜhᴜhᴜmakŭt. Varsatc aɪ(d) kâm wᴜtcǎ rsânak ap atava ᴜtcᴜ
our ones.   Up there   small   kâm (tree)   under   spring   there   they   placed

siatcokam ĭtcokakĭta kontûk tairsk tahiwoa. Wᴜtcom tatcoĭp
magician   my darkness   I was   press   sitting.   Before   thinking

sᴜtatkĭm kᴜsĭm kota sʿhâtkai-ĭ nymasĭtatc kontak âĭmᴜlᴜkatc sʿâhâta-
adjusting   difficulties I was   quickly   me early morning   I was   haunts his   cause

tctahĭmûk katatc sʿâhâtatctahĭmûk vapatckatc sʿâhâtatctahĭmûk rsotakĭ
to dislike   bow his   cause to dislike   reed his   cause to dislike   water

enemy's magician. May he not like his bow and arrows. In drinking,
may he swallow but his image reflected in the water. May he grasp
the branches of trees and fall under them exhausted. I sent my young
men east, west, and toward the center. The scout to the east saw the
freshly broken grass trodden by the enemy. He sent a messenger to
inform us of his discovery and to state that he would report as soon as
darkness fell. Hastening to make ready, those in the lead rushed forward. The scout to the west ran in, telling of the discovery of signs
in a canyon in that direction. I sent two experienced men to investigate; they moved carefully forward and discovered a camp of Apaches.
Like birds my young men swept down upon and surrounded the
enemy. I sent my white power and my blue to aid them. After

vasĭpĭtc	siwᴜtcă	olĭnûk	tcᴜ.	Kota	ita-ak	ᴜta	am	vataprs	ᴜ-ᴜkᴜtak pa.
drink	very	under	hold	put.	It was jumped	in	there	fall his	shadow swallow.

Avaot	osᴜkatc	mamhaktcᶜ	hᴜk	isipᴜĭ	kotak	wᴜtcâ	am	kᴜrskai-ĭpop
It was	tree	his branch	that	grasp	it was	under	there	fall exhausted

kontak	hap	tcoi-ĭkam	tcᴜm	nyᴜi-ĭtâk	ĭm	sia-al	woĭ	wâpâĭ-ĭtcotkᶜ	hoᴊĭ-
I was	that	sort	then	saw	in	east	toward	sent running	sun-

nyĭk	woĭ	wâpâĭ-ĭtcotkᶜ	ᴜta	wâpâĭ-ĭtc.	Hᴜk	âĭtkᶜ	kâĭ	hᴜ-ᴜkĭa	rsârs	kota
set toward	sent running	in	race.	That	after	not	yet any	moves	it was

sia-al	takĭŏ	tcᴜt	ta-ak	iakᴜrsk	hastco	wâpâkam	kᴜĭkmiakatc	o-ok	ĭn
east	direction from	flew	here fall	what	hairy	traces	take	in

ĭrsoᴊ(d).	Kota	am	tcom	nyᴜĭk	nyi-ĭmĭk(i)	am	wᴜs	tcᴜkaitam	ᴜtatkᶜ
throw.	It was	there	before	seen	my relatives	there	all	prompt one	felt

am	pi-ĭtcivĭx	tcᴜ.	Kota	hodon	takĭŏ	tcᴜt	ta-ak	iakᴜrskaipᴜny	akit.
there not allow each other	see.	It was	sunset	direction from	flew	here told	fall me	told.

Hᴜmakâ	rsakĭk	isĭpĭtcimĭm	tcoĭ-ĭk	am	âsûtakowoĭm	tcoĭ-ĭk	am	âsûta-
One	canyon	turn	like	there	end of hill may touch	like	there	may be

hama	tcoĭ-ĭk.	Avaot	kᴜs	kâmak(ĭ)	tcokŭt	makai	kontak	hap	tcoĭ-ĭkam
sitting	like.	It was kind	gray	owl	magician	I was	that	sort

mamtcĭk	ap	imûk	rᴊᴜrᴊoᴜ	kotap	sĭnhâĭ-itam	ᴜtatkᶜ	worsanyĭk	wᴜkatc
guess	there (	)	cry	I was	friendly	felt	arose	around

pitcĭmĭtahĭmûk	ha-akĭa	stcohokmomkatc	maĭ-ĭrsk	ap	woak	opam	tcivĭak
going	many	darkness with	covered	there	throw	home-	came ward

nyᴜ	akĭt.	Kotak	ᴜta	hux	isikᴜĭrsk	kᴜkiwoa	kᴜny	viapâkᴜ-ᴜlka.
me	told.	It was	in	already	stand firmly on	stand	my	sons.

Tcᴜwᴜᴊâ	mᴜtᴜtam	o-ofĭk	ta-atam	ᴜwᴜpâkĭtkᶜ	nᴜnyĭk	tam	ap	ᴜiawa
Land	running	birds	flying	assume form	fly	on	there	alight

kavap(ûk)ᶜ	itcᴜᴀᴜlĭtkᶜ	hᴜkatc	ap	inûk	ap	tatkᶜ.	Kaoᴊ	hᴜs	tândâm nyᴜ
reed	lengthen	with it	there inclose there	wrestle.	It was kind of	white	me

piahakŭt	kontûk	tcᴜx	ihimtcotkᶜ	hᴜkatc	ap	âĭmᴜlkatc	hokĭt	ap	tarsk
instrument	I was	bound	go	with it	there	ground his	edge	there	set

hap	tâta.	Kaoᴊ	kᴜs	tcᴜtak(ĭ)	nyᴜ	piahakŭt	kontak	tcᴜx	ihimtcotkᶜ
that	make.	It was kind of	blue	me	instrument	I was	bound	pushed

hᴜkatc	ap	âĭmᴜlkatc	hokĭt	ap	tarsk	hap	tâta.	Anta	am	vam	hap
with it	there	haunts his	edge	there	set	that	make.	I	there	more	that

inytcok	pia-atco	pᴜx	imyᴜ	mᴜlᴜnâkĭ.	Kaoᴊ	taprs	katatc	kontᴜk	pᴜk
same way as before	nothing	take	me	turn around.	It was	his	bow	I was	catch

ĭm	tcᴜwᴜᴊ	sᶜᴜtdaftcotkᶜ	kᴜrsk	kai-ipop.	Amtcᴜt	mamtcᴜk	am	hat-
in	land	center	fall	exhausted.	There from	guess	there	make

destroying these Apaches I went on, but killed only an old woman.[a]
I took their bows and then fell exhausted.   Next I sent the swiftest
young men to carry home the news of victory to the old men and
women.   With the news that I bring, the earth, the thunder, the night,
the mountain, and the trees rejoice.

You may think this over, my relatives.   The taking of life brings
serious thoughts of the waste; the celebration of victory may become
unpleasantly riotous.

---

cotcoa kᴜs tcotcoaatcmakam nyᴜ vipiâpka kota ki-ĭk ap rsârs.   Ata
stand kind of   swiftest   me   youths   it was four there renewals. They
them

mᴜlifkai kai-ĭtc kᴜlĭ vi-ĭkam âks vi-ĭkam.   Konyak âĭtcʿ kᴜs sʿap-
came running notify old man remainder old remainder.   I was   after kind good
                                       woman

tahatkam nyᴜ moa-a oa-atc antavaiĭ oapa.   Tak hᴜkatc hᴜk tcᴜwᴜʇ
feelings   me killing held I was had brought. That with that   land

am ᴜta sipᴜpᴜtkʿ ᴜtcᴜ.   Tak hᴜkatc stcohokmom am ᴜta sikikĭfk
there in   roared self stay. That with it   night   there in   shake

ᴜtcᴜ tâta-ak am ᴜta sirsarsafk ᴜtcotcoa.   O-os tcotcĭm am ᴜta
self stay mountain there in echoed   stand.   Trees standing there in

simokofk ᴜtcotcoa.   Sʿha-ap hap hᴜmsâ ᴜlĭtkʿ tatcoa nanûkâ tcoi-ĭkam
shaking   stand.   Way   that you   thought desire different   sorts

inyi-ĭmikĭ kotc hᴜmo hap patma tâtan hᴜk paʇ rsâĭka natc apahâpta
my relatives we now   that lazy   make that bad slave   we   proper

kaihâkĭm kai-ĭtc.
noise   said.

---

a " An arrow without feathers."

We have come thus far, my brothers. In the east there is White Gopher, who is skillful with his teeth. He was friendly and came to me after coming out to the surface four times on the journey. Looking in all directions he saw that a plan had been formed, in accordance with which he slowly approached the enemy, appearing at the surface four times during the journey. He gnawed the power of the enemy and sank their springs. He saw that the wind of the enemy was strong and he cut it up. He gnawed in short pieces their clouds. They had

---

Iat	tava	tcʊtcka	nanʊkâ	tcoi-ĭkam	nyi-ĭmĭk(ĭ).	Ava	ĭm	sia-lĭk
Here	we	came	various	classes	my relatives.	It	was in	east

takĭŏ	kʊ	tânĵâm	Tcʊfhâ.	Kotpkᶜ	hastco	ski-ĭtckatkam	kontak	hap
direction	kind of	white	gopher.	He is	what	gnawer	I was	that

tcoi-ĭkam	mamtcʊk	ap	imʊk	rsârsoa	kotap	sĭnyhâĭ-ikʊĭ-itam	ʊtatkᶜ
sort	guess	there	my	cry	it was	friendly	felt

amtcʊt	ku	tânĵâm	utcohokĭk	woak	hʊk	âĭtkᶜ	ap	ki-ĭkap
there from	kind of	white	itself darkened	lay	that	after	there	four

nâ-âkanûk	makai	nata	tcʊmûk	hokĭt	an	tahiwoa.	Am	a-ai
appearances	magician	fire	all over	edges	about	sitting.	There	four

nyʊnhâk	tcʊm	nyʊĭk	âvak	makai	vâkĭta	tânâttc	katc.	Kot	hʊk
directions looking	then	saw	it was	magician	trail	whitish	lay.	That	that

âĭtkᶜ	am	kʊ	tûntâm	utcohokĭk	woak	hʊk	âĭtkᶜ	ap	ki-ĭkap
after	there	kind of	white	itself darkened	throw	that	after	there	four

nâ-âkanûk	ap	sûpapak(ĭ)	tcʊmâ-âk	nyʊ	âapûta.	Âvak	tcʊwʊt	ap
appearances	there	slowly	covered	my	enemy.	It was	land	there

katc	toa-ak	ap	kʊktcᶜ	tcom	sᶜʊnaki-ĭtc	kux	ʊ-ʊlĭt	kotak	am
lay	mountain	there	standing	it	hanging	standing	he believes	he was	there

sirsâ-ârspaɩ	ki-ĭkoamia.	Âvak	rsârsânûkam	rʒotak(ĭ)	tâta-atc	tcom
short	bitten off.	It was	springs	waters	put it	it

sᶜʊnaki-ĭtc	wutc	ʊ-ʊlĭt	tak	am	siki-ĭkarsahimûk	am	sitco-otcpĭt.
hanging	laying	believes	that	there	continue biting	there	sink it.

Âvak	huwʊɩkatc	âva	tcom	tcoviomatkᶜ	ʊ-ʊlĭt	tak	am	sirsâ-ârspaɩ
It was	wind lay	it was	it	like land	thought	that	there	short

ki-ĭkoamia.	Âvak	tcʊʌakikatc	âva	tcom	stcova-akûpatkᶜ
bitten off.	It was	clouds his	it was	it	very sprinkle

ʊ-ʊlĭt	tak	am	sirsâ-ârspaɩ	ki-ĭkoamia.	Âvak	hʊmatckam
he thought	that	there	short	bitten off.	It was	people

hʊk	tam	ap	âimututam	vatcom	skʊ-ʊk	tcʊ-ʊtc	kat
that	on	there	haunts	not	good	dreams	he

ʊ-ʊlĭt	tan(d)ʊlĭm	haitco	nyʊĭtatkᶜ	ʊ-ulit	tak	am	sirsâ-ârspal
thought	brightly	something	false seeing	he thought	that	there	short

ki-ĭkoamia.	Âvak	hʊmatckam	hʊk	tam	ap	âimututam
bitten off.	It was	people	that	on	there	haunts

vatcom	sᶜapʊkam	kat	kia-atkam,	rsʊl	ta-atam	vapu(k)
not	best	bow	string,	straight	flying	reed

dreams and shining power, good bows and arrows, but all these he cut
in pieces. Gathering all their possessions, he brought them with him,
rising to the surface of the ground four times on his journey. Leaving
all that he brought, he went home, making four appearances at the
surface on his way. The land roared and rejoiced with him for what
he had done.

In the south is Blue Coyote, upon whom I called for assistance. He
was friendly to me and came running, circling around, howling, four
times on the journey. When he arrived he approved of my plan. He
cast his blue darkness upon the enemy and slowly reached their place,
after circling around, howling, four times on the way. He sucked in
the power of the enemy, their springs, trees, winds, clouds, dreams,

---

tcoi-ĭta   rsakûtcĭtkᶜ   u-ulit   tak   am   sirsâ-ârspal   ki-ĭkoamia.   An
clean   had grasped   he thought   that   there   short   bitten off.   About

wukatc   katcĭm   nanûkâ   tcoi-ĭtckatc   si-ĭnasĭk   supapak(i)   kaʌoɽkatkᶜ
around   lay   different   belongings   gathered   slowly   ground

puk   opam   ha-akok   i-iwoa.   Ap   opam   ku   tântâm   utcohokĭk
took   homeward   turn   around.   There homeward   kind of   white   itself darkened

woak   âĭtkᶜ   ap   ki-ĭkap   mâ-âkan   makai   nata   tcumûk   hokĭt   am
placed   after   there   four   appearances   magician   fire   all   edges over about

takûtâ.   Smakaitkam   â-âtam   sivakssĭtk   tam   tarsûwoa.   Vi-ĭkam
release.   Expert magician   people   a prepared place   top   sat.   Remainder
                              with something
                              spread to sit on

supapak(ĭ)   kaʌoɽkatkᶜ   pux   am   opam   ku   tânɽâm   utcohokĭk   woak
slowly   grouped   catch there   homeward   kind of   white   his darkness   throw

âĭtkᶜ   ap   ki-ĭkap   mâ-âkan   uʌâĭ-ĭkŭt   tcumâ-â.   Huk   hukatc
after   there   four   appearances   his bed   come.   That   with

sᶜhai-ĭtcokm   utatkᶜ   kot   huk   hukatc   huk   tcuwuɽ   am   uta   sipuputk
conceit   felt   he   that   with   that   land   there   in   roar

utcu.   Ĭm   katcĭm   takĭŏ   kus   tcutak(ĭ)   tuwumukaɽ   wotᶜpkᶜ   hastco
placed.   In   laying   direction   kind of   blue   our with to   expert   what

tcokok   sᶜhokimutam   kontak   hap   tcoi-ĭkam   mamutcuk   ap   imûk
made   carnivorous   I was   that   sort   guess   there   my

rsârsoa   kotap   sĭnyhâĭ-ikuĭ-itam   utatkᶜ   amtcut   kus   stcutak(ĭ)
cry   it   friendly   felt   there from   kind of   blue

utcohokĭk   woak   huk   âĭtkᶜ   ap   ki-ĭkhâ   sikâl   mutkᶜ   hihinakhĭmûk
his itself   throw   that   after   there   four   round   run   shouting
darkened

makai   nata   tcumûk   hokĭtan   tcuɽakiwoa.   Am   a-ai   nyunhâk   tcum
magician   fire   everywhere   edges   thud.   There   four   directions   then
                                                                looking

nyuĭ.   Âvak   makai   vâkĭta   tânâtcᶜ   katc.   Kotuk   âĭtkᶜ   kus   stcutak(i)
saw.   It was   magician   trail   whitish   lay.   It was   after   kind of   blue

utcohokĭk   woak   huk   âĭtkᶜ   ki-ĭkhâ   sikâl   mutkᶜ   hihinakĭmk   ap
his itself darkened   throw   that   after   four times   around   run   shouting   there

supapak(ĭ)   tcumâ-âk   nyu   â-aputa.   Âvak   tcuwuɽ   ap   katc
slowly   covered   me   enemy.   It was   land   there   lay

toa-ak   ap   kuxtc   tcom   sᶜunaki-ĭtc   kux   u-ulĭt   kotak   am   sihafw(u).
mountain   there   stand   it   hanging   stand   he thought   it was there   inhale.

Âvak   rsârsanûkam   rsorsok(ĭ)   tâta-atc   tcom   sᶜunaki-ĭtc   wukatc   os
It was   springs   waters   placed   it   hanging   round   tree

ap   kukam   tcom   sᶜunaki-ĭtc   tcotck   u-ulĭt   tak   am   sihâfw(u).
there   standing   it   hanging   stand   he thought   that   there   inhale.

Âvak   huwuɽkatc   âva   tcom   tcoviomatkᶜ   u-ulĭt   tak   am   sihafw(u).
It was   wind his   it was   it   cause to blow   thought   that   there   inhale.

and magic power, also their bows and arrows. Gathering up their other possessions he turned toward home. Enveloped in his blue darkness he came to me, circling around, howling, four times on the journey. Leaving all that he brought, he went home, traveling through his blue darkness and circling around, howling, four times on the way. He rejoiced at his deeds, jumping in the four directions, and in the morning all rejoiced with him.

In the west is Black Kangaroo Mouse, an expert thief, upon whom I called for help. He was friendly to me, and enveloped me in his mantle of darkness, making four halts on the way. After surveying the situation he approved of my plan. Sending forth his black darkness he pushed his way through it to the enemy, making four stops on the way. He opened the sack containing the most prized magic prop-

---

Âvak tcuvakikatc tcom stcova-akᴜpatkᶜ ᴜ-ᴜlĭt tak am sihafw(u).
It was clouds his it sprinkle thought that there inhale.

Âvak hᴜmatckam hᴜk tam ap âĭmᴜtᴜtam vatcom skᴜ-ᴜk
It was people that on there haunts it was good

tcᴜ-ᴜtckatvk ᴜ-ᴜlĭt tanᶁam haĭtco nᶁᴜitatkᶜ ᴜ-ᴜlĭt tak am sihâfw(u).
dream thought white thing seen thought that there inhale.

Âvak hᴜmatckam hᴜk tam ap âĭmᴜtᴜᶁam vatcom sᶜapᴜkam kat
It was people that on there haunts it was best bow

kia-atkam rᴣᴜɹ ta-atam vapᴜkᶜ tcoi-ĭta rᴣakᴜtcĭtkᶜ ᴜ ᴜlĭt tak
string straight flying reed clean had grasped he thought that

am sihâfw(u). An wᴜkatc katcĭm nanûkâ tcoi-ĭtckatc sinasĭk
there inhale. About round lay different belongings gathered

sᴜpapak(ĭ) kawoɹkatkᶜ pᴜk ha-ahâk i-iwoa. Ap opam kus
slowly grouped take turned back. There homeward kind of

stcᴜtak(ĭ) ᴜtcohokĭk woak hᴜk âĭtkᶜ ap ki-ĭkhâ sikaɹ mᴜtkᶜ
blue itself darkened throw that after there four round run

makai nata hokĭt an tâkûta. Smakaitkam â-âtam isivakssĭtk
magician fire edge about release. Expert musician people a prepared place with something spread to sit on

tam tarsᴜwoa. Vi-ĭkam sᴜpapak(ĭ) kawoɹkatkᶜ pᴜk opam kᴜs
on placed. Remainder slowly grouped take homeward kind of

stcᴜtak(ĭ) ᴜtcohokĭk woak âĭtkᶜ ap ki-ĭkhâ sikaɹ mᴜtkᶜ
blue itself darkened throw after there four round run

hihinakhimûk ᴜᴧâĭkᴜt tcᴜmâ-â. Hᴜkatc sᶜhai-ĭtcokam utatkᶜtcᶜ am
shouting his bed covered. With conceit felt there

a-aip tcᴜᶁakiwoa. Hᴜkatc hᴜk sia-aɹ tcotcĭm am ᴜta
all directions thud. With that east standing there in

sirsarsafᴜktcᶜ tcotc. Ĭm hotĭnyĭk takĭŏ kᴜs tcok nahakĭâ.
echoed stand. In sunset direction kind of black kangaroo mouse.

Wotpk hastcos ᴜskam kontak hap tcoĭ-ĭkam mamᴜtcᴜk ap imûk
Expert something robber I was that sort guess there my

rᴣârsoa kotak sĭnyhâĭ-ikᴜĭ-itam utatkᶜ amtcᴜt kᴜs stcok ᴜtcohokĭk
cry it was friendly felt there from kind of black itself darkened

woak âĭtkᶜ ap ki-ĭkhâ tahiwoak makai nata tcᴜmûk hokĭt an
throw after there four sitting magician fire covered edges about

tahiwoa. Am a-ai nynᴜhâk tcom nᶁᴜĭk âvak makai vâkĭta
sit. There all directions looking then saw it was magician trail

sitânâɹûtc katc. Kot hᴜk âĭtkᶜ kᴜs stcok ᴜtcohokĭk woak
brightly lay. It that after kind of black itself darkened throw

hᴜk âĭtkᶜ am ki-ĭkhâ tahiwoak ap sᴜpapak(ĭ) tcᴜmâ-â hᴜk
that after there four sitting there slowly covered that

erty of the enemy, though the sack was tied in many places, and took
from it the blue necklaces, blue earrings, down, and everything of that
nature before turning homeward. Enveloped in his yellow darkness
he reached me after four rests. Leaving all at the council ground he
went to his home, halting four times on the way. Rejoicing, he jumped
about, and the night rustled like the fluttering of leaves in sympathy
with him.

I called on Owl, above, for assistance. He was friendly to me and
came, sailing four times on the way. He looked about him and saw
my plan. In accordance with this he slowly reached the enemy after
sailing four times. He cut the power of the enemy, their springs,
their trees, and their dreams. He grasped their bows and arrows and

nyʋ â-apûta. Âva ĭt noarsamĭtc vatcom ha-akĭa ʋtam
my enemy. It was this bag was it many on top of another

hawolk ʋ-ʋlĭt tak am siki-ĭkassahimûk âĭtkᶜ am mawoak am
tied he thought that there bit off after there reach there

pʋĭ kʋs stcʋtak(ĭ) payoka tcʋkĭtaɟakatc. Kʋs skʋ-ʋk vi-ĭk
take kind of blue necklace hoard. Kind of good down

tcʋkĭtaɟakatc. An wʋkatc katcĭm nanûkâ tcoĭ-ĭtckatc si-inasĭk
hoard. About round laying different belongings gathered

sʋpapak(ĭ) kawoɽkatkᶜ pʋk opam ha-ahâk i-iwoa. Ap opam kʋs
slowly grouped take homeward turned back. There homeward kind of

stcok ʋtcohokĭk woak âĭtkᶜ ap ki-ĭkhâ tahiwoak makai nata tcʋmûk
black itself darkened throw after there four sitting magician fire everywhere

hokit an takĭtâ. Smakaitkam â-âtam isivakûsĭtkᶜ tam tarsʋwoa.
edges about release. Expert magician people seat on placed.

Vi-ĭkam sʋpapak(ĭ) kawoɽkatkᶜ pʋk am opam kʋs stcok ʋtcohokĭk
Remainder slowly grouped take there homeward kind of black itself darkened

woak âĭtkᶜ am ki-ĭkhâ tahiwoak ʋʌâĭkût tcʋmâ-â. Hʋkatc sᶜhaitcom
throw after there four sit his bed covered. With conceit

ʋtatkᶜ am a-aip tahiwop kʋk hʋkatc stcohokomom am ʋta si
felt there all directions sits that with darkness there in

rsamoñtc katc. Âva ĭt tam kʋs stcohokomom sikǎlktc katc. Âvak
rustling lay. It was this on kind of darkness round lay. It was

uta sᶜiâ-âmp ʋolĭntcᶜ kʋtânɟâm ʋ-ʋt vaohotam kontak hap tcoĭ-ĭkam
in right being held kind of white blood sucker I was that sort

mamûtcʋk ap imûk rsârsoâ tap sĭnyhâĭ-ĭkʋĭ-ĭtam ʋtatkᶜ amtcʋt
guess there my cry friendly felt there from

ki-ĭkhâ ikâmalwoak makai nata tcʋmûkᶜ tam ʋnakia. Am a-ai
four thin fly magician fire covered on hang. There all

nyʋnhâk tcom nyʋĭk âva makai vâkĭta tânâttc katc. Tʋk âĭtkᶜ
directions then saw it was magician trail brightly lay. That after
looking

am ki-ĭkhâ ikâmalwoak ap sʋpapak(ĭ) tcʋmâ-âk hʋk nyʋâpûta.
there four thin fly there slowly covered that me enemy.

Âvak tcʋwuɟ katc toa-akatc tcom sᶜʋnaki-ĭtc kʋk ʋ-ʋlĭt tak am
It was land lay mountain it hanging stand thought that there

sirsâ-ârspâɽ ki-ĭkomia. Rsârsânûkam rsorsok(ĭ) tâtoatc, os kʋrsatc
very short bit off. Springs waters his placed, tree plant his

tcotcom sĭs ʋnaki-ĭstc ʋ-ʋlĭt tak am sirsâ-ârspâɽ ki-ĭkomia.
standing very hanging thought that there short bit off.

Hʋmatckam hʋk tam ap âimutuɟam vatcom sĭs kʋ-ʋk tcʋtckatkᶜ
People that on there haunts was it very good dreamed

ʋ-ʋlĭt tak am sirsâ-ârspâɽ ki-ikomia. Vatcom sᶜapʋkam kat kiatkam
thought that there very short bit off. Was it good-best bow stringed

bit them in twain. He bit off their flesh and sinews, and in their bones made holes. From the things collected he made a belt from a bow-string and turned homeward. He came through his gray mist in four flights. Leaving all that he had secured in my behalf, he reached his home in four flights. At early dawn he rejoiced in his success and the darkness rattled with him.

You may think this over, my relatives. The taking of life brings serious thoughts of the waste; the celebration of victory may become unpleasantly riotous.

---

rsuɪ ta-atam vapûk(ᴜ) tcoĭ-ĭta rsaktcĭtkᶜ ᴜ-ᴜlĭt tak am sirsâ-ârspâ
straight flying reed clean had grasped thought that there very short

ki-ikomia. Am vak hᴜk tcohokatc ahava ki-ikomia. Katatc isi
bit off. There enter that flesh his then bit off. Bow his very

kiahontûk â-âtc kahaitcᴜtckarsk ap koapatkᶜ ap kĭrsa-atkᶜ ap opam
relaxed bones his perforate there wig there bark dress there turn

kᴜ tânɹâm ᴜtcohokĭk woak hᴜk âĭtkᶜ ap ki-ĭkhâ ikâmalwoak svaosĭm
kind of whitish itself darkened throw that after there four thin fly damp

isĭtckĭ. Makai nata tcᴜmûkᶜ hokĭt an takĭtâ. Smakaitkam â-âtam
rattling. Magician fire cover edges about release. Expert magician people

isivakssitk tam tarsᴜwoa. Vi-ĭkam sᴜpapak(ĭ) kawoɪkatk pᴜk am
a prepared place on sitting. Remainder slowly grouped take there
with something
spread to sit on

opam kᴜ tânɹâm ᴜtcohokĭk woak âĭtkᶜ am ki-ĭkhâ ikâmᴜlᴜwoak
homeward kind of whitish itself darkened throw after there four times thin fly

sᴜvaosĭm isĭtckĭm ᴜʌâĭkût tcᴜmâ-â. Hᴜkatc sᶜhaĭtcokûm ᴜtatktc
damp rattling his bed arrive. With conceit felt

am a-ai tai-ĭnyok âva hᴜkatc stcohokomom am ᴜta sisticᶜktckatc.
there all directions flying it was with darkness there in rattling lay.

S ha-ap hapûkᶜ hᴜmsa ᴜlĭtkᶜ tatcoa nanûkâ tcoĭkam nyi-imĭkĭ kotc
Way that you think plan different class my relatives we

hᴜmo hap patmatâtan hᴜk pat rsûĭka natc apahâpta kaihâkĭm kaĭtc.
now that lazy make that bad slave way proper noise said.

SACATON

b TCO'KŬT NAK, HOLDING A CALENDAR STICK

a ANTONIO AZUL

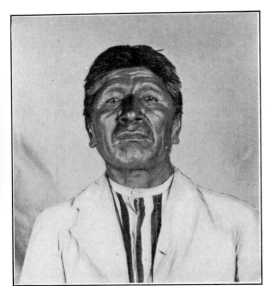

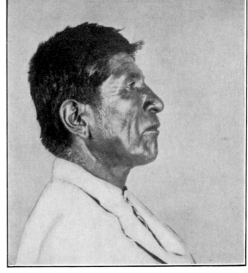

c KÂEMÂ-Â

THREE OF THE AUTHOR'S PIMA INFORMANTS

CASA GRANDE RUIN

a SANTAN (FROM THE WEST)

b RUIN BELOW SANTAN (FROM THE WEST)

c SWEETWATER (FROM THE SOUTHWEST)

a CASA BLANCA (FROM THE WEST)

b SCHOOLHOUSE RUINS

CASA BLANCA AND RUINS OF FIRST SCHOOLHOUSE

b ARROW-BUSH INCLOSED KITCHEN

c FIREPLACES

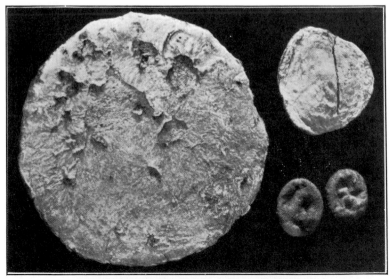

a FOURTEEN-POUND WHEAT LOAF; CORN BREAD; DOUGHNUTS

PIMA BREAD, KITCHEN, AND FIREPLACES

b CAT'S CLAW (ACACIA GREGGII)

a IRONWOOD (OLNEYA TESOTA)

IRONWOOD AND CAT'S CLAW

a HA'NÛM CACTUS (OPUNTIA ARBORESCENS)

b SAGUARO FOREST (CEREUS GIGANTEUS)

TWO VARIETIES OF CACTUS

d UNBRANCHED SAGUARO (CEREUS GIGANTEUS)

a CREOSOTE BUSH (LARREA MEXICANA)   *b* OKATILLA (FOUQUIERA SPLENDENS)
c SAGUARO (CEREUS GIGANTEUS), IN BACKGOUND

CHARACTERISTIC DESERT VEGETATION

a MESQUITE (PROSOPIS VELUTINA)

b PALOVERDE (PARKINSONIA TORREYANA)

MESQUITE AND PALOVERDE

a PIMA FIELDS

b KWAHADK' VILLAGE

c HOHOKAM FIELDS

FIELDS AND VILLAGE IN PIMERIA

CHOLLA CACTUS (OPUNTIA BIGELOVII ENGELM.)

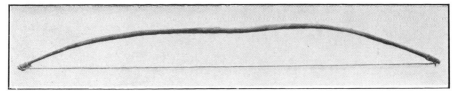

a WAR BOW

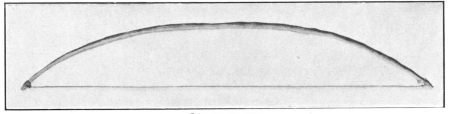

b HUNTING BOW

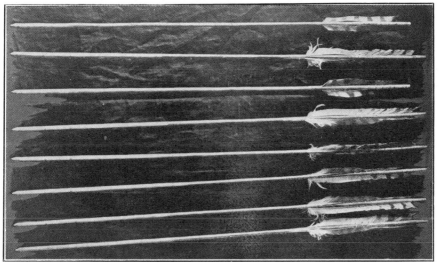

c HUNTING ARROWS

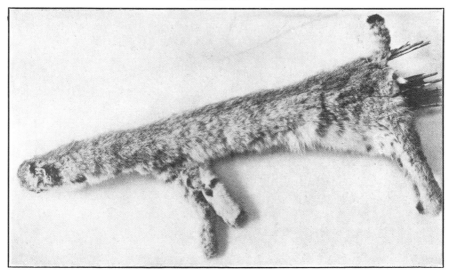

d QUIVER OF WILD-CAT SKIN

PIMA WEAPONS

a   *b*   *c*   *d*   *e*

A 'MÍNA

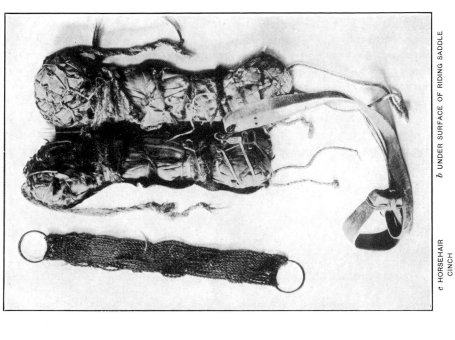

a UPPER SURFACE OF RIDING SADDLE

b UNDER SURFACE OF RIDING SADDLE

c HORSEHAIR CINCH

RIDING SADDLE AND CINCH

a SKÂSŎWALĬK HILLS CLAY PIT

c CLAY PIT NEAR THE GILA

b SCREENING CLAY AT PIT

CLAY PITS

a ROLLING CLAY

b SMOOTHING SURFACE AFTER APPLYING COIL

c SUPPORTING VESSEL ON LOOSE SAND

d DECORATING EXTERIOR

PIMA WOMAN MAKING POTTERY

b BEAN POT   *a* COOKING POT

c CANTEEN   *d* CANTEEN

e DOUBLE-NECKED CANTEEN

POTTERY—POTS AND CANTEENS

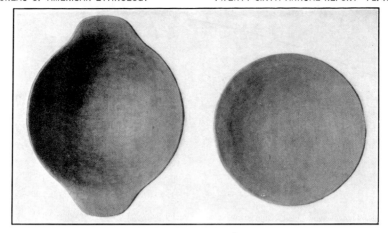

a PARCHING PAN b TORTILLA BAKING PLATE

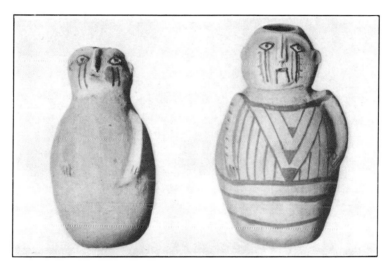

d EFFIGY VASES

c PLATE e CUP f PLATE

POTTERY—PAN, PLATES, VASES, CUP

a ANCIENT SPOON   *b* NEW SPOON

c BOWL

d COILED BOWLS

e DECORATED BOWLS

POTTERY—SPOONS AND BOWLS

a ARROW BUSH (PLUCHEA BOREALIS)

b BA3CHARIS GLUTENOSA

c CRUCIFIXION THORN (HOLOCANTHA EMORYI) SURROUNDED BY SALTBUSHES

CHARACTERISTIC DESERT VEGETATION

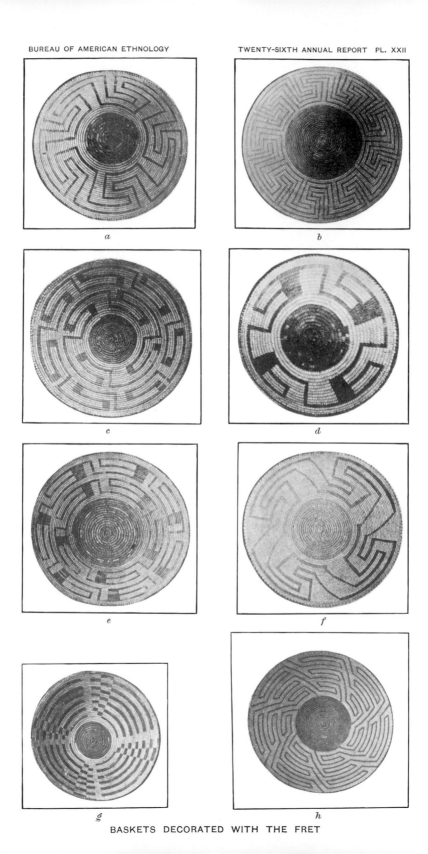

BASKETS DECORATED WITH THE FRET

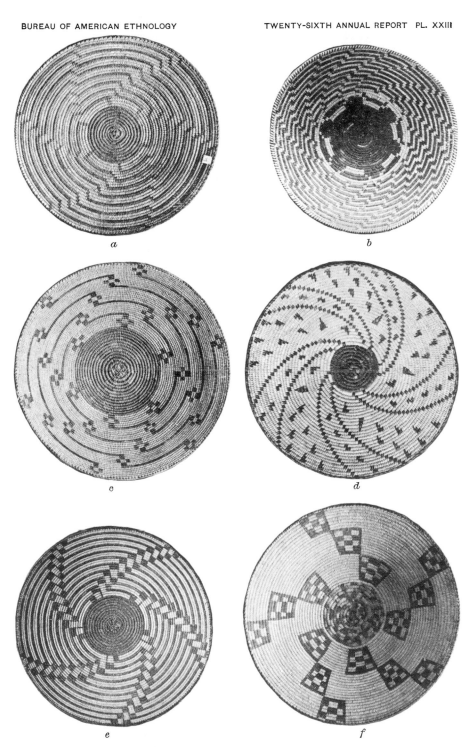

BASKETS DECORATED WITH THE FRET

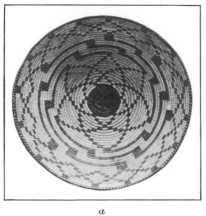

a

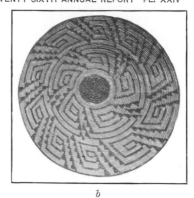

b

c

d

e

f

BASKETS

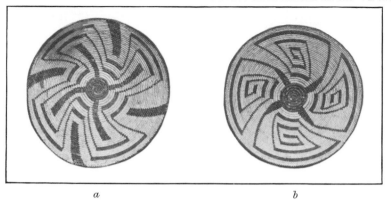

a   b

c   d

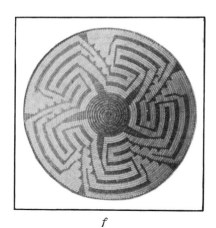

e   f

BASKETS

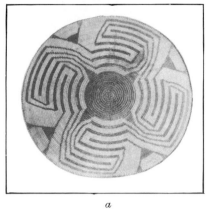

a

b

c

d

e

f

BASKETS

a

b

c

d

e

f

BASKETS

a

b

c

d

e

f

BASKETS DECORATED WITH FLOWER-LIKE PATTERNS

BASKETS, UPRIGHT FORMS

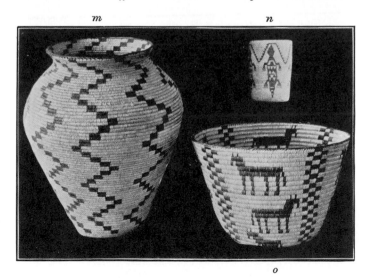

BASKETS, UPRIGHT FORMS

a   *b*

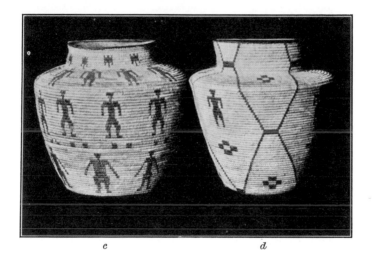

c   *d*

e   *f*

BASKETS, UPRIGHT FORMS

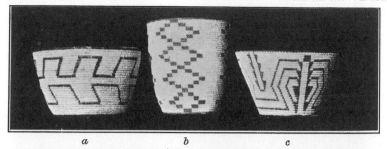

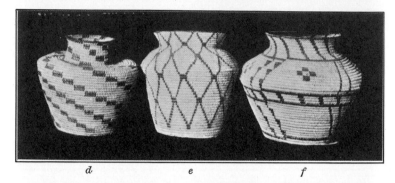

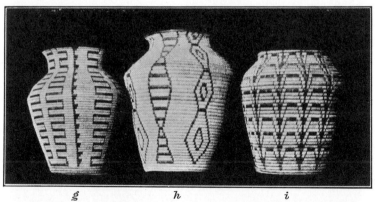

BASKETS, VARIANTS OF UPRIGHT FORMS

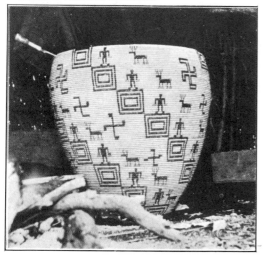

a

b

c

d

YAVAPAI BASKETS

a LOADING THE KIÂHÂ

b RISING WITH THE LOAD

c THE LOAD IN POSITION

d REMOVING THE LOAD

WOMAN WITH KIÂHÂ

a FRAMEWORK OF HOUSE

d SHED FRAME

b BLANKET DOOR

f STOREHOUSE AND WAGON SHED

c EARTH-COVERED HOUSES

e SHED DOOR

HOUSES AND SHEDS

ARROW-BUSH KITCHEN AND PIMA WOMAN

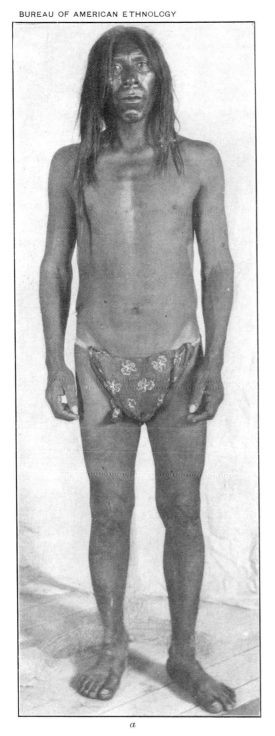
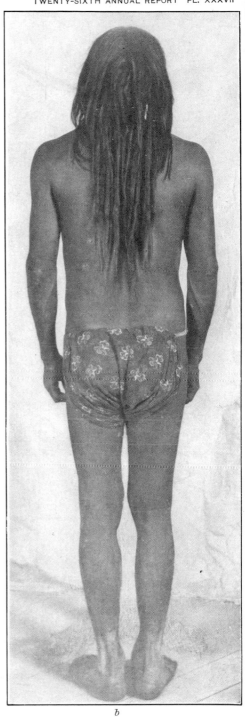

a   *b*

PIMA MAN, SHOWING COSTUME WORN IN HOT WEATHER

a

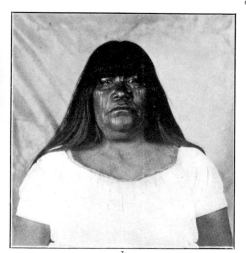

b

d

c

PIMA WOMEN, SHOWING MODES OF HAIRDRESSING AND FACE PAINTING

a CEMETERY AT SACATON

b CEMETERY AT STATANYIK

c GRAVE AT STATANYIK

CEMETERIES AND GRAVE

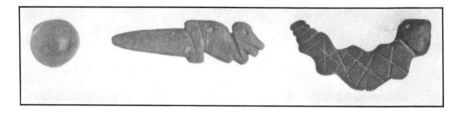

OBJECTS FROM HÂHÂTESUMIEHĬN SHRINE

a CEREMONIAL HILL NEAR DOUBLE BUTTES

b HÂHÂTESUMIEHĬN SHRINE

c SHRINE NEAR DOUBLE BUTTES

CEREMONIAL HILL AND SHRINES

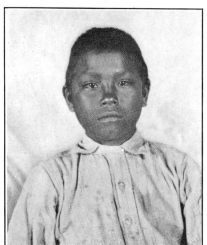

PIMA MEN AND BOY

a PANHOP

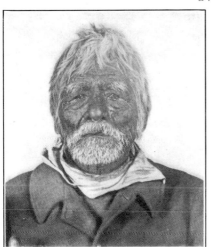

b MARICOPA ANTOINE

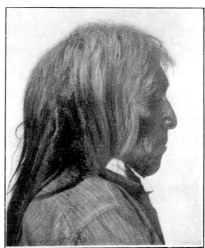

c KOSPITO

ELDERLY PIMA MEN

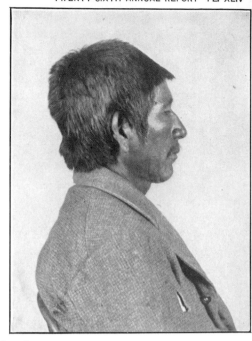

a VI-CÛK-RÂ-E-HĬN

b KÂ'MÂL TKÂK, THIN LEATHER

PIMA MEN

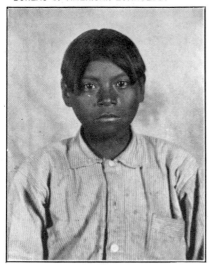

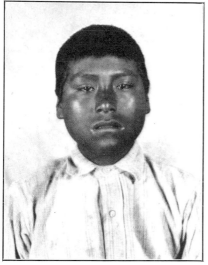
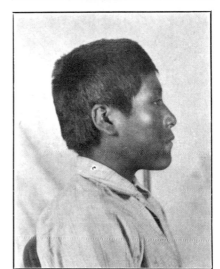

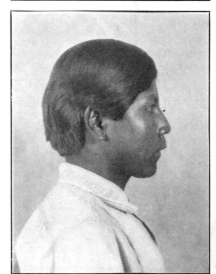

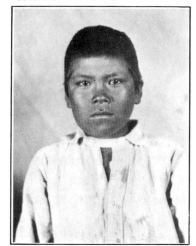
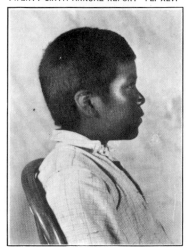
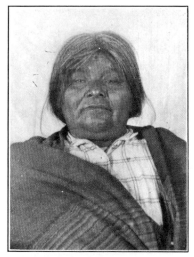

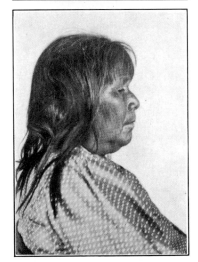

PIMA BOY AND WOMEN

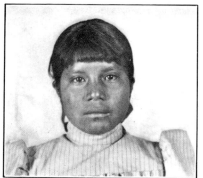
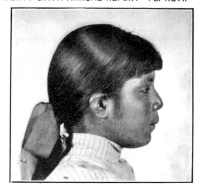
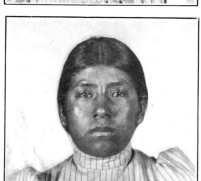
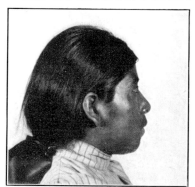
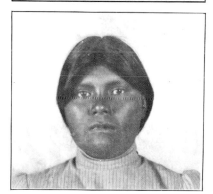
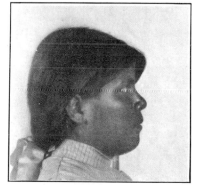
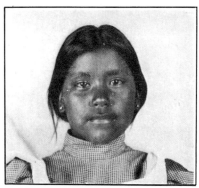
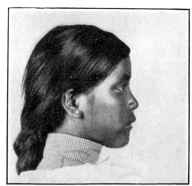

PIMA GIRLS

CITATION SOURCES

The editor has provided the following list of sources for Russell's citations in both the text and footnotes of the original volume. The list is arranged according to text page numbers, including the letter notation where it is employed as a key to footnotes.

19a	Mowry 1864: 30	34a	Brinton 1885a
19b	Velarde 1856: 345	34b	Mallery 1877, 1886, 1893
20a	Gatschet 1877: I: 156	35a	Mooney 1898
20b	Shea 1859–1862: V;	35b	Mallery 1893: 227; Seaver
	Smith 1862b		1827: 70
20c	Browne 1869a: 110, 290;	35c	Clark 1885: 211; Mooney 1898:
	Chapman 1859 (see Bailey 1859:		142
	559); [Nentvig] 1894: 128, 129;	36a	Baegert 1864–1865: 388
	Rusling 1874: 369; Whipple,	36b	United States. *Department of*
	Ewbank, and Turner 1855: 123		*Agriculture. Weather Bureau*
21a	Font 1775–1776a: 35		1901: I: 289
23a	[Nentvig] 1894: 192	37a	Mallery 1893: 271
24b	Bartlett 1854: II: 248	43a	Alegre 1841–1842: II: 218
24c	Cushing 1890: 155	47a	Bancroft 1889: 501; Cremony
24d	Sedelmayr 1856: 847		1868: 148; Ives 1861: 45;
24e	Bandelier 1884: 80, 81; 1892:		Mowry 1858b: 588
	463, 464	48b	Bancroft 1889: 514. The
26a	Garcés 1900: II: 386–387		one-armed trader who sold his
28a	Bancroft 1889: 362		store to Ammi White was Silas
29a	Font 1775–1776a: 48–52;		St. John. The capture of White by
	Pfefferkorn 1794–1795: I: 6		the Confederates is documented,
30	Cooke 1848: 557–558; Emory		among other places, in Barrett
	1848a; Johnston 1848		(1897).
30a	Pattie 1833	50b	Browne 1869a: 121
30b	Browne 1869a: 118	51a	Collins 1863: 239; Walker
31	Couts 1846–1849		1860c: 168
31a	Bancroft 1889: 479	52b	Bancroft 1889: 536
31b	Bartlett 1854	54b	Bourke 1891: 191–200
31c	Parke 1855a: 5	55a	Carlos Montezuma was a
31d	Bailey 1859: 556; Ruggles		Yavapai. He ultimately died and
	1867: 163		was buried on the Ft. McDowell
31e	Mowry 1860b: 723		Reservation in Arizona. For a
32a	Browne 1969a: 19		somewhat fictionalized account
32b	Bancroft 1889: 548		of his life, see Arnold (1951).
32c	Mowry 1860: 727	56b	United States. *Department of*
32d	Poston 1864: 386		*Agriculture. Weather Bureau*
33a	Lippincott 1900: 10		1901: I: 292

58b	Cremony 1868: 117		(Mange 1954: 84–87). The
59a	Jackson 1884a: 6		AGN manuscript is cited in
59c	Whittemore and Cook 1893		Bolton (1913: 54).
60b	Goodfellow 1887	83a	Evermann and Rutter 1895;
60c	Kate 1892: 119		Garcés 1900: II: 142; Jordon
62b	Emory 1848a: 86		1900
67a	The manuscript in the	84a	John J. Thornber, from an

67a The manuscript in the Hemenway Collection, copied by Bandelier and attributed by him to Father Kino, is doubtless that of Martín Bernal (1856). It is signed by Martín Bernal, Kino, and others, but the former is actually the author. It has appeared in translated form (Martín Bernal 1966), the shortage of pinole being mentioned on page 42. Bolton (1960: 371) refers to the same shortage in his biography of Kino.

I have been unable to locate the "Hemenway Collection," although it may refer to the Hemenway materials now in the possession of the Museum of the American Indian, Heye Foundation, in New York City.

84a John J. Thornber, from an unpublished source
85a Emory 1848a: 84
86a Emory 1848a: 85
86b Lippincott 1900: 36
87a Hodge 1893: 324
87b Blake 1902: 710
87c See note 82a
87d Garcés 1854: 235
90a Browne 1869a: 110
91a Garcés 1900: I: 170; Heintzelman 1857: 36
92a Brinton 1885b
93a [Nentvig] 1894: 129
94a Walker 1860b: 720
95a Bourke 1890: 210
96c Bartlett 1854: II: 237
103d Mason 1896: 524
104a Edward Palmer, from an unpublished source
104b Mason 1889: 184
111b Cushing 1890: 179
116a Venegas 1759: I: 99
125a Langenbeck 1895: 60
141a Bartlett 1854: II: 236
143a Mason 1895: 251; 1896: 471
144a Bandelier 1892: 426
148a Bartlett 1854: II: 225; Emory 1848a: 85
149a Bartlett 1854: II: 229
149b Bartlett 1854: II: 225
153c Froebel 1857–1858: II: 440
153d Barrows 1901: 755 (see Jenks 1901: 755)
154a Bartlett 1854: II: 233
155a Emory 1848a: 85
165a Mowry 1864: 30. Schoolcraft (1851–1857: III: 297–299) publishes a translation by Buckingham Smith of a small portion of a manuscript by Francisco Garcés (1775–1776) located by Smith in the *Archivo General y Público de la Nación* in Mexico City. It has been published once in Spanish (Garcés 1854: 326–330) and additionally, in a second version, in English translation (Garcés

67b Pfefferkorn 1794–1795: II: 132
71a McGee 1898: 212
72a Baegert 1864–1865: 363; Garcés 1854: 438; Venegas 1759: I: 82
74a [Harrington] 1889: 30
76a Venegas 1759: I: 45
76b Arricivita 1792: 396; Buschmann 1857a: 321, 322; Duflot de Mofras 1844: I: 208
77a Poston 1865a: 153
79a Edward Palmer, from an unpublished source
80a John J. Thornber, from an unpublished source
80b Albert K. Fisher, from an unpublished source
82a Schoolcraft (1851–1857: III: 301–303) publishes a translation by Buckingham Smith of a small portion of a manuscript by Juan M. Mange (1693–1721) located by Smith in the *Archivo General y Público de la Nación* in Mexico City. It has been published in Spanish twice (Mange 1856: 282–284; 1926: 252–254) and in English translation an additional time

1900: II: 373–388). A third version of the same diary has also been translated into English (Garcés 1965: 72–74). The AGN copy of the manuscript is cited in Bolton (1913: 26).

167a   Whipple, Ewbank, and Turner 1855: 52. Volume "II" as cited in Russell should be volume "III."

169a   Lumholtz 1900: 189

175a   Culin 1898: 738

176a   Culin 1898: 739

180a   Culin 1898: 742

182a   Rusling 1874: 361

187a   Bourke 1896: 114

187b   Cushing 1896: 335

188a   Whipple, Ewbank, and Turner 1855: 35

188b   Alegre 1841–1842: II: 217

195a   Bourke 1889: 184

196a   Poston 1865a: 153

196b   [Nentvig] 1894: 129

197b   Villa-Señor y Sánchez 1746–1748: I: 396

198a   Emory 1848a: 84; Froebel 1857–1858: II: 448, 449; Johnston 1848: 600. Schoolcraft (1851–1857: III: 299–301) publishes a translation by Buckingham Smith of a small portion of a manuscript by Pedro Font (1775–1776b) located by Smith in the *Archivo General y Público de la Nación* in Mexico City. The so-called "short diary" (in contrast to Font 1775–1776a), has subsequently been published in Spanish once (Font 1913: 18, 20, 22) and in English translation twice (Font 1913: 19, 21, 23; 1930b: 214–217). The AGN manuscript is cited in Bolton (1913: 26), but another copy is in the Bancroft Library, University of California,

Berkeley. For the Mange manuscript translated in Schoolcraft (1851–1857: III: 301–303), see note 82a.

198b   Poston 1865a: 152

199a   Browne 1869a: 84

200a   Garcés 1900: II: 449

201a   Mowry 1858b: 587

202a   Whipple, Ewbank, and Turner 1855: 30

204a   Bourke 1891: 203

212a   Font 1775–1776a: 23–24a

216a   Bourke 1889: 178

217   The Latin on this page, written in more prudish times, translates: "She carried the coyote on her shoulders, but when she had gone only a few steps, the coyote exclaimed, 'Stop! Stop! I am hurting. Let me down a little while.'

"When she had done what he requested he was able to copulate with her, doing this shameful thing to the woman. Then he took her home with him and repeated the act."

221a   Bandelier 1892: 462–463

239a   Bourke 1889: 178

239b   Matthews 1883: 216

240a   Emory 1848a: 83

252a   Bourke 1889: 181; Garcés 1900: I: 122

252b   Matthews 1883: 224

257a   Venegas 1759: I: 98, 100

260a   Lumholtz 1900: 63

269   Buschmann 1857a: 367; Gallatin 1848: 129; Hervás y Panduro 1787: 124–125; Latham 1850: 390–393; Mühlenpfordt 1844: 225; Pfefferkorn 1794–1795: II: *passim*; Schoolcraft 1851–1857: III: 461; Scouler 1841: 248; Whipple, Ewbank, and Turner 1855: 94.

BIBLIOGRAPHY

Alegre, Francisco J.
1841–   *Historia de la Compañía de Jesús en Nueva-España.* Three volumes.
1842   Edited by Carlos M. Bustamante. México, Impr. de J. M. Lara.
1956–   *Historia de la provincia de la Compañía de Jesús de Nueva España.*
1960   Four volumes. Edited by Ernest J. Burrus and Felix Zubillaga. Rome,
        Institutum Historicum, S.J.

Anonymous
1862   Vocabulary of the Eudeve. A dialect of the Pima language, spoken in
        Sonora. *The Historical Magazine,* Vol. 6, no. 1 (January), pp. 18–19.
        New York, Charles B. Richardson & Co.; London, Trübner & Co.

Arizona. *University of Arizona. Arizona State Museum.*
n.d.   "Calendar stick." One-page mimeographed account of a Papago calendar
        stick, 1842–1938. Tucson, Arizona State Museum.

Arizona. *University of Arizona. Bureau of Ethnic Research.*
1971   *Political organization and business management in the Gila River Indian
        Community.* Tucson, The University of Arizona, Bureau of Ethnic
        Research.

Arnold, Oren
1951   *Savage son.* Albuquerque, University of New Mexico Press.

Arricivita, Juan D.
1792   *Crónica seráfica y apostólica del colegio de propaganda fide de la Santa
        Cruz de Querétaro en la Nueva España.* México, Por D.F. de Zúñiga
        y Ontiveros.

Baegert, Jakob
1772   *Nachrichten von der Amerikanischen Halbinsel Californien . . .* Mann-
        heim, Churfürstl. hof- und academiebuchdr.
1864–   An account of the aboriginal inhabitants of the California peninsula.
1865   Translated by Charles Rau. *Annual Report of the Board of Regents of
        the Smithsonian Institution for 1863 (House Miscellaneous Documents,*
        no. 83, 38th Congress, 1st session), pp. 352–369, and *Annual Report of
        the Board of Regents of the Smithsonian Institution for 1864,* pp. 378–
        399. Washington, Government Printing Office.
1882   An account of the aboriginal inhabitants of the California peninsula.
        Translated by Charles Rau. In *Articles on anthropological subjects con-
        tributed to the annual reports of the Smithsonian Institution from 1863
        to 1877,* pp. 2–41. Washington, Smithsonian Institution.
1942   *Noticias de la península americana de California.* Translated by Pedro
        R. Hendrichs. México, Antigua Librería Robredo José Porrúa e Hijos.
1952   *Observations in Lower California.* Translated by M. M. Brandenburg
        and Carl L. Baumann. Berkeley, University of California Press.

[443]

Bahr, Donald M.
  1971   Who were the Hohokam? The evidence from Pima-Papago myths.
          Ethnohistory, Vol. 18, no. 3 (Summer), pp. 245–266. Tucson, American
          Society for Ethnohistory.
Bahr, Donald M.; Juan Gregorio, David Lopez and Albert Alvarez
  1973   *Piman shamanism and staying sickness* (ká:cim múmkidag). Tucson,
          The University of Arizona Press.
Bailey, G.
  1858a   [Letter to Charles E. Mix, Commissioner of Indian Affairs, November 4,
          1858.] *Report of the Commissioner of Indian Affairs, accompanying the
          Annual Report of the Secretary of the Interior, for the year 1858*, pp.
          202–208. Washington, Wm. A. Harris, printer.
  1858b   [Same.] *Report of the Commissioner of Indian Affairs* [for 1858] *(House
          Executive Documents*, no. 2, 35th Congress, 2nd session), pp. 554–560.
          Washington, James B. Steedman, printer.
  1859   [Same.] *Senate Executive Documents*, no. 1, part 1, 35th Congress,
          2nd session, pp. 554–560. Washington, William A. Harris, printer.
Bancroft, Hubert H.
  1886   The native races [of the Pacific states]. Vol. 3. *The works of Hubert Howe
          Bancroft*, Vol. 3. San Francisco, The History Company.
  1889   History of Arizona and New Mexico, 1530–1888. *The Works of Hubert
          Howe Bancroft*, Vol. 17. San Francisco, The History Company.
Bandelier, Adolph F. A.
  1884   Reports by A. F. Bandelier on his investigations in New Mexico during
          the years 1883–84. *Annual Report of the Executive Committee of the
          Archaeological Institute of America*, Vol. 5, pp. 55–98. Cambridge,
          John Wilson and Son.
  1892   Final report of investigations among the Indians of the southwestern
          United States, carried on mainly in the years from 1880 to 1885. Part II.
          Papers of the Archaeological Institute of America, American Series,
          no. 4. Cambridge, University Press.
Barrett, James
  1897   [Letter to Major E. A. Rigg, March 19, 1862]. *War of the Rebellion:
          a compilation of the official records of the Union and Confederate armies*,
          series 1, Vol. 50, part 1, p. 940. Washington, Government Printing Office.
Barrows, David P.
  1901   (See Jenks 1901).
Bartlett, John R.
  1854   *Personal narrative of explorations and incidents in Texas, New Mexico,
          California, Sonora, and Chihuahua.* Two volumes. New York and
          London, D. Appleton and Company.
  1965   [*Same.*] Chicago, Rio Grande Press, Inc.
Beals, Ralph L.
  1934   *Material culture of the Pima, Papago, and Western Apache.* Berkeley,
          U.S. Department of the Interior, National Park Service, Field Division
          of Education.
Blake, William P.
  1901   The caliche of southern Arizona. *The Engineering and Mining Journal*,
          Vol. 72, no. 19 (November 9), pp. 601–602. New York, The Engineering
          and Mining Journal, Inc.
  1902   The caliche of southern Arizona: an example of deposition by the vadose
          circulation. *Transactions of the American Institute of Mining Engineers*,
          Vol. 31, pp. 220–226. New York, The Institute.
Bolton, Herbert E.
  1913   Guide to materials for the history of the United States in the principal
          archives of Mexico. *Publications of the Carnegie Institution of Washing-
          ton*, no. 163. Washington.

1960   *Rim of christendom.* New York, Russell & Russell.

Bourke, John G.
1889   Notes on the cosmogony and theogeny of the Mojave Indians of the Rio Colorado, Arizona. *The Journal of American Folk-Lore,* Vol. 2, no. 6 (July-September), pp. 169–189. Boston [etc., etc.], American Folk-Lore Society.
1890   Notes on Apache mythology. *The Journal of American Folk-Lore,* Vol. 3, no. 10 (July-September), pp. 209–212. Boston [etc., etc.], American Folk-Lore Society.
1891   *On the border with Crook.* New York, Charles Scribner's Sons.
1896   Notes on the language and folk-usage of the Rio Grande Valley. *The Journal of American Folk-Lore,* Vol. 9, no. 33 (April-June), pp. 81–116. Boston [etc., etc.], American Folk-Lore Society.
1962   *On the border with Crook.* Chicago, Rio Grande Press, Inc.
1969   [*Same; indexed.*] Glorieta, New Mexico, Rio Grande Press, Inc.

Breazeale, James F.
1923   *The Pima and his basket.* Tucson, Arizona Archaeological and Historical Society.
1927   A tale from a calendar stick. *Progressive Arizona;* Vol. 5, no. 4 (October), pp. 13–14, 30. Tucson, Ward Shelby Publications, Inc.
1951   Ho-ho-kum days in Pimeria. In *My calendar stick,* by James F. Breazeale, pp. 126–127. N.p., n.p.

Brennan, José Lewis
1958   "Gold placer of Quijotoa, Ariz." Edited by Bernard L. Fontana. Mimeographed; 15 pages. Tucson, Bernard L. and Hazel M. Fontana.
1959   José Lewis Brennan's account of Papago "customs and other references." Edited by Bernard L. Fontana. *Ethnohistory,* Vol. 6, no. 3 (Summer), pp. 226–237. Bloomington, American Indian Ethnohistoric Conference.

Brinton, Daniel G.
1885a   The Lenâpé and their legends . . . *Library of Aboriginal American Literature,* no. 5. Philadelphia, D. G. Brinton.
1885b   *The lineal measures of the semi-civilized nations of Mexico and Central America.* Philadelphia.

Brown, Herbert
1906   A Pima-Maricopa ceremony. *American Anthropologist,* Vol. 8, no. 4 (October-December), pp. 688–690. Lancaster, American Anthropological Association.

Browne, John R.
1864–   A tour through Arizona . . . *Harper's New Monthly Magazine,* Vol. 29,
1865   no. 11 (October), pp. 553–574; no. 12 (November), pp. 689–711; Vol. 30, no. 1 (December), pp. 22–33; no. 2 (January), pp. 137–149; no. 3 (February), pp. 283–293; and no. 4 (March), pp. 409–423. New York, Harper and Brothers.
1869a   *Adventures in the Apache country: a tour through Arizona and Sonora, with notes on the silver regions of Nevada.* New York, Harper and Brothers.
1869b   [*Same.*] London, S. Low, Son, and Marston.
1871a   [*Same.*] New York, Harper and Brothers.
1871b   Reisen und Abenteur im Apachenlande. Translated by H. Hertz. *Bibliothek geographischer Reisen und Entdeckungen alterer und neuerer Zeit,* Vol. 6. Jena, H. Costenoble.
1878   [*Same as 1869a.*] New York, Harper and Brothers.
1950   *A tour through Arizona, 1864, or adventures in the Apache country.* Limited edition. Tucson, Arizona Silhouettes.
1951   [*Same.*] Trade edition. Tucson, Arizona Silhouettes.

Buschmann, Johann C. E.
  1857a   Die Pima-sprache und die sprache der Koloschen. *Abhandlungen der Königlichen Akademie der Wissenschaften zu Berlin aus dem Jahre 1856,* part 3, pp. 321–432. Berlin.
  1857b   [*Same.*] Berlin, Gedruckt in der Druckerei der Königlichen Akademie der Wissenschaften; in Commission bei F. Dümmler's Verlags-Buchhandlung.

Cain, H. Thomas
  1962   *Pima Indian basketry.* Phoenix, Heard Museum of Anthropology and Primitive Arts.

Castetter, Edward F., and Willis H. Bell
  1942   Pima and Papago Indian agriculture. *Inter-Americana Studies,* Vol. 1. Albuquerque, University of New Mexico Press.

Chapman, A. B.
  1858   *See* Bailey 1859.

Clark, William P.
  1885   *The Indian sign language* . . . Philadelphia, L. R. Hamersly & Company.

Collins, James L.
  1862   Report of the superintendent of New Mexico Indian affairs. *Report of the Commissioner of Indian Affairs* [for 1862] *(House Executive Documents,* no. 1, Vol. 2, 37th Congress, 3rd session), pp. 382–386. Washington, Government Printing Office.
  1863   Report of the superintendent of New Mexico Indian Affairs. *Report of the Commissioner of Indian Affairs for the year 1862,* pp. 238–242. Washington, Government Printing Office.

Cooke, Philip St. George
  1848   Report of Lieut. Col. P. St. George Cooke of his march from Santa Fe, New Mexico, to San Diego, Upper California. *House Executive Documents,* no. 41, pp. 549–563, 30th Congress, 1st session. Washington, Wendell and Van Benthuysen, printers.
  1849   Journal of the march of the Mormon battalion . . . *Senate Documents,* no. 2, pp. 2–85, 31st Congress, special session, 1849. Washington, printed at the Union Office.
  1878   *The conquest of New Mexico and California.* New York, G. P. Putnam's Sons.
  1938   Cooke's journal of the march of the Mormon battalion. In *Southwest Historical Series,* edited by Ralph P. Bieber, Vol. 7, pp. 65–240. Glendale, Arthur H. Clark Company.
  1964   *The conquest of New Mexico and California.* Chicago, Rio Grande Press, Inc.

Cormack, Charles W.
  1968   "Social structure and economic production on an Arizona Indian reservation." Unpublished Ph.D. dissertation, Department of Anthropology, The University of Arizona, Tucson.

Couts, Cave J.
  1846–   "Diary." Ms., scribe's copy, Bancroft Library, University of California,
  1849   Berkeley.
  1961   *Hepah, California! The journal of Cave Johnson Couts* . . . Edited by Henry F. Dobyns. Tucson, Arizona Pioneers' Historical Society.

Cremony, John C.
  1868   *Life among the Apaches.* San Francisco, A. Roman and Company.
  1951   [*Same.*] Tucson, Arizona Silhouettes.
  1969   [*Same.*] Glorieta, New Mexico, Rio Grande Press, Inc.

Culin, Stewart
  1898   Chess and playing-cards. *Report of the U.S. National Museum for 1896,* pp. 665–942. Washington, Government Printing Office.

1907   Games of the North American Indians. *Annual Report of the Bureau of American Ethnology,* Vol. 24, pp. 3–846. Washington, Government Printing Office.

Curtin, Leonora S. M.
1949   *By the prophet of the earth.* Santa Fe, San Vincente Foundation, Inc.

Curtis, Edward S.
1907–   *The North American Indian.* 20 volumes. Seattle, E. S. Curtis; Cam-
1930   bridge, Massachusetts, The University Press.
1909   Village tribes of the desert land. *Scribner's Magazine,* Vol. 45, no. 3 (March), pp. 275–287. New York, Charles Scribner's Sons.

Cushing, Frank H.
1890   Preliminary notes on the origin, working hypothesis and preliminary researches of the Hemenway southwestern archaeological expedition. *Congrès International des Americanistes,* 7me session (Berlin, 1888), pp. 151–194. Berlin, Libraire W. H. Kühl.
1896   Outlines of Zuni creation myths. *Annual Report of the Bureau of American Ethnology,* Vol. 13, pp. 321–447. Washington, Government Printing Office.

DiPeso, Charles C.
1956   The upper Pima of San Cayctano del Tumacacori. *The Amerind Foundation, Inc.,* no. 7. Dragoon, Arizona.

Douglas, Frederic H.
1930   Pima Indian close coiled basketry. *Denver Art Museum Leaflet Series,* no. 5, pp. 17–20. Denver.
1939   A Pima wood bowl. *Material Culture Notes,* no. 11, pp. 43–46. Denver, Denver Art Museum. [Reprinted in 1969 on pp. 60–64 of a revised edition.]
1953   Five Pima pots. *Material Culture Notes,* no. 18, pp. 83–86. Denver, Denver Art Museum. [Reprinted in 1969 on pp. 110–113 of a revised edition.]

Drucker, Philip
1941   Culture element distributions: XVII: Yuman-Piman. *Anthropological Records,* Vol. 6, no. 3. Berkeley and Los Angeles, University of California.

Duclos, Antoinette S.
1939   Rhythm that comes from the earth. *Desert Magazine,* Vol. 2, no. 4 (February), pp. 12–14. El Centro, California, Desert Publishing Company.

Duflot de Mofras, Eugène
1844   *Exploration du territoire de l'Orégon, des Californies et de la Mer Vermeille* . . . Two volumes. Paris, A. Bertrand.
1937   *Duflot de Mofras' travels on the Pacific coast* . . . Two volumes. Translated and edited by Marguerite Eyer Wilbur. Santa Ana, California, Fine Arts Press.
1968   *Exploration du territoire de l'Orégon, des Californies et de la Mer Vermeille* . . . Two volumes. Microcard edition. Louisville, LCP.

Emory, William H.
1848a   Notes of a military reconnaissance, from Ft. Leavenworth, in Missouri, to San Diego, in California . . . *House Executive Documents,* no. 41, pp. 5–126, 30th Congress, 1st session. Washington, Wendell and Van Benthuysen, printers.
1848b   [*Same.*] *Senate Executive Documents,* no. 7, pp. 5–126, 30th Congress, 1st session. Washington, Wendell and Van Benthuysen, printers.
1848c   [*Same as 1848b,* separately published, includes more illustrations.] New York, H. Long and Brother.
1848d   Major Emory's narrative. In *Notes of travel in California,* pp. 79–311. Dublin, J. M'Glashan; New York, Appleton and Company.
1951   *Lieutenant Emory reports.* Introduction by Ross Calvin. Albuquerque, University of New Mexico Press.

Evermann, B. W., and Cloud Rutter
1895   The fishes of the Colorado basin. *Bulletin of the U.S. Fish Commission*,
        Vol. 14 (1894), pp. 473–486. Washington, Government Printing Office.
Ezell, Paul H.
1957   The conditions of Hispanic-Piman contacts on the Gila River. *América
        Indígena*, Vol. 17, no. 2 (April), pp. 163–191. México, Instituto Indi-
        genista Interamericano.
1961   The hispanic acculturation of the Gila River Pimas. *Memoirs of the
        American Anthropological Association*, no. 90. Menasha, Wisconsin.
1963   Is there a Hohokam-Pima culture continuum? *American Antiquity*,
        Vol. 29, no. 1 (July), pp. 61–66. Salt Lake City, Society for American
        Archaeology.
Ferdon, Edwin N., Jr.
1967   The Hohokam "ball court," an alternative view of its function. *The Kiva*,
        Vol. 33, no. 1 (October), pp. 1–14. Tucson, Arizona Archaeological
        and Historical Society.
Field, Clark
1969   Pima basketry. *Arizona Archaeologist*, no. 4, pp. 21–33. Phoenix, Ari-
        zona Archaeological Society, Inc.
Font, Pedro
1775–   "Diario que formó el P. P.^{dor} Ap.^{co} Fr. Pedro Font . . . en el viage que
1776a   hizo à Monterey." Ms., original in the John Carter Brown Library,
        Providence, Rhode Island.
1775–   "Diario que forma el P. Fr. Pedro Font Pd.^{or} Ap.^{co} del Colegio de la
1776b   Sta Cruz de Querétaro, sacado del borrador que escribo en el camino,
        del viage que hizo à Monterey y Puerte de Sn Francisco . . ." Horcasitas,
        September 29, 1775 — Horcasitas, June 23, 1776. Copies in the *Archivo
        General y Pública de la Nación*, Mexico City [see Bolton 1913; 26] and
        in the Bancroft Library, University of California, Berkeley.
1913   Diary of Pedro Font. Translated and edited by Frederick J. Teggart.
        Publications of the Academy of Pacific Coast History, Vol. 3, no. 1
        (March). Berkeley, University of California.
1930a   Diary kept by the Father Preacher Fray Pedro Font . . . during the
        journey which he made to Monterey. In *Anza's California expeditions*,
        translated and edited by Herbert E. Bolton, Vol. 4, pp. xiii–534. Berkeley,
        University of California Press.
1930b   Font's short diary. In *Anza's California expeditions*, translated by Herbert
        E. Bolton, Vol. 3, pp. 201–307. Berkeley, University of California Press.
Fontana, Bernard L.; William J. Robinson, Charles W. Cormack and Ernest E.
        Leavitt, Jr.
1962   *Papago Indian pottery*. Seattle, University of Washington Press.
Froebel, Julius
1857–   *Aus Amerika*. Two volumes. Leipzig, J. J. Weber.
1858
1859   *Seven years' travel in Central America, northern Mexico, and the Far
        West of the United States*. London, Richard Bentley.
1861   *À travers l'Amérique*. Three volumes. Brussels and Leipzig, A. Lacroix,
        Verboeckhoven and Company; Paris, E. Jung-Treuttel.
Gallatin, Albert
1848   Hale's Indians of north-west America, and vocabularies of North Amer-
        ica. *Transactions of the American Ethnological Society*, Vol. 2, pp.
        xxiii–130. New York, Bartlett and Welford.
Garcés, Francisco T. H.
1775–   "Diario y derrotero que siguió el M.R.P. Fr. Francisco Garcés en su

1776   viaje hecho desde Octubre de 1775 hasta 17 de Setiembre de 1776, al Rio Colorado para reconocer las naciones que habitan sus márgenes, y a los pueblos del Moqui del Nuevo-México." Manuscript in the *Archivo General y Público de la Nación*, México [see Bolton 1913: 26].

1854   [*Same.*] *Documentos para la Historia de México*, 2nd series, Vol. 1, article 4, pp. 225–374. México, F. Escalante y Comp.

1900   *On the trail of a Spanish pioneer*. Two volumes. Translated by Elliott Coues. New York, F. P. Harper.

1965   *A record of travels in Arizona and California, 1775–1776*. Translated and edited by John Galvin. San Francisco, John Howell Books.

Gatschet, Albert S.

1877   The Indian languages of the Pacific states and territories. *Magazine of American History*, Vol. 1, no. 3 (March), pp. 147–171. New York and Chicago, A. S. Barnes and Company.

Goodfellow, G. E.

1877   The Sonora earthquake. *Science*, Vol. 10, no. 236 (August 12), pp. 81–82. New York, The Science Company.

Grossman, Frederick E.

1873   The Pima Indians of Arizona. *Annual Report of the Smithsonian Institution for 1871*, pp. 407–419. Washington, Government Printing Office.

1958   Three Pima fables. *The Kiva*, Vol. 24, no. 1 (October), p. 24. Tucson, Arizona Archaeological and Historical Society.

Hackenberg, Robert A.

1962   Economic alternatives in arid lands: a case study of the Pima and Papago Indians. *Ethnology*, Vol. 1, no. 2 (April), pp. 186–196. Pittsburgh, University of Pittsburgh.

1964   Changing patterns of Pima land use. *Contributions of the Committee of Desert and Arid Zone Research of the Southwest and Rocky Mountain Division of the American Association for the Advancement of Science*, no. 7, pp. 6–15. Lubbock, Texas Technological College.

Hall, Sharlot M.

1907   The story of a Pima record rod. *Out West*, Vol. 26, no. 5 (May), pp. 413–423. Los Angeles, Out West Magazine Company.

Halseth, Odd S.

1933   Archaeology in the making. *Masterkey*, Vol. 7, no. 2 (March), pp. 37–40. Los Angeles, Southwest Museum.

Hamilton, James H.

1948   "A history of the Presbyterian church among the Pima and Papago Indians of Arizona." Unpublished Master's thesis, The University of Arizona, Tucson.

[Harrington, H. H.]

1889   Report of the chemist. *First Annual Report of the Texas Agricultural Experiment Station for the Year 1888*, pp. 21–34. College Station, Texas.

Haury, Emil W.

1967   The Hohokam, first masters of the American desert. *National Geographic*, Vol. 131, no. 5 (May), pp. 670–701. Washington, National Geographic Society.

Hayden, Carl, compiler

1965   A history of the Pima Indians and the San Carlos irrigation project. *Senate Documents*, no. 11, 89th Congress, 1st session. Washington, Government Printing Office.

Hayden, Julian D.

1959   Notes on Pima pottery making. *The Kiva*, Vol. 24, no. 3 (February), pp. 10–16. Tucson, Arizona Archaeological and Historical Society.

Hayden, Julian D. (cont.)
1970   Of Hohokam origins and other matters. *American Antiquity,* Vol. 35, no. 1 (January), pp. 87–93. Salt Lake City, Society for American Archaeology.
Heintzelman, Samuel P.
1857   [Report to Major E. D. Townsend, Asst. Adj. Gen. U.S.A., Pacific Division, July 15, 1853.] *Indian affairs on the Pacific (House Executive Documents,* no. 76, 34th Congress, 3rd session), pp. 43–58. Washington, Cornelius Wendell, printer.
Hervás y Panduro, Lorenzo
1787   *Saggio practico delle lingue con prolegomeni . . .* Cesena, Gregorio Biasini all'insegna di Pallade.
Herzog, George
1936a   A comparison of Pueblo and Pima musical styles. *Journal of American Folk-Lore,* Vol. 49, no. 194 (Oct.-Dec.), pp. 283–417. New York, American Folk-Lore Society.
1936b   Note on Pima moieties. *American Anthropologist,* Vol. 38, no. 3 (July-September), pp. 520–521. Menasha, Wisconsin, American Anthropological Association.
1940   A Pima dromedary basket. *The Masterkey,* Vol. 14, no. 3 (May), pp. 98–101. Los Angeles, Southwest Museum.
1960   Culture change and language: shifts in the Pima vocabulary. In *Language, culture, and personality: essays in memory of Edward Sapir,* edited by Leslie Spier, A. Irving Hallowell and Stanley S. Newman, pp. 66–74. Menasha, Wisconsin, Sapir Memorial Publication Fund.
Hill, W. W.
1936   Notes on Pima land law and tenure. *American Anthropologist,* Vol. 38, no. 4 (October-December), pp. 586–589. Menasha, Wisconsin, American Anthropological Association.
1938   Note on the Pima berdache. *American Anthropolgist,* Vol. 40, no. 2 (April-June), pp. 338–340. Menasha, Wisconsin, American Anthropological Association.
Hine, Robert V.
1968   *Bartlett's west. Drawing on the Mexican boundary.* New Haven, Yale University Press.
Hodge, Frederick W.
1893   Prehistoric irrigation in Arizona. *American Anthropologist,* Vol. 6, no. 3 (July), pp. 323–330. Washington, Anthropological Society of Washington.
1903   Frank Russell. *American Anthropologist,* Vol. 5, no. 4 (October-December), pp. 737–738. Lancaster, American Anthropological Association, Anthropological Society of Washington and the American Ethnological Society of New York.
Hrdlička, Aleš
1906   Notes on the Pima of Arizona. *American Anthropologist,* Vol. 8, no. 1 (January-March), pp. 39–46. Lancaster, American Anthropological Association.
Ives, Joseph C.
1861   Report upon the Colorado River of the west. *House Executive Documents,* no. 90, 36th Congress, 1st session. Washington, Government Printing Office.
Jackson, A. H.
1884a   [Report of the Agent for the Pima, Maricopa, and Papago Indians to Hiram Price, Commissioner of Indian Affairs, August 14, 1884.] *Annual report of the Commissioner of Indian Affairs to the Secretary of the*

Interior for the Year 1884, pp. 5–7. Washington, Government Printing Office.

1884b   [*Same.*] *Report of the Commissioner of Indian Affairs* [for 1884] *(House Executive Documents,* no. 1, part 5, 48th Congress, 2nd session), pp. 49–51. Washington, Government Printing Office.

Jenks, Albert E.
1901   Review of *The ethno-botany of the Coahuila Indians of Southern California,* by David P. Barrows. *American Anthropologist,* n.s., Vol. 3, no. 4 (October-December), pp. 754–756. New York, G. P. Putnam's Sons.

Johnston, Abraham R.
1848   Journal of Captain A. R. Johnston, first dragoons. *House Executive Documents,* no. 41, pp. 567–614, 30th Congress, 1st session. Washington, Wendell and Van Benthuysen, printers.

Jordan, David S.
1900   [Footnote concerning fish in the Gila River.] *In* Benavide's memorial, 1630, translated by Mrs. Edward E. Ayer, annotated by Frederick W. Hodge, part 3, pp. 435–444, *Land of Sunshine,* Vol. 13, no. 6 (December), p. 436. Los Angeles, Land of Sunshine Publishing Company.

Kate, Herman F. C. ten
1892   Somatological observations on Indians of the Southwest. *Journal of American Ethnology and Archaeology,* Vol. 3, pp. 119–144. Boston and New York, Houghton, Mifflin and Company.

Kelly, William H.
1967   *A study of southern Arizona school-age children, 1966–1967.* Tucson, The University of Arizona, Bureau of Ethnic Research.

Kilcrease, A. T.
1939   Ninety-five years of history of the Papago Indians. Southwestern Monuments Monthly Report, April, pp. 297–310. [Coolidge, Arizona?], U.S. Department of the Interior, National Park Service. [Also see Papago Tribe of Arizona and others 1972: A1-A11.]

Kissell, Mary L.
1916   Basketry of the Papago and Pima. *Anthropological Papers of the American Museum of Natural History,* Vol. 17, part 4, pp. 115–264. New York.

1972   *Basketry of the Papago and Pima Indians.* Glorieta, New Mexico, Rio Grande Press, Inc.

Kneale, Albert H.
1950   *Indian agent.* Caldwell, Idaho, Caxton Printers.

Kroeber, Henriette R.
1908   Pima tales. *American Anthropologist,* Vol. 10, no. 1 (January-March), pp. 231–235. Lancaster, American Anthropological Association.

Krueger, Darrell W.
1971   "The political integration of the United States Indians: a case study of the Gila River Reservation." Unpublished Ph.D. dissertation, Department of Government, The University of Arizona, Tucson.

Langenbeck, Karl
1895   *The chemistry of pottery.* Easton, Pennsylvania, Chemical Publishing Company.

Latham, Robert G.
1850   *The natural history of the varieties of man.* London, J. Van Voorst.
1860   *Opuscula. Essays, chiefly philosophical and ethnographical.* London, Williams and Norgate; [etc., etc.].

Lay, Permelia R.
1972   Reviving an ancient art. *Design,* Vol. 74, no. 2 (Winter), pp. 29–32. Indianapolis, Review Publishing Co., Inc.

Lippincott, Joseph B.
1900   Storage of water on Gila River, Arizona. *Water Supply and Irrigation Papers of the U.S. Geological Survey,* no. 33. Washington, Government Printing Office.

Lloyd, J. William
1911   *Aw-aw-tam Indian nights.* Westfield, New Jersey, The Lloyd Group.

Lumholtz, Carl S.
1900   Symbolism of the Huichol Indians. *Memoirs of the American Museum of Natural History,* Vol. 3, *Anthropological Series,* Vol. 2, part 1. New York.

1912   *New trails in Mexico.* New York, Charles Scribner's Sons; London and Leipsic, T. Fisher Unwin.

1971   *New trails in Mexico.* New introduction. Glorieta, New Mexico, Rio Grande Press, Inc.

McClintock, James H.
1918   The friendly Pima of southern Arizona plains. *Arizona: the New State Magazine,* Vol. 8, nos. 5, 6, 7 (August), pp. 5–7. Phoenix, State Publishing Company.

McGee, William J.
1898   The Seri Indians. *Annual Report of the Bureau of American Ethnology,* Vol. 17, part 1, pp. 1–344*. Washington, Government Printing Office.

1971   *The Seri Indians of Bahia Kino and Sonora, Mexico.* Glorieta, New Mexico, Rio Grande Press, Inc.

Mallery, Garrick
1877   A calendar of the Dakota nation. *Bulletin of the U.S. Geological and Geographical Survey of the Territories,* Vol. 3, no. 1, article 1 (April), pp. 3–25. Washington, Government Printing Office.

1886   On the pictographs of the North American Indians. *Annual Report of the Bureau of American Ethnology,* Vol. 4, pp. 1–256. Washington, Government Printing Office.

1893   Picture-writing of the American Indians. *Annual Report of the Bureau of American Ethnology,* Vol. 10. Washington, Government Printing Office.

Mange, Juan M.
1693–   "Luz de Tierra Yncógnita en la América Septentrional de todos los
1721   Viajes de Tierra, Ríos, y Naciones . . . desde fines del año de 1693 hasta el de 1721." Original Spanish manuscript in the *Archivo General y Público de la Nación,* México [see Bolton 1913: 54].

1856   Historia de la Pimería Alta. *Documentos para la Historia de México,* 4th series, Vol. 1, pp. 226–402. México, Imprenta de Vicente García Torres.

1926   Luz de tierra incognita. *Publicaciones del Archivo General de la Nación,* Vol. 10. México, Talleres Graficos de la Nación.

1954   *Luz de tierra incognita.* Translated by Harry J. Karns and associates. Tucson, Arizona Silhouettes.

Martín Bernal, Cristóbal
1856   Relación del estado de Pimería que remite el Pe. Visitador Horacio Polici: y es copia de Carta que le escribe el Capitan Dn. Christóval Martín Bernal. *Documentos para la Historia de México,* 3rd series, Vol. 16, pp. 797–799. México.

1966   Diary of Lieutenant Christóbal Martín Bernal. Translated by Fay J. Smith. In *Father Kino in Arizona,* by Fay J. Smith, John Kessell and Francis J. Fox, pp. 35–47. Phoenix, Arizona Historical Foundation.

Mason, Otis T.
1889   Cradles of the American aborigines. *Report of the U.S. National Museum for 1887,* pp. 161–212. Washington, Government Printing Office.

1895   The origins of invention: a study of industry among primitive peoples. *The Contemporary Science Series,* edited by Havelock Ellis, Vol. 28. London, W. Scott, Ltd.

1915   *The origins of invention: a study of industry among primitive peoples.* London, Walter Scott Publ. Co., Ltd.; New York, Charles Scribner's Sons.

Matthews, Washington
1883   A part of the Navajo's mythology. *The American Antiquarian and Oriental Journal,* Vol. 5, no. 3 (July), pp. 207–224. Chicago, Jameson and Morse.

Mohave County Miner *(newspaper)*
1903   Death of a Harvard professor. November 7, p. 3, col. 1. Kingman, Arizona.

Mooney, James
1898   Calendar history of the Kiowa Indians. *Annual Report of the Bureau of American Ethnology,* Vol. 17, part 1, pp. 129–443. Washington, Government Printing Office.

Mowry, Sylvester
1857   [Report to James W. Denver, Commissioner of Indian Affairs, November 10, 1857.] *Annual Report of the Commissioner of Indian Affairs* [for 1857] *(House Executive Documents,* no. 2, 35th Congress, 1st session), pp. 584–593. Washington, James B. Steedman, printer.

1858a   *[Same.] Report of the Commissioner of Indian Affairs, accompanying the Annual Report of the Secretary of the Interior, for the year 1857,* pp. 296–305. Washington, William A. Harris, printer.

1858b   *[Same.] Annual Report of the Commissioner of Indian Affairs* [for 1857] *(Senate Executive Documents,* no. 11, 35th Congress, 1st session) pp. 584–593. Washington, William A. Harris, printer.

1859   *The geography and resources of Arizona & Sonora.* Washington, American Geographical and Statistical Society [H. Polkinhorn, printer].

1860a   [Report to Alfred B. Greenwood, Commissioner of Indian Affairs, November 21, 1859.] *Report of the Commissioner of Indian Affairs, accompanying the Annual Report of the Secretary of the Interior, for the year 1859,* pp. 353–362. Washington, George W. Bowman, printer.

1860b   *[Same.] Report of the Commissioner of Indian Affairs* [for 1859] *(Senate Executive Documents,* no. 2, Vol. 1, 36th Congress, 1st session), pp. 721–730. Washington, George W. Bowman, printer.

1863   *[Same as 1859.]* 2nd edition. San Francisco and New York, A. Roman and Company.

1864   *Arizona and Sonora: the geography, history, and resources of the silver region of North America.* 3rd edition. New York, Harper and Brothers.

1866   *[Same as 1864.]* New York, Harper and Brothers.

Mühlenpfordt, Eduard
1844   *Versuch einer getreun schilderung der republic Mejico, bezonders in bezeihung auf geographie, ethnographie und statistik . . .* Two volumes. Hannover, C. F. Kius.

Neff, Mary L.
1912   Pima and Papago legends. *Journal of American Folk-Lore,* Vol. 25, no. 95 (January-March), pp. 51–65. Lancaster and New York, American Folk-Lore Society.

[Nentvig, Juan]
1863   *Rudo ensayo, tentativa de una prevencional descripcion geographica de la provincia de Sonora, sus terminos y confines . . .* San Augustin de la Florida [Albany, Munsell, printer].

1894   Rudo ensayo. Translated by Eusebio Guitéras. *Records of the American Catholic Historical Society of Philadelphia,* Vol. 5, no. 2 (June), pp. 109–264. Philadelphia.

1951   *[Same as 1894.]* Tucson, Arizona Silhouettes.

Padfield, Harland; Peter Hemingway and Philip Greenfeld
    1966   The Pima-Papago educational population: a census and analysis. *Journal of American Indian Education,* Vol. 6, no. 2 (October), pp. 1–24. Tempe, College of Education, Arizona State University.
Papago Tribe of Arizona; Bureau of Indian Affairs, Papago Agency; U.S. Public Health Service
    1972   *Facts about the Papago Indian Reservation and the Papago people.* Sells, Arizona, n.p.
Parke, John G.
    1855a   Report of explorations for that portion of a railroad route near the thirty-second parallel of north latitude lying between Dona Ana, on the Rio Grande, and Pimas villages, on the Gila. *Senate Executive Documents,* no. 78, Vol. 13, part 2, 33rd Congress, 2nd session (Vol. 2, report 5, pp. 1–22). Washington, Beverley Tucker, printer.
    1855b   [*Same.*] *House Executive Documents,* no. 91, Vol. 11, no. 2, 33rd Congress, 2nd session (Vol. 2, report 5, pp. 1–22). Washington, Beverley Tucker, printer.
    1857a   Report of explorations for railroad routes from San Francisco Bay to Los Angeles, California, west of the Coast Range, and from the Pimas villages on the Gila River to the Rio Grande, near the 32nd parallel of north latitude. *Senate Executive Documents,* no. 78, Vol. 13, part 7, 33rd Congress, 2nd session (Vol. 7, part 1, pp. 1–42). Washington, Beverley Tucker, printer.
    1857b   [*Same.*] *House Executive Documents,* no. 91, Vol. 11, part 7, 33rd Congress, 2nd session (Vol. 7, part 1, pp. 1–42). Washington, Beverley Tucker, printer.
Parsons, Elsie C.
    1928   Notes on the Pima. *American Anthropologist,* Vol. 30, no. 3 (July–September), pp. 445–464. Menasha, Wisconsin, American Anthropological Association.
Pattie, James O.
    1833   *The personal narrative of James O. Pattie . . .* Edited by Timothy Flint. Cincinnati, E. H. Flint.
    1847   *The hunters of Kentucky.* New York, W. H. Graham.
    1905   [*Same as 1833.*] Cleveland, A. H. Clark Company.
    1930   [*Same as 1833.*] Chicago, R. R. Donnelley and Sons Company.
    1962   [*Same as 1833.*] Philadelphia, Lippincott.
    1966   [*Same as 1833.*] Ann Arbor, University Microfilms.
Pfefferkorn, Ignaz
    1794–   *Beschreibung der Landschaft Sonora samt andern merkwürdigen Nach-*
    1795   *richten von den innern Theilen Neu-Spaniens und Reise aus Amerika bis in Deutschland.* Two volumes. Köln am Rhein, Auf Kosten des Verfassers gedrukt in Langenschen Buchhandlung.
    1949   Sonora, a description of the province. Translated by Theodore Treutlein. *Coronado Cuarto Centennial Publications, 1540–1940,* Vol. 12. Albuquerque, University of New Mexico Press.
Poston, Charles D.
    1863   [Report to William P. Dole, Commissioner of Indian Affairs, April 1, 1863.] *Report of the Commissioner of Indian Affairs* [for 1863] (*House Executive Documents,* no. 1, 38th Congress, 1st session), pp. 503–510. Washington, Government Printing Office.
    1864   [*Same.*] *Report of the Commissioner of Indian Affairs, for the year 1863,* pp. 383–390. Washington, Government Printing Office.
    1865a   [Report to William P. Dole, Commissioner of Indian Affairs, September 30, 1864.] *Report of the Commissioner of Indian Affairs, for the year 1864,* pp. 150–158. Washington, Government Printing Office.

1865b   [*Same.*] *Report of the Commissioner of Indian Affairs* [for 1864] *(House Executive Documents,* no. 1, 38th Congress, 2nd session), pp. 294–302. Washington, Government Printing Office.

Robinson, Bert
1954   *The basket weavers of Arizona.* Albuquerque, The University of New Mexico Press.
1955   Akimoel Awatam. *Arizona Highways,* Vol. 31, no. 7 (July), pp. 30–39. Phoenix, Arizona Highway Department.

Ruggles, Levi
1867   [Report to George W. Dent, Arizona Superintendent of Indian Affairs, June 20, 1867]. *House Executive Documents,* no. 1, 40th Congress, 2nd session, pp. 161–165. Washington, Government Printing Office.
1868   [*Same.*] *Annual Report on Indian Affairs* [for 1867] *by the Acting Commissioner,* pp. 161–165. Washington, Government Printing Office.

Rusling, James F.
1874   *Across America; or, the great west and the Pacific coast.* New York, Sheldon and Company.

Russell, Frank
1897   Review of *The history of mankind,* by Friedrich Ratzel. *The American Naturalist,* Vol. 31, no. 138 (December), pp. 1062–1064. Philadelphia, The Edwards and Docker Company.
1898a   An Apache medicine dance. *American Anthropologist,* Vol. 11, no. 12 (December), pp. 367–372. Washington, Anthropological Society of Washington.
1898b   "A study of a collection of Eskimo crania from Labrador, with observations on the prevailing system of craniometry." Unpublished Ph.D. dissertation, Harvard University, Cambridge.
1898c   *Explorations in the far north. Being the report of an expedition under the auspices of the University of Iowa during the years 1892, '93, and '94.* [Iowa City?], The University.
1898d   Gauging cranial capacity with water. *American Anthropologist,* Vol. 11, no. 2 (February), pp. 52–53. Washington, Anthropological Society of Washington.
1898e   Myths of the Jicarilla Apaches. *Journal of American Folk-Lore,* Vol. 11, no. 43 (October December), pp. 253–272. Boston and New York, Houghton, Mifflin and Company; [etc., etc.].
1898f   Review of *The import of the totem,* by Alice C. Fletcher. *The American Naturalist,* Vol. 32, no. 373 (January), pp. 54–55. Boston, Ginn and Company.
1898g   Review of *The races of Europe,* by Joseph Deniker. *The American Naturalist,* Vol. 32, no. 375 (March), pp. 203–205. Boston, Ginn and Company.
1898h   Reviews of recent literature. Anthropology. *The American Naturalist,* Vol. 32, no. 380 (August), pp. 586–587. Boston, Ginn and Company.
1899a   Human remains from the Trenton gravels. *The American Naturalist,* Vol. 33, no. 386 (February), pp. 143–155. Boston, Ginn and Company.
1899b   Review of *Man past and present,* by A. H. Keane. *The American Naturalist,* Vol. 33, no. 393 (September), pp. 738–740. Boston, Ginn and Company.
1899c   Review of *The races of Europe,* by W. Z. Ripley. *The American Naturalist,* Vol. 33, no. 394 (October), pp. 827–831. Boston, Ginn and Company.
1899d   Review of *Der Ursprung der afrikanischen Kulturen,* by L. Frobenius. *The American Naturalist,* Vol. 33, no. 387 (March), pp. 255–256. Boston, Ginn and Company.

Russell, Frank (cont.)
1899e   Reviews of recent literature. Anthropology. *The American Naturalist,*
         Vol. 33, no. 385 (January), pp. 63–65; no. 386 (February), pp. 158–160;
         no. 388 (April), pp. 333–334; no. 389 (May), pp. 425–428; no. 390
         (June), pp. 514–518; and no. 391 (July), pp. 609–611. Boston, Ginn
         and Company.
1900a   Athabascan myths. *Journal of American Folk-Lore,* Vol. 13, no. 48
         (January-March), pp. 11–18. Boston and New York, Houghton, Mifflin
         and Company; [etc., etc.].
1900b   Physical structure of the Labrador Eskimos and the New England
         Indians. *Scientific American Supplement,* Vol. 49, no. 1254 (January 13),
         pp. 20106–07. New York, Munn and Company.
1900c   Review of *The races of man,* by Joseph Deniker. *The American Natural-*
         ist, Vol. 34, no. 402 (June), pp. 521–522. Boston, Ginn and Company.
1900d   Reviews of recent literature. Anthropology. *The American Naturalist,*
         Vol. 34, no. 402 (June), pp. 521–522. Boston, Ginn and Company.
1900e   Studies in cranial variation. *The American Naturalist,* Vol. 34, no. 405
         (September), pp. 737–745. Boston, Ginn and Company.
1901a   Laboratory outlines in somatology. *American Anthropologist,* Vol. 3,
         no. 1 (January-March), pp. 28–50. New York, Anthropological and
         Ethnological Societies of America.
1901b   A new instrument for measuring torsion. *The American Naturalist,*
         Vol. 35, no. 412 (April), pp. 299–300. Boston, Ginn and Company.
1901c   Review of *The North Americans of yesterday,* by F. S. Dellenbaugh.
         The American Naturalist, Vol. 35, no. 414 (June), pp. 501–503. Boston,
         Ginn and Company.
1901d   Review of *The Seri Indians,* by W. J. McGee. *The American Naturalist,*
         Vol. 35, no. 418 (October), pp. 853–854. Boston, Ginn and Company.
1901e   Reviews of recent literature. Anthropology. *The American Naturalist,*
         Vol. 35, no. 413 (May), pp. 399–401. Boston, Ginn and Company.
1902   Know, then, thyself. *Journal of American Folk-Lore,* Vol. 15, no. 56
         (January-March), pp. 1–13. Boston and New York, Houghton, Mifflin
         and Company; [etc., etc.].
1903a   Anthropology in American secondary schools and after. *Education,*
         Vol. 23, no. 9 (May), pp. 530–537. Boston, The Palmer Company.
1903b   Pima annals. *American Anthropologist,* Vol. 5, no. 1 (January-March),
         pp. 76–80. Lancaster, American Anthropological Association, Anthro-
         pological Society of Washington and the American Ethnological Society
         of New York.
1903c   A Pima constitution; with notes by Frank Russell. *Journal of American*
         Folk-Lore, Vol. 16, no. 63 (October-December), pp. 222–228. Boston
         and New York, Houghton, Mifflin and Company; [etc., etc.].
1903d   Review of *A manual for physical measurements, for use in normal*
         schools, by W. W. Hastings. *American Anthropologist,* Vol. 5, no. 1
         (January-March), p. 133. Lancaster, American Anthropological Asso-
         ciation, Anthropological Society of Washington and the American Ethno-
         logical Society of New York.
1908   The Pima Indians. *Annual Report of the Bureau of American Ethnology,*
         Vol. 26, pp. 3–389. Washington, Government Printing Office.
1909   Pima myths. *Out West,* Vol. 30, no. 5 (May), pp. 485–495; no. 6 (June),
         pp. 571–582; Vol. 32, no. 1 (July), pp. 643–646; no. 3 (September),
         pp. 828–834; no. 4 (November), pp. 890–895. Los Angeles, Out West
         Magazine Company.
1967   Pima Indian subsistence. In *The North American Indians; a sourcebook,*
         edited by Roger C. Owen, James J. F. Deetz and Anthony D. Fisher,
         pp. 443–452. New York, Macmillan.

Russell, Frank, and Henry M. Huxley
1899   A comparative study of the physical structure of the Labrador Eskimos and the New England Indians. *Proceedings of the American Association for the Advancement of Science,* Vol. 48, pp. 365–379. Easton.

Schoolcraft, Henry R.
1851–   *Historical and statistical information respecting the history, condition and*
1857   *prospects of the Indian tribes of the United States.* Six volumes. Philadelphia, Lippincott.
1954   Index to Schoolcraft's "Indian tribes of the United States." Compiled by Frances S. Nichols. *Bulletin of the U.S. Bureau of American Ethnology,* no. 152. Washington, Government Printing Office.

Scouler, John
1841   Observations on the indigeneous tribes of the N.W. coast of America. *Journal of the Royal Geographical Society of London,* Vol. 11, pp. 215–251. London.

Seaver, James E.
1824   *A narrative of the life of Mrs. Mary Jemison* . . . Canandaigua, [New York], Printed by J. D. Bemis and Company.
1826   [*Same as 1824.*] Howden, England, Printed for R. Parkin.
1827   [*Same as 1824.*] London, Longman, etc.
1834   *Interesting narrative of Mary Jemison.* Buffalo, n.p.
1842a   *De-he-wa-mis: or, A narrative of the life of Mary Jemison* . . . Batavia, New York, W. Seaver and Son.
1842b   [*Same as 1824.*] Otley, William Walker.
1842c   [*Same as 1824.*] Utica, G. Cunningham; Woodland & Donaldson, printers.
1844   [*Same as 1842a.*] 3rd edition. Batavia, New York, W. Seaver and Son.
1847   [*Same as 1842a.*] Devon, S. Thorne; [etc., etc.].
1856   *Life of Mary Jemison: Deh-he-wä-mis.* 4th edition. New York and Auburn, Miller, Orton & Mulligan; Rochester, D. M. Dewey.
1859   [*Same as 1856.*] New York, C. M. Saxton.
1860   [*Same as 1856.*] New York, C. M. Saxton, Barker & Company.
1877   [*Same as 1856.*] 5th edition, with appendix. Buffalo, New York, Printing house of Matthews and Warren.
1880   [*Same as 1856.*] Buffalo, New York, Matthews Brothers and Bryant.
1898   [*Same as 1856.*] New York, G. P. Putnam's Sons.
1910   [*Same as 1856.*] New York and London, G. P. Putnam's Sons.
1918   *A narrative of the life of Mary Jemison* . . . 20th edition. New York, The American Scenic and Historic Preservation Society.
1925   [*Same as 1918.*] 22nd edition. New York, The American Scenic and Historic Preservation Society.
1929   [*Same as 1824.*] New York, Random House.
1932   [*Same as 1918.*] Edition of 1932. New York, The American Scenic and Historic Preservation Society.
1942   [*Same as 1918.*] Edition of 1942. New York, The American Scenic and Historic Preservation Society.

Sedelmayr, Jacobo
1856   Relación. *Documentos para la historia de Mexico,* 3rd series, Vol. 4, pp. 843–859. México, Imprenta de Vicente García Torres. [This is the published version of the 1746 draft of the *relación.*]
1939   Sedelmayr's relacion of 1746. Translated by Ronald L. Ives. *Bulletin of the Bureau of American Ethnology,* no. 123, *Anthropological Papers,* no. 9, pp. 101–117. Washington, Government Printing Office.
1955   *Jacobo Sedelmayr.* Translated by Peter M. Dunne, pp. 14–53. Tucson, Arizona Pioneers' Historical Society. [This is the translated version into English of the 1744 draft of the *relación.*]

Shaw, Anna M.
  1968   *Pima Indian legends.* Tucson, The University of Arizona Press.
  1974   *Pima past.* Tucson, The University of Arizona Press.
Shea, John D. G.
  1859–   *Shea's library of American linguistics.* Series 1, nos. 1–13; Series 2,
  1874   nos. 1–2. New York, Cramoisy Press.
Simpson, Ruth D.
  1946   Those who have gone still live: the Hohokam since 1400 A.D. *The
          Masterkey,* Vol. 20, no. 3 (May), pp. 73–80. Los Angeles, Southwest
          Museum.
Smith, Buckingham, editor
  1862a   *Arte de la lengua Névome que se dice Pima, propia de Sonora; con la
          doctrina christiana y confesionario añadidos.* San Augustin de la Florida
          [Albany, Munsell, printer].
  1862b   Grammar of the Pima or Nevome, a language of Sonora, from a manu-
          script of the XVIII century. *Shea's Library of American Linguistics,*
          Vol. 5. New York, Cramoisy Press.
  1970   [*Same as 1862b.*] New York, AMS Press, Inc.
Smith, F. M.
  1930   Educational facilities are offered Indian youths. *Progressive Arizona,*
          Vol. 10, no. 3 (March), pp. 18–19, 26. Tucson, Ward Shelby Publica-
          tions, Inc.
Smith, [Mrs.] White Mountain
  1942   Time marches on in Pimeria. *Desert Magazine,* Vol. 5, no. 6 (April),
          pp. 22–24. El Centro, California, Desert Publishing Company.
Smith, William N.
  1945   The Papago game of "gince goot." *The Masterkey,* Vol. 19, no. 6
          (November), pp. 194–197. Los Angeles, Southwest Museum.
Southworth, C. H.
  1931   A Pima calendar stick. *Arizona Historical Review,* Vol. 4, no. 2 (July),
          pp. 45–52. Phoenix, Arizona State Historian.
Spicer, Edward H.
  1962   *Cycles of conquest.* Tucson, The University of Arizona Press.
Steen, Charlie R.
  1943   Some notes on the use of tobacco and cane pipes by the Pimas of the
          Gila valley. *American Anthropologist,* Vol. 45, no. 4 (October-Decem-
          ber), pp. 641–642. Menasha, Wisconsin, American Anthropological
          Association.
  1946   Notes on some 19th century Pima burials. *The Kiva,* Vol. 12, no. 1
          (November), pp. 6–10. Tucson, Arizona Archaeological and Historical
          Society.
Tanner, Clara L., and Ernest E. Leavitt, Jr.
  1965   Papago burden baskets in the Arizona State Museum. *The Kiva,* Vol. 30,
          no. 3 (February), pp. 57–76. Tucson, Arizona Archaeological and
          Historical Society.
Underhill, Ruth M.
  1938   A Papago calendar record. *The University of New Mexico Bulletin,*
          no. 322, *Anthropological Series,* Vol. 2, no. 5. Albuquerque, University
          of New Mexico Press.
  1939   Social organization of the Papago Indians. *Columbia University Contri-
          butions to Anthropology,* Vol. 30. New York, Columbia University Press.
  n.d.   The Papago Indians of Arizona and their relatives the Pima. *Sherman
          Pamphlets,* no. 3. Riverside, California, Department of the Interior,
          Bureau of Indian Affairs, Branch of Education.

United States. *Department of Agriculture, Weather Bureau.*
1901   *Report to the chief of the weather bureau.* Two volumes. Washington, Government Printing Office.
Van Valkenburgh, Richard F.
1946   We found the hidden shrine of old makai. *Desert Magazine*, Vol. 9, no. 11 (September), pp. 20–22. El Centro, California, Desert Press, Inc.
Van Willigen, John
1970   Contemporary Pima house construction practices. *The Kiva*, Vol. 36, no. 1 (Fall), pp. 1–10. Tucson, Arizona Archaeological and Historical Society.
Velarde, Luis
1856   Descripcion del sitio, longitud y latitud de las naciones de la Pimería y sus adyacentes septentionales, y seno california y otros noticias y observaciones. *Documentos para la Historia de México*, 4th series, Vol. 1, pp. 344–357. México, Imprenta de Vicente García Torres.
1926   [*Same.*] In *Luz de tierra incognita*, by Juan M. Mange, *Publicaciones del Archivo General de la Nación*, Vol. 10, pp. 297–307. México, Talleres Graficos de la Nación.
1954   This is the description of the site, longitude, and latitude of the nations of the Pimería and its northern adjoining nations, the land of California. It also contains other news and observations . . . In *Luz de tierra incógnita*, by Juan M. Manje, translated by Harry J. Karns and associates, pp. 221–234. Tucson, Arizona Silhouettes.
Venegas, Miguel
1757   *Noticia de la California y de su conquista temporal y espiritual hasta el tiempo presente.* Three volumes. Madrid, La viuda de M. Fernandez.
1759   *A natural and civil history of California . . .* Two volumes. London, J. Rivington and J. Fletcher.
1761–   *Natuurlyke en burgerlyke histoire van California.* Two volumes. Trans-
1762   lated by J. J. D. Haerlem, Johannes Enschedé.
1767   *Histoire naturelle et civile de la Californie . . .* Three volumes. Translated by M. A. Eidous. Paris, Durand.
1769–   *Natürliche und bürgerliche geschichte von Californien . . .* Three volumes
1770   in one. Translated by Johan C. Adelung. Lemgo, Meyer.
1777   *Natuurlyke en burgerlyke histoire van California . . .* Two volumes. Translated by J. J. D. Amsterdam, J. van Gulik.
1943–   *Noticia de la California y de su conquista temporal y espiritual hasta el*
1944   *tiempo presente.* Three volumes. Edited by Andrés M. Burriel. México, Editorial Layac.
1966   *A natural and civil history of California . . .* Ann Arbor, University Microfilms.
Villa-Señor y Sánchez, José A. de
1746–   *Theatro americano . . .* Two volumes. México, La viuda de D. J. Bernardo
1748   de Hogal.
Walker, John
1860a   [Report to James L. Collins, Superintendent of New Mexico Indian Affairs, September 28, 1859.] *Report of the Commissioner of Indian Affairs, accompanying the Annual Report of the Secretary of the Interior, for the year 1859*, pp. 351–353. Washington, George W. Bowman, printer.
1860b   [*Same.*] *Report of Commissioner of Indian Affairs* [for 1859] *(Senate Executive Documents*, no. 2, Vol. 1, 36th Congress, 1st session), pp. 719–721. Washington, George W. Bowman, printer.
1860c   [Report to James L. Collins, New Mexico Superintendent of Indian

Walker, John (cont.)
> Affairs, September 6, 1860.] *Report of the Commissioner of Indian Affairs accompanying the Annual Report of the Secretary of the Interior for the year 1860,* pp. 167–169. Washington, George W. Bowman, printer.
> 1860d   [*Same.*] *Report of Commissioner of Indian Affairs* [for 1860] *(House Executive Documents,* no. 1, 36th Congress, 2nd session), pp. 391–393. Washington, George W. Bowman, printer.

Walton, Eda L., and T. T. Waterman
> 1925   American Indian poetry. *American Anthropologist,* Vol. 27, no. 1 (January-March), pp. 25–52. Menasha, Wisconsin, American Anthropological Association.

Weaver, Thomas
> 1974   Social and economic change in the context of Pima-Maricopa history. In *Proceedings of the 40th International Congress of Americanists,* based on a presentation at the meeting of this organization on September 5, 1972, Rome, Italy.

Webb, George
> 1959   *A Pima remembers.* Tucson, The University of Arizona Press.

Wetzler, Lewis
> 1949   "History of the Pimas." Unpublished Ph.D. dissertation, University of California, Berkeley.

Whipple, Amiel W.; Thomas Ewbank, and William W. Turner.
> 1855   Report upon the Indian tribes. *Reports of explorations and surveys, to ascertain the most practicable and economical route for a railroad from the Mississippi River to the Pacific Ocean,* Vol. 3, *Route near the thirty-fifth parallel . . . in 1853 and 1854 (Senate Executive Documents,* no. 78, Vol. 13, part 3, 33rd Congress, 2nd session). Washington, Beverley Tucker, printer.
> 1856   [*Same.*] *House Executive Documents,* no. 91, Vol. 11, part 3, 33rd Congress, 2nd session (Vol. 3). Washington, A. O. P. Nicholson.

Whittemore, Isaac T., and Charles H. Cook
> 1893   *Among the Pimas — or the mission to the Pima and Maricopa Indians.* Albany, Ladies' Union Mission School Association.

Willenbrink, Antonine
> 1935   *Notes on the Pima Indian language.* N.p., The Franciscan Fathers of California.

Winter, Joseph
> 1973   Cultural modifications of the Gila Pima: A.D. 1697–1846. *Ethnohistory,* Vol. 20, no. 1 (Winter), pp. 65–77. Tucson, American Society for Ethnohistory.

Woodward, Arthur
> 1933   A man's way. *The Masterkey,* Vol. 7, no. 6 (November), pp. 165–167. Los Angeles, Southwest Museum.
> 1938   Indian humor. *The Masterkey,* Vol. 12, no. 5 (September), pp. 194–196. Los Angeles, Southwest Museum.
> 1949   Historical notes on the Pima. *The Masterkey,* Vol. 23, no. 5 (September), pp. 144–147. Los Angeles, Southwest Museum.

INDEX